PENGUIN BOOKS

# INDIA IN THE PERSIANATE AGE

Richard M. Eaton has over a long and varied career published a number of ground-breaking books on India before 1800, including major works on the social roles of Sufis, slavery, Indian biography, the growth of Muslim societies along Bengal's eastern frontiers, the social history of the Deccan, and the place of Islam in the sub-continent's history. *India in the Persianate Age* draws on a lifetime of teaching and research. He is Professor of History at the University of Arizona.

T0322261

*For family, friends old and new, villagers, farm-hands, musicians, and in memory of fields of golden grain, horses, cows, and dogs (Sadie and Cam), at 100 Lovers Lane, Bainbridge*

# RICHARD M. EATON

# India in the Persianate Age

## *1000–1765*

PENGUIN BOOKS

PENGUIN BOOKS

UK | USA | Canada | Ireland | Australia
India | New Zealand | South Africa

Penguin Books is part of the Penguin Random House group of companies
whose addresses can be found at global.penguinrandomhouse.com.

First published by Allen Lane 2019
Published in Penguin Books 2020

007

Text copyright © Richard M. Eaton, 2019

The moral right of the author has been asserted

Set in 9.35/12.51 pt Sabon LT Std
Typeset by Jouve (UK), Milton Keynes
Printed and bound in Great Britain by Clays Ltd, Elcograf S.p.A.

A CIP catalogue record for this book is available from the British Library

ISBN: 978-0-141-98539-8

# Contents

CONTENTS

# List of Illustrations

# List of Maps

# Acknowledgements

Books of this sort germinate, grow and ripen in mysterious ways. Yet one thing is clear. Over years of teaching, reading, and immersing myself in fieldwork in India, Pakistan and Bangladesh, many colleagues and friends, perhaps unbeknown to them, helped shape my thinking about South Asian history generally, and about this book in particular. Those to whom I am especially indebted include Said Arjomand, Akeel Bilgrami, Jerry Brennig, Carl Ernst, Munis Faruqui, Barry Flood, Stewart Gordon, Najaf Haider, Harbans Mukhia, Laura Parodi, Shelly Pollock, Ajay Rao, Rajat Ray, Ronit Ricci, Francis Robinson, Samira Sheikh, David Shulman, Ramya Sreenivasan, Audrey Truschke, Phil Wagoner, and André Wink. I also wish to thank those who offered useful comments at talks I gave at the University of California at Berkeley, Vanderbilt University, Jahangirnagar University, Cambridge University's Trinity College, St Andrews University, and Yale University. For sharpening my focus on what this book is really about, I owe special thanks to Özlem Ayse Özgür. I alone, however, am responsible for any mistakes that might remain.

For his sound advice and steadfast support, I am deeply grateful to Simon Winder and his talented team at Penguin. Linden Lawson's meticulous copyediting proved immensely valuable. In different ways, many others helped me in this project. For their warm hospitality in Hyderabad (Deccan), I thank V. K. Bawa and Frauke Quader; in Bangalore, Amar Kumar; and in Dhaka, Perween Hasan. I thank Gail Bernstein for commenting on early drafts, Lois Kain for her expert work in preparing the maps, and the staffs at the University of Arizona Main Library and the Chillicothe & Ross County Public Library for their able assistance. I am also grateful to my dean, J. P. Jones, for generously granting me sufficient leave time to complete this project.

That might never have happened, however, were it not for the tranquility and the fellowship of my sister Beth's lovely farm in the Appalachian foothills. The following chapters were drafted in the walnut-panelled hallway of her rambling, nineteenth-century farmhouse, surrounded by fields of corn and soybeans. It was a delightful place to work – inscribed on the brick and stone hearth was an old Scottish adage: 'East, West, Hame's Best'. On occasion, I might spot an eagle soaring high in the skies outside, or hear the sound of horses galloping along the pasture fence that lay only a few meters beyond the hallway's big front door. I dedicate this book to those treasured days.

# India in the Persianate Age

# Introduction

## STEREOTYPES AND CHALLENGES

This book focuses on South Asian history from roughly 1000 to the late eighteenth century, one of the most compelling, consequential and controversial periods in India's long history. While providing a broad overview of the subcontinent during this period, the book also seeks to challenge lingering stereotypes that have taken hold in recent decades.

One such stereotype is that India had remained a largely stagnant civilization until stimulated by European rule in the eighteenth century. In contrast, the current volume paints a picture of India's repeated self-transformation during these eight centuries. It was between the eleventh and eighteenth centuries, after all, that India witnessed, among other things, the disappearance of Buddhism, the appearance of the Sikh religion, the growth of the world's largest Muslim society, the transform-ation of vast tracts of land from jungle to fields of grain and the integration of tribal clans into the Hindu social order as castes. This era also witnessed India's emergence as the world's industrial powerhouse, based on the export of manufactured textiles. The notion that India merely stood still for eight centuries is, to say the least, mistaken.

Another stereotype addressed in this volume is the notion of India as a self-contained and territorially bounded essence, historically isolated from outside. Rather, this book stresses South Asia's contacts with the societies and cultures of Central Asia, Africa, East Asia, South-east Asia and, especially, the Middle East. In fact, most of the historical changes mentioned above cannot be understood without situating India in the context of its relations with neighbouring peoples.

A third and related stereotype is that of India as an essentially self-generated Hindu and Sanskritic civilization that evolved on its own, rather than a hybridized composite produced from protracted interaction with other peoples and cultures. The present volume affords an excellent opportunity to examine this theme since its chronological scope covers the period of South Asia's intense contact with other regions, particularly with the Iranian plateau, with Persian culture and with Islam. Indeed, the period extending from *c*.1000 to *c*.1800 is conventionally referred to as India's 'Muslim period', inaugurated by a 'Muslim conquest' of India. But there is good reason to question such characterizations.

Consider an analogous world-historical encounter. By the early sixteenth century Spanish conquistadors had sailed across the Atlantic Ocean, established large empires in Central and South America, planted new colonies there, forcibly uprooted native American religious and political institutions and conducted a vigorous, state-sponsored programme of Christianizing the continent's native populations, as a result of which the vast majority of the region's peoples are Roman Catholic today. Yet historians never refer to this great historical moment as a 'Christian conquest' of America. Rather, it is conventionally understood as the 'Spanish conquest'. But generations of historians have referred to the equally momentous events that took place in India towards the end of the twelfth century not as a Turkish conquest but as 'the Muslim conquest', even though the Sanskrit term typically used by contemporary Indians to describe the conquerors was not 'Muslim' but 'Turk' (*turushka*). Further complicating the idea of some religion-based 'clash of civilizations' is the fact that Muslims who had already settled in north India – specifically, in early-thirteenth-century Benares – fought with Indian dynasties against these invading Turks.[1] So a key question that should be asked at the start is: what explains the very different ways in which the American and Indian cases are conventionally characterized? Why is religion foregrounded in one, but not in the other? What hidden assumptions lurk behind our continued use of such different categories when we refer to these otherwise comparable encounters?

Much is at stake in these questions. First, the notion of a 'Muslim conquest' may well result from the inappropriate application of present-day understandings of religion to earlier times, as though religions had always been self-contained and closed belief systems, impervious to change over time and making totalizing claims on people's identities. Then there are political issues. Ever since the end of British imperial rule in 1947, the two largest states in South Asia, India and Pakistan, have remained bitter rivals, with one of them making Islam a state religion and, at least initially, the sole criterion of its national identity. As Pakistan's President Zia-ul-Haq stated in 1981, 'Take Islam out of Pakistan and make it a secular state; it would collapse.'[2] It is, then, hardly surprising that the three wars fought by these now nuclear states have only reinforced the notion of religion as the primary force that had 'always' divided South Asia's inhabitants.

Of course, the idea of cultural alterity, or 'otherness', long predated the creation of the two states. Think of the figures of speech found in two very different literary traditions, the Persian and the Sanskrit. From the mid eleventh century a dynasty of Central Asian Turks, the Ghaznavids, ruled over much of the Punjab from Lahore. However, their Indian rivals identified them in their inscriptions and texts not as Muslims but as the 'Lords of the Horses', an apparent reference to their dependence on cavalry warfare and their control over trade routes leading to Central Asia, a major source of war-horses. That is, these Turks were understood as powerful but familiar rivals in north India's crowded stage of contending lineages. But then in the late twelfth century another Turkish group, the Ghurids, would sweep away both the Ghaznavids and north India's martial clans, later called Rajputs, and put them on a path to eventually establishing the Delhi sultanate (1206–1526), a sultanate being, of course, a kingdom ruled by a sultan. Unlike the Ghaznavids, however, these later Turks had not yet been assimilated as one of north India's many ruling houses: on the contrary, they were wholly alien and unfamiliar, not to mention destructive. Accordingly, a contemporary Sanskrit epic, the *Prthviraj-vijaya*, lustily stigmatized them as outright 'barbarians' (*mlechha*s), 'demon-men' (*nararaksasam*), enemies of cows and 'given to eating foul foods'.[3] Yet, as destructive and alien as they were, the Ghurid Turks – like their Ghaznavid predecessors – were not identified by their religion. As the historian Cynthia Talbot notes, the image of Muslims in contemporary Indian texts 'oscillated depending on the prevailing political conditions: in times of military conflict and radically fluctuating spheres of influence, the rhetoric was often negative in tone; whereas long-established Muslim rulers were conceptually assimilated into the Sanskritic political imagination'.[4]

That said, the authors of the Persian chronicles, unlike their Indian counterparts, certainly did see the world through the lens of religion: people were either Muslim believers or infidels. But, we must ask, for whom did these writers speak? It is one thing for a pious chronicler to colour an event in ways that conformed to – or violated – his own sense of a properly ordered world. However, how culturally different communities actually interacted with one another, or what sorts of political and social modi vivendi they reached, can be another thing altogether. This means that, while Persian chronicles are indispensable in reconstructing India's history in our period, it would be a mistake to rely on that genre alone. Hence the present volume parts company with British-period historians of India, who obsessively adhered to written data to the exclusion of other kinds of evidence and placed excessive trust in Persian chronicles, which for them formed an unshakeable basis for the reconstruction of India's post-eleventh-century past. Not surprisingly, British histories of India written during the Raj tended to reproduce the very believer-vs-infidel mindset of the chroniclers whose Persian texts they used.

Another reason why many nineteenth- and early-twentieth-century historians replicated the religiously defined worldview of medieval Persian chroniclers relates to Britain's rationale for occupying India. The British came to justify the Raj on the grounds that they had introduced India to an enlightened era of sound and just government, a position logically requiring that rulers immediately preceding them be construed as despotic and unjust. Perhaps the clearest case of history-writing in service of the Raj is the work of Sir Henry M. Elliot, whose translations of Indo-Persian chronicles, *Bibliographical Index to the Historians of Muhammedan India*, first appeared in 1850. Elliot sought to use such chronicles to show readers how destructive Muslim rulers had been before the arrival of British rule. As he wrote in the Preface:

> The few glimpses ... we have of Hindus slain for disputing with
> Muhammadans, of general prohibitions against processions, worship,
> and ablutions, and of other intolerant measures, of idols mutilated, of
> temples razed, of forcible conversions and marriages, of proscriptions

and confiscations, of murders and massacres, and of the sensuality and drunkenness of the tyrants who enjoined them, show us that this picture is not overcharged.[5]

Elliot presents the advent of European rule, by contrast, as a period 'when a more stirring and eventful era of India's History commences; and when the full light of European truth and discernment begins to shed its beams upon the obscurity of the past'. Therefore, he concludes, reading translations of Indo-Persian chronicles – which he characterized as dull, prejudiced, ignorant and superficial – 'will make our native subjects more sensible of the immense advantages accruing to them under the mildness and equity of our rule'.[6] Within seven years, India would be consumed by the horrific Revolt of 1857 and its brutal suppression by British troops. Nonetheless, the rhetoric of the Raj's 'mildness and equity', in contrast to the 'Muhammadan' tyranny said to have preceded it, would prevail throughout Britain's occupation of India.

Other factors also inclined the British to see Indian history through the lens of religion. Students of South Asian history are aware of the charge that European rulers had deployed classic 'divide-and-rule' measures as a strategy for governing India. Already in the late eighteenth century, as the East India Company was gaining a political toehold on parts of South Asia, Governor General Warren Hastings established a legal system in which Muslims and non-Muslims were tried by separate law codes; henceforth, Muslims and non-Muslims would constitute juridically separate communities. The British then went on to establish a formidable array of publications – decennial census reports, district gazetteers, ethnographic surveys, etc. – that pigeonholed Indians into separate, watertight compartments using religion as a principal category. All this, so the argument goes, had the insidious effect of enhancing – some would even say creating – cultural divisions in an otherwise relatively harmonious Indian society.

Consider, too, how religion dominated European notions of Indian time. Comprehensive histories of India published in the nineteenth and twentieth centuries were typically divided into three periods: ancient, medieval and modern. The scheme dates at least to the 1817 publication of James Mill's *The History of British India*, which divided India's history into Hindu, 'Mahomedan' and British eras.[7] This tidy, tripartite scheme was actually a transposition on to India of the same ancient–medieval–modern scheme by which, ever since the Renaissance, Europeans had periodized their own history. In the South Asian case, however, those three temporal units were made to correspond to three culturally defined and supposedly homogeneous communities that had successively ruled most of the subcontinent. Formulated in this way, the system posited two great ruptures in Indian time. The first, which defined the transition from 'ancient' to 'medieval', implied a descent from an earlier Hindu 'golden' age to one of 'Mahomedan' tyranny. To India's British rulers, this decline corresponded to Europe's fall from an earlier age of Greco-Roman splendour to its own medieval period, initiated by the so-called 'Dark Ages'. Implicitly, then, the appearance of Muslim Turks in India was analogous to that of the Visigoths or Vandals in Rome: all were construed as alien outsiders whose armed intrusions had violated a sacred realm. Such a formulation allowed British imperialists to imagine India's second great historical rupture – the transition from 'medieval' times (i.e. Muslim rule) to modernity (i.e. British rule) – as having validated the coming of European governance as a blessing for a benighted land. By this self-serving formulation, Britain had liberated India from eight centuries of 'Muhammadan' stagnation.

While Indian Muslims in the modern period certainly did not share this view of India's middle period, many did see the advent of Islam as a transformative moment in India's history. Early leaders of the Pakistan movement, seeking a historical basis for justifying the creation of a separate Muslim state in post-British South Asia, propounded the so-called 'two-nation' theory. According to this understanding, India's Muslims had comprised a homogeneous and self-aware community objectively distinct from India's non-Muslims ever since the eighth century, when the earliest known Muslim community had appeared in the region. Therefore, the creation of an Islamic state merely acknowledged constitutionally what was held to have been a social reality for over a thousand years. In this way, too, Muhammad bin Qasim, the eighth-century Arab conqueror of Sind, in today's Pakistan, could be conjured up as a proto-nationalist figure, even as Pakistan's 'first citizen'.[8]

Conversely, in their efforts to locate their own moments of glory in India's past, many Hindu nationalists of the first half of the twentieth century imagined rebels against pre-colonial 'Muslim' states as heroes who were, in some small or inchoate way, struggling on behalf of an India-wide, pan-Hindu collectivity. Thus in the early twentieth century, during the twilight years of the Raj, two opposing nationalist narratives emerged, both driven by religion. And since any form of nationalism selectively picks and chooses from its past in order to endow the present with meaning, if not inevitability, both Hindus and Muslims politicized South Asia's history, in particular the eight centuries prior to the British arrival. One community's heroes became the other's villains, and vice versa, while both narratives interpreted the past in order to explain the present and justify an imagined future. India's 'medieval' history, in short, became a political football.

Although British rulers, Indian nationalists and Muslim separatists were motivated by very different agendas, each understood India's middle period as one in which religion comprised the fundamental building block of community identity, with the Muslim presence in India looming especially large in South Asia's collective consciousness. This is clearly reflected in the tradition of history-writing since the nineteenth century. In book after book, the tendency has been to list events, kings, battles and literary and religious texts in chronological order, each of them neatly divided into separate Hindu and Muslim compartments.[9] India was thus given two Procrustean beds, one Muslim and one Hindu, into one or the other of which nearly everything had to fit – architecture, dress, art, literature, language, and so on.[10] The British art historian Percy Brown, for example, could publish a two-volume study on Indian architecture, one volume covering the 'Buddhist and Hindu periods' and another the 'Muslim period.'

The reading of history in terms of mutually exclusive religions has, however, come at enormous cost. For one thing it has made it difficult to account for, or even to see, larger cultural processes. Consider the earliest genre of Hindi literature – the so-called *premakhyan*s, or Sufi romances – which appeared in the eastern Gangetic plain between the fourteenth and sixteenth centuries. This literature was composed originally in the Persian script by Sufis who narrated the seeker's mystical quest for union with God, but it did so using characters who were ostensibly Hindu in name and cultural/religious practice, in a landscape saturated with Indian deities, mythology, flora and fauna. Failing to fall neatly into either Hindu or Muslim categories, this literary genre baffled Ramchandra Shukla and other early-twentieth-century nationalist writers, who engaged in long and fruitless debates over whether or not this literature was truly Indian.[11]

The convention of seeing India mainly in terms of religion, and of dividing its history into three religiously defined units of time, is thus well entrenched. Although the present volume covers what historians in the tradition of James Mill labelled the 'Muslim' age, the aim is nonetheless to narrate this period on its own terms, and not to project on to it today's values or biases. For not only did India's socio-cultural landscape differ vastly from that of today: the conceptual categories by which peoples of earlier times understood that landscape did too. We might start, then, by rethinking the notion of a 'Muslim' conquest and, indeed, the proper place of religion in India's history during this period. But if religion is not to serve as the key to India's past, what might?

## TWO TRANSREGIONAL WORLDS: SANSKRIT AND PERSIANATE

Western Civilization, Dar al-Islam ('the abode of Islam'), Christendom, the Motherland, the Free World, the Promised Land, the Third World, the Middle Kingdom – these are just some of the terms in which people have imagined geographical space, attempting in each instance to impose culture or ideology on to territory. It can be a vexed enterprise. In recent years the Sanskritist and historian Sheldon Pollock, suggesting a very different way of thinking about cultural space, coined the term 'Sanskrit cosmopolis', referring to the diffusion of Indian culture across a vast swathe of Southern Asia between the fourth century and the fourteenth.[12] Sanskrit place names alone attest to the geographical sweep of a culturally connected zone between Afghanistan's Kandahar (Skt Gandhara) and the South-east Asian city state of Singapore (Skt Singhapura).

For Pollock, what characterized this Sanskrit world was not religion but the ideas elaborated in the entire corpus of Sanskrit texts that, between the fourth and fourteenth centuries, circulated above and across the world of vernacular, regional tongues. Sanskrit, like only a few others, was a language that travelled: it was not a 'language of place'. Not being identified with a particular ethnic or linguistic group or with a particular region, Sanskrit was transregional by nature, or, as Pollock puts it, 'a language of the gods in the world of men'. Texts composed in Sanskrit embraced everything from rules of grammar to styles of kingship, architecture, proper comportment, the goals of life, the regulation of society, the acquisition of power and wealth, and much more. The circulation of these texts and of the people who carried them created a network of shared idioms and styles that made similar claims about aesthetics, polity, kingly virtue, learning and the universality of dominion. Fundamentally, the Sanskrit world – that is, the vast sweep of territory in which such texts circulated and were considered normative – was concerned with defining and preserving moral and social order.

Moreover, this cultural formation expanded over much of Asia not by force of arms but by emulation, and without any governing centre or fortified frontiers. It was thus comparable to the Hellenized world that embraced the Mediterranean basin and the Middle East after Alexander the Great. For that world, too, was a cultural zone without political borders, in which people of many ethnic or religious backgrounds readily subscribed to the prestige of Greek language, sculpture, drama, cuisine, architecture and so on, but without paying taxes to a Greek official or submitting to the might of Greek soldiers. We may contrast this 'cosmopolis' idea with any classical empire, such as the Roman, with its centralized governing structure, sharp distinction between citizens and non-citizens, fortified frontiers and reliance on the hard power of coercive force as opposed to the soft power of models that encourage emulation.

The Sanskrit world that Pollock describes was, however, only one such formation to have appeared in South Asian history. From about the eleventh to the nineteenth centuries a similar, Persianate world embraced much of West, Central and South Asia. Both expanded and flourished well beyond the land of their origin, giving them a transregional, 'placeless' quality. Both were grounded in a prestige language

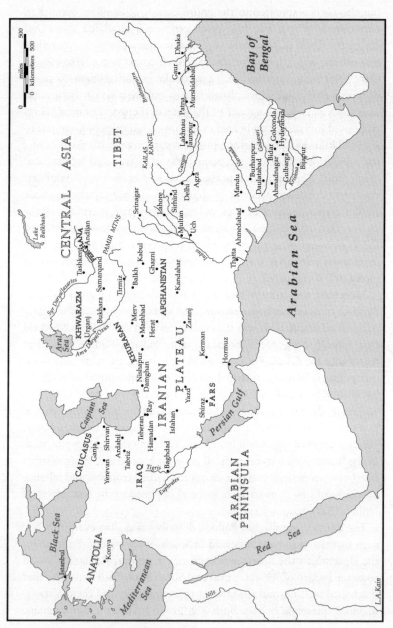

The Persianate world, 900–1900

and literature that conferred elite status on its users. Both articulated a model of worldly power – specifically, universal dominion. And while both elaborated, discussed and critiqued religious traditions, neither was grounded in a religion, but rather transcended the claims of any of them. Decoupled from particular religious systems, both of these transregional traditions could and did spread over great expanses of territory, and were embraced by peoples of varied ethnic and religious backgrounds. Fundamentally – and this is the underlying theme of this book – much of India's history between 1000 and 1800 can be understood in terms of the prolonged and multifaceted interaction between the Sanskrit and Persianate worlds.

But what exactly is the Persianate world, and how did it evolve?[13] Several centuries after the Arab conquest of the Iranian plateau in the seventh century, Persian-speakers gradually recovered a rich but largely submerged pre-Islamic Persian civilization. The linguistic dimension of this movement saw the emergence of New Persian – a hybrid of the indigenous Middle Persian of Iran's Sasanian period (AD 224–651) and the Arabic brought to the Iranian plateau in the course of the Arab conquest. This new language appeared first in spoken form across the Iranian plateau and deep into Central Asia. A written form using a modified Arabic script emerged in the ninth and tenth centuries, when Persian writers in present-day north-eastern Iran, western Afghanistan and Central Asia began appropriating the cultural heritage of both Arab Islam and pre-Islamic Iran.

Initially, at least, these developments were promoted and patronized by the court of the Samanid kings in Central Asia (819–999). Based in Bukhara (in today's southern Uzbekistan), the Samanid domain straddled major trade routes connecting the Iranian plateau with the Mediterranean to the west, India to the south and, via the Silk Road, China to the east. Bukhara thus lay in a commercially vibrant zone. It was also multilingual, as Arabic and Turkish were both commonly used there, as was, until the eleventh century, Sogdian. But New Persian (henceforth simply 'Persian') was now the lingua franca, having replaced the region's indigenous Iranian languages and dialects.

As with the Sanskrit texts, from the eleventh century onwards a large corpus of imaginative literature in Persian began to circulate widely through West, Central and South Asia. A case in point is the cycle of epics based on the historical Alexander penned by such luminaries as Firdausi (d. 1020) in Iran, Nizami (d. 1209) in Georgia, Amir Khusrau (d. 1325) in India and Jami (d. 1492) in Afghanistan. Although composed a great distance apart, and circulating over an even wider one that spanned many vernacular cultures, these works enabled diverse peoples to imagine and inhabit a single cosmopolitan space enlivened by Alexander's real – or imagined – exploits.[14] Such works of literature helped knit together a 'Persianate world' across West, Central and South Asia. However, like Sanskrit texts, Persian literature had no single geographical or political centre, especially after the thirteenth century when Mongol invaders overran Central Asia and northern Iran, destabilizing their courts. From that point on, peoples in far-flung regions such as the Caucasus or India might retain everyday use of their local languages while cultivating, and even producing, great works of Persian literature.[15] By the fourteenth century Persian had become a vibrant and prestigious literary language, a widely used medium in state bureaucracies, and the principal contact tongue for inter-regional diplomacy along the Silk Road between Anatolia and East Asia. In Mongol-dominated China, it served not only as a lingua franca but as the official foreign language. The Venetian merchant-traveller Marco Polo (d. 1324) mainly used Persian in China, as he did, in fact, throughout his travels on the Silk Road. So did his near-contemporary and even greater globetrotter Ibn Battuta (d. 1377), who travelled many of the same pan-Asian circuits in fourteenth-century Asia.[16]

Of particular relevance for understanding India's changed political order after the late twelfth century is what Persian writers had to say about power and authority. Crucially, the same culturally diverse milieu that had nurtured the literary and bureaucratic use of Persian under Samanid patronage also shaped a particular conception of a universal ruler or 'sultan', the title preferred by such men throughout the Persianate world. Occupying a political space above all ethnic groups and religious communities, this figure was understood as both universal and supreme: he occupied unlimited sovereign space and commanded the loyalty of all lesser political actors. The crystallization of the idea of the sultan in the tenth and eleventh centuries resulted from two factors in particular: the steady decline of the Abbasid cali-phate in Baghdad, which in theory ruled over the entire eastern Islamic world, including Central Asia; and the infiltration of waves of Turkish-speakers from eastern Asia into urbanized Central Asia and northern Iran. Some came as military recruits, others as pastoral nomadic migrants, others as powerful confederations of warriors. To accommodate these new realities, political thought in South-west Asia underwent drastic revisions. In particular, spiritual and political authority split into separate spheres, with the caliph retaining his reli-gious authority and the sultan exercising effective political power. Making the best of a bad situation, a leading theologian of the time, Abu Hamid al-Ghazali (d. 1111), pronounced that *any* government was lawful so long as its ruler, or sultan, acknowledged the caliph's authority in spiritual matters. Reciprocally, caliphs accepted the sec-ular authority of upstart sultans under the fiction of having appointed them to their office.

Stoking memories of pre-Islamic Iran, poets and chroniclers endowed these sultans with the same pretentions to absolutist rule as pre-Islamic Persian emperors. In the early twelfth century the histor-ian Ibn Balkhi conceived of kingship in that earlier age as based on the supreme principle of justice, for, he wrote, every king had taught his heir apparent the following maxim:

> There is no kingdom without an army, no army without wealth, no wealth without material prosperity, and no material prosperity with-out justice.[17]

Persian scholars such as Ibn Balkhi made no attempt to yoke state power to Islam or to any other religious tradition; instead, it was jus-tice that bound their world together. Notably, long before Renaissance or Enlightenment thinkers in Europe began theorizing the separation of Church and State, intellectuals in eleventh- and twelfth-century Iran and Central Asia were already doing precisely that. Such a secu-larist conception of government would have far-reaching implications for rulers styling themselves sultans in areas as ethnically diverse as India. In fact, by the time it reached India, the term 'sultan' had become so detached from ethnicity or religion that Hindu rulers, aspiring to the most powerful titles then available to them, adopted it. In 1347 Marappa, one of the founders of the Deccan kingdom of Vijayanagara, declared himself 'sultan among Indian kings' (*hinduraya-suratalah*), a title used also by his earliest successors.[18]

India's eventual inclusion in this expanding Persianate world was thus facilitated by, among other things, a ruling ideology that had co-opted the political authority of a caliph, embraced the principle of universal justice and accommodated cultural diversity. Such an inclusivist political ideology happened to be well suited for governing a north Indian society that was itself extraordinarily diverse religiously, linguistically and socially. Moreover, the elevation of justice, not religion, as the measure of proper governance allowed Persianized states to flourish throughout India, notwithstanding a ruler's own religion. As argued by Ziya al-Din Barani (d. *c.* 1357), a leading historian and theorist of the early Delhi sultanate, whereas any country could flourish under a non-Muslim ruler as long he was just, no country ruled by a Muslim would flourish if he was unjust.[19]

What is perhaps most remarkable about the Persianate world, however, is how readily its core ideas diffused not only within Indian territories governed by Persianized states such as the Delhi sultanate, but also into territories lying *beyond* such states. A distinctively Persianate ideology privileging the notion of justice and connecting economy, morality and politics infiltrated peninsular India even while that region was governed by independent Hindu rulers. At some point in the twelfth or thirteenth centuries the Telugu poet Baddena, writing at the Kakatiya court at Warangal in southern India, penned these striking lines:

> To acquire wealth: make the people prosper. To make the people prosper: justice is the means. O Kirti Narayana! They say that justice is the treasury of kings.[20]

In linking wealth, prosperity and justice, this terse aphorism seems to paraphrase Ibn Balkhi. Moreover, it is clear that the idea of justice, so central to Persian political thought, had been freely borrowed by Baddena and not imposed from without.[21] Like Mongol rulers on the Iranian plateau, Baddena had assimilated a Persianate vision of political and moral order, even though he lived very far from the Delhi sultanate.

Apart from political ideology, other aspects of Persian culture spread throughout South Asia after the thirteenth-century Turkish conquest of north India, including styles of architecture, dress, music, courtly comportment, cuisine and, especially, vocabulary. As the geographical reach of Persian letters expanded, so did the production of dictionaries, whose compilers sought to make literature produced in different parts of the Persophone world mutually comprehensible; by the nineteenth century, many more Persian-language dictionaries had been produced in India than in Iran, suggesting how thoroughly India had been absorbed into that world. Indeed, by the fourteenth century Persian had already become the most widely used language for governance across South Asia, as Indians filled the vast revenue and judicial bureaucracies in the Delhi sultanate and its successor states, and later in the Mughal empire (1526–1858) and its successors. As a result, a wide range of Persian words infiltrated the vocabulary of many of South Asia's major regional languages.

All of which brings us back to the theme of periodization, and the rationale for this book's chronological borders of 1000 and 1765. Recent generations of historians of India have rightly eschewed the old tripartite Hindu–Muslim–British scheme and have reverted to its European predecessor, the ancient-medieval-modern one. But the precise meaning of these timespans, especially the second, has remained elusive. Instead of giving substance to the term 'medieval', historians have produced a host of high-quality regional studies covering the whole or part of the period 1000–1800 – e.g. on Bengal, Gujarat, Malabar, Orissa, the Punjab, the Deccan plateau, the Delhi region, the Tamil country. As a result, the term 'medieval' when applied to India as a whole has become something of an orphan – repeatedly invoked, but lacking meaning. As the historian Daud Ali notes:

> the category of medieval has gradually been evacuated of any definitive substance in most national historiographies, in favour of a sort of cacophony of regional isolates simply holding the fort until the cavalry arrives.[22]

By 'the cavalry' Ali appears to mean some new conceptual handle or idea that might confer meaning on the term 'medieval', other than that of a religiously defined Muslim era.

I argue that there is such a handle. As it happens, the period of India's history conventionally labelled 'medieval' coincides with the eastward diffusion of Persianate culture across almost all the Indian subcontinent and its interaction with its Sanskrit counterpart. The story of this interaction – the encounter between the Persian and Sanskrit worlds – is both rich and complex. It is the subject of this book.

# I

# The Growth of Turkic Power,
## 1000–1300

## A TALE OF TWO RAIDS: 1022, 1025

In the early second millennium, within only three years of each other, two armies marching from opposite directions raided north India. Neither would remain to govern or colonize conquered territory. Although both expeditions were successful in their own ways, they harboured different objectives, had different martial traditions and were informed by very different political systems. The two invasions also suggest why the opening of the second millennium marked a major transition in India's long history.

The first of the two raids was led by a general acting on the authority of Rajendra I (r. 1014–44), maharaja of the Chola empire (848–1279) towards the extreme southern end of the Indian peninsula. In 1022 his army marched 1,600 kilometres north from the Cholas' royal and ceremonial capital of Tanjavur, moving along India's eastern coast. After subduing kings in Orissa, Chola warriors defeated rulers in the western and the south-central districts of the Ganges delta. Then, in a fiercely fought pitched battle, they defeated Mahipala, maharaja of the Pala empire (c.750–1161), at the time the dominant power in India's easternmost region of Bengal. The southerners crowned their victory by carrying off a bronze image of the deity Śiva, which they seized from a royal temple that Mahipala had presumably patronized [see Fig. 1]. In the course of this long campaign, the invaders also took from the Kalinga raja of Orissa images of Bhairava, Bhairavi and Kali. These, together with precious gems looted from the Pala king, were taken down to the Chola capital as war booty.[1]

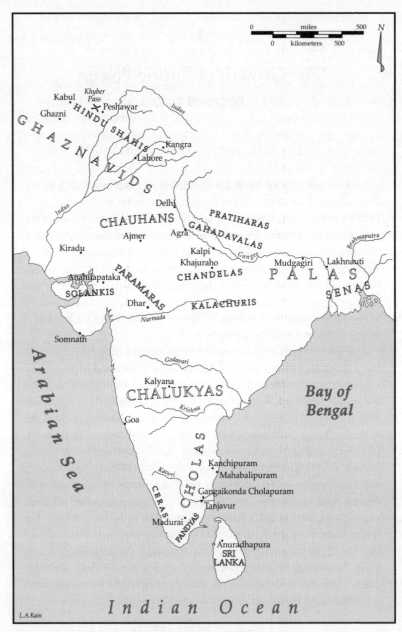

Major Indian dynasties, 975–1200

Before leaving the delta, however, Chola officers directed an operation unusual for military campaigns: they arranged for water from the Ganges River to be collected in pots and carried on the army's long march back to Tanjavur. In the Godavari River delta, midway between Bengal and the Chola heartland, Rajendra, who had been consolidating Chola rule in coastal districts north of his capital, joined the victorious army. From there, the combined forces triumphantly returned to Tanjavur. The Cholas were at this time nearing the zenith of their might and glory; they would soon become the dominant power in the eastern Indian Ocean, their influence stretching across the Bay of Bengal to Sumatra. In their own estimation, they occupied the centre of the earthly and cosmic worlds.

In October 1025, not long after Rajendra Chola's return from his conquests in Bengal, the son of a Turkish-speaking Central Asian slave marched out of Ghazni in eastern Afghanistan with 30,000 cavalry behind him. Heading south-east through the craggy ravines of the Sulaiman Mountains, he and his troops descended from the Afghan plateau into the low, lush Indus valley. Like his Chola contemporaries, Sultan Mahmud of Ghazni (r. 997–1030) planned to attack a specific north Indian target – the wealthy temple of Somnath, an important pilgrimage site on the shores of the Arabian Sea on Gujarat's southern coast. Built of stone a hundred years earlier and situated in a fortress that was surrounded by the sea on three sides, the temple of Somnath, like that of Mahipala in Bengal, was dedicated to the god Śiva. In December 1025, having crossed the Indus and marched across western India's forbidding Thar Desert, Mahmud reached the site, successfully besieged the fortress and plundered the famous temple of its riches. He also ordered its Śiva image to be broken up and its pieces taken back to Ghazni, his capital, to be set in a floor and walked upon.[2]

This was not Mahmud's first raid on north India. The sultan had already launched more than a dozen, beginning with an attack in 1001 on Peshawar, at the foot of the strategic Khyber Pass which connects the Afghan highlands with the Indus valley. Almost annually, similar offensives took place against prominent cities of the Punjab and the upper Ganges valley. In each of them, Mahmud's men brought plundered wealth back through the mountain passes leading to Ghazni.

What distinguished the Somnath raid from the others, however, was the way in which it captured the imagination of Persian chroniclers: those contemporary with the raid hailed Mahmud as an arch-iconoclast, piously responding to Islam's prohibition against image-worship. Subsequent chroniclers even lionized him as the founder of Turkish rule and of Islamic sovereignty in South Asia, although in fact he was neither of these.

In striking contrast to Persian chronicles, which made so much of Mahmud's raid on Somnath, Sanskrit inscriptions recorded by local Hindus made no mention of it at all. On the contrary, accounts dating to the months and years after the raid convey a sense of undisturbed business as usual for both the temple and the bustling seaport of Somnath, a major commercial entrepôt that imported war-horses from the Persian Gulf and exported locally produced textiles to markets around the Arabian Sea. Twelve years after the attack, a king from the Goa region recorded performing a pilgrimage to the temple, but he failed to mention Mahmud's raid. Another inscription dated 1169 mentioned repairs made to the temple owing to normal deterioration, but again without mentioning Mahmud's raid. In 1216 Somnath's overlords fortified the temple to protect it not from attacks by invaders from beyond the Khyber Pass, but from those by Hindu rulers in neighbouring Malwa; apparently, such attacks were so frequent as to require precautionary measures.[3] The silence of contemporary Hindu sources regarding Mahmud's raid suggests that in Somnath itself it was either forgotten altogether or viewed as just another unfortunate attack by an outsider, and hence unremarkable.

In fact, the demonization of Mahmud and the portrayal of his raid on Somnath as an assault on Indian religion by Muslim invaders dates only from the early 1840s. In 1842 the British East India Company suffered the annihilation of an entire army of some 16,000 in the First Afghan War (1839–42). Seeking to regain face among their Hindu subjects after this humiliating defeat, the British contrived a bit of self-serving fiction, namely that Mahmud, after sacking the temple of Somnath, carried off a pair of the temple's gates on his way back to Afghanistan. By 'discovering' these fictitious gates in Mahmud's former capital of Ghazni, and by 'restoring' them to their rightful owners in India, British officials hoped to be admired for heroically rectifying what they construed as a heinous wrong that had caused centuries of distress among India's Hindus. Though intended to win the latters' gratitude while distracting all Indians from Britain's catastrophic defeat just beyond the Khyber, this bit of colonial mischief has stoked Hindus' ill-feeling toward Muslims ever since.[4] From this point on, Mahmud's 1025 sacking of Somnath acquired a distinct notoriety, especially in the early twentieth century when nationalist leaders drew on history to identify clear-cut heroes and villains for the purpose of mobilizing political mass movements. By contrast, Rajendra Chola's raid on Bengal remained largely forgotten outside the Chola country.

On the surface, the military operations of Rajendra Chola and Mahmud of Ghazni would seem to have had much in common: both armies marched some 1,600 kilometres with a view to attacking and plundering specific north Indian sites; neither had any intent of occupation, annexation or permanent government; and both desecrated royal temples, carrying off plundered images to their respective capitals. But the differences between the two invasions are far more important than their similarities, since they highlight radically different political cultures in early-eleventh-century South Asia. The older of these two political cultures was informed by a body of Sanskrit texts that had circulated across India for many centuries before the rise of Chola power in south India. The other culture, informed by an analogous body of Persian texts, had come into being only two centuries before Mahmud's day.

## POLITICAL CULTURE IN THE SANSKRIT WORLD

The culture that had informed Rajendra Chola's political actions, including his raid on Bengal, was derived from Sanskrit treatises on power, wealth and rulership. It presumed a political universe crowded with little kings, bigger kings and emperors – that is, kings of kings. It also presumed a world of shifting political sands, where rulers had neither permanent enemies nor permanent allies. In conducting the business of warfare, therefore, classical Indian thought recommended that enemies not be annihilated, but rather co-opted and transformed into loyal subordinates[5] who could be put to use as allies against future enemies. Thus the same inscription that describes the Chola raid on Bengal records that when Rajendra returned from his victorious northern expedition:

> He [then] entered his own [capital] town, which by its prosperity despised all the merits of the abode of the gods – his lotus feet [all along] being worshipped by the kings of high birth who had been subdued [by him].6

In reality, of the eight kings that Rajendra or his generals are said to have fought on this expedition, one was killed in battle, two others fled the battlefield and the rest were 'conquered'. These defeated kings – or at least, the five who survived the Chola invasion – were not executed or publicly humiliated. Instead, they became loyal vassals.

Such an outcome conformed to well-defined norms of inter-state politics long canonized in classical Indian thought.[7] According to these norms, territory was imagined as something like a large chessboard on which kings manoeuvred with allies and against rivals with a view to creating an idealized political space called the Circle of States, or *mandala*. The term referred to a series of concentric circles, where one's own capital and heartland was at the centre, surrounded by a second circle of one's allies, and a third circle of one's enemies. Beyond that lay a fourth circle occupied by one's enemies' enemies, understood as potential allies with whom a king endeavoured to ally himself. With all of India's major dynastic houses playing by the same geostrategic rules, the result was not only intense political jockeying and perpetual conflict, but overall stalemate and equilibrium.[8] No single dynastic house could achieve lasting dominance over large tracts of territory within India, much less over South Asia as a whole. Indeed, it is hardly surprising that the game of chess itself originated in India around the sixth century, just when these geopolitical ideas were taking hold.[9]

Rajendra's father Rajaraja (r. 985–1014) is widely acclaimed as the greatest of Chola emperors, as judged by his conquests and the literature and art he patronized, including his building of one of the grandest temples in south India, the Rajarajeśvaram (or Brihadeśwara) Temple in his capital of Tanjavur. The temple was designed to replicate cosmic space and to situate itself at the centre of that space; one of its names is 'Daksinameru', or the southern Mt Meru – that is, the axis of the universe.[10] Much of the wealth necessary for patronizing the king's cultural projects derived from his successful deployment of the *mandala* strategy on India's geopolitical chessboard. From the Cholas' heartland in the fertile Kaveri delta, Rajaraja had waged a series of victorious military campaigns, defeating in turn the Pandya kings of Madurai to his south and the Cera kings of Kerala to his west. Since these two dynasties had been allied with the Buddhist kings of Sri Lanka, Rajaraja launched a naval expedition to the island kingdom and sacked its ancient capital of Anuradhapura, making him the first Indian king to embark on overseas conquests. Just as importantly, these conquests validated Rajaraja's claims to being a universal emperor (*chakravartin*) since, according to classical Indian political thought, such an emperor had to perform a *digvijaya*, or 'conquest of the quarters' – that is, kingdoms to the south, west, north and east.

In 1014, when Rajaraja died, Rajendra, who had been co-emperor at the end of his father's reign, became Chola emperor in his own right. One of Rajendra's inscriptions records that he soon thereafter 'turned his attention to the conquest of the quarters [*digvijaya*] backed by a powerful army'. In 1017 he launched a fresh invasion of Sri Lanka, conquering the entire island, of which his father had occupied only the northern portion. The next year he reconquered the Pandya king to his south and the raja of Kerala to his west. In 1021 he attacked the Chalukyas of Kalyana, an ascendant dynasty based in the heart of the Deccan plateau. Having defeated that house, Rajendra returned to his capital before moving his army towards Bengal, thereby continuing his clockwise *digvijaya*. But the inscription discloses another rationale for the expedition to Bengal. 'This light of the Solar race [Rajendra],' it says,

> laughing at Bhagiratha who had brought down the Ganga [to the earth from heaven] by the power of [his] austerities, wished to sanctify his own country with the waters of the Ganga [i.e. the Ganges] carried thither through the strength of [his] arm. Accordingly [he]

ordered the commander of the army who had powerful battalions [under his control], who was the resort of heroism [and] the foremost of diplomats – to subdue the enemy kings occupying [the country on] the banks of that [river].[11]

This passage refers to a Hindu myth, visually narrated in a stunning seventh-century seaside bas-relief at Mahabalipuram (or Mamallapuram, near modern Chennai), according to which the ascetic Bhagiratha, by performing rigorous austerities, induced the great god Śiva to water the parched earth by bringing the Ganges down from heaven. The parallel between Bhagiratha and Rajendra is clear: if an ascetic had mythically brought the river down from heaven to earth, King Rajendra would ritually bring it down from north India to Tanjavur.

Rajendra attached great importance to his raid on Bengal and the pots of Ganges water that he brought south to his capital. Not only did he assume the title Gangaikonda-Chola ('the Chola who took the Ganges River'), but he built a new capital in the Kaveri delta named Gangaikonda Cholapuram, or 'the city of the Chola who took the Ganges'. This he embellished with a colossal temple to Śiva whose central, nine-storey shrine soars to a height of fifty-six metres. Inside, he had a well dug for the sacred Ganges water into which was placed a statue of a lion, a Chola dynastic symbol. Completed in 1035, the temple served to publicize Rajendra's military successes in conquering not just neighbouring kingdoms, but – symbolically – all India. Standing on either side of the main temple are two shrines, called Northern and Southern Kailash, which refer to the sacred Himalayan mountain in which dwells Śiva himself, the Lord of the Universe. By, as it were, bringing this mountain into the heart of the temple precincts, the Chola monarch architecturally asserted both his affinity with the great god and his claim to universal sovereignty. Ritually, the Ganges, too, was relocated to the heart of Rajendra's empire – a striking instance of how India's sacred landscape could be metaphorically manipulated to serve a political purpose.

The invasions of Sri Lanka by Rajendra Chola and his father also led to the extension of Indian influence across the Bay of Bengal and on to the mainland and islands of South-east Asia. In fact, with their maritime contacts stretching as far as the South China Sea, the Cholas were the most outward-looking Indian state in their day, joining Arabs, Persians, Malays and Chinese in a transregional commercial system. Around 1025 Rajendra Chola embarked on a grand naval campaign against the kingdom of Śrivijaya, which ruled over much of the Malay peninsula and Sumatra. Since the Cholas had maintained diplomatic contact with China since 1015, their subsequent control of the Straits of Malacca, together with the tributary suzerainty they exercised over Śrivijaya, enabled direct Indo-Chinese maritime trade, unmediated by Śrivijaya authorities. In effect, the territories under Śrivijaya's rule became incorporated within the Chola kingdom's *mandala*, or circle of tributary states, the legacy of which survives today in the ordinary term for the Tamil coast: Coromandel, a corruption of 'Chola mandala'.

The *mandala* theory not only informed inter-state relations, however. Its logic also sowed the seeds of decline for its participant states. Since bestowing land on vassals was understood as a mark of royal dignity, the greater a king's pretensions to imperial grandeur or universal dominion, the more land and authority he was obliged to bestow on courtiers or vassals. But this was ultimately a self-defeating enterprise, as is seen in the case of the Chalukya kings of Kalyana (974–1190), the Cholas' principal rivals for control of the Deccan plateau. From the mid twelfth century on, that dynasty's subordinate rulers increasingly appear in inscriptions bearing exalted titles and enjoying powers to grant land, dispose of local revenues, wage war and administer civil and criminal justice. Mere generals were given the most prestigious insignia of royalty, such as the white umbrella, the great drum and the fly-whisk. Although in theory the Chalukya emperor remained the supreme bestower of such honours, over time even this prerogative was delegated to feudal lords in his confidence.[12] Ultimately, ceding so much authority only encouraged larger feudatory lineages to assert their autonomy from their imperial overlords, a process that effectively hollowed out the Chalukya crown to an empty shell. By the end of the twelfth century the dynasty's most prominent vassal states – the Hoysalas in southern Karnataka, the Kakatiyas in Andhra, the Yadavas in upland Maharashtra – had all emerged as independent kingdoms. The pattern was repeated across the subcontinent.[13] By the eleventh century not only was India as a whole divided into many dynastic houses, but those houses were further internally divided, as vassals and smaller chieftains built up their own courts, replicating in miniaturized form the rituals and retinues of their overlords.

These political ideas were closely intertwined with religion, inasmuch as sovereign rule over royal territory was formally invested in a patron deity – usually a form of Śiva or Vishnu – in relation to whom a king was conceived as a mere servant. The king honoured his Cosmic Overlord by patronizing Brahmin priests to interact with the deity and by sponsoring the construction of monumental temples in which that deity's image was housed. Such ideas radically transformed India's built landscape, which by the tenth century had become dotted with royal temples. Situated in a king's capital city, these structures were typically richly endowed, elaborately carved and often covered with gold. But such magnificent monuments carried risks for their royal patrons. Since they visually expressed a king's claims to legitimate authority, royal temples were also highly charged political institutions, and as such were subject to attack by enemy kings who, wanting to expand their own circle of tributary rulers, sought to desecrate the most visible sign of a king's sovereignty – his temple. Someśvara III (r. 1127–39), an emperor of the Deccan plateau's Chalukya dynasty, bluntly made the case for such action: 'The enemy's capital city should be burned – the palace of the king, beautiful buildings, palaces of princes, ministers and high-ranking officers, temples, streets with shops, horse and elephant stables.'[14]

Gujarat's temple of Somnath, as noted above, had been fortified in 1216 to protect it from attacks by Hindu rulers in neighbouring Malwa. Recorded instances of Indian kings attacking the temples of their political rivals date from at least the eighth century, when Bengali troops destroyed what they thought was the image of Vishnu Vaikuntha, Kashmir's state deity under King Lalitaditya (r. 724–60). In the early ninth century Govinda III, a king of the Deccan's Rashtrakuta dynasty (753–982), invaded and occupied Kanchipuram in the Tamil country. Intimidated by this action, the king of nearby Sri Lanka sent Govinda several (probably Buddhist) images that the

Rashtrakuta king then installed in a Śiva temple in his capital. At about the same time the Pandya King Śrimara Śrivallabha (r. 815–62) also invaded Sri Lanka and took back to his capital at Madurai, in India's extreme south, a golden Buddha image – a symbol of the integrity of the Sinhalese state – that had been installed in the island kingdom's Jewel Palace. In the early tenth century, King Herambapala of north India's Pratihara dynasty (c.750–1036) seized a solid-gold image of Vishnu Vaikuntha when he defeated the king of Kangra, in the Himalayan foothills. By mid-century the same image had been seized from the Pratiharas by the Chandela King Yasovarman (r. 925–45), who installed it in the Lakshmana Temple of Khajuraho, the Chandelas' capital in north-central India. In the mid eleventh century the Chola King Rajadhiraja (r. 1044–52), Rajendra's son, defeated the Chalukyas and raided their capital, Kalyana, in the central Deccan plateau, taking a large black stone door guardian to his capital in Tanjavur, where it was displayed as a trophy of war.[15] In the late eleventh century, the Kashmiri King Harsha (r. 1089–1111) raised the plundering of enemy temples to an institutionalized activity. In the late twelfth and early thirteenth centuries, kings of the Paramara dynasty (800–1327) attacked and plundered Jain temples in Gujarat.[16] Although the dominant pattern here was one of looting and carrying off the images of state deities, we also hear of Hindu kings destroying their enemies' temples. In the early tenth century, the Rashtrakuta monarch Indra III (r. 914–29) not only demolished the temple of Kalapriya (at Kalpi near the Jamuna River), patronized by the Rashtrakutas' deadly enemies the Pratiharas, but took special delight in recording the fact.[17]

Rajendra Chola's seizure of the Śiva image from the Palas of Bengal in 1022, then, was hardly unique. In order to sever the links between a defeated king and the visible manifestation of his divine patron, it was necessary to carry off images or in other ways desecrate his royal temples. Consequently, a high level of inter-state violence between the ninth and thirteenth centuries inevitably accompanied efforts to create idealized *mandala*s and to transform neighbouring enemies into subordinate vassals. Conquest of the quarters was built into the politics of the day.

## POLITICAL CULTURE IN THE
## PERSIANATE WORLD

If Rajendra Chola's raid on Bengal had operated within the world of the *mandala*, the *digvijaya* and South Asia's sacred geography, Mahmud of Ghazni's 1025 raid on Somnath – like his sixteen previous raids on northern India – was driven by very different ideas. The core of Mahmud's forces was composed of Turkish slaves or *mamluks*, who, as young men typically captured in war and separated from their kin groups, had been recruited to eastern Afghanistan from Central Asia on account of their exceptional military skills. They were 'Turks' inasmuch as their native language was Turkish, dialects of which in the eleventh century were spoken from the western frontiers of China across Central Asia to the Oxus River (Turkish-speakers would not occupy Anatolia – that is, most of present-day Turkey – until several centuries later). And they were slaves inasmuch as they were attached neither to their natal kin nor to land, but to their masters, who were typically state officials. But, because they were entrusted with weapons and lived in close quarters with their masters, this type of 'elite' or 'military' slavery differed fundamentally from the plantation slavery typical of the early modern Atlantic world.

The kingdom that Mahmud inherited, the Ghaznavid sultanate (975–1187), had arisen from its declining parent Samanid kingdom in Central Asia (819–999) at a time when this sort of military slavery was already a well-established institution. In 962 the Samanid commander-in-chief, Alptigin, abandoned the court in Bukhara and carved out a semi-independent state with its capital in Ghazni, in eastern Afghanistan. He was succeeded in 975 by his slave Sabuktigin, who, after consolidating his rule as an independent sovereign, launched a number of raids on the ruler of Peshawar in the northwestern corner of the Indus valley. On his death in 997, Sabuktigin was succeeded not by another slave but by his own son, Mahmud, thereby launching a new dynasty at Ghazni.

Like their Samanid predecessors, the Ghaznavid sultans continued to recruit Turkish slaves and freemen from Central Asia, where cavalry warfare, together with the breeding and herding of horses, had been woven into the fabric of pastoral life. Even young boys acquired exceptional riding skills, including shooting arrows at full gallop. Writing in the ninth century, the Arab historian al-Jahiz captured the awe with which outsiders viewed these fighters:

> If a thousand of their [Turks'] horse join battle and let off a single shower of arrows, they can mow down a thousand [Arabs'] horse. No army can withstand this kind of assault. The Kharajites and the Bedouin have no skill worth mentioning in shooting from horseback, but the Turk can shoot at beasts, birds, hoops, men, sitting quarry, dummies and birds on the wing, and do so at full gallop to fore or to rear, to left or to right, upwards or downwards, loosing ten arrows before the Kharajite can nock one ... and if they do turn their back, they are to be feared as much as deadly poison and sudden death; for their arrows hit the mark as much when they are retreating as when they are advancing.[18]

By contrast, Indian archers in Mahmud's day were for the most part infantrymen, mounted archery not being widespread. Additionally, a shortage of extensive pastures and competition from sedentary agriculture in India drastically reduced the supply of war-horses.[19] This was never an issue in Central Asia. Moreover, by inhabiting the heart of the vast, intercommunicating zone between China and the Mediterranean basin, the peoples of Central Asia readily adopted both offensive and defensive military technologies that passed along the trade routes connecting the two ends of Eurasia. These included not only the most efficient technologies associated with horsemanship, such as iron stirrups or heavy saddles, but also siege equipment such as the trebuchet, which was used for hurling large missiles, or mortar for cementing masonry in the bastions and curtain walls of forts.

Central Asian Turks and north Indian warrior clans also inherited very different conceptions of political territory. North Indian ruling lineages were organized in large, patrilineal kin groups which were dispersed on to ancestral lands and controlled the peasant society that produced the land's surplus wealth. This link between land and kin inclined such clans to identify strongly with particular, ancestral territories. As pastoralists in Central Asia, Turks had also been organized into lineage groups, but their kin ties had been distorted by the institution of military slavery, which detached them from their clans and took them into unfamiliar households in eastern Afghanistan or Khurasan – that is, the Persian-speaking region embracing today's north-eastern Iran, western Afghanistan and the territory up to the Oxus. Whether as mobile pastoral nomads in Central Asia or as uprooted slaves serving sultanates in Khurasan or Afghanistan, Turks had little or no attachments to ancestral lands. This inclined them to envision political space as open and unbounded, which helps explain the elastic, expansive nature of sultanates, in India or elsewhere. By contrast, states of eleventh-century north India, such as Rajendra Chola's empire in the south, were rooted in the ideology of the *mandala*, with its fixed centre based on a maharaja's palace or royal temple, surrounded by concentric circles populated by allies and enemies.

What gave the Ghaznavid Turks their special character, and perhaps their clearest contrast with contemporary Indian states, were the geostrategic forces driving their continued raids on north India in the early eleventh century. Those raids aimed not at appropriating territory but at plundering wealthy cities and their temples, especially for gold or silver. Taken back to Ghazni, this bullion was typically melted down into coins to finance campaigns in Central Asia and Iran, where the annexation of land was very much the objective. Cash was also needed for purchasing war-horses, slaves and manufactured goods, and for paying the salaries of Mahmud's army and administrative hierarchy. As this hierarchy was elaborated, and as the size of the army grew with the addition of more mercenaries or slaves, ever more cash was needed to pay them. This in turn required still more raw treasure, readily acquired by launching more raids, for which still more troops were needed. The result was a self-catalysing cycle that was inherently expansive and predatory, based above all on mobile wealth. The raids also reversed historic patterns in the transregional flow of precious metals.[20] Whereas for centuries such metals had poured into India, mainly in payment for textiles and spices, after the early eleventh century the bulk of precious metals began flowing from India to Central Asia and the Middle East, both for trade and for maintaining Ghaznavid armies in those regions. In 1009 alone Mahmud seized seventy million minted coins, amounting to 136 metric tons of silver, from the mountain fortress of Kangra in modern Himachal Pradesh.[21]

The transregional circulation of wealth through Central Asia, the Iranian plateau and north India was the material counterpart to a growing canon of Persian texts that spread through those same regions. By elaborating distinctive norms of kingship, governance, courtly etiquette, social comportment, Sufi piety, poetry, art, architecture and so on, these texts provided the ideological scaffolding that sustained an emerging Persianate world. At the same time, royal courts, regional political centres, the lodges or shrines of Sufi shaikhs (venerated religious leaders) and schools (*madrasas* or *maktabs*) provided the institutional bases from and through which such texts circulated. From the days of Mahmud of Ghazni on, these networks spread across ever greater stretches of territory. And, as this happened, an urbane, literate and transregional Persianate culture defined by an evolving literary canon was superimposed over a number of vernacular ones.[22] The prestige associated with this culture also attracted non-Persian-speaking peoples into its field of influence. In particular, from the ninth century confederations of Turkish-speaking pastoralists migrated westwards from the fringes of western China into Central Asia and the eastern rim of the Iranian plateau, which included Khurasan and Afghanistan. As these nomadic or semi-nomadic peoples encountered Persian-speaking peoples of Central Asian oasis towns and their rural hinterlands, they rapidly assimilated both the Persian language and the broader Persianate culture associated with that region's agrarian and urban classes. Whenever they achieved positions of power – thanks to their equestrian and fighting skills – these Persianized Turks lavishly patronized the entire gamut of Persian culture, not least in order to earn political legitimacy for themselves in an expanding Persianate world.

It was the Ghaznavid sultans, successors to Mahmud, who initiated the diffusion of Persian culture into north India. In 1040 Mahmud's son Mas'ud (r. 1030–40) launched an expedition to recover the city of Merv (in modern Turkmenistan) from another confederation of Persianized Turks that would soon dominate the Middle East – the Seljuqs (1037–1194). He failed to do so, and the defeated sultan was forced to flee across the Indus before being assassinated by one of his own men. Having lost their realm in Iran and Central Asia to Seljuq power, Mas'ud's successors then focused their energies on south-eastern

Afghanistan and north-west India, with Lahore serving as their base in the Punjab. After several decades of instability, the second half of the eleventh century saw the relatively steady reign of Sultan Ibrahim (r. 1059–99), who resumed the dynasty's earlier policy of raiding deep in the Gangetic plain, even capturing Agra in the late 1080s.[23] But eighteen years after his death his dynasty's old nemesis, the Seljuqs, struck from the west, sacking Ghazni in 1117 and reducing the Ghaznavid sultan, Bahram Shah (r. 1117–57), to a tributary vassal. In 1135 the Seljuks struck again, forcing Bahram Shah to take temporary refuge in Lahore. The final blow to the Ghaznavids' splendid capital came in 1150, when a deadly feud broke out between Bahram Shah and one of the Ghaznavids' former vassals – the ruler of Ghur, in mountainous central Afghanistan – who burned the city to the ground. For seven days Ghazni was plundered, with a reported 60,000 slain and many splendid palaces, schools and mosques destroyed, justly giving the Ghurid chieftain the sobriquet *Jahan-suz*, 'one who sets the world ablaze'. Also lost in that attack was the library of the great philosopher and polymath Ibn Sina (Avicenna, d. 1037), which had been brought to Ghazni from Isfahan in 1034.[24] The city never regained its former glory. A severely weakened Ghaznavid state now fell back on Lahore, which became the dynasty's capital until 1186, when it too was overrun by the rulers of Ghur.

Deprived of their direct ties with Central Asia – and with it their access to Turkish slaves, mercenaries and war-horses – the later Ghaznavids lost their wider, imperial vision and acquired the character of a regional, north Indian state. They were certainly not seen as menacing aliens who might have posed a civilizational threat to Indian culture. Contemporary Sanskrit inscriptions refer to the Ghaznavids not as Muslims but as *turushka*s (Turks), an ethnic term, or as *hammira*s, a Sanskritized rendering of *amir* (Arabic for commander), an official title.[25] For their part, in the eleventh and twelfth centuries Ghaznavid rulers in India issued coins from Lahore bearing the same legends that had appeared on those of their Indian predecessors, the Hindu Shahi dynasty (*c.*850–1002). These included Śiva's bull Nandi and the Sanskrit phrase *śri samanta deva* (Honourable Chief Commander) inscribed in Devanagari script.[26] Such measures point to the later Ghaznavids' investment in establishing cultural and monetary continuity with north Indian kingdoms. Moreover, despite the dynasty's rhetoric about defending Sunni Islam, religion posed no bar to military recruitment, as Indians had always been prominent in Ghaznavid armies. In 1033 Mahmud of Ghazni gave the command of his army stationed in Lahore to a Hindu general, and in Ghazni itself Indian military contingents had their own commanders, inhabited their own quarter of the city, and were generally considered more reliable soldiers than the Turks.[27]

Crucially, the Ghaznavids brought to the Punjab the entire gamut of Persianate institutions and practices that would define the political economy of much of India for centuries to come. Inherited from the creative ferment of tenth-century Khurasan and Central Asia under the Samanid rulers of Bukhara, these included: the elaboration of a ranked and salaried bureaucracy tied to the state's land revenue and military systems; the institution of elite, or military, slavery; an elaboration of the office of 'sultan'; the courtly patronage of Persian arts, crafts and literature; and a tradition of spiritually powerful holy men, or Sufis, whose relations with royal power were ambivalent, to say the least.

The first of these, the institution of a salaried bureaucracy, was based on the principle of state-run revenue assignments known as *iqta*'s, which were defined units of land whose revenues were collected by the assignee, or *iqta'dar*. From these revenues the *iqta'dar* was required to recruit, train, equip and command a stipulated number of troops who would be available to the sultan on demand. The state's revenue and military systems were thus tightly integrated. *Iqta'* lands were assigned to free nobles as well as to high-ranking slaves who enjoyed the special confidence of the sultan. Although the *iqta'* system had evolved in Iraq and western Iran in the ninth and tenth centuries, Ghaznavid rulers do not appear to have used it until the late eleventh century, when they could no longer rely on war booty to finance government operations, as they had done in the dynasty's early days.[28]

The institution of military slavery was also inherited from earlier practice in Iraq. From the ninth century, rulers in Baghdad had recruited Turks in Central Asia to serve the Abbasid caliphate (750–1258), entrusting them with both military and administrative responsibilities. As young men uprooted from their natal communities and recruited for service in a distant court, military slaves embodied a deep paradox. Having no traceable genealogy in a Persian-ordered universe where purity of blood translated into high status, they were lowly non-persons. But as well-trained elite soldiers given arms and close proximity to a ruling dynasty, they possessed power, wealth and the opportunity for advancement. For courts plagued with internal factionalism, it made strategic sense to stabilize central authority by recruiting powerful outsiders from Central Asia's vast military labour market, and to place them under the tutelage of trusted state officers. These masters trained, equipped, fed and socialized their slave charges into a sultanate's culture. As kinless aliens, they were rendered totally dependent on their masters, enhancing their presumed loyalty to the state. As the institution matured, ties of mutual trust and affection evolved; slaves close to a royal household were understood as fictive sons who might be praised even above biological sons for their loyalty and dedication.[29] For these reasons, from the tenth century to the fourteenth, thousands of Central Asian Turks were recruited to serve not only the Arab Abbasid dynasty in Baghdad but, in far greater numbers, native Persian dynasties such as the Samanids in Bukhara, and later the Ghaznavids and their client chieftains.

Overarching the entire political system loomed the sultan, an absolute sovereign whose political authority in the ninth and tenth centuries grew in tandem with the decline of that of the caliph in Baghdad. By the dawn of the eleventh century, sultanates evolved a de facto separation of religion and state. As the successor to the Prophet of Islam, the caliph still possessed religious authority, but sultans – or *amir*s or *malik*s, as they were called before 1002[30] – now held effective political authority. Moreover, since these political developments coincided with the revival of Persian culture in the Samanid court, Persian writers and theorists in Bukhara and elsewhere on the Iranian plateau endowed the office of sultan with the absolutist trappings of the ancient pre-Islamic Persian *shahanshah*, or 'king of kings', a title revived in western Iran by rulers of the Buyid dynasty (934–1062). In courtly discourse, the sultan *was* the state, while the world, as the political theorist Fakhr al-Din Razi (d. 1209) metaphorically put it, 'is a garden, whose gardener is the state'.[31]

But the sultan was not the only claimant to worldly authority. Also emerging amidst a declining caliphal state in Baghdad and the flores-cence of Persian culture in Samanid Central Asia was a substantial body of literature that had grown up around vivid and charismatic spiritual personalities, Sufi shaikhs, who had played a key role in assimilating Turkish groups to Sunni Islam as the latter migrated through Central Asia into Khurasan and Iran. Sufis sought a direct experience of divine reality and postulated a vision of authority that sometimes complemented and sometimes opposed that of royal courts. Sultans certainly possessed power, reinforced by all the pomp and glory inherited from pre-Islamic Persian imperial traditions. But, in a discourse challenging such claims, Sufi texts suggested that rulers were entrusted with only a temporary lease of earthly authority, granted to them through the grace of some spiritually powerful shaikh. Possessing a special nearness to God, it was shaikhs, not princes or kings, who had the better claim to being God's true repre-sentatives on earth. From this perspective, all things in God's creation were understood as dependent on a hierarchy of spiritually powerful Sufis, or 'God's unruly friends', as they have been characterized.[32] Such a view, needless to say, was difficult to reconcile with the courtly vision of an all-powerful sultan and his flock of tax-paying subjects.

Whether arriving as invaders or immigrants, then, Persianized Turks brought to India two competing visions of legitimate authority and power: a Sufi discourse that circulated mainly among Muslims, and a courtly discourse that claimed validity across all communities. Both of them, however, sharply contrasted with India's chessboard-world of the *mandala* and the *digvijaya*, which so preoccupied north India's warrior clans as to blind them to the storm clouds that, by the end of the twelfth century, were gathering beyond the Khyber Pass.

## THE GHURID CONQUEST OF NORTH INDIA, 1192–1206

For most of the twelfth century, the Seljuqs and Ghaznavids ruled over Khurasan and Afghanistan respectively. But this changed in the latter part of that century when the Ghaznavids' steady decline cre-ated a power vacuum in eastern Afghanistan and the Punjab. That

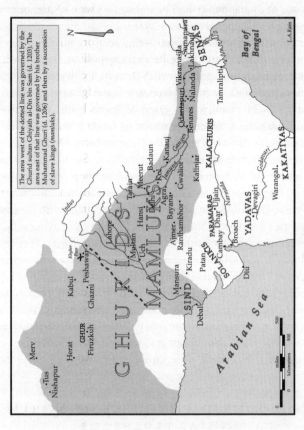

The area west of the dotted line was governed by the Ghurid sultan Ghiyath al-Din bin Sam (d. 1203). The area east of that line was governed by his brother Muhammad Ghuri (d. 1206) and then by a succession of slave kings (*mamluks*).

Ghurids and Mamluks, 1175–1290

vacuum would be filled not by the Ghaznavids' historic rivals, the Seljuqs, but by one of their own former client states – Ghur, a kingdom centred in the remote and rugged heart of Afghanistan's Hindu Kush Mountains. Rising from obscurity in the mid twelfth century, chieftains of this kingdom would soon roll over the Ghaznavids on their way to defeating the dominant martial lineage of northern Rajasthan, the Chauhans, thereby paving the way for the establishment of the Delhi sultanate (1206–1526).

Whereas the Ghaznavid ruling family had originated as Turkish slaves who cultivated and patronized cosmopolitan Persian culture, the Ghurids were free, pastoral chieftains in a culturally marginalized and geographically remote backwater of Afghanistan. They had been converted to Islam only a few generations before they abruptly broke out of their mountain strongholds on to the plains of India, adhering until the late twelfth century to an obscure but zealous sect, the Karramiya, considered deviant by mainline Sunni Muslims. Ethnically they were of eastern Iranian origin, but their dialect of Persian was so distinct from that of contemporary Iran or Khurasan that the Ghaznavid sultan Mas'ud needed the help of interpreters when he campaigned in their territory.[33]

The chiefs of Ghur would not remain obscure for long, however. In the mid twelfth century they burst on to the world stage, building with astonishing speed a multicultural empire that straddled both sides of the Hindu Kush range. To the east, their capture of Ghazni in 1148 marked their first toehold on the north-western rim of the subcontinent. To the west, in Khurasan, they seized from the Seljuqs the cosmopolitan city of Herat in 1175, and in 1201 the oasis cities of Merv, Tus and Nishapur. Two brothers co-governed the sultanate during its rapid expansion in the last quarter of the twelfth century. The senior partner, Sultan Ghiyath al-Din bin Sam (r. 1163–1203), ruled from the Ghurid capital of Firuzkuh in west-central Afghanistan and focused on first conquering and then governing the great Khurasani cities long associated with urban Persian culture: Herat, Nishapur, Tus and Merv. His aspirations to appropriate this culture are seen in his renovation of Herat's congregational mosque, next to which lies his own mausoleum. A culturally rich and cosmopolitan city, Herat at this time was reported to have had 12,000 shops, 6,000 baths and

444,000 households[34] – figures that, though probably inflated, would have far surpassed contemporary Paris's estimated population of 110,000.

Ghiyath al-Din's younger brother and junior partner in this diarchy was Shihab al-Din bin Sam, or Mu'izz al-Din, commonly known as Muhammad of Ghur, or simply Muhammad Ghuri (r. 1173–1206). He governed Ghazni in eastern Afghanistan and for more than three decades used that city as a base for launching military and political operations in north India. These began in 1175, when he marched through the Kurram Pass to the middle Indus valley and attacked the Isma'ili Muslim community in Multan. Three years later he advanced into Gujarat, sacking the Śiva temple at Kiradu. Up to this point, the sultan was following Mahmud of Ghazni's policy of a century and a half earlier, raiding Indian sites for plunder in order to finance his dynasty's imperial ambitions to the west. But his intentions soon turned to seizing and holding territory in upper India. In 1176 he captured Peshawar and secured the Khyber Pass, giving him direct access to the Indian plains from his base in Ghazni. In 1181 he attacked but failed to capture Lahore, capital of the last Ghaznavid sultan, Khusrau Malik (r. 1160–86). The next year he secured his southern flank to India by seizing the Sindi port of Debal. In 1186 he successfully took Lahore, finally extinguishing the Ghaznavid dynasty. Then in 1191 he engaged the Chauhan maharaja, Prithviraj III, at Tarain, 120 kilometres north of Delhi. Here the sultan suffered his first defeat, as well as a wound to his arm caused by an Indian spear.

Muhammad Ghuri spent the next year regrouping in Ghazni. There he prepared for a return engagement with Prithviraj, training his cavalrymen and their horses to combat the Chauhans by having them attack mock elephants made of mud and wood.[35] In 1192 the two armies fought a rematch, again at Tarain, where the sultan carried the day and Prithviraj was captured.[36] Over the next ten years Muhammad Ghuri's armies attacked and annexed political centres across the whole of north India – Meerut, Hansi, Delhi, Kol (modern Aligarh), Benares, Ajmer, Bayana, Ujjain, Badaun, Kanauj, Gwalior and Kalinjar.[37] Meanwhile, having evolved so quickly from a remote mountain chiefdom to a sprawling sultanate spanning north India, Afghanistan and Khurasan, the Ghurid leaders shed their former provincial identity and adopted a more cosmopolitan posture, embracing both the substance and the trappings of the Persianate bureaucratic and centralized state. This included proclaiming their sovereignty at the Friday prayer and using the imperial umbrella (*chatr*) and kettledrums (*naubat*), both of them Persianate symbols of political authority. They also discarded the modest title of *malik al-jabal*, 'king of the mountains'. Ghiyath al-Din now grandly styled himself 'the most exalted sultan' (*sultan al-a'zam*) and Muhammad Ghuri 'the great sultan' (*sultan al-mu'azzam*). Finally, in 1199 they embraced Sunni Islam, abandoning their earlier adherence to a provincial Islamic sect.[38]

What motivated the Ghurids to appear so suddenly in this manner, and what explains their remarkable success? An obvious factor was the power vacuum created by the decline of their two powerful neighbours: to the west, the Seljuq Turks of Khurasan, and to the east their former overlords, the Ghaznavids. Later Indo-Muslim chroniclers – and in their turn, British colonial historians – construed Ghurid operations in north India as motivated by the ideals of Islamic holy war (*ghaza*). But no contemporary inscription, coin or chronicle identified Muhammd Ghuri or other Ghurids as holy warriors.[39] Moreover, the sultan's raids in India were initially targeted not at Hindu states but at Muslim ones – Isma'ilis in Multan and the Ghaznavids in Lahore. Yet the sultan's armies clearly aimed at overthrowing ruling Hindu houses and annexing their territory following raids on Delhi and regional capitals in the modern districts of Ajmer, Patiala, Karnal, Aligarh and Benares – all of them seized in 1193–94. To this end, their armies destroyed Hindu temples patronized by defeated rulers, which followed the traditional Indian practice of desecrating royal temples of defeated monarchs, thereby detaching enemy rulers from the most visible sign of their former sovereignty.[40] On the other hand, the construction of large congregational mosques on some of these same sites signalled an intention to replace the authority of a defeated enemy with a new tradition of governance.

The governing structure that Muhammad Ghuri established in north India suggests yet another motivation for the conquest. Although he and his brother Ghiyath al-Din shared their kingdom's sovereignty, they governed their respective domains very differently. To the west, in newly conquered territories in Khurasan, Ghiyath al-Din planted members of the Ghurid clan as his governors. By contrast, Muhammad Ghuri excluded his clan members from administering the annexed territories in India, preferring instead Turkish slaves personally loyal to him, together with reinstated Indian rulers under the authority of those slaves. As men uprooted from their native lands and kinfolk, these slaves had entered the sultan's household as fictive sons utterly dependent on their master-sovereign. Although Ghiyath al-Din also held slaves, they were not placed in responsible administrative or military positions. It seems likely, then, that Muhammad Ghuri's momentous invasions in India were driven, at least in part, by a desire to carve out a semi-autonomous domain for himself, where he would not have to share rulership with collateral branches of his own clan.[41] Shortly after defeating Prithviraj III Chauhan in 1192, Muhammad Ghuri ordered his slave Qutb al-Din Aibek to push further east. This resulted in the conquest of Delhi, with both that city and the old Ghaznavid capital of Lahore placed under Aibek's governorship. The sultan's other most trusted slaves continued to expand and consolidate Ghurid authority across the Indo-Gangetic plain from their respective bases – Taj al-Din Yildiz in the strategic zone between Ghazni and the Indus valley, Baha al-Din Tughril in Bayana (in eastern Rajasthan) and Nasir al-Din Qubacha in Sind.

Having violently annexed so much north Indian territory, Muhammad Ghuri sought to minimize the disruption of the conquest by establishing continuities with the pre-conquest order. At the local level of political authority, landed elites appear to have remained in office, since no contemporary inscriptions suggest that they had been displaced.[42] At the upper level, leading political figures were also maintained in power. Whereas the Chauhan raja Prithviraj III had been captured in 1192 and soon thereafter put to death, his son was installed as a tributary king to the Ghurids, ruling over both Ajmer and the formidable hill fort of Ranthambhor. Although Prithviraj's brother revolted shortly after the conquest, his nephew Govindaraja remained loyal to the Ghurids, for which he was rewarded with a robe of honour. The Chauhan prince reciprocated by sending Muhammad Ghuri a series of exotic golden sculptures, which were forwarded first to Ghazni and then to the Ghurids' court in Firuzkuh in the Afghan highlands.[43] By such measures the Chauhan line was allowed to continue, albeit subordinate to the Ghurid victors. Similarly, in 1196 the Ghurids redefined the Parihara raja of Gwalior as a subordinate ruler at that strategic fort. In Benares, leaders of the Gahadavala dynasty (late eleventh to mid thirteenth centuries) were reinstated in power, also as tributary kings. And in 1201–02, when the sultan's armies stormed Anahilapataka (Patan) in Gujarat, the defeated raja of the Solanki dynasty (mid tenth to late thirteenth centuries) was restored to power, again as a tributary king to the Ghurids.[44] In short, the sultan positioned himself as an overlord reigning over a circle of Indian authorities identified in the Persian sources by such royal titles as *rai*s, *rana*s or *thakur*s. Symbolizing his new political status in India, Muhammad Ghuri seems to have sent to his subordinate Indian rulers signet rings with his name engraved in Sanskrit.[45] Members of the former Indian ruling classes would thereby have been folded into a larger imperial order that adhered to Persianate ideologies and institutions. Yet, viewed from below, India's first sultan effectively established a classical Indian *mandala*, or circle of sovereignty, with himself at its centre.

Circulating through many hands, the words and images stamped on Ghurid coins served as one of the few ways the new rulers could communicate their political ideology to their subjects. Significantly, the sprawling new state adopted a Janus-faced policy of projecting two different self-images to its different constituencies. Coins issued from Ghazni and circulating in the western, Muslim districts of the Ghurid empire conformed to the numismatic standards of the Islamic world. These carried no images, only Arabic calligraphy, with Muhammad Ghuri bearing the title *sultan al-mu'azzam*, 'the great sultan'. By contrast, coins issued from India followed north Indian standards of weight and metallic purity while maintaining the same iconographic programme used by the defeated Chauhan lineage. These coins depict a bull on one side and a horseman carrying a spear on the other, features that had appeared on the coins of north Indian dynasties for centuries. On the coins' reverse side Muhammad Ghuri's name appeared in Devanagari script, prefaced with the Sanskrit honorific title *śri*. Some of his coins even included an image of the Hindu goddess Lakshmi, while on the reverse side the sultan's name, again in

Devanagari script, was preceded by either *śri* or *hammira*, a Sanskritized form of the Arabic *amir* [see Fig. 2]. Apart from projecting an image of political continuity with north India's defeated dynasties, the new government was also aware of the conservative instincts of India's merchant classes, which resisted new coinage types. Issuing coins with familiar metallic purity, weight, script and images was therefore vital for avoiding disruptions in commerce.[46]

In 1196 Muhammad Ghuri ceased directing operations in India and joined his elder brother in campaigns in Afghanistan and Khurasan, succeeding him as supreme sultan when Ghiyath al-Din died in 1203. Events beyond the Khyber, however, soon threw north India into a crisis of authority. In 1204 Muhammad Ghuri suffered a crushing military defeat at the hands of Turkish rivals in Khurasan, as a result of which Ghurid power there, and then in Afghanistan itself, all but vanished. In 1206 the sultan was assassinated while offering evening prayers. With the Ghurid state now in disarray, his senior slaves in India, cut adrift from Firuzkuh after their master's death, asserted separate claims to sovereign authority. Yet, as former slaves of Muhammad Ghuri with no blood connection with the Ghurid dynastic house, none of them had any legal right to rule over the others. Moreover, during the last ten years of Muhammad Ghuri's reign while he was absent from India, his slaves had conducted military campaigns without their master's direct supervision. In doing so, they acquired a host of local clients and dependants, while becoming fiercely competitive with each other.

Although the launching of the Delhi sultanate as a unified state is customarily dated from 1206, when Muhammad Ghuri died, what actually occurred in that year was the outbreak of protracted civil wars among the late sultan's principal slave commanders. Aibek, Tughril, Qubacha and Yildiz all became legally manumitted on their master's death; moreover, their mutual rivalries, dormant as long as their master was alive, now broke out into the open. Nobody at the time could have predicted that Delhi, under Aibek, would ultimately emerge as north India's pre-eminent capital, or that the Delhi sultanate would become India's pre-eminent state. Even when Aibek died in 1210, north India remained fragmented by these civil wars: Sind and Multan were held by Qubacha, Lahore by Yildiz and Bengal by the political descendants of its conqueror, Bakhtiyar Khalaji.[47] Especially intense was the struggle between Qubacha and Yildiz over Multan and Lahore, and, after 1216, between Qubacha and the rulers in Delhi for control of the whole of north India. Indeed, between 1206 and 1228 an outside observer might well have concluded that the flourishing court of Nasir al-Din Qubacha at Uch, and not that at Delhi, would most likely become the prime centre of Turkish power in north India. During his long reign, Qubacha sought to create an Indus valley–Arabian Sea maritime circuit, centred on his court at Uch. His port of Mansura, in the Indus delta, was connected commercially with the Gujarati ports of Diu, Broach and Cambay, and with Arabian ports in Aden and Muscat, while to the north he maintained overland commercial ties with Lahore and Kabul. And, like his rivals and fellow slaves, Qubacha adorned his court with the brightest luminaries he could find: Sufi shaikhs, artisans of all sorts and historians commissioned to place his reign in larger geographical and chronological frameworks.[48]

In Delhi itself, meanwhile, just four years after the succession crisis precipitated by Muhammad Ghuri's death, another one broke out when Aibek was killed in a freak polo accident. If the crisis of 1206 had arisen over which one of Sultan Muhammad Ghuri's slave commanders would succeed their master, that of 1210 centred on whether Aibek would be succeeded by his natural son or by one of his own slaves. The deeper issue was the very nature of kingship in north India. Would the throne of Delhi follow the Persian model of hereditary monarchy, in which a single royal family was sovereign, generation after generation? Or would it follow the early Ghaznavid tradition, in which kingship devolved to a sovereign's slave, and then to the slave of that slave? And if the latter, then which of the master's slaves would inherit the master's patrimony?

## THE DELHI SULTANATE UNDER THE MAMLUKS, OR SLAVE KINGS

In Delhi, these issues were settled when Aibek's favourite slave, Iltutmish, defeated both his fellow slave cohorts and his former master's son, Aram Shah, after which he claimed the throne. However, a contradiction lies at the heart of Iltutmish's momentous reign, which lasted from 1210 to 1236. Though himself a slave – indeed, a slave of a slave – Iltutmish assiduously endeavoured to establish the Delhi sultanate as a hereditary monarchy, endowed with all the trappings of Persian imperial symbolism and rituals. This effort began immediately on the death of Aibek, whose own son, Aram Shah, had staked a claim to the throne. But Iltutmish confronted and defeated the party of Turks loyal to Aram Shah, who died in the conflict. Then, in an attempt to defuse the bad press surrounding his usurpation of power and his killing of Aibek's son, Iltutmish married Aibek's daughter. This made him the son-in-law of his deceased master – not quite the same as a direct descendant of Aibek, but a close approximation thereof.[49]

Although doubts about the legality of Iltutmish's rise to power lingered for at least another century, in the short run a string of military victories over his rivals in north India quelled such grumbling. Five years after Aibek's death a bitter dispute broke out between Iltutmish and Yildiz over who had the better claim to royal authority. Not only had Yildiz been a favourite slave of Sultan Muhammad Ghuri, but that sultan had manumitted him and given him the throne of Ghazni and was even said to have adopted him as his son. So in 1215, when he marched from his base in Lahore down to Delhi to challenge Iltutmish, Yildiz confronted the latter with the words, 'You know that I am fitter than you to rule the kingdom of Hindustan . . . for I am in the position of a son to the late king . . . I am as good as a descendant of the kings of Iran . . . As for you, you are but a slave of the slaves of the king.' To which Iltutmish retorted:

> O reputed king and son of kings. You know that today the dominion of the world is enjoyed by him who possesses greater strength. The principle of hereditary succession is now extinct; long ago Destiny abolished the custom . . . You cannot take the world through inheritance and boasting; you can take it only by wielding the sword in battle.[50]

In their own battle, Yildiz was defeated and killed. In 1217 Iltutmish then seized Lahore from Qubacha, and in 1225 Bengal from its independent Khalaji rulers. In 1226 he reconquered from recalcitrant Indian rajas the fortress of Ranthambhor, claimed at the time to be so impregnable as to have defied attacks by some seventy kings through the ages. Finally, a year later he defeated and killed Qubacha, bringing both Sind and the southern Punjab under his control. In sum, by 1227 Iltutmish had brought the northern and southern Punjab, Sind, Bengal and eastern Rajasthan under Delhi's sway.

In addition to these stunning military victories, three developments originating beyond India further contributed to Iltutmish's consolidation of power, and to the Delhi sultanate's growing prestige and authority. First, in 1215 Ghurid influence in Afghanistan, already greatly diminished for nearly a decade, was altogether extinguished by a rival Central Asian sultanate, that of Khwarazm (1077-1231). Thus ended the novel experiment of a wider, Perso-Indian empire that, based in the remote mountain fastness of central Afghanistan, had briefly straddled the Iranian plateau and north India. With the Ghurids eliminated from the political scene, the fiction of north India's slave sultanates being part of a larger, Afghan-based empire had ended; Iltutmish now governed his kingdom from within India, as an Indian sovereign. An autonomous Delhi sultanate had become realized.

Second, during the years 1219-21 Genghis Khan, the founder of the Mongol empire in eastern Asia, burst into western Asia. Offended by the insolent behaviour of the same ruler of Khwarazm who a few years earlier had annihilated the Ghurids, the Mongol leader personally marched across Asia to punish the impudent monarch. In the course of this expedition, Mongol cavalry inflicted fire and fury throughout Central Asia and Khurasan, driving many thousands of terrified town-dwellers and semi-nomadic peoples into India, where they sought and found refuge. It was a propitious moment both for them and for Iltutmish, who needed men skilled in civil and military affairs in order to govern his fledgling kingdom. The influx of a host of refugees in search of a stable state with a successful and generous Muslim ruler boosted the sultan's claims to being precisely that sort of sovereign. For Iltutmish and the youthful Delhi sultanate, then, the Mongol holocaust in Central Asia proved a timely boon, unlike the catastrophe it represented for millions in Asia and the Middle East.

And third, in 1229 the Abbasid caliph in Baghdad, still technically the supreme sovereign over the various sultanates of the eastern Islamic world, sent a robe of investiture to Iltutmish, confirming his position as India's only legitimate Muslim monarch. This deed of recognition carried much symbolic weight for the throngs of refugees who had fled from the pagan Mongols and sought a secure state ruled by a Muslim. The period 1215–29, then, marked the emergence of the Delhi sultanate as the dominant power in north India. At the same time, Delhi itself swelled to become one of the world's major cities. A contemporary traveller estimated that it contained twenty-one neighbourhoods, gardens stretching some twenty kilometres, 1,000 *madrasa*s, seventy hospitals, 2,000 inns, extensive bazaars, numerous public baths and reservoirs.[51] The city also claimed one of the most stunning minarets on earth – the Qutb Minar, begun by Aibek around 1195.

What did the contours of the Delhi sultanate's society in the thirteenth century look like? Contemporary Persian chronicles present a simple picture of a monolithic ruling class of 'Muslims' superimposed over an equally monolithic subject class of 'Hindus'. But a closer reading of these same sources, together with Sanskrit ones and material culture, suggests a more textured picture. First, the ruling class was far from monolithic. The ethnicity of Turkish slaves, the earliest generation of whom dated to the Ghurid invasions of India, survived well into the thirteenth century. For a time, even Persian-speaking secretaries had to master Turkish in order to function.[52] There persisted, moreover, deep cultural tensions between native Persian-speakers – whether from Iran, Khurasan or Central Asia – and ethnic Turks. Nizam al-Din Auliya (d. 1325), Delhi's renowned Sufi shaikh, characterized Turks as rude, bellicose and vain, reflecting a view, prevalent among many native Persians of the day, that Turks were uncultured boors who had illegitimately monopolized power and privilege.[53] Such animosities were amplified by the asymmetrical power relations between ethnic Turks and Persians, often depicted in the literature as 'men of the sword' and 'men of the pen' respectively. The latter had inherited a deep attachment to the nobility of blood and hereditary authority, whether in the form of landed aristocracies or dynastic kingship. And yet, as writers employed in the sultanate's secretarial establishment,

Persians found themselves having to serve powerful Turkish commanders who, as slaves, were anything but high-born. Legally, in fact, they were only commodities.

Moreover, not all ethnic Turks were military slaves, as streams of free-born Turks also flowed into India following repeated Mongol devastations of their Central Asian homelands. Nor were all the commanders, whether slave or free-born, ethnic Turks. Some had come from the interior of Iran, others from the oasis towns of Khurasan and Central Asia. And others were Khalaji tribesmen, humble pastoralists from southern Afghanistan. We also hear of remnants of north India's old military aristocracy – men described as *thakur*s and *rana*s – who served in the sultanate's armed forces, and of other Indians promoted even to the rank of senior slaves of the sultan. Muslims of the early sultanate were also divided along religious lines. While patronizing clerics of both the Shafi'i and Hanafi legal traditions, Iltutmish marginalized charismatic Sufi shaikhs whose popularity among commoners might have posed a threat to the court's authority. This was because many rural Muslims felt a closer bond to Sufi shaikhs who had no formal connection with the court than they did to state-appointed clerics who held high offices, much less to ethnically alien slave commanders posted in their regions.[54]

In addition, Sultan Iltutmish, for all his rhetoric of being India's sole legitimate Muslim ruler, continued to issue coins with the old bull-and-horseman motif and a Sanskritized form of his name and title: *Suratana Śri Samsadina*, the latter referring to his given name, Shams al-Din. He also enlarged Delhi's Qutb mosque by three times in order to accommodate the many immigrants from beyond the Khyber who had flocked to Delhi during his reign. And he added three storeys to the city's famous minaret, the Qutb Minar. Notably, he placed a seven-metre iron pillar in the centre of the mosque's oldest courtyard, on a direct axis with its main prayer chamber. Originally installed in a Vishnu temple to announce the military victories of a fourth- or fifth-century Indian king, the pillar was now associated with Iltutmish and his own victories. In transplanting the pillar in this way, the sultan broke with Islamic architectural conventions while conforming to Indian political traditions. For in 1164, within living memory of Iltutmish's installation of the Vishnu pillar in Delhi's great mosque, Vigraharaja IV Chauhan (r. 1150–64) recorded his own conquests on the same stone pillar on which the emperor Ashoka had published an edict back in the third century BC.[55]

Iltutmish's death in 1236 plunged the sultanate into another crisis of governance. The issue, again, was whether the state would continue to be run by slaves (or former slaves), as had been the case in the days of Muhammad Ghuri, Aibek and Iltutmish himself, or whether it would become a hereditary monarchy on the Persian model, with Iltutmish the dynastic founder. The sultan clearly intended the latter outcome, and in fact four of his children did succeed to the throne. However, whereas most of Iltutmish's senior slaves remained loyal to the late sultan's offspring owing to their long association with the court, the loyalty of his junior slaves – younger men more recently recruited for royal service – was more dubious. Several months after Iltutmish's eldest son, Rukn al-Din, acceded to the throne, junior slaves deposed him and replaced him with his sister, Raziyya. Much admired by modern historians as the only Indian woman to rule over Delhi until Prime Minister Indira Gandhi (d. 1984), Sultana Raziyya (r. 1236–40), despite adopting the dress and persona of a male, failed to overcome the same opposition that her elder brother had faced. In 1240 her father's junior slaves deposed and replaced her with another brother, Bahram Shah, who lasted several years before being replaced by Rukn al-Din's son, 'Ala al-Din Mas'ud Shah. He, too, reigned two years before being replaced in 1246 by yet another of Iltutmish's sons, Nasir al-Din Mahmud Shah (r. 1246–66). By this time most of Iltutmish's senior slaves had died off, and a new cohort of slaves had emerged who were loyal only to their own patrons, whether slave or free, and not necessarily to the family of Iltutmish.[56]

As a mode of governance, then, the institution of hereditary monarchy, launched so hopefully by Iltutmish, fared little better than had that of elite slavery. In fact, what preserved Sultan Nasir al-Din Mahmud on the throne for two decades was not his strength of character, but dissensions among the remaining corps of military slaves and, more importantly, the growing influence of one exceptionally powerful slave, Ulugh Khan. A Central Asian Turk who had been purchased and brought to India towards the end of Iltutmish's reign, Ulugh Khan would eventually rise to the throne himself as Sultan Ghiyath al-Din Balban. But first, during the twenty years of Nasir al-Din's reign, he served as the sultan's deputy, or 'viceroy' (*na'ib*), the virtual power behind the throne.[57] In order to enhance his personal clout, Ulugh Khan recruited his own corps of Turkish slaves, supplemented by a large body of free Afghans. This further complicated an already socially complex ruling class, as high-born Persian-speaking 'men-of-the-pen' tended to stereotype Afghans as fierce, uncultured brutes, much as they had earlier stereotyped ethnic Turks. Yet Ulugh Khan's policy of creating a personal support base composed of uprooted outsiders was hardly unique in the history of the Delhi sultanate. Empowering people of humble origins and placing them in contexts alien to their social background ensured their dependence on their masters. As a Central Asian Turk who himself had experienced the life of a deracinated outsider in the court of Delhi, Ulugh Khan clearly understood the merits of this strategy.

In 1266 Nasir al-Din died, and Ulugh Khan, who may well have had a hand in his master's demise, rose to power as Sultan Balban (r. 1266–87). Many themes from Iltutmish's reign were now repeated: a high-ranking slave would manoeuvre himself into a position to seize supreme power; more Mongol invasions would drive streams of traumatized and uprooted Khurasani and Central Asian refugees into India; such invasions would justify keeping the state on a nearly permanent war footing; and Sultan Balban, once secure on the throne in 1266, would endeavour to shake off his slave identity and establish a dynasty. But in this he proved no more successful than his former master. His first son and chosen successor predeceased the sultan by several years, having died fighting the Mongols. Balban then selected as his successor his second son, Bughra Khan, whom he had appointed governor of Bengal. But on the sultan's demise in 1287, Bughra Khan preferred to rule that distant and ever-rebellious province as an independent king rather than involve himself in Delhi's affairs. In the end, Balban was succeeded by Bughra Khan's son and grandson, but the two together lasted only three years before a clan of outsiders, the Khalajis, swept aside the short-lived house of Balban and established a new dynasty that would rule the sultanate from 1290 to 1320.

Balban's reign saw the perennial tension between elite slavery and hereditary monarchy come to a head. He continued to recruit elite slaves, whom he appointed as governors and military commanders, but this only perpetuated an institution that he otherwise sought to replace by grooming his sons to succeed him. Even though he preferred to have his own bloodline continue in royal succession, he could not relinquish the strategic advantage of having a body of kinless outsiders wholly dependent upon his patronage. But in the end, it was the slave institution that ultimately disappeared, and here, too, Balban's actions played a role. With the dying-off of the senior slaves who, like himself, had formerly served Iltutmish, Balban allowed the children of those slaves to inherit the offices of their fathers. They did so, moreover, as free men. Despite their 'low' social origins, some even took on the pretensions of high-born aristocrats. But by this time the core rationale of the slave system had become irredeemably eroded. By default, after Balban's reign the Delhi sultanate would be ruled as a hereditary monarchy under a succession of dynastic houses.

Balban's most lasting legacy was to extend the sultanate's authority not only to urban centres beyond Delhi, but into the north Indian countryside too. As regional commanders sought to consolidate their individual power bases in the provinces – either as agents of Delhi's authority, or as independent actors seeking protection *from* that authority – they inevitably made alliances with local chieftains and other remnants of India's old ruling aristocracy, including the latter's dependants. This had the effect of simultaneously indigenizing and deepening the roots of Delhi's authority in rural areas. Balban also enlisted woodcutters to accompany his military campaigns, in order to clear the thick forests between the Jamuna and the Ganges. In this he aimed both to remove the physical cover of suspected rebels and to open up new lands for arable agriculture, which in turn expanded the agrarian economy and the state's revenue base. Finally, the sultan recruited Afghans from beyond the Khyber and resettled them on the newly reclaimed forest lands. These policies encouraged the emergence of rural networks of commercial exchange that linked the countryside more tightly with urban centres. Such market towns, or *qasbah*s, would provide the true foundation of the sultanate, firmly rooting it in India's economy, society and culture. By the early fourteenth century, the areas most directly affected by Balban's forest-clearing operations had become so prosperous that their revenues were reserved for the state, and not entrusted to nobles.[58]

Further deepening the sultanate's moral authority were the activities of Sufi shaikhs who comprised the informal ranks of Muslim piety in thirteenth-century north India. Many such men had joined the tide of migrants who, dislodged from their homelands in Khurasan or Central Asia, arrived in India from the 1220s on. By mid-century, mystical fraternities centred on the lodges of charismatic shaikhs had begun to appear throughout north India, especially in areas distant from Delhi. Among the more illustrious names were Jalal al-Din Tabrizi (d. 1244/5) in Bengal, Farid al-Din Ganj-i Shakar (d. 1265) in the western Punjab, Baha al-Haq Zakaria (d. 1267) in the southern Punjab and Khwaja Gurg (d. 1301) in eastern Uttar Pradesh. Such figures espoused open disdain for the glitter and corruption of this world, which they viewed as a moral disaster zone to be transcended by arduous austerities and mystical practices. Furthermore, members of Delhi's court and conservative clerics harboured suspicions about men who claimed esoteric knowledge and a special relationship with God, both of which were denied to ordinary humans. Conflicting political positions also divided the court and such Sufis. Despite their possession of worldly might, sultans could only envy the popularity of charismatic shaikhs who were widely believed to possess miraculous powers such as the ability to predict the future, cure the sick or provide physical protection to travellers in certain regions. Especially after 1258, when Mongol troops razed Baghdad and abolished the Abbasid caliphate, such shaikhs seemed to offer religious direction in a world that otherwise lacked a moral centre. In effect, they provided a spiritual counterpart to the political safe haven that the Delhi sultanate had given uprooted refugees arriving from beyond the Khyber.

At the centre of power in Delhi, meanwhile, conservative thinkers such as Ziya al-Din Barani (d. c.1357) complained that Hindus of that city enjoyed a social status as high as or even higher than Muslims:

> And in their Capital [Delhi], Muslim kings not only allow but are pleased with the fact that infidels, polytheists, idol-worshippers and cow-dung [*sargin*] worshippers build houses like palaces, wear clothes of brocade and ride Arab horses caparisoned with gold and silver

ornaments ... They take Musalmans into their service and make
them run before their horses; the poor Musalmans beg of them at their
doors; and in the capital of Islam ... they are called *rai*s [great rulers],
*rana*s [minor rulers], *thakur*s [warriors], *saha*s [bankers], *mehta*s
[clerks], and *pandit*s [priests].

He then considered non-Muslim religious practices under sultanate
rule:

> In their capital [Delhi] and in the cities of the Musalmans the customs
> of infidelity are openly practiced, idols are publicly worshipped ...
> they also adorn their idols and celebrate their rejoicings during their
> festivals with the beat of drums and *dhol*s [a two-sided drum] and
> with singing and dancing. By merely paying a few *tanka*s and the poll-
> tax [*jizya*] they are able to continue the traditions of infidelity[59]

Barani's pointed remarks allow several inferences. First, under the sultanate's rule high-status Indians continued to enjoy their traditional
social privileges, and Hindu religious practices flourished. Second,
conservative members of Delhi's Muslim intelligentsia were appalled
at such things. And third, by adopting a pragmatic live-and-let-live
policy regarding religious pluralism, rulers prioritized socio-political
stability over narrowly interpreted religious dictates. That is to say,
sultans ignored the rantings of conservative intellectuals such as Barani.

It is more difficult to know how the sultanate's non-Muslim subjects assessed their rulers and their claims to legitimate authority. But
clues can be found in contemporary inscriptions that were *not* patronized by the sultanate, or even known to its officers. A striking example
is in Sanskrit and is dated 1276, in the middle of Balban's reign,
recording the construction of a well in Palam, not far from Delhi.
The state took no part in authorizing or financing the well, which
had been patronized by a Hindu landholder, Thakur Udadhara, to
benefit local villagers and to accumulate religious merit for himself.
He and the inscription's Brahmin author, Pandit Yogishvara, therefore had no discernible motive for flattering ruling authorities. In any
event, since the inscription was composed in Sanskrit and not in the
court language of Persian, it was presumably not intended to be read
by government officials. It is therefore likely that its references to

ruling authorities reflected the candid views of the patron and the village community for which the well had been built.

The text conformed to a format found in inscriptions sponsored by Hindu courts throughout India. Pandit Yogishvara preceded the particulars regarding the well with a flowery panegyric to the reigning monarch identical to those that Brahmins had for centuries been using for their Hindu royal patrons. He mentions not only the reigning sovereign, Sultan Balban, but the entire line of rulers, both Turkish and Indian, who had reigned over the Delhi region in the preceding several centuries:

> Salutation to Ganapati. Om. Salutation to Śiva . . .
>
> The land of Hariyanaka [upper India] was first enjoyed by the Tomaras and then by the Cauhanas. It is now ruled by the Shaka ['Scythian', or Central Asian] kings. First came Shahabadina [Shihab al-Din (i.e. Muhammad) Ghuri], then Khudavadina [Qutb al-Din Aibek], master of the earth . . .
>
> In his [Sultan Balban's] kingdom, abounding in benign rule, extending from Gauda [Bengal] to Gajjana [Ghazni], from the Dravida region [south India] and from the Setubandha [to the north] where the entire region was filled with inner content, the earth bore vernal floral charms produced by the rays of the innumerable precious stones and corals which dropped on it from the crowns of the bent heads of the rulers who came from every direction for his service. He, whose legions daily traversed for a bath the earth both eastward to the confluence of the Ganges with the [Bay of Bengal] and westward to the confluence of the Indus with the sea . . . The dust raised by the hooves of whose cavalry marching ahead of his army stops the enemies in front.
>
> He, the central gem in the pearl necklace of the seven-sea-girt earth, Nayaka Śri Hammira Gayasidina [Ghiyath al-Din Balban], the king and the emperor reigns supreme . . . When he went forth on a military expedition, the Gaudas [Bengalis] abdicated their glory; the Andhras through fear sought the shelter of holes, the Keralas forsook their pleasures; the Karnatas hid themselves in caves; the Maharashtras gave up their places; the Gurjjaras resigned their vigour . . .
>
> The earth being now supported by this sovereign, Śesha, altogether forsaking his duty of supporting the weight of the globe, has betaken

himself to the great bed of Vishnu; and Vishnu himself, for the sake of protection, taking Lakshmi on his breast, and relinquishing all worries, sleeps in peace on the ocean of milk.[60]

By 1276, Hindu subjects living near Delhi had evidently integrated the sultanate's ruling authority into their historical memory and their understanding of political legitimacy. As masters of north India, the Tomara dynasty (early eleventh century to 1152) was followed by the Chauhans (late tenth century to 1192), who were seamlessly followed by the Turks (Scythians), namely Muhammad Ghuri, Aibek and their successors. Balban himself is entitled 'Nayaka Śri Hammira' – *nayaka* being Sanskrit for a powerful lord. The author sees no sharp break, much less a civilizational rupture, between Indian and Turkish rule. One dynasty simply succeeds another, as Balban's reign is smoothly accommodated within conventional Sanskrit tropes of powerful and worthy rulers. The author's hyperbole regarding the sultan's success in smashing his rivals could have been applied to any number of Indian monarchs of that day or earlier, while the sultan's sovereign domain is generously (though inaccurately) said to have extended from Bengal to eastern Afghanistan, and deep into south India. Most poignant is the statement that under Balban's benign rule India enjoyed such stability and contentment that even Vishnu – the great god who appears periodically in various incarnations to rescue human affairs in times of distress – could sleep peacefully on an ocean of milk, without a care in the world.

The inscription's bombastic rhetoric praising Sultan Balban takes us full-circle to the beginning of this chapter, which discussed Rajendra Chola's 1022 attack on Bengal. Two and a half centuries before Pandit Yogishvara spoke of 'the crowns of the bent heads of the rulers who came from every direction for his service' when referring to Balban, a Tamil poet had described Rajendra's victories in terms of 'his lotus feet [all along] being worshipped by the kings of high birth who had been subdued [by him].' Rhetorically, the two statements are virtually interchangeable. Their only notable difference is that, whereas the Tamil poet was a paid servant of the Chola court, Pandit Yogishvara had no official connection with the Delhi sultanate. From this 'worm's-eye' perspective of Delhi's ruling class, it meant nothing that the sultan was Muslim and Yogishvara a Hindu; what mattered was that the people who produced this text viewed their rulers in Delhi as legitimate and protective.

From the vantage point of a more distant, bird's-eye perspective, however, the inscription suggests how far the Persian and the Sanskrit worlds had already begun to overlap and even penetrate each other. Even though Balban's chroniclers might clothe his regime in a Persianate discourse of worldly power or in an Islamic one of pious rectitude, unbeknownst to the court, and located only twelve kilometres from his palace, the sultan and his regime were perceived – literally inscribed – within a Sanskrit discourse of worldly power and moral authority.

## CONCLUSION

In assessing the impact of the conquest on north India's subject population, one must distinguish the rhetoric of conquest from the practices of conquerors and rulers. Many contemporary chroniclers were themselves immigrants or their near-descendants, who had been traumatized by the destructive invasions of their native Central Asia by pagan Mongols. They consequently looked to Delhi as a safe haven for themselves and for Islam.[61] They also trumpeted a narrative of Muslim invaders triumphantly vanquishing a mass of Indian infidels. But such rhetoric stood at odds with the practice of the Delhi sultanate's rulers, who needed to govern a huge population accustomed to their own ways of managing affairs. Overruling objections from their more conservative Muslim advisers, they followed the policies of their Ghaznavid and Ghurid predecessors by integrating defeated Indian elites into their political systems and aligning their coinage with indigenous numismatic traditions. Although Brahmins who had been attached to the courts or temples of north India's defeated ruling houses lost their institutional bases, the many who were not so affiliated continued their traditional vocation as local priests. As long as sultanate officials were seen as preserving the social order, Brahmins such as Pandit Yogishvara appear to have given their assent to Delhi's rule.

The most immediate consequence of the conquest was that the larger dynastic houses of northern India, together with their courts and the temples that housed their patron deities, were either annihilated or assimilated to the new order, depending on the extent to which they resisted the new dispensation. Second, attacks by Bakhtiyar Khalaji on large monastic establishments in present-day Bihar (i.e. Odantapuri, Vikramaśila and Nalanda) hastened a long-term decline of Buddhism in eastern India, a decline that had already taken place in the rest of South Asia.[62] As early as the seventh century Chinese pilgrims had noted a drop in the number of monasteries in Bihar and Bengal, the centre of India's once-vibrant Buddhist tradition and home of the historic Buddha (d. *c.*400 BC).[63] From the seventh to the twelfth centuries these monasteries continued to shrink in number, and became increasingly scholastic in nature, some of them accommodating thousands of monks. Whereas Indian monasteries had originally relied on the Buddhist lay population for material support, over many centuries the laity had become progressively absorbed in Hindu society, while the Buddha himself became popularly transformed into an incarnation of Vishnu. Detached, then, from lay support, the great academic monasteries of Bihar and Bengal grew increasingly dependent on royal patronage and on income from large, accumulated land holdings.[64] In the early thirteenth century these remaining Buddhist institutions received a crippling blow from invading Turks, who probably viewed them simply as big landowners with no significant lay constituency. Within several hundred years they would be largely abandoned.[65]

Third, the Turkish conquest and the advent of the Delhi sultanate opened up new opportunities for north India's merchant communities. The sultanate's commercial integration with the Middle East greatly augmented international trade, thereby expanding the reach of merchants at every level, from long-distance brokers to local retailers in *qasbah*s. Such trade certainly existed before the Turkish conquest, as is suggested by the image of Śiva's trident on Ghurid coins struck in Firuzkuh during the 1160s.[66] But from the end of the twelfth century, when the Ghurids integrated north India, Afghanistan and Khurasan under a single political umbrella, India's trade with the lands beyond the Khyber increased exponentially. Most importantly, with the consolidation of the Delhi sultanate in Iltutmish's reign, silver no longer left India as plunder, as had been the case in early Ghaznavid times. Since Delhi's rulers now had a stake in enriching their realm, they eagerly resumed normal trade with Central Asia and the Middle East, as a result of which precious metals once again flowed in from those lands. This allowed the sultanate to mint and circulate unprecedented levels of silver-based coinage, most notably under Iltutmish, who established a stable currency based on the silver *tanka*, to which the modern rupee can be traced.[67] The increased amount of circulating cash not only facilitated the pace and volume of commercial transactions, but enabled the state to elaborate a ranked political hierarchy.

Fourth, the establishment of the Delhi sultanate opened up India to a rapid influx of Persian culture, with far-reaching consequences. By a coincidence of some note, the period of Ghaznavid and Ghurid contact with India, stretching from *c*.1000 to 1206, synchronized with what the British Orientalist E. G. Browne calls the 'Persian Renaissance'. By that he refers to the flowering of Persian literary activity seen first in Central Asia and Khurasan from the tenth century, and then across the entire Persian-speaking world, reaching its zenith in eleventh-century Ghazni, in eastern Afghanistan.[68] It was in tenth-century Central Asia under the patronage of the Ghaznavids' parent dynasty, the Samanid rulers of Bukhara, that modern Persian first achieved literary status. Under them the poet Rudaki (d. 940/41), celebrated as the father of modern Persian literature, penned thousands of verses. The Samanids also patronized the historian Bal'ami (d. 974), who adapted for the Persian-speaking world an abridged version of the *Universal History* of Tabari (d. 923), who had previously chronicled the early Muslim centuries in Arabic. And in the dynasty's twilight years, the epic poet Firdausi began writing the *Shah-nama* ('Book of Kings'). Completed in 1010 under Mahmud of Ghazni's patronage, this vast literary canvas glorified pre-Islamic Iranian history and mythology, even giving Alexander the Great Persian descent. If, then, Bal'ami had appropriated for the Persianate world the legacy of early Islam, Firdausi did the same for the legacies of both pre-Islamic Iran and Greek imperialism.[69] He also limited the *Shah-nama*'s Arabic vocabulary to just 4 per cent or 5 per cent of the total, a move that, given the epic poem's immense popularity for generations of Persian-speakers, contributed greatly to consolidating the modern Persian language.[70] Finally, the *Shah-nama* helped define political and cultural ideals across the Persophone world. In India, the epic would be foundational for newly independent sultans, who commissioned royal editions of the text or reworked imitations of it for their libraries.

What enabled this Persian Renaissance was the political economy of courtly patronage. Across Central Asia and the Iranian plateau, artists and literati from the tenth century on circulated from court to court along well-travelled networks that over time expanded in reach and increased in density, giving the Persian world its institutional infrastructure. Just as these ambitious and talented men sought livelihoods from courtly patronage, rulers desired the prestige and cultural capital that patronizing gifted literary or artistic luminaries could bring to their courts. By the early eleventh century Mahmud of Ghazni, awash with silver plundered from India, was attracting to his court the brightest stars in the galaxy of Persian literati. These included, in addition to Firdausi, such celebrated poets as 'Unsuri (d. 1040), Farrukhi Sistani (d. 1037), Manuchehri (d. 1040), and the first Persianized intellectual to engage with Indian culture in all its dimensions, the polymath al-Biruni (d. 1048). Slightly later Sana'i (d. 1131), the first of the great mystical poets in Persian literature, was patronized by one of Mahmud's royal successors in Ghazni, Bahram Shah.[71] Mahmud also brought back to Ghazni entire libraries of Persian literature plundered from his conquests in Iran. Importantly, he created the position of official court poet laureate (*amir al-shu'ara*).[72] Continued by his successors, this office helped secure the nexus between Persian literature and court culture.

Although the Ghaznavids' last capital and centre of Persian patronage had shifted from eastern Afghanistan to Lahore in the later twelfth century, by the early thirteenth century Delhi was India's pre-eminent magnet, attracting Persianate literati, artists and artisans. This resulted, in part, from Iltutmish's defeat of Muhammad Ghuri's former slaves in the bitter struggle over hegemony in north India. Soon thereafter, and continuing throughout the middle decades of the thirteenth century, the Mongol catastrophe in Central Asia and Khurasan drove thousands of uprooted scholars, soldiers, administrators, Sufis and artisans into the welcoming arms of the fledgling Delhi sultanate. By then a substantial canon of Persian literary works had already emerged[73] that would now spread throughout South Asia, which soon became a major centre in its own right for the production, and not just the reception, of Persianate culture. Over the course of the next six centuries, India – not Iran – would become the world's principal centre for the production of Persian dictionaries.[74] The first major anthology of Persian poetry would be compiled not in Central Asia or the Iranian plateau, but in southern Punjab at the court of Muhammad Ghuri's former slave, Nasir al-Din Qubacha.[75]

In its earliest encounter with South Asia and the Sanskrit world, then, Persianate learning was brought to India in the vessel of courtly patronage. This would soon change, however, as Persianate culture engaged more closely with that of Sanskrit and with India's vernacular communities. At the same time, even if the Delhi sultanate was never the unified monolith that its chroniclers might have imagined, the state established by Aibek and consolidated by Iltutmish planted in India the *idea* of the sultanate as a new and powerful system of governance. This idea would prove to be contagious, as various actors sought to replicate it in regions very far from Delhi. It is that story to which we now turn.

# 2

# The Diffusion of Sultanate Systems, 1200–1400

## IMPERIAL EXPANSION ACROSS THE VINDHYAS

With their tallest peaks barely exceeding 700 metres, the Vindhya Mountains that span west-central India are hardly imposing. They certainly cannot compete with the Sulaiman Mountains on South Asia's north-west frontier with Afghanistan, which reach 3,800 metres, much less the snow-capped Himalayas on India's frontier with Tibet, with peaks at 8,800 metres. Rather, the importance of this 1,000-kilometre-long discontinuous range, which runs east to west just north of the Narmada River, lies in its historic role of demarcating the Indo-Gangetic plain – or 'Hindustan', in early Arabic and Persian sources – from the Deccan plateau to the south. Its craggy ravines, dense forests and reputedly fierce tribes rendered the terrain inaccessible, or even impassable. Historically, few states straddled both sides of these mountains, and few invasions were launched from one side to the other.[1]

Despite the topographical barriers, rulers of the early Delhi sultanate were well aware of the rich states lying to the Vindhyas' south. Occupying the north-western plateau was the Yadava dynasty of kings (1175–1318), with their capital located in Devagiri, a formidable natural stronghold. The eastern Deccan was dominated by the Kakatiya kings (1163–1323), who ruled from Warangal, a classically designed capital encircled by three concentric walls. In the Kannada-speaking country further south, kings of the Hoysala dynasty (1190–1346) ruled over the south-western plateau from their capital, Dwarasamudra (modern Halebid). Already in the mid thirteenth century, officials in Delhi coveted these wealthy states. Before becoming sultan himself, Balban had urged Sultan Nasir al-Din to undertake military campaigns deep into India's interior – not out of greed, nor with a view to annexing territory, but to use its wealth to finance the defence of north India from Mongol invasions.[2] For the threat of Mongol attacks did not end with Genghis Khan's initial invasions of India in the 1220s; they continued throughout the thirteenth and deep into the fourteenth centuries. Balban well understood the importance of stationing garrisons in the frontier towns of the Punjab and in the passes leading from the Afghan highlands to the Indus plain below. It would be the court's far-sighted geopolitical vision that spared India from the devastation sustained by the peoples of China, Central Asia, Russia and the Middle East.

Delhi's expansion into the Deccan, however, did not commence with Balban's reign. After his death in 1286, Balban's short-lived dynasty succumbed to a *coup d'état* led by the Khalajis. Their leader, the mild-mannered Jalal al-Din Khalaji, had already reached his late seventies when his kinsmen seized power in 1290. But he was soon overwhelmed by the rapid ascent of his own nephew and son-in law, 'Ala al-Din Khalaji (r. 1296–1316). Ambitious and talented, 'Ala al-Din used his *iqta'* in Kara – near Allahabad in the central Ganges region – as a power base for launching a series of unauthorized raids to the south, in lands hitherto untouched by Delhi's influence. In 1292, just two years after the Khalajis had come to power, he led a contingent of swift cavalry that raided Malwa, the region located immediately north of the Vindhya Mountains. His appetite whetted by this success, two years later his cavalry made a daring, lightning raid still further south. Passing over the Vindhya Mountains, he crossed the Narmada and surprised Devagiri, the Yadava capital. After extorting an immense booty from the city's unsuspecting rulers, the Khalaji prince returned to Delhi and used the plundered wealth to win the military services of numerous freelance soldiers. By now, though, he also had royal ambitions of his own. In July 1296 'Ala al-Din treacherously murdered his father-in-law, crowned himself sultan and promptly appeased Delhi's stunned population with the loot he had hauled back from Devagiri.

Having opened the door to peninsular India, between 1297 and

1311 Sultan 'Ala al-Din Khalaji launched repeated raids on the Deccan, most of them led by his African slave eunuch, Malik Kafur. Like Mahmud of Ghazni's raids on north India two centuries earlier, these were aimed at plunder, not the annexation of territory. But whereas Mahmud's booty was used to finance conquests far to the west, 'Ala al-Din's Deccan raids were aimed at financing north India's defence from Mongol invasions, just as Balban had recommended. Like Mahmud's raids, too, those of 'Ala al-Din were launched nearly every other year over the span of a decade, penetrating ever deeper into the peninsula: Gujarat in 1297, northern Rajasthan in 1299–1301, southern Rajasthan in 1302–03, Malwa in 1305, Maharashtra in 1307, Andhra in 1309 and both Karnataka and Madurai in 1311. In these campaigns Khalaji armies pressed their military advantages to the hilt. Their cavalries of mounted archers were supplied with powerful war-horses imported from Central Asia, and their engineers possessed the world's most advanced siege technology: trebuchets, smaller siege engines (tension-powered ballistas), wooden parapets and long earthen ramps for filling up moats, enabling besiegers to breach a fort's curtain walls.

Sultan 'Ala al-din Khalaji's reign stands out not only for its aggressive raids in peninsular India, but also for its equally aggressive domestic policies. All matters that the state could conceivably touch – administrative, economic, social – were carefully monitored and controlled to a degree perhaps never before seen in India. Disguised as 'news reporters', spies apprised the royal court of the activities of state servants throughout the realm, including even market transactions. The sultan prohibited the consumption and sale of wine and liquors. He abolished tax-free land grants and charitable endowments, transferring the management of lands that had supported such grants to the central government. He banned extravagant banqueting among noble families and took measures to control marital relations between them. He increased his land revenue to 50 per cent of the harvest, the legal maximum in Islamic law. Unlike any of his predecessors in Delhi, the sultan based these taxes on the actual measurement of cultivated fields. He fixed the price of grain and established royal granaries. He required that cultivators sell their grain only to licensed merchants, and that grain carriers be licensed and registered with the state. As a result of such stringent reforms, the price of grain remained stable during the whole of his twenty-five-year reign, whether or not the monsoon rains arrived in any given season.[3] The sultan justified these sweeping measures on the grounds that only a stable and prosperous economy could defend the country from the Mongol armies that periodically broke through the Afghan hills and threatened the Indo-Gangetic plain. Notably, no rural rebellions were recorded during his reign.[4]

'Ala al-Din Khalaji's death in 1316 again raised the question of whether the sultanate would continue to be run by a succession of slaves, or by the sultan's blood descendants. The late sultan's favourite slave general, Malik Kafur, enthroned 'Ala al-Din's child and for a month ruled as regent before being slain by another of 'Ala al-Din's sons, Mubarak Khan, who crowned himself as Sultan Qutb al-Din Mubarak Khalaji (r. 1316–20). Meanwhile, the Deccan states previously humbled by 'Ala al-Din took advantage of the turmoil in Delhi by withholding their annual tribute. In response, the new sultan personally marched south in 1318 and, departing from his father's policy of transforming defeated monarchs into tribute-paying vassals, overthrew the Yadava dynasty and annexed its territories to the sultanate. Governors were appointed throughout former Yadava territory, strategic forts were garrisoned, Delhi's revenue system was established, and the sultanate's coinage was minted at Devagiri, now made the provincial capital.

Qutb al-Din Mubarak also built a grand congregational mosque in Devagiri, the Deccan's earliest surviving Islamic monument. Consisting of a spacious courtyard with colonnades on three sides and a prayer hall on its western side, the mosque comprised 177 columns that were stripped from nearby Jain and Hindu temples, brought to the site and stacked end on end, giving the interior its great height. Apart from serving as a house of worship, the monument projected Delhi's political presence in this distant province by replicating the metropolitan style of mosques that earlier sultans of Delhi had built in the north: Ajmer, Kaman, Khatu and Delhi. All these structures featured spacious central courtyards encircled by pillared aisles on three sides, a monumental projecting entrance, and a corbelled dome over the prayer hall, supported by reused pillars similarly stacked. In addition, the engaged corner towers of Devagiri's mosque resembled miniaturized replicas of the most iconic symbol of contemporary Delhi – the famous Qutb Minar – giving visual evidence of Delhi's imperial presence in the Deccan plateau.

In 1320, Khalaji forces annexed the provincial town of Bijapur, some 350 kilometres south of Devagiri, and raised a mosque there named after its new governor, Karim al-Din. Built under the supervision of a local Hindu architect, this mosque closely engaged with the local culture, as the placement of its reused columns adhered to long-established principles of Hindu temple design. Stone-cutters visually connected the new, Khalaji era with the former Yadava age by continuing the same diamond motif on the upper half of the mosque's Mecca-facing prayer niche as was found on the niche's lower half, a reused door jamb of a temple sanctum. The prayer niche's upper half also contains the Arabic verse, 'let there be no compulsion in religion' (Qur'an 2:256), suggesting the new regime's non-coercive public posture vis-à-vis the region's non-Muslim population. The Devagiri and Bijapur mosques thus reflect two distinct faces of Khalaji authority in the Deccan: whereas the former projected an image of Delhi's imperial power and grandeur, the latter conveyed a desire to connect the new regime with local elites and their cultural traditions.[5]

In north India, meanwhile, Qutb al-Din Mubarak's style of governance diverged sharply from that of his father. Brittle and uncompromising, 'Ala al-Din's nearly totalitarian regime was followed by laxity in all respects. Qutb al-Din reportedly opened the jails, gave his army six months' pay, abolished many taxes, restored to rural elites the land grants his father had resumed, allowed merchants to return to their former corrupt practices and relaxed his father's price controls, which in turn led to consumer price inflation. The sultan himself grew ever more vainglorious and debauched. Ultimately his favourite slave, a Gujarati convert to Islam named Khusrau Khan, assassinated him and usurped the throne under the title Nasir al-Din Khusrau Shah. But the new ruler's prohibition of cow slaughter alienated many Muslim nobles, who after just four months transferred their loyalty to Ghiyath al-Din Tughluq, a popular and experienced commander who had repulsed several Mongol invasions in the Punjab.[6] In 1320 Ghiyath al-Din, his Turkish kinsmen and his battle-hardened army invaded Delhi and swept the usurper from power. Finding no surviving sons of 'Ala al-Din to place on the throne, Khusrau Shah having massacred them all, the army proclaimed the septuagenarian Ghiyath al-Din Tughluq the new sultan.

The kingdom the Tughluqs inherited was far from unified. Although the Punjab was firmly under their control, the sultanate's presence in Gujarat was limited to just a few garrisons. Bengal, still ruled by Balban's descendants, was virtually independent. Across Rajasthan powerful chieftains had reasserted their independence. Delhi's grip on the Deccan was minimal at best. Maharashtra remained nominally part of the sultanate, but to the east the Kakatiya raja had ceased paying tribute. Moreover, the continuing Mongol threat created a demand for more treasure to defend the north-west frontier. Accordingly, one of the new sultan's first initiatives was to send his son, Ulugh Khan, on a two-year expedition across the Vindhya Mountains in an effort to reassert the sultanate's political presence there. His mission was twofold: to shore up the sultanate's shaky grip on Devagiri and the western plateau, and to punish the eastern plateau's Kakatiya rulers for allowing their tribute to fall in arrears. The prince's expedition, however, was to end with the annexation of the entire northern half of the Deccan.

In 1321 Prince Ulugh Khan marched out of Delhi and headed south. After joining forces with Turkish troops already garrisoned in Devagiri, he proceeded east into Andhra to confront Pratapa Rudra, the Kakatiya maharaja. From the Tughluq perspective the expedition was completely successful: the Kakatiya kingdom was extinguished, its territory annexed to Delhi, and its former capital of Warangal renamed 'Sultanpur'. Defeated and dethroned, Pratapa Rudra was to be escorted to north India to appear in the newly built capital of Tughluqabad, located in the southern quarters of modern Delhi. There he would personally submit to Sultan Ghiyath al-Din Tughluq. But he never reached the capital; in fact, he never left the Deccan. Rather than face the humiliation of attending Ghiyath al-Din's court, the proud Kakatiya maharaja committed suicide by the banks of the Narmada.[7]

Ulugh Khan, meanwhile, occupied himself with asserting Delhi's presence in the Kakatiyas' former capital. Seeing the great Svayambhu Śiva temple in the heart of the citadel, the most imposing in the

Kakatiya realm, the prince would have understood that the icon of the god was also the emblem of the Kakatiya state and the source of its authority. Aiming to eradicate that authority, he dismantled the edifice to its foundations. But because he planned to redefine the temple plaza's purpose, he scrupulously preserved its four majestic *torana*s, or ritual gateways, which, standing at the four cardinal directions just beyond the plaza, gave that zone a clear and emphatic focus. Near the plaza's centre he raised a large congregational mosque, using materials from the destroyed temple, and not far to the west he built a royal audience hall. Locally known as the Khush Mahal, this structure's battered, heavy walls and horseshoe interior arches reveal a distinctively Tughluq aesthetic [see Fig. 3]. Indeed, it remains the best-preserved Tughluq palace in India, asserting Delhi's presence in the eastern Deccan just as Devagiri's congregational mosque did in the western plateau.

While Ulugh Khan was preoccupied with his Deccan campaign, Sultan Ghiyath al-Din had marched down the Gangetic valley to reassert Delhi's grip on Bengal, whose rulers had also seized on the Khalaji–Tughluq transition to assert their autonomy. With that mission accomplished, the king began his return march to Delhi. By that time Ulugh Khan, having already returned to the capital from his Deccan campaigns, arranged for a triumphal reception to celebrate his father's successful mission in Bengal. However, the canopy that had been specially arranged for the royal reception collapsed just as the sultan passed beneath it, killing him instantly. For several centuries gossip lingered in Delhi that the fatal mishap had been arranged by the ambitious and impatient Ulugh Khan, thus facilitating his own accession to Delhi's throne as Sultan Muhammad bin Tughluq (r. 1325–51).[8]

The new sultan's reign was filled with contradictions that astonished contemporary observers and have continued to perplex historians down to modern times. In 1326, just three years after he had so purposefully demolished the great Śiva temple in Warangal, the sultan issued an inscription authorizing the restoration of public worship in another Śiva temple in Kalyana, a town located in the heart of the Deccan, within the sultanate's administered territory. Owing to damages the temple had sustained in an unspecified local

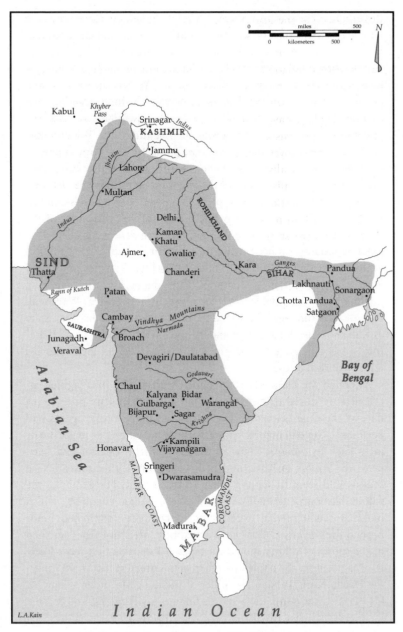

India in the time of Muhammad bin Tughluq, 1325–51

disturbance, the governor there, Khwaja Ahmad, conferred with the temple trustees and arranged for its repair and the formal reinstallation of its image. Everything about the inscription regarding this temple shows how thoroughly Muhammad bin Tughluq's government sought to accommodate local society. Written in Sanskrit and dated according to the Hindu (Śaka) calendar, the inscription referred to the sultan by the classical Indian title *maharajadhiraja śri-suratana*, 'great king of kings and prosperous sultan', and to the Tughluq governor of the Deccan as *mahapradhana*, 'great minister'.[9] Such imperial titles had been used in this city for centuries, for Kalyana had formerly been the capital of one of the mightiest empires in the Deccan's history: the Chalukya (974–1190). Muhammad bin Tughluq's destruction of the Warangal temple while prince and his patronage of the Kalyana temple while sultan did not, however, reflect his alleged bipolar personality. Rather, the two cases indicate how a temple's political environment dictated official policy towards it. Temples associated with enemy kings whose territories lay in the path of the advancing Tughluq army were liable to be destroyed, as happened at Warangal. But any structure brought within the orbit of sovereign territory, such as Kalyana's Śiva temple, was understood as state property and therefore subject to government protection, provided its local patrons remained loyal to the state.

Although the Delhi sultanate under Muhammad bin Tughluq attained a territorial extent greater than any Indian state prior to his day, by the time he died in 1351 nearly all his territorial gains had been lost. To contemporary observers the rebellions in major provinces such as Malwa, Gujarat, Bengal and the Deccan had been provoked by his quixotic and rash behaviour. Other measures he took would seem to support such an assessment. For example, the sultan harboured grandiose schemes of foreign conquest, which included sending huge expeditions to conquer unspecified lands beyond the Khyber. On one such expedition, an entire army perished in the snows of a lofty mountain range – a debacle that most likely gave to posterity the name of Afghanistan's greatest mountain range, the Hindu Kush, Persian for 'killer of Indians'.[10] In order to pay for his extravagant coronation and to finance his domestic and foreign conquests, he raised the land revenue in the richest lands near the capital. But such measures only reduced villagers to flight or beggary, leading to uncultivated fields, lower grain harvests and even famine. Infuriated that cultivators would simply abandon their lands without contributing to the public welfare, the sultan resorted to hunting down peasants like animals.

The sultan's bold initiative in currency manipulation similarly resulted in failure. Having heard that the Chinese under Mongol rule had experimented with a token currency, using paper backed up by precious metal, he launched a similar initiative. Needing silver to pay his sizeable army of 370,000, in 1330–32 he ordered his mint to issue brass or copper coins that were nominally equivalent in value to silver ones. But as Gresham's Law would have predicted, people paid their taxes in the cheaper coins, while merchants demanded payments in silver, which they then hoarded, driving silver coinage out of circulation. All this impoverished the state treasury, enriched the merchant and banking classes and infuriated the sultan.

There were still more failures. In 1327, having remodelled the old Yadava capital of Devagiri, the sultan ordered a tenth of Delhi's population to migrate south and settle in that city, which he renamed Daulatabad and proclaimed the state's new co-capital. He evidently reasoned that creating a co-capital for governing an enormous state straddling both sides of the Vindhyas would be administratively efficient. But implementing the scheme proved disastrous. Although rest houses and shade trees were established along a new road connecting the two cities, many died making the arduous, forty-day, thousand-kilometre trek south. The political fallout of this initiative ultimately proved fatal, as most of the transplanted migrants bitterly resented their forced removal from north India. After only several decades, this resentment would erupt into outright rebellion against a ruler whom many saw as a tyrant.

In 1334 Ibn Battuta (d. 1377), the Moroccan globetrotter whose journeys would take him through much of Eurasia and Africa, reached Delhi. On hearing reports of Sultan Muhammad bin Tughluq's lavish generosity, the newcomer prudently borrowed a considerable sum from moneylenders so that he could present the sultan with an assortment of gifts. True to his reputation, the sultan returned the favour with gifts of far greater value, including several thousand silver dinars, fully furnished living quarters in Delhi and the post of a judgeship that carried a handsome annual salary of 5,000 dinars. Such generosity also extended to the wider public. Six years after Ibn Battuta's arrival, he abolished all taxes beyond legal alms and distributed food to the people of Delhi for six months. At court he would patiently hear the complaints of distressed people. The Moroccan recorded flamboyant displays of the sultan's devotion to justice, a cherished Persianate ideal. On one occasion, the son of a noble filed a complaint that he had been unjustly struck by the sultan. The *qazi* (judge) hearing this case decreed that the sultan should either give the boy monetary compensation or allow the youth to retaliate in kind. Ibn Battuta reports: 'That day I saw that the sultan came back to his court, sent for the boy and gave him a cane saying, "I call upon you by my head, you must strike me just as I struck you." The boy took hold of the stick and struck the emperor twenty-one strokes so that his cap [*kulah*] flew off.'[11]

Yet the sultan could also act with astonishing brutality. 'Of all the people,' continues Ibn Battuta, 'this king loves most to make presents and also to shed blood. His door is never free from an indigent person who is to be enriched and from a living person who is to be killed. Stories of his generosity and bravery as well as his cruelty and severity towards the offenders have obtained great currency among the people.'[12] Although conversant in several languages, famously intelligent and fond of debating the finer points of law with learned courtiers, the sultan also rushed impetuously into new projects. Then, when his advisers or the wider public would not or could not catch up with his ideas, he would react with outbursts of terrible cruelty. Having spent eight years in the sultan's service at Delhi, and sensing the danger of attending such an unpredictable patron any longer, in 1342 Ibn Battuta seized an opportunity to escape.

As it turned out, Ibn Battuta left Delhi just in time, as opposition to the sultan's daring policies was mounting throughout the realm. With some provinces seething in discontent, or already in open revolt, the Moroccan traveller's hasty departure – first from Delhi, then from India altogether – resembled a man escaping a house on fire.

## SETTLERS, SHAIKHS AND THE DIFFUSION OF SULTANATE INSTITUTIONS

Two outstanding themes of fourteenth-century India were the expansion and contraction of the Delhi sultanate's political frontiers and, more quietly, the diffusion of institutions, norms and tastes informed by the circulation of Persian texts. The two processes were not unrelated. The spread of Persianate culture accompanied the establishment of new urban centres, which in turn followed the sultanate's annexation of new territories.

Sizeable settlements to the south and east of Delhi began to appear in the second half of the thirteenth century after Sultan Balban's punitive raids against rebels in those regions. In the course of these raids, Balban cleared the jungles of present-day Rohilkhand, enlarging the agrarian base that could support both migrants from north India and refugees arriving from beyond the Khyber Pass displaced by Mongol invasions. In the more arid Punjab to the west of Delhi, it was a technological innovation that helped increase agricultural production. Already by the twelfth century, and possibly earlier, the Punjab had seen the introduction of the Persian wheel, a mechanical device for raising water from open wells. Powered by draught animals and using wheels, gears, a crankshaft and buckets, the device could raise water from depths of ten to twenty metres, distributing it over the land through troughs and channels. The technology considerably expanded the production of the Punjab's primary grain crop, wheat, which in turn sustained growing urban settlements in Delhi's western and southern hinterlands.

Called *qasbah*s in the original sources, settlements established in thirteenth- and fourteenth-century north India were typically walled towns garrisoned by troops sent out from Delhi and placed under the control of trusted governors. Such a site was Chanderi, in present-day northern Madhya Pradesh. Established in the fourteenth century and defended by several hundred soldiers supported by light cavalry, this walled and fortified town guarded the routes from Delhi leading south to Gujarat and the Deccan.[13] In nearby Gwalior, another such frontier *qasbah*, some 600 cavalry were deployed.[14] Among the most strategically significant of such frontier towns was Kara. Located at the intersection of both overland and riverine routes in the central Ganges valley, this town served as a staging point for operations directed east into the Bengal delta or south into central India. It was also a major gathering point for tribute in the form of elephants sent to Delhi from Bengal or Orissa.[15]

The sultanate's authority beyond Delhi was further deepened by the *iqta'* institution. Although intended to decentralize government by allowing *iqta'dars* to collect their salaries from their land assignments, thereby sparing central authorities from sending cash salaries across dangerous roads to reach provincial officers, the practice had a more subtle consequence. Whereas *iqta'*s in older regions near Delhi were generally given to trusted men from families with generations of service to the sultanate, those on the political frontier were often awarded to Indian officials who had served defeated regimes. Politically and culturally, then, the institution helped indigenize the sultanate, since it assimilated local elites as petty *iqta'dars*. This not only accommodated Indians to a ruling power whose historical roots lay beyond the Khyber Pass: it also exposed them to sensibilities carried by the circulation of Persian texts at the local, *qasbah* level. The influx of Persianized Turks from Central Asia and the Iranian plateau further contributed to the diffusion of Persianate culture and the sultanate's authority. These included literati, engineers, artisans of all sorts, soldiers and administrators already familiar with Persianate governance. The arrival of such immigrants proved a boon for Delhi's rulers, who made every effort to welcome them, as is suggested by the lavish gifts with which Sultan Muhammad bin Tughluq welcomed Ibn Battuta to his court.

Finally, in nearly every provincial centre of the sultanate there resided a Sufi shaikh who belonged to one or another spiritual order, each order cultivating a distinctive regimen of spiritual techniques or exercises aimed at attaining a heightened awareness of the divine presence. Literature composed by these provincial shaikhs suggests the presence of small, distant and sometimes beleaguered rural communities of Muslims engaged in small-town life or farming.[16] Yet shaikhs residing in such *qasbah*s were very much connected to metropolitan Delhi. Just as the sultanate's central administration sent governors to provincial towns, so too did prominent Sufis in Delhi send their leading disciples; there they were often patronized by those same governors. In this way, networks of Sufi shaikhs overlapped those of the sultanate's government.

In the late thirteenth and early fourteenth centuries, during the Delhi sultanate's most expansive phase, the capital's leading Sufi was Shaikh Nizam al-Din Auliya, a renowned and highly revered figure whose tomb-shrine in Delhi continues to be a central focus for Sufi practices today. His followers included not only adherents of the Chishti path of spiritual discipline, as supervised by the shaikh himself, but also the cream of Delhi's intellectual elite. His *khanaqah* – a Sufi's residence and locus of teaching – thus emerged as a major hub from which his disciples were sent to the sultanate's far-flung provinces. During Qutb al-Din Mubarak Khalaji's reign, for example, the shaikh sent his disciple Maulana Yusuf down to Chanderi; subsequently, the soldiers garrisoned there became loyal followers of Yusuf's Sufi master in Delhi.[17] Nizam al-Din also extended Chishti networks by sending his own cloaks (*khirqa*s) to designated followers living in the frontier town of Kara, further down the Ganges valley. Having been worn by the shaikh himself, a *khirqa* conveyed to its recipient the authority, prestige and charisma of a Sufi master. The passing of such robes from shaikhs to disciples thereby strengthened spiritual networks across space and spiritual lineages across time.

Among Nizam al-Din Auliya's most prominent disciples were the two principal Persian poets in India at the time, Amir Hasan and Amir Khusrau, and the leading historian, Ziya al-Din Barani. As writers whose works enjoyed wide circulation, the three men were in effect publicists for Shaikh Nizam al-Din and his order and, indirectly, for the policies and ideology of the sultanate that patronized them. This implicit alliance between Sufis and the sultanate in the fourteenth century contrasts with the situation prior to Balban's reign (1266–87), when the court in Delhi marginalized or even coerced Sufi shaikhs and their institutions. The court's informal affiliation with the Chishti order, in particular, had a further effect of indigenizing the sultanate since the major shrines of that order were all located *within* India, unlike the foundational shrines of most other orders in

India, which were located in Central Asia or the Middle East. This made India itself the spiritual home of Chishti Sufism. Seeking to establish their legitimacy both as Muslims and as Indians, Delhi's rulers consequently turned to prominent Chishti shaikhs for blessings and support.

The charismatic authority of eminent Sufi shaikhs, however, was a double-edged sword. Just as Sufis could help transmit Delhi's political authority to its far-flung provinces, Sufis patronized by provincial authorities could be enlisted to bless their patrons' rebellions *against* Delhi. Such revolts, after all, were integral to the nature of a sultanate, since any powerful governor or *iqta'dar* could, under the right circumstances, turn his province or land assignment into the nucleus of a new sultanate. Everybody knew that India's first sultanate, the Ghaznavids, had been launched in eastern Afghanistan by a powerful *iqta'dar* of the Samanid state who had declared his independence from his overlord in Bukhara. It was now India's turn to experience such splintering, notably in Bengal and the Deccan.

## THE EARLY BENGAL SULTANATE

Bengal is a low-lying floodplain laced with numerous rivers and channels, making overland communication and transportation extremely difficult. By the eighth century large, regionally based imperial systems had emerged in the greater delta region, some of them, such as the Palas (750–1161) and Chandras (c.825–1035), patronizing Buddhism and others a revitalized Brahmanism, in particular the Senas (c. 1097–1223). The latter, after wresting their independence from their Pala overlords, consolidated their base in western Bengal and then moved into the eastern hinterland. By the early thirteenth century, the centre of civilization and social power in eastern India had moved from Bihar to Bengal, while royal patronage had shifted from a mainly Buddhist to a mainly Hindu orientation. By this time, too, the granting of land to Brahmins who officiated at court rituals had become a kingly duty. As elsewhere in India, kings of the Sena dynasty sought to replicate cosmic order by building monumental stone temples housing an image of their patron overlord.

In 1204, amidst the rapid rise of Ghurid power in upper India, Muhammad Bakhtiyar Khalaji, a client of Muhammad Ghuri, over- threw Bengal's last Sena monarch. The invader's 10,000 horsemen had overwhelmed the local population, while his propaganda left lit- tle doubt regarding the basis of his power. Upon establishing his capital in Lakhnauti, Bakhtiyar Khalaji struck a gold coin in the name of Muhammad Ghuri that depicted a Turkish cavalryman charging at full gallop and holding a mace in his hand. It bore the Sanskrit phrase, 'On the conquest of Gaur' (i.e. Bengal). Silver coins struck over the next decade bore a similar horseman image, commu- nicating to the local population a message of brute force. Imposing monuments in the south-western delta dating to the late thirteenth century, such as the Minar of Chhota Pandua or the mosque of Zafar Khan, also announced the presence of Bengal's new rulers, making no concessions to the aesthetic sensibilities of the delta's conquered population. In the decades immediately following Bakhtiyar Khalaji's conquest, Bengal's provincial masters sought to reproduce in this dis- tant, forested delta the political and cultural vision of north India's new rulers.

Aided by the delta's great distance from Delhi, however, the sultan- ate's governors in Bengal repeatedly asserted their independence from their north Indian overlords. As early as 1213, Delhi's governor in Bengal not only proclaimed his autonomy from north India, but even declared himself the right-hand defender of the caliph in Baghdad. In response, Sultan Iltutmish invaded and re-annexed the province. To drive home his own superior claims to association with the caliph the sultan, while still in Bengal, arranged to receive from the caliph in Baghdad a robe of honour, which arrived under a red canopy of state. But Mongol invasions from beyond the Khyber kept the sultans of Delhi preoccupied with defending their north-western flank, enabling subsequent rulers of Bengal repeatedly to assert their independence. As this happened, they adopted ever more exalted titles on their coins and public monuments. In 1281 Balban ruthlessly stamped out one revolt, hunting down and publicly executing his rebel governor in Bengal. Yet within a week of Balban's death in 1287, his own son, who had been left behind to govern the turbulent province, declared his independence from Delhi. And when the latter's son rose to the

Bengal throne in 1291 as Sultan Rukn al-Din Kaikaus (r. 1291–1300), the new ruler emphatically defied Delhi's claims to authority by assuming the inflated title of 'the great Sultan, master of the necks of nations, the king of the kings of Turks and Persians, the lord of the crown, and the seal', as well as 'the right hand of the viceregent of God'. He even styled himself 'the shadow of God', an honorific derived from ancient Persian imperial usage.

Exasperated with its wayward province, Delhi temporarily ceased mounting costly operations to keep it within its grip. Indeed, the founder of Delhi's Khalaji dynasty, Sultan Jalal al-Din (r. 1290–96), indicated his disdain for the delta by rounding up 1,000 criminals from the Delhi region, loading them on to boats and floating them down to the Ganges delta where they could be set free.[18] Within a century of its conquest, then, Bengal had passed from being a prized possession of the Delhi sultanate, whose capture had occasioned the minting of gold commemorative coins, to a dumping ground for the capital's social undesirables. We also see in this incident an early manifestation of the sort of north Indian, or, more precisely, Punjabi chauvinism towards the Bengal delta that would be echoed in the aftermath of the Mughal conquest of the region in the late sixteenth century.

During the earlier part of Sultan Muhammad bin Tughluq's reign, however, Bengal was once again brought under Delhi's control, governed from the delta's three major cities: Lakhnauti in the north-west, Satgaon in the south-west and Sonargaon in the east. But midway through the sultan's turbulent reign, local rulers in the delta again managed to assert their independence from Delhi. A key player in this drama, Shams al-Din Ilyas, had begun his career in Delhi, but after running foul of the mercurial sultan he fled to Bengal where he took up service with the Tughluq governor of Satgaon. When that governor died in 1338, Ilyas seized power and declared his independence. Four years later, after defeating his rivals in the delta's other major cities, he proclaimed himself sultan of the whole delta, which he ruled until his death in 1357.

Just as Sufi shaikhs associated with Shaikh Nizam al-Din Auliya had helped plant Delhi's authority in Bengal, disciples of those same shaikhs helped legitimate Ilyas Shah's rebellion against Delhi. As a young man, the Bengal-born Akhi Siraj al-Din (d. 1357) had travelled to Delhi where he studied with Nizam al-Din Auliya, returning periodically to his homeland with other servants of his master in Delhi, thereby strengthening the spiritual links between the capital and Bengal. When Nizam al-Din died in 1325, Siraj al-Din returned to the delta, where he inducted others into the Chishti order. Among these was another native Bengali, Shaikh 'Ala al-Haq (d. 1398), who developed close ties with Sultan Shams al-Din Ilyas Shah soon after the latter had severed his political ties with Delhi.[19] From this point on, the sultan and the Sufi formed a mutually supportive relationship. The latter's son, Nur Qutb-i 'Alam (d. 1459), attached his fortunes even more firmly to the fate of the Bengal sultanate, seeing himself as its principal spiritual adviser.

One of Ilyas Shah's first acts as sultan was to move his capital from the old provincial capital of Lakhnauti to the new site of Pandua. Though only thirty kilometres from Lakhnauti, the new capital symbolized his determination to sever all ties with his former overlords in Delhi. Twice in the 1350s Delhi tried but failed to reconquer the delta. Then, for the next two centuries, Bengal was at last left undisturbed by north Indian armies. This long period of political independence contributed to the growth of a distinct Bengali regional identity. Already in the late thirteenth century, Marco Polo had mentioned 'Bangala', a place he had apparently heard of from his informants and which he understood as being distinct from India, for he described it as 'tolerably close to India', and its people as speaking 'a peculiar language'.[20] An historian of the mid fourteenth century referred to Shams al-Din Ilyas Shah as the 'sultan of the Bengalis' and as 'king of Bengal'.[21]

Through the medium of architecture, Sikandar Shah (r. 1357–89), the son and successor of the dynasty's founder, made the most dramatic statement defying Delhi. Completed in 1375 in the capital of Pandua, the Adina mosque signalled both the delta's political distance from its former masters in Delhi and its patron's imperial pretensions. With its immense courtyard surrounded by a screen of arches, and bearing no fewer than 370 domed bays, this structure surpassed in size any edifice built in Delhi. It also broke from Delhi's architectural tradition by asserting its indigenous character. The motifs of its many prayer niches reveal a successful adaptation, and appreciation, of the aesthetic traditions of the delta's former Pala and Sena rulers.[22] On the other hand, it went over the heads of Delhi stylistically, conveying an imperial aura that recalls the grand style of pre-Islamic Persia. The shadowing effect produced by the alternating recesses and projections on the exterior of the multi-storeyed western wall resembles the external façade of the Taq-i Kisra palace of Iran's Sasanian dynasty (AD 225–641), located in Ctesiphon near modern Baghdad. The mosque's central nave, moreover, was covered with a huge barrel vault, an unusual feature having no antecedent in India, but which had also been used in the Taq-i Kisra. Finally, whereas Bengal's earlier rulers had been content with being merely first among 'kings of the East', Sultan Sikandar Shah – whose very name, 'Alexander', associated him with imperialism – portrayed himself in the mosque's inscription as the most perfect among the kings of Arabia and Iran, without even mentioning the kings of South Asia, where he was actually ruling.[23]

## SULTANATES OF THE DECCAN: THE BAHMANIS AND VIJAYANAGARA

The Deccan in the fourteenth century witnessed a pattern similar to that of Bengal: the political expansion of the Delhi sultanate, the diffusion of Persianate culture, and rebellion followed by the establishment of not one but two independent regional sultanates.

In 1342, as his caravan lumbered southwards from Delhi to the Tughluqs' co-capital of Daulatabad, Ibn Battuta described the road he was using as 'bordered with willow trees and others in such a manner that a man going along it imagines he is walking through a garden; and at every mile there are three postal stations . . . At every station [*dawa*] is to be found all that a traveller needs.'[24] Such a description indicates Muhammad bin Tughluq's earnest attempts to link north India politically with the Deccan. But the Moroccan also recorded that those roads were infested with bandits, armed tribal groups and other miscreants, suggesting the sultan's failure to build the sort of transport and communication infrastructure that is essential for any large state. The ever-resilient world traveller did manage to wriggle out of dangerous encounters with bandits on the road to Daulatabad, as he did many other times in his global travels. But there is no doubting the fragility of the lifeline that linked the Deccan to Delhi, suggesting that the sultanate's attempt to annex the plateau was doomed from the start.

The Tughluq rulers inherited from their Khalaji predecessors two distinct ways of governing newly conquered regions: direct rule and indirect rule – a strategy not unlike nineteenth-century India, where British imperialists divided conquered territory into directly administered provinces and indirectly ruled 'princely states'. In the annexed regions of the northern Deccan, stretching from the Vindhya Mountains down to the Krishna River, Muhammad bin Tughluq imposed a colonial idea – that is, a tightly controlled direct rule, symbolized by the name-change of the Deccan's provincial capital from Devagiri to Daulatabad, meaning 'city of government'. The idea was to plant colonies of northern immigrants, establish mints and strike coins on the same standard as those of Delhi, and partition the land into revenue parcels assigned to trusted *iqta'dar*s. Whereas many of these men were colonists from the north, administrators co-opted local society wherever possible by redefining as *iqta'dar*s those native chieftains who already occupied the land.

To the south of the Krishna, by contrast, the Tughluqs established an imperial idea, a system of indirect rule. Here they planted no colonists, appointed no governors, established no mints and made no effort to reach the base of the agrarian society, remaining content to identify powerful figures at the top of local political hierarchies and redefine them as tribute-paying chiefs, designated by the Perso-Arabic term *amir*, 'commander'. Annual tribute, not regular taxes, was what they expected from territories south of the Krishna. By the end of Muhammad bin Tughluq's reign, however, some tributary states were teetering on the verge of collapse. This was true of the Hoysala rajas, who had been conquered by Malik Kafur in 1311. But their capital, Dwarasamudra, lay some 650 kilometres south of Daulatabad, putting them practically beyond the Tughluqs' reach. What is more, Malik Kafur's looting of the Hoysala capital had so crippled the dynasty's credibility across the south-western Deccan that its client-chieftains were soon commanding their own armies and carving out autonomous regions of effective control.[25]

Among the strongmen who emerged in this politically volatile environment were the five sons of Sangama, an obscure chieftain who seems to have been in Hoysala service in south-eastern Karnataka in the early fourteenth century. Already in 1313 one of his sons had emerged in the records as a politically active chieftain. By 1327, the same year the Tughluqs established direct administration in the northern Deccan, another of his sons, Muddamma, asserted his authority in the present Mysore District. In the next decade, both the Sangama brothers and the Tughluqs were picking up the pieces of the disintegrating Hoysala state, with Muhammad bin Tughluq co-opting chieftains formerly subordinate to the Hoysalas and installing them over their territories as Tughluq *amir*s. Ibn Battuta met three sons of one of those chieftains who had died resisting Delhi's authority. The sultan had made all of them imperial *amir*s, the Moroccan reported, 'in consideration of their good descent and [the] noble conduct of their father'.[26] Sometime in the 1320s another of Sangama's sons, Harihara, was enlisted in Tughluq imperial service as an *amir*, at least nominally. Although a contemporary observer called him a 'renegade' (*murtadd*), referring to his subsequent renunciation of former association with Tughluq authority,[27] his loyal service in the Delhi sultanate persisted in folk memory. A Sanskrit chronicle composed around 1580 states that Muhammad bin Tughluq had 'bestowed' the entire Karnataka country (i.e. the south-western Deccan) on Harihara and his brother Bukka because the sultan, in his wisdom, had recognized the two men as eminently trustworthy and deserving of imperial patronage.[28]

However, the entire edifice of Tughluq authority south of the Vindhyas, both direct and indirect, began to crumble in 1336 when a Telugu-speaking chieftain of obscure origins led a successful uprising in Sultanpur, the Kakatiyas' former capital of Warangal, which Prince Ulugh Khan had seized only thirteen years earlier. The imperial governor of the city was forced to flee, which permanently ended the sultanate's control over the eastern Deccan, while other rebellions arose across the rest of the plateau. In that same year, Bukka asserted his autonomous control over parts of modern Kolar District. By 1339

Harihara had begun styling himself 'Lord of the Oceans of East and West', referring to his control over widely dispersed regions of the southern plateau between the Coromandel and Malabar coasts.[29] In 1342 Ibn Battuta identified him as the overlord of the port of Honavar in northern Malabar. Significantly, he made no reference to Harihara's former loyalty to the Tughluqs.[30]

By early 1344 most of Karnataka had accepted the Sangamas' rule amidst the continued crumbling of both Hoysala and Tughluq authority. In February 1346 all Sangama's sons gathered at the important Śaiva centre of Śringeri (in modern Chikmagalur District), where they celebrated Harihara's coast-to-coast conquests. This meeting anticipated the final collapse of Tughluq authority on the plateau, the disappearance of the Hoysala house altogether – their last inscriptions were issued just two months later – and the formation of a new state, Vijayanagara, which would have an illustrious place in Indian history. Finally, in February 1347 one of the brothers, Marappa, declared the Sangama family's principal deity to be Virupaksha, a form of Śiva. He also publicly presented himself as, among other titles, 'sultan', or in its Kannada formulation, 'Sultan among Indian kings' (*hindu-raya-suratalah*).[31] In 1352, his brother Bukka adopted the same title, as did Harihara two years later, in an apparent arrangement of joint rule. In 1354 Bukka reaffirmed Virupaksha as the Sangama family deity, implicitly making that god the fledgling kingdom's state deity. In 1355 he styled himself simply as 'sultan', instead of the earlier 'Sultan among Indian kings'.[32] When Harihara died in 1357, Bukka became the sole ruler of the new kingdom, now identified as Vijayanagara, 'City of Victory'. The next year he added grandiose Sanskrit imperial titles to his name; in 1374 he even sent an ambassador to Ming China.[33] Such was the meteoric rise of Vijayanagara, a hybridized sultanate-like state that would soon sprawl over nearly the entire southern half of the peninsula, and whose four dynasties, the Sangamas being the first, would survive down to the mid seventeenth century.

Meanwhile, a similar drama was playing out to the north of the Krishna. Although the Tughluq revolution of 1320 had overthrown the Khalaji rulers in Delhi, many former Khalajis remained entrenched as local administrators in Tughluq service. This was especially true in the Deccan, where such officers viewed the new dynastic house as usurpers. Among these was one Zafar Khan and his three brothers, who were nephews of a former high official in the deposed Khalaji court. In 1339, just when Harihara and his brothers emerged as dominant players amidst the chaos of the crumbling Hoysala dynasty further south, Zafar Khan and his brothers joined an anti-Tughluq uprising in which the forts of Gulbarga, Bidar and Sagar were all briefly seized. In addition to former Khalaji officers, Daulatabad's settler-colonists who had migrated from north India since 1327 – many of them forced to move against their will – felt increasingly alienated by Muhammad bin Tughluq's high-handed governance of his Deccan province. In 1344 the sultan dismissed Daulatabad's popular governor, to whom Deccanis had looked to defend them against the sultan's increasingly erratic and arbitrary actions. Things came to a head the next year, when 1,500 cavalrymen and a large number of commanders were ordered to be transferred from Daulatabad to Gujarat. Aware that the transfer amounted to a death penalty, given what the sultan had done under similar circumstances in the neighbouring Tughluq province of Malwa, these cavalrymen and officers openly rebelled, seizing and executing those government officers who had been sent to investigate them. The year 1345 was also the last that imperial coins were minted anywhere in the Deccan, indicating the demise of Tughluq rule across the entire plateau. Two years later Zafar Khan triumphantly strode into Daulatabad's great mosque, where he was crowned Sultan 'Ala al-Din Hasan Bahman Shah.

In short, in 1347 two independent kingdoms had emerged on either side of the Krishna, each founded by a family of obscure origins. The realm of 'Ala al-Din Bahman, known eponymously as the Bahmani kingdom, covered the northern Deccan, where the Tughluqs had exercised a direct colonial rule. To the south of the river, the Sangama brothers based themselves in the new capital of Vijayanagara and ruled over territory vacated first by the Hoysalas and then by the Tughluqs. In the brief span of just eight years, between 1339 and 1347, the founders of these two dynasties had radically redrawn the plateau's political map. Upon expelling Tughluq power from the Deccan, the Sangamas and the Bahmanis both established new, transregional states that sprawled across the plateau's three vernacular zones: the

Marathi, the Telugu and the Kannada. The two ruling families also styled themselves 'sultans'. By using this title, which denoted supreme power in Persianate political discourse, the dynasties expressed not only their claims to political independence and supremacy but also their aim to participate in the wider Persianate world.

If these two states shared similar political origins, having arisen from simultaneous rebellions against their Tughluq overlords in Delhi, they differed vastly in how they legitimized their claims to rule. For the Bahmanis, as with other former provinces of the Delhi sultanate, the blessings of a Sufi shaikh were considered essential for ensuring a new state's prosperity and legitimacy. According to Deccani sources, Shaikh Nizam al-Din Auliya himself had implicitly lent his blessings to the Bahmani enterprise, even though the state would not emerge until several decades after his death. In an anecdote current in the Deccan in the late 1500s, the great Chishti shaikh of Delhi had just finished a meeting with Sultan Muhammad bin Tughluq at his *khanaqah* in Delhi when he found Zafar Khan, the future founder of the Deccan's Bahmani sultanate, waiting outside. 'One sultan has left my door,' the shaikh is reported to have remarked, 'another is waiting there.'[34] The anecdote illustrates the theme of an eminent shaikh predicting future kingship for some man, with that 'prediction' serving as a veiled form of appointment to royal power. For in the discourse of Sufism, sovereign authority was in fact held by these spiritually powerful shaikhs. In the words of 'Isami, a contemporary chronicler who witnessed the launching of the Bahmani state, 'Although there might be a monarch in every country, yet it is actually under the protection of a fakir [i.e. a Sufi].'[35] By this logic, such shaikhs effectively leased political sovereignty to kings and charged them with the messy business of worldly governance while they themselves withdrew to a life of austerity, spiritual discipline and teaching.

However, a shaikh's prediction of kingship was no guarantee of a sultanate's well-being. As in Bengal, independent rulers in the Deccan needed the continuing legitimacy underwritten by a resident Chishti shaikh spiritually descended from Shaikh Nizam al-Din Auliya. 'Isami recorded that with the latter's death in 1325, the city and empire of Delhi had sunk to desolation, tyranny and turmoil. But the

Deccan, he maintained, suffered no such fate. Because one of Nizam al-Din's leading disciples, Burhan al-Din Gharib, had migrated down to Daulatabad in 1329, the city prospered thanks to the shaikh's radiant, beneficent presence.[36] When Burhan al-Din died in 1337, that protective presence passed to his leading disciple, Shaikh Zain al-Din Shirazi (d. 1369), by whose actions the newly launched Bahmani state was transformed from a rebel movement into a legitimate Indo-Islamic kingdom. The very robe worn by the Prophet Muhammad on the night he ascended into Paradise – a robe subsequently passed on through twenty-three generations of holy men until finally received by Zain al-Din – was allegedly bestowed upon Zafar Khan when he was crowned sultan in 1347.[37]

Sultan 'Ala al-Din Bahman Shah's earliest successors to the throne sought the support of other Sufi shaikhs, one of whom, Shaikh Siraj al-Din Junaidi (d. 1379/80), shifted his residence from Daulatabad to Gulbarga when the Bahmani capital moved there. The shaikh presented a robe and turban to each of the first three Bahmani sultans during their respective coronations. Sufi shaikhs thus played roles fundamental to the diffusion of sultanate systems in the Deccan, as elsewhere in India. Whereas Khalaji and early Tughluq invasions beyond the Vindhya Mountains had lacked any moral basis, being undertaken simply for booty or tribute, the extension of the Sufis' notion of spiritual sovereignty lent moral legitimacy to the planting of a sultanate's political authority. No longer available for plunder with impunity, such land – its people, its produce and its fixed assets (including Hindu temples) – now merited state protection. In classical Islamic discourse, the presence and blessings of great Sufi shaikhs could transform yesterday's Abode of War (*Dar al-Harb*) into today's Abode of Peace (*Dar al-Islam*), thereby legitimizing the transplantation of Indo-Muslim rulership from one region to another within South Asia. As vessels into which divine favour was believed to have been poured, great shaikhs thus exercised a quasi-political dominion over the lands in which they resided. If Shaikh Burhan al-Din Gharib's arrival in colonial Daulatabad had inaugurated Delhi's legitimate rule of the Deccan, legitimate independent rule there began when Shaikh Zain al-Din Shirazi bestowed the mantle of the Prophet on 'Ala al-Din Hasan Bahman Shah in 1347.

To the south of the Krishna, meanwhile, the new state of Vijayanagara asserted very different claims to legitimate rule. Its authority was based on a goddess cult that had emerged as early as the seventh century on the southern banks of the Tungabhadra River, a major tributary of the Krishna. At that time the site was known simply as Pampa's *tirtha* – or the 'crossing' of the river goddess Pampa – where passing chieftains would halt and make votive offerings during military campaigns. By the ninth century the first stone temple had appeared at the site, dedicated evidently to this goddess. By the early eleventh century, donations were being made to the male deity Mahakala Deva, the violent aspect of Śiva. By the twelfth century, a temple complex dedicated to Virupaksha, who represented Śiva's more universal and benign aspect, had emerged. Unlike the earlier phase, when she was merely protected by Mahakala Deva, to whom she was in no way subordinate, the river goddess Pampa was now reduced to a subordinate status as Virupaksha's consort. Moreover, south Indian texts had begun describing Pampa's marriage to Virupaksha in terms paralleling the all-Indian story of Śiva's marriage to the goddess Parvati.[38]

In this way, over the course of 500 years a regional shrine had gradually become Sanskritized, as a local river goddess was pulled up into, and transformed by, the big world of pan-Indian Śiva-worship. At the same time, the site grew ever more important as a pilgrimage centre. From the thirteenth century on, politically ambitious or already dominant rulers in the area had begun cultivating closer ties with the shrine and its deities, whereas in earlier days only passing chieftains had done so. In the early fourteenth century, the short-lived kingdom of Kampili tried to reap the ritual and political benefits of an expanding goddess-cum-Śiva shrine by building a state near the site. But in 1327 Sultan Muhammad bin Tughluq crushed that fledgling kingdom. Soon thereafter, though, the Sangama brothers proclaimed themselves to be the site's 'protectors'. And when those chieftains established their capital at the site, by then called Vijayanagara, their family deity Virupaksha was elevated to the status of state deity. Important state documents now bore the 'signature' of this deity, while the Sangama kings heaped lavish architectural patronage on his temple complex by the banks of the Tungabhadra [see Fig. 4]. Hundreds of copper-plate inscriptions recording land grants state that the donation was carried out 'in the presence of Virupaksha on the banks of the Tungabhadra River' and conclude with a large 'signature' of the god 'Śri Virupaksha', written in Kannada script. As owner of all state land within his kingdom, the deity in this way participated in formal transactions and attested to their validity.

From the moment of its launching, then, Vijayanagara was a culturally hybridized kingdom. Its religious origins and legal foundations were embedded in a state cult focused on a local form of the great god Śiva, just as the Kakatiya kingdom had been grounded on one devoted to another form of that deity. On the other hand, the kingdom's ruling institutions, architecture and its wider, transregional posture suggest a desire to assimilate the ideals and idioms of the Persianate world. Vijayanagara's system of land revenue assignments, called *nayamkara*, required high-ranking officials, or *nayakas*, to combine military and tax-collecting duties. Having no known precedent in earlier kingdoms of the Deccan, the *nayamkara* institution was apparently modelled on that of the *iqta'* used by the Tughluqs and their political descendants in the Deccan, the Bahmani sultans. Vijayanagara also incorporated and lavishly displayed Persianate architectural motifs – arches, domes, vaulted arcades, squinches, and so on – together with the image of the sultan as a supreme king of kings.[39] Paralleling Turko-Mongol political traditions, claims to sovereignty at Vijayanagara were extended to all male members of the ruling family, meaning that royal successions were marked by tensions and sometimes violent conflict.[40]

# THE EARLY KASHMIR SULTANATE

Directly north of Delhi, protected by massive walls of snowcapped mountains, lies the fertile and densely populated valley of Kashmir, an oval-shaped plain approximately 145 kilometres long and forty wide. For centuries, the valley's physical properties have enchanted its visitors: 'A garden of perpetual spring' is how the Mughal administrator Abu'l-fazl characterized it. Surrounded on all sides by towering mountains attaining 5,500 metres in height, the valley – 1,800 metres above sea level – is watered by the Jhelum River, which springs from the valley floor and flows gently westwards until it plunges through a narrow gorge in the Pir Panjal Mountains, which form the valley's western edge. After cutting through this range, the river turns abruptly south, eventually forming the westernmost of the five rivers that flow over the Punjab; in all, it drops over 1,000 metres from its headwaters in the Kashmir valley to the plains of the Punjab.

These topographical features helped shape the course of Kashmiri culture and history. For centuries, Hindu rulers in the secluded valley had enjoyed freedom from outside invaders; formidable mountains to the south, east or north could block incursions from those sides. Incursions were rare and logistically difficult even from the valley's western side, where the Jhelum cuts through a narrow defile at Baramulla, the so-called 'gateway to the Kashmir valley'. In the eighth century Arabs tried to invade the valley at least once, possibly twice, but failed. Mahmud of Ghazni attacked Kashmir twice – in 1015 and 1021 – but turned back both times owing to severe snowstorms. Muhammad Ghuri and his slave commanders made no attempt to conquer Kashmir when they swept over the Indo-Gangetic plain in the late twelfth century. After the Delhi sultanate was established at the beginning of the thirteenth century, sultans never attacked the valley, focusing instead on the flat, physically accessible Indo-Gangetic plain.

The same isolation that protected Kashmir from repeated invasions also made it a secure haven for refugees fleeing other regions. Among these was a Tibetan Buddhist prince, Rinchana, who reached the valley in 1320 after fleeing nearby Ladakh, where he had led a failed rebellion against his royal uncle. This was shortly after a Mongol chieftain, Zulju, had successfully invaded and devastated Kashmir – a notable exception to the string of failed attempts to penetrate the valley. In the chaos following the Mongol invasion and the flight of the Hindu raja Suhadeva (r. 1301–20), Rinchana seized power and declared himself king (r. 1320–23). Soon thereafter the latter appointed as his chief minister another outsider to the valley, Shah Mir; probably of Iranian origin, Shah Mir had migrated to Kashmir in 1313 and risen to high office in Suhadeva's government. In 1339 he attained sovereign power after winning a palace struggle, thereby launching Kashmir's first dynasty of Muslim sultans. With his reign, a more definitive Iranian influence took hold in the valley, as seen, for example, in the sultan's replacing the Hindu Śaka calendar with a Zoroastrian one that had been launched in Iran by the last Sasanian emperor in AD 632.[41] Shah Mir also fixed the state's land revenue demand at just one-sixth of the annual harvest, while abolishing various other taxes. Since Rinchana and Shah Mir had broken the influence of powerful feudatories, the valley's Brahmins acquiesced in such measures. Nor did Brahmins view the sultans as threatening their own status, especially when Kashmir's new rulers married into the families of neighbouring rajas and – more importantly – made Brahmins their partners in governance.[42]

The mid fourteenth century saw a burst of the dynasty's territorial expansion, as Shah Mir's grandson, Shihab al-Din (r. 1355–73), became the first Kashmiri ruler since the eighth century to launch military campaigns beyond the valley, annexing Baltistan to the north, Ladakh to the east and Jammu to the south. But these campaigns came at great cost to the state's treasury. The sultan's Hindu finance minister even suggested increasing the state's coinage by melting down a brass image of the Buddha – a measure that Shihab al-Din, shocked at the proposal, refused.[43] Meanwhile, Persian culture continued to flow into the valley, as seen in the state's increasing patronage of Persian literature relative to Sanskrit works, whether produced at the court or beyond. Through it all, the actual management of the sultanate's governance remained firmly in the hands of Brahmin ministers and administrators.

Sultan Shihab al-Din was succeeded by his brother Qutb al-Din (r. 1373–89), in whose reign another prominent migrant reached Kashmir, Saiyid 'Ali Hamadani (d. 1384). Though brief, this Sufi's stay in the valley would have far-reaching consequences. Like Shah Mir, 'Ali Hamadani had come from Iran, and, like Rinchana, he arrived as a refugee – in his case, as a consequence of the rise of Timur, the great Central Asian warlord who between 1360 and 1405 would conquer most of the eastern Muslim world. Fearing sectarian persecution from Timur's army, which campaigned across the Iranian plateau between 1380 and 1386, 'Ali Hamadani left western Iran accompanied by a host of *saiyid*s, men claiming descent from the Prophet Muhammad. In 1381 he found refuge in Kashmir, where Sultan Qutb al-Din warmly greeted him and his companions, allegedly numbering some 700. These men then set up a network of intercommunicating *khanaqah*s throughout the valley. 'Ali Hamadani also maintained close ties with the sultan, giving him his own headgear (*kulah-i mubarak*) to wear underneath his crown.[44] Although the shaikh left the valley only several years after his arrival, he had established Kashmir as a place of refuge for other Sufis coming from Central Asia or Iran. As Timur's assaults across western Asia continued during the reign of Qutb al-Din's successor Sultan Sikandar (r. 1389–1413), still more waves of immigrants reached the valley, including 'Ali Hamadani's son, Muhammad Hamadani. Towards the end of the fourteenth century Sultan Sikandar patronized the construction of a shrine for Saiyid 'Ali Hamadani, known as the Khanaqah-i Mu'alla, which stands on the banks of the Jhelum in Srinagar's old city. Although rebuilt several times over the centuries, this elegant structure, with its sloping pyramidal roofs made of cedar and its delicately carved eaves, is a superb example of traditional Kashmiri architecture.

In Kashmir's volatile fourteenth century, the valley kingdom thus saw the end of the indigenous Lohara dynasty (1003–1320), Mongol invasion, and the fitful beginnings of the Kashmir sultanate. The latter part of that century also saw a remarkable female poet, Lalla (also called Laleshwari, or Lal Ded, d. 1392), who further unsettled Kashmir's existing socio-religious order. Following a pattern of Indian religious reformers going back at least to the time of the Buddha, Lalla severed social ties with her marital family and wandered for extended periods of time in a quest for truth. An ardent devotee of Śiva, she described achieving liberation from the endless cycle of reincarnation that underlies much of Indian thought:

> I, Lalla, entered by the garden-gate of mine own mind,
> And there (O joy!) saw Siva with Shakti sealed in one;
> And there itself I merged in the Lake of Immortal Bliss.
> Now while alive I am unchained from the wheel of birth and death,
> What can the world do unto me?[45]

She also boldly challenged the norms of conventional religion. Declaring that images and temples are only stone, Lalla – though herself born into a Brahmin household – threw down the challenge: 'Whom will you worship, O stubborn Pandit?'[46] For centuries, Lalla's poems were cherished, committed to memory and handed down orally among the masses of Kashmir's rural society.[47] Indeed, her verses comprise the earliest specimens of vernacular Kashmiri language and literature.[48] Moreover, like other devotional poets who began to appear throughout South Asia from the fourteenth century on, Lalla sought, found and preached a social reality lying beyond conventionally understood religious communities.[49]

Several points stand out regarding the growth of sultanate institutions in fourteenth-century Kashmir. First, such institutions did not derive from any political connection with the Delhi sultanate, as was the case in regions such as Bengal, Gujarat or the Deccan. Consequently, the Kashmir sultanate did not inherit a tradition of military slavery or of slave rulers, as did some other Indian sultanates. Nor did it mint the kind of coinage that appeared in the Delhi sultanate from its earliest days. Brahmins continued to run government affairs after the valley's transition to a sultanate form of rulership, and Sanskrit – not Persian – remained the official language. Although Kashmir's fourteenth century had opened with a Hindu dynasty and closed with a Muslim one, the valley experienced no serious rupture in its governing institutions during this transition. It would pioneer its own style of Indian sultanate.

## THE DECLINE OF THE TUGHLUQ EMPIRE

Although the Delhi sultanate was still in its ascendency of wealth and power at the turn of the fourteenth century, by mid-century the state was on the wane. On nearly all its frontiers Sultan Muhammad bin Tughluq's patchwork empire experienced rebellions, most dramatically in Gujarat. Topographically, this region is far less uniform than the Bengal delta, the valley of Kashmir, or even the Deccan plateau. Gujarat's long coastline jutting into the Arabian Sea for centuries exposed the region to outsiders who came as invaders, settlers and, especially, merchants. The latter integrated Gujarat with wider Indian Ocean networks of trade, making it one of the most globalized regions in the world – in contrast to the nearly hermetically sealed

Kashmir. Unlike Gujarat's coastal areas, the hinterland of the Saurashtra peninsula is an arid and hilly mix of desert and scrubland, and hence a mainly pastoral region. Historically, nomadic herding communities moved in from Rajasthan to the north-east and from Sind to the north-west. Eastern Gujarat features a fertile north–south corridor of rich farmland, capable of producing surplus food and cash crops, especially cotton. These geographical differences engendered distinctive occupational specialists: cosmopolitan merchants along the coasts, pastoral nomads in Saurashtra, and grain-producing agriculturalists in the eastern corridor. Yet despite their differences, Gujarat's subregions were historically interdependent. Rulers in the eastern corridor, for example, took measures to enhance region-wide security with a view to promoting coastal trade.[50]

From the mid tenth to the mid thirteenth centuries, kings of the Solanki dynasty ruled over most of the region from their capital, Anahilapataka, in eastern Gujarat. Theirs was a period of unprecedented prosperity for the many seaports that dotted the coastline along Saurashtra and both sides of the Gulf of Cambay. Already in 916 the port of Chaul, just south of modern Mumbai, had a community of 10,000 people descended from mixed marriages of Arab merchants and local women.[51] As early as 971, a congregational mosque was built to accommodate the many foreign merchants who had taken up residence in the great commercial entrepôt of Cambay.[52] The cosmopolitan nature of coastal Gujarat is captured in a thirteenth-century inscription at Veraval, the site of the temple of Somnath and one of the more important pilgrimage centres in western India. As noted in the preceding chapter, contemporary Sanskrit inscriptions convey a business-as-usual atmosphere at this commercially important site, notwithstanding Mahmud of Ghazni's plundering the temple in 1026. More than two centuries later, in 1264, a Sanskrit and Arabic bilingual inscription at the same site records the construction of a mosque patronized by an Iranian merchant from the Persian Gulf named Nur al-Din Firuz. The Arabic text refers to the deity worshipped in the mosque as Allah, and describes Nur al-Din as 'the king [*sultan*] of sea-men, the king of the kings of traders' and 'the sun of Islam and the Muslims'. By contrast, the Sanskrit text identifies the deity worshiped in the mosque as Viśvanatha ('lord of the universe'),

Śunyarupa ('one whose form is of the void') and Viśvarupa ('having various forms'). It identifies the prophet of Islam as a *bodhaka* – that is, 'preceptor', 'elder' or 'wise man', and the mosque's patron, Nur al-Din Firuz, as a *dharma-bhandaya*, or 'supporter of *dharma*' – that is, cosmic/social order as understood in classical Indian thought.[53]

While the inscription's Arabic text reflects the perspective of the mosque's Muslim patron, its Sanskrit counterpart reveals that of the proximate Hindu population, which identified the supreme deity of Islam with Viśvanatha, the prophet of Islam with an Indian *bodhaka*, and Nur al-Din Firuz with a 'supporter of *dharma*'. Informing these theological representations was the context in which the inscription appeared. In order to build the mosque, Nur al-Din needed the approval of the temple's trustees, who apparently controlled the land he acquired. Since merchants and customs houses paid taxes to the temple, both the temple priests and the town's governing classes would have approved the project. They all had a shared interest in attracting long-distance merchants such as Nur al-Din to trade, settle and worship in the town. The particulars of Hindu and Muslim theology were accordingly adjusted to ensure that cash kept moving and that all would profit.

Of course, wealthy commercial or pilgrimage centres such as Veraval also attracted outside invaders. In 1216, the Solanki overlords of Somnath had to fortify the temple to protect it from attacks by Hindu rulers in neighbouring Malwa. In 1243, when the Solanki rulers were overthrown by one of their own former vassal clans, the Vaghelas, these new rulers moved quickly to ensure the security of routes leading to and between prosperous coastal towns such as Veraval. But by the early fourteenth century, outsiders more distant than Malwa had cast their eyes on those towns. From Delhi, 'Ala al-Din Khalaji's generals launched their first invasion of Gujarat in 1297, and by 1306 they had swept away the Vaghela dynasty altogether. Revealing their intention not to plunder but to govern the region, the Khalajis replaced the topmost layer of the former Vaghela rulers with their own governor, renamed the former Vaghela capital Patan, built a large congregational mosque there, and garrisoned strategic forts with mainly Afghan soldiers. They also allowed native landholders to retain their former positions, so long as they paid taxes to their new overlords. Finally, they made conciliatory gestures toward the Jains, one of Gujarat's largest and most prosperous trading communities, by restoring and patronizing their temples.

When Sultan Muhammad bin Tughluq rose to power in 1325, however, Delhi took steps to impose a more direct rule over Gujarat. In Patan, the sultan replaced the province's single governor with two chief officers, one for the army and another for finance, and took several major land assignments (*iqta'*) under his personal control. Architecturally, the clearest statement of the regime's presence was its patronage of one of India's most imposing mosques built in this period – the congregational mosque of Cambay, the most commercially vibrant of Gujarat's seaports in the thirteenth and early fourteenth centuries. Located at the head of the gulf bearing its name, Cambay directly linked the maritime world of the Indian Ocean with Gujarat's rich, eastern agricultural zone, and beyond that with overland routes leading up to Delhi. Given that Tughluq power was based on its cavalries, and that Cambay was the principal seaport through which Delhi imported its war-horses – thousands arrived annually from across the Arabian Sea – the city was also of vital strategic importance. At one point, the Tughluq officer who patronized the city's congregational mosque had held the post of Superintendent of the Royal Stable,[54] suggesting the overlap of Tughluq imperial power, commerce, access to war-horses and piety. Visually projecting that nexus, the mosque loomed over the city's bustling harbour, architecturally imposing itself on its visitors. Ibn Battuta praised the seaport as 'one of the most beautiful cities as regards the artistic architecture of its houses and the construction of its mosques'.[55]

By the 1330s, however, Muhammad bin Tughluq's seemingly arbitrary policies of reshuffling his appointees, which involved the dismissal of even experienced officers, created an atmosphere of insecurity throughout the realm. In peripheral provinces, where sheer distance from Delhi worked against the government's ability to impose its will, rebellion always threatened. As new territories were annexed by the Khalajis and Tughluqs, large numbers of Afghans were garrisoned in frontier forts as high-ranking officers and ordinary soldiers. But by the late 1330s, when these elements threatened sedition – not only in Gujarat, but also in Malwa and the Deccan – the sultan sent in Indian and older, Turkish, regiments to stabilize matters.[56] In Gujarat a group of Afghans challenged and defeated an imperial army in Baroda in 1344 and then marched directly on Cambay, which also fell under its control. At this moment a certain Taghi, a former high-ranking officer whom the sultan had capriciously dismissed from his court, was being held in Cambay, about to be exiled to Yemen. But when the rebels seized control of the city, they liberated Taghi and went on to declare an independent sultanate in central Gujarat.

Resolving to take matters into his own hands, in January 1345 the sultan left Delhi for good, destined to spend his last six years tirelessly suppressing rebellions in both Gujarat and the Deccan. After first recovering Cambay and making Broach his headquarters, he moved on Daulatabad in an unsuccessful effort to quash the Deccan uprising. While still there, in early 1346 he received the news that Taghi and a large force of rebels had seized Gujarat's provincial capital of Patan and were on their way to Cambay. By the time the sultan returned to Gujarat, Taghi had already seized Cambay and was besieging Broach. But on the sultan's arrival, Taghi retreated into the Gujarat hinterland and defiantly executed the Tughluq provincial governor, whom he had been holding hostage after seizing Patan. For the next year the sultan pursued Taghi, who continued to elude imperial troops in both eastern Gujarat and Saurashtra. In September 1347, the sultan received the grim tidings that his army in the Deccan had been completely routed. This only stiffened his resolve to capture Taghi, who soon joined forces with rebellious chiefs at the fort of Junagadh, in central Saurashtra. Although the chieftains holding that fort submitted to the sultan in 1349, Taghi once again escaped, this time fleeing westwards to Sind. Since that region had never been annexed to the Delhi sultanate, the sultan hoped both to capture the fugitive rebel and to return to Delhi having added a new province to his realm, compensating for the loss of the Deccan.

But this was not to happen. In mid 1350, just as his officers were drawing up plans to cross the desolate Rann of Kutch – the huge salt marsh separating the Saurashtra peninsula from the mouth of the Indus – the sultan was stricken with a violent fever. By December he had recovered sufficiently to start moving his army towards Thatta, the capital of the Samma chieftain then ruling lower Sind. But in March 1351, with his army within just forty kilometres of the Sindi capital whose fort he was about to besiege, the sultan died. Tughluq fortunes had reached a low point from which they never fully recovered. As the late sultan's army hastily returned to Delhi, the rebel Taghi was still at large, Sind remained unconquered, Gujarat slipped into a state of semi-autonomy and the Deccan had achieved complete independence.

## CONCLUSION

Although Sultan Muhammad bin Tughluq ruled the Delhi sultanate for only twenty-six years, the spectre of this towering and complex figure loomed over the entire fourteenth century. When he came to power in 1325, the sultanate had reached the height of its might, prestige and cultural florescence. By that time, the state no longer relied on recruiting luminaries from beyond the Khyber, since a class of India-born intellectuals had emerged within the Delhi sultanate. The most famous of these, the brilliant poet Amir Khusrau, was just as proud of his Indian heritage as he was skilled at turning a Persian verse. Nor were the Khalaji or Tughluq courts the sole foci of intellectual talent: men of letters attached themselves to the *khanaqah*s of charismatic Sufi shaikhs across all of north India.

Underlying the prosperity and power of the Khalajis and Tughluqs in the fourteenth century was the minting of precious metals that had been plundered from Indian capitals in the preceding century – first under the Ghurids, and then under Iltutmish, Balban and their respective successors. The entire period from 1192 to 1325 had seen a self-sustaining cycle whereby plundered specie was converted to minted money to purchase foreign war-horses, pay troops and defend the north-west frontier from Mongol incursions. But by the 1340s, when the peak of Tughluq power coincided with the middle of Muhammad bin Tughluq's extravagant reign, that treasure had become exhausted. Regions once well integrated into the Tughluqs' revenue system rose in open rebellion against central authority and would soon emerge as independent sultanates. The first of these secessions occurred in Bengal, led by Shams al-Din Ilyas Shah in 1342. This was followed just five years later by the loss of the sultanate's Deccan dependencies and the appearance of the independent Bahmani and Vijayanagara kingdoms. Fiscally, the sultanate's loss of Bengal and the Deccan led to a silver famine that hindered its ability to purchase war-horses or pay its troops at the same levels as previously.[57]

But even as former provinces such as Bengal, the Deccan and ultimately Gujarat pulled away from Delhi's direct rule, the ideology and institutions of the sultanate form of polity, which had crystallized in Central Asia under Samanid monarchs in the tenth century, continued to flourish in these regions. These included, most importantly, a Persianized conception of the universal monarch, the sultan, assisted by a salaried class of intermediaries standing between the primary producers of agrarian wealth and a centralized state apparatus; the division of sovereign territory into units of land whose revenues were used by those intermediaries to recruit, train and command designated numbers of cavalry; and a commitment to the idea and ideal of justice (*'adl, 'adalat*) as the fundamental justification for wielding worldly power.

Elaborating such core ideas, together with the aesthetic and moral order that underpinned them, was a growing canon of Persian texts that circulated widely across South Asia. Some of the genres and representative authors comprising the canon at this time included works of epic poetry (Firdausi), Sufism (Sana'i, 'Attar, Rumi, Hujwiri), morality (Hafiz, Sa'di, Tusi, Amir Khusrau), romance literature (Nizami), science (Ibn Sina), history (Ibn Balkhi, Bayhaqi) and politics (Nizam al-Mulk). Transmitted through ever-widening networks of literati, Sufi shaikhs, mercenaries, artists, merchants and so on, these texts moved within the sovereign territories of established sultanates, as well as, increasingly, lands that had never been exposed to direct sultanate rule. Yet across South Asia, one can see the uneven penetration of the core ideas that constituted the Persianate world. Kashmir, landlocked and secluded in its mountain fastness, had never been conquered by a Persianized state such as the Delhi sultanate. Yet, in the course of the fourteenth century, it assimilated many of the ideas that informed those states.

Towards the very end of the fourteenth century, however, much of

South Asia would be subjected to dramatic changes after the destruction of Delhi and the virtual decapitation of the sultanate owing to the devastating invasion by the Central Asian warlord Timur. Although the state had been in decline ever since the 1340s, its near-collapse, catalysed by Timur's invasion, set in motion a new series of historical forces that altered the course of India's history for ever.

# 3
# Timur's Invasion and Legacy,
## 1400–1550

From jigging veins of rhyming mother-wits,
And such conceits as clownage keeps in pay,
We'll lead you to the stately tent of war,
Where you shall hear the Scythian Tamburlaine
Threatening the world with high astounding terms,
And scourging kingdoms with his conquering sword.
View but his picture in this tragic glass,
And then applaud his fortunes as you please.

## OVERVIEW

Above is the brief prologue that, in late 1587, introduced an audience in Elizabethan London to the first performance of *Tamburlaine*, Christopher Marlowe's bold new play. No audience in England had heard anything like it before. In point of form, its author had broken radically with literary convention, and he knew it. The play's very first lines airily dismiss the entire legacy of Renaissance drama – its 'jigging veins of rhyming mother-wits' – as mere clowning. Now, for the first time, audiences would hear blank verse, freed from rhymes, in the very iambic pentameter that William Shakespeare would soon deploy in his own plays.

*Tamburlaine* was so popular – the 1594–5 season saw fourteen performances – that Marlowe had to write a sequel to it. But its significance lies not just in its vivid language, its blank verse, or its complex character development. Most striking was the larger-than-life 'Tamburlaine' himself, whom Marlowe presented as a cold-blooded

Machiavellian warrior. Exulting in his barbarism and cruelty, Marlowe's hero is determined to crush, subdue or win over any and all opponents in his singular quest to conquer the world. We thus see him feeding scraps to a defeated king placed in a cage, or using the king's live body as a footstool, or driving a chariot pulled by a team of defeated monarchs, harnessed like horses in their traces. In his unchecked excess, Marlowe's Tamburlaine must defy and master not just men, but also the gods, as at one point he even burns a copy of the Qur'an. Indeed, this hubristic figure, depicted by Rembrandt in the mid seventeenth century [see Fig. 5], probably planted in Europe's collective subconscious the archetypal Asian tyrant that emerged in nineteenth- and twentieth-century scholarship as the 'Oriental despot' anticipated by Marx or Weber and elaborated by Karl Wittfogel. Later, in the twentieth and twenty-first centuries, that same archetype – violent, authoritarian and above all, Muslim – would be incarnated in some Euro-American quarters in figures such as Ayatollah Khomeini, Muammar Gaddafi or Saddam Husain.

Marlowe's outrageous protagonist is very loosely based on the historical Timur (1336–1405), a remarkably successful warlord and one of history's most astonishing figures. 'Tamerlane' is a European corruption of the Persian *Timur-i lang*, or 'Timur the lame', in reference to a limp acquired from a crippling wound suffered in his youth. Like Marlowe's character, the historical Timur rose from humble beginnings in a clan of pastoral nomads in Central Asia. He happened to reach adulthood in the mid fourteenth century just as the last successor states to the Mongol empire in Iran and Central Asia had crumbled into a collection of feuding principalities. Timur sought to unify this politically fragmented region by creating, in effect, a neo-Mongol empire. Although himself an ethnic Turk unrelated to Genghis Khan, he married a princess descended from the great Mongol empire-builder and on this basis proudly titled himself *gurkan*, or 'imperial son-in-law'.

Politically, Timur emerged around 1360 as the head of a minor tribe in the region of Samarqand, then a vibrant oasis town on the Silk Road between China and the Mediterranean basin, surrounded by semi-arid lands ideally suited for pastoral nomadism. Rich oasis towns such as Samarqand were inhabited mainly by Persian-speaking communities of Sunni Muslims – artisans, merchants, officials, religious clerics, scholars – while their surrounding hinterlands were populated chiefly by Persianized Turks. Recently integrated into Muslim life, these clans of nomadic or semi-nomadic pastoralists had mastered horse warfare, and as such were powerful players in Central Asian politics. Timur's career began by negotiating the balance between peoples inhabiting these two mutually interdependent ecological and cultural niches: the pastoral and the sedentary. In the 1360s he manoeuvred his way through a maze of local tribal politics, forging alliances with other clans while expanding both commercial and political linkages within Central Asia. A natural leader endowed with personal charisma and military genius, he repeatedly transformed rivals and would-be enemies into allies, thereby building up formidable armies of mounted archers.

By 1370 Timur dominated Samarqand, which he ruled through a Mongol puppet khan by exploiting his 'imperial son-in-law' status. Several years later he annexed the rich and fabled Ferghana valley in present-day Tajikistan [see Maps 1 or 5]. In 1383 he marched southwards in a series of campaigns that over the next decade ravaged the entire Iranian plateau, either destroying or subjugating such centres of high Persian culture as Herat, Zaranj, Tabriz, Isfahan and Shiraz. While systematically using terror tactics against recalcitrant urban populations, Timur spared cities that submitted to his armies, sending literati, artisans and artists back to Samarqand to adorn his capital with spectacular works of architecture. In the 1390s he campaigned across western Iran and Iraq, sacking Baghdad in 1393. His armies then turned north to the Caucasus, subduing chieftains and destroying cities of the Golden Horde in Crimea and the Don and Volga valleys, briefly occupying Moscow in 1395. In 1400 he seized Tiflis, reducing the Georgian monarch to a vassal. From there he pressed south to Syria, capturing Aleppo and Damascus. In 1402 he marched on Anatolia, defeating the main army of the fledgling Ottoman state near Ankara, where he captured the hapless Sultan Bayazid I. By this time Timur had acquired such a fearsome reputation that he secured the submission of both the Byzantine emperor and Egypt's Mamluk sultan without investing either Constantinople or Cairo. In 1404 he returned in triumph to his capital at Samarqand, where he received a host of foreign emissaries while preparing for what would have been the capstone to his grandiose plan of recreating Genghis Khan's Mongol imperium – the conquest of China. In early 1405 his armies had barely left Samarqand, however, when he was overtaken by a brief sickness and died.

His failure to conquer China notwithstanding, in one important respect Timur accomplished what the Mongols themselves had repeatedly attempted but failed to do – namely, invade India and sack Delhi. In the thirteenth and early fourteenth centuries the sultans of Delhi had prudently garrisoned soldiers in the mountain passes leading from Afghanistan to the Punjab, thereby thwarting Mongol attempts to invade India. But by the end of the fourteenth century the sovereign territory of the Tughluqs had shrunk drastically following numerous mid-century rebellions. In 1351 Muhammad bin Tughluq was succeeded by his cousin Firuz Shah Tughluq (r. 1351–88), who led several failed expeditions to reconquer Bengal, although he did reduce both Orissa and Sind to tributary states in 1361 and 1363 respectively. He also managed to stabilize what little remained of the Delhi sultanate. To enhance irrigation and expand cultivation in Delhi's immediate hinterland, he oversaw the construction of a number of major canals in the Punjab; he promoted education by building *madrasa*s in Delhi; he established hospitals to provide treatment for the poor; and he adorned Delhi with rest-houses, gardens, water tanks and wells. But he also relaxed some of the sounder administrative practices of the system he had inherited. Whereas revenue assignments (*iqta*'s) had formerly reverted to the crown upon the death of their holders, under Firuz they became inheritable by their holders' descendants, thereby creating a powerful landed gentry with vested interests in permanent holdings in the countryside. This policy, accompanied by a decline in land-tax collection, considerably weakened the state's central power. Worse, the ten years following Firuz's death in 1388 saw a rapid succession of five weak sultans, putting the city and the sultanate in a fatally vulnerable state. The fifth of these rulers, one of Firuz's grandsons, would prove no match for Timur, a world-conqueror who had already swept over many of the most populous and fabled cities on earth.

In the late summer of 1398, having conquered the Iranian plateau and placed loyal governors in its principal cities, Timur marched through Afghanistan and, bypassing Kashmir, crossed the Indus that September. Encountering little resistance, his cavalry rolled across the Punjab to Panipat, some sixty-five kilometres north of the capital, where he met and crushed a Tughluq cavalry of 10,000, only a quarter the size of the sultanate's army of just several decades earlier. For about a month Timur plundered Delhi with impunity, massacring a reported 80,000 inhabitants and so thoroughly ruining the built landscape that it took the city nearly a century to recover. Unlike Muhammad Ghuri and his slave generals two centuries earlier, however, Timur had no intention of remaining in India, or of integrating the remnants of the sultanate's territories into his sprawling empire. Instead, like a violent storm that disappears as suddenly as it appears, in January 1399 he quit India, hauling back to Samarqand an immense amount of booty; elephants taken from this expedition were used to transport quarried stone for his ambitious construction projects there.

Although the Delhi sultanate survived Timur's destructive onslaught, and even experienced something of a revival in the late 1400s, it would never regain the power or prestige it had enjoyed in the days of Muhammad bin Tughluq. In reality, Timur's invasion inaugurated what has been called India's 'long fifteenth century', that is, the period bracketed on the front end by Timur's invasion in 1398–9, and on the back end by the advent of Mughal rule (1526–1858). The founder of the Mughal dynasty, Babur (r. 1526–30), was a direct descendant of Timur and claimed the right to govern north India as his legal patrimony. One might therefore think of the period 1398–1526 as a long interregnum between the planting of the idea of Timurid rule in India by Timur himself, and its eventual realization by Babur.

There are good reasons to regard this as a coherent era in India's history. Although the Delhi sultanate had unified much of South Asia by the early fourteenth century, Timur's invasion at the end of that century shattered the sultanate as a stable political or cultural entity – even if such status had only ever been imperfectly realized. By 1400 the northern two-thirds of the subcontinent had become a patchwork quilt of independent kingdoms, as former Tughluq governors, or their sons, rebranded themselves as independent sultans ruling sovereign states. Politically, then, Timur's invasion accelerated a process of devolution that had already begun in the mid fourteenth century with the breakaway of former provinces such as Bengal or the Deccan. As ever more former Tughluq provinces became independent sultanates, horizons were lowered, and a wider, pan-Indian world, at least in a political sense, vanished.

Much conventional historiography portrays the long fifteenth century as a dreary period when the stage lights in the theatre of history seem to have dimmed while onlookers are forced to sit in darkness, waiting for the curtain to rise to reveal the dazzling dawn of the Mughal era, when India would once again see a large, centralized empire. But in fact it was one of India's most vibrant and creative eras. The fragmentation of northern India catalysed by Timur's invasion meant, among other things, increasing demands for literary and military specialists, as throngs of competing chieftains and warlords sought to fill power vacuums created by the collapse of Delhi's authority. Instead of a single, centralized locus of patronage, dozens of smaller such centres now mushroomed across north India's landscape, each headed by an aspiring state-builder.

The present chapter therefore explores three interconnected themes that characterize India's long fifteenth century: the emergence of regional courts in territories formerly under the Delhi sultanate's rule; the emerging idea of 'Rajput' as a social category; and the rise of vernacular literatures and its significance.

## UPPER INDIA

Nowhere were the effects of Timur's invasion more acutely felt than in the heartland of the former Tughluq domain – the wide, densely populated Indo-Gangetic plain that extended from the Punjab through the upper and mid-Gangetic basin to the Bengal delta. The career of Khizr Khan, a Punjabi chieftain belonging to the Khokar clan, illustrates the transition to an increasingly polycentric north India. Sultan Firuz Tughluq (r. 1351–88) had earlier appointed this chieftain as his governor of Multan. But when Timur's army sacked Delhi in 1398–9, Khizr Khan shrewdly ingratiated himself with the

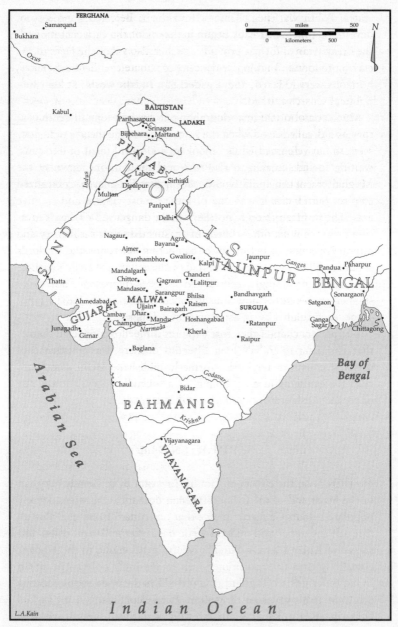

Fifteenth-century north India

Central Asian warlord. His efforts paid off. Before leaving India, Timur made the Khokar chieftain governor of the Punjabi cities of Lahore, Multan and Dipalpur. Khizr Khan also visited Timur's capital at Samarqand to negotiate the annual tribute that he would send to his treasury. Then in 1414, shortly after the death of the last Tughluq monarch and nearly a decade after Timur's death, he managed to wrest control of Delhi itself and launch his own dynasty of monarchs, the so-called Saiyid dynasty (1414–51). Yet even then he refrained from using sovereign titles, preferring instead to rule as the viceroy of Timur's son and successor, Shah Rukh of Herat (r. 1405–47), to whom he regularly sent tribute. This was one way that Timur's legacy lingered on in northern India.

In the early fifteenth century, however, the danger to Delhi no longer came from the west, but from the newly formed sultanate of Jaunpur to the east. Lying in present-day Uttar Pradesh and Bihar, between the rump Delhi sultanate under Khizr Khan's successors and Bengal, the kingdom of Jaunpur emerged from a former Tughluq province that attained independence soon after Timur had left India. It was founded by of one of Sultan Firuz Tughluq's eunuch slaves, the Ethiopia-born Malik Sarwar, whom the sultan had sent to quell rebels in the Jaunpur region. By 1394, however, after his master's death but before Timur's invasion, Sarwar had already established virtual independence from Delhi. Then, soon after Timur left India, Sarwar's adopted son and successor declared his formal independence, thereby establishing the Sharqi dynasty of Jaunpur (1399–1483), so-called because Malik Sarwar had been titled *malik-i sharq*, 'king of the East'. The new state was an immediate beneficiary of Timur's invasion, absorbing many of Delhi's traumatized scholars, artisans, artists and craftsmen who had managed to escape likely enslavement by fleeing eastwards. This explains why the Tughluqs' architectural style – a robust, militaristic vocabulary of battered walls, scant ornamentation, engaged corner towers and monumental gateways – figures so prominently in Jaunpur's early structures, such as the city's grand Atala mosque (1408).

The sovereigns of Jaunpur, which straddles the middle Ganges and its tributaries, enjoyed ready access to war-elephants, large herds of which roamed the jungles of Bihar and Bengal. Moreover, because the central Gangetic plain was being rapidly converted from forest to rice paddy, the Sharqis' sovereign territory could support a growing population. The region was therefore something of a frontier zone, with small colonies of Muslim farmers surrounded by larger populations of non-Muslims. The sultanate's strategic weakness, however, was that it lay far from the great trade routes that brought war-horses from Central Asia to India. Jaunpur therefore lacked easy access to the most important military commodity in premodern South Asia, since war-horses were generally more reliable and efficacious in combat than elephants, even if less fearsome. Partly for this reason Jaunpur's rulers sought to take over what remained of the Delhi sultanate, for Delhi, unlike Jaunpur, was well positioned to acquire the long strings of war-horses that wound their way from beyond the Khyber Pass to Indian markets. By the mid fifteenth century, moreover, the tiny kingdom of Delhi ruled by the Saiyid sultans had shrunk to but a shadow of its former self. As was wittily said of the dynasty's last monarch, Sultan 'Alam Shah (r. 1445–51), 'the kingdom of the king of the world [*shah-i 'alam*, i.e. 'Alam Shah] extends from Delhi to Palam'.[1] Since the latter is located near New Delhi's international airport, the dictum refers to an area spanning a mere thirteen kilometres! What little remained of Sultan Muhammad Tughluq's once-mighty empire had literally become a joke, and Delhi itself a minor but tempting target for ambitious neighbours.

But after 'Alam Shah, Delhi saw a new dynasty of sultans, the Lodi rulers (1451–1526), under whose reign the old Delhi sultanate experienced something of a renewed lease of life. Moreover, the rise of this dynasty in the heart of the broad Delhi plain – historically, north India's geopolitical cockpit – reveals a prominent feature of the long fifteenth century: the immigration and settlement of ethnic Afghans across the breadth of upper India. For centuries, Afghans had played a central role as merchants and transporters, responding to the subcontinent's insatiable demand for Central Asian war-horses. Throughout those centuries, caravans had moved horses from Bukhara and other collection points south and east across the rugged Afghan mountains and through the several passes in the Sulaiman range that led down to the Punjab plains, thence to north India's horse markets. These caravans were necessarily well armed, for reasons made clear by the

English scholar Simon Digby. Recalling his days as a youth in India in the late 1930s and early 1940s, Digby writes:

> I saw the last survivors of these horse caravans, great processions with thousands of men, with women and children marching beside their Bactrian camels, when I was a young man, though by that time the route had changed to the Khyber further north [rather than the Gomal Pass further south], and they mainly engaged in the trade of dry fruit from Gilgit. They were still a formidable armed entity on the march, with very small boys carrying rifles, women unveiled and sometimes also armed – altogether several thousand people. The caravans going into the north Indian plains in the fourteenth and fifteenth centuries had to be sufficiently powerful in their arms and their fighting tactics to be able to defeat any local ruler who would rather confiscate their horses and other goods than pay for them.[2]

Having once settled down in upper India, many Afghan horse-merchants parlayed their commercial connections – and their access to Afghan warriors – into power, a process facilitated by north India's fragmented, post-Timurid political landscape. Throughout the first half of the fifteenth century, rulers of the Saiyid dynasty relied on the support of well-connected Afghans to fend off attacks from the sultans of Jaunpur. This inevitably drew Afghans deeper into north India's political affairs, giving them secure footholds on an unstable geo-political chessboard. The founder of the Lodi dynasty, Bahlul Lodi (r. 1451–89), first reached India from Afghanistan with a long caravan of horses, for which the Saiyid government paid him with a land assignment instead of cash. That land soon became his political base. Later he was appointed governor of the Punjabi city of Sirhind. In 1451, with the abdication of the last Saiyid ruler, Sultan 'Alam Shah (the 'king of the world'), Bahlul emerged well positioned to become sultan himself. Then, as sovereign of Delhi, he recruited more Afghans as commanders and cavalrymen to defend the city from its hostile neighbours, in particular the sultans of Jaunpur. One of those sultans, Jaunpur's Husain Shah Sharqi (r. 1458–83), repeatedly challenged Bahlul Lodi for the control of Delhi. But in 1483 Bahlul counter-attacked, seized Jaunpur and drove Husain Shah into exile in Bihar.

Notwithstanding the strategic advantage of their relative proximity to Afghanistan and its horse-suppliers, Bahlul Lodi and his successors, Sikandar (r. 1489–1517) and Ibrahim (r. 1517–26), had constantly to cut deals with other Afghan clans. Since all Afghans were bound by codes of honour obliging them to take revenge on perceived infringements to their dignity, Lodi chieftains were constrained in their efforts to create a hierarchically ordered monarchy of the sort set up by their Khalaji or Tughluq predecessors. Once established in Delhi, Bahlul Lodi appealed to Pashtun chiefs back in Afghanistan to migrate with their men to India in order to provide manpower for his fledgling kingdom, promising to share his possessions with them as brothers. In response, his kinsmen reportedly descended from the Afghan mountains 'like ants and locusts', according to one chronicler, and were rewarded with *iqta*'s over which they enjoyed considerable autonomy. Nor did the sultan have a throne erected for himself; rather, so we are told, he 'shared the carpet with his peers'.[3] Bahlul's successors did try to centralize power somewhat: his son Sikandar arrogated the right to choose which son of a deceased *iqta'dar*'s progeny might inherit land and soldiers. And Ibrahim, the dynasty's third and last sultan, went further by requiring his Afghan kinsmen in the sultanate to observe proper court ceremonies. But such measures threatened the cohesion of the Lodi state, which in Bahlul's day had been governed as a confederation of loosely aligned chieftains with only tenuous loyalty to Delhi.

Although Bahlul Lodi had invoked Afghan sentiment and culture to attract his kinsmen to India, and although the Lodi regime was dominated by ethnic Afghans, calling the Lodis an 'Afghan' dynasty is not fully accurate. None of the three Lodi sultans enjoyed a monopoly of Afghan talent in India, since Afghan immigrants had settled across the entire Indo-Gangetic plain, especially in the Sharqi sultanate of Jaunpur. The Lodis even employed non-Afghans to check their Afghan rivals. Some Afghans residing within Lodi territory and theoretically loyal to the Lodi cause actually opposed the regime. In fact, the fateful 1526 invasion of India by Babur – the event that would overthrow the Lodis and establish the Mughal empire – was launched after Afghan chieftains in Lodi-administered Punjab had invited that Central Asian prince, then ruler of Kabul, to intervene in Delhi's affairs.

## BENGAL

Apart from catalysing the emergence of new states, Timur's invasion also gave rise to regional cultures in former Tughluq provinces. But in the case of Bengal, a former Tughluq governor, Shams al-Din Ilyas Shah, had established the delta's first independent dynasty nearly sixty years before Timur sacked Delhi. During this prolonged period of autonomy, which covered the latter half of the fourteenth century, Bengal's ancient class of Hindu aristocrats rose to prominence in the state's government. By the end of that century, elements of the delta's native ruling class had gained so much authority as to unsettle the Bengal sultanate's elite Sufi shaikhs, champions of a reformed and purified Islam.[4] The most important of these native nobles was Raja Ganesh, a powerful Bengali landholder whose family had enjoyed prominent status in the delta for four centuries. In 1410 the high-born patrician audaciously usurped power and for five years governed the kingdom through a succession of Muslim puppet-sultans. In 1415 he went so far as to enthrone his own son, a lad of only twelve years named Jadu, while continuing to govern as regent. But Ganesh never sought to revive the Brahmanically defined model of kingship of classical Indian tradition. Rather, a compromise formula was worked out between political brokers for the court's Muslim and non-Muslim factions, whereby young Jadu was allowed to rule on condition that he convert to Islam, which he did, reigning as Sultan Jalal al-Din Muhammad (r. 1415–32). Soon after his enthronement, coins bearing his name were simultaneously issued from Bengal's principal urban centres – Pandua, Chittagong, Sonargaon and Satgaon – suggesting a calculated attempt by Raja Ganesh to ensure the acceptance of his son's accession throughout the delta.[5]

Yet this arrangement only infuriated elite Sufis attached to Bengal's royal court. One of them, Shaikh Nur Qutb-i 'Alam, even wrote to the Sharqi sultan of neighbouring Jaunpur, imploring him to invade the kingdom and 'liberate' Bengal for 'Islam'. Although the sultan did send an army towards Bengal, it seems to have turned back when placated with gold. Amidst the chaos in the sultanate's capital at Pandua, meanwhile, things remained far from settled in Bengal's hinterland, where remnants of pre-sultanate ruling houses on the eastern frontier seized the moment to assert their independence. For a single year, 1417–18, no sultanate coins appeared anywhere in the delta, while in the extreme eastern and south-eastern sectors two successive Hindu kings rose in rebellion. But in the following two years the sultanate, now firmly under seventeen-year-old Jalal al-Din's rule, with his father still acting as regent, managed to suppress this rebellion and reassert its authority across the delta.[6]

The Raja Ganesh episode showed that, despite the vigorous objections of conservative sections of the Muslim elite, Bengali Hindus would henceforth be assimilated in the sultanate's ruling structure. Raja Ganesh refused to support the restoration of an explicitly Hindu polity anywhere in the delta. Of course, he operated under severe restraints, being able to retain his considerable influence only by merging his interests with those of the existing state, and by conciliating powerful Muslim classes at the capital. In the following years, as Jalal al-Din Muhammad grew to maturity, the sultan became ever bolder in asserting his claims to a specifically Islamic ruling ideology. He became a devoted follower of Shaikh Nur Qutb al-'Alam, Pandua's leading Chishti shaikh and the same man who had so strenuously opposed Raja Ganesh's coup. The sultan also rebuilt mosques demolished by his father, patronized a religious college in Mecca, obtained recognition from the Mamluk sultan of Egypt (the most prestigious ruler in the Middle East since the destruction of Baghdad in 1258), and stamped the Islamic confession of faith on his coins, a custom that had disappeared from Bengal several centuries earlier.[7] In 1427, after ruling for a dozen years, he went so far as to proclaim himself the 'caliph of Allah in the universe'.[8] One can only marvel at the audacity of a convert to the religion claiming the loftiest title in the Sunni world, second only to that of the Prophet himself.

Even while strenuously posturing as a correct Muslim, Sultan Jalal al-Din grounded himself and his regime in Bengali culture. He minted silver coins depicting the image of a lion, an animal possessing a wide symbolic range that included not only Persian imperial kingship, but also the cosmic vehicle of the goddess popularly manifested as Chandi, in whose name anti-sultanate rebellions had been waged in eastern Bengal shortly after Jalal al-Din came to power.

A contemporary Chinese traveller reported that, although Persian was understood by some in the court, the language in universal use there was Bengali – an observation indicating the triumph of the local vernacular at the highest level of officialdom.[9] And, as with the Adina mosque, architecture again suggests the state's nativist orientation. Starting with Jalal al-Din's reign, Bengali mosques adopted local structural elements and motifs: single-domed brick buildings with engaged corner towers, curved cornices and extensive terracotta ornamentation. The last feature was a throwback to Bengali Buddhist shrines dating to at least the eighth century, such as that seen at Somapura (Paharpur) in present-day northern Bangladesh. The curved cornice appeared in Bengali architecture for the first time in what is believed to be Jalal al-Din's own tomb, the Eklakhi Mausoleum (1432), which was inspired by the familiar thatched bamboo hut found throughout rural Bengal. The curved roofs of these ordinary dwellings, formed by the natural bend of a bamboo structure under the weight of thatching, allow water to drain from their upper surfaces in a part of India notorious for its heavy rainfall. This Bengali folk motif was now translated from bamboo and thatching into brick, used for both temples and mosques.

This nativist trend became even more pronounced in the reigns of Sultan 'Ala al-Din Husain Shah (1493–1519) and his son Nasir al-Din Nusrat Shah (1519–32). Under the former monarch, Hindus pervaded the state's government, serving in such important posts as chief minister, chief of bodyguards, master of the mint, private physician and private secretary to the sultan. State-sponsored brick and stone mosques built in native styles proliferated throughout the delta – more than 100 of them appearing between 1450 and 1550, far more than in any other period in Bengal's premodern history. At the same time, the court lent vigorous support to literature written in vernacular Bengali. Sultan Rukn al-Din Barbak (r. 1459–74) patronized the writing of the *Sri Krsna-Vijaya* by Maladhara Basu, and the courts of 'Ala al-Din Husain Shah and Nasir al-Din Nusrat Shah patronized the writing of the *Manasa-Vijaya* by Vipra Das, the *Padma-Purana* by Vijaya Gupta, the *Krsna-Mangala* by Yasoraj Khan and translations (from Sanskrit) of portions of the great epic *Mahabharata*, made by Vijaya Pandita and Kavindra Paramesvara.[10] The state's patronage of local culture stemmed partly from strategic assessments made in the wake of the upheavals of the Raja Ganesh period, and partly from the delta's protracted political and cultural isolation from north India.

Yet royal patronage was also selective. With the apparent aim of deepening the roots of their political authority, the sultans of Bengal patronized folk architecture as opposed to classical Indian styles, popular Bengali literature rather than Sanskrit treatises, and Vaishnava Bengali officials instead of Śakta Brahmins. This was doubtless due to the long association of Śiva worship with Hindu kingship, not just in Bengal but throughout India. Prior to the advent of Persianate sultanates in India, many Hindu kings had patronized one or another manifestation of Śiva, understood as the Cosmic Overlord protecting a maharaja's sovereign domain. This prior association made Persianate courts in Bengal and elsewhere wary of Śaiva culture, which would explain why the above-mentioned Bengali works were mainly Vaishnava in orientation. At the same time, royal coinage dispensed with the bombast of earlier periods, when Bengali sultans associated themselves with Alexander the Great or Arab caliphs. As is clear from the writing on his coins, Sultan Nasir al-Din Nusrat Shah was sultan simply because his father had been one; no further justification seemed necessary. Secure in their power, and with domination by faroff Delhi but a hazy memory, the sultans of Bengal confidently fashioned themselves as Bengali kings.

This sort of interaction between Persianate and Sanskritic cultures was in some ways unique to the delta. We find a very different variation on this same theme in the isolated valley of Kashmir.

# KASHMIR

Like many conquerors before him, Timur bypassed the Kashmir valley during his invasion of India, fixing his sights on the Tughluq capital of Delhi. In the autumn of 1398 his army had already marched across Afghanistan and was moving through the passes leading to the upper Indus valley. Yet his reputation for wholesale massacres of great cities had preceded his arrival in India, which is why Kashmir's

Sultan Sikandar (r. 1389-1413), on hearing that the Central Asian warlord was nearing his neighbourhood, rushed envoys to Timur's camp bearing gifts and fervent pledges of loyalty. Although Timur only wanted Sikandar's formal appearance, and no cash, his unscrupulous envoys caused the Kashmiri court to understand that it would have to furnish horses and a large sum of money. Puritanical and influential Muslims in Srinagar seized this moment to advance their religious agenda. One of these was Saiyid Muhammad Hamadani, a revered shaikh who, like his father 'Ali Hamadani, had migrated from Iran. Also influential was a group of Muslim clerics, the Baihaqi saiyids. In order to meet Timur's alleged financial demands, the latter urged the sultan to demolish Hindu temples and convert their images to bullion. The sultan's chief minister, Suha Bhatta, himself a zealous convert to Islam, persuaded Sikandar to destroy at least four major temple complexes in the valley – Parihaspura, Bijbehara, Tripureśvara and Martand – which earned the sultan the title *butshikan*, 'temple-destroyer'.[11] Sikandar also undermined the influence of the valley's powerful class of Brahmins by revoking their tax-free holdings and destroying their Sanskrit books.[12] Owing to such coercive measures, plus his imposition of the discriminatory *jizya* tax on non-Muslims, the charge of anti-Hindu bigotry has ever since clung to Sikandar's memory.[13] But not to that of his son.

There is a proverb that an apple never falls far from the tree; that is, a son tends to inherit his father's character. But in the case of Sikandar's son Zain al-'Abidin (r. 1420–70), the apple fell nowhere near the tree. After a brief period when his weak-willed elder brother ruled the valley, Zain al-'Abidin deposed his sibling and in 1420, with military help from allies in the Punjab, rose to power in Srinagar. His fifty-year reign, unlike Sikandar's fractious, intolerant rule, has been remembered as a golden age in Kashmir. The sultan's love of the valley's land, its literary heritage and its religious traditions comes through very clearly in contemporary literary works. One of his court poets, the Sanskrit scholar Śrivara, recorded an instance in which he and the sultan climbed high in the Pir Panjal Mountains to visit a lake sacred to the god Vishnu. After being rowed to the centre of the lake, the sultan asked the poet to relate the legends associated with it. As snow began to fall, the sultan reclined in the boat and listened as the poet recited verses from a famous Vaishnava Sanskrit work. 'Hearing the songs from the Gitagovinda from me,' recalled the poet:

> a wondrous sentiment raining down the devotion of Visnu Govinda arose for the king. The melodious tune struck up by both our voices echoed from the thickets [on the bank] as if repeated in refrain by the *gandharvas* [heavenly beings] staying there out of veneration to the king. Suddenly, gods showered forth flowers in the form of snowfall upon the king as he moved about on the lake, as if pleased at his devotion.[14]

As in Bengal, Kashmir's sultans showed a clear affinity for Vaishnava Hinduism. In both sultanates Muslim rulers patronized Vaishnava literature, admired Vaishnava poetry and consorted with Vaishnava personalities.

There are other reasons why Zain al-'Abidin's reign has been treasured in subsequent memory. The sultan recovered neighbouring territories that, though annexed by his grandfather Shihab al-Din, had asserted de facto independence in the intervening years. These included Baltistan and Ladakh to the north and east of the valley, and the upper Indus region to the west. He exchanged embassies or gifts with potentates beyond Kashmir, both in India and the Middle East. He improved the state's infrastructure by building bridges and digging irrigation canals. He encouraged villagers to settle in urban centres and take up a range of handicraft industries – for example, glasswork, woodwork, carpets and shawls – that have made Kashmir world-famous ever since. He gave encouragement to foreign architects such as Sadr al-Din Khurasani, who developed the design of wooden buildings that thereafter defined Kashmir's built landscape.[15] He regulated commodity prices, and was the valley's first sultan to inscribe his name on coins certain to have been minted in Kashmir. He was also the first local sultan to mint silver coins, suggesting his regime's economic stability and administrative centralization.[16] Finally, he eased taxes on the rural classes and, by abolishing the poll tax on non-Muslims, reversed one of his father's most contentious policies.

Zain al-'Abidin's most interesting initiatives, however, lay in his court's patronage of literature. It was in Kashmir, especially during this king's reign, that the Sanskrit and Persian literary worlds engaged with one another with an intensity not seen in India before. The sultan patronized not only literary production in both languages, but also bi-directional translation projects between them. Modern scholars have marvelled at how a small and isolated valley in the Himalaya range so far from India's main political centres had become such an important cultural hub for the entire subcontinent. For more than four centuries Sanskrit scholars there dominated the discourse on poetics while making unique contributions in the disciplines of Sanskrit grammar and logic.[17] Sanskrit also served as the language used both for everyday government administration and for literary expression. Zain al-'Abidin continued the Kashmir court's tradition of patronizing Sanskrit literature by commissioning the poets Jonaraja (d. 1459) and his student Śrivara (fl. 1459–86) to write supplements to the *Rajatarangini*, the renowned Sanskrit text chronicling Kashmir's history composed in the mid twelfth century by the poet Kalhana. In his reign, too, a manuscript of one of the earliest works of India's sacred literature, the *Atharvaveda*, was brought from Karnataka to Kashmir and recited by Brahmin priests.[18]

Sultan Zain al-'Abidin's court also patronized the translation of numerous Sanskrit classics into Persian, as well as Persian classics into Sanskrit. The *Mahabharata*, the *Kathasaritsagara* by Somadeva, the *Daśavatara* by Ksemendra, the *Rajatarangini* (possibly only Kalhana's), the *Hatakeśvara Samhita* and the *Prthviraj-vijaya* by Jayanaka were all translated from Sanskrit to Persian.[19] In the opposite direction, the Sanskrit scholar Bhattavarta used Firdausi's great epic poem the *Shah-nama* as a model for his Sanskrit *Jainavilasa*, which also contains the sayings of Sultan Zain al-'Abidin.[20] And the court poet Śrivara translated from Persian into Sanskrit the immensely popular *Yusuf va Zuleikha*, composed by the Persian mystical poet 'Abd al-Rahman Jami in 1483.[21] Śrivara's Sanskrit version of this Persian classic, his *Katha-kautuka*, appeared in the Kashmir court in 1505, just a few decades after Jami had composed the Persian original in Herat, some 1,100 kilometres to the west. This indicates, notes the literary historian David Shulman, 'both the astonishing rapidity of cultural transmission in fifteenth-century Kashmir and the intricate interpenetration there of parallel linguistic cultures'.[22] Nor was this sort of Sanskrit–Persian bilingualism confined to the Kashmir court. Both languages were used in manuscripts found in regional Sufi shrines and in inscriptions inscribed on fifteenth- and sixteenth-century Muslim gravestones.[23]

Zain al-'Abidin's reign thus witnessed a singular moment in the braided history of the Sanskrit and Persian worlds. While cultivating both literary traditions, this sultan's long reign also bridged the transition from an era of Sanskrit literary dominance to one of sustained production of original Persian literature, promoted both at the state level and in the hinterland. Much of it pertained to the life and career of Saiyid 'Ali Hamadani, the renowned shaikh whose memory became more hallowed with each passing decade. By the time of Zain al-'Abidin's reign there had emerged an integrated network of Sufi shrines in the valley's countryside, most of them focused on Sufi migrants from Iran or Central Asia who considered Shaikh Hamadani their spiritual head. From this time on, Sufi shaikhs or minor members of Kashmir's rural gentry authored many saintly biographies and local histories in Persian.[24]

Finally, Zain al-'Abidin was the first Kashmiri ruler to establish Persian as the state's official language, which it would remain until the end of the nineteenth century. Brahmins, long accustomed to serving both Hindu and Muslim rulers in the medium of Sanskrit, quickly switched to using India's other transregional language, which they avidly cultivated for the next five centuries. Many of them formed the main body of Kashmir's *karkun*s, later known as the Kashmir Pandits, who formed the class of secretaries, clerks and accountants and retained their prominent position in government and letters up to the mid twentieth century.[25] Meanwhile, generations of Kashmiri-speakers memorized and passed on orally the Kashmiri poetry of revered religious figures such as the mystics Lalla or Shaikh Nur al-Din (d. 1440). But except for a short period during Zain al-'Abidin's reign, ordinary Kashmiri was never patronized by the court, either in pre-sultanate or in sultanate times.[26] Instead, Persian acquired a certain double persona. Like Sanskrit, it possessed high status as a transregional and prestigious language. Brahmins read the classics of Persian literature – the works of Rumi, Firdausi, Nizami, etc. – in local schools or *maktab*s, which they often ran.[27] At the same time, from Zain al-'Abidin's day Persian, not Kashmiri, attained the status of the valley's regional written language.[28] In discussing the literary productions of his fifteenth-century contemporaries, the poet Śrivara referenced a type of locally written literature that he characterized as *deśa*, or 'regional'. He was not referring to works composed in Kashmiri, far less in Sanskrit, but to those in Persian.[29] Elsewhere in India it was the local vernacular tongue that emerged as a region's written medium, whether for documentary or for literary purposes. Only in Kashmir did Persian function both as a prestigious, trans-regional medium and as the valley's written medium.

## GUJARAT

Unlike Kashmir or Bengal, Gujarat had been politically well integrated with the Tughluq empire ever since Sultan 'Ala al-Din Khalaji annexed this commercially rich region in the early fourteenth century. Basing themselves in the province's eastern corridor that leads to upper India, the Delhi sultanate's governors were well positioned to profit from the caravans transiting from the seaports to India's interior, and courtiers paid substantial bribes to be appointed provincial governors or commanders of strategic Gujarati forts.[30] Merchants and rulers, moreover, were mutually dependent. The former needed the security, the stable currency and the predictable taxation that the state could provide, while rulers required the silver, the horses and the arms that could be obtained from merchants. By the late fourteenth century, though, Tughluq rulers had become displeased with their governor in Gujarat over his failure to remit taxes to the central administration. They also feared that he had set down local roots and had built up a provincial army composed mainly of local soldiers. Keeping provincial rulers loyal to the political centre being a perennial metropolitan anxiety, in 1392 Zafar Khan, the son of a peasant convert to Islam and a former confident of Sultan Firuz Tughluq, was sent down to restore central rule in the wayward province. After confronting and defeating the former governor, the khan managed to pacify the province's strategically important eastern corridor leading to the sea, though he spent the rest of his life battling recalcitrant chieftains both in the mountains to the east and in the Saurashtra peninsula to the west.[31]

Only a few years after Zafar Khan had taken up office in Gujarat, however, Timur invaded India, weakening – or even wrecking – Delhi's grip on its remaining provinces. After a period of uncertainty, in 1407 Zafar Khan declared his independence from Delhi and titled himself Muzaffar Shah (r. 1407–11), sultan of the new sovereign state of Gujarat. Independence from Delhi now led to many of the same consequences in Gujarat as it had in Bengal. When Timur invaded India the region had been mainly pastoral, punctuated by scattered, commercially rich towns. Ensconced in well-defended forts or within walled, commercially active towns, merchant-princes had made ad hoc alliances with pastoral chieftains. But with the appearance of Muzaffar Shah's independent sultanate, a fully developed court society evolved in which the regional sultan presided over a host of petty chieftains.[32] Yet Gujarat was slow to emerge as a self-conscious, coherent region. The new state was not truly consolidated until the reign of Muzaffar Shah's successor and grandson Ahmad Shah (r. 1411–42), who in his first year as sovereign built Ahmedabad. Named after himself, the new capital lay in the heart of the busy corridor that connected the maritime hub of Cambay with routes leading north to the Indian interior. With Delhi no longer draining wealth from the province, coast and hinterland became even more mutually dependent, to the advantage of each. Agriculture was intensified in the more prosperous eastern districts, which soon became some of the leading engines of textile manufacturing in the world. Although Gujarati block-printed cotton goods exported to markets in Egypt can be dated to at least as early as the eleventh century, under the sultans the volume of these exports increased exponentially. The exports also facilitated the importation of silver and war-horses, which in turn enabled the sultans to maintain a standing army at a time when most Indian states were raising mercenary armies on an ad hoc basis.

Dominating the second half of the fifteenth century in Gujarat was the sultanate's sixth ruler, Mahmud Begada (r. 1458–1511), who established centralized control over all the province's subregions. Several strategic objectives guided his policies. The first was to protect and extend trade between the commercially active coastal cities and the agrarian hinterland. This he did by ensuring safe overland trade routes, imposing uniform and stable rates of taxation, establishing a standard silver coin, the *mahmudi*, and maintaining a formidable navy. The *mahmudi*, which became one of the most stable currencies in fifteenth-century India, is by far the most common coin that survives from Gujarat's sultanate period, largely because so many merchants invested their trust in it. As for his navy, Mahmud built some of the largest ships then plying the Arabian Sea. In a 1508 naval engagement off the port of Chaul, his ships meted out to the Portuguese their first defeat in the Indian Ocean.[33]

Another of Mahmud Begada's objectives was to colonize forested regions and bring undeveloped land into cultivation. To pacify the Sabarmati valley – the strategic north–south corridor connecting Rajasthan with the Gulf of Cambay – he settled charismatic religious figures among refractory Kanbi and Koli communities. To stabilize the province's turbulent eastern flank, in 1483 he built and made as his new capital the fort of Champaner, which abutted the mountains that had provided refuge for state rebels. Here the sultan granted courtiers permanent land holdings to encourage their long-term interest in clearing and developing the land for agricultural purposes. To the west, the Saurashtra peninsula and Kutch remained frontier zones, populated by pastoral communities that had been immigrating from Rajasthan or Sind. In 1472 he annexed the stronghold of Junagadh in Saurashtra, which even before the rise of the Gujarat sultanate had held out against Delhi's repeated attempts to subdue the region.[34] In all these subregions, Mahmud Begada aimed to control, or at least pacify, the various clans of armed pastoralists that for centuries had been migrating into Gujarat from the north and north-west. Some, arriving with their cattle and their martial traditions, had been driven out of Sind in the thirteenth century by famine. Others had been drawn to western Gujarat by the sultanate's offers of tax relief to clear scrublands. However they arrived, the regime sought to play one group off against another by offering protection to some if they would suppress threats from others. Meanwhile, the clans and their chiefs redefined themselves in ways that disguised their obscure origins. To this end they built fortified settlements and set up petty courts where their chiefs patronized Brahmins and poets, who in turn provided their patrons with respectable genealogies or even royal pedigree, thereby masking their former identity as livestock-herding chieftains.[35]

Mahmud Begada's attempts to ensure the security of pilgrimage routes led to the flourishing of different religious traditions in what has been called a 'religious marketplace' in fifteenth-century Gujarat.[36] Pilgrimage sites such as Girnar hill in Saurashtra hosted multiple religious institutions side by side – Jain, Sufi, Nath, Śaiva and Vaishnava. Merchants were especially prominent among followers of popular forms of Vaishnava devotion, to which ruling authorities in Gujarat, like those in Bengal and Kashmir, were favourably disposed. Jain communities, which had been active in Gujarat since the fourth century, thrived from the earliest days of the Delhi sultanate's rule in the province, undertaking such critical tasks as managing the mint for the sultans.[37] The atmosphere of cultural pluralism promoted by Mahmud Begada is reflected in some remarkable works of contemporary literature. In his panegyric *Rajavinodamahakavya*, the fifteenth-century Sanskrit poet Udayaraja portrayed the sultan as an ideal warrior of the *kshatriya* class, even a *chakravartin* ('universal conqueror'). Never referred to as Muslim, the sultan was seamlessly woven into classical Indian tropes of kingship, such as his descent from a long line of Indian rulers traceable to the Solar dynasty of *kshatriya* warriors. Mahmud Begada's court, writes Udayaraja, was blessed both by Saraswati, the goddess of learning, and by Lakshmi, the goddess of wealth.[38]

## MALWA

In 1391, just seven years before Timur launched his India campaign, four governors were sent out from Delhi to bring order to the provinces of an unsteady Tughluq empire. Each would establish an independent sultanate soon after the Turkish warlord sacked Delhi. Khizr Khan founded the Saiyid dynasty of rulers in Delhi, Malik Sarwar the Sharqi sultanate of Jaunpur and Zafar Khan the Gujarat sultanate. The fourth governor, Dilawar Khan Ghuri, was posted to Malwa, the rich though landlocked tableland in west-central India north of the Narmada. When Timur began sacking Delhi in December 1398, the last Tughluq sultan, not a paragon of courage, quietly slipped out of Tughluqabad fort and fled to Gujarat. He had hoped that Zafar Khan would help him reclaim his capital. When such assistance was not forthcoming, the fugitive king moved on to Malwa, where Dilawar Khan hosted him for several years. So long as the royal exile was his guest, Dilawar Khan tactfully refrained from declaring his independence. But as soon as the erstwhile sultan had taken his leave, Dilawar declared himself sovereign and built congregational mosques in what would be the core cities of the Malwa sultanate: Ujjain, Lalitpur, Mandu and Dhar. Meanwhile his son, Alp Khan, busied himself strengthening the fort of Mandu. Situated in a spectacular natural setting some thirty-five kilometres south of Dhar, this would soon become one of the architectural gems of medieval India. Jutting out from the Vindhya Mountains, its southern side sharply dropping 400 metres to the Nimar plain below, the city stretches along a jagged-edged plateau about twenty-five kilometres north of the Narmada. This would be Alp Khan's new capital when he succeeded to his father's throne as Sultan Hoshang Shah (r. 1406–35).

The new sultan, however, was challenged by Zafar Khan of Gujarat, now reigning as Sultan Muzaffar, who not only invaded Malwa but captured and held Hoshang Shah prisoner for a year. When finally released, the humiliated sovereign vowed revenge, as would his successors, making Gujarat the lasting enemy of Malwa. To defend his kingdom from Gujarat, Hoshang made several strategic moves. First, although Malwa, like Jaunpur, did not have ready access to war-horses, it was well positioned to acquire elephants that roamed the heavily forested jungles to the east. In 1420 Hoshang seized the fort of Kherla, located some 300 kilometres east of Mandu, and installed as its chieftain a vassal who would pay an annual tribute in elephants. Second, he began recruiting soldiers from the eastern Gangetic valley, or Purbiya. Later known as 'Purbiya Rajputs', these men would form a central component of Malwa's army. They also settled undeveloped tracts of the Nimar plain, south of Mandu.

On Hoshang Shah's death in 1435, his son briefly occupied the throne but was outmanoeuvred by the son of Hoshang's *vazir* (chief minister), who in 1436 was crowned Sultan Mahmud Shah Khalaji (r. 1436–69). Descended from the Khalaji rulers of Delhi, Mahmud

Shah continued his predecessor's policies of strengthening the state with mercenaries and war-elephants. In 1440 he marched some 600 kilometres east from Mandu to Bandhavgarh, a major entrepôt for elephants in present-day Umaria District, Madhya Pradesh. From there he moved into the Surguja region of northern Chattisgarh, which remained a permanent source of the sultanate's war-elephants. These he deployed to exert Malwa's control over much of Rajasthan.

Meanwhile, the affairs of the Saiyid dynasty in Delhi had reached such a pitiful state that a delegation of disgruntled clerics invited Mahmud Shah to invade their capital and even take the throne for himself. In 1442 Malwa's sultan accepted the challenge and, although his battle with Delhi's army was inconclusive, along the way he demonstrated sufficient power and largesse to attract the leaders of prominent clans to his vassalage, including those of Nagaur, Ajmer and the guardians of a number of forts in Mewar. When the powerful raja of Chittor, Rana Kumbha, expelled his younger stepbrother owing to a conflict between their households, the latter sought and was given refuge by Mahmud Shah, who granted him land assignments near Malwa's border with Mewar. By exploiting such internal dissensions, the sultan was able to assert Malwa's authority across much of Rajasthan. In the 1440s he seized Bayana and Ajmer, reinforced his grip on Ranthambhor, conquered Mandalgarh and regained his kingdom's control over Gagraun (in Jhalawar District, Rajasthan).[39]

Malwa's history highlights three interconnected themes of India's long fifteenth century: the strategic importance of elephants in inter-state warfare; the exploitation of inter-household conflicts by outside powers as a strategy of territorial expansion; and the importance of India's vast military labour market. All three helped Mahmud Shah create what amounted to a classic Circle of Kings, or *mandala*. Surrounding his political core (Mandu and Dhar) was a ring of inner provinces governed by his own courtiers (Ujjain, Sarangpur, Bhilsa, Hoshangabad), which were encircled in turn by a belt of states governed by allies (Ranthambhor, Mandasor, Gagraun, Chanderi and Kherla), beyond which lay a distant circle of tributary states (Ajmer, Bayana, Kalpi, Raipur, Ratanpur, Bairagarh, Baglana).[40] This elegantly constructed geopolitical system suggests how far a Tughluq successor state had succumbed to Indian understandings of inter-state politics.

Instead of a centralized polity in which a sultan enjoyed uniform authority throughout his realm, assisted by a cadre of personally loyal nobles, Malwa under Mahmud Shah Khalaji approximated to the classical Indian model of a polycentric state in which power and authority, being distributed unevenly among semi-sovereign allies, gradually diminished the further one moved from the core.

And yet, even while acting according to traditionally Indian political norms, the ruling class avidly participated in the Persianate cultural sphere. The language of the sultanate's civil administration was Persian, and three of the four Persian dictionaries compiled in fifteenth-century India were composed in Malwa.[41] It was by producing such normative texts that this isolated regional court asserted its claims to literary and linguistic status within the larger Persianate world.[42] Sultan Mahmud Shah Khalaji certainly imagined himself a major player in that world – and even beyond. An inscription in Dhar dated 1455 described him as:

> A king of graceful countenance, Sultan of the world,
> Visitors bowing at his door step were the Great Khan and the Emperor
>   of China.
> 'Ala al-Din va'l-Dunya Abu'l-Muzaffar
> Triumphed over his enemies with the help of God,
> So in that era, with Mahmud as the king of the world,
> The world flourished like heaven, thanks to his justice ['adl].[43]

This was not entirely hyberbole. In early 1466 the sultan actually did receive a mission from a claimant to the office of caliph of Islam residing in Cairo. The envoy brought a black robe of investiture representing the sultan's formal 'appointment' as a legitimate ruler in the eyes of Islam. Two years later, the visit of another foreign mission linked Mahmud Shah directly with the legacy of Timur. In January 1468 he received an emissary from Abu Sa'id Mirza (r. 1424–69), Timur's great-grandson, who then ruled the heartland of his ancestor's former empire. The gifts Mahmud Shah presented to the envoy projected an image not of a great conqueror, but of a connoisseur of high Persianate culture: a book of wisdom, a ruby cup, a carnelian plate, a turquoise dish, an alabaster basin, a crystal tray, fine silks and cottons, amber, musk, talking birds and some horses and slaves.[44]

Mahmud Shah's architectural projects at Mandu also suggest his desire to participate in Timur's resplendent world, especially when contrasted with those in nearby Dhar, which had been patronized by governors of the Delhi sultanate. In the early fourteenth century Sultan 'Ala al-Din Khalaji's first governor in Dhar had built a structure known today as the 'Kamal Maula' mosque.[45] Stylistically mimicking Delhi's iconic Qutb mosque, it symbolized Dhar's inclusion in the Delhi sultanate's political orbit. A century later, in 1405, the last Tughluq governor in Dhar installed an iron pillar in a nearby mosque known as the 'Lat Masjid', making visual reference to a similar pillar that Sultan Iltutmish had placed before Delhi's Qutb mosque.[46] Mahmud Shah, on the other hand, looked westwards. Near Samarqand, one of Timur's inscriptions boldly proclaims: 'If you challenge our power, look at our buildings.'[47] Timurid architecture was characterized by imposing, free-standing structures meant to be seen from afar, complex vaulting techniques supporting large dome chambers on high drums, exterior surfaces richly decorated with glazed and unglazed brick, and geometric patterning using interlocking star and polygon patterns [see Fig. 7]. The style also featured ensembles of buildings, made by grouping together such features as a *madrasa*, a tomb, a mosque, a Sufi hospice, a palace or a garden. The effect was an integrated complex of monuments and open space. Established by Timur and elaborated by his successors in Central Asia and Iran, this aesthetic vision diffused across India with the quickening circulation of diplomats, pilgrims, merchants, adventurers, literati and artisans throughout the Persianate world.

In the heart of Mandu, Mahmud Shah Khalaji constructed precisely such an integrated complex, the first to be seen in India. Consisting of three monuments and an open square, all of them set in a single row in similarly sized square units, the ensemble asserted Mandu's transformation from a provincial backwater to a world-class centre of Timurid-style power. The first in the ensemble is a large congregational mosque that Hoshang Shah had begun shortly before his death in 1435, and which Mahmud Shah spent the first eighteen years of his reign completing. To its west is an elegant tomb made entirely of white marble that he built for Hoshang Shah. To the east of the mosque, separated by a spacious square, is the ensemble's most ambitious and imposing structure. Known as the 'Ashrafi Mahal', this is a *madrasa*-cum-dynastic tomb complex that was begun in 1441 and was still under construction twenty-seven years later. Although nearly entirely ruined today, its design can be reconstructed from notices by visitors and a resident chronicler. Its ground level incorporated a *madrasa* and a *khanaqah* with cells built into all four sides of its base. Standing on one part of the base was a tomb for three royal graves, its large dome rising to a height of twenty-seven metres above ground level, and its walls richly decorated by Iranian craftsmen working with green- and cobalt-striped jasper, red cornelian, agate, white alabaster and black marble. It also contained a great hall in white marble with carved doorways, windows and cornices decorated in mosaics of precious stones and friezes of blue and yellow glazed tiles. On all four corners stood circular structures, the most imposing being a seven-storeyed tower measuring fifteen metres in diameter at its base and rising to a height of forty-five metres, or two-thirds the height of Delhi's Qutb Minar.[48] In short, unlike the sultanates of Bengal or Gujarat, where patrons continued or revived indigenous building traditions, Malwa's architects experimented with forms having no local precedents.[49] If Timur had taken Indian architects with him to Samarqand, where he developed his distinctive style, a generation later architects from Khurasan had brought that style to the heart of India.[50]

Following Mahmud Shah's reign, however, the kingdom began a steady decline. His son and successor, the eccentric Sultan Ghiyath al-Din Shah (r. 1469–1501), withdrew altogether from politics and governance. Protected by a palace guard of 500 Ethiopian slave women dressed in men's attire, the sultan ardently devoted himself to the pursuit of pleasure. He is best known for patronizing a remarkable cookbook, the *Ni'mat-nama* ('Book of Delights'), which is not just a catalogue of Mandu's culinary traditions, but an epicurean's digest of pleasures, including detailed instructions for preparing perfumes, medical remedies, aphrodisiacs, betel nut and so on.[51] Depicted in paintings wearing dainty slippers and a formidable moustache, the *bon vivant* Ghiyath al-Din neglected his father's shrewd policy of constructing and maintaining an outer belt of tributary states. To the west, he failed to challenge the annexation of Champaner by Gujarat's Mahmud Begada, and to the north he left uncontested the occupation of the forts of Kalpi and Bayana by Delhi's Bahlul Lodi.

The kingdom's core, meanwhile, fell under the domination of powerful chiefs who recruited ever-larger numbers of soldiers from the east, the so-called Purbiya Rajputs, on whom the kingdom had become militarily dependent.

Malwa thus presents a curious hybrid, inhabiting several worlds simultaneously. Important Sanskrit literature was produced during Mahmud Khalaji's reign, including a copy of the *Kalpa Sutra*, a revered work on Jain rituals that maps a path for crossing life's river of rebirths. Completed at Mandu in 1439, the *Kalpa Sutra* is also one of India's earliest manuscripts bearing dated miniature paintings.[52] In fact, most of the styles of Rajasthan's famous miniature tradition evolved from copies of this text that were produced either in Mandu or in the state's hinterland.[53] This was probably due to the prominent role that powerful warrior chiefs linked to courts in Rajasthan played in Malwa's political system. In 1463, while accompanying the sultan on a military campaign, Mahmud Khalaji's chief treasurer, also a Jain, composed another important Sanskrit work, the *Buddhi Sagar*.[54] Because Jains were so prominent in managing the government's accounting and revenue departments, and because the government relied so heavily on wealthy Jain merchants for financing its projects, the state actively supported its Jain community. It was similarly invested in indigenous military systems. Lacking access both to warhorses and to Turko-Iranian military labour, rulers recruited war-elephants from the forests to the east and military labour from Rajasthan and the eastern Gangetic plain. By the time of the sultanate's last dynasty, Sultan Mahmud II (r. 1511–31), 40,000 men later identified as Rajputs were in state service, most of them recruited from the eastern Gangetic plain, or Purbiya.

## EMERGING IDENTITIES: THE IDEA OF 'RAJPUT'

It was only from the sixteenth century that the word 'Rajput' became securely associated with territorially based, closed clans claiming deep genealogical roots and nurturing a warrior ethos of heroism and martyrdom.[55] In inscriptions from western and central India dating from the eleventh to the fourteenth centuries, the Sanskrit term *rajaputra*, 'a king's son', appears simply as a title indicating a rank or official position, but not one that was inheritable by subsequent generations or associated with martial heroism.[56] In those earlier centuries, kings received military service from subordinate chieftains, called *ranaka*s or *thakura*s, in return for gifts of land that the latter gave to their own cavalry commanders, called *rauta*s, a term derived from *rajaputra*. In Persian sources dating to the early thirteenth century these commanders are called *rawat*, also derived from *rajaputra*.[57] In the early fifteenth century, the label 'Rajput' was still associated with successful military service performed by men who had taken up soldiering on behalf of a deserving king. But by the end of that century, the word was well on the way to referencing entire aristocratic lineages bearing a martial ethos of courage, heroism and martyrdom. Such lineages included the Chauhans of Ajmer, the Tomaras of Delhi, the Gahadavalas of Kanauj and the Chandelas of Kalinjar.

An early phase in the crystallization of Rajput identities is seen in the career of a fourteenth-century soldier known as Muhammad Shah in Persian sources and Mahimasahi in Sanskrit sources.[58] Revealing the fluidity of social categories and the ease with which men could move between them, an early-fifteenth-century Sanskrit text, the *Hammira-Mahakavya*, portrays Muhammad Shah/Mahimasahi as transitioning from an ethnic Mongol, to an Indian Muslim, and finally to a *kshatriya* warrior. Recruited from Central Asia, he joined the Delhi sultanate service in the late thirteenth century and participated in that state's successful invasion of Gujarat in 1299. But when he and other Mongol retainers unsuccessfully rebelled against their commanding officers in the course of this campaign, they took refuge in the fabled fort of Ranthambhor in eastern Rajasthan, then controlled by Hammira, the last ruler of the Chauhan lineage. In March 1301 the sultan of Delhi, 'Ala al-Din Khalaji, besieged this fort, and when its defenders foresaw their inevitable doom Muhammad Shah entered his quarters inside the fort, massacred his entire family, and gallantly sallied forth against the sultan's forces with the intent of sacrificing his life in one final, desperate struggle. Afterwards, 'Ala al-Din Khalaji discovered his former retainer lying wounded on the battlefield. Although the sultan offered to have his wounds healed if he would once again pledge loyalty to Delhi, Muhammad Shah refused, declaring instead his devotion to the Chauhan cause, whereupon he was executed.

Although the Sanskrit text identifies Muhammad Shah as a *kshatriya* and not a Rajput, his actions – exhibiting loyalty, courage and heroic martyrdom – were those that would later be acknowledged as characteristically Rajput. By killing off his own family when the defenders at Ranthambhor found their cause to be doomed, Muhammad Shah engaged in the ritual of *jauhar* – the destruction of elite women in order to prevent their falling into enemy hands. Only then did he hurl himself before the Delhi sultanate's overwhelming force, expecting certain death. Composed in the early fifteenth century, about a century after the events it describes, the *Hammira-Mahakavya* thus appears to capture a moment when the idea of Rajput was evolving. The early-modern and modern ideology of martial heroism and martyrdom was clearly already in place, even if the term *rajaputra* was still an open social category, accessible even to an outsider such as Muhammad Shah, and not yet a closed, kin-based one. The career of Muhammad Shah as related in the *Hammira-Mahakavya* typifies the sort of accounts that circulated orally in fifteenth-century western India and celebrated the heroic exploits of single individuals. In the following century bards patronized by chieftains aspiring to be kings would weave such personal stories into connected narratives and genealogies that served to bind together members of whole clans. When such clans were mapped on to territory as kingdoms, those genealogies provided historical depth for ruling houses that could then trace their origins back to common founder-heroes. At that point, the ideology of martial prowess and martyrdom associated with earlier warrior-heroes such as Muhammad Shah was projected on to the entire clan, which in turn would self-identify as Rajput.

Several factors appear to have shaped this development, one of which was military in nature. After Timur left India, intensified conflict on India's fragmented political chessboard created greater demands for military labour. Such demands were met by the emergence of an India-wide military labour market, which became a prominent feature of South Asia's social landscape from at least the

Fig. 1: Bronze image of Śiva as Nataraja, Pala dynasty (c.750–1161). Śiva temple, Śri
Amirthakadeśvara, Mela Kadambur, South Arcot, Chidambaram. Seized from
Bengal by Rajendra Chola, c.1022.

Fig. 2:
(*Above*): Silver coin of Ajaya Raja II Chauhan (r. *c*.1110–35)
(*Below*): Gold coin of Muhammad Ghuri (r. 1192–1206)

Fig. 3: Warangal fort: interior of Tughluq audience hall, the so-called 'Khush Mahal' (1323)

Fig. 4: Vijayanagara (modern Hampi): northern gateway to the Virupaksha Temple (established twelfth century)

Fig. 5: Emperor Timur (d. 1405) enthroned. Pen and wash in Indian ink on Japanese paper, by Rembrandt van Rijn (1606–69)

Fig. 6: Bidar: the madrasa of Mahmud Gawan (completed 1472)

Fig. 7: Shahr-i Sabz, Uzbekistan: the Aq Saray, palace of Timur (completed 1396)

Fig. 8: Yadgir: wrought-iron cannon on a hill in the centre of the fort (late 1550s)

Fig. 9: Calicut: Mishkal Mosque (said to date to the fourteenth century, subsequently renovated)

Fig. 10: Raichur: Krishna Raya with female attendants, depicted on a frieze in the Naurangi Darwaza's inner courtyard (1520)

Fig. 11: Detail of Surjan Singh submitting to Akbar, from a painting by Mukund in the *Akbar-nama* (*c*.1595)

fifteenth century until the early nineteenth, when British colonial rulers demilitarized Indian society.[59] Since no state during India's long fifteenth century could ever achieve a monopoly of armed force, rulers were uneasily aware that armed villagers were as free to become rebels as they were to be recruited into their own military forces.[60] Consequently, states and warlords alike competed for access to the countryside's vast reservoir of armed peasants.[61] They were normally recruited on an ad hoc, seasonal basis, with warrior–villagers typically spending part of the year in military service and the remainder working the fields in their home villages. Middlemen or entrepreneurs called *jama'dar*s negotiated deals that were agreeable both to those who hired the mercenaries and to the local chiefs, or *zamindar*s, who had access to those labour pools. From the standpoint of the recruits themselves – especially those living along the economic margins – serving a distant warlord or sovereign seasonally was a prudent survival strategy, since such service provided income, if only a meagre one, for themselves and their families. Pre-colonial India thus teemed with armed recruits roaming the countryside with their middlemen or commanders, responding to the shifting supply and demand of the military labour market.

From the late fifteenth century rulers of the Jaunpur sultanate (1394–1483) had taken many peasant-soldiers of the eastern Gangetic plain into their armed forces. But in 1483, when the Lodi sultans of Delhi extinguished the Jaunpur regime and annexed its former territory, Jaunpur's former recruits were forced to find military service further afield and deeper in India's interior, especially in Malwa. These men were employed by warlords who, based in strongholds such as Raisen (near Bhopal, Madhya Pradesh), supplied them to emergent states or existing kingdoms in Rajasthan or Malwa. There they were known as 'Purbiya Rajputs', a name indicating their origins in the eastern Gangetic plain, or 'Purbiya'. Notably, in the fluid social context of India's long fifteenth century, terms such as 'Rajput' or 'Afghan' had not yet become fixed ethnic identities, but merely indicated one's military affiliation. Men adopted the cultural identity associated with the particular military tradition into which they had been integrated, so that, in this instance, 'Purbiyas' recruited by brokers and employers who identified themselves as Rajputs became

'Purbiya Rajputs'. In this way, the military labour market itself was a major generator of ethnic identities.[62]

Rajput status was also claimed by martial clans of pastoral nomads in northern and western India as those clans evolved into royal lineages and became displaced on to territories as petty states. This could be a very long process, taking several centuries to complete. Between the thirteenth and fifteenth centuries, nomadic clans steadily moved within proximity of settled and socially stratified agrarian realms with a large class of peasant cultivators at their base, and royal courts, Brahmin priests and state-sponsored temples at their apex. In northern Gujarat and Saurashtra martial pastoralists migrating from the north and west settled down and carved out agrarian territories over which they claimed sovereign authority. Their pastoralist kinship organization then weakened as their chiefs shed aspects of their pastoralist pasts, adopted prestigious titles, acquired courts, styled themselves kings and claimed patrilineal lines of descent linked to prestigious lineages.

In Gujarat, as in Rajasthan, genealogy proved essential for making such claims. To this end, local bards composed ballads or chronicles that presented their patrons as ideal warriors who protected Brahmins, cows and vassals, as opposed to the livestock-herding chieftains that they actually were, or had once been. As people who created and preserved the genealogies, local bards therefore played critical roles in brokering for their clients socio-cultural transitions to a claimed Rajput status.[63] A similar thing was happening in the Thar Desert region, where from the fourteenth century onwards mobile pastoral groups gradually evolved into landed, sedentary and agrarian clans. Once again, it was bards and poets, patronized by little kings, who transformed a clan's ancestors from celebrated cattle-herders or cattle-rustlers to celebrated protectors of cattle-herding communities.[64] The difference was subtle but critical, since such revised narratives retained an echo of a pastoral nomadic past while repositioning a clan's dynastic founder from pastoralist to non-pastoralist. The term 'Rajput', in short, had become a prestigious title available for adoption by upwardly mobile clans in the process of becoming sedentary.[65]

By one mechanism or another, a process of 'Rajputization' occurred in new states that emerged from the turmoil following Timur's invasion of 1398, especially in Gujarat, Malwa and Rajasthan.

## WRITING IN VERNACULAR LANGUAGES

It was also in the long fifteenth century that across much of South Asia vernacular, spoken languages appeared in written form, for both documentary and expressive purposes. This 'vernacular revolution', however, did not displace India's older, transregional literary traditions, Sanskrit and Persian, but occurred alongside and in dialogue with them.

Like the emergence of regional and Rajput identities, the appearance of vernacular literatures was associated with the Delhi sultanate's diminished status following Timur's invasion. As Delhi's authority receded, former imperial governors, lesser regional chiefs and local warlords all asserted themselves politically. Larger players such as the sultans of Bengal, Jaunpur, Gujarat or Malwa could do this by patronizing imposing works of architecture or by maintaining substantial numbers of armed retainers. But smaller chiefs or warlords, possessing fewer resources, had fewer options. Just to survive amidst a patchwork of mutually hostile states meant spending much of their limited resources on recruiting mercenaries from India's military labour market. On the other hand, what small but ambitious warlords could feasibly manage was to build up large households and attain local renown by patronizing the best and the brightest literati they could find. These would be poets, singers or bards who composed and propagated literary works intended for as wide a circulation as possible within their patron's realm. But because such states might be of modest size, the literature was likely to be composed in the spoken language and dialect specific to a state's sovereign domain. These could be songs extolling their patron's generosity or power, genealogies, biographies, hagiographies, popular narratives dedicated to a political patron or, most commonly, vernacular adaptations either of Persian classical genres such as romance literature, or of Sanskrit classical genres such as courtly epics. In creative ways, then, India's two transregional literary traditions were effectively reinvented in ways that could be intelligible in the more fragmented political and social world that had emerged in the wake of Timur's invasion.[66]

As an illustration of this process, ever since 1394 north India's Tomar lineage had controlled the fort of Gwalior, 320 kilometres south of Delhi. But by the fifteenth century that fort's ruler, Dungar Singh Tomar (r. 1427–59), had to face pressure from two Tughluq successor states that coveted this strategically located fort – the Saiyid sultans of Delhi to the north, and the Khalaji sultans of Malwa to the south. The beleaguered Dungar Singh managed to keep the two powers at bay by paying tribute to them both. He also patronized abridged and modified vernacular versions of India's classic Sanskrit epics, the *Mahabharata* and the *Ramayana* – the former in 1435 and the latter in 1443. These were the first extant versions of the great epics to appear in the dialect of Hindavi later known as Brajbhasha, referring to the dialect of Braj, that is, the region of the upper Ganges in western Uttar Pradesh associated with the hero and Hindu god Krishna.[67] Composed by the poet Vishnudas, the epics appear to have been originally sung at Dungar Singh's court, where they were written down and, like other vernacular works of the period, tailored to suit the values and ambitions of their patron. Thus, the hero of Vishnudas's *Mahabharata* is not Arjuna or Yudhishthira as in the Sanskrit epic, but the muscular Bhima – an appropriate model for an aspiring but hard-pressed king. Similarly, in his version of the *Ramayana*, abridged to only a sixth of the Sanskrit original, Vishnudas narrates episodes that stress royal splendour, courageous combat, and one of the most common themes of fifteenth century north India: renewing or breaking former alliances and forging new ones.[68]

Another illustration of India's literary vitality in the long fifteenth century is seen in the Hindavi Sufi romance, or *premakhyan* (love story).[69] Composed in eastern India between the late fourteenth and mid sixteenth centuries, these stories narrate a princely hero's quest for romantic love, a metaphor for the quest for union with God.[70] Although the poets of this genre were thoroughly familiar with classic Persian romance literature by poets such as Nizami Ganjavi (d. 1209), they were also immersed in local Hindavi culture and its own traditions of storytelling. For a poet such as Muhammad Jayasi (d. 1542), India was home, and his references to stepwells, temples, yogis, Jains, white-clad sadhus, Śiva-worshippers and so on all served to valorize that home.[71] The patrons of this literature, moreover, were Turkish or Afghan local rulers or regional warlords who had become transformed by the Indian culture that surrounded them.[72] Herein lies the contrast between a *premakhyan* like Jayasi's *Padmavat* (1540) and courtly narratives of the early Delhi sultanate era. Whereas poets of that time had represented north India as a stage for enacting triumphal narratives of conquest, and indigenous warrior clans as infidels to be conquered and subdued, Jayasi reverses this opposition. In narrating 'Ala al-Din Khalaji's conquest of the fort of Chittor (1303), the poet identifies himself not with the victorious sultan but with the doomed Indians who resisted the invading Turks. For him, the Indians' annihilation at Chittor becomes a metaphor for the Sufis' ultimate mystical quest, namely annihilation of the self (*fana'*) by way of achieving an abiding presence of God.[73]

Owing to their need for official records, regional courts also stimulated the use of written vernacular languages. In 1513 the sultan of Malwa was issuing public decrees in Hindavi. In some states, local administration was conducted on a bilingual basis, with records kept in both Persian and the local vernacular, which in north India might be Hindavi, written in *nagari*, the script of Sanskrit. By the early 1500s, the Lodi Afghans of Delhi were issuing bilingual documents in Persian and Hindavi.[74] In the Deccan (see Chapter Four), ruling authorities of the sultanates of Golconda (1497–1687) and Bijapur (1490–1686) realized that the most efficient way of managing their judicial and revenue bureaucracies was to employ the same class of skilled, literate administrators that had been serving the Deccan's ruling authorities for centuries. In Golconda these were mostly Brahmins. Whereas that state's royal edicts of the sixteenth century had been issued in Persian only, by the early seventeenth century such documents were typically issued in both Persian and Telugu. By the end of the seventeenth century, they were issued entirely in Telugu, with brief Persian summaries appearing only on their reverse sides.[75] Moreover, because the state's sovereign territory roughly coincided with Telugu-speaking Telangana and the Andhra coast, the kingdom's ruling classes tended to imagine their sovereign realm as a Telugu one, and the rulers themselves as

Telugu sultans.[76] Consequently, they vigorously patronized the production of Telugu literature, just as the sultans of Bengal, whose sovereign territory likewise coincided roughly with a Bengali-speaking region, did the production of Bengali literature. Sultan Ibrahim Qutb Shah (r. 1550–80) was known in Telugu sources as *Ibharama cakravarti* ('emperor Ibrahim'), a ruler so thoroughly steeped in Telugu aesthetics that he would sit, as one court poet put it, 'floating on waves of bliss' listening to the *Mahabharata* recited to him in its classical Telugu version.[77]

The same was true in the western Deccan. Early in their history, the sultans of Bijapur began collecting revenue and administering justice in written Marathi, not Persian. The change came abruptly in 1535, when Sultan Ibrahim 'Adil Shah I (r. 1534–58) ordered that all public revenue and judicial records, formerly recorded in Persian, be kept in Marathi and placed under Brahmin management.[78] Royal decrees (*farman*s) were still written in Persian, but vernacular Marathi was used for orders (*khurdkhat*s) issued by crown bureaucrats or landholders, letters (*misali*s) issued by mid-level bureaucrats or police chiefs, letters of assurance (*qaul-nama*s) issued by higher authorities to lower ones, and judgments (*mahzar*s) issued by judicial assemblies.[79] In particular, courts administered or acknowledged by the state became arenas for repeated face-to-face disputations. A single case might be taken from court to court, from locale to locale and from level to level along the socio-political spectrum, in each case involving diverse peoples of various castes, classes and religions. Since the language in which local cases were litigated was vernacular Marathi, the very act of engaging in public disputation had the deeper effect of forging a larger, discursive community around that language, both as spoken in the courts and as recorded by them.[80] Regional states such as the sultanate of Bijapur thus created a political and judicial framework that in turn allowed for the emergence of a public, vernacular space.

Further contributing to the creation of such a space was the spread of paper-making technology, which Persianized Turks had introduced to north India from Central Asia in the thirteenth century; with the growth of the Delhi sultanate in the fourteenth century it diffused across South Asia. By the time that Timur sacked Delhi in 1398–9, it had already reached that sultanate's provinces, so that in the fifteenth century, when they had become regional states, this revolutionary technology was already available for use. Around 1590 the Bengali poet Mukundaram noted the presence of whole communities of Muslim paper-makers (*kagaji*) in Bengali cities.[81] The link between paper production and Indo-Persianate governance is suggested by the name of an ancient town called Kaghdhipura ('paper town'), located very near Daulatabad, the oldest centre of Persianate government in the Deccan.[82] Almost everywhere it went, paper-making technology gradually displaced other media such as copperplate, palm leaf or stone. It is true that earlier courts such as the Chalukyas (974–1190) and the Yadavas (1175–1318) had patronized the writing of vernacular Marathi and Kannada inscriptions and expository treatises, and that as early as the tenth century both languages were used for documentary purposes.[83] But given the cumbersome and expensive technology of communication in those earlier, pre-paper centuries, such texts – even when committed to memory and transmitted orally – did not circulate far beyond elite groups.[84] Paper, by contrast, being cheaper to produce and easier to handle, enjoyed a much greater velocity of movement and a far wider circulation than any other media then in use. This allowed it to penetrate deeper in the social order and bring greater numbers of people belonging to different social classes into closer communication both with each other and with the state. It is revealing that the ordinary words for 'paper' and 'pen' in many South Asian vernacular tongues are derived from two Perso-Arabic words, *kaghaz* and *qalam* respectively, suggesting not only the new technology's path of transmission from Central Asia to South Asia, but also the deep impact that it had made on the peoples of India.

If the emergence of a public, vernacular space was stimulated by the diffusion of paper-technology and the use of local languages in regional administration, both revenue and judicial, that space also expanded as a result of forces coming 'from below', in the form of popular devotional movements. Although powerful waves of popular religiosity, or *bhakti*, can be traced as far back as sixth-century south India, in the long fifteenth century they swept across the whole of India. Because it entailed a direct encounter with the divine – unmediated by ritual, learning or priests – *bhakti* presented a formidable challenge to the more ritually oriented Vedic traditions preserved by Brahmin elites. Privileging personal experience over ritual, *bhakti* celebrated mutual companionship among fellow devotees, including both sexes and all social strata. Moved by a direct engagement with divine reality, people turned to both poetry and song, the natural vehicles of *bhakti*, which invariably appeared in the spoken tongues of India's various subregions, composed by poets popularly venerated as saints.[85] Writing in Hindavi, these included such powerful voices as Kabir (d. *c.*1518), Raidas (d. *c.*1520), Mirabai (d. 1557) and Surdas (d. 1573); in Bengali, Chaitanya (d. 1533); in Punjabi, Nanak (d. 1539); in Gujarati, Narsinh Mehta (d. 1488); and in Marathi, Namdev (d. 1350) and Eknath (d. 1599).[86]

In different ways, then, regional courts, the advent of paper-technology and the '*bhakti* public sphere' all served to stimulate the spate of vernacular works that appeared in India's long fifteenth century. This momentous outcome compares with a nearly simultaneous development in Europe, where vernacular literatures were beginning to displace the hegemony of Latin for both documentary and discursive purposes.

# CONCLUSION

Persian chronicles compiled in the fourteenth century convey the impression of the Delhi sultanate's sovereign territory as a politically uniform terrain. Even if reality never did match such a monolithic vision, it was at least possible to imagine the sultanate in such terms. But Timur's sack of Delhi upended all that, setting off a chain reaction of processes that would define the long fifteenth century.

First, Timur's invasion was followed by former Tughluq governors declaring their independence from Delhi and setting down roots in their respective regions, a process already begun in Bengal and the Deccan when those regions were lost to Delhi in the mid fourteenth century. Second, the shrinking of Delhi's political authority disrupted overland trade routes that carried caravans of war-horses from Central Asia to north India. As a result, independent rulers were forced to rely less on cavalry and more on war-elephants, to which they had ready access, together with manpower recruited not from upper India or points west, but from India's own military labour markets, especially the lower Ganges region, or Purbiya.

Third, new groups were staking claims to high social or political status. In the late fifteenth century, when Jaunpur was conquered by a partially revived Delhi sultanate under the Lodi sultans, Purbiya's military manpower was contracted by brokers in central India for labour further west, in particular in Malwa. As soldiers from eastern India serving in Rajasthan and Malwa, these men acquired the identity of Purbiya Rajputs, and finally of Rajputs, a process suggesting how the military labour market itself enabled the assimilation of new groups into this emerging ethnic category. In Gujarat, as tribal and pastoral communities migrated into or near more hierarchical, agrarian societies, they too claimed Rajput identities, seeking valorization for their claims to aristocratic, or even royal, status. Bardic poets facilitated these efforts by celebrating the warrior ideals of those communities and by linking the ancestors of their chiefs with prestigious *kshatriya* lineages.

Fourth, the post-Timur era saw ceaseless alliance-building and alliance-shifting at multiple levels – between households, between chieftains and between states. In a world made less secure by the loss of an imperial centre, many were left to their own devices politically. Clients sought patrons, patrons sought allies. Political capital was measured by the cash in one's treasury, the size of one's household and the number of women serving as collateral in negotiating alliances with other parties. No alliance was iron-clad, and no agreement final; anything could be negotiated or renegotiated. This made for a volatile political environment, for neither allies nor enemies were permanent. Military service was often no more than a temporary arrangement made on a face-to-face basis, with no stabilizing mechanism that might guarantee contractual agreements. With political loyalties so thin on the ground, patrons and clients alike were constantly forging and abandoning alliances. The flow of troops from one contractor to another could make or break a kingdom.[87]

Fifth, the era witnessed an extraordinary spurt in the use of written vernacular languages, both for literature and for governmental record-keeping. In the politically fragmented world of post-Timur north India, newly formed sovereign states and politically emergent communities patronized literary works in the tongue of their immediate locale. Vernacular literatures also channelled the torrent of devotional poetry that swept over the land, composed by *bhakti* poets who exuberantly celebrated an unmediated presence of the divine. Yet the emergence of written vernaculars did not displace Sanskrit or Persian. Upwardly mobile chieftains, aspiring to claw their way into the world of classical Indian kingship, sought the prestige associated with Sanskrit.[88] In Gujarat, Sanskrit texts were patronized both by the sultan and by chieftains challenging him. In the 1460s the Sanskrit poet Udayaraja produced a lengthy panegyric of Sultan Mahmud Begada, the *Rajavinoda*.[89] Yet at about the same time, the poet Gangadhara wrote Sanskrit plays at the courts of two chieftains – one in Champaner, the other in Junagadh – whom he lionized as mighty *kshatriya* warriors, even while advising them to submit to the sultan's greater power.[90] Further north, the Rajput chieftain of Gwalior, Dungar Singh Tomar, sent two Sanskrit treatises on music to Sultan Zain al-'Abidin of Kashmir, who famously patronized both Sanskrit and Persian literary works, and even bidirectional translations between the two cosmopolitan traditions.[91] Operating across the whole of western India, Jain merchants or high-ranking administrators commissioned the production of Sanskrit texts and biographies.

Persian also flourished in this age of growing vernacularism, but, as with Sanskrit, it was put to new uses. Although the age of grand, pan-Indian chronicles had ended with Timur's invasion, Sufi shaikhs everywhere continued to produce treatises and biographies in Persian, and provincial courts from Kashmir to the Deccan to patronize provincial histories in the language. In fact, as Persian grew progressively provincialized in the decades following Timur, it also became more firmly rooted in India's linguistic landscape. Considerable Persian vocabulary entered regional Indian languages at the very time that those languages were achieving literary status.[92] More Persian dictionaries were produced in India in the fifteenth century than in Iran, or for that matter in the entire world outside India. Although multilingual, these dictionaries used Persian as their medium, that is, the language to which others were made to relate. The large number of Persian dictionaries produced at India's provincial courts suggests a need for some pan-Indian cultural centre of reference that might fill the void created by the loss of Delhi as a political one.[93]

Finally, the sort of restless movement that was occurring at the linguistic level – the appearance of written vernaculars, the translations of Sanskrit texts into regional tongues, the new roles played by both Sanskrit and Persian – reflect what was simultaneously happening at the social level. Jains had become well integrated into sultanate courts as administrators, financiers and mint-masters.[94] Fifteenth-century Sanskrit texts reveal the normality of Hindu princes, even those of the *kshatriya* class, serving Muslim rulers and fighting non-Muslim antagonists in performing that service.[95] Conversely, Sufi romance stories of the *premakhyan* genre show the extent to which Persianate society in post-Timur upper India had absorbed Indian sensibilities.

Developments in Bengal epitomize the growing fluidity between the Sanskrit and Persianate worlds. In his *Sri Caitanya Bhagavat*, a popular Bengali Vaishnava work composed in the 1540s, the poet Vrindavan Das referred to the Bengal king as *raja*, not sultan. Another Vaishnava poet, Jayananda, referred in his *Caitanya-Mangala* to the sultan not only as *raja* but as *iśvara* ('god'), and even as Indra, the Vedic king of gods.[96] During their installation ceremonies, the sultans of Bengal sent for water from Ganga Sagar, the ancient holy site where the old Ganges River emptied into the Bay of Bengal; they then washed themselves in that holy water in the manner of earlier Hindu sovereigns.[97] And in their public architecture, those sultans yielded so much to local conceptions of form and medium that, as one art historian observes, 'the country, originally possessed by the invaders, now possessed them'.[98]

# 4

# The Deccan and the South,
## 1400–1650

## LINKS TO THE PERSIANATE WORLD

When Timur raided north India in mid December 1398, Delhi's poorer classes had little choice but to remain and face the devastation. But many of the city's elites, well aware of the warlord's prior conquests and possessing sufficient resources, hastily packed their things and escaped before the storm broke. Among these was Muhammad Gisudaraz (d. 1422), who would become the most famous Sufi shaikh of the Deccan plateau. His tomb in Gulbarga, then the Bahmani sultanate's capital, remains today the Deccan's most popular Sufi shrine.[1]

Gisudaraz had actually grown up in the Deccan, as his family migrated there around 1327 when Sultan Muhammad bin Tughluq transferred a large part of Delhi's population to the new imperial co-capital of Daulatabad. Seven years later, while still in his teens, he returned to Delhi with his mother and elder brother, his father having died in Daulatabad. In the Tughluq capital he gained stature as a public figure and a prominent shaikh in the Chishti tradition. But just as Timur was about to capture Delhi, he and more than seventy of his disciples and camp-followers abandoned the city and headed south. It had been sixty-three years since he left the Deccan for Delhi. Now a venerable shaikh acclaimed throughout north India, he was returning with the immediate aim of visiting his father's grave site in Daulatabad, the city of his boyhood.[2] He and his considerable entourage finally reached the Deccan in the summer of 1399.

Considering it a boon that such a distinguished shaikh had fallen into his lap, the Bahmani ruler, Sultan Firuz (r. 1397–1422), personally rode up to Daulatabad to greet the newcomer and invite him to settle

Peninsular India, 1565

near his palace in Gulbarga. The shaikh agreed, but over time their relationship soured. Following a bitter falling-out, Gisudaraz was finally obliged to shift his residence to a site at a considerable distance from the Bahmani citadel, ostensibly because the large crowds attending his *khanaqah* had caused a security threat to the capital. Firuz also considered the shaikh deficient in the very branches of knowledge in which he claimed to excel, such as rhetoric and geometry.

The rift between the Sufi and the court widened further when it was learnt that Gisudaraz had been teaching lessons on a highly controversial text, the *Fusus al-hikam*, authored by the Spanish-Arab mystic Ibn al-'Arabi (d. 1240). The sultan sent a secretary to the shaikh's *khanaqah* to investigate and report on how Gisudaraz was using this text. But upon attending the discourses, the secretary became spellbound himself and enrolled as one of the shaikh's disciples, much to the court's dismay. Matters became political, however, when the shaikh refused to support Firuz's plan to be succeeded by his son, widely considered a weak and dissipated prince. In fact, the shaikh predicted that Firuz would be succeeded by his own brother, Ahmad, a mystically inclined prince who had shown personal veneration for the shaikh. Ultimately, Firuz accepted the political reality that the kingdom's *amir*s preferred such an outcome, and in late 1422 Ahmad was crowned sultan. Ten days later Firuz died, as did Gisudaraz a month afterwards.

The tortuous relationship between Gisudaraz and Firuz Bahmani points to a fundamental conflict between spiritual and royal authority. Having founded or inherited dominion over newly conquered territory, sultans sought the support of men whose blessings were thought to lend moral legitimacy to their rule. However, Sufis were popularly regarded as ocupying a moral plane above the sultan's world of glitter, corruption and violence, making it problematic for them to consort with royal courts. Indeed, the greater a shaikh's popular esteem, the more obliged he might feel to reject courtly patronage. Further complicating matters, sultans could be deeply jealous of a Sufi's popularity, as is suggested by Firuz's demand that Gisudaraz relocate his residence on the pretext that the throngs of people attending the shaikh's musical and teaching sessions posed a security threat. Relations between Sufis and royal courts could be vexed, to say the least.

Firuz Bahmani's relations with Timur were another matter altogether. Like other Indian monarchs, the Deccani sultan held in awe his towering contemporary, at that time the world's most powerful ruler and most lavish patron of Persian arts. From Bengal to the Balkans, Timur's dazzling court at Samarqand had set a transregional standard for imperial splendour. Shortly after Timur sacked Delhi, Firuz prudently rushed ambassadors and gifts to the Turkish conqueror, enlisting himself as the warlord's most faithful servant, doubtless hoping that he would not put the Deccan on his to-do list. In response, Timur addressed Firuz as 'son' and sent him a belt, a gilded sword, four royal robes, a Turkish slave and four splendid horses, items typical of the material gifts that circulated within, and helped constitute, the Persianate world.[3] In a gratuitous gesture, Timur also offered Firuz sovereignty over Gujarat and Malwa, two former Tughluq provinces and now independent sultanates that the warlord had not even bothered to conquer.

Even before receiving Timur's gifts, Firuz had embarked on an ambitious programme of Persianizing his court. In each year of his reign he had sent ships from his principal seaports on the Arabian Sea – Goa, Dabhol and Chaul – to the Persian Gulf to recruit Persian-speaking men of letters, administrators, soldiers and artisans. In 1399, only months after Timur sacked Delhi, he began building a new palace city, Firuzabad, twenty-seven kilometres south of Gulbarga. There, the sultan would emulate Timur's aesthetic vision, just as Sultan Mahmud Khalaji would do in Malwa's capital at Mandu. Between 1379 and 1396, shortly before launching his India campaign, Timur had built the most grandiose of his own architectural projects – the Aq Saray ('White Palace') in Shahr-i Sabz, the warlord's birthplace south of Samarqand [see Fig. 7]. On the spandrels of this structure there appeared the image of a pair of lions, an ancient symbol of Persian royalty.[4] News of this monument probably reached Firuz as he was planning Firuzabad, for the two lions also appeared on the spandrels of the city's western gateway, built just three years after the completion of the Aq Saray palace.[5]

Upon succeeding his brother Firuz in 1422, Sultan Ahmad Bahmani (r. 1422–36) transferred the state's capital from Gulbarga to Bidar. Located in the heart of the plateau at the junction of the Deccan's three major subregions – the Kannada-speaking south-west, the Telugu-speaking east and the Marathi-speaking west and north-west – the site was well suited as the capital of a state aspiring to transregional, imperial status. Moreover, with Delhi still largely ruined since Timur's invasion several decades earlier, Bidar would lay claim to being India's most imposing imperial centre, at least architecturally. In contrast to the low, squat arches found at Gulbarga, the tall arches and graceful spandrels of Bidar's Royal Chamber recall the sweeping vision of Timurid Samarqand. Those spandrels also repeat the same lion and sun motifs seen on the Aq Saray palace and at Firuzabad. Like Timur's palaces, Bidar's Hall of Public Audience was adorned with a profusion of blue, yellow, green and white glazed tiles.

Stylistically, Bidar's most Timurid-looking monument is the *madrasa*, patronized by the renowned Mahmud Gawan (d. 1481). A high-born merchant prince from Iran's Caspian Sea region, Gawan had joined the throngs of so-called 'Westerners' (Persian *gharbian*) who had been migrating to the Deccan from the Middle East ever since the Bahmani revolt against Muhammad bin Tughluq in 1347. Having severed their ties with Delhi, the Bahmanis now looked across the Arabian Sea for administrative talent and war-horses. Reaching the port of Dabhol in 1453, Mahmud Gawan, forty-one years of age and with considerable commercial and political experience behind him, was exactly the sort of person the regime wished to recruit. He easily convinced Dabhol's governor that he was no ordinary horse merchant, but a cosmopolitan Iranian who had already travelled through Anatolia, Syria, Egypt and Central Asia and had declined offers to serve as minister in courts in both Iraq and Khurasan. Upon reaching the Bahmani capital he was interviewed by Sultan Ahmad II Bahmani (r. 1436–58), who made him an *amir* with a command of 1,000 cavalrymen. In 1458, after suppressing a minor rebellion in the eastern plateau, he was promoted to chief minister of the whole kingdom with the title 'prince of merchants' (*malik al-tujjar*), an office whose name indicates the importance the kingdom attached to trade with the outside world. In 1466 he was made regent for two successive boy monarchs and entrusted with supervising the administration of all the kingdom's provinces, which then stretched from the Arabian Sea to the Bay of Bengal.

Boasting personal and commercial connections from the Balkans to India, the cosmopolitan *vazir* was determined to put Bidar on the world map. This is seen in his voluminous correspondence, which he maintained with luminaries all over the Persianate world, including the Ottoman sultan Mehmet II, who had conquered Constantinople the same year Gawan reached India. In these letters he sought to attract the brightest scholars of that world, for which purpose he built his famous *madrasa*, completed in 1472 and located just beyond the citadel in the heart of the city. Although a quarter of it is missing today owing to damage by lightning, the brilliant glazed tiles covering the minaret and eastern façade, the sweeping arches, the vaulting and the structure's sheer monumentality reflect Timur's aesthetic vision [see Fig. 6]. Standing before this remarkable structure, one can easily imagine oneself in Herat, Bukhara or Samarqand.

To the south, meanwhile, Vijayanagara's ruling class had begun absorbing Persianate ideas and practices even before waves of Timurid culture washed over India in the early fifteenth century. From its founding in 1347, as we have seen, the state's rulers styled themselves 'sultan among Indian kings' (*hindu-raya-suratrana*), a title used a century later by even minor Hindu chieftains in the Andhra country.[6] By 1355 Vijayanagara's rulers were referring to themselves simply as 'sultan' several decades before they began using Sanskrit imperial titles such as *rajadhiraja* ('king of kings') or *rajaparamesvara* ('supreme king').[7] In 1442 they established direct contact with the Timurid court when Timur's son and successor, Shah Rukh (r. 1405–47), sent an envoy on a diplomatic mission to important courts in south India. Sailing from the Persian Gulf, the envoy, 'Abd al-Razzaq, first reached Calicut, the commercially important city state on India's Malabar coast. When Vijayanagara's King Deva Raya II (r. 1422–46) learnt of this, he summoned the Timurid ambassador to his court, where he gave his guest two private audiences a week and a generous allotment of gifts and cash, letting it be known how pleased he was that 'the great Padishah' (Shah Rukh) had sent him an emissary. What most impressed 'Abd al-Razzaq in his report on the Vijayanagara court was the apparel he saw. The king, he noted, wore a tunic of Chinese silk locally known by a variation of the Persian term *qaba*. Made of cotton or silk, this long-sleeved pullover had first appeared in Iran in

the eleventh and twelfth centuries. Subsequent visitors to Vijayanagara noted that royalty and members of the nobility also wore tall,
brocaded, brimless headgear whose name derived from another Persian word – *kulah*. Both the headgear and the name for it had come
from Iran. By adopting the title of 'sultan' and wearing garments and
headgear then fashionable in the cosmopolitan Timurid world, members of Vijayanagara's ruling class showed their desire to participate
in that world.[8]

Vijayanagara was drawn into the Persianate cultural orbit in other
ways too. By the late fourteenth century, the capital had grown far
beyond the temple complexes that hug the banks of the Tungabhadra,
constituting the city's Sacred Centre. Measuring thirty-nine kilometres in circumference, the city's walls were extended southwards,
snaking through the maze of jumbled granite boulders that define the
area's extraordinary, moonlike landscape [see Fig. 4]. Several kilometres south of the city's Sacred Centre, these walls embraced the
Royal Centre, where the kingdom's ruling household and governing
classes presided over cycles of elaborate political rituals. The participants in the processions central to those rituals – elephants, horses,
warriors, entertainers, musicians, dancers, and so on – are vividly represented in the exuberant bas-relief figures that cover the outer surfaces
of several prominent monuments.[9] In contrast to the city's Sacred Centre,
most of those in the Royal Centre lavishly incorporate the architectural vocabulary of the Persianate world – domes, pointed arches,
cross-vaultings and stucco reliefs – as seen in such structures as the
so-called 'Elephant Stables', the 'Queen's Bath', the 'Lotus Mahal' and
in numerous gateways, watchtowers and water pavilions. At the heart
of the capital's Royal Centre stands a great audience hall of 100 columns, forty metres square, whose design closely adheres to those
found in Persianate courts elsewhere in India and the Iranian plateau,
the forerunner of which reaches back to the Hall of a Hundred Columns in Persepolis (fifth century BC), capital of the ancient Persian
empire. Serving as a stage for enacting courtly rituals, receiving foreign emissaries and displaying the court's cosmopolitan identity, the
Royal Centre made manifest the rulers' claims to being sultans among
Indian kings.

Commerce and military concerns also linked Vijayanagara with the Persianate world. The base of the capital's great ceremonial platform known as the Mahanavami Dibba, built in stages between the fourteenth and early sixteenth centuries, is adorned with bas-relief panels that depict, among others, foreign merchants. Appearing to be Turks from Central Asia, these men lead their horses to be received by the king and his attendants.[10] Such images point to the state's chronic dependence on war-horses imported from the Persian Gulf region and its active participation in maritime commercial networks. Far more numerous than foreign merchants were the Muslim soldiers recruited into the state's army. In 1430 Deva Raya II employed 10,000 Turkish troops in his armed forces, and in 1535 Rama Raya (d. 1565) recruited 3,000 Iranian and Turkish troops.[11] Tombs and mosques located in the urban core north-east of the Royal Centre indicate where they and their officers were settled. Krishna Raya (r. 1509–29) so valued his Muslim soldiers that in his 1520 invasion of Raichur he placed them in the vanguard of his troops.[12] And in the capital itself, we find sculptures of Turkic – and presumably Muslim – warriors guarding the precincts of the city's Hindu temples. On a free-standing hall in the walled compound of the city's Vitthala Temple, the city's most politically important temple in the sixteenth century, such warriors are depicted, three-quarters human in size, riding rearing lion-like beasts and armed with diverse weapons.[13]

## SUCCESSORS TO THE BAHMANI STATE

The Bahmani court's efforts to recruit talent from the Persian-speaking world came at heavy cost. As more so-called Westerners – ethnic Persians and Turks – arrived from across the Arabian Sea and acquired positions of influence, the kingdom's native Muslims, the Deccanis, felt increasingly embittered and alienated. This class was descended from north Indian immigrants who, such as Gisudaraz's parents, had settled in the Deccan from the 1320s, when the Tughluqs established Daulatabad as their empire-wide co-capital. Born in the Deccan, this class spoke indigenous languages in addition to an early form of Hindavi called Dakani. And, to a far greater extent than Westerners, they had adopted the plateau as their natural home.

During their successful struggle against the Tughluq regime in Delhi, they had positioned themselves against north Indians. But after achieving independence from Delhi, their rivals became the Westerners, whom they viewed as interlopers who had been given preferential treatment by the court. The differences between the two groups were therefore both political and cultural. By the mid fifteenth century a de facto apartheid system had emerged. In Bidar's Hall of Public Audience, Westerners attending court stood to the right-hand side of the throne and the Deccanis to the left. While on military campaigns, the two factions continuously clashed, each side blaming the other for insubordination, cowardice, even treason.

As prime minister, Mahmud Gawan had addressed these tensions by decreasing the influence of both Deccani and Westerner *amir*s. To minimize quarrelling over lands coveted by either faction he increased the size of those controlled directly by the court; he also forbade *amir*s to have charge of more than a single fort. But the minister's many months away from the capital directing military campaigns only gave his enemies opportunities to conspire behind his back, as one chronicler put it, 'like wounded vipers, writhing in the torment of jealousy'.[14] Gawan himself wrote: 'Out of sheer malice they would kill each other and make me the object of all the wrongs which it is in their power to perpetrate.'[15] In this vicious atmosphere the minister, himself a Westerner, became the object of conspiracies hatched by disaffected Deccanis. In 1481 members of that faction plied his seal-bearer with gifts and then gave him a blank sheet of paper that required Gawan's seal. Told that it was only a routine document, the seal-bearer obligingly stamped it. The conspirators then filled in the document with treasonous words purporting to be Gawan's, inviting a foreign power to invade the kingdom and share the spoils with him. When the sultan was shown the authenticated document he flew into a rage, summoned his minister to court, and forthwith had him beheaded for treason.

From this point on, the Bahmani kingdom fell into a downward spiral from which it never recovered. The deep and intractable Deccani–Westerner rift, and the poisonous intrigues and destructive civil wars it spawned, ultimately undermined the state's stability. On the one hand, the court was obliged to patronize the Deccanis inasmuch as they were descended from the northern settlers who, having rebelled against Muhammad bin Tughluq, had launched the dynasty. But in order to earn a coveted place in the cosmopolitan Timurid world, rulers in Bidar felt equally obliged to recruit immigrants from the Middle East or Central Asia. In the end, the Deccanis and Westerners represented not just two competing political factions, but two different conceptions of state and society. Each class being legitimate in its own way, neither could be dislodged. Mahmud Gawan's policy of politically balancing the two classes proved an impossible juggling act: no administrative measure could resolve the ideological rift.

Within a decade of Mahmud Gawan's execution, the Bahmani kingdom began to disintegrate into five successor states, as provincial governors scrambled to assert their independence. The first to do so was Malik Ahmad, who founded the Nizam Shahi dynasty of Ahmadnagar (1490-1636). He was the son of one of the last Bahmani prime ministers, a staunchly partisan Deccani who in the 1480s had aggrandized all power and reduced the sultan to a puppet, exacerbating the perennial Westerner–Deccani conflict. In 1486 he was assassinated, and four years later Malik Ahmad, embittered by the politics of the court and the murder of his father, declared his independence at the fort of Junnar in Maharashtra, where he had been governor. He also established a new capital named after himself, Ahmadnagar, soon to become one of the Deccan's most important centres of artistic patronage.

Variations on this pattern were now repeated throughout the plateau. To the north, Fath Allah 'Imad al-Mulk (r. 1490-1504), the governor of the Bahmani province of Berar, also grew disgusted with the deteriorating affairs in Bidar and in 1490 declared his independence, founding the 'Imad Shah sultanate (1490-1574) with the fort of Elichpur his capital. About the same time Yusuf 'Adil Khan (r. 1490-1510), the provincial governor of Bijapur, asserted his de facto independence. An immigrant from Ottoman Anatolia, Yusuf declared Shi'ism Bijapur's state religion in 1503, shortly after Iran's new Safavid regime (1501-1736) had done the same. Yet he never imposed his faith on Bijapur's subjects. His son and successor Isma'il (r. 1510-34), by contrast, was far more zealous. Brought up by an aunt who had migrated directly from Iran, Isma'il seldom spoke Dakani, the language of the Deccani class, and employed only Westerners, banishing all Deccanis from his court. Clearly, the same ethnic poison that had killed the Bahmani parent state had infected its political offspring. In 1519 Isma'il had the Friday prayers offered for Iran's Safavid family and ordered his entire army to imitate the Safavid courtly custom of wearing scarlet caps with twelve points, symbolizing the imams of 'Twelver' Shi'ism. Isma'il's son Ibrahim 'Adil Shah I, however, identified himself and his regime with his native Deccan and embraced Sunni Islam, the sect of most Deccani Muslims. In a move more dramatically expressing his identification with the plateau's history and culture, he explicitly invoked the memory of the Kalyana Chalukyas (974–1190), one of the peninsula's most illustrious imperial dynasties. Bijapur itself had once been an important Chalukya provincial centre known by its Sanskrit name, Vijayapura. The sultan referenced the past by placing Chalukya inscription tablets and a stunning ensemble of twenty-four Chalukya columns in conspicuous locations in his citadel's grand gateway, the kingdom's most public space.[16]

Ibrahim 'Adil Shah's son and successor 'Ali 'Adil Shah I (r. 1558–80), however, reoriented the dynasty's sectarian affiliation back to Shi'ism. No zealot himself, he was actually a serious intellectual and free-thinker. While on tours or on military campaigns he would take cartloads of books with him for his personal use. He invited Portuguese clerics to his capital so that he could learn about Christian tenets.[17] His crowning intellectual achievement was to author a remarkable text, the *Nujum al-'ulum*, or 'Stars of the Sciences', which, composed in Persian but replete with Dakani words, drew on Indic, Islamic, Greek and Turkic traditions to render a comprehensive vision of medieval Deccani courtly knowledge. Blending astrology, incantations, conjuring, talismans, omens, the interpretation of dreams, alchemy, poetry, music and martial skills, the text aimed at transforming a culturally diverse and politically divided body of courtiers into a cohesive whole. It was also lavishly illustrated with miniature paintings that artfully blended the Persianate and Sanskrit worlds. The planet Mars, for example, is depicted as a hero wearing a leopard helmet, which is associated with Rustam, the most celebrated hero of Persian mythology. But he also holds a trident, associated with the god Śiva. In another painting, the text depicts an anthropomorphic image of the sun drawn in Central Asian style, driving a chariot across the sky like the god Helios in Greek mythology. But the figure also holds a conch shell and a mace, which are associated with the god Vishnu.[18] The text's royal author thus emerges as a thoroughly cosmopolitan figure, epitomizing the degree to which the Deccan plateau had, by the mid sixteenth century, become a crossroads of diverse cultural traditions.

In the Bahmanis' former capital of Bidar itself, the last Bahmani prime minister, Qasim Barid (d. 1505), established the Barid Shahi dynasty more or less by default, as he found himself effectively marooned in the old Bahmani capital, abandoned by rebellious provincial governors who, one by one, had withdrawn their support for the central government. Although the sultanate of Bidar (c.1490–1619) inherited the substantial fortifications and outworks of the last Bahmani capital, together with the palaces and audience halls that recalled the formerly united kingdom, it was also the smallest and weakest of that kingdom's five successor states.

Finally, in the eastern Deccan another migrant from Iran, Sultan Quli (r. 1497–1543), had been appointed Bahmani governor of Telangana in 1496 with the title Qutb al-Mulk. But he soon asserted his independence, founding the Qutb Shahi dynasty, with his capital at the famous hill fort of Golconda. On the death of Sultan Quli Qutb Shah in 1543, his son Jamshid (r. 1543–50) blinded his elder brother and seized the throne. Anticipating the same fate for himself, Jamshid's younger brother Ibrahim prudently fled south to the court of Vijayanagara, where he spent seven years as a guest of that state's autocrat, Rama Raya, immersing himself in Telugu poetry and his host's courtly culture. When Jamshid died in 1550, a coalition of Telugu and Westerner commanders met at the fort of Koilkonda (100 kilometres south-west of Hyderabad), where they resolved to invite Prince Ibrahim to return to Golconda and rule the kingdom.[19] Ibrahim accepted the invitation and marched from Vijayanagara to Koilkonda, from where he was escorted to the Qutb Shahi throne.

Golconda's hybridized culture is seen in the remarkable career of 'Abd al-Qadir Amin Khan (fl. 1568–83), a prominent *amir* and a Deccani with long-standing family roots in India.[20] At Patancheru, thirty kilometres north-west of Hyderabad, he patronized the construction of a mosque and a tomb for himself, the latter bearing an elegant Persian inscription indicating his humility, his piety and his devotion to a local Sufi shaikh. At the same time, he employed a Brahmin as his personal secretary and established a tax-free village (*agraharam*), 'Aminpuram', for the support of traditional Brahmin priests. He was also an enthusiastic patron of Telugu literature, commissioning a Telugu adaptation of part of the *Mahabharata* epic. Titled the *Yayati Caritramu*, this is the first known work that sought to 'purify' Telugu of its Sanskrit loan words, and as such compares with the *Shahnama*, in which the epic poet Firdausi had endeavoured to do the same for modern Persian by minimizing his work's use of Arabic loan words. There is even evidence that the Telugu poet was inspired by Firdausi's example.[21]

The cultural achievements that appeared in the reigns of Golconda's Sultan Ibrahim Qutb Shah and Bijapur's 'Ali 'Adil Shah I were not isolated phenomena. The entire period from 1565 to the Mughal conquest in the 1680s enjoyed unprecedented peace, prosperity and artistic florescence. It was a golden age for the principal Deccani sultanates, whose great wealth, based especially on the production and export of textile fabrics, astonished foreign visitors. In the imagination of Europeans – and later, of Americans – Golconda in particular became synonymous with fabulous wealth, thanks to European merchants who travelled to that city's bazaars and gave glowing accounts of the fine diamonds taken from nearby mines.[22] The best evidence of Deccan-wide prosperity is the significant urbanization that took place in this period. Older cities such as Daulatabad were greatly enlarged to accommodate growing urban populations, while entirely new cities also appeared – most prominently Hyderabad, which Ibrahim's successor, Sultan Muhammad Quli Qutb Shah (r. 1580–1612), founded in 1591.

Located several kilometres from Golconda fort and centred on the famous Charminar monument, Hyderabad is often called an 'Islamic city'. But in reality, its layout and design reflect the aesthetic sensibilities of the new social classes that had attained prominence in the late-sixteenth-century eastern Deccan. One of those groups, the *nayakwari*s, were Telugu-speaking Hindu warriors whose political prominence dates back to the Kakatiya period. Although *nayakwari* families maintained strong ties to particular ancestral locales, the more successful among them enjoyed a good deal of mobility, moving easily from one chieftain or court to another, offering their military service in exchange for estates where they could maintain their troops. As suppliers of soldiers to would-be patrons, they served in the Deccan's military labour market, which operated much like its counterpart in contemporary north India. As a class, Telangana's *nayakwari*s were thoroughly familiar with Persianate courtly practices and had adopted Persianate military and administrative technology.[23]

Another prominent group in sixteenth-century Golconda were the Niyogis. These were worldly-oriented Telugu Brahmins who had given up their caste's traditional priestly roles to assume salaried political and administrative appointments in the Qutb Shahi sultanate. Whereas most of them served as village accountants, maintaining official records such as tax ledgers, others kept records for towns, or served as governors, diplomats to neighbouring states, or court advisers. The prosperity of the Qutb Shahi sultanate depended upon its ability to recruit talent from all its four most powerful constituent groups – Deccanis, Westerners, *nayakwari* warriors and Niyogi Brahmins – and the willingness of their members to act in concert with one another politically, as happened when *nayakwari*s and Westerners collaborated in raising Ibrahim Qutb Shah to power.

Given the prominence of Niyogi Brahmins and *nayakwari*s in Golconda's ruling structure, it is not surprising that, when planning his new city of Hyderabad near Golconda fort, Sultan Muhammad Quli Qutb Shah drew upon the aesthetic and material legacy of Telangana's most important regional dynasty. These were the Kakatiya kings, who had established their capital at Warangal towards the end of the twelfth century. Located 140 kilometres north-east of Golconda, Warangal is South Asia's best surviving example of a city replicating classical Indian conceptions of the world – that is, a great circular continent divided in four quarters and surrounded by a series of ring-shaped oceans, with the cosmic mountain Meru, where Śiva dwells, lying at its centre. At Warangal, the area within the inner, stone wall replicated the central continent, in the middle of which stood a great temple that was dedicated to Śiva and represented Mount Meru. Beyond the stone wall lay a moat representing a cosmic sea, with a second, outer wall and moat corresponding to the sea surrounding a second, ring-shaped continent and another sea. Standing at cardinal directions around the temple precincts, four majestic ceremonial gateways symbolized the sources of four rivers that flow outwards from Mount Meru, defining the universe's four quarters.

Although Warangal's Śiva temple had been demolished by the Tughluq prince Ulugh Khan when he seized the city in 1323, Qutb Shahi authorities in Golconda were well aware of Warangal's cosmographic plan and its homology between Śiva as the lord of the universe and the Kakatiya king as lord of the human realm. The Qutb Shahis had ruled Warangal throughout the sixteenth century, and Telugu histories of the Kakatiyas had begun to appear from around 1550. Telugu verses praising Ibrahim Qutb Shah specifically connected that sultan with Mount Meru, identifying him as a *chakravartin* ('world-conqueror') who had crossed the seven seas and circled the seven continents of classic Indian mythology. All this suggests that for Qutb Shahi elites – whether *nayakwari*, Westerner, Niyogi Brahmin or Deccani – Warangal's open plaza and four ceremonial gateways carried rich memories of the Kakatiya past and were powerfully redolent of imperial domination.

The physical parallels between Warangal and Hyderabad are also striking.[24] Both cities were built on a plain seven kilometres south-east of a former capital and hill fort – Hanamkonda and Golconda respectively. Like Warangal, Hyderabad was laid out on a four-quartered plan produced by four avenues extending in cardinal directions from a distinctive structure that indicated the crossing point of those four avenues. Both cities featured a broad, open plaza defined by four lofty gateways, or *torana*s, located immediately north of that central crossing point. At Warangal these are the central plaza's four ceremonial gateways, and in Hyderabad, four great portals, the 'Char Kaman'. In both cities a palace complex was situated immediately west of the plaza, with which it was axially aligned. At Warangal, that palace was the well-preserved Tughluq audience hall, the so-called 'Khush Mahal' [see Fig. 3], and at Hyderabad it was the Qutb Shahi royal palace, subsequently destroyed. Most strikingly, in Warangal a simple, two-storeyed open-pillared structure, a *chaubara*, stands to the south-west of the plaza in the precise centre of the fort where Warangal's four roads meet. Taking the idea of Warangal's *chaubara* as marking the centre of the Kakatiya capital, Muhammad Quli built to the south of Hyderabad's plaza what has become the most iconic monument of the Deccan, the famous Charminar, which marks both the city's centre and the intersection of its principal avenues. Far more complex and sophisticated than Warangal's *chaubara*, the Charminar features spacious arches, a domed chamber, two upper storeys, a mezzanine, arcades with views looking outwards, four tall minarets and at the topmost level a sumptuously decorated mosque.

As Hyderabad was established in 1591, corresponding to the year 1000 in the Islamic calendar, the city's founding also inaugurated the second millennium of Islam. This would explain an important difference between these two structures: whereas Warangal's *chaubara* is aligned with the cardinal directions, the Charminar is aligned with Mecca, which at Hyderabad's latitude turns the structure ten degrees clockwise from cardinal directions. On the other hand, at the interior apex of the Charminar's uppermost storey is a large solar lotus – the iconic Indian symbol of life and energy – with twelve smaller lotuses placed around it in the manner of the zodiac. In this way, the Charminar combined Indic and Persianate forms, while it was set in a city whose layout had been inspired by the memory of Telangana's most famous regional dynasty, the Kakatiyas of Warangal. The monument may be understood, then, as one of India's most eloquent visual representations of the interpenetration of the Indic and Persianate worlds.

## POLITICAL AND CULTURAL EVOLUTION AT VIJAYANAGARA

Long before Sultan Muhammad Quli Qutb Shah began planning the city of Hyderabad, royal patrons in the sprawling kingdom of Vijayanagara had already built the monumental temple complexes that, in popular imagination, remain iconic images of that state. In their metropolitan capital, kings regularly sponsored huge public processions and ceremonies taking place over several days that were enacted in elaborately built structures near their palaces or in the city's temple complexes. Long chariot streets, tanks, multi-pillar halls and colonnades lining inner enclosure walls – all were prominent features of these complexes.

The capital's oldest temple complexes appeared in its Sacred Centre, the well-defined quarter near the southern banks of the Tunga-bhadra, originating with the one dedicated to the goddess Pampa and a form of Śiva locally called Virupaksha [see Fig. 4]. Here, pro-gressively greater Tamil influence can be seen in a cluster of temples associated with the first four Sangama rulers, spanning the period from the mid fourteenth to the early fifteenth centuries. This is read-ily understandable, since very early in the kingdom's history, between 1352 and 1371, royal armies from the upland plateau conquered most of the fertile and prosperous Tamil country to the south and east of the dry interior that formed the core of the Vijayanagara state. Pro-longed contact between Vijayanagara's political centre and its wealthy coastal provinces led, among other things, to the imperial city's grad-ual assimilation of the rich heritage of classical Tamil architecture, including such elements as heavily carved pyramidal entrance towers with their distinctive barrel-vaulted roofs.

Vijayanagara's conquests in India's deep south also had religious and ideological consequences. From the mid fourteenth century through to the mid sixteenth, as an increasingly diverse range of peoples and cultures were brought under its rule, the state evolved an ever more synthesized, cosmopolitan courtly style.[25] We have noted the extent to which the kingdom's elite classes had been assimilated into an expand-ing Persianate world. Eschewing the status of a regional kingdom, Vijayanagara also patronized a range of religious traditions that included Śaiva, Vaishnava and Jain, together with Islamic institutions. The Sangama brothers, who had founded the state in 1347, declared their official deity to be Virupaksha. Down to the mid sixteenth cen-tury, the kingdom's official documents continued to be authenticated in the presence of the icon representing that god in the city's Virupak-sha temple. From the early fifteenth century onwards, however, ruling authorities gave increasing patronage to the god Vishnu in his various manifestations, or *avatar*s. The trend began with Deva Raya I, who built the Ramachandra Temple, a magnificent structure dedicated to the Vaishnava deity Rama, in the heart of the Royal Centre. In build-ing this temple, the king made efficient use of the city's mythic landscape, inasmuch as the Tungabhadra next to which it stands, together with the hills to the north and east of the Royal Centre, are all associated with an important episode in the *Ramayana* epic. This is the Kishkindha section, in which Rama meets and secures the help of monkey heroes in his quest to rescue his abducted wife, Sita. However, even though the mythic associations of Rama with Vijayanagara's landscape had probably preceded the founding of the capital, the Sangama founders of the dynasty never mentioned Rama in their inscriptions, patronizing Virupaksha instead.

As a solution to this growing tension over which deity would be recognized as the dynasty's Cosmic Overlord – the Śaiva god Virupaksha or the Vaishnava god Rama – recent research has proposed that, throughout the fifteenth century, Vijayanagara's rulers practised a hybrid royal theology. Kings presented themselves as ideal *devotees* of Śiva in the form of Virupaksha, but as ideal *kings* in the manner of Rama, an *avatar* of Vishnu.[26] But in the late fifteenth century when the Sangama house was overthrown by Saluva Narasimha (r. 1485–91), a warlord based at the stronghold of Chandragiri on the northern Tamil plain, the new king openly favoured the Vaishnava deity Venkateśvara, the lord of the popular shrine at Tirupati in southern Andhra. From Narasimha's reign on, south India's pilgrimage centre at Tirupati grew dramatically in importance, both for the general population and for the state's rulers. Whereas before the Vijayanagara period only 150 inscriptions at Tirupati referred to the shrine's benefactors, that figure rose to 480 in the short period between 1509 and 1542, when the state had attained its height of cultural and political influence. Vijayanagara's most famous monarch, Krishna Raya, made Venkateśvara his patron deity and visited Tirupati seven times. His successor, Achyuta Raya (r. 1529–42), performed several coronation ceremonies, the first of which occurred at Tirupati in the presence of Venkateśvara.[27] In 1544 the state altogether ceased authenticating official documents before the Śaiva god Virupaksha, as it had been doing for nearly two centuries; from then on, they were authenticated before another Vaishnava deity, Vitthala, locally identified with Krishna.[28] This change in sectarian affiliation is also reflected in the state's minted gold coins. Between 1377 and 1424, following Vijayanagara's conquest of the Tamil coastal area, state coins bore mixed Śaiva and Vaishnava images, whereas after 1509 most of the coins' motifs were exclusively Vaishnava in nature.[29]

It was in this last phase of metropolitan Vijayanagara's historical evolution, the first half of the sixteenth century, that its theology most closely matched its imperial ambitions. Having expanded over most of the southern portion of the Indian peninsula, its sovereigns incorporated in the heart of their capital temples dedicated to cults specific to regions they had conquered, or which they aspired to conquer. The city's temple complex dedicated to Balakrishna – the god Krishna as an infant – was specially built in the Sacred Centre to commemorate Krishna Raya's 1513 victory over the Gajapati raja at Udayagiri near the Andhra coast. It also houses the Krishna image that was taken from Udayagiri to Vijayanagara. Similarly, the Vitthala Temple complex, the bulk of which dates to the early sixteenth century, reproduces in the imperial capital the worship of Vitthala, which had been centred in Pandharpur, 280 kilometres north-west of Vijayanagara. In 1534 Achyuta Raya built the capital city's Tiruvengalanatha Temple, which replicates the Venkateśvara Temple at Tirupati, located 120 kilometres north-west of modern Chennai. In this manner, the later kings gathered into their imperial centre ritual representations of the state's most important constituent sovereign territories, or (as in the case of Pandharpur) would-be territories: Virupaksha for the state's core in Karnataka, Venkateśvara for the Tamil and southern Andhra country, Balakrishna for the coastal districts and Vitthala for the northern Deccan. The state's imperial pantheon, made visual in its capital's built landscape, thus fused its theology with its sovereign territory.

Vijayanagara's economic history also experienced dramatic changes between the fourteenth and sixteenth centuries. Two distinct periods of the kingdom's economic growth are seen in the pattern of reservoir construction, projects that were essential to agrarian life in a region as arid as the Deccan plateau. During the century between the state's founding in 1347 and 1450, thirty-five reservoirs were built in its core region, and twenty more in the first half of the sixteenth century. Between these two peaks of reservoir-construction, however, there was a lull from 1450 to 1500, when only three reservoirs are known to have been constructed on the plateau.[30] Nor were any major temples built at this time, or many stone or copperplate inscriptions issued. Whereas the state continuously minted gold and copper coins between 1347 and 1446, only copper coins were issued for the next several decades, and for the next four decades after that no new coins appeared at all.[31]

This dramatic decline in cultural and economic activity is associated with a period of devastating drought-induced famines that struck the Deccan in the fifteenth century, which in turn triggered a marked decline in agricultural production, land revenue and population. This was exacerbated by the state's chronic inability to harmonize the agrarian economy of the dry, upland plateau with the highly commercialized economy of the Tamil coast. Until the early 1500s, the plateau and coast practically lived in two separate economic worlds, as is seen in patterns of textile production and consumption. Along the coast, the port of Pulicat had emerged in the fifteenth century as a major centre for the export of textiles produced in both the Coromandel low country and the Kaveri delta. By the early sixteenth century, Pulicat's annual textile exports to the South-east Asian port of Malacca were estimated to be worth 175,000 Portuguese *cruzados*,[32] reflecting the integration of the heavily commercialized coastal region with the trading world of the wider Indian Ocean. The boom had also improved the lives of Tamil weavers, who in the course of the fifteenth and sixteenth centuries won the right to ride in palanquins and blow conch shells on ritual occasions, a sure sign of their rising social status.[33]

Notably, the Coromandel coast's manufacturing and commercial boom in the late fifteenth century coincided with the economic stagnation in Vijayanagara's agrarian heartland. Although the court itself appears to have been consuming increasing amounts of cloth in this period, much of it produced on the Coromandel coast, the kingdom's upland core region proved unable to profit fiscally from the coastal boom. In 1513 coastal weaving communities even induced the government to rescind an order that would have increased taxes on their looms.[34] The court's inability to impose and collect taxes on such a crucial sector of the economy points to the central government's structural weakness with respect to its rich coastal provinces. An early sign of this came in the form of a major tax revolt. In 1429 communities of cultivators and artisans in the Kaveri delta, which Vijayanagara had conquered and annexed sixty years earlier, rose up in a widespread rebellion protesting the oppressive taxes imposed by imperial administrators.[35] After that revolt, Vijayanagara's central administration maintained only a loose grip over its Tamil province.[36] As a result, the state's core upland region failed to benefit from the economic boom then occurring in the Tamil country. As one historian remarks, 'the Kaveri milch-cow of resources for a central Vijayanagara exchequer proved difficult to milk'.[37]

What is more, the rich Coromandel coast and its considerable wealth soon served as a power base for a succession of military commanders who would shape the state's destiny. The pattern had already begun in the reign of Deva Raya II, who had granted considerable autonomy to powerful military commanders after the Kaveri delta tax revolt of 1429. In 1456 Saluva Narasimha began making generous endowments to the nearby Tirupati Temple complex, already the most important pilgrimage centre in south India. In the 1470s, gathering supporters through his military prowess and his continued patronage of the Tirupati shrine, he seized control over the entire Coromandel coast from the hill fort of Udayagiri in modern Nellore District down to Rameśwaram, adjacent to Sri Lanka. Although he remained for some time nominally subordinate to his royal overlord in the capital, in 1485 he became the first Vijayanagara general to overthrow the state's ruling Sangama dynasty and establish a new one, the Saluva.

A violent pattern had now set in. In 1505 the son and successor of the new dynasty's founder was himself overthrown by Tuluva Vira Narasimha (r. 1505–9), the son of Saluva Narasimha's chief minister. He then founded Vijayanagara's third dynasty, the Tuluvas. In 1509 he was succeeded by his half-brother Krishna Raya, the most famous of the kingdom's rulers. Krishna Raya is celebrated for an unbroken string of military conquests that brought enormous wealth to the capital and helped end the state's half-century of economic stagnation. The victories began in 1509, when at Koilkonda, 100 kilometres southwest of Hyderabad, he defeated the last remnant of Bahmani power, Sultan Mahmud along with Yusuf 'Adil Khan, the founder of the fledgling sultanate of Bijapur. The king then led his armies southwards and seized Penukonda, Śrirangapattanam and Śivasamudram from the chiefs of the powerful Ummattur family. In 1513, turning to the southern Andhra coast, he reconquered the fort of Udayagiri, which had fallen into the hands of the Gajapati kings of Orissa. Two years later his armies took from the Gajapatis the fort of Kondavidu in the Krishna delta. In 1517 he took Vijayavada and Kondapalli, also in that delta, and then Rajahmundry, further up the coast in the Godavari delta. With the help of Portuguese mercenary musketeers, in 1520 he reconquered from Bijapur the rich Raichur region, an area that, lying between the Krishna and Tungabhadra Rivers, his Sangama predecessors had perennially contested with the Bahmani sultans. In 1523 he penetrated further north and seized, but chose not to hold, Gulbarga.

Thus ended fourteen years of uninterrupted military success. Especially notable was the king's brief capture of Gulbarga, the Bahmanis' second capital and a venerable site of Persianate culture in the Deccan. While he had the city in his grasp, Krishna Raya provocatively 'appointed' one of the sons of the last Bahmani sultan as the new Bahmani ruler – even though that state was by then defunct – and styled himself 'the one who brings about the (re)establishment of Yavana [Turkish] rule'. This insolent gesture was probably made in retaliation for the Bahmanis' reduction of Vijayanagara to tributary status for most of the first half of the fifteenth century. The boast also affirmed that he, Krishna Raya, now claimed to be the political arbiter of the entire Deccan, capable of establishing – or in this case, renewing – Turkish power. Never before had a ruler of Vijayanagara so brazenly intruded in the affairs of the northern Deccan. Once back in his capital and securely in power, Krishna Raya refrained from planting his kinsmen in central ministries or in command of major forts. Rather, he continued the state's earlier practice of hiring large numbers of mercenary troops – Deccani and Westerner cavalry, Portuguese gunners – and of placing Brahmins, not kinsmen, in command of the kingdom's prominent forts. Such measures were aimed at checking the power of quasi-independent warlords. After all, he was well aware of the pattern whereby earlier warlords, including his own half-brother Vira Narasimha, had used major forts as power bases to launch new dynasties.

Accompanying Krishna Raya on his military campaigns was Rama Raya, a chieftain of the Aravidu clan whose performance so impressed the king that he gave him his daughter in marriage. Born in 1484 in Kurnool District, south-western Andhra, Rama Raya began his career in the service of Quli Qutb Shah, the founder of the sultanate at Golconda. That the son of a prominent Vijayanagara general could so readily enrol in Golconda's service suggests that in the Deccan, as in north India in this age, loyalty to family, faction or paymaster counted far more than loyalty to land, religion or ethnic group. But his service at Golconda lasted only three years. In 1515 Golconda's neighbour to the west, Bijapur, invaded some districts that were under his charge, and instead of defending his fort he fled back to Golconda. Considering this an act of cowardice, the sultan dismissed the Telugu warrior, who then took up service with Krishna Raya. Once in Vijayanagara's service, Rama Raya systematically gathered power around himself, his immediate family and his extended lineage, the Aravidu clan. Although Krishna Raya had named his other half-brother, Achyuta Raya, his successor, when the king died in 1529 Rama Raya tried to subvert his father-in-law's choice by having the late king's infant son proclaimed king and himself regent. Although the attempted power-grab was blocked by the kingdom's nobility, Rama Raya exploited his position as minister and his marital connection with the late Krishna Raya by arranging that the command of key forts in the heartland – Adoni, Kurnool and Nandyal – be transferred to his Aravidu kinsmen. This marked an important step in Vijayanagara's transition to a patrimonial state. Also, like Saluva Narasimha before him, Rama Raya showered lavish patronage on the shrine of Venkateśvara at Tirupati, which had earlier proved such a useful stepping stone to the throne. Whereas Achyuta Raya had granted forty-three villages for the benefit of the shrine at Tirupati, Rama Raya bestowed sixty.[38]

Rama Raya also benefited from political events to the north of the Krishna. In 1535, Sultan Ibrahim 'Adil Shah I of Bijapur dismissed all but 400 of his Westerner troops and replaced them with Deccanis. In another instance of elite mobility across the plateau, Rama Raya recruited the 3,000 Westerners dismissed by the sultan, most of them Shi'i immigrants from Iran.[39] When Achyuta Raya died in 1542 and was succeeded by his youthful son, the kingdom's regent attempted to seize the throne for himself by wiping out nearly the entire ruling Tuluva family. This heinous act so alienated the nobility that Rama Raya, who had fled to one of his estates during the chaos in the capital, suddenly emerged as the rallying point for the kingdom's salvation. In a rare public display of their covert power, the queens of the royal harem ordered the nobles to hand over the city to Rama Raya, who in the meantime had consolidated his grip over the major forts of the interior uplands. Gathering together large armies from these regions, in 1543 he triumphantly marched up to the capital, where he was hailed as a political saviour.

Riding by Rama Raya's side through the city's gates were his two brothers and Sadaśiva, the sole remnant of the ruling Tuluva dynasty to have escaped the violence of the preceding months. The sixteen-year old, a nephew of Krishna Raya whom Rama Raya had spirited off to an interior fort during the turmoil in the capital, would now serve as Rama Raya's ticket to supreme power. Forgoing the more perilous path of seizing the throne for himself, Rama Raya chose the easier one of organizing Sadaśiva's formal coronation, with himself as regent. This arrangement lasted until 1550, when Sadaśiva tried to assert himself, to which the regent responded by simply imprisoning his charge, allowing him but one public appearance a year. By now Vijayanagara had become a fully patrimonial state, as Rama Raya appointed his own Aravidu kinsmen as commanders of its principal forts, as high officials at court, and as governors over territories as distant as Sri Lanka. In 1562, he even discontinued the formality of allowing the hapless Sadaśiva his annual public viewing. Though stopping just short of having himself crowned, Rama Raya had emerged as the state's supreme autocrat.[40]

To legitimize his power-grab, Rama Raya associated himself and his family with the long-defunct but once mighty and still prestigious Chalukya dynasty, which had ruled over the entire plateau between 973 and 1183 from its capital in Kalyana, in the heart of the Deccan. As in north India, where upwardly mobile chieftains employed specialists to support their claims to Rajput status, court poets and genealogists substantiated the claims that Rama Raya and his Aravidu kinsmen were directly descended from the Chalukya kings of

Kalyana. As early as the 1540s, in the early days of his ascent to power, Rama Raya's family members were praised with titles such as 'Founder of the kingdom of Kalyana', 'Born in the Chalukya line' and even 'Chalukya emperor'. Subsequent Telugu poets not only claimed that Rama Raya had descended from the Kalyana Chalukya emperors, but assigned him exalted titles such as 'Radiant king of Kalyana', 'Lord of the excellent city of Kalyana' and 'The one who captured the city of Kalyana'.[41] Of course such claims had no basis in fact since Kalyana, located 300 kilometres north of Vijayanagara, had for more than two centuries been under the rule of the Tughluqs, the Bahmanis and, in Rama Raya's own day, the sultanate of Bidar.

Rama Raya's preoccupation with the Chalukya dynasty and its ancient capital of Kalyana did not stop with titular claims. For more than twenty years, mixing high-handed diplomacy with outright warfare, he worked to ensure that whichever northern sultan he was at the moment allied with also controlled Kalyana, as though that sultan were an intermediary vassal between himself and the former Chalukya capital. Because his own army was larger than that of any of the five northern sultanates, and because those mutually hostile kingdoms were often at war with one another, Rama Raya was able to play them off against each other. This he did from 1543 to 1565 with consummate skill, becoming ever more arrogant and audacious as he methodically humbled one proud sultan after another. In particular, Sultan Husain Nizam Shah of Ahmadnagar was brought to his knees, on one occasion being compelled to eat *pan* (betel nut) from the autocrat's own hand. While returning to his capital after a second occasion of humiliating that ruler, Rama Raya gratuitously plundered and annexed several districts belonging to Golconda, and even some belonging to his current ally, 'Ali 'Adil Shah I of Bijapur.

But this time, the scheming octogenarian had overplayed his hand. Four northern sultanates – Ahmadnagar, Bijapur, Golconda and Bidar – suspended their mutual hostilities and combined their forces to challenge the grand army of Vijayanagara. Gathering in December 1564 in the town of Talikota, just north of the Krishna, the four armies forded that river and in late January 1565 engaged an enormous Vijayanagara army near the river's southern shores. The momentous Battle of Talikota would be Rama Raya's last. During the conflict he suffered a spear wound that dislodged him from his horse. Snatched by the trunk of one of the coalition's elephants, he was taken at once to the tent of Sultan Husain Nizam Shah who, confronting his bitter adversary for the last time, ordered him to be beheaded on the spot. His head was then stuffed with straw and displayed to his troops on the tip of a spear. Demoralized, the Vijayanagara army now completely disintegrated. Rama Raya's brother Tirumala, blinded in one eye, rushed from the battlefield to the capital, where he released Sadaśiva from prison, picked up his family and hastily quit the city just before the advancing allies reached it.

While Tirumala and Sadaśiva were busy transferring the capital to the fort of Penukonda 200 kilometres to the south-east and reconstituting the state there, the victorious allies spent the next six months looting the Vijayanagara metropolis. The once-great city now lost its eminence, as well as most of its population. Wandering about the desolate site several years after the great battle, the Venetian traveller Cesare Federici described the place as 'not altogether destroyed, yet the houses stand still, but emptie, and there is dwelling in them nothing as is reported, but Tygres and other wild beasts'.[42]

## GUNPOWDER TECHNOLOGY IN THE DECCAN

The drama that played out between Vijayanagara and its northern adversaries took place against the backdrop of a military revolution – or, as some historians would say, *the* military revolution.[43] The term conventionally refers to the socio-political transformations that occurred in early modern Europe following the advent of large siege cannon capable of smashing the tall, vertical walls of medieval forts. It is widely assumed that such technologies and transformations first appeared in Europe and then diffused to the rest of the world in the early period of European colonialism, the sixteenth and seventeenth centuries. However, the presence of gun-ports built into the walls of forts at Bidar, Kalyana and Raichur indicate that as early as the 1460s cannon were being used defensively in the heart of the plateau. In the early 1470s the Bahmani minister Mahmud Gawan directed military operations in which he seems to have referred to the use of siege cannon. By the beginning of the sixteenth century, Portuguese merchant-soldiers who had just entered the Indian Ocean reported the presence of artillery in cities along India's western coast. And in 1510, when Portuguese naval squadrons captured the strategic seaport of Goa from the sultan of Bijapur, they found the arsenal in that city well stocked with munitions, including adaptations of some of their own firearm technology that had been captured from a naval engagement several years earlier. In the decades preceding 1510, Bijapur's military engineers in Goa had been assimilating firearm technologies from both Mamluk and Ottoman, as well as European sources. Indeed, Afonso de Albuquerque (d. 1515), the viceroy and mastermind of the Portuguese enterprise in the Indian Ocean region, was so impressed with the weaponry manufactured at Goa that he reported to the king of Portugal in 1513 that Muslim gunsmiths there were making firearms of higher quality than those produced in Germany, which the Portuguese had considered the finest anywhere. Albuquerque even sent to Lisbon one of these master gunsmiths, together with samples of heavy cannon made in Goa, with the idea that Portuguese engineers might learn munitions techniques from him.[44] Such evidence of technologies moving from India to Europe instead of vice versa challenges the conventional image of Europe as the undisputed font of military technology in the early modern era, and of the rest of the world as its passive recipients.

The first time such techniques were put to use on an Indian battlefield, both defensively and offensively, was at Raichur.[45] Located in the fertile tract between the Krishna and the Tungabhadra Rivers, the fortress had long been contested between Vijayanagara and the Bahmani sultans. In the early sixteenth century this fort, defended by 200 heavy cannon positioned along its curtain walls, passed from Bahmani to Bijapuri control. Then in May 1520 Krishna Raya, owing to a dispute with Bijapur's Isma'il 'Adil Khan (r. 1510–34), besieged the place, seeking to dismantle its walls with pickaxes and crowbars, for he possessed very few firearms of his own. After the siege had dragged on for weeks with no resolution, news reached the Vijayanagara camp that Isma'il had mobilized Bijapur's army to relieve the fort. So Krishna Raya suspended the siege and took 27,600 cavalry up to the Krishna, where he confronted a Bijapuri army of 18,000 cavalry, 150 war-elephants and 400 heavy field cannon. Upon crossing the river, Isma'il arranged his entire cannon in a single line and ill-advisedly fired all of them at once into Krishna Raya's massed heavy cavalry. Although the latter's front lines broke, Vijayanagara's remaining cavalry divisions swiftly circled behind Bijapur's artillery-men before they had time to reload their ordnance. This caused panic in the rest of Isma'il's army, which Vijayanagara's archers drove back towards and into the river with great loss of life. The sultan himself barely escaped the debacle. Then, returning to Raichur fort to resume his siege, Krishna Raya was joined by a contingent of Portuguese mercenary sharpshooters, one of whom shot and killed the fort's governor with a matchlock gun. The next day, 15 June 1520, the dispirited defenders surrendered the fort. The Vijayanagara army thus prevailed against Bijapur both in a pitched battle by the Krishna and at the siege of Raichur.[46]

Two points stand out regarding the Battle of Raichur. First, the side that possessed what might seem the superior military technology – the 200 cannon defending the fort, and the 400 field cannon at the pitched battle – lost to an army using pickaxes and crowbars at the fort, and mounted archers at the pitched battle. Given the apparent advantages of gunpowder technology, such an outcome might seem counter-intuitive. But in both venues, Bijapur's forces lost because of their faulty use of firearms. At the fort their cannon, placed on immobile carriages and fixed in their gun-ports, were unable to be easily manoeuvred in any direction, severely reducing their effectiveness. And at the Krishna, instead of firing their cannon in an orderly sequence of staggered volleys, Isma'il's artillerymen launched them all at once, enabling Krishna Raya's remaining ranks of cavalry to attack the Bijapuris from the rear.

Second, the two armies drew exactly opposite conclusions from the battle's outcome. Krishna Raya, though impressed with the matchlocks used by his Portuguese mercenaries, failed to see firearms as the way of the future. Both in the pitched battle by the river and at the besieged fort he had prevailed against Bijapur's artillery without making significant use of firearms, which seems to have reinforced the king's confidence in the efficacy of the conventional technologies and tactics of the day. There is no evidence that he followed up his victories by establishing an arsenal or a matchlock foundry in Vijayanagara. Nor did he or his successors ever mount cannon on the walls of their capital or provincial forts, or in other ways adapt their defensive systems to accommodate gunpowder technology. To the contrary, his victories at Raichur and other sites throughout southern India had the effect of lulling Krishna Raya and his commanders into a state of complacency, with the result that Vijayanagara's military system stagnated. Apart from hiring some foreign mercenaries adept at using handguns, for the rest of its existence the state of Vijayanagara failed to take gunpowder technology very seriously.

Bijapur, by contrast, responded quite differently to the battle's outcome, suggesting that the assimilation of new technologies can be a slow, painful process of trial and error, in the course of which failures can be as important as successes. Leaders in Bijapur understood from their twin failures at Raichur that, despite the advances in cannon technology they had made at their Goa arsenal, they needed to learn much more about the development and deployment of firearms, both defensively and offensively. They therefore launched an accelerated drive to pioneer new gunpowder technologies. Strategically, they aimed to control the wide tract of territory lying before their forts, thereby preventing attackers from approaching their walls with siege equipment. To accomplish this, their engineers replaced the fixed, relatively immobile breech-loading wrought-iron cannon on their forts with large, wrought-iron or cast bronze muzzle-loaders that could be manoeuvred both laterally and vertically. From the Ottomans they adopted the technique of the trunnion – that is, the pivot projecting from a cannon's sides, enabling a gun to be moved up or down. And from the small swivel guns that the Portuguese had placed on the gunwales of their ships, they took the idea of mounting a much larger cannon on a cubic block of granite set on an iron pin, enabling the gun to move horizontally [see Fig. 8]. Engineers soon improved on this by replacing the unwieldy granite block with an iron swivel fork. Much of this pioneering experimentation took place in the late 1550s at the hill fort of Yadgir, 150 kilometres south-west of Hyderabad.[47]

By 1560, huge cannon ranging from two to five metres in length – with the longest of them exceeding nine metres – began appearing mounted on the bastions of forts across the northern plateau. Others were placed on tall, free-standing platforms as high as twenty-seven metres above ground level, giving them 360-degree coverage of the surrounding plains. To accommodate the new guns, forts across the northern Deccan were considerably modified: curtain walls were strengthened, while bastions were equipped with prominent gun-mounts for the big swivel guns. Realizing the superiority of the new technology, Bijapur's neighbours – Ahmadnagar, Golconda and Bidar – soon engaged in a frenzy of activity to modernize their own forts. Of the Deccan's seventy-four dated bastions built in the six-teenth and seventeenth centuries and capable of carrying the new guns, nearly half appeared during the thirty years between 1560 and 1590. At the same time, engineers in the northern Deccan also devel-oped larger and more efficient cannon designed for use in pitched battles.[48]

Inasmuch as the battlefield is the ultimate test for new weapon systems, the Battle of Talikota of 1565 exposed the wide gap in mili-tary technology that had opened up between the northern and southern Deccan since 1520. The outcome of that battle, in which a coalition of northern sultanates completely routed the Vijayanagara army, lay in good part in the latter's victory at Raichur forty-five years earlier. After defeating Bijapuri forces at both Raichur fort and the Krishna river, Krishna Raya not only failed to integrate the new gunpowder technology into his armed forces; he also exhibited bla-tant contempt for his adversary, Isma'il 'Adil Khan, promising to return to him all the spoils of his victory on the condition that he first come to his court and kiss his foot. When the sultan refused to suffer such a humiliation, the arrogant king marched up to Bijapur and forced Isma'il to withdraw into the countryside for several days while his forces occupied and plundered the 'Adil Shahi capital. Par-ticipating in these manoeuvres – and evidently taking notes on how to treat the northern sultanates – was Krishna Raya's son-in-law Rama Raya. Forty-five years later Rama Raya would lead Vijayana-gara's army to catastrophic defeat at the Battle of Talikota. Although the southern kingdom's forces did possess firepower in that battle, the more efficient use of field artillery by the northern sultanates car-ried the day. In a tactic resembling that earlier used by the Ottomans against the Safavid rulers of Iran, the coalition forces fastened together 600 cannon of different calibres in three rows, with 200 heavy cannon in the front row, intermediate cannon in the middle and swivel cannon at the back. Masking the artillery were several thousand archers, who showered arrows on Rama Raya's advancing infantry. When the infantry came within close range, the archers withdrew while the gunners fired two devastating volleys: the first with cannon balls, the second with copper coins that functioned like shrapnel. This repulse decided the outcome. With the Vijayanagara army thrown into disarray and with Rama Raya himself captured and executed, the allies marched straight from the battlefield to loot metropolitan Vijayanagara, which lay defenceless before them.

The innovations in military technology pioneered in the northern Deccan and used with such effect at Talikota found no parallel anywhere in contemporary India, or, for that matter, the world. In Europe, when the advent of cannon enabled attackers to batter down stone walls, defenders of cities or forts responded by building lower, slanting walls so as to give incoming projectiles less of a target to hit, while adding angled, arrow-shaped bastions – the so-called *trace italienne* – to cover blind spots along the walls. In the Deccan, by contrast, engineers built bastions with higher profiles than those they replaced, complete with gun platforms on which their huge swivel cannon could be mounted in order to dominate the countryside. The idea was not to minimize the damage that enemy fire could inflict on a fort, which was the European approach, but to prevent besiegers from approaching close enough to fire at all. The reason that states in the Deccan took this path followed from the region's unique topography, with its many hilltops spiking up from an otherwise flat plateau. For centuries prior to the advent of gunpowder, Deccanis had taken advantage of the plateau's naturally hilly terrain by building forts on its many promontories. Being easier to defend than plains forts, hill forts enabled chieftains to control the surrounding countryside by using both the stick of coercion – that is, a fort's garrisoned cavalry – and the carrot of holding, or withholding, grain stored in their granaries. Power itself was therefore understood in terms of seizing prominent heights in order to dominate the peoples below. With this background, when firearms reached the Deccan, it seemed natural to adapt the new gunpowder technologies to serve a familiar strategy, which meant building upwards and placing larger cannon on higher positions.

## CULTURAL PRODUCTION IN THE GUNPOWDER AGE

As modernized forts began to appear across the plateau, the balance of military advantage tipped from attackers to defenders. Besieging armies found it difficult or impossible to seize reconstituted forts, which thereafter virtually ceased changing hands. For the first time since the emergence of the five sultanates in the early sixteenth century, the Deccan's internal frontiers stabilized. As this occurred, the cultural production of the northern sultanates grew in quantity and became more differentiated in quality. For example, for the first seven or eight decades of their independent existence, the Deccan's four principal sultanates used existing stocks of Bahmani and Vijayanagara coins, which remained in circulation during that period. But then, between 1578 and 1584 – shortly after the northern Deccan's internal borders had stabilized – each of the region's sultanates began minting its own coins, reflecting an awareness of, and a desire to express, their distinctive identities. A similar thing happened regarding architecture, art and literature produced after the mid sixteenth century.

Shortly after the Battle of Talikota, the Nizam Shahi sultanate of Ahmadnagar saw a surge of cultural production, beginning with an illustrated chronicle, the *Ta'rif-i Husain Shahi*, that narrated the famous battle. In the reign of Husain's son Murtaza Nizam Shah (1565–88) there appeared architectural gems such as the Damri mosque (1568), which was delicately carved from brown-grey basalt, and the elegant Farah Bakhsh Bagh pavilion. In the reign of Sultan Burhan Nizam Shah II (1591–5), a new and distinctive school of drawing appeared using simple ink and line drawing, combined with technical effects such as stippling and shading. That ruler also patronized the first history of the Nizam Shahi dynasty, the *Burhan-i ma'athir*, which reflected an awareness of Ahmadnagar's distinct identity among Deccani states.

Cultural production at Bijapur, like that at Ahmadnagar, did not peak until the latter sixteenth century and continued well into the seventeenth. Miniature painting came into its own there with the illustrations for the *Nujum al-'ulum*, an extraordinary text composed in 1570 by Sultan 'Ali 'Adil Shah I himself. Whether in architecture, literature, music or painting, Sultan Ibrahim II's reign (1580–1627) witnessed Bijapur's high point in cultural achievement. Ibrahim was also an author, having composed a book on music, the *Kitab-i Nauras* ('Book of the Nine Emotions'), which reveals his eclectic religious sensibilities and his personal devotion to Saraswati, the Hindu goddess of literature and the arts. It was in the latter half of the seventeenth century, too, that Bijapuri architecture evolved a distinctive style that included broad arches, domes with carved lotus petals around their drums, delicate plasterwork, finely carved brackets, bulbous turrets and relief ornaments featuring pendants from stone chains. Outstanding examples include 'Ali 'Adil Shah I's congregational mosque (begun 1576), the Anda Masjid (1608), the Mihtar Mahal (early 1600s) and, most remarkably, the Ibrahim Rauza (*c.*1627–35), Sultan Ibrahim II's sumptuously carved tomb complex.

The same pattern holds for the other Deccani sultanates. In Bidar, 'Ali Barid Shah (1543–80) patronized the construction of the Rangin Mahal ('coloured palace'), in the heart of the former Bahmani court. Adorning this structure's arch is inlaid mother-of-pearl worked into polished black basalt, an aesthetic that prefigured the production of Bidriware, a kind of metalwork in which sheets of silver or brass floral or geometric motifs were inlaid into a blackened alloy of zinc and copper. This craftwork was singularly associated with Bidar, after which it was named, and was used for trays, incense burners, basins and especially water pipes, or *huqqa*. The latter proliferated in the late sixteenth century, along with the widespread use of tobacco, an American product recently introduced via Portuguese maritime contact with India. The Bidriware *huqqa* thus bears witness to the interplay of both global and regional forces. Just as Bijapuri engineers had responded to the introduction of Portuguese swivel guns by developing a new kind of cannon that involved redesigning their forts, so also Bidari metalworkers addressed the introduction of American tobacco by adapting their own craft traditions, as with Bidriware water pipes, to a growing demand for the plant.

In the easternmost sultanate of Golconda, Ibrahim Qutb Shah cultivated and promoted a distinctively regional culture informed by Telugu language and literature and a revived consciousness of Telangana's past history. Ibrahim patronized the construction of large tanks for storing water from dammed-up streams, which were essential for sustaining agriculture in the dry, upland eastern plateau. It was a practice that stretched back to the region's Kakatiya kings. As noted above, Kakatiya traditions had also found expression in the layout of the Qutb Shahis' greatest legacy to subsequent history, the city of Hyderabad, with its incomparable gem, the Charminar monument. At the same time, for their mosques and tombs these kings evolved a style that included nearly spheroid domes with the forms of lotus petals at their base, plaster and carved stone, and minarets with miniaturized, bulbous domes.

In sum, by the 1570s and 1580s newly designed forts had given defenders a strategic advantage over besiegers in each of the sultanates of the northern Deccan. This, in turn, lowered the level of inter-state warfare, froze inter-state boundaries and allowed the sultanates to devote their energies to patronizing cultural projects that were both distinctive and remarkable.

## VIJAYANAGARA'S SUCCESSORS AND SOUTH INDIA

After the Battle of Talikota, the peninsula south of the Krishna evolved along very different lines from those of the northern Deccan. Following Rama Raya's disastrous defeat and death on the battlefield, his brother, Tirumala, rescued the imprisoned king, Sadasiva – together with courtiers, government officials, the harem, military personnel and 1,500 elephants laden with treasure[49] – and set out to relocate the capital in more secure territory. This was the fort of Penukonda, 200 kilometres south-east of their abandoned metropolis. But the disruptions caused by the shock of defeat had plunged the empire into a state of chaos that persisted for the next six years, during which Sadasiva, the last Tuluva emperor, mysteriously died. Tirumala's efforts to pick up the pieces of the stricken state were further stymied by domestic turmoil, including a bitter dispute with his nephew, Rama Raya's son, over leadership of the Aravidu clan. By 1570, however, Tirumala felt sufficiently secure to crown himself the first Aravidu monarch of a reconstituted state of Vijayanagara, to be succeeded two years later by his son Śriranga I (r. 1572–85).

Prior to the Battle of Talikota, the empire had sprawled over the entire peninsula south of the Krishna, excepting the Malabar coast. But after the calamitous events of 1565, most of Vijayanagara's former territory gradually fell under the control of either its enemies to the north or its own vassals to the south. In 1592 the state's capital was again relocated, from Penukonda to the stronghold of Chandragiri, another 200 kilometres to the south-east. The site was not only more distant from the northern sultanates; it also lay within just ten kilometres of one of the most popular temple-shrines in south India – that of Venkateśvara, near Tirupati. The Aravidu rulers (1570–1669) were well aware that kings of Vijayanagara's two preceding dynasties – the Saluva and Tuluva – had both legitimized their rise to power in good measure by lavishly patronizing this key pilgrimage centre.[50] The Aravidus would do the same.

Owing to increasing pressure from the sultans of Bijapur and Golconda, however, after 1604 the dynasty was compelled periodically to shift its capital eighty kilometres further south, to Vellore. In 1623 Sultan Ibrahim 'Adil Shah II of Bijapur captured Kurnool, a stronghold strategically located near the juncture of the Krishna and Tungabhadra Rivers. Ten years later his successor, Muhammad 'Adil Shah (r. 1627–57), invaded Vijayanagara's former capital of Penukonda. In 1635 his generals seized Ikkeri, a former Vijayanagara dependency whose ruler moved his capital further south to Bednur. In 1638 they captured Bangalore, and several years later besieged Vellore. Stimulated by their ancient rivalry with Bijapur, as well as their own appetite for expansion, the rulers of Golconda launched assaults on Vijayanagara territory in the eastern Deccan, in 1642 capturing all the forts along the Andhra coast down to Pulicat. In the following year, their forces took the powerful stronghold of Udayagiri, 100 kilometres inland from the Coromandel coast. In 1644 Bijapur captured Bankapur in the western Deccan. As the two sultanates now found themselves competing for much of the same territory, in 1646 they agreed that any further spoils seized from Vijayanagara would be divided between them on a two-to-one basis in favour of Bijapur – a ratio indicating the latter's greater power.

As Vijayanagara's centre of gravity migrated deeper into the peninsula, its rulers became ever more dependent for support on their tributary vassals to the south.[51] In the wake of the empire's much earlier annexations made by Krishna Raya and Achyuta Raya, local administration had been left to military chieftains known as 'nayakas'. Some of these were Telugu warriors appointed as regional governors by the Vijayanagara emperor; others were local chiefs whom the central government recognized as tributary vassals. Two important Telugu *nayaka* lineages in the Tamil-speaking South, those of Madurai and Tanjavur, claimed direct links either to Krishna Raya or Achyuta Raya, while a third, that of Jinji (or Gingee) in the northern part of the Tamil zone, did not emerge until the 1590s. In the Kannada-speaking south-western plateau, the *nayaka* lineage of Ikkeri (later, Bednur) is traceable to a local chieftain whose authority had been recognized by the Vijayanagara court shortly before 1565. Further south, the Wodeyar ruling lineage of Mysore was similarly descended from a local chieftain who had been a tributary vassal of Achyuta Raya.

The debacle at Talikota, however, forced Tirumala and his Aravidu successors to confront powerful centrifugal forces, since the chaos that followed that battle tested the loyalty of all these *nayaka*s. The third Aravidu monarch, Venkata II (r. 1585–1614), proved the most successful of the dynasty's rulers in maintaining some of the integrity, though not the glory, of the old empire. Although recapturing Vijayanagara's original capital lay well beyond his reach, the emperor did manage to recover key forts that had been seized by Golconda after 1565. For a while he even succeeded in restoring the Krishna as his northern frontier with that sultanate. To the south, he brought rebellious vassals in Kolar and Vellore back into line. But Venkata II had no sons, and his death in 1614 plunged the crippled state into a bitter, four-year succession struggle, with different *nayaka*s supporting different sides in the conflict. Worse still, the instability triggered by this war alienated the larger *nayaka* houses, some of which altogether ceased sending their annual tribute to their Aravidu overlord. This was also when Bijapur and Golconda began launching their aggressive southward campaigns. Nonetheless, a reconstituted Vijayanagara state under the Aravidus managed to limp along well into the seventeenth century, aided not least by the mutual rivalries and nearly constant warfare among its nominally dependent *nayaka* vassals.

Between 1570 and about 1650 those *nayaka* states – in particular the three in the Tamil country (Jinji, Tanjavur and Madurai) – evolved a distinctive style of articulating their political authority. The old Vijayanagara empire had celebrated and practised classic norms of Indian kingship, which included sponsoring Vedic sacrifices, protecting the Hindu social order and donating land to Brahmins, understood as ritually superior to the rulers. By contrast, the *nayaka*s of the Tamil zone were proud of their humble, Śudra origins and even inverted the classic conception of social order by placing Brahmins in a position subordinate to themselves. Moreover, as seen in contemporary Telugu literature patronized by these courts, their conception of kingship was structured around profligate expenditures on deities, courtesans, Brahmins, poets and, most conspicuously, on adorning and feeding their own bodies. Rather than supporting Brahmins with donations of land, they fed them on a vast scale: one text claimed that the *nayaka* of Tanjavur would not eat his breakfast until he had fed 12,000 Brahmins. Nor did these *nayaka*s present themselves in managerial or bureaucratic roles, devoting themselves instead to elaborate rounds of ritual. Contemporary texts focus especially on their sexual prowess, with their conquests of hosts of women effectively substituting for the warrior ideal of conquering other lands. For them, the symbolism of kingship replaced its substance. Put differently, symbolism had become the substance of kingship.[52]

Even though these states functioned as de facto successors to the old Vijayanagara empire, the *nayaka*s of the southern peninsula refrained from proclaiming their outright independence from their nominal Aravidu overlords. Mysore's Wodeyar lineage of rulers went the furthest in the latter direction. In 1610 Raja Wodeyar (r. 1578–1617) seized Vijayanagara's provincial capital of Śrirangapattanam from the Aravidu governor, marking a decisive break from imperial authority. And yet, although his successors adopted grandiose titles such as 'supreme lord of kings of great kings' and 'emperor of Karnataka', they continued to acknowledge Vijayanagara's formal overlordship in their inscriptions. By the end of the seventeenth century, by which time the Aravidu dynasty had come to an end, Mysore's rulers had even adopted Vijayanagara's imperial boar seal, suggesting the enduring prestige of the old empire, as well as the Wodeyars' self-image as its rightful heirs.[53]

Perhaps the most tortured imperial–vassal relationship was that between the Aravidu court and the *nayaka* of Madurai, near the peninsula's southern extremity. Because the Aravidu sovereign at Chandragiri no longer possessed the requisite power to serve as a proper overlord, by the late sixteenth century Madurai's *nayaka*s looked to Vijayanagara's 'golden age' as an alternative source of their own legitimacy. A courtly Telugu text of *c*.1600, the *Rayavacakamu*, sees Madurai's political authority as deriving not from its nominal Aravidu overlord in Chandragiri, whom the text never even mentions, but directly from the glorious reign of Krishna Raya, who had died some seven decades earlier. More fundamentally, the *nayaka*s of Madurai looked for political inspiration to that emperor's great capital: metropolitan Vijayanagara.[54] At the time of the text's composition, Vijayanagara lay largely abandoned, a ghost city. But in the early sixteenth century, the empire's glory days, it had been a sprawling megalopolis with an estimated population of between 300,000 and 400,000, making it at the time one of the largest cities in the world.[55] More than that, it was so ideologically charged that it functioned rather like a political talisman. Apart from its vast wealth and architectural grandeur, its urban core had served as a stage on which magnificent political ceremonies were periodically enacted, thereby empowering those who possessed the thriving metropolis. As such, the site was not merely the centre of the state's power: it was the *source* of its power. Imperial dynasts had derived their political authority by simply ruling over, and from, the great city. But the catastrophe of 1565 severed the bonds between city, ruling dynasty and the mandate to rule. Not only were the empire's Tuluva rulers succeeded by a different dynasty, the Aravidus: more importantly, by abandoning the partially ruined city for sites deeper in the peninsula's interior, this new dynasty had become physically detached from the source of the empire's former legitimacy. The Aravidus were aware of this, of course, for they rather wistfully referred to their new capitals in Penukonda and Chandragiri as 'Vijayanagara'.

As a consequence of these drastically altered political realities, south India's *nayaka* rulers of the late sixteenth and seventeenth centuries exhibited a chronic ambivalence about their loyalty to Vijayanagara's Aravidu kings. If they treasured the memory of the great metropolitan capital, their loyalty to the current dynasty was often lukewarm, perfunctory and grudging. A series of dramatic events in the mid 1640s, described by an eyewitness, illustrates not only the *nayaka*s' uncertain relationship towards their nominal over-lords, but also the intensity of their mutual rivalries, their penchant for ritual and symbolism over substance, and the means by which the sultanates of Bijapur and Golconda would ultimately dominate nearly the entire peninsula. Our source is a report to Rome filed by Balthazar da Costa, a Jesuit missionary who served in Madurai from 1640 to 1670. He knew the terrain well, having travelled throughout the Tamil country for three decades. He also had friends in Madurai's court and disciples in its armies.[56]

By 1640, da Costa tells us, the *nayaka* of Madurai, Tirumala, had ceased paying tribute to the aged Aravidu king of Vijayanagara, Venkata III (r. 1630–42), who did nothing about it. But the king's son, Śriranga III (r. 1642–72), resolved to claim the arrears as soon as his father died and he came to power, both of which happened in 1642. Reflecting his weak position with respect to his subordinate vassals, however, the prince could not be crowned without the consent of his principal *nayaka*s, and not all of them were willing to give it. Nonetheless, Śriranga III's representative in Madurai pressed Tirumala for payment of his arrears of tribute. When Madurai's *nayaka* prevaricated, the king wrote insulting letters to his recalcitrant vassal, swearing that if the arrears were not paid he would flay the *nayaka* alive and from his skin make a drum to be beaten during processions as a warning to other vassals. Such bombastic threats drove Tirumala to enlist Brahmin sorcerers to practise incantations intended to kill his meddle-some overlord. But seeing that witchcraft had no effect on Śriranga III's life, Tirumala decided in 1645 to form an anti-Aravidu league with the *nayaka*s of neighbouring Tanjavur and Jinji. For this purpose he proposed to host a trilateral conference of the three rulers.

Tirumala ordered three pavilions to be built nearly a kilometre from each other in a wooded area at the point where his kingdom's frontiers met those of both Tanjavur and Jinji. When all was ready, he marched to his pavilion with an army of 30,000 infantry and cavalry, supported by many elephants and oxen. His army was ordered to remain on Madurai's territory while he occupied the pavilion specially built for him. The *nayaka* of Tanjavur came to the site with an equally large army, which camped on its own territory. Several days later the *nayaka* of Jinji arrived, but with only 10,000 men since his northern border met territory ruled directly by Śriranga III, and he felt it necessary to guard his domain from a possible invasion by his overlord's army. After Brahmin priests consulted their auguries to determine the most auspicious time for their meeting, at the appointed hour on a particular Friday in August 1645, writes da Costa:

> Tirumala Nayak mounted a magnificent elephant richly caparisoned with a saddle cloth of crimson velvet studded with pearls, and tusks sheathed in gold plates. He wore a rich robe embroidered with gold thread with a turban of the same material, and earrings consisting of eight large pearls, while his necklace and bracelets were of the best diamonds. To guide his elephant, he held in his right hand the 'angusam' [*ankuśa*, iron hook] of which the handle was inlaid with precious stones. On the same elephant sitting behind him was his nephew, dressed in the same style, who presented him with betel. He was preceded by the arms and insignia and followed by the file of elephants mounted by his chief nobles and captains, all dressed in rich garments and wearing huge pendants, earrings, and necklaces. The cavalry brought up the rear while the rest of the army marched past accompanied by the music of numberless martial instruments. It was an imposing and majestic procession well worth seeing.[57]

Late that afternoon Tirumala and his magnificent retinue arrived at the meeting place, as did the two other *nayaka*s on their respective elephants, which were also richly decorated. In a scene indicating the supreme necessity of preserving their relative status, the three men conversed for about half an hour without ever dismounting from their elephants. Given the ties between elephants and royal authority in Indian culture,[58] none of them could have stepped to the ground without appearing to have relinquished his kingly status. Doing so would also have acknowledged his inferiority vis-à-vis the other *nayaka*s. The next day, Tirumala invited his guests to his pavilion for a magnificent banquet, followed by dances that continued far into the night. Had it not been for a fire that broke out in the Tanjavur *nayaka*'s pavilion the next day, that ruler would have hosted another such entertainment the following evening.

The three men ultimately reconvened in Tanjavur where, after another round of sumptuous banquets, they finally got down to the business of determining how best to deal with their nominal but still-dangerous overlord. Noting that Śriranga III could not be crowned without their consent, Tirumala urged deposing him and setting up a more pliable sovereign. After all, he argued, if the king were permitted to pressure his own state of Madurai, would he not soon be pressuring the other states he nominally ruled? The *nayaka* of Tanjavur, however, fearing the power that Śriranga still possessed, and apprehensive of the devastation to his lands that a war would cause, urged Tirumala to pay his arrears. The latter retorted that doing so would only enhance the king's ability to crush all the *nayaka*s, and that the prudent course would be to stand united and attack Śriranga III while he was still relatively weak. Although the *nayaka* of Jinji accepted this argument, that of Tanjavur only pretended to accept it, for he secretly intended to assist the Aravidu monarch.

Śriranga III was very much aware of these intrigues against him, thanks to spies planted in the courts of all his *nayaka*s. He was especially angered at Tirumala's resort to black magic to kill him. So he sent his cavalry into the territory of the *nayaka* nearest his southern frontier, that of Jinji, who immediately left the trilateral conference to confront and repulse his overlord's troops. In the course of this new struggle, Jinji's military units intercepted a convoy carrying 100,000 *cruzados* that the *nayaka* of Tanjavur had secretly sent to the king, a perfidious act that naturally stirred Jinji's enmity with Tanjavur. Yet Tirumala engaged in behaviour even more duplicitous, secretly urging Golconda's Sultan 'Abd Allah Qutb Shah (r. 1626–72), whose territory lay directly north of the remnants of Vijayanagara territory, to seize as much of Śriranga III's domain as possible while the Aravidu ruler was preoccupied with Jinji. The sultan did as encouraged, taking

Chandragiri in April 1646 and advancing from there to Vellore, then the Aravidu capital, which he besieged. In a state of desperation, Sriranga III threatened that he himself would ally with Golconda if his *nayaka*s would not come to his aid. In these circumstances, all three *nayaka*s outwardly agreed to aid the king, and in May 1646, after peace had been concluded with Golconda, the king, then in Tanjavur, received the three Tamil rulers with honours.

The intrigues did not end there, however. To avoid a clash with 'Abd Allah Qutb Shah of Golconda, whose armies were in the vicinity and still advancing south, the *nayaka* of Tanjavur abandoned his alliance with Madurai and allied himself with the Golconda sultan. To counter this, Tirumala invited the sultan of Bijapur to send troops to his defence, aiming to exploit Bijapur's rivalry with Golconda in order to pursue his own – Madurai's – rivalry with Tanjavur. But the strategy backfired. Once Bijapur's 17,000 troops reached the Tamil country, their commanders came to an agreement with Golconda whereby Bijapur would continue the siege of Jinji while Golconda's troops withdrew to consolidate earlier conquests. In December 1648 the *nayaka* of Jinji, in despair, surrendered his capital to Bijapur, whose armies continued south. Early the next year both Tanjavur and Madurai were forced to accept Bijapur's overlordship.

Amidst these realignments of power in the peninsula, meanwhile, Sriranga III had become a king without a kingdom, forced to move about as a guest at the court of one or another of his nominal vassals. For a while he was maintained by Tirumala in the court of Madurai, until late 1647 when he settled in that of the *nayaka* of Tanjavur. But when the latter gradually decreased his royal guest's allowance, Sriranga III took the hint and, with his court, settled in nearby forests. He next arranged to repair to the Kannada country as a guest of another notional vassal, Kanthirava Narasaraja (r. 1638–59), the Wodeyar king of Mysore. But by this time his stature had diminished appreciably. As he passed through Tanjavur and Madurai en route to the Kannada country in late 1648, the *nayaka*s of those places – still his nominal vassals – took no more notice of him than had he been an ordinary traveller.[59]

The advance of Golconda and Bijapur into India's southern extremities was thus assisted by the duplicity of *nayaka*s who were technically vassals of the Aravidu house, the avowed enemy of the northern sultanates, but who repeatedly invited those two sultanates to intervene in their own affairs. Indeed, the political and diplomatic behaviour of these states harks back to India's ancient theory of the Circle of Kings, the *mandala*, which recommends that a king create a ring of loyal, subordinate vassals around his territorial core, and then connive with his enemies' enemies, construed as potential allies, to defeat and transform them into new allies. By the seventeenth century, however, this practice, derived from classical Sanskrit texts, had become mingled with other courtly practices derived from the Persianate world. Across the southern peninsula, courtiers in the *nayaka* states had inherited from the old Vijayanagara empire Persian-style clothing, including long tunics and coloured cloaks. This is suggested both by contemporary paintings and by the evidence of Dutch envoys, who remarked on the 'Moorish' dress they saw in local courts.[60] Moreover, the same Persianate system of military-service tenures that had been fundamental to the old Vijayanagara empire appears to have been inherited by the *nayaka*s of Madurai.[61] Mysore's Wodeyar rulers even used the Persianate title 'Sultan among Indian kings', just as Vijayanagara's emperors had done.[62]

To the west of Mysore and the Tamil country is a formidable mountain range, the Western Ghats, beyond which lie a hilly lowland and a lush, tropical coastal strip laced with rivers and channels that flow from the mountainous interior. This is Malabar. Hugging the shores of south-west India and stretching 300 kilometres in length and averaging sixty kilometres in width, the Malabar coast bore remarkable similarities to a contemporary coastal area on the opposite side of the planet. The Dutch colony of Manhattan – now the heart of New York City – flourished owing to its commercial connections with the wider world. Although geologically attached to North America, for four decades (1624–64) this 'island at the centre of the world' had served as a nexus through which beaver pelts extracted from the American interior were shipped to the Netherlands, garnering immense profits for Dutch merchants on both sides of the ocean.[63] And in the process, Manhattan emerged as a free-trade zone, an ethnic melting pot, an experiment in self-government and religious tolerance, a socially fluid frontier and a shipping hub linked to a network of ports dotting the shores of the North and South Atlantic Oceans. Indeed, the quest for North American furs by Dutch merchants was driven by the same forces that had already sent their compatriots – and before them, Portuguese mariners – into the Indian Ocean in search of commodities even more valuable than beaver pelts: spices, and especially Malabar pepper, highly prized as a food seasoning.

For at least 1,500 years Malabar had been the world's principal source of this 'black gold', as the Dutch called the spice, drawing to its shores long-distance merchants from as far away as the Mediterranean basin and the South China Sea. This coastal strip also exported other widely coveted tropical products to eager markets overseas: ginger, cardamom, cinnamon, aromatic woods and hard woods. Already in the first century AD Romans worried about the drain of hard currency going to feed their countrymen's seemingly insatiable demand for Indian luxuries, especially pepper. By the thirteenth century China had become the world's largest consumer of black pepper, with Hangzhou alone consuming more than 4,300 kilograms a day, if Marco Polo is to be believed. The Venetian also estimated that, for every boatload of pepper that reached the Mediterranean world, 100 went to China's busy port of Quanzhou.[64]

Linked to distant transoceanic markets but cut off geographically and politically from the rest of India, Malabar was, like Dutch Manhattan, something of an island at the centre of the world. Although Vijayanagara had held a loose sort of sovereignty over part of its northernmost coast in order to import war-horses, the rest of Malabar, unlike south India's *nayaka* states, was never ruled by Vijayanagara or by any other of the peninsula's great empires. Ever since the twelfth century it had been divided into a handful of rival houses that, reigning from coastal ports, maintained only a formal sovereignty over their respective hinterlands. The most important such city states included, from north to south: Cannanore, Calicut, Cochin and Kollam. Inhibiting the rulers' authority was the economic and military influence of a powerful martial aristocracy, the Nairs (or Nayars), who served the rulers as elite warriors. Because the Nairs also held superior rights to the coast's rich hinterland, and because Brahmins collected dues on temple lands, Malabar's coastal kings, unlike the rulers of India's agrarian states, were unable to impose land taxes in areas over which they claimed sovereignty. But they did have an alternative source of income. Owing to strict taboos barring high-caste Hindus from seafaring, the region's lucrative overseas export sector was handled entirely by foreigners – first Romans, then Jews, Christians, Tamils, Gujaratis, Sinhalese, Malays, Chinese, Persians and, especially, Arabs. Such an arrangement met local kings' need for revenue, the bulk of which was derived from taxing the export of locally produced commodities that the entire world seemed to crave.[65] Foreign traders, writes a classical Tamil poet, 'arrive with gold and leave with pepper'.[66]

This singular political and commercial structure partly accounts for Malabar's demographic profile, unique among modern India's subregions. By the early twenty-first century a little more than half its population was Hindu, with the remainder divided almost equally between Muslims and Christians. The latter are composed mainly of Syrian Christians, so called owing to their presumed Middle Eastern origins and their use of the Syriac language for liturgical purposes. They trace themselves back to Jesus's apostle Thomas, who is thought to have reached Malabar in the mid first century and founded churches in at least seven coastal cities, all of which were centres of spice exports. By the thirteenth and fourteenth centuries local Christians appeared as pepper-brokers and port revenue officers in southern Malabar, especially Kollam, and, by the fifteenth century, as ship owners, brokers and merchants in Cochin, Kayamkulam and Kodungallur (Cranganur). By this time, too, the community had acquired a substantial base in Malabar's interior. Many Syrian Christians were recruited as warriors in service to Hindu lords in southern Malabar's pepper-growing interior, in this respect functioning as a separate caste, much like the Nairs. In fact, ruling houses gave these warriors titles and land grants, and a status equal to that of the Nairs. They endorsed the offices of Syrian Christians' chief clerics and endowed and protected Christian churches in the same way that they patronized Hindu temples. For their part, the Christians adopted many Hindu rituals, were given access to Hindu temples, and until the late sixteenth century intermarried with the Nair community. Leading Christian clerics even took part in the trappings of Malabari kingship, such as travelling with large entourages of elite warriors (*chavers*) sworn to die protecting their patron.[67]

Meanwhile, from at least the ninth century onwards, Arab Muslims began to play a prominent role in Malabar's overseas commerce. By the eleventh century, Arab brokers controlled the long-distance spice trade between India and China and dominated the maritime trade between India and the Middle East. Owing to Malabar's central position in the Indian Ocean and the natural rhythm of that ocean's two annual sailing seasons, the south-western and north-eastern monsoons, Arab mariners found Malabar's ports to be natural sites for the supply, trans-shipment and warehousing of commercial goods. As a result, communities of Arab merchants, the *pardesi*s (foreigners), put down permanent roots along the coast, conducting long-distance trade with kinfolk or trusted partners in ports across the entire Indian Ocean, especially the Arabian Sea. By the fourteenth and fifteenth centuries Muslims dominated overseas trade in Malabar's central and northern sectors as pepper cultivation spread northwards. By then one port in particular, Calicut, had become Malabar's premier site for exporting pepper throughout the Indian Ocean region. In the 1340s Ibn Battuta saw thirteen large Chinese junks anchored beside the city. Although Calicut had no natural harbour, the Moroccan globetrotter considered it one of the world's largest seaports.[68] He attributed the city's prosperity to the scrupulous attention that Calicut's ruler, the so-called Zamorin, gave to the security of merchants and their property. The Zamorin – from *samudra raja*, or 'king of the seas' – not only protected his resident merchants: he also fostered a climate of religious tolerance, even letting Muslims build their mosques with tiled roofs, a privilege allowed for no other structures in the kingdom except royal palaces or Hindu temples.

Under such favourable circumstances Malabar's Muslim community – especially in Calicut, but along the northern coast generally – flourished and swelled in numbers as low-caste labourers such as dock-workers, shipbuilders and other communities ancillary to the maritime trade converted to Islam, and as the residents from overseas increasingly intermarried with the local society. This new, hybridized Arabo-Malayali community, called the Mappilas, spoke Malayalam, dressed like the Nairs, except for their caps and beards, and practised matrilineal inheritance, again like the Nairs.[69] Reflecting their historic ties to the Arab maritime world – especially the Red Sea region, a hub for shipping goods to the Mediterranean zone – Malabar's Muslims followed the Shafi'i branch of Islamic law, the same one followed by the peoples of Yemen and the Horn of Africa. By contrast, Muslims across north India and the Deccan followed the Hanafi school, then dominant across Anatolia, the Iranian plateau, Afghanistan and Central Asia – that is to say, the Persianate world. A similar pattern is seen in Mappila architecture, which reflects local Malayali, not Persianate, traditions. Rather than the pointed arches, domes, minarets and vaulted ceilings that are associated with the Persianate visual vocabulary, Malabar's older mosques – and also its older Syrian Christian churches – feature the same multi-tiered roofs, sloped wooden window panels and elaborate gables that are found on the coast's traditional palaces and Hindu temples [see Fig. 9]. Indicating the coastal region's relative isolation from the rest of the peninsula, these characteristically Malabari architectural features are not found elsewhere in India.

At the very end of the fifteenth century Malabar's society was upended by the abrupt arrival of Portuguese mariners driven by Roman Catholic crusading zeal and a quest for direct, maritime access to Indian spices, in particular pepper. Vasco da Gama's pioneering voyage from Lisbon to Calicut in 1498 was followed by a second one led by Pedro Cabral. Shortly after reaching Calicut in 1500, Cabral seized a Muslim cargo ship, provoking a mob attack on a Portuguese warehouse in which a number of Portuguese died. Cabral retaliated by seizing five nearby merchant ships and slaying their crews. He then spent a full day bombarding the city before sailing down to Cochin. Since that city's ruler viewed the Portuguese as a counterbalance to his rival, the Zamorin of Calicut, he allowed Cabral to establish a fortified trading post under his protection. This marked the first European toehold on Indian territory. In 1502 Vasco da Gama, returning to Calicut with twenty ships and nearly 1,000 men, sank a merchant ship sailing from Mecca, drowning 700 pilgrims, and then demanded that the Zamorin expel all Muslim merchants from the city. When the Zamorin refused to comply, da Gama also bombarded the city and then sailed down to Cochin, where he stationed a flotilla of ships at the post established by Cabral. This violent and monopolistic approach to trade quickly internationalized warfare on the Indian Ocean. In 1508, warships of Mamluk Egypt joined those of the sultanate of Gujarat to defeat a Portuguese fleet near Chaul (forty kilometres south of Mumbai), and nine years later an Ottoman fleet prevented the Portuguese from conquering the Red Sea port of Jiddah.

The sixteenth century thus saw an entirely new relationship between Malabar and the outside world, which in turn led to profound changes within Malayali society. In the course of that century the Syrian Christians would face mounting pressure to align their theology, liturgy, rites, ecclesiastical structure and socio-cultural practices with those of the Roman Catholic Church. This provoked powerful resistance, culminating in 1665 with the emergence of two rival communities. One followed Roman Catholic authority as mediated by European missionary bishops, and the other – the 'Jacobite' or 'Orthodox' Syrians – adhered to the authority of prelates in Antioch, as mediated by hereditary Malayali archdeacons.[70]

Malabar's Muslim society was no less transformed by this sudden European intrusion. The Portuguese intervention led to the nearly complete withdrawal of Malabar's resident community of foreign (*pardesi*) Arab merchants. This, in turn, created a space for indigenous Mappilas to expand their own operations, which they did by establishing transoceanic commercial networks and dodging Portuguese patrols, or by sending consignments of pepper overland to the sultanate of Gujarat, a sworn enemy of the Portuguese, and exporting them from Gujarati ports. Second, Portuguese assaults galvanized the Mappilas into a unified community and instilled in them a mentality of holy war directed at the Portuguese. This appeal to militancy was made explicit in an Arabic text that, composed in the 1580s and widely circulated in Malabar, identified the Portuguese not as infidels (*kuffar*) but as 'Franks' (*al-frange*), a term meant to evoke memories of the Crusades several centuries earlier.[71]

In sum, the advent of Portuguese operations in early-sixteenth-century Malabar, soon followed by similar operations elsewhere on Indian shores, exposed local communities to a style of commerce that was entirely new to them. This was the idea of armed trade, symbolized by the cannon carried on Portuguese caravels and the string of fortified trading posts that appeared along much of the Indian Ocean rim. Nonetheless, to label the centuries following 1498 the 'Vasco da Gama epoch', as some have suggested, is surely an exaggeration. By 1600, after a full century of doggedly pursuing commercial monopolies, Europeans were buying only 10 per cent of Malabar's pepper production, estimated at about 10,000 metric tons a year.[72] What is more, the Portuguese could never keep northern Europeans from discovering the knowledge they had painstakingly gathered regarding the winds, currents and ports of the South Atlantic and Indian Oceans.

## CONCLUSION

Between 1347 and 1565 Vijayanagara had often been at war with the Bahmani sultanate and the latter's sixteenth-century successor states. Because the ruling houses of Vijayanagara and its northern neighbours adhered to different religious traditions, many modern historians have construed the Krishna as a civilizational frontier dividing the Deccan into a Muslim north and a Hindu south. In part, this idea is a legacy of historian Robert Sewell who, writing in 1900, first brought Vijayanagara's history to the attention of the reading public. Sewell famously described that state as a 'Hindu bulwark against Muhammadan conquests',[73] thereby contributing to an enduring trope of religiously defined territorial separatism in the plateau. Sewell's book was published when India's nationalist movement was in full swing, and when Indian historians were looking to the country's past for evidence of successful states whose memory might mobilize British India's population for the nationalist cause. Inasmuch as Indian nationalism for many meant Hindu nationalism, Sewell's communalized characterization of Vijayanagara found a receptive audience.

But Sewell's 'bulwark' thesis reads history backwards, projecting into the past an early-twentieth-century preoccupation with religious identity and motives. Nor is his thesis sustained by evidence: in fact, it is contradicted by evidence. Peninsular India in the fifteenth and sixteenth centuries was not so much a sacred realm, far less a zone of two mutually exclusive sacred realms, as it was a crossroads. As in contemporary north India, peoples in the fifteenth- to the seventeenth-century Deccan circulated through overlapping religious, political and commercial networks. Long-distance merchants such as Mahmud Gawan brought horses, precious metals and other goods from the coasts inland and textiles and spices from the interior to the coasts. Jain, Hindu and Muslim pilgrims moved in all directions. Sufis, ascetics and lay seekers circulated from place to place, or from person to person, pursuing salvation, wisdom or more mundane goals. Adventurers and men of arms comprising the plateau's military labour market moved from court to court seeking promising rulers, commanders or chieftains to whom they might offer their service. None of these people appear to have experienced any civilizational barrier of the sort that Sewell posited – certainly not the 10,000 Turkish archers that Deva Raya II recruited to serve at Vijayanagara. And certainly not the Qutb Shahi prince Ibrahim, who fled south to Rama Raya's court in Vijayanagara to escape treachery in Golconda, or even Rama Raya himself, whose first patron was Golconda's Sultan Quli Qutb Shah. As a region where loyalties frequently shifted and alliances were always subject to renegotiation, the peninsula differed little from north India, which experienced a similarly high degree of mobility of goods, peoples and ideas across borders.

Peninsular India, then, is best understood in this period as a single, interconnected zone, a perspective illustrated by the ways in which ordinary people used coinage. When the Bahmani and Vijayanagara kingdoms were established in the mid fourteenth century, both states minted their own coins, which initially circulated only within their respective realms. In the north, the Bahmanis introduced a currency system inherited from that of their parent state, the Delhi sultanate, which was based on the gold *dinar* and *tanka*, together with a silver *tanka*. To the south, Vijayanagara issued a gold coin, the *hon*, which had derived ultimately from the Chalukya dynasty of kings, whose realm spanned the entire plateau in the tenth to the twelfth centuries. In effect, the Bahmanis introduced a coinage system whose historical roots were alien to the plateau, whereas the kings of Vijayanagara issued coins with a long-standing, indigenous pedigree. Merchants and consumers in both realms consequently invested more trust in the *hon* than they did in Bahmani coinage. In the reign of the Bahmanis' second sultan, Muhammad Shah I (r. 1358–75), money-changers would melt down locally minted gold *dinar*s and *tanka*s and send the bulk bullion across the Krishna to Vijayanagara, where it was re-struck as Vijayanagara *hon*s or its smaller denominations.[74] The newly minted coins then found their way back north to Bahmani territory, where they were used for commercial transactions. Throughout the fifteenth and sixteenth centuries, twice as much Vijayanagara coinage circulated in the Bahmani state as did the Bahmanis' own coins. In fact, more Vijayanagara coins circulated in the Bahmani kingdom than in Vijayanagara itself. Yet the southern coins never completely drove the Bahmanis' coins out of circulation, since the two systems were used by different social communities. Wealthier elites used the larger-denomination gold and silver Bahmani coins for international trade and official salaries, whereas commoners in both rural and urban areas used the smaller, more versatile and more familiar Vijayanagara coins for local purchases and payments.

After the collapse of the Bahmani state in the early sixteenth century, its coins continued to circulate until the 1580s, when Ahmadnagar, Bijapur and Golconda began articulating their separate identities by issuing their own silver coins. Yet throughout this period Vijayanagara's *hon*s still circulated in the northern Deccan. In fact, they were in such demand that from 1513 onwards the northern sultanates, succumbing to reality, began assessing agricultural and commercial taxes in the *hon*, and not exclusively in their own *dinar*s or *tanka*s. Even after 1565, when the Vijayanagara state was severely crippled following the Battle of Talikota, Bijapur, Golconda and Ahmadnagar not only continued using the Vijayanagara coins in their official transactions, but from the 1580s they began minting their own *hon*s, thereafter the only type of coin mentioned in sultanate inscriptions. These coins bore the same standard of weight and purity as the old Vijayanagara-minted coins, the only difference being that the Sanskrit titles and images of Hindu deities of the old coins were replaced by Persian lettering.

But even this compromise was not accepted by the peoples living within the sultanates' frontiers. As the older, 'genuine' Vijayanagara *hon*s became rarer with the passage of time, their intrinsic value increased relative to that of the sultanate's newer *hon*s. In their normal transactions, people therefore preferred using the *hon*s that had earlier been minted in Vijayanagara. Nonetheless, the sultanates tried to enforce the use of their own, newer *hon*s. In 1654 'Adil Shahi authorities in Bijapur ordered the confiscation of the property of anybody who used the older *hon*s minted by the defunct Vijayanagara state instead of Bijapur's *hon*s. But such royal edicts evidently failed. Within several decades of that order, even the Muslim functionaries of a Qutb Shahi mosque were insisting that an annual grant made for their maintenance be made not in Golconda's minted *hon*s, but in 'genuine' *hon*s – that is, the currency minted by Vijayanagara over a century earlier, bearing Sanskrit lettering and images of Hindu deities.[75]

Notwithstanding the bombastic rhetoric sometimes found in contemporary Persian chronicles regarding Vijayanagara's 'infidels', or twenty-first-century talk of a Hindu–Muslim 'clash of civilizations' in the premodern Deccan, ordinary people actually living at that time experienced the plateau as a single economic zone that transcended both political frontiers and cultural difference. Their preference for the *hon* also speaks to a deep continuity over time, as merchants, producers and consumers across the peninsula preferred to use a familiar medium of economic exchange traceable to the Chalukya maharajas of Kalyana. This should not be surprising, for in the late fifteenth and early sixteenth centuries ruling elites on both sides of the Krishna were actively reviving the memory of the Chalukya past. In Vijayanagara, government officials – probably Rama Raya himself – ordered a large, Chalukya-period stepped tank to be disassembled and transported from its original site to the Vijayanagara capital, where it was laboriously reassembled in the heart of the city's Royal Centre. Meanwhile, Bijapur's Sultan Ibrahim I (r. 1534–58) installed Chalukya-period stone inscriptions and an ensemble of Chalukya-period columns in the main gateway to his capital's citadel, while at the fort of Kalyana – the Chalukyas' former capital – his grandson Sultan Ibrahim II built a palace around a carefully preserved Chalukya-period temple.[76]

Such evidence speaks of a deeper trend in the Deccan's cultural history, namely a progressive interpenetration of the Sanskrit and

Persianate worlds between the fourteenth and sixteenth centuries. At the time of the Khalaji and Tughluq invasions of the Deccan in the early fourteenth century, these two worlds had remained quite distinct, sustained by two different literary traditions. But by the sixteenth century their mutual intermingling had proceeded to a remarkable extent. One sees this, for example, in a frieze that runs along the cornice of a gateway at Raichur which Vijayanagara's Krishna Raya built when he seized that fort from Bijapur's control in 1520. In the centre is an image of Krishna Raya seated in royal splendour and at ease, surrounded by female attendants [see Fig. 10]. Since the entire frieze narrates well-known stories from the *Ramayana* epic, the king is contextually associated with Rama, its divine hero. But unlike the panel depicting Rama, Krishna Raya also appears wearing tall, conical headgear called *kullayi* in Telugu (*kulah* in Persian). This item of apparel had migrated to India from Iran, where it was associated with high social status, even royalty. With whom, then, is Krishna Raya to be identified – a Hindu deity, a Persian nobleman, or both?

The ambiguity conveyed in this single image, like the assimilation of the headgear's Persian name into the Telugu language, captures how a sixteenth-century Deccani monarch could draw from two discourses of power and civilization simultaneously. It is a phenomenon that will bear closer scrutiny in the following chapters.

# 5

# The Consolidation of Mughal Rule, 1526–1605

## OVERVIEW

The rise of the Mughal empire centres on the career of an extraordinary personality, Zahir al-Din Babur (d. 1530). Deprived of his father's kingdom in the Central Asian highlands, Babur famously descended on the plains of India from his base in Kabul and, in a celebrated battle fought in 1526, defeated Ibrahim Lodi, the last ruler of the last dynasty of Delhi sultans. He then went on to launch India's most splendid empire, which at its height would dominate nearly all of South Asia. Babur's place in Indian history is rendered even more vivid thanks to his very personal and self-revealing memoir, the *Baburnama*, which combines elements of a diary, a gazetteer, a chronicle and a father's advice to his son. Much of this fascinating text was drafted by lamplight or a flickering campfire before being packed in saddlebags, as Babur and his men rode from Samarqand to Kabul, and then on to Delhi [see Map 5].

Much larger themes lie behind this tale. Babur's mother was directly descended from Genghis Khan and, although she was separated from her illustrious ancestor by fourteen generations, that ancestry explains the name by which outsiders would call the dynasty launched by her son: the word 'Mughal' is simply Persian for 'Mongol'. But Babur identified more powerfully with his father's political and cultural inheritance. As his father was a great-great-grandson of Timur, Babur was much closer in descent to the storied warlord of Samarqand than he was to the founder of the Mongol empire. Moreover, during the century following his death in 1405, Timur's descendants continued to rule parts of Central Asia and the Iranian plateau, where they upheld their forebear's tradition of generously patronizing the Persianate arts. For Babur was, first and foremost, a proud Timurid. As destructive as Timur's sack of Delhi had been – bitter memories of which certainly lingered on in north India – Babur prized his Timurid ancestry. He would doubtless have preferred to govern a kingdom from Timur's city of Samarqand than to spend his remaining days in the plains of north India, about which he had little good to say. Hindustan, he flatly declares in his memoirs, did not possess much charm. 'There is no beauty in its people,' he grumbled, 'no graceful social intercourse, no poetic talent or understanding, no etiquette, nobility, or manliness. The arts and crafts have no harmony or symmetry. There are no good horses, meat, grapes, melons, or other fruit. There is no ice, cold water, good food or bread in the markets. There are no baths and no madrasas. There are no candles, torches, or candlesticks.'[1]

As dismayed as he was over north India's lack of melons or good horses, Babur was much impressed with the country's wealth. Immediately upon seizing control of Delhi, he addressed his weary, homesick kinsmen and retainers, imploring them to abandon thoughts of marching back to Afghanistan. 'For some years', he reminded them:

> we have struggled, experienced difficulties, traversed long distances, led the army, and cast ourselves and our soldiers into the dangers of war and battle; through God's grace we have defeated such numerous enemies and taken such vast realms. What now compels us to throw away for no reason at all the realms we have taken at such cost? Shall we go back to Kabul and remain poverty-stricken? Let no one who supports me say such things henceforth. Let no one who cannot endure and is bound to leave be dissuaded from leaving.[2]

Having secured a foothold on the Indo-Gangetic plain, Babur sent letters back to Central Asia urging his kinsmen and their supporters to come and settle in India. For in the end, Babur understood his conquests in terms of reclaiming a piece of his Timurid patrimony. Although Timur had returned to Samarqand after sacking Delhi, for some time afterwards he continued to exercise an indirect rule in the Punjab. What history has called the 'Mughal' empire, then, was in the eyes of its founder an attempt to restore Timurid rule in north India after a lapse of more than a century.

Babur's conquest also represented an historic moment in the relations between two very different ecological worlds. Central Asia's semi-pastoral culture was based on rearing livestock and mastering horse-based warfare, and it assessed wealth largely in terms of movable assets: sheep, horses, goats, camels. The Indian world Babur encountered, by contrast, was one of ploughs and bullocks, a sedentary and agrarian society that understood wealth mainly in terms of fixed resources: harvested grain, manufactured goods, precious metals. If the kingdom that Babur established in India was initially a transplant of Central Asia's semi-pastoral oasis culture, his descendants would root the state ever more deeply in India's agrarian economy, its socio-religious culture and its political life. Evolving gradually over several centuries, this process is often overlooked by historians seeking to capture the character of the Mughal empire in static essences such as 'centralized bureaucratic state', 'Oriental despotism', 'feudal kingdom' or 'Islamic empire'. No such facile characterization is satisfactory, not least because that empire was never static: its history was one of a progressive fusion of two very different worlds.

That said, Babur's Indian kingdom was never purely agrarian, just as the Central Asian world of his youth and early manhood was never purely pastoral. Although the broad grasslands north of Afghanistan's Hindu Kush Mountains were ideally suited for nomadic pastoralism, for centuries Turko-Mongol pastoral culture had interacted with that of Persianized oasis towns and cosmopolitan cities such as Samarqand or Bukhara. Babur's native Ferghana valley was itself a fertile region of sedentary agriculture and urban settlement, in close touch with the great centres of Persian cultural production. His own parentage epitomized the mixing of pastoral, Mongol–Timurid with sedentary, Persianate culture. When sitting with his Turco-Mongol kinsmen or retainers, Babur's father would wear a Mongol cap. But when holding court in the small principality he governed in the Ferghana valley, he would wear a turban in the fashion of a member of the Persianized ruling elite.[3] Such headgear was associated with the more urbanized, socially stratified and literary Persianate world. Notwithstanding this mixed Mongol and Timurid/Persianate inheritance, it is telling that the Mughals understood themselves as Timurids – or, more precisely, 'Indo-Timurids', indicating the prestige they associated with Timur's career and legacy, and more broadly with Persianate culture, in contrast to the Mongols' lingering association with the devastation that had driven so many Central Asians from their homelands in the thirteenth century.

By the time the processes Babur set in motion came to an end, the Mughals had shed all but a few trappings of their former pastoral and semi-nomadic identity, and become a thoroughly agrarian state. A kingdom originally run by a mainly foreign governing class – ethnically Turko-Mongol, Persianate in literary and aesthetic traditions, Sunni Muslim by religion, Timurid in dynastic identity – would put down roots and, in the course of the sixteenth and seventeenth centuries, become an essentially Indian polity.[4]

## BABUR

Babur was just eleven years old in 1494 when, on his father's death, he ascended the throne of Ferghana, a small Central Asian principality 350 kilometres east of Samarqand, the jewel of Timurid Central Asia. From the very start, young Babur faced fierce resistance from his nobles and even his uncles, who tried to replace him with his more malleable younger brother. Nonetheless, when only fifteen he managed to seize control of Timur's former capital of Samarqand. It proved a brief reign, however, for within just a few months he lost the city to a rival while trying to recover his base at Ferghana, which hostile elements had meanwhile snatched from his grasp. Finding himself now with no territory to rule, he spent several dismal years wandering about hills and valleys seeking kinsmen and supporters. In 1501 he made a second attempt at Samarqand, but was repulsed this time by a powerful confederation of ascendant Uzbeks, Turkish-speakers ethnically distinct from Timur's Chagatai lineage of Turko-Mongols. One by one, Uzbek armies commanded by Muhammad Shaybani Khan (r. 1500–10) overthrew Babur's kinsmen in the successor states of Timur's former empire. Shaybani Khan had seized Samarqand just a year before Babur's second attempt to recover the city, and in several years' time he would take other flourishing centres of Persianate culture formerly under Timurid control, notably Bukhara. For his part, Babur was reduced to utter destitution, accompanied by a small band of loyal retainers and his mother, Qutlugh Nigar Khanum, who in their worst times was given the use of the only tent they possessed.

In 1504, sensing the futility of ever recovering his patrimony in Central Asia, Babur, his mother and 300 lightly armed men marched southwards across the snowy passes of Afghanistan's Hindu Kush Mountains in search of a base safely distant from the growing Uzbek threat. They set their sights on Kabul, then ruled by an unpopular strongman generally considered a usurper, enabling Babur to capture the city in fairly short order. Kabul straddled several strategic crossroads: east–west caravan trade routes linking north India with Iran, and north–south routes linking India with Central Asia. Through this choke-point long caravans of Central Asian war-horses were sent through the mountain passes leading to India's horse markets, on which so many states vitally depended for their cavalries. Making their way through Kabul from the opposite direction were caravans of Indian textiles and spices destined for markets in Iran, Central Asia and beyond. The Afghan city therefore presented an ideal staging site for raids across the Khyber into India.

As early as 1505 Babur waged his first such expedition in the Punjab, then held by Afghan chieftains nominally loyal to Sultan Sikandar Lodi (r. 1489–1517). But events in Central Asia and Iran awakened his dormant ambition to recover Samarqand from Uzbek control. Timur's immediate successors had shifted their capital to Herat, at the time a brilliant centre of Persianate culture. In 1506, however, the city's last Timurid ruler died, and a year later it, too, was taken by Uzbek Turks. Especially distressing was that the Uzbeks had seized and imprisoned Babur's female relatives, including his sister Khanzada, his only full sibling, who was forced to marry his perennial nemesis, Shaybani Khan. These events not only humiliated and embittered Babur, they also left him the sole reigning Timurid anywhere in Timur's former empire. Many of the remaining Timurid princes and their retainers, their own hopes dashed by the ascendant Uzbeks, now took refuge with him at Kabul. Aware that the survival of Timur's legacy rested on his shoulders, in 1508 Babur adopted the exalted Persian title *padshah*, or 'supreme king'. With so many disenfranchised Timurids looking to him for political leadership, his fading hopes of recovering his Central Asian patrimony were suddenly rekindled. Moreover, he would have a powerful ally in such an undertaking. Shah Isma'il Safavi (r. 1501–24), the charismatic and seemingly invincible founder of Iran's Safavid dynasty (1501–1736), was just then consolidating his authority across the Iranian plateau. Alarmed by Shaybani Khan's 1507 conquest of Herat, Isma'il defeated an Uzbek army in 1510, resulting in the death of Shaybani Khan and the fall of Herat to the Safavids. He also freed Babur's imprisoned relatives, leading to Babur's joyful reunion with his sister Khanzada.

With his long-standing Uzbek adversary out of the way, a grateful and indebted Babur collaborated with Shah Isma'il in a joint project of conquering Uzbek territories for their respective kingdoms. Safavid assistance also helped Babur recover Samarqand, if only briefly. But collaboration came at a price. Isma'il's self-proclaimed semidivine status horrified Babur's fellow Sunni Muslims, who considered the shah a dangerous heretic. And in return for receiving material assistance from Isma'il, Babur had to act as his junior partner, which involved wearing the Safavids' twelve-pointed headgear, indicating the wearer's identity as an ardent member of Shi'ism's dominant Twelver sect. Babur was painfully aware that he appeared to have renounced his Sunni identity and become a Shi'i. Moreover, having recently proclaimed himself a *padshah*, it was especially humiliating publicly to acknowledge his subservient status to the Iranian shah, whose name was proclaimed on Samarqand's coins and in its mosques. In the end, the city's Sunni population rejected both Shi'ism and nominal Iranian sovereignty, preferring instead another Uzbek overlord to Babur, who yet again proved unable to hold on to Samarqand. It is due to his long record of suffering at the hands of his Uzbek and other enemies that Babur's memoirs are pervaded by themes of defeat, humiliation, displacement and exile.[5]

In 1514, abandoning the possibility of ever regaining Samarqand, Babur returned to his base in Kabul and again began to look to the north Indian plain, this time not as an object of plunder, but as territory for building a sovereign domain large and stable enough to preserve the threatened Timurid house from extinction. This was his foremost objective. Moreover, the only way a warlord could recruit and retain armed followers was by demonstrating success in obtaining and distributing resources from sedentary societies, and he was aware that in India, a land of fabulous wealth, the Lodis' governing structure was rapidly crumbling. In 1517 Sikandar Lodi had died and was succeeded by his son Ibrahim, who unwisely replaced senior nobles in his service with younger men who were supposedly loyal but were also less experienced. When Babur's expeditions of 1519 and 1520 took him as far as the Punjab's Chenab River, some of those recently dismissed senior Lodi nobles, including the governor of the Punjab and even the sultan's own uncle, began to see the Mughal commander as a viable alternative to the unpopular Ibrahim. In 1524 they invited him to invade and assume sovereign rule. Again he entered the Punjab, this time with the intent of challenging Sultan Ibrahim Lodi. But on reaching Lahore and Dipalpur, he found that he could not trust the Lodi turncoats nominally under his command, and so he returned to Kabul.

In late 1525 Babur, aged forty-two, launched his fifth and final invasion of India, marching from Kabul at the head of an army of 8,000 men, composed of subordinate Timurid princes and their retainers, Pashtun allies from south-eastern Afghanistan and artillery and matchlock contingents advised by Turkish officers from Anatolia. Crossing the Indus in mid December, his force faced little resistance as it advanced across the Punjab, where Lodi authority had already collapsed. By April 1526 he reached Panipat, sixty-five kilometres north-west of Delhi, and secured his defences. On the twenty-first he was met by a Lodi force much larger than his own, but far less disciplined. The Mughals also possessed the relatively new technology of matchlock and cannon firepower, which Ibrahim lacked. Most importantly, Babur deployed the same flanking cavalry tactics that Uzbek cavalries had used to defeat him decades earlier in his struggles over Samarqand. By midday, the decisive Battle of Panipat had left Sultan Ibrahim dead on the battlefield, with no obstacle standing between Babur and Delhi. Far from plundering that city as his Timurid ancestor had done, however, Babur took care to secure its palaces, guarantee the safety of its population, arrange for a pension

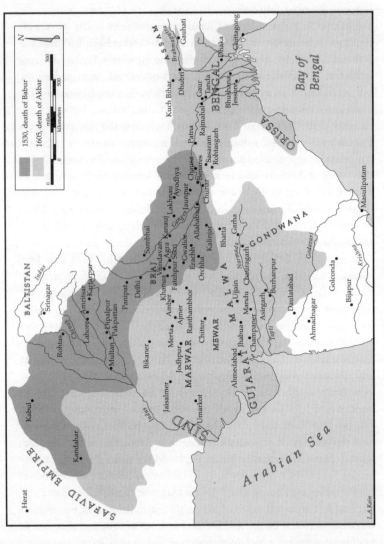

The Mughal empire to the mid seventeenth century

for the mother of the slain Lodi sultan, and pay his respects to the shrines of the city's most prominent Sufi saints – the Chishti shaikhs Qutb al-Din Bakhtiyar Kaki (d. 1236) and Nizam al-Din Auliya. Such measures signalled that the Mughals not only would remain in north India, but that they would patronize the same 'invisible sovereigns' as had several centuries of Delhi's rulers, thereby establishing a spiritual continuity between themselves and previous Delhi-based dynasties. There was no going back to Samarqand. India would be Babur's home and the seat of his kingdom, which he was determined to pass on to his descendants.

From Delhi, Babur sent his son Humayun down to Agra, the Lodi capital since 1506, in order to secure the defeated regime's treasury and government palaces. Several days later he joined his son in Agra and, making that city his own capital, set himself to governing the fledgling kingdom. He soon realized, however, that he had stepped into a fierce struggle between two large ethno-political blocs contending for supremacy over the fertile north Indian plain: Afghans and Rajputs. The founding of Lodi rule in the mid fifteenth century had seen many Afghans pour through the mountain passes and become rooted in north India's socio-political landscape as long-distance horse merchants, cavalrymen, petty traders and landholders. Challenging them for hegemony across northern and western India were confederations of martial lineages that, by the fifteenth and sixteenth centuries, had become organized by common descent lines, like their Afghan rivals. But whereas the Afghans' identification of clan with territory had become distorted by migration from their ancestral homelands, Rajput lineages tended to be displaced on to territory. In the early sixteenth century, one lineage in particular was making a bid for supremacy over north India and the Delhi sultanate itself – the Sisodiyas, based in Mewar in southern Rajasthan and led by the renowned Rana Sanga (r. 1508–28). In fact, at the very time that Babur was waging his final, decisive invasion of north India, Rana Sanga was preparing for his own assault on Delhi.

In 1527, only a year after defeating Sultan Ibrahim Lodi, Babur confronted Rana Sanga at Khanua, sixty-five kilometres west of Agra. The Sisodiya raja had under his command some 80,000 cavalry, augmented by contingents of surviving Afghans recently defeated by Babur, including Ibrahim Lodi's brother Mahmud, who made common cause in trying to expel the Mughals from India. Although vastly outnumbered in cavalry, the Mughals again carried the day, and again the opposing commander, this time Rana Sanga, was killed in action. Babur's memoirs reveal much about his state of mind before and after this battle. Although up to this point he had regularly participated in rousing drinking parties with his men, on the eve of his contest with Rana Sanga the new sovereign of Delhi and Agra solemnly vowed to renounce wine. Associating alcohol with his lower self, he felt it necessary first to subdue his baser part in order to gird himself for the approaching contest. And since Rana Sanga's was a mainly non-Muslim army, Babur expressed his ideas in religious terms, comparing the breaking of wine goblets with the breaking of Hindu images. On achieving victory over Rana Sanga, he referred to his army as an 'army of Islam' and himself as a *ghazi*, or 'holy warrior', a title he now added to his seal.[6] Immediately after the contest, though, the title disappeared from his vocabulary.

After his twin victories at Panipat and Khanua, Babur swiftly moved to consolidate his authority in a strip of territory stretching from eastern Afghanistan through the central Punjab to the mid-Gangetic plain. For personnel and models of governance he drew on his Central Asian and Timurid past, placing Turks and Mongols in the kingdom's governing core. Although he was thoroughly conversant in Persian as a medium of cosmopolitan culture, his principal supporters were fellow Turkish-speakers. Having spent nearly his entire life leading a steppe-based band of warriors, he saw himself as the first among equals, very much in the tradition of Bahlul, the founder of the Lodi dynasty. Like his ancestor Timur, he governed on a personal and informal basis: men who had sworn allegiance to him received his unqualified protection and shared in any booty gained from successful military expeditions. But equally, men who had broken sworn compacts of loyalty were subject to severe punishments. For Babur, like Timur, was capable of inflicting severe cruelty, such as impaling defeated enemies or erecting towers filled with their skulls. Above all, although he held neither India nor Indians in very high regard, he was pragmatic, being well aware of his precarious position as an outsider in a large and politically volatile land. He was therefore quick to reach agreements with the Sisodiya lineage after defeating Rana Sanga at Khanua, as he did with other Rajput leaders in Awadh, Malwa and the Punjab.

The dynastic change in north India from Lodi to Mughal was accompanied by a change in royal patronage of Sufi orders. The dominant Sufi order in Babur's homeland, the Naqshbandis, had been led by the eminent Shaikh Ubaid Allah Ahrar (d. 1490) who, thanks to the lavish patronage heaped on him by Timurid princes, also happened to be the largest single landowner in Central Asia. Babur's father had been one of his many disciples, and Babur himself, while still a young man in Central Asia, once dreamt that Shaikh Ahrar appeared before him and allowed him to seize Samarqand, which he actually did soon after that dream. From his capital in Agra, Babur maintained close ties with Naqshbandi shaikhs in Central Asia, even though Chishti shaikhs were then dominant in Delhi, thanks to patronage by the erstwhile Lodi regime. At the Battle of Panipat, Delhi's leading Chishti shaikh of the day, 'Abd al-Quddus Gangohi, had prayed for the success of his Lodi patrons. But when the latter were defeated, the Mughal victors captured the shaikh and forced him to walk the sixty-five kilometres back to Delhi.[7] Babur's attitude to living Chishtis who had opposed him obviously differed from his respect for the shrines of revered Chishti saints.

Although he reigned in India for just under four years, Babur left a solid foundation for his descendants to build on: a ruling structure dominated by Mongols and Turks, a court guided by a Timurid ruling ideology, the spiritual direction of Naqshbandi shaikhs, and durable ties between India and the Persianate world. He left no grand monuments, apart from mosques at Panipat, Sambhal and Ayodhya, but he did bequeath to his successors a refined aesthetic sensibility and a fascination with the natural world, as is graphically reflected in his memoirs. He established gardens nearly everywhere that he could, recreating in India the same green, symmetrical and carefully laid-out spaces that might recall a Central Asian oasis. One of his first acts upon seizing Agra was to plant Afghan melons and grapes in his 'Garden of the Eight Paradises'. Although surviving today only in fragments, the garden's interlocking canals and raised walkways introduced to India the Timurid, and ultimately Persianate, scheme of a walled-in garden divided into quarters.[8] And his *Babur-nama* gave subsequent dynastic rulers – most immediately, his son Humayun – a narrative lesson on proper governance and leadership. Its gazetteer quality also sketched out the idea, more fully developed later in the dynasty's history, that, to rule a kingdom, its peoples and places must be identified, located and enumerated.

## HUMAYUN

Although repeatedly dismayed with his behaviour, in the end Babur favoured Humayun over his younger sons to manage the newly won kingdom. On one occasion, when Humayun lay seriously ill, he even vowed to offer his own life for that of his ailing son. Upon praying while thrice circumambulating Humayun's bed, he sensed that Humayun's illness had passed. He was right about that, but soon thereafter Babur himself was stricken by a severe illness to which he succumbed in December 1530. According to his wishes, he was buried in a magnificent garden he had earlier laid out on a Kabul hillside.

In what were reportedly his last words, Babur admonished Humayun to do nothing against his brothers, even though they might deserve it.[9] Humayun steadfastly followed this advice, despite being betrayed time and again by his half-brothers Kamran, 'Askari and Hindal – especially Kamran. One reason for his brothers' frequent deceits lay in the Turko-Mongol tradition of collective sovereignty that Babur had inherited. In this theory, territorial sovereignty was shared collectively by a clan's male members, meaning that a ruler's nearest male relations had equal claims on succeeding to supreme rulership on his death. This explains why, when Babur was a youth in Ferghana and Samarqand, his closest relatives had also been his foremost political rivals. And it explains why, even though most of his successors on the Mughal throne preferred to be succeeded by their eldest son, younger sons fiercely challenged that idea; and why, from the sixteenth to the early eighteenth centuries, succession disputes were often bloody, fratricidal affairs. The idea of collective sovereignty also accounts for the practice of distributing large tracts of sovereign territory to royal princes to be governed on a semi-independent and semi-permanent basis. Accordingly, Babur had assigned to each of his sons separate territories to govern as semi-independent rulers – Humayun in Badakhshan, Kamran in Kandahar and Kabul, and 'Askari in Multan.[10] As soon as Humayun assumed sovereign authority, his brothers began plotting to take over the kingdom. Kamran, in particular, occupied Punjab from his base in Kabul, where he began drawing to his service officers formerly loyal to his father.

Meanwhile, Humayun marched eastwards to confront rebellious Afghans who had been driven down the Gangetic plain in the course of Babur's initial conquest. Near Lakhnau he engaged and defeated Ibrahim Lodi's brother Mahmud, who had declared himself sultan after Ibrahim's defeat at Panipat. Then he heard that the powerful ruler of Gujarat, Sultan Bahadur, was planning to invade Mughal territories with the aid of the Portuguese, who had recently established a number of trading posts along India's western shores. So in 1535 he turned to the south-west and confronted the Gujarat ruler. Although he managed to capture the strategic fort of Champaner, Humayun failed to pursue the fleeing Bahadur, much less advance further and annex the whole province. Instead, he abandoned his Gujarat campaign in order to resume his drive against Afghans, whose numbers continued to grow in the eastern Gangetic region, and who had allied themselves with remnants of the defeated Lodis.

Many of these soldiers regrouped around one of the most brilliant warriors of the age, the Afghan chieftain Sher Khan Sur. In point of military talent, he and Humayun differed profoundly. Whereas the former was strategically gifted and bold, the latter was inept and excessively cautious. Whereas the Afghan chieftain was self-disciplined, Humayun indulged in protracted bouts with wine or drugs. Sher Khan's career also suggests how Afghans had become rooted in the north Indian countryside since the mid fifteenth century. Born as Farid Khan in 1486 in present-day Haryana, he was known in his youth as Sher Khan owing to his reputation for courage, for *shir* is Persian for lion (or tiger). But because he belonged to the Sur clan, a marginal Afghan lineage unrelated to the politically dominant Lodis, he lacked ready access to upper India's rich agrarian resources. At some point between 1501 and 1511 he became a freelance soldier in the Jaunpur region. But it was further down the Gangetic plain, in western Bihar, that he built up a political base. There he recruited Afghans who had formerly served the Lodis before their defeat by Babur, and also local villagers who, when agricultural labour was in low demand, constituted the region's pool of available military labour. Through non-Afghan middlemen, whose friendship and confidence he cultivated, Sher Khan was able to acquire local manpower to which he would otherwise have had no access. He then commanded these men with a combination of generosity and strict discipline: soldiers received regular monthly salaries but were subjected to systematic military drills.

The key to tapping into India's military labour market, in Bihar as elsewhere, was access to cash. To this end, Sher Khan shrewdly gave refuge to a wealthy and respectable widow who belonged to one of the most powerful clans in the former Lodi regime. From her wealth he bulked up the number of troops under his command while placating the Mughal governor of Jaunpur to his west with tribute. This enabled him to mount a bold invasion eastwards. Skirting the defences of Sultan Ghiyath al-Din Mahmud Shah (r. 1532–38) of Bengal, he dashed straight to the latter's capital of Gaur. Overwhelmed, the sultan was forced to concede all territories west of Rajmahal and to pay Sher Khan an annual tribute of 900,000 *tanka*s, cash that enabled the Afghan warlord to augment his armies still further. In 1537, when the sultan failed to pay his annual tribute, Sher Khan sent his generals into the delta and toppled his regime. After capturing the Bengal sultanate's considerable treasure, Sher Khan commanded 40,000 cavalry, 1,500 war-elephants, 300 boats and 200,000 infantry. This gave him the confidence to crown himself sultan, adopt the sovereign title of Sher Shah Sur, and undertake the ultimate goal of overthrowing the new Mughal dynasty.[11]

Meanwhile, Humayun continued to pursue rebellious Afghans across upper India, marching from Bihar to Bengal. In response, Sher Shah merely melted into Bihar's interior, allowing the Mughal sovereign to occupy Bengal's capital of Gaur in 1538. But just then, Humayun's younger half-brother Hindal audaciously stormed the Mughal capital of Agra and declared himself king. Such treachery did not stop there. With Humayun still in distant Bengal and the whole of upper India in turmoil, Kamran marched down from the Punjab, ostensibly to assist Humayun in his struggles with Afghans, but actually to cut a deal with Hindal to divide up the new kingdom and rid them both of their elder brother. In 1539, when Humayun heard this news he hastily moved towards upper India, even though that year's monsoon rains had already submerged much of the Bengal delta. His luck then passed from bad to worse. At Chausa, by the Ganges in western Bihar, Sher Shah seized the moment to pounce upon Humayun, thoroughly outmanoeuvring and decimating his army. The Mughal monarch barely managed to escape with his life, swimming across the river with the help of an air-filled animal skin.[12]

The hapless Humayun then returned to Agra and, perhaps recalling his father's dying admonition, generously pardoned his brothers for their treasonous behaviour. Yet even as news arrived of Sher Shah's steady advance up the Gangetic plain towards Agra, the brothers could not agree on a common strategy. Ultimately, Kamran withdrew to Lahore, where he again raised an independent army. In May 1540, Humayun confronted Sher Shah at Kanauj, but owing to strategic military blunders he was again defeated and forced to retreat to Lahore. Sensing total victory, and with none of Babur's sons able to challenge him, Sher Shah rejected Humayun's offer to let him rule all Hindustan except the Punjab. The Afghan then drove the Mughals out of Lahore. Kamran and 'Askari still governed in Afghanistan, but Humayun and his youngest half-brother Hindal were left with no sovereign domain at all.

The Mughals having vacated the entire Indo-Gangetic plain, Sher Shah now set himself up in Delhi as Hindustan's sole sovereign and founder of a new ruling house, the Sur dynasty (1540–56). For five years, until his untimely death in 1545, he governed a realm renowned for its stability, prosperity and orderly government. As king, he brought to the art of governance the same discipline that as warlord he had brought to recruiting, training and commanding his army. To ensure a predictable flow of revenue to the royal centre, he systemized the measurement of agricultural lands, something that had been introduced only sporadically by previous rulers of the Delhi sultanate, notably 'Ala al-Din Khalaji. He also stabilized his regime's economy by establishing a trimetallic currency based on the silver *rupiya*, which he issued at a standard weight of 178 grains, complemented by the gold *mohur* and the copper *dam*. This standardized silver coin anticipated the modern rupee, found in states of South and South-east Asia today. Well aware of India's strategic need for commerce with Central Asia, especially for importing war-horses, he renovated and extended one of the most famous roads in Asia – the Grand Trunk Road linking Sonargaon in eastern Bengal with Peshawar in western Punjab, with further extensions to Kabul. Because so many of his governing traditions have survived into modern times, the Republic of India issued a postage stamp in his honour in 1970, as did Pakistan in 1991.

Sher Shah's most visible legacy lies in his architectural projects. In Delhi, he made considerable alterations and additions to the Purana Qila, the palace–citadel complex that Humayun had begun building in 1533. There he patronized the construction of an elaborately decorated mosque, whose façade of articulated entrance archway and alternating red sandstone and white marble recalls the entranceway of the Alai Darwaza in Delhi's Qutb Minar complex, suggesting Sher Shah's intention to link himself visually to Sultan 'Ala al-Din Khalaji, the mightiest of Delhi's sultans. He also built a pair of imposing forts: Rohtas in western Punjab near the city of Jhelum, and Rohtasgarh in the Son valley, south-western Bihar. Finally, in Sasaram, his original political base 115 kilometres east of Benares, he built for himself a large three-storeyed domed octagonal mausoleum. Standing in the middle of an artificial lake, this massive structure rises to forty-six metres, surpassing in size the tomb of any previous Indian ruler. Nearby, his son and successor, Islam Shah Sur (r. 1545–54), began an even larger octagonal tomb for himself, but it was never completed. The scale of these tombs probably motivated subsequent Mughal rulers to build ever more monumental tomb complexes for themselves – most spectacularly, the Taj Mahal – by outperforming their former Afghan adversaries.[13]

For the fourteen years when Sher Shah and his son enjoyed north India's political limelight, Humayun was driven off the stage entirely. During the first period of Sher Shah's reign, the fugitive Mughal roamed across Sind and Rajasthan seeking allies and troops with which to reclaim his lost kingdom. But Sher Shah had pressured

Humayun's potential Rajput allies into refusing his overtures. Meanwhile, his brothers had become politically divided: Kamran and 'Askari remained in Afghanistan, aloof and still opposed to their older brother, while Hindal, formerly so disloyal, joined the royal camp. In 1541 Humayun even married the daughter of Hindal's tutor. The next year he and his party crossed the scorching Thar Desert en route to Sind under extremely stressful circumstances. When the horse his pregnant wife was riding died, Humayun gave her his own horse and rode a camel. Matters improved later that year when the party reached Umarkot, in Sind. The amir of that province, one of Humayun's appointees who had earlier served Babur, helped his guest gather horses and arms. It was also there that Humayun's wife Hamida gave birth to the king's first son, the future emperor Akbar. The next year, they crossed the Indus and headed north-west towards Kandahar where Humayun, ever sanguine about his siblings' loyalty, planned to rally his brothers in a bid to recover his throne from Sher Shah. But Hindal, already sent ahead to Kandahar, was arrested by Kamran for refusing to have the Friday prayers read in the latter's name. Kamran also sent 'Askari from Kabul with an army to confront the advancing Humayun. Under these circumstances, and with no better options in sight, the fugitive monarch avoided all his brothers and marched westwards toward Iran, where he hoped to secure help from the Safavid monarch. Since it was December and travel would be difficult in the snow and bitter cold, the infant Akbar was left in Kandahar in the care of 'Askari's wife. With Hamida and just forty men, Humayun undertook the arduous trip across western Afghanistan. In one snowy night they were so weakened from hunger that Humayun ordered a horse to be killed, and the party was reduced to eating boiled horsemeat in their helmets – another of Humayun's many low points.

After a month they finally reached Herat, where their Iranian hosts gave them a warm welcome. The city had succeeded Samarqand as the Timurid capital soon after Timur's death in 1405, and it was still ruled by a Timurid prince when Babur visited it a century later. When Humayun and his party arrived, it was held by Shah Tahmasp (r. 1524–76), the second ruler of Iran's Safavid dynasty. Under both Timurid and Safavid rule, Herat had flourished as a major centre of

Persianate culture, with its magnificent Timurid monuments and the studio of the brilliant miniature artist, Behzad, who had died nearly a decade earlier. When shown that artist's work, Humayun made it known that, should he regain his Indian kingdom, he would patronize Behzad's pupils. In July 1544 Humayun reached the Safavid capital of Qazvin, where he had his first audience with Shah Tahmasp. The Iranian monarch, however, pressured his fugitive guest to convert to Islam's Shi'i sect, which Shah Isma'il had recently imposed across the Iranian plateau. Aware that he stood little chance of acquiring material assistance without acceding to his host's demands, Humayun went through the formalities of showing his Shi'i allegiance, just as his father had done when in similar straits. Swallowing his pride, he also agreed to hand over the city of Kandahar, in return for which Shah Tahmasp provided him with 10,000 cavalrymen for recovering his Indian kingdom.

In the spring of 1545 a combined Mughal–Safavid force marched into Afghanistan, taking first Kandahar from 'Askari and then Kabul from Kamran, although both brothers evaded capture. Humayun's next steps would both re-establish Mughal rule and define Mughal culture. First, in the course of the Afghan campaigns the infant Akbar was joyfully reunited with his parents, guaranteeing the continuance of the Mughal dynasty. Second, by reconfirming the tax-free land holdings of Naqshbandi shaikhs, the Sufi order traditionally favoured by Timurid princes, Humayun consolidated his grip on Kabul. What had been his father's base for conquering Hindustan would now be his own for reconquering it. And third, he acted on his resolve, sworn while in Behzad's studio in Herat, to promote Persian culture by recruiting and patronizing the brightest artistic and literary luminaries he could find. Some of them accompanied Humayun on his return to India; others migrated after he had regained his kingdom.

Humayun's return to power, however, would take time. Although his old nemesis, Sher Shah, had been killed in a cannon accident in May 1545, the Afghan ruler's son Islam Shah quickly consolidated his grip over Hindustan, while Kamran and 'Askari continued to challenge their elder brother for dominance of eastern Afghanistan. In 1548 Humayun defeated Kamran in battle, after which he hosted a grand feast of reconciliation for all his brothers. But Kamran and

'Askari again took up arms against him. Several years later he managed to capture 'Askari, whom he exiled, but his younger brother
Hindal – of late such a loyal ally – was killed by Kamran's forces. In
1553 Humayun for a last time captured Kamran, yet he could not
bring himself to have his troublesome brother executed. Instead, he
had him blinded and sent off to Mecca. The next year, with the issue
of his brothers finally settled, Humayun began to reoccupy territory
in the Punjab, assisted by the expert military leadership of Bairam
Khan, a former servant of Babur who had joined the royal camp during Humayun's long period of wandering. Also favouring his cause
was the political chaos then gripping Delhi, as five successive rulers
of Sher Shah Sur's dynasty rose to power during the year following
Islam Shah's death in 1554. The sudden collapse of the Sur house
appears to have energized Humayun and concentrated his focus in
ways seldom seen earlier in his career. In July 1555 he and his troops
triumphantly entered Delhi.

Restored at last to his throne, Humayun acted vigorously to re-
establish his authority after a fifteen-year absence. He also redefined
the nature of Mughal kingship in ways that departed from his
father's 'first-among-equals' style of governance. Acting within the
Timurid tradition, Babur had given his sons separate, semi-independent
regions to govern. But Humayun's long and painful experience with
his brothers set a precedent for how subsequent Mughals, having
attained the throne, would deal with their own brothers. Notwithstanding his mild temperament and his father's admonitions to
show kindness to his brothers, Humayun's actions marked a crucial
step in making succession to the Mughal throne a bloody fraternal
struggle.

Humayun's problems with his brothers also led him to embrace a
more centralized notion of royal authority, which was elaborately
enacted in courtly rituals derived from his fascination with astrology
and cosmology.[14] These rituals were set under a tent and on a carpet
bearing a geocentric model of the universe, with concentric circles
corresponding to the planets, the sun and the moon, each assigned a
distinctive colour, with different classes of courtiers seated within
spaces associated with particular planets. The tent above the carpet
resembled a round horoscope, with the twelve zodiac signs and stars

indicated by holes in the tent's inner cover. Since the carpet and tent could be easily folded and carried around, the scheme was ideally suited for a court that was itself mobile – a practice reflecting the Mughals' pastoral–nomadic origins. These rituals were carried over to Humayun's royal palace in Delhi's Purana Qila, which was said to have had seven rooms, each dedicated to a planet. Every day of the week, the king would hold court in the room corresponding to that day's planetary ruler, wearing robes in colours corresponding to that planet.[15]

Central to Humayun's courtly style was his identification with the sun, which was coloured gold on his courtly carpet and placed in the middle of the planetary spheres. He also greeted the rising sun every morning, showing his face to the public just as the sun showed itself to the king. The custom corresponded to a traditional Indian rite whereby a king would appear each morning for viewing by his subjects, seated icon-like in a small, raised pavilion called a *jharokha*, which projected from a royal palace's exterior walls. Whereas the entire rite would be carried over by Akbar, complete with the *jharokha*, we already perceive its antecedents in Humayun's daily ritual, suggesting an early stage in the progressive Indianization of the Mughals' political culture. This is also seen in the king's marriage to the daughter of an Indian Muslim landholder rather than to a Central Asian Timurid, and his encouraging his nobles to do the same. Finally, Humayun confirmed, rather than rescinded, key administrative initiatives undertaken by his bitter rival, Sher Shah. These included the Afghan king's trimetallic currency system based on a standardized silver *rupiya* and his division of the kingdom's administration into fixed territorial units, or *sarkar*s, subdivided in districts, or *pargana*s. From Sher Shah's administration on, revenue and judicial officers were posted at both *sarkar* and *pargana* levels, thereby ensuring an orderly system of land-revenue assessment and collection. Further, to centralize his administration, Humayun designated as much revenue-producing land as possible as *khalisa*, or land administered directly by the state, rather than by nobles.

In short, many of the ideological and institutional foundations of Mughal rule commonly associated with the reign of Akbar (r. 1556–1605) were already in place during Humayun's turbulent reign, or during the interregnum of Sher Shah and his successors. Tragically, however, notwithstanding the many travails suffered in regaining his kingdom, Humayun lived for only six months after restoring Mughal rule. In late January 1556, he accidently fell from the staircase of his library in the Purana Qila and died shortly thereafter. Once again, the Indo-Timurid project was thrown into turmoil.

## AKBAR'S EARLY YEARS

No succession struggle followed Humayun's death. At the time, Akbar was thirteen and already in the capital of Delhi, whereas his half-brother Mirza Hakim was a two-year old child and in distant Kabul. It was apparent, moreover, that Akbar was blessed with a gift for memory and remarkable intelligence, even though his tutors were unable to teach him to read or write, as he was apparently dyslexic. Fortuitously, the young heir was placed under the regency of Bairam Khan, whose competent generalship had facilitated Humayun's restoration of Mughal rule. On the other hand, his father's short tenure after the restoration had given him little opportunity to consolidate his rule, as a result of which the countryside in upper India still abounded with disaffected Afghans. In late 1556 Hemu, a Hindu general who had formerly served the dislodged Afghan regime, seized Delhi and set himself up as the city's 'liberator' and new sovereign. Bairam Khan met Hemu at the historic battlefield at Panipat, using the youthful Akbar to rally support for the Mughal cause. He also allowed his charge, barely fourteen years of age, his first taste of military combat, even letting him behead Hemu so that he could claim the title of *ghazi*.[16] Thanks to Bairam Khan's exertions so early in Akbar's reign, Hemu's uprising had been quashed, and the heartland of upper India had fallen securely under Mughal control. The last two prominent princes of Sher Shah's dynasty, Sikandar and Ibrahim, were soon defeated and driven away, while the stronghold of Gwalior, 100 kilometres south of Agra, was secured after a two-year siege.

In response, many Afghans simply packed up and moved further down the Ganges valley, settling in Bihar and Bengal. In order to put pressure on those elements, the Mughals decamped their court from

Delhi to Agra, Humayun's capital before his exile from India. It was here that Akbar, now in his late teens, began to find his voice as an independent ruler. In 1560 he managed to extract himself from Bairam Khan's control by suggesting that he do the pious thing and perform the pilgrimage to Mecca. It was an old ploy. The appeal to piety left the veteran counsellor and commander no choice but to leave India and Mughal service. But before the young king could fully assert himself, his former wet-nurse, Maham Anga, stepped into the vacuum as Akbar's de facto regent. This woman enjoyed immense prestige within the Mughal household, as her husband had played a critical role in rescuing Humayun in a humiliating debacle caused by Sher Shah. But she overplayed her hand by promoting her own son, the ambitions Adham Khan, who in 1562 recklessly assassinated the kingdom's leading minister of state. This so enraged the nineteen-year-old Akbar that, although the youth was his own foster-brother, he threw him over a palace balcony to his death. When a grief-stricken Maham Anga died shortly afterwards, Akbar ordered stately tombs to be built over both their graves – a politically astute move as the young king sought to assert his autonomy in a faction-ridden Mughal household. At the same time, he restored relations with the household of Bairam Khan, whom he had manoeuvred out of India altogether, by marrying one of the latter's widows. He also adopted into his household one of Bairam Khan's sons, a four-year-old child who would ultimately emerge as one of the most powerful nobles in Akbar's court: Khan-i Khanan. Akbar already understood that a successful sovereign had to build up a large household of loyal dependants who represented a broad cross-section of the realm's political and ethnic constituencies.

Yet the Mughals were still surrounded by enemies. Powerful Afghan chiefs held considerable territory from the central Ganges valley through Bihar to Bengal, and in Malwa. Rajput lineages dominated Rajasthan, while further south lay the rich and powerful state of Gujarat. For many disaffected parties uprooted by the return of Mughal power, the sultanate of Gujarat offered an attractive refuge and source of patronage. Among those parties were Uzbek Turks, Babur's old enemies who, as Sunni Muslims, resented the influence of Shi'i officers who had accompanied Humayun's return from Iran. In the mid 1560s disaffected Uzbeks rebelled in eastern India, rallying around Akbar's half-brother Mirza Hakim when he marched to Lahore from his base in Kabul. In response, Akbar first advanced to Lahore, driving Hakim back to Kabul. Then he routed the Uzbeks rebelling in the central Ganges valley. But exerting pressure in eastern India only drove more disaffected elements, especially Afghans and Uzbeks, into Gujarat. The conquest of this wealthy state thus became an early objective in Akbar's efforts to consolidate his rule over north India.

## EMERGING IDENTITIES: RAJPUTS

However, lying between upper India and Gujarat, and controlling the major trade routes passing between the two regions, was Rajasthan, the hilly, semi-arid tract home to powerful warrior lineages known since Akbar's day as Rajputs. Despite the occasional successful siege of one of its famous strongholds, neither the slave sultans nor the Khalajis, Tughluqs, Lodis or Surs had been able to subdue these chieftains, much less annex their territories. Nor had any of the sultans of Delhi enlisted into their service Rajasthan's major warrior lineages, who for centuries had remained Delhi's obdurate focs. The mutual enmity had continued with Babur's 1527 defeat of Rana Sanga at Khanua, a debacle still within living memory when Akbar rose to power. In view of this background, Akbar's signature policy of integrating these lineages into Mughal service was all the more dramatic. This bold break with the past had far-reaching consequences for both Mughals and Rajputs.

Akbar's Rajput policy, however, did not result from any grand, premeditated strategy. Rather, it began as a response to the internal politics of one of the Rajput lineages, the Kachwaha clan, based in the state of Amber in northern Rajasthan. In 1534 the clan's head, Puran Mal, died with no adult heir and was succeeded by his younger brother, Bharmal. Puran Mal, however, did have a son who by the early 1560s had come of age and challenged Bharmal's right to rule Amber. Feeling this pressure from within his own clan, Bharmal approached Akbar for material support, offering in exchange his daughter in marriage. The king agreed to the proposal. In 1562 the Kachwaha chieftain entered Mughal service, with Akbar assuring him of support in maintaining his position in the Kachwaha political order, while his family entered the royal household. Besides his daughter, Bharmal also sent his son Bhagwant Das and his grandson Man Singh (1550–1614) to the court in Agra. For several generations thereafter, the ruling clan continued to give its daughters to the Mughal court, thereby making the chiefs of these clans the uncles, cousins or even fathers-in-law of Mughal emperors. The intimate connection between the two courts had far-reaching results. Not only did Kachwaha rulers quickly rise in rank and stature in the Mughal court, but their position within their own clan was greatly enhanced by Akbar's confirmation of their political leadership. Akbar's support also enhanced the position of the Kachwahas as a whole – and hence Amber state – in the hierarchy of Rajasthan's other Rajput lineages.

Neighbouring clans soon realized the political wisdom of attaching themselves to the expanding Mughal state, a visibly rising star in north Indian politics. Around 1564 the Rathor raja of Merta, in western Rajasthan, submitted to Akbar and gave him his daughter in marriage. Mughal support now gave this lineage, a junior branch of the Rathors of Jodhpur, a political edge over local rivals. The same pattern continued across Rajasthan. In 1569 the Hada Rajputs surrendered the stronghold of Ranthambhor in order to gain Mughal backing for leverage vis-à-vis their own kinsmen in south-eastern Rajasthan. About the same time, the Baghela Rajputs of Bhatta surrendered the fort of Kalinjar to Akbar. The next year the Rathors of Bikaner submitted to Mughal power, as did the Bhatis of Jaisalmer. In 1583 Udai Singh of the Rathor clan of Jodhpur was recognized as the ruler of Marwar, in western Rajasthan, initiating that powerful house's collaboration with Mughals. Driving these arrangements, though, was not just the incentive of courtly patronage. The clans of Rajasthan well understood that refusal to engage with the Mughals would bring the stick of military confrontation. Alone among the Rajput clans, the Sisodiyas of Mewar in southern Rajasthan, north India's pre-eminent warrior lineage, obstinately refused to negotiate with the Mughals. In response, Akbar in 1568 led a four-month siege of the Sisodiyas' principal stronghold of Chittor, which ultimately fell to the Mughals, but only after a spectacular *jauhar* in which the fort's defenders, foreseeing their doom, killed their women and gallantly sallied forth to meet their deaths. In all, some 30,000 defenders of the fort were killed, although its ruler, Rana Pratap, managed to escape. For decades, he and the Sisodiya house would continue to resist Mughal domination, whereas nearly every other Rajput lineage had acknowledged Mughal overlordship.

Both sides gained from the partnership. For their part, Rajputs received high-ranking positions in Akbar's imperial service, which had the effect of transforming what had been parochial, regional clans into elite players empowered to operate on an all-India stage. To gain this new mobility and status, moreover, Rajputs did not have to sacrifice their autonomy within their native lands, as they were free to continue managing their own courts and internal affairs, a major concession. Moreover, whereas the land assignments, or *jagirs*, of other imperial officers were regularly rotated around the empire, Rajputs were allowed to continue administering their ancestral lands as 'native' (*watan*) *jagirs*. Mughal support also gave those clans that entered the imperial orbit considerable bargaining strength with local rivals, which is what had induced Bharmal to ally himself with Akbar. Finally, Rajputs were guaranteed religious freedom; there was no pressure on them to convert to Islam. In fact, a warrior ethos common to both the Mughals and the Rajputs superseded religious identities, enabling Muslims to be included as fellow Rajputs within the latter's scheme of socio-political hierarchy. As the historian Norman Ziegler notes, the category of 'Muslim' within a Rajput kin group did not include all Muslims, 'but only those who were warriors and who possessed sovereignty and power equal to or greater than the Hindu Rajput. The Muslim emperor in particular held a position of high rank and esteem, and the traditions often equate him with Ram, the pre-eminent Ksatriya cultural hero of the Hindu Rajput.'[17] In this way, both Muslims and the Mughal imperium could be conceptually assimilated into the Rajput world.

For their part, the Mughals received regular tribute payments from Rajput houses, in addition to the right to circulate their own coinage in Rajput domains, to regulate succession to Rajput houses, to incorporate Rajput princesses in the Mughal harem, and to enjoy safe passage for merchants and pilgrims passing through Rajasthan to Gujarat. Akbar's inclusion of Rajput warriors in the Mughal army also served a political purpose. Just as Rajput chiefs such as Bharmal saw Mughal allies as a counterweight to the influence of their own kinsmen, Akbar regarded his Rajput allies as counterweights to Uzbek Turks, a potentially unruly faction in his service that he had inherited from his father. Moreover, from the Mughal perspective, the alliance had pacified Rajasthan after centuries of turbulence, rendering it no longer a breeding ground for revolt, as it had been under the Delhi sultans. The alliance's ultimate consequence, however, was to fuse Rajput and Mughal cultures and, more generally, the Sanskritic and Persianate worlds, which would be reflected in north Indian architectural and artistic traditions of the seventeenth and eighteenth centuries.

In these high-stakes political negotiations, the direction in which women were moved from household to household defined asymmetric power relations between Akbar's court and Rajput lineages, and also between Rajput clans themselves. Just as higher-ranking Rajput clans received women from the households of minor clans, the incorporation of Rajput women into the imperial harem defined the Mughals as overlords of consenting Rajput houses. Only the Sisodiya clan of Mewar in southern Rajasthan, proudly claiming pre-eminence among Rajput clans, refused to send its women to the Mughal harem, resulting in the siege and mass suicide at Chittor. Because Akbar saw the incorporation of women of prominent royal houses into the Mughal household as a tool of empire-building, the size of his harem grew with that of the empire – contemporary estimates of the number of his wives range from 300 to 5,000.[18] This had the effect of swelling the Mughal court into a huge, multi-ethnic and women-centred world, with the Rajput element in the imperial harem steadily gaining in influence relative to that of other ethnicities.

To be sure, the Rajputs and the Mughals did not view these political arrangements in exactly the same way. Consider the surrender of the fort of Ranthambhor by the Hada Rajput chieftain, Surjan, in 1569. A miniature painting in the *Akbar-nama*, the official chronicle of the emperor's reign, shows Surjan submissively bowing down to a seated Akbar, guided by a court servant [see Fig. 11]. In the accompanying text the chronicle's author, Abu'l-fazl, boasts of how easily the fort had fallen, comparing Akbar's feat with that of 'Ala al-Din Khalaji, who had captured it in 1301. By contrast, a nearly contemporary Sanskrit biography of Surjan portrays Akbar as having been so pleased with Surjan's courageous conduct that he offered him three territories in return for this single fort, suggesting that the siege's outcome had actually been a victory for the Rajput chieftain. This text, the *Surjanacarita*, also has a different take on Surjan's subsequent employment with the Mughals. Like other Rajputs who capitulated to Mughal overlordship, he went on to have a successful, prestigious career. After serving as a Mughal governor of Garha in central India, he was given charge of Chunar fort by the Ganges near Benares. He also took part in Akbar's last campaign against the emperor's half-brother, Mirza Hakim, and died holding a high rank in Mughal service. Yet the *Surjanacarita* ignores all this, emphasizing instead the chieftain's piety and his pilgrimages to important Hindu sites, as though he had transcended his earlier, merely military service for something more worthy.[19]

Other Rajput houses resolved these asymmetrical relationships by imagining that they, not the Mughals, were the dominant player. As the grandson of Bharmal Kachwaha, Man Singh grew up steeped in the tradition of his clan's service to the Mughals, entering imperial service in 1572 at just twelve years of age. His career shows how imperial service could expand the political horizons of an otherwise provincial lineage absorbed in inter-clan struggles within Rajasthan. Man Singh led campaigns against Rajput houses that remained outside the Mughal fold, notably the obdurate Sisodiyas and their chieftain Rana Pratap in the Battle of Haldighati (1576). He also fought Afghans in Kabul, led a Mughal army in its capture of the stronghold of Rohtas in Bihar, and another army against Afghan chiefs in Orissa. Through it all, he smoothly navigated between two political and cultural worlds. A eulogistic biography, the *Manacharit Raso* by Narottam Kavi (*c.*1600), celebrated his military career under Akbar, proudly listing the many Turkish groups that served under his command, even attributing the empire's territorial expansion to Man Singh himself, and not to Akbar![20] Similarly, the Persian section of a bilingual inscription gives Akbar fulsome praise, while Man Singh is mentioned as merely having built 'a strong building'. In the inscription's Sanskrit section, by contrast, Man Singh is given exalted titles, including 'king of kings', while Akbar is not mentioned at all.[21]

The pattern of Mughal–Rajput mutual accommodation is also seen in Man Singh's religious patronage. As one of the most popular *avatar*s of Vishnu, Krishna had been an important object of devotional traditions in Bengal, owing especially to the exertions of the charismatic Bengali saint and ecstatic mystic Chaitanya (d. 1533). Already in the 1530s itinerant religious mendicants from Bengal had established places of Krishna worship in Braj, a region located along the Jamuna valley in the western part of modern Uttar Pradesh, closely identified with the life of Krishna. After inheriting the leadership of the Kachwaha lineage upon the death of his father, to whom Akbar had granted land in Braj, Man Singh patronized the construction of a major monument in this region, the Govinda Deva Temple in Vrindavan.[22] Dedicated to Krishna and completed in 1590, this was the largest Hindu structure built in north India since the thirteenth century. Its long barrel vault, dome, squinches, cross-vaulting and intersecting arcuated corridors not only employ distinctly Persian architectural features, but create a sense of open space not previously seen in Mughal architecture [see Fig. 12].[23] While demonstrating Man Singh's participation in the Persianate world and the Mughal imperium, the Govinda Deva Temple also points to Akbar's desire to associate the empire with Vaishnava Hinduism, as the sultanates of Kashmir, Bengal and Gujarat had earlier done (see Chapter Three).[24] At the same time, by patronizing the construction of this temple, Man Singh was acting like a traditional Hindu king, even though he had no administrative or juridical authority in Vrindavan, since both taxation and justice were handled by local Mughal officials.[25]

Man Singh behaved similarly in his manner of conquering territories and communicating those conquests to his home constituents. In 1594 Akbar appointed him governor of Bengal, where he was charged with subduing Afghan and native chiefs. One of these, Kedar Rai, was the Hindu chief of Bhushana in the eastern delta, whose tutelary deity was the goddess Shila Mata. Upon defeating this chief in 1596, Man Singh seized the deity's image and later installed it inside his own kingdom's Amber fort. No break in ritual had occurred, since the Brahmin priests who had officiated at the temple in Bengal were brought to Rajasthan to continue performing these duties. But politically, Kedar Rai was left with neither sovereign domain nor protective goddess, whereas Man Singh had practically replaced Kedar Rai as the deity's new sovereign patron.[26]

If the character of the Mughal state had been transformed by Akbar's Rajput policy, the meaning of 'Rajput' was also consolidated at this time. Lineages in Rajasthan that had traditionally identified themselves as *kshatriya* (warriors) began calling themselves Rajputs only in the sixteenth century.[27] Although few written accounts of the Rajput past survive from the period before Akbar's reign, from the mid sixteenth century on, just when Akbar was engaging intensely with Rajasthan's warrior lineages, a number of such narratives appeared in Sanskrit and in dialects of early Hindavi. Since the Mughals had brought from the Persianate world a keen sense of genealogy and the purity of blood as a mark of one's cultural identity, a clan's partnership with Akbar intensified a preoccupation with its own genealogy and purity of descent.[28] But Rajputs were not just responding to the Mughals' tradition of history-writing or genealogy-keeping. There were also practical considerations. Since only the Mughals could confirm legitimate succession to Rajput kingship, those clans needed detailed genealogies stating their origins and their exact lines of descent. Rajput rulers therefore patronized poets, bards and genealogists who compiled geneaologies and poems celebrating the heroic deeds of a clan's collective past. This had the effect not only of sharpening the boundaries between Rajput clans, but also – because there were fierce struggles with other peoples in the region – of shaping the identity of Rajputs as against non-Rajputs. Rajput lineages now closed ranks into sharply defined social units.[29]

Moreover, at this time the ideology of martyrdom, sacrifice and honour – an ethos present in north-west India since at least the thirteenth century – became securely associated with 'Rajput'. This indicated a final stage in the term's evolution from at least the eleventh century, when it simply referred to a military position open to persons of any caste or religion. Catalysing this later understanding was an early Hindavi text dating to the 1590s, the *Prithviraj Raso*.

This widely read work celebrated the career of the Chauhan king Prithviraj III, whose army famously engaged that of Muhammad Ghuri at the Battle of Tarain in 1192. The *Raso* transformed the actual loser of that battle, Prithviraj, into a larger-than-life hero. More importantly, it anachronistically identified each of Prithviraj's subordinate officers as ancestors of the leading Rajput clans of Akbar's day, while also characterizing those officers as embodying the essence of chivalry, courage and martial prowess. In this way, the text effectively collapsed three distinct time periods into one: the ancient epic past of the *Mahabharata*, with its *kshatriya* heroes; the late twelfth century, when Prithviraj fought Muhammad Ghuri; and the late-sixteenth-century world of the Mughal court, with which Rajput lineages were then closely engaged. Precisely because it encompassed such a large number of warrior lineages and offered them a shared history, the *Raso* contributed to the consolidation of an aristocratic Rajput identity, beginning in the late sixteenth century.[30]

## MUGHAL EXPANSION UNDER AKBAR

While enrolling Rajput warriors into his service, Akbar and his advisers refined and elaborated the decimal military organization they had inherited from Delhi sultanate, Timurid and Mongol traditions. By 1574 a rationalized system had emerged in which all state servants were classified into fixed ranks pegged to specified salaries and duties, and in most cases to specified assignments of land, or *jagirs*, from whose revenues they were expected to recruit, train and support specified numbers of mounted cavalry. This was new. Whereas appointments and pay under previous regimes had been rather ad hoc, officers were now assigned a numerical rank, or *mansab*, which could rise or fall according to assessments of the performance of the rank-holder, or *mansabdar*. The number associated with each rank originally ranged anywhere from ten to 10,000, indicating how many soldiers a given *mansabdar* was expected to maintain. Soon, however, ranks were expressed in two numbers: the first, *zat*, was the *mansabdar*'s personal salary; and the second, *sawar*, the number of cavalrymen that the *mansabdar* was expected to recruit, train, pay and command. The system therefore required matching a *mansabdar*'s rank with a *jagir* sufficient in size to support his required level of troops. *Jagirs* were also uninheritable and temporary, as both *mansabdars* and their land assignments were regularly rotated through the realm every few years.

By maintaining a corps of state servants who were dependent upon and personally loyal to the regime, and by keeping tight control over those servants' powers and responsibilities, Akbar sought to prevent any one ethnic faction of his nobility from becoming dominant. Afghans, only recently dislodged from power in upper India, were suspect among available fighting groups. So were the Uzbeks, who had driven Babur from Central Asia and had rebelled against Mughal authority early in Abkar's reign. Even many in his own Timurid lineage had rallied around his younger half-brother Mirza Hakim in Kabul. To counteract these politically destabilizing trends, Akbar wanted his nobles to transcend their particular ethnic identities and to consider themselves as loyal servants of the state. This involved transforming the warrior–aristocratic values of his many retainers, regardless of their ethnic or cultural origins, and redirecting their ideas of honour from personal, lineage or sectarian pride to a more impersonal, imperial pride. The numerically based *mansab* system was intended to do precisely this, since a *mansabdar*'s promotion or demotion was in principle based solely on his accomplishments or failures in the imperial service, not on his genealogy or ethnic identity. The effects of such promotions or demotions, moreover, were publicly displayed according to where one stood in the court's assembly halls, since highly ranked *mansabdars* were positioned closer to the seated emperor, while lower-ranked officials stood at a greater distance.[31] From Akbar's time on, therefore, we see a certain tension between the ideal of ethnic or lineage pride, extolled in both Persianate and Rajput discourses, and the ideal of a rank-based meritocracy, which was the essense of the *mansabdari* system.

Further serving to create a cohesive and socially inclusive service corps, the court circulated among its *mansabdars* a common core of Persian works on ethics and morality. Imperial servants were urged to read, most importantly, the *Akhlaq-i Nasiri* by the Khurasani political theorist Nasir al-Din Tusi (d. 1274), but also the theology of al-Ghazali (d. 1111), the Sufi poetry of Rumi (d. 1273), and the *Kalila wa Dimna*, the immensely popular collection of practical wisdom in the accessible form of animal fables. The point of promoting these classics from the Persian literary canon was to construct a model of masculine virtue that could transcend law, caste and religion, thereby providing a moral framework that was independent of the court's Sunni Muslim clerical establishment.[32] The circulation of these texts among Akbar's multicultural nobility also helped assimilate the ruling elite into the Persianate world.

In the 1560s and 1570s, while consolidating his nobility politically and ideologically, Akbar led or sent armies in all directions on an astonishing string of conquests and annexations across northern India. To the south, he twice sent armies into Malwa. When an invasion launched in 1561 proved inconclusive, a second invasion the following year resulted in that region's annexation to the nascent empire. In 1564 his forces invaded and annexed the kingdom of Gondwana, a hilly and heavily forested tract to the east of Malwa that was home to herds of wild elephants. This gave Akbar access to plentiful supplies of war-elephants, whose use in his armies reflect the Mughals' growing reliance on classical Indian military traditions. The 1560s also saw the pacification of Rajasthan, where the emperor's carrot-and-stick Rajput policy served the geostrategic aim of connecting the still-unconquered maritime world of Gujarat with the agrarian-rich Mughal heartland in upper India. With the important forts of Chittor and Ranthambhor in Mughal hands by 1568, and with most of the rest of Rajasthan under indirect control, Akbar turned his attention to the sultanate of Gujarat.

As a first step towards realizing this objective, in 1571 Akbar moved his capital westwards from Agra to the town of Sikri, the residence of a venerable Chishti Sufi, Shaikh Salim, whose prayers entreating divine intervention were believed to have facilitated the birth of Akbar's first son, named Salim in his honour. From Sikri, the emperor then planned his operations in Gujarat. In 1572 he occupied the regional capital of Ahmedabad, legally annexed the province and returned to his new capital, which he renamed Fatehpur Sikri in commemoration of his victorious Gujarat campaign (Fatehpur means 'city of victory'). But the following year, when a combination of Afghans,

Rajputs and Turks in Gujarat resisted the new arrangement, Akbar raced back to Ahmedabad in an astonishing eleven-day blitz over a distance that normally took caravans several months to traverse, and reconquered the province. Yet the Mughals' grip on it remained shaky. Although Muzzafar II, the last Gujarat sultan, had been imprisoned in Agra, ten years later he managed to escape and mobilize sufficient support to regain his throne. Only in 1584 did the Mughals finally sweep him away and achieve full authority in Gujarat.

Meanwhile, Akbar had turned his attention towards the equally rich province of Bengal. Ever since Babur's day numerous Afghan migrants had fled upper India and put down roots in Bengali society. The Bengal sultan Nasir al-Din Nusrat Shah had actively encouraged the build-up of Afghans in Bihar with a view to creating a buffer zone between himself and the new Mughal state. Even more Afghans poured into the delta region during Humayun's reign, and in 1564 their leader Taj Khan Karrani (r. 1564–5) launched an Indo-Afghan dynasty there. Keenly aware of Akbar's successes in Rajasthan and Gujarat, Taj Khan's successor Sultan Sulaiman Karrani (r. 1565–72) prudently adopted a posture of outward submission to the Mughals, even arranging that Akbar's name be included on his coins and in the sermons of his mosques. But when Sulaiman died in late 1572, his son and successor Daud made no pretence of loyalty to the Mughals, striking coins and having the Friday sermon read in his own name. In response, in 1574 Akbar led a large army down the Ganges valley, routing Afghan defenders at Patna. From there one of his generals, Mun'im Khan, led an army of 20,000 to the Afghans' capital of Tanda, which he easily seized and declared 'liberated'. But while Mun'im Khan was reorganizing the region's revenue administration, assisted by his renowned revenue officer Todar Mal, the Afghans melted into Bengal's heavily forested eastern sector and merged with local society, patronizing Bengali language, architecture and literature.[33] It took the Mughals another thirty-six years to root out Indo-Afghan resistance and establish lasting authority there.

Hindering the advance of Mughal authority in Bengal was the disaffection of many officers regarding new regulations that Akbar had instituted. In 1574, aiming to prevent officials from receiving pay for cavalry they were not maintaining, he ordered all *mansabdars* to brand and present for imperial review the precise number of horses they were required to have according to their numerical rank. He also centralized the empire's fiscal administration by converting imperial territories into crown lands.[34] Such measures naturally provoked resentment among the nobles, and in 1579 rebellious officers plundered the fortress at Tanda, executed the Mughal governor and set up a 'revolutionary government' among themselves. For several years, imperial authority in Bengal utterly vanished. Although the regime soon restored order in western Bengal, from 1583 the vast eastern hinterland was dominated by a coalition of twelve chieftains (*bara bhuyan*) that the Mughals would spend the next decade pursuing. It was ultimately Raja Man Singh – chief of the Rajput Kachwaha lineage – who in 1602 planted Mughal authority in the heart of the eastern delta by establishing Dhaka, hitherto a remote outpost, as his military headquarters. From this point on, the momentum towards the delta's complete annexation was irreversible.

Contributing to Bengal's rebellion of 1579–82 was the political emergence of Mirza Hakim, Akbar's half-brother and independent ruler of Kabul. Officers in Bengal, resentful of the emperor's new regulations, had rallied around Akbar's younger brother, and in response the prince, emboldened by this unexpected show of support, marched down to Lahore. Akbar, instead of dealing personally with the Bengal rebellion, in 1581 moved his whole army north to confront his half-brother. One reason for this response was the need to regain control of the vital trade routes leading from Kabul to Delhi and Agra. When Mirza Hakim retreated beyond the Khyber Pass, Akbar pursued him all the way to Kabul. Then, when his sibling fled with his troops to a nearby mountain, the emperor entered the city unopposed and for seven days occupied the throne of his grandfather and father in its ancient citadel. Rather than pursue his treasonous brother any further, a confident Akbar declared his sister Bakht al-Nissa Begum the legal governor of Kabul, in this way asserting de facto sovereignty over the strategic province. When Mirza Hakim died several years later, the emperor simply handed over the region's administration to some Rajput officers. Like Gujarat and Bengal, Kabul had been annexed.

Akbar's brush with Mirza Hakim highlighted the empire's

vulnerability from the north-west. Though unreliable and unpredictable, the emperor's half-brother had at least provided a buffer between the Uzbeks and the Mughal heartland. But with him gone, Akbar needed to keep a closer watch on the turbulent north-west and the ever-dangerous Uzbeks – once his grandfather's nemesis, and now his own. So in 1586 he moved his capital for a third time, abandoning Fatehpur Sikri for the historic city of Lahore. Meanwhile, Raja Man Singh was sent to Kabul as governor, and in 1588 the emperor himself made a second trip there. The next year he sent his minister Raja Birbal on a failed mission to suppress the Roshaniyya, a millenarian movement then raging among frontier Afghans of the Yusufzai lineage. In an attempt to subdue the uprising, the Mughals launched still more expeditionary forces from both Kabul and Lahore. They also built and garrisoned forts throughout the frontier region with a view to stabilizing imperial authority there. Further north, in 1585 Akbar sent an army into the valley of Kashmir, whose Shi'i king was defeated the following year. Three years later Akbar made a state visit to the valley's capital of Srinagar, formalizing Kashmir's annexation to the empire. Finally, the emperor turned his attention southwards towards Sind, the land of his birth, which was then governed by Mirza Jani Beg Tarkhan, an independent Timurid prince. In 1586 the Mughal governor of Multan invaded the region without success, but another assault in 1590 succeeded. Several years later the mirza formally submitted to Akbar in Lahore and was made imperial *mansabdar* of Thatta, the capital of Sind. In short, the Lahore phase of Akbar's reign, spanning the period from 1586 to 1598, witnessed a significant projection of Mughal power throughout the Indus valley and far into the mountainous zones to the north and north-west. By the end of the century the empire had embraced the entire Indo-Gangetic plain plus Kashmir and eastern Afghanistan.

How can one explain this extraordinary series of victories and annexations? New military technologies and tactics that the Mughals brought to India certainly played a role. Following Central Asian tradition, Akbar's armies, like those of Babur and Humayun, were built around mounted archers.[35] Numbering 12,000 when he came to power, by 1581 his cavalry had swollen to 50,000. Whereas many of these men had been recruited from beyond the Khyber Pass, the Rajput share of ordinary troopers in Mughal service steadily increased. Some Turkish and Iranian nobles commanded units composed mainly of Rajputs and, by the end of Akbar's reign, Kachwaha *mansabdar*s alone commanded more than 26,000 ordinary cavalrymen in Mughal service.[36] Enlisting India's finest cavalries surely played a part in Akbar's military successes. Also important was his use of firearms technology and tactics, such as placing field cannon between carts tied together to prevent opposing cavalry from breaking through Mughal lines. Though always secondary to cavalry, war-elephants were also incorporated into his armies. In pitched battles, Mughal forces were deployed in multiple divisions. Mounted archers would open a battle by probing and provoking the enemy, followed by a strategic retreat aimed at drawing the enemy to charge the Mughal centre. Supported by artillery, war-elephants and infantry, the centre would face the enemy directly while the right and left wings of mounted archers swiftly outflanked and surrounded their opponents.

Rather than mounting pitched battles, however, the Mughals often deployed the more subtle tactic of sowing and exploiting internal dissensions within enemy camps.[37] In his 1574 campaign in Bengal, the veteran general Mun'im Khan became bogged down for months in unfamiliar jungle terrain, while his 20,000 troops came close to desertion from lack of interest in fighting so far from upper India. In these circumstances, the commander's colleague Todar Mal recommended that 'the method to restrain the faction was to send money by one who was loyal and smooth-tongued'. By such tactics, wrote Akbar's chronicler Abu'l-fazl, 'the dust of disturbance [*fitna*] was laid', later noting with satisfaction that the chosen approach had 'quieted the slaves to gold'.[38] With a large part of the Bengal sultan's forces thus bribed over to Mughal service, the Bengal army had been hollowed out from within. Such transfers of manpower were enabled by India's military labour market, which operated not on the basis of ethnic or political loyalties, primordial or otherwise, but on cash and the highest bidder. Because Akbar had greater access to financial resources than the sultan of Bengal, the scales necessarily tipped to the Mughals' advantage.

Once an adversary's army was prepared to surrender, Akbar conformed to the classical Indian practice of not annihilating his adversary but of honourably including him in the imperial orbit. Accordingly, when Sultan Daud Khan Karrani of Bengal realized the futility of continued opposition, he appeared before Mun'im Khan in April 1575 and partook of a formal 'banquet of reconciliation', as Abu'l-fazl called it. Displaying warm affection, the Mughal general advanced to the edge of a carpet laid out in a ceremonial tent specially arranged for the occasion. There he greeted the defeated king. Daud ungirded his sword and set it aside. Mun'im Khan then presented the Afghan with a Mughal sword, an embroidered belt and a cloak. Whether or not Akbar had actually worn the cloak, by donning it Daud Khan had become symbolically incorporated into the body of the emperor, a political rite the Bengali ruler would have well understood since his predecessors on the Bengal throne had followed the same practice.[39] Adorned with Mughal regalia, Daud then turned in the direction of Akbar's capital in Fatehpur Sikri and solemnly prostrated himself.[40]

A more interesting question is how the common people of defeated states accepted imperial rule. Well before the advent of the Mughal age, Indian bards, poets and chroniclers had prepared the ideological ground for the acceptance of an imperial overlord such as Akbar. In the fourteenth century, Indians referred to the Tughluq sultans using variations of the Sanskrit *sarvabhauma*, or 'universal ruler'.[41] From about the same time a hybridized Persianate and Indic notion of universal kingship became widely known and accepted among the masses, as political and proto-historical works that included warrior tales and retellings of epic stories began to appear in vernacular languages.[42] In the early fifteenth century the poet Vidyapati, writing in an early vernacular tongue of eastern India, compared the court of Sultan Ibrahim Sharqi (r. 1401–40) in Jaunpur with heaven, imagining his court as existing above the whole universe, and the king (Persian: *padshah*) as supreme, with none but God (Sanskrit: *karatara*) above him.[43] Vidyapati further wrote of chieftains (*rajaputa*) from such diverse and far-flung regions as Andhra, Bengal, Orissa and even the Tamil south all coming to Jaunpur and submitting to the overlord, Sultan Ibrahim, in their own languages. The poet here articulated in vernacular speech the essence of universal empire, an idea into which Akbar would insert himself more than a century later.

In addition to the formal submission by defeated rulers and the general population's acceptance of the ideology of overlordship, the expansion of Mughal power entailed political negotiations and compromises at the local, grass-roots level. [44] Across all India, Akbar's success lay not so much in his superior use of military force as in how his officers co-opted political agents, intervened and mediated in local conflicts, and generated credit among conquered populations. Even as major political actors such as Todar Mal or Mun'im Khan were cutting deals at the level of high politics, low-ranking imperial servants on the leading edge of the empire's expanding frontier deepened the roots of Mughal authority by sharing the perquisites of sovereignty with local power holders. In Gujarat, for example, while appointing their own local judges (*qazi*), police commissioners (*kotwal*) and revenue functionaries (*mutassadi*), the Mughals also recruited petty officers from among the existing service gentry of scribal Brahmins. Proficient in both Persian and Gujarati, these Brahmins kept records of goods and merchants coming to the customs houses in bilingual registers. By helping the Mughals realize taxes and by advancing loans to Mughal officials, local merchants – together with the scribal Brahmins – implicitly co-shared Mughal authority with the imperial court.[45]

Indeed, soon after Akbar's conquest of Gujarat, the Mughals began to grant revenue-collection rights to local parties, especially local gentry and merchants, including them in the imperial system by giving them emblems, honours and insignia such as elephants, horses, royal robes and turbans.[46] Both ritually and practically, then, local actors became empowered. But such empowerment created a certain paradox, since each new perquisite granted to some local notable meant that one more tiny chip of imperial sovereignty had been effectively transferred from the centre to the periphery.[47] This fact must inform our understanding of the growth of Mughal power. The Mughal empire was not a Leviathan state, and its extraordinary expansion in Akbar's reign was anything but the relentless advance of a mighty juggernaut that simply rolled over and crushed its opponents. Although the Mughals propagated such a notion in their official chronicles, their courtly ceremonies and their imposing architecture, power was in reality distributed across the entire social body, becoming progressively more diffused as the state incorporated ever more territory.

## AKBAR'S RELIGIOUS IDEAS

Akbar's views and policies regarding institutional religions evolved throughout his lifetime, swinging from one position to another in ways that puzzled or shocked contemporary observers. Both in his own day and in modern times he has been called everything from a strict Muslim to an apostate, from a free-thinker to a crypto-Hindu, from a Zoroastrian to a proto-Christian, from an atheist to a radical innovator, even a prophet. Each of these assessments contains a degree of truth, depending on which phase of his long forty-nine-year reign one considers. But through it all, the one constant was the emperor's unquenchable curiosity regarding all things religious. This was abetted by his awareness that the turn of the first Islamic millennium, 1000 AH (AD 1591), would occur in the thirty-fifth year of his reign. Because that year also saw the height of his political successes and the maturity of his courtly style, some of his courtiers viewed Akbar as a millennial figure – as did the emperor himself for a while.

As a youth, Akbar had received a sound religious training by both Shi'i and Sunni tutors, but as an adult he looked back with regret on his life before the age of twenty-one, confessing that in those days he had 'persecuted men into conformity with my faith and deemed it Islam'.[48] But after his twenty-first year he experienced what he called an internal bitterness, acknowledging that his soul had been 'seized with exceeding sorrow'.[49] Thus began a rocky spiritual ride. This was also when he began marrying the daughters of Rajput chiefs and placing those women on a social par with other women of the court, contributing to the growing diffusion of Rajput values in Mughal culture. Changes in official policies regarding non-Muslims soon followed. In 1563, also when aged twenty-one, he abolished pilgrimage taxes on non-Muslim institutions. The next year he abolished the *jizya* tax on non-Muslims, a measure to which earlier Muslim rulers had paid lip service but seldom enforced. The effect was to treat all Mughal subjects, regardless of religion, on a basis of legal equality before the state. He also banned the killing of cows and peacocks. In 1565 he went further by actively supporting Hindu institutions, establishing a grant that maintained the Govinda Deva Temple at

Vrindavan.[50] On the other hand, his bloody conquest of the Rajput fort of Chittor in 1568 was immediately followed by a 'victory declaration' (*fath-nama*) in which the emperor, flushed with victory, boasted of engaging in *jihad*, of occupying a fort belonging to infidels, and of 'establishing Islam' there.[51]

However, just a few years later, around 1571, Akbar fell under the influence of the Spanish-Arab mystic Ibn al-'Arabi, whose pantheistic doctrines seem to have led him to reject the narrow, scripturalist understandings of Islam as promoted by his own state-supported clerics. His commitment to the more liberal-minded Chishti school of Sufism also deepened. Ever since 1562 he made annual pilgrimages to the shrine of the founder of the Chishti Sufi tradition in India, Shaikh Mu'in al-Din Chishti (d. 1236), located in Ajmer, 350 kilometres west of Fatehpur Sikri. Some of those visits he made by foot across the scorching sands of Rajasthan. By 1577 he was practising arduous physical austerities unique to the Chishti order. It was at about this time, too, that he established in his court a so-called 'House of Worship' (*'ibadat-khana*), in which he presided over formal debates between Muslims, Brahmins, Jains, Zoroastrians and Christians. Lasting late into the night, these soirées often saw Jesuit Fathers pose knotty theological questions to Muslim clerics, with the emperor apparently enjoying the spectacle of those clerics being discomfited.

These inter-faith debates led Akbar to conclude, however, that all religions were either equally true or equally false, a position that provoked condemnation among Muslim clerics and dismay among the delegation of Jesuit Fathers at his court, who had been hoping for his conversion.[52] Matters came to a head in May 1578 when, in the midst of a hunting expedition in the Punjab, the emperor suddenly fell unconscious, which his friend and adviser Abu'l-fazl attributed to some spiritual experience. Upon recovery, he halted the hunt and freed the animals that had been caught by the beaters. At about the same time he adopted a vegetarian diet and shortened his hair in the manner of religious ascetics.[53] But then, about a month after the hunting incident, informed that his ancestor Timur had occasionally read the Friday sermon in the Samarqand mosque, Akbar mounted the pulpit of Fatehpur Sikri's royal mosque and began to do the same. In the midst of the sermon, however, he suddenly broke into a fit of stammering and trembling. Unable to continue, he stepped down and handed over the duties to a cleric.[54]

The problem evidently shadowing Akbar in those tumultuous months was how to reconcile imperial and religious authority, and perhaps, ultimately, how best to articulate his own sovereign identity. Several issues were now forcing a break with Sunni opinion. One of these was his multiple marriages, for which his Muslim jurists believed there was no legal basis. A particularly bitter controversy arose when one of his judges ordered the execution of a Brahmin who had allegedly cursed the Prophet of Islam. Akbar was infuriated when he heard of this, especially when advised that Muslim rulers were legally obliged to protect their non-Muslim subjects, even if they committed the act of which the Brahmin was accused. In response, the emperor exiled the judge to Mecca. In August 1579 he went further by issuing an order proclaiming his own ultimate authority in interpreting all matters pertaining to Islam, adopting for himself such grandiose titles as 'commander of the faithful', 'shadow of God' and 'king of Islam'.[55] Later that year, he even considered substituting his own name for that of the Prophet Muhammad in the Islamic credo, but he abandoned the idea when it caused commotion.[56] For many of his Muslim subjects this was simply too much. In 1580, with rumours of Akbar's religious excesses circulating throughout the realm, one disgruntled cleric urged the emperor's half-brother Mirza Hakim in Kabul to seize the throne, which triggered the emperor's long and eventful expedition to the north-west frontier.

During that march to Afghanistan, launched in early 1581, Akbar's religious thinking made another sharp turn. When his army reached Peshawar, at the base of the Khyber Pass, he assured the son of Shaikh Bayazid, founder of the militant illuminationist Roshaniyya cult in eastern Afghanistan, that he was perfectly free to practise his religion. Learning of this, Father Monserrate, a member of the first Jesuit mission to Akbar's court who was accompanying the expedition, remarked that 'the King cared little that in allowing everyone to follow his religion he was in reality violating all'.[57] Yet Akbar was still seen publicly offering prayers in a mosque in the Khyber Pass, and he still maintained his white tent where he supposedly performed his prayers in private. But on the return trip, after having driven his brother out of

Kabul and reasserted his authority there, the white tent was nowhere to be seen, an absence the emperor pretended not to notice.[58] This was also when he confided to Father Monserrate that he was not a Muslim, adding that he would allow his sons to follow whatever religion they might choose.[59] The timing of this notable confession suggests that, with his brother eliminated as a potential focus of Islamic revolt, the emperor felt free to follow his own religious instincts. Moreover, it was clear to him by now that his earlier claims to Islamic leadership had proved fruitless: to pious Muslims they were deeply offensive, while to his non-Muslim subjects they were meaningless.

All this was happening while powerful millennial currents regarding an anticipated End of the World and Day of Judgment were roiling in Christian and Muslim societies.[60] People in both faith traditions had been looking expectantly for signs of the apocalypse, or even claiming to be personally heralding a new age of justice that would follow the present age of injustice and chaos. In 1501, nearly a decade after millennial expectations had helped drive Christopher Columbus on his famous voyage westwards from Spain, Shah Isma'il had launched Iran's Safavid dynasty, claiming to be a messiah figure and identifying himself variously with Alexander, 'Ali and even God. His Turkoman tribal followers, members of a rustic Sufi tradition of which Isma'il was leader, believed him to be invincible, even immortal. Such potent beliefs propelled him and his ardent followers to embark on a vast campaign of 'world conquest' that would include the entire Iranian plateau, eastern Anatolia, Iraq, western Afghanistan and much of Central Asia.

Instead of first proclaiming himself a millennial sovereign and then embarking on a programme of territorial conquest, as Shah Isma'il had done, Akbar projected himself as a saintly and messianic figure only after having conquered much of northern India. Apocalyptic ideas were clearly on his mind when he marched to Kabul to confront Mirza Hakim. In conversations with Father Monserrate during that march he made detailed inquiries about the Last Judgment, whether Christ would be the Judge, when it would occur, and what sort of signs would precede that day. Monserrate replied that such signs would include wars and rebellions, and that 'these things we see happening very frequently in our time'.[61] Upon returning to his capital,

Akbar once again overhauled his sovereign identity, combining a saintly and a messianic persona in ways that recall what Iran's Shah Isma'il had done earlier in the century. According to his courtier and private critic Badauni, the emperor believed that Islam would last only 1,000 years – until 1000 AH, corresponding to AD 1591 – at which point he would be free to abjure the religion altogether. His chronicler Abu'l-fazl, on the other hand, asserted that Akbar had been born to inaugurate the second Islamic millennium,[62] a claim the emperor evidently acted upon ten years before its arrival. In 1582, or 990 AH, he decreed that for the next ten years all coins of the realm would bear the same date, 1000 AH.[63] In 1585 he ordered the minting of coins bearing only the words *Allahu akbar jalla jalaluhu*, or 'God is great, splendid is His Glory' – an ambiguous legend that could also be read as 'Akbar is God', with the word for glory also matching part of the emperor's given name, Jalal.[64] But in 1591, when the Islamic millennium actually did arrive, his coins ceased referring to the millennium altogether and began using instead a solar calendar based on the date of his accession.

His ten-year flirtation with millennial sovereignty having passed, Akbar now reverted to his predominant identity as a sacred king. In the early 1580s he had propounded a religious concoction, dubbed the Din-i Ilahi, or 'divine faith', which the Jesuits at his court judged an eclectic brew drawn from all existing systems. At its core was the emperor's self-fashioning as the spiritual guide for his subjects. Despite what his Muslim adversaries or Jesuit interlocutors might have thought, Akbar's principal ideologue, Abu'l-fazl, implied that his patron did not oppose Islam or any other religion, but rather that, as the most sacred sovereign on earth, he was simply above all religions.[65] He had fashioned himself not as a *Muslim* ruler, but as the ruler of all humanity.[66] In addition, the Jesuits noticed that the emperor had begun showing increasing favour to Hindus, and that he was venerating the rising sun every dawn from the highest point of his palace roof.[67] He had also memorized the 1,001 Sanskrit names of the sun.[68]

As a result of these shifts in Akbar's religious ideology, the Jesuit delegation, now very discouraged, gradually withdrew from participating in the emperor's debates in the House of Worship, grudgingly concluding that he would never accept baptism. This, in turn, left the field open to increasing Hindu influence, not only in the debates in the House of Worship, but throughout the court. Some twenty Hindu chieftains, mainly Rajputs, were now admitted to the innermost parts of Akbar's palace, a privilege not allowed even to Muslim courtiers.[69] Meanwhile, the emperor adopted the political rituals of a traditional Indian raja, presenting himself to both public and private audiences seated in a *jharokha*. Finally, in view of the many peoples and cultures encompassed in his sprawling realm, Akbar and Abu'l-fazl promulgated a policy of *sulh-i kull*. Variously understood as 'perfect reconciliation', 'universal toleration', 'peace with all' or 'complete civility', this appears to have been a product of Akbar's inclusivist religious outlook, which not only acknowledged the presence of cultural diversity in Mughal India but challenged his subjects to engage with new sources of knowledge, even if they conflicted with the traditions of their own community.[70] There is even indirect evidence that, with the coming of the Islamic millennium in 1591, Akbar's adventurous leanings led him to order the suppression of formal Islamic rites, including the prohibition of public prayer and the destruction of at least one congregational mosque. But these decrees do not appear to have been carried out. By 1601, just four years before his death, he had evidently backed off from authorizing such destabilizing measures. In fact, he seems to have resumed practising the external rites of Islam, if only to silence his conservative critics.[71]

If Akbar's stance on religion shifted over time, his governing policies remained more stable. Early in his reign, he replaced the Delhi sultanate's notion of a single, all-powerful minister, or *vazir*, with four central ministries: finance under a chief *diwan*, army under a *mir bakhshi*, the royal household under a *khan-i saman*, and the judiciary under a *qazi al-quzat* (or *sadr-i jahan*). These four offices were replicated in each of the empire's fourteen provinces, co-ordinated by a governor. To maximize control over state revenue functions, towards the end of his reign he made provincial *diwan*s answerable to the imperial *diwan*, instead of, as formerly, to provincial governors. Unlike territories governed by tributary vassals, territories under direct rule were administered by the *zabt* system, according to which land revenue was collected in cash at rates calculated according to which crop was sown, the size of cropped land and soil types.

For administering justice, provincial judges appointed district-level judges (*qazi, shiqdar*), who judged civil and criminal cases on the basis of the Islamic *shari'a*. Cases involving non-Muslims were normally decided by village councils (*panchayat*) according to local custom, although Mughal judges also adjudicated such cases on the basis of local custom, not Islamic law.[72] All this testifies to the care Akbar gave to upholding the principle of justice, an ideal inherited from centuries of Persianate discourse and practice.[73] Capital cases and important civil cases were normally conducted by the emperor himself, who alone could issue a death penalty. Punishments, moreover, were not meted out until he had given his orders a third time. Even in such cases, Akbar was capable of compassion. On one occasion, a prisoner who had been convicted of desertion from the army was handed over to him for an order of execution. The prisoner pleaded that his life be spared on the grounds that he possessed marvellous powers of a certain nature. When the emperor asked what those powers might be, the prisoner replied that he could sing beautifully. So Akbar commanded that he sing. 'The wretched fellow', writes a European observer:

> then began to sing in a voice so discordant and absurd that everyone began to laugh and murmur, and the King himself could scarcely control his smiles. When the guilty man perceived this he put in, 'Pardon me this poor performance, O King. For these guards of yours dragged me along so roughly and cruelly, on a hot and dusty road, and pummelled me so brutally with their fists, that my throat is full of dust, and my voice so husky that I cannot do myself justice in singing.'[74]

Appreciating the man's wit, Akbar pardoned both him and his companions.

## CONCLUSION

Between Babur's arrival in Delhi in 1526 and Akbar's death in 1605, the Mughal dynasty had become rooted in the heart of north India. In the intervening period, three monarchs consolidated their rule in a great swathe of territory where the regime's governing institutions and cultural traditions became firmly established. Yet the state that Babur founded differed vastly from the one Akbar left behind. Having captured Ibrahim Lodi's capital and treasury, Babur did little more than replace the defeated Afghans with his own people, without substantially altering the Lodis' governing structure. After Babur's brief reign, his son Humayun was driven from India before he could consolidate his rule. Ironically, it was another Indo-Afghan, the capable Sher Shah Sur (r. 1540–45), who established many of the administrative traditions that Humayun and his son Akbar would then inherit and elaborate. In his long, nearly half-century reign, Akbar put in place the empire's most enduring ruling institutions, while the dynasty's character completed its transition from a mobile ruling group steeped in semi-pastoral Central Asian traditions to a sedentary empire based on the economic, political and cultural traditions of agrarian India.

One aspect of this transition was the abandonment, under Akbar, of the theory of co-sovereignty, a Mongol legacy traceable to Genghis Khan (r. 1206–27) and later incorporated into Timurid practice. In that theory, each and every prince sharing the blood of a ruling monarch could in principle lay claim to the empire's sovereignty in whole or in part. Accordingly, the states launched by both Genghis Khan and Timur were, on the death of a sovereign, liable to territorial division among their lineal heirs. Luckily for him, Babur had no brothers competing for his newly won kingdom in north India. But, following Mongol–Timurid practice, he parcelled out parts of his kingdom to his four sons. Humayun consequently spent years struggling with his three brothers, each of whom claimed a share of their father's sovereign legacy, if not the whole of it. Similarly, rule over Kabul by Akbar's younger brother Mirza Hakim was also a remnant of the old Mongol tradition, since Humayun had divided his realm between Hakim in Kabul and Akbar in Hindustan. It was only in 1585, after his younger brother had died, that Akbar reimagined the empire as an indivisible state to be handed down to a single heir, while all princes would be rotated around the empire as high-ranking *mansabdar*s, like other nobles.

This new conception of the Mughal state meant that princes, acutely aware of the winner-take-all nature of any future succession struggle, would devote their entire adult lives to building up enormous households, learning political skills, gaining military experience and establishing allies on an empire-wide basis in preparation for the contest that would inevitably follow a sovereign's demise. Such a strategy not only guaranteed the empire's territorial unity and integrity from one sovereign to the next; it also meant that the best-'networked' prince would become the new emperor, since in any given pool of contenders the prince winning the empire would probably be the most competent militarily, politically and administratively. On the other hand, the system implied that succession disputes would be more intense and violent, since siblings knew that in the aftermath of such succession struggles the losers would be eliminated, whether by blinding, exile or execution. For the winner, meanwhile, it would be necessary to reintegrate back into the empire's governing structure the former supporters of losing contenders.[75] Much Mughal history from 1585 to the early eighteenth century flowed from this revised notion of the state.

The Mughals' first seven decades also witnessed the elaboration of a multi-stranded ruling ideology. One strand was the tradition of sacred kingship traceable to Timur, who in his own day was widely seen as the expected messiah, a descendant of 'Ali, and the Lord of the Conjunction (sahib-i qiran).[76] The millennial aspect of the Mughals' ruling ideology was most pronounced under Akbar between 1581 and 1591, the turn of the first Islamic millennium. Accordingly, he commissioned a chronicle, The Millennial History, which declared him to be the 'Renewer of the Second Millennium'.[77] Belief in astrology and the influence of planets formed another ideological strand, with both Humayun and Akbar matching the colour of their robes with the planet associated with a given day. Like their Delhi sultanate predecessors, the first three Mughals all believed deeply in the spiritual authority of Sufi masters, whom they patronized both in life and in revered memory. Although Babur had brought the Central Asian Naqshbandi tradition with him to north India, he soon turned to patronizing the indigenous Shattari order, as did Humayun. Akbar, for his part, fell under the spell of India's most important indigenous order, the Chishti, which had been so closely associated with Tughluq imperialism in the fourteenth century. But, unlike any of his royal predecessors in India, Akbar not only patronized Chishti institutions: he went further and projected himself as an enlightened Sufi master for all his subjects, reinforced by his association with the sun and hints of divine illumination.

Another strand of the Mughals' ruling ideology grew out of Akbar's political alliance with Rajput chieftains and the incorporation of Rajput women in Akbar's household. This contained Rajput ideas of rulership, reflected in the *jharokha* institution and the Rajputs' aesthetic vision, prominently projected in the architecture of Akbar's second capital, Fatehpur Sikri. At different points in his career, then, Akbar variously fashioned himself as a Sufi master, a solar and even divine emanation, a renewer of the second Islamic millennium, a Timurid prince and a traditional Indian sovereign. That last element, visible ever since he first began integrating Rajput chieftains into his ruling structure, became more pronounced after 1585 with the death of Mirza Hakim, who had presented himself as a traditional, Central Asian prince very much in the mould of his grandfather, Babur. Entrenched in Kabul, he continued to use the Turco-Mongol legal system and to circulate the Timurid currency, the *shahrukhi*. Once he disappeared from the scene, however, Akbar felt free to define the empire not only as a unitary state, but as a more forthrightly Indian one. This change is especially clear when one contrasts Babur's memoir, the *Babur-nama*, with Abu'l-fazl's history of Akbar's reign, the *Akbar-nama*. Although Babur had dwelt at length on India's flora and fauna, he showed very little interest in the cultures of India, dismissing its peoples as 'infidels'. By contrast, Abu'l-fazl characterizes Indians as 'seekers of God, kindhearted, friendly to strangers, congenial, and pleasant. They are fond of knowledge, inclined toward austerities, committed to justice, content, hardworking, skilled, loyal, honest and trustworthy.'[78] In short, the *Akbar-nama* affirms the empire's multi-ethnic and multi-religious character, promoting Akbar as a committed guardian of India's cultural diversity.[79]

By the time of his death in 1605, Akbar was able to bequeath to his son Salim a consolidated state with well-ordered administrative institutions and a hybridized ruling ideology suited to India's diverse society. To the south, the five successor states to the Bahmani sultanate (1347–1528) had narrowed to four, and would soon become just three as Akbar's successors continued to exert pressure on the Deccan. At the same time, successor states to Vijayanagara had emerged in the interior of southern India, while European trading companies began planting commercial enclaves along India's shores a century after the Portuguese Estado da India established its first coastal toehold in 1500. Whereas India's north, Deccan and coastal regions had evolved more or less separately prior to 1605, after Akbar they were brought into much tighter relations with each other – a topic to which we now turn.

# 6

# India under Jahangir and Shah
# Jahan, 1605–1658

## JAHANGIR

Of his three sons, Akbar favoured his firstborn, Salim, to succeed him. Yet Salim, even while being groomed for the throne, felt excluded from what he deemed his proper share of royal authority. He was especially jealous of the attention that his father showered on his principal adviser and friend, Abu'l-fazl. Already in the early 1590s, he began showing signs of impatience for full sovereign power, picking fights with his younger brothers and engaging in excesses and follies that Abu'l-fazl would bring to Akbar's attention. This only created tensions between father and son, while intensifying the prince's hostility towards Abu'l-fazl . Matters came to a head in 1599 when, while his father was campaigning in the Deccan, Salim gathered supporters and made an impetuous strike on Agra, where the imperial treasure was stored. When Akbar's mother scolded the wayward prince, Salim, ashamed and unable to challenge his dear grandmother, dashed back to his base in Allahabad. In 1601, after Akbar had returned to Agra, he again marched towards the capital, pretending to pay respects to his father. But he turned away, intimidated by the prospect of actually confronting him. Yet when he returned to Allahabad, he followed the urgings of his advisers and set up his own court. He even assumied imperial titles.

A crisis occurred when Akbar recalled Abu'l-fazl, then campaigning in the Deccan. Fearing that the powerful minister might advise Akbar to take stern measures against him, possibly even barring his succession to power, Salim took the drastic step of arranging for Abu'l-fazl's assassination. In August 1602, while marching north, Akbar's

244

devoted friend was cut down by Bir Singh Bundela, the Rajput chieftain of Orchha, who was then in rebellion against the Mughals. A deeply anguished Akbar now sent another senior Mughal female, Salim's stepmother Sultana Salima Begam, to Allahabad to persuade his son to return to court. The prince again yielded to this soft diplomacy, and in April 1603 the emperor and heir apparent had an emotional reconciliation.

But it was short-lived. The emperor's feckless attempts to check his rebellious son only worsened relations between the two men. First, he allowed Salim's younger brother Daniyal the honour of using, while on campaign, the red tents that were normally reserved for the sovereign's sole use. Worse, he tried to temper his son's excesses by driving a wedge between Salim and Salim's own son Khusrau, whom he promoted to high rank. This began as early as 1594, when Khusrau was only seven years of age. The emperor also insisted on keeping his grandson under his personal charge instead of leaving him in Salim's household. Such measures only made the prince more frustrated and rebellious. In 1603, when Akbar sent Salim to reduce the Sisodiya chieftains of Mewar, the last major Rajput lineage to resist partnership with the Mughals, he refused to advance far from the court, fearing that, should his ageing father die, his brother Daniyal would be in a better position than he to claim the throne. Akbar finally relented and allowed him to return to his base in Allahabad, which he did in November 1603, only to set up an independent court once again.

By this time Salim's son Khusrau was seventeen and, thanks to his grandfather's promotions, had built up a substantial household of his own. Moreover, Khusrau was the nephew of Raja Man Singh and the son-in-law of Akbar's foster-brother Aziz Koka, two of the most powerful nobles in the realm, both of whom supported the young prince. In April 1604 Daniyal, Akbar's only surviving son after Salim, died of alcoholism, which considerably narrowed the number of possible successors to the throne. Four months later, when Salim was in Agra for the ceremonies after the death of Akbar's mother, the emperor reprimanded him for his many acts of disloyalty, even humiliating his thirty-five-year-old son by confining him in a room for ten days without access to wine or opium, for both of which he had developed a fondness, if not a dependency. All this kindled in

Khusrau thoughts that he himself, and not his father, should right-fully succeed to the throne. In September 1605, during an elephant fight that the emperor staged for courtly entertainment, Salim and his son had an ugly, vicious quarrel. Everybody, however, understood the quarrel's real meaning, for Akbar's health was then rapidly declining, and opposing factions were lining up behind his two likely succes-sors. Despite Aziz Koka's and Man Singh's backing of Khusrau, it became clear that Akbar would never agree to his grandson's succes-sion. Consequently, when the emperor died a month later, Salim ascended the throne without a struggle, adopting as his imperial title Jahangir, 'world-conqueror'.

Notwithstanding an emotional reconciliation between Khusrau and his father, shortly after his accession to power, a wary Jahangir confined his son in Agra in a state of virtual detention, cut off from the outer world and deprived of the ability to forge alliances with would-be supporters. But, having tasted the dynasty's practice of princely networking during the last years of Akbar's reign, and hav-ing nearly gained the throne for himself, young Khusrau chafed at his deplorable fate. So, by a ruse, he managed to escape his confinement and with a core of followers rode towards the Punjab in search of potential allies. He was now in open rebellion. By plundering impe-rial convoys and using their cash to buy new supporters, Khusrau gathered a growing, though ragtag army of 10,000. When he reached Lahore, however, the governor refused to open the city's gates for him. Meanwhile, his father and the imperial army pursued and easily defeated his hastily organized force. Khusrau fled towards Kabul, but was captured near the Chenab and brought back to Lahore. On 1 May 1606 the fugitive rebel was dragged, weeping and in chains, before his father in a garden just outside the city. But the new emperor was not about to show leniency. Khusrau's supporters were impaled along both sides of a road, while their miserable leader was placed on an elephant and mockingly made to receive his supporters' 'homage' as they writhed in agony.

From Lahore Jahangir continued marching north-west to Kabul, for the shah of Iran had recently tried to reconquer the contested city of Kandahar, which Akbar had recovered from Safavid control in 1594. In Kabul Jahangir unchained Khusrau, unaware that his son had been secretly plotting another rebellion. When the plot was discovered, Jahangir executed its ringleaders and partially blinded his son. Secure in power at last, Jahangir made shrewd choices about whom to patronize, and to what degree. He enlisted into his service Bir Singh Bundela as a reward for assassinating Abu'l-fazl. To appease his former enemies in Akbar's court, and perhaps also to assuage his guilt, he promoted Abu'l-fazl's son. In the same way, powerful nobles who had backed Khusrau for the succession were reintegrated into the imperial fold. Aziz Koka retained all his former titles and, although Raja Man Singh was removed as governor of Bengal, his son Jagat was promoted. Showing continuity with his father's pattern of patronage, Jahangir generously supported the family of Shaikh Salim Chishti, in whose village Akbar had established his capital Fatehpur Sikri, and to whom Jahangir owed his princely name.

The course of Jahangir's life was changed for ever in March 1611 when the emperor met a striking woman named Mihr al-Nissa. He was immediately smitten, notwithstanding that his harem was already stocked with seventeen wives and numerous concubines. Their marriage several months later created one of the most extraordinary marital partnerships in Mughal history. Nur Jahan, as the emperor would title her, was already a mature woman of thirty-four and the mother of a young girl from an earlier marriage. She was also the daughter of a high-ranking Iranian immigrant, I'timad al-Daula, who had served Akbar and was now in Jahangir's court, together with his son Asaf Khan. From all reports, Nur Jahan was a capable, independent and intelligent woman of uncommon beauty. In a contemporary painting depicting her loading a musket, her posture and her strong, angular body language suggest anything but a delicate wallflower [see Fig. 13]. In fact, she was an excellent shot. In a single day in 1617 she killed four tigers from atop an elephant, firing only six bullets without a single miss.[1]

Within months of her marriage, Nur Jahan began to exercise considerable influence at court, arranging high positions for her family members and associates. A powerful clique soon formed around her, consisting of herself, her father I'timad al-Daula, her brother Asaf Khan and Jahangir's third son, Khurram. Already nineteen years old when Nur Jahan and Jahangir were married, Khurram was brought into Nur Jahan's clique by virtue of his marriage to Asaf Khan's daughter, the future Mumtaz Mahal. Of the emperor's immediate family, he was by far the most disciplined. He refused even to touch wine – the bane of many Mughals – until he was twenty-four, and then only because his father had urged it on him. Since Nur Jahan had no children with the emperor, it was Khurram on whom the clique fixed their sights to succeed Jahangir, in preference to the disgraced and partially blinded Khusrau, the dull and incompetent second son Parviz, or the much younger and totally untested Shahryar.

The ascendance of Khurram – the future emperor Shah Jahan – was associated with the Mughals' fraught relations with the one major Rajput house that Akbar had failed to absorb into his imperial orbit: the Sisodiyas of Mewar in southern Rajasthan. Ever since the Mughals had defeated them at the Battle of Haldighati, the clan's leader Rana Pratap, who escaped the battlefield, had led a protracted guerrilla war against Akbar. Over the next several decades he even recovered much Sisodiya territory that Akbar had seized, except the important stronghold of Chittor. During the first six years of his reign Jahangir repeatedly sent armies into Mewar against Rana Pratap's son and successor Amar Singh. But the results were inconclusive, if not outright failures. Finally, in 1614 the emperor dispatched the veteran general Aziz Koka into Mewar, assisted by the twenty-two-year-old Khurram, his first major military assignment. However, the two had a falling-out that ended with the prince placing the senior general in confinement. Having a free hand, Khurram prosecuted a vigorous campaign against Amar Singh, who, with his forces thinning and famine threatening, finally offered peace negotiations. With a view to integrating this last major Rajput holdout into the Mughal system, Khurram treated his adversary with dignity and respect.

The agreement concluded in 1615 between Khurram and Amar was exceptional in the history of Mughal–Rajput relations. The Sisodiyas were exempted from entering into matrimonial relations with the Mughals; they were not obliged to send their ruling head to the imperial court; and no Sisodiya territory was placed under Mughal administration. In addition, Jahangir made two gestures of goodwill towards these ancient adversaries. First, he returned the historic fort of Chittor to the Sisodiya house, on the condition that it never again be fully inhabited. And, second, he ordered that two life-size equestrian statues of Amar Singh and his son Karan Singh be carved from marble and placed in Agra's most important palace garden. It was a politically astute move. While acknowledging the unique importance of the Sisodiya clan by monumentalizing its two leading political figures in the heart of Mughal power and authority, the statues visibly displayed the Sisodiyas' obeisance to Mughal authority since they were placed immediately below the *jharokha* in which the Mughal emperor would sit above his subjects.[2]

Jahangir also inherited the perennial north Indian ambition, going back to the days of Ashoka (r. 268–232 BC), of conquering the Deccan plateau, thereby bringing territories both north and south of the Vindhya Mountains under the sway of a single, northern sovereign. Both 'Ala al-Din Khalaji and Muhammad bin Tughluq had been seized by this ambition. In Mughal times Akbar was the first to chip away at the Deccan's north-western corner, conquering and occupying Asirgarh and Burhanpur in Khandesh, and the Nizam Shahi capital of Ahmadnagar (though not its territory). Early in Jahangir's reign, Mughal generals waged no fewer than five major campaigns south of the Vindhyas, with no decisive breakthrough. Finally, the veteran commander 'Abd al-Rahim Khan-i Khanan (d. 1627) deployed the Mughals' vast financial resources to bribe independent chieftains and officers of Bijapur and Ahmadnagar to the Mughal cause, followed by decisive battlefield victories in early 1616 that brought territories between the Tapti and Godavari Rivers into Mughal possession. A year later Prince Khurram reached Burhanpur, by then the Mughals' staging point for subsequent Deccan operations. From there he sent envoys to the sultan of Bijapur to negotiate a treaty formally ceding to the Mughals the territories that Khan-i Khanan had recently conquered. Khurram then proceeded to the imperial court in Mandu, where in October 1617 Nur Jahan hosted a grand feast to celebrate his recent triumphs, even though in reality he had only formalized territorial gains already made by Khan-i Khanan. Jahangir also used that occasion to raise his son's rank to an unprecedented *mansab* of 30,000/30,000 and to confer on him the lofty title Shah Jahan, 'king of the world'.

The Mandu celebrations marked the zenith of the cohesiveness and political influence of Nur Jahan's clique. Thereafter serious splits developed, followed by a headlong train of events that would end with a new emperor. It began with the first signs of Jahangir's deteriorating health. For years the emperor had been consuming twenty cups of doubly distilled spirits daily, which by 1616 had caused so much trembling in his hands that he needed assistance drinking.[3] In 1618 he began suffering from shortness of breath. By 1623 he was no longer physically able to write his memoir, which he entrusted to the chronicler Mu'tamad Khan.[4] While empowering Nur Jahan, Jahangir's worsening condition also made urgent the issue of succession at the very time that Khurram, the clique's favourite candidate, was growing arrogant, thanks to his Deccan successes and his father's favours. This only made Nur Jahan more jealous of her authority as she gradually grew threatened by, and estranged from, her headstrong stepson.

Aware that she could never exercise the same influence through Khurram that she could through her husband, Nur Jahan began looking for an alternative candidate for the impending succession. Her ace card in this delicate game was her daughter from her first marriage, Ladli, whom she would marry off to any prince she could manipulate. Initially, she set her hopes on the still-imprisoned and partially blind Khusrau, even offering him freedom if he would marry the girl. But Khusrau refused, stubbornly preferring life in confinement with his devoted wife to accepting his stepmother's offer. The queen then focused on marrying Ladli to Jahangir's youngest surviving son, the sixteen-year-old Shahryar. Although the lad was widely dismissed as an inexperienced lightweight, in late 1620 his marriage took place, and immediately the queen's clique began to crumble. Her father I'timad al-Daula, for years the pillar of the clique, died soon after the marriage ceremonies had concluded, while her brother Asaf Khan stoutly supported Khurram, to whom his own daughter Arjomand Banu was married. With brother and sister now backing different princes, and Nur Jahan's new son-in-law by far the weaker of the two, the queen became ever more isolated, even as her influence over her failing husband continued to grow.

To prevent Khurram from participating in a succession struggle, the queen persuaded Jahangir to send him back south to resume his Deccan operations. But Khurram, wary of her designs, refused to go unless his imprisoned brother Khusrau, whom he regarded as his only viable rival, be transferred to his custody. Content with having both rivals to Shahryar away from the court, Nur Jahan got the emperor to approve Khurram's request. In December 1620 the prince left the court at Lahore with 40,000 troops and headed for Burhanpur. Once in the Deccan, however, Khurram learnt that Jahangir had fallen seriously ill and, anticipating his father's death, arranged for Khusrau's murder. Refusing to believe Khurram's claim that he had died from colic, in 1622 Jahangir reassigned Khurram's *jagir*s in a manner the prince considered punitive. In response, the unruly Khurram went into open rebellion, marching directly north towards Agra, with the Mughal treasury his target. In an imperial order bearing her own seal, the queen then summoned the veteran commander Mahabat Khan from virtual exile in Afghanistan, raised his rank to 6,000/5,000 and sent him to check the rebellious prince. In March 1623 an army under his command soundly defeated Khurram between Delhi and Agra. Mahabat Khan then pursued Khurram in a great pan-India sweep as the fugitive prince first moved south to Mandu, then east through Golconda's territory to Masulipatam on the Andhra coast, then north through Orissa and into Bengal. Swinging back up the Gangetic plain, in mid 1624 Khurram was again defeated by Mahabat Khan near Allahabad. Once more he returned to the Deccan where, having run out of options, he begged for the court's full pardon. In early 1626 Nur Jahan replied that he would first have to surrender several forts – Rohtas in Bihar and Asirgarh in Khandesh – and as a sign of good faith, send to the court two of his sons: ten-year-old Dara Shukoh and eight-year-old Aurangzeb. Khurram complied, and in June 1626 the two boys reached Lahore, where they were placed under the queen's care.

Khurram's three-year traipse through the subcontinent reveals much about the nature of Mughal politics at the highest level. Whereas a prince might acquire the skills of political networking in a gradual way while serving as a governor or field commander, in the midst of rebellion he had to learn them very quickly to survive. Prince Khusrau had failed that test. In a rebellion lasting less than a month in early 1606, he had only begun frantically forging alliances before he was captured, blinded and imprisoned. Prince Khurram, by contrast, had passed the test, but not without enduring great hardships. In November 1623, by the time he reached the Andhra coast with the imperial army in hot pursuit, he had been reduced to just 4,500 cavalry, 10,000 infantry and 500 elephants.[5] But because he managed to stay just beyond the reach of the imperial forces, he had three full years to build up broad political networks across a wide expanse stretching from Gujarat to Bengal, and from Allahabad to the northern Deccan. Everywhere he went, he gained the support of groups either previously opposed to the Mughals or poorly integrated into imperial networks. In Bengal and Bihar, for example, he paid respects to important Sufi shrines, to which he distributed large sums of money, which won him favour.[6] He also recruited landed chiefs – especially Indo-Afghans, who had a long history of opposition to Mughal rule – to join him in defeating the Mughal governor of Bengal.[7] Such intense political activity placed Khurram in a far better position than any rival both to win the succession struggle when it finally arrived, and also to govern successfully once he had gained the throne.

Another lesson to draw from Khurram's three-year rebellion is the court's benign response to it. Once he fulfilled the conditions imposed on him for a pardon, he was fully rehabilitated into the imperial structure. His reconciliation with Jahangir recalls Jahangir's own with Akbar after he, as Prince Salim, had similarly rebelled against imperial authority. For such reasons Mughal succession struggles, while disastrous for their losers and disruptive for many in the short term, could in the long run be restorative for the empire as a whole. New elites and political networks were invariably swept into power with their victors, thereby replenishing the entire system.[8]

## THE VIEW FROM THE FRONTIER

Jahangir's India amounted to much more than the palace intrigues and battles that fill the pages of contemporary chronicles, or the courtly gossip that so fascinated contemporary European visitors. A very different picture emerges if one steps away from the courtly centre and considers the empire's political margins. In these porous frontier zones, the imperial presence was but a shadow of its imposing profile in Agra or Lahore. In the first place, such zones were hardly empty spaces that the empire simply occupied. Rather, they were filled with peoples of varied cultural backgrounds who had their own political traditions and leaders. Many of them, moreover, participated in India's vast military labour market. Armed villagers might sell their martial services to the highest bidder, but would remain in service only as long as their salaries were forthcoming. How, then, did the Mughals integrate such politically fluid, often volatile, zones into their cultural and political system? With what success? We get glimpses from a detailed memoir left by Mirza Nathan, a junior imperial officer who was posted on the Mughals' eastern frontier between 1607 and 1624, spanning most of Jahangir's reign.

At an auspicious hour on 4 July 1607, Emperor Jahangir sat in his *jharokha* in Agra watching while, below him, a mighty flotilla of warships commanded by Admiral Ihtiman Khan set sail down the Jamuna. Announcing the great military enterprise, artillery was fired with thunderous noise. 'The conquest of Bengal', wrote Mirza Nathan, the admiral's son, 'had assumed a practical shape, as was desired by all the nobles of the State.'[9] Akbar had begun the conquest several decades earlier, planting the first toeholds of imperial authority in the delta's north-western and western quarters when he accepted the surrender of Sultan Daud Khan Karrani in 1575. But the task of subduing the entire delta remained far from complete, as the region's dense jungles and ever-shifting maze of waterways afforded protection for indigenous peoples and an ideal refuge for those resisting Mughal suzerainty. When Jahangir came to power, Bengal's central, northern and eastern quarters were seething with well-armed warlords, most of them Indo-Afghans, who had carved out independent kingdoms fiercely opposed to Mughal intrusions. Socially, the region was a mix of communities: independent Kuch tribes in the northern mountains, ethnic Assamese in the broad, upper Brahmaputra valley, Bengali-speakers in the delta's flat central and eastern districts, and ethnic Arakanese who, settled in the Chittagong region, regularly made predatory raids in the southern delta. In addition, thousands of Portuguese adventurers who had abandoned service to Lisbon effectively joined eastern India's thriving military labour market by selling their services to whichever warlord could make them the best offer. Some even set up their own petty kingdoms.

Such was the turbulent, swampy realm that Ihtiman Khan's flotilla entered, having sailed down the Jamuna and the Ganges. The admiral was first met by Bengal's new governor, Islam Khan Chishti (1608–13), who commanded large numbers of cavalry, infantry, elephants and war-boats of his own. These were quartered in the provincial capital of Rajmahal, in the delta's north-western corner. In 1610 the governor would transfer the provincial capital from Rajmahal to Dhaka, in the heart of the delta, dramatizing the Mughals' determination to subdue and annex the delta's unsettled central and eastern quarters. The fleet sent down from Agra consisted of 295 war-boats, seventy of them equipped with heavy cannon. It was also an amphibious operation, with Ihtiman Khan commanding 770 cavalry, 3,000 infantry and eighty elephants. But co-ordinating river and land operations was always difficult, given the logistical problem of moving men, animals and supplies through Bengal's dense forest tracts. On one occasion Mirza Nathan describes getting lost with his men in a swamp, wandering about 'in that deep water in the whirlpool of perplexity'.[10] He spoke of 'wallowing perpetually in mud like buffaloes',[11] and tells of a Mughal army moving against Arakanese forces in the Chittagong area 'through a jungle route which was impassable even for an ant'. Along the way, he continued:

> not only others but even the Khan himself cleared jungles with his own hands and he proceeded onward till he arrived at a place where the boats could not ply any farther. A small gondola was carried with the Khan with very great difficulty. The horses also could not be taken farther. The elephants proceeded with very great difficulty. The scarcity of food became so great that a seer of oil could not be procured for Rs. 15 . . . The state of all other things may be imagined from this.[12]

Dealing with the Mughals' human adversaries was as challenging as coping with the natural environment. On one occasion Arakanese raiders on 300 boats audaciously sailed from the Bay of Bengal to the Dhaka region, where they captured villagers and carried them off into slavery. Portuguese raiders took 1,500 villagers for the same purpose.[13]

Ultimately, the conquest of eastern Bengal, like that of other regions, was a political process. Islam Khan treated the delta's warlords as Akbar and Jahangir had treated the Rajputs: while carrying a big stick, whenever possible he bestowed honours on them and confirmed them in their existing possessions, insisting only that they or their close family members serve the provincial court in Dhaka. The governor thus confronted Raja Satrajit, the king of Bhushana (in modern Faridpur District, Bangladesh), with a large army but offered him his own territory as *jagir* if he would enlist in Mughal service. After initially resisting, the raja ultimately submitted, in exchange for which the governor honoured him by calling him 'son' (*farzand*). Similarly, after an initial show of force, Islam Khan met the warlord of modern Jessore, Pratapaditya, at an agreed spot where the governor presented his adversary with a horse, a grand robe of honour and a bejewelled sword-belt. 'Thus,' records Mirza Nathan, 'he was converted into a loyal officer.'[14]

An important objective of such ceremonies was to draw chieftains to the Mughal cause, on the assumption that smaller actors looked to their more powerful neighbours for political cues. Pratapaditya agreed to send his son with 400 war-boats to join the imperial fleet, while he himself contributed 20,000 infantry and 500 war-boats, together with more than 30,000 kilos of gunpowder. All these were combined with imperial forces with a view to confronting an even bigger warlord, Musa Khan, ruler of an immense tract of the eastern delta and considered the chief of east Bengal's so-called 'twelve chiefs' (*bara bhuyan*).[15] In effect, the governor offered carrots to large chieftains, enabling them to apply sticks to still larger chieftains.

In Bengal's northernmost region, Kuch Bihar and Kamrup (western Assam), the Mughals faced tough resistance in thickly forested terrain inhabited by peoples very different from the mainly Hindu, hierarchically structured peasant society of the western delta, which for centuries had been well integrated into the Bengal sultanate (1342–1574). Kuch society, by contrast, consisted of clan-based tribes whose cultivators paid tribute to a king, not in cash or crops but in rotational corvée labour, rendering service to him for one of every four years. The region had never evolved bureaucratic land-revenue systems as found in monetized and agrarian tracts such as western

Bengal. Only in the sixteenth century had Kuch agriculture begun shifting from the hoe to the plough, adopting with it the sedentary life associated with the cultivation of wet rice.

In early 1613, having already subdued the 'twelve chieftains' of lower Bengal, Islam Khan sent a large force of musketeers, cavalry-men, war-boats, elephants and cash up the Brahmaputra valley into the Kuch country. Upon besieging and seizing Dhubri, an important fortress on the western banks of the Brahmaputra, the imperial forces pushed on, driving the Kuch raja into Kamrup, where he finally submitted to Mughal authority and was sent off to Dhaka in order, as Mirza Nathan put it, 'to learn the court etiquettes'.[16] By mid 1613 the Mughals had annexed both Kuch Bihar and Kamrup, bringing both regions under direct imperial administration. The land was divided into revenue circles, taxes were levied on the peasantry, and agents were sent to collect the newly imposed revenue demand. The Mughals also required that local militias be paid out of the general land tax, thus transforming a corvée-based militia system into a salaried army under the authority of a distant governor. Mughal revenue farmers who had contracted to pay the government's land tax squeezed the peasantry for their own profit by raising taxes in their revenue circles. The whole system was supported by tax burdens imposed on a peasantry unfamiliar with a monetized economy. Such conditions led to serious peasant revolts in 1614, followed the next year by a full-scale Mughal invasion in which imperial stockades recently seized by the rebels were retaken by force.[17]

But Mughal rule along the Bengal frontier was always constrained by the region's politically porous, sponge-like character. Local authorities, whether natives or imperial appointees, had options: if their overlords on one side of the frontier were oppressive or simply too demanding, they could – and did – cast their eyes to the other side. Apart from the Mughals, these might be Indo-Afghans, forest chieftains, renegade Portuguese, Ahom rajas or Arakanese, among others.[18] Similarly, cultivators had to be treated fairly lest they flee their lands, leaving revenue authorities with nothing to tax. This would explain why government assessors sent to recently annexed Jessore were instructed to prepare revenue registers 'to the satisfaction of the ryots [cultivators]'.[19] Islam Khan instructed his commanders to offer enemy chieftains, in exchange for submission, the hope of having their territory transformed into *jagir*, with themselves named the *jagirdar*, or *jagir*-holder.[20] Mirza Yusuf Barlas, the chief minister of Raja Ananta Manik, warlord of the Noakhali region in south-eastern Bengal, accepted an imperial *mansab* of 500/300 in return for submission to the Mughals.[21] The imperial governor well understood the empire's relatively weak position along its furthest peripheries, where offers of honours, land or a rank in the Mughal *mansabdari* system were more effectual than the application of brute force.

On frontiers such as eastern Bengal the Mughals used various mechanisms to promote cohesiveness among their own culturally mixed imperial corps. The Islamic religion was certainly not among these; in fact, state officials were punished for promoting Islam among non-Muslim subjects. When Islam Khan learnt that an officer of his had converted the son of one of Bengal's notorious 'twelve chiefs', he had him censured and transferred from his *jagir*.[22] More important for this purpose, and more subtle, was the substance and political symbolism of salt, great quantities of which had been loaded on to the flotilla of boats bound for Bengal in July 1607. For the Mughals, salt possessed a deep cultural significance since it defined patron–client relations. From the emperor down to the lowest servant, individuals and groups were intrinsically linked vertically by mutual obligations of protection and dependency expressed by the giving and receiving of the mineral: the giver of salt pledged to protect a recipient, and the latter swore undying loyalty to the giver. The symbolism of salt also bound together members of the imperial corps horizontally, as it expressed corporate solidarity, especially at times when the group felt itself mortally endangered. In 1615, during an imperial invasion of Assam, Mughal troops once found themselves surrounded by the army of the Ahom raja. The commanding officer and his comrades wrapped their heads in shrouds and, preparing for death rather than surrender, cried out to the Assamese: 'As we have taken the salt of Jahangir, we consider martyrdom to be our blessings for both the worlds.'[23] Such declarations were not just metaphorical. After Musa Khan finally submitted to Mughal power in Bengal, the Afghan warlord Khwaja Usman became the Mughals' most redoubtable opponent and leader of the resistance to imperial rule in the delta. When he was killed in battle in 1612, his Indo-Afghan support-ers formalized their surrender by presenting elephants to the Mughal general, who in turn gave robes of honour to the relatives of Usman Khan and shawls to 400 Afghan commanders. Then, preceding a grand feast organized for their former enemies, the Mughals distrib-uted the salt the emperor to all the Afghans.[24] It was, in effect, the political and ideological 'glue' cementing the loyalty of these former enemies to the Mughal order.

Also serving to promote solidarity within Mughal service were Rajput practices that, by the time Jahangir came to power, had thor-oughly saturated Mughal culture. In Dhaka, governor Islam Khan had a *jharokha* built into the side of his palace four metres above ground level, overlooking the courtyard. Seated in the *jharokha*, he would review both military and non-military personnel, who in turn paid him their respects, standing in fixed positions according to their *mansab*.[25] When Jahangir learnt of this he sternly rebuked the gover-nor, on the grounds that it too closely approximated his own imperial *jharokha* in Agra. The governor was ordered that his *jharokha* could be no higher than half a man's height above the ground and that nobody could pay obeisance there or remain standing while attend-ing the governor.[26] Here one sees not just an assertion of an imperial prerogative over that of a provincial governor. The larger point is that first Akbar, then Jahangir and now Jahangir's governors had all taken an originally Rajput political institution and made it their own. Even more strikingly, by the early seventeenth century the tradition of *jauhar* had found its way into the practices of officers and ordinary troopers in Bengal, indicating the Mughals' assimilation of an ethos of martial heroism and honour that by this time had become associ-ated with Rajput lineages. In 1617 Bengal's ex-governor, Qasim Khan Chishti, and his allies were besieged in a fort near Dhaka and, when it became clear that they would not survive the battle, they destroyed all their women in the terrifying rite of *jauhar*.[27] Somewhat later, Mirza Nathan twice ordered his men to commit the rite of *jauhar* should their situation in the heat of battle likewise become so desperate.[28]

The diffusion of Rajput institutions in Mughal culture is partly explained by the incorporation of Rajput women in the Mughal harem and Rajput youths in Mughal households, which had begun in the early decades of Akbar's reign. Children born of Rajput women in the imperial harem were treated as full members of the Mughal dynasty and eligible for inheriting the throne. This meant that, although Jahangir's paternal grandfather was Humayun, his maternal grandfather was Raja Bharmal, leader of the Kachwaha Rajput lineage. Jahangir's mother, Harkha,[29] entitled Mariam al-Zamani, was the sister of Raja Bharmal's son and successor, Bhagwant Das. Jahangir himself, then, was biologically half Rajput. He, in turn, married the daughters of prominent Rajput rulers who had submitted to Mughal overlordship. Seven of his seventeen wives before Nur Jahan had come from Rajput lineages: two from Amber, and one each from Jodhpur, Jaisalmer, Jhabua, Bikaner and Orchha.[30] His son Khurram, the future Shah Jahan, was born of one of these Rajputs – Jagat Gosain Begum, the daughter of Udai Singh of Jodhpur. Shah Jahan was therefore three-quarters Rajput by blood. Since Rajput mothers imparted their inherited culture to their offspring, the Mughal harem became a site for the diffusion of Rajput values at the heart of the imperial system. The Mughal connection with Rajputs, then, was more than political. It was biological and cultural, as Rajput institutions, introduced at the upper end of the Mughal order, percolated downwards, gradually diffusing among the officer corps. In addition, many officers and troopers in Mughal service were themselves Rajputs, which also served to lend a Rajput ethos to imperial armies.

## THE DECCAN: AFRICANS AND MARATHAS

One of the most arresting portraits commissioned by Jahangir is the deeply allegorical painting of himself standing on a globe that rests on the horns of a bull, which in turn stands on a great fish – symbols of kingship drawn from Hindu lore [see Fig. 14]. All around the emperor are seen images representing his highest aspirations. Cherubs in the sky offer him a sword and arrows. To one side is an elaborate crown above a roundel in which is inscribed his own name and those of each of his royal ancestors reaching back to Timur. Above the crown flutters a bird of paradise. To the emperor's other side is a golden scale of justice hanging from a chain with golden bells. The chain is suspended between the globe and a javelin, against which rests a musket. In the centre of the painting, wearing a white turban, a crimson gown and impeccably white slippers, is Jahangir himself, drawing a reverse-curved bow and aiming his arrow at the severed head of his most hated enemy, Malik Ambar (d. 1626), which rests on the tip of the javelin. Perched on Ambar's bare head is an owl, a symbol of darkness. All around the head are inscriptions that speak of the emperor's contempt for Malik Ambar – 'The head of the night-coloured servant has become the house of the owl'; 'Ambar the owl, which fled the light, has been driven from the world by your [Jahangir's] enemy-smiting arrow.'[31]

The painting was completed c.1616, another bad year in a series of bad years for Mughal military operations in the Deccan. From the start of his reign, Jahangir had sent army after army south to fulfil his father's dream of annexing the plateau to the empire. Between 1608 and 1612 he launched four major invasions led by his best generals, but all were repulsed by armies loyal to Ahmadnagar, one of the three remaining major sultanates of the plateau. Although the kingdom's Nizam Shahi house was headed by a series of weak, puppet sultans and the capital of Ahmadnagar was occupied by Mughal forces, the state was kept alive by two powerful groups: Maratha warrior lineages and the so-called Habshis – natives of east Africa recruited as military slaves. Malik Ambar, a disciplined leader and master tactician, was a member of the latter group. His career is important, not just because he and his Deccan forces managed to check India's mightiest armies for two decades, but also for what it reveals about the place of Africans in Indian history, and about military slavery itself.

From at least the fifteenth century, cotton goods manufactured in Gujarat and the western Deccan had been reaching the Ethiopian highlands in exchange for African exports of gold, ivory and, especially, slaves. Since the Christians who ruled Ethiopia could not legally enslave other Christians, they captured pagan Africans and sold them to Arab or Gujarati merchants for Indian textiles. The captives were then sent to slave markets along African or Middle Eastern coasts, where they were purchased, converted to Islam and then became either domestic servants or were given military training and resold to other buyers. As with any type of slavery, military slaves were severed from their natal kin group, rendering them dependent upon their owners. And, as with military slavery under the Ghaznavid and Ghurid dynasties, it was assumed that, as uprooted outsiders with no local kin network, these men would be reliably loyal to the state their masters served. Ever since the fourteenth century, the sultanates of the Deccan had been weakened by incessant struggles between the ruling class's Deccani and Westerner factions. Recruiting military labour unaffiliated ethnically or politically with either group was therefore considered a practical way to neutralize intractable domestic strife.

Masters fed, housed and educated their African slaves, receiving in return unswerving loyalty, which is why courts were willing to entrust their Habshi slaves with such important positions as governors, seal-bearers, bodyguards and commanders, as well as ordinary troopers. But the status of African slaves in the Deccan was never permanent. On the death of their masters, they typically became freedmen and served as freelancers in the service of powerful commanders, thereby exchanging a master–slave relationship for a patron–client one. While the humbler sorts sought out and served commanders as paid troopers, the more talented ex-slaves managed to attract their own troopers (often other ex-slaves), obtain land assignments and enter a sultanate's official hierarchy as ranked commanders or *amir*s. Because their ties with Africa had been permanently severed, these men necessarily adopted the Deccan as their home, readily embracing the local culture and becoming fiercely loyal to the region and its political systems.

This is what happened to Malik Ambar. Born in 1548 in the pagan countryside surrounding the Ethiopian highlands, he turned up in the slave markets of the Red Sea, was taken to Baghdad and sold to a prominent merchant who educated him, converted him to Islam and changed his name from 'Chapu' to 'Ambar'. From Baghdad he reached the Deccan in the early 1570s, having been purchased by the *peshwa* (prime minister) of the Nizam Shahi sultanate of Ahmadnagar. When the *peshwa* died in 1574/5 Ambar was freed by his master's widow and became a freelancer. He also acquired a wife. For a while he served the sultan of Bijapur, who gave him the title 'Malik', and in 1595, having acquired a contingent of his own troops, he entered the service of a Habshi commander in the Nizam Shahi state. In 1600 its capital, Ahmadnagar, fell to Mughal forces – but not the countryside, which teemed with troops formerly employed by the sultanate. Foremost among those picking up the pieces of the fragmented kingdom was Malik Ambar, whose cavalry swiftly grew to 7,000 men. Upon finding a prince of Ahmadnagar's royal house, he promoted the youth's cause as the future sovereign of a reconstituted Nizam Shahi state. He also married his daughter to him and presided over his coronation as Sultan Murtaza Nizam Shah II (r. 1600–10), who for the next ten years would reign as the first of Malik Ambar's two puppet sultans, with Ambar himself actually managing the state as *peshwa* and commanding its armies. Ambar's repeated successes against Jahangir's forces – and the source of the emperor's frustration, as revealed in the miniature painting – lay in his mastery of guerrilla tactics. Avoiding pitched battles against the Mughals' formidable armies, Ambar harassed Mughal supply lines, launched surprise night attacks and drew imperial forces into wooded hills and rugged ravines where they could be ambushed by light cavalry.

Between 1600 and 1627, when Malik Ambar held undisputed control over the Ahmadnagar sultanate's military and civil affairs, the kingdom acquired a distinctly African character. By 1610 he commanded an army of 50,000, a fifth of whom were Africans.[32] Habshis entered India in considerable numbers as military slaves, some of whom, after attaining their freedom, would purchase large numbers of their own Habshi slaves. This had become an established pattern. Just as Malik Ambar had arrived in the Deccan as one of 1,000 slaves of Chengiz Khan, who was then *peshwa* of Ahmadnagar, Chengiz Khan himself had earlier come to the Deccan as a Habshi slave. These men could experience a remarkable degree of upward mobility, moving from slaves to freelancers, to commanders, and finally to slave owners. Their experience recalls the pattern found in thirteenth-century north India, where a freed slave such as Balban acquired his own slaves and eventually went on to seize control of the Delhi sultanate. The difference was that Malik Ambar never declared himself sultan, preferring to maintain a puppet sovereign so as not to upset

Nizam Shahi dynastic continuity, much as Rama Raya, a century earlier, had retained Sadaśiva to uphold Vijayanagara's Tuluva dynasty.

Malik Ambar could not have held off sustained Mughal pressure without the substantial contributions of Maratha warrior clans that, together with Habshi slaves, had also been recruited into Ahmadnagar's state system. Alongside the Africans, the Marathas' swift and light cavalry units stoutly resisted the Mughals' cumbersome armies, which they occasionally pursued as far as the imperial headquarters at Burhanpur. The emergence of such units in the Deccan's sultanates had a deep history. Like the Delhi sultans before them, the Mughals easily recruited war-horses and cavalrymen from Central Asia, owing to north India's proximity to that region's military labour markets and abundant pasture lands. But the Deccan sultanates, cut off by hostile Mughal territory from inner Asia's military labour markets and horse pastures, had to find alternatives. Either they could import warrior-slaves native to East Africa and war-horses from the Persian Gulf, or they could recruit both cavalrymen and horses from their own locality, thereby tapping into the Deccan's military labour market.

They actually did both. Beginning with the Bahmani dynasty (1347–1518), the sultans of the Deccan understood that in order to access the grass-roots source of local wealth – the surplus grains produced by the cultivating classes – they had to recruit hereditary territorial chiefs, or *deshmukh*s, who were native to the plateau. The sultans also needed a reliable source of military labour. The *deshmukh*s not only collected revenue, adjudicated disputes and provided ritual leadership in the lands they controlled: they also recruited troops from among their own villager–clients, who formed the region's military labour market. They would then make these recruits available to a sultan, who in return gave the *deshmukh*s documents (*sanad*s) that formalized their rights to specified lands. Sultan Ibrahim 'Adil Shah I recruited 30,000 Maratha cavalry for service in the sultanate of Bijapur. He also introduced the practice of enlisting *bargir*s, Maratha cavalrymen whose horses were supplied by the state.[33] Many leading Maratha clans had risen to prominence in tandem with the rise of the sultanates themselves. The Shinde lineage of Kanerkhed had served the Bahmani sultans as *siledar*s, that is, cavalrymen who furnished their own horses. The Mane lineage of Mhasvad did the same for the sultans of Bijapur. As rewards for their military service, those sultans made the Nimbalkar lineage of Nimlak and the Ghatge lineage of Malavdi *sardeshmukh*s, that is, 'heads of *deshmukh*s'.[34] The rights to lands inherited by Shivaji (r. 1674–80), who would found the Maratha kingdom later in the seventeenth century, were initially conferred on his father, Shahji, by the sultans of Ahmadnagar and Bijapur in return for his service to those states. It was the *sanad* from the court that gave a *deshmukh* authority over his own kinsmen and the state's backing if they opposed him, as they often did. As a result, the history of Maharashtra and the Maratha polity is essentially the history of these *deshmukh* families.[35]

Under Malik Ambar's leadership, then, the Ahmadnagar sultanate had actually become a joint Habshi–Maratha enterprise. Building on earlier sultanate methods of recruitment, the units of Maratha cavalry in Malik Ambar's service grew from 10,000 in 1609 to 50,000 in 1624.[36] In the end, however, it was the Maratha component that would have the more lasting consequences for Indian history. Few Ethiopian females were brought to India, meaning that the Habshi population there could never be self-replicating. Furthermore, the collapse of the Nizam Shahi sultanate ended the patronage system by which African military slaves had been recruited to India. By contrast, the number of fighters that *deshmukh* families could recruit on behalf of the sultans eventually enabled them not only to surpass the Habshis in importance, but to replace the sultanates that had initially recruited them. In short, the rise of Maratha power – such an important socio-political development between the late seventeenth and early nineteenth centuries – was deeply rooted in the Marathas' prior patronage by the region's sultanates.

# EMERGING IDENTITIES: THE IDEA OF 'SIKH'

Especially between the fourteenth and seventeenth centuries, poets across India, writing in the spoken languages of the people, aspired for direct experience of ultimate reality unmediated by liturgy, elaborate rituals, book learning or intercession by institutionalized specialists such as Brahmin priests or Muslim clerics. Some poets focused on fervent devotion – *bhakti* – to a loving, personal deity who possessed attributes that were manifested in visible form. Such devotion was expressed by outward forms of piety such as reciting or singing verses of adoration addressed directly to the deity, or making pilgrimages to a temple in which the deity's image was enshrined. Other poets conceived of the deity as a formless, eternal, all-pervading consciousness that both created and inhabited reality, but which was not manifested with attributes and could not be represented in images. Both kinds of devotion were animated by the promise of liberation for all sincere devotees, regardless of caste or gender, meaning that the verses of *bhakti* poet-saints often carried, at least implicitly, a message of protest against socio-religious inequality. From at least the late nineteenth century on, it was common to refer to the collective aspirations and deeds of these poets as constituting a '*bhakti* movement'. This phrase, however, suggests a monolithic and self-conscious historical phenomenon possessing a well-considered goal, such as a 'nationalist movement'. An alternative model is the notion of a '*bhakti* network', in which the voices of disparate poets echoed or resonated with one another across time and space, but without there ever having been a coherent or collectively organized 'movement'.[37]

In the Punjab, such a voice was heard in the words of Guru Nanak (1469–1539). Unlike other poet-saints of pre-colonial India, however, Guru Nanak actually did initiate a movement – indeed, a new and original religious tradition: Sikhism. Born in 1469, Nanak belonged to the rural Punjab's upper-caste Khatri community. His father had learnt Persian to get a job as a *patwari*, or village accountant in the service of a village headman, working in the lower rungs of the Delhi sultanate's revenue system during the Lodi dynasty's final, chaotic days. As a young man, Nanak became a householder and found a job as a rural grain merchant. But he was living in unsettled times; he was thirty-six in 1505 when Babur launched the first of his five raids on north India. The political landscape was collapsing, and to him the moral landscape looked no better. As a rural official who witnessed plenty of corruption first-hand, he concluded that he was living in the *kaliyuga*, that is, a time of moral decay when *dharma*, codes of proper conduct, had vanished. It seemed to him that neither

Hindu nor Muslim ideals were being upheld. According to one tradition, a holy man came to him and so 'subdued his mind' that he gave
away all his granary's assets, together with his personal property,
and abandoned his wife and children.[38] He then undertook a series of
long trips that included, within the Punjab, sites important for yogi
ascetics as well as Sufi centres in Multan and Pakpattan. He also
made more distant travels within and beyond India before finally
returning to the Punjab and settling down at Kartarpur, on the banks
of the Ravi River. Here he famously declared his distance from both
Hindu and Islamic institutions, gathering a group of followers who
would hear and accept his message. Nanak returned from his wan-
derings and began his career as a spiritual teacher around 1524, just
a few years before Babur swept away the last Lodi sultan and established the Mughal empire, meaning that north India witnessed the
launching of two new dispensations – one spiritual, one political – at
nearly the same time.

Like other *bhakti* poets, Nanak challenged the hierarchal order of
the caste system and delivered a message of liberation from the cycle of
births and rebirths fundamental to classical Indian thought, preaching
that liberation was offered to all, regardless of caste or gender. And,
like most devotional poets, he composed his verses in the common
language of the people, in his case Punjabi, with a view to reaching a
broader public. He saw no merit in making pilgrimages or in worshipp-
ing images. For him the Supreme God is a formless, eternal being who,
both transcendent and immanent, created not only the observable
reality but also the very deities that head the Hindu pantheon: Brahma,
Vishnu, Śiva. He would not worship such derivative, created deities,
much less their many incarnations or *avatar*s. To his followers at
Kartarpur, Nanak preached a distinctive doctrine of meditation on the
name and the word of God, together with an active, ethical engagement with society; there would be no retreating from the world in the
manner of monks or ascetics. Release from the bonds of karma (the
theory of action and its consequences), and the cycle of repeated
rebirths to which karma gives rise, could result only from the grace of
God, together with one's individual effort and piety. That is to say, the
law of karma might explain the social position into which one is born,
but it could also be annulled by the grace (*hukm*) of God.[39]

Nanak, who soon acquired the title *guru*, or 'teacher', understood his teachings as constituting a decisive break with existing religious traditions, which is why he took measures to institutionalize his work so as to ensure its survival for subsequent generations. He modified a thirty-five-character script that had existed from before his day, and used it for his own verses – hence the script's name of Gurmukhi, 'from the mouth of the Guru'. Just as the Arabic script was associated with Islam, and Devanagari with classical Hindu scriptures, the use of this distinctive script was intended to ensure the unique nature of Guru Nanak's teachings. Written scriptures also served to stabilize the new community, since they could provide focus, cohesion and permanence across space and time. Indeed, the Sikhs (from the San-skrit *shishya*, 'disciple'), being a community that coalesced around a holy book, present a clear instance of a 'scriptural community'. Guru Nanak took further steps to stabilize his fledgling following. He established three daily prayers (dawn, sunset and day's end), and in order to eradicate distinctions of caste and gender he instituted a communal kitchen open to all followers. He engaged in collective singing of his own verses in a sacred meeting place, initially called a *dharmsal*, and admitted followers through a formal initiation rite. He also took great care in selecting a successor, both to institutional-ize the authority of his position and to ensure its continuance in succeeding generations. By choosing someone who was not a member of his own family, moreover, he implicitly rejected a dynastic prin-ciple for the tradition's future leadership.[40]

That said, the religion founded by Guru Nanak, like any when viewed across historical time, did not fail to evolve after the death of its founder in 1539. Some fluidity is seen, for example, in the different terms by which the community was known – for example, Nanak-panth, Gurmukh-panth, Nirmal-panth, Gursikh. The same is true of the growth of the movement's holy book, the Guru Granth Sahib. Originating in a volume of Guru Nanak's own hymns that were passed on to his first successor, Guru Angad (1539–52), the book continued to grow during the sixteenth century.[41] This was a time when devotional verses of poet-saints across northern India were being compiled in anthologies. The so-called Fatehpur manuscript, compiled in Rajasthan in 1582, included the verses of Surdas (d. 1573) and thirty-five other poet-saints such as Kabir (d. c.1518), Namdev (d. c.1350), and Ravidas (d. 1540).[42] Similarly, the third Sikh Guru, Amar Das (1552–74), collected surviving verses by Guru Nanak and included them in a two-volume holy book, the Adi Granth, to which he added hymns and couplets of more than a dozen non-Sikh poet-saints – most prominently Kabir, Namdev, Ravidas and the Chishti Sufi Shaikh Farid al-Din Ganj-i Shakar (d. 1265) – evidently because their thought conformed to Sikh theological and ethical principles.[43] Apart from the Adi Granth, however, from the late sixteenth century there circulated oral narratives of Guru Nanak's life, the *janam-sakhi*s, which freely borrowed themes from tales of Hindu deities (*Purana*s), Sufi saints (*tazkira*s), and the Buddha (*Jataka*s). This sort of diversity suggests the malleability of Sikh identity in the sixteenth century, and the lack of a fixed image of the religion's founder, whose life appears in these stories to have been fashioned, at least in part, by the fluid cultural universe of early Mughal Punjab.[44]

The Sikh community grew rapidly in the sixteenth century. Nanak's earliest followers had been fellow Khatris engaged in petty trade, shopkeeping, or lower-level civil service in the Lodi or Mughal bureaucracies. But as the movement grew, it experienced a significant influx of Jat cultivators.[45] The Jats first appear in recorded history in eighth-century Sind, where they were described as cattle-herding tribes that lacked a sense of social hierarchy. By the eleventh century they had migrated up the lower Indus to the Multan region of southern Punjab, where they were described as 'cattle-owners, low Sudra people'. By the thirteenth century they had moved further north into the central Punjab, and by the late sixteenth century they had abandoned pastoralism for agriculture, becoming dominant landholders in nearly half of Mughal Punjab. Their adoption of agriculture was assisted by the introduction of the Persian wheel (see p. 73), which enhanced the land's capacity for producing food crops.[46] The Jats' transformation from nomadic pastoralism to field agriculture progressed to the point that, by the 1650s, the word 'Jat' had become virtually synonymous with 'villager', or even 'cultivator'. Yet their elevation in economic status had not been accompanied by a commensurate rise in caste status in the Hindu social hierarchy. They also appear to have retained an egalitarian social outlook from their pastoralist days. As an open community that espoused social as well as religious equality, the Sikh movement was therefore well positioned to absorb a significant influx of Jats.

The growth in the Sikh religion also saw changes in ritual. Guru Amar Das established festival days and distinctive ceremonies for a Sikh's birth, marriage and death. Even though Guru Nanak had rejected the idea of pilgrimages, Guru Amar Das built a well of eighty-four steps in his village of Goindwal, which became the Sikhs' first pilgrimage centre. Before his death in 1574, he had begun excavating a great tank on a plot of 500 *bigha*s (a unit of land area) given to him by Akbar. Completed by the next guru, Ram Das (1574–81), the tank would become known as Amritsar, 'the nectar of immortality'. Eventually the town that grew up around the tank would be known by that name, too, as it became the primary seat of Sikh authority.[47] As the community grew across the Punjab and even beyond, Guru Amar Das began sending personal representatives (*masand*s) to look after distant congregations and to bring annual offerings to Amritsar. This organizational elaboration was followed by attempts to standardize the Sikhs' canonical scripture. The fifth guru, Arjan (1581–1606), updated the Adi Granth by adding his own verses and those of Guru Amar Das to the two-volume body that had been collected by Guru Ram Das. He then supervised the compilation of an authoritative text, completed in 1604. This was done, in part, to commit to writing hymns that in his day were available mainly in oral form, and partly to protect the purity of Sikh verses from interpolations by the guru's rivals.[48] The result was to stabilize the scriptural foundation of the Sikh religion. To strengthen its institutional and ritual basis, Guru Arjun enlarged Amritsar's great tank, paved it with bricks and – most prominently – in 1589 built in its middle the famous Harmandir, popularly known as the Golden Temple. Apart from being one of India's greatest architectural triumphs, the Harmandir made Amritsar the Sikh faith's primary ritual focus, since it was here that the Adi Granth was placed for continuous reading, highlighting that scripture's role as the heart and soul of Sikhdom. Notably, the Harmandir's distinctive design and architectural style clearly set this structure apart from mosques and Hindu temples of the day, boldly asserting the autonomy of its faith community from India's other religious traditions [see Fig. 15]. It even appears that Akbar – who had a brief but cordial meeting with Guru Arjan when passing through the Punjab in 1598[49] – allowed the latter to manage the city of Amritsar, effectively placing it outside the Mughal administrative framework, a 'state within a state'.[50]

In the sixteenth century, the growth of the Sikh movement attracted little if any attention at the Mughal court. But this changed soon after Jahangir came to the throne in 1605. Because the new emperor's eldest son, Khusrau, had contested his father's claim to succeed Akbar, he was detained immediately upon Jahangir's accession. But in April 1606 the headstrong prince managed to escape confinement in Agra and dashed straight for the Punjab in a desperate search for support to overthrow his newly crowned father. When his hastily assembled army reached Tarn Tarun, a settlement south of Amritsar, which Guru Arjan had established, the guru responded favourably to Khusrau's call for supporters, notwithstanding the fact that the emperor was advancing towards the Punjab in hot pursuit of his rebellious son. Jahangir himself relates what took place next:

> Khusrau happened to halt at the place where he [Guru Arjun] was, and he came out and did homage to him. He behaved to Khusrau in certain special ways, and made on his forehead a fingermark in saffron, which the Indians (Hinduwan) call *qashqa* [*tika*], and is considered auspicious. When this came to my ears and I clearly understood his folly, I ordered them to produce him [Arjun] ... and having confiscated his property commanded that he should be put to death.[51]

Jahangir ordered the execution not out of any animus against Sikhism, which in any event he failed to recognize as a separate religion, but because of the guru's apparent support for a state rebel.[52]

Guru Arjun's execution posed a major crisis for the Sikh community. The late guru had personally acquired both spiritual and temporal authority and had done more to institutionalize the Sikh religion than anybody since Guru Nanak. His absence therefore not only left the Sikhs momentarily leaderless: it set them on a collision course with the Mughal empire. The guru's son and successor Guru Hargobind (1606–44) reacted by girding himself with two swords that symbolized spiritual and temporal authority, indicating an ethos of militancy hitherto alien to Sikh tradition. He also built a fort to defend Amritsar, another sign of the community's more militant profile. Finally, he adopted the trappings of royalty, building opposite Amritsar's Harmandir a high platform called the Akal Takht, 'immortal throne', where he conducted worldly business in a court-like atmosphere. When suspicious officials reported these activities to the imperial court, Jahangir ordered that the guru be detained in Gwalior fort, where the Mughals' political prisoners were held. Although he was released several years later, Sikh–Mughal relations were poisoned for decades to come.

## ASSESSING JAHANGIR

Jahangir's reign falls into two distinct phases. From his coronation to 1622, the emperor remained active in the state's administrative and military affairs, ruling after 1611 in virtual partnership with Nur Jahan. The latter issued land grants to women under her own seal, struck coins in her own name and sat in the *jharokha* of her palace, while below her nobles presented themselves and received her orders. Her name and title were jointly attached on all imperial documents receiving Jahangir's signature.[53] But in the last five years of his life, from 1622 to his death in 1627, the emperor became so incapacitated by drink and opium that Nur Jahan took many administrative matters into her own hands. The extent of her influence in this latter phase of Jahangir's reign is suggested by Francisco Pelsaert, a Dutch East Company commercial officer serving in Agra from 1621 to 1627. 'When the King comes home in the evening from hunting,' he wrote:

> he takes his seat in his Ghusalkhana [private audience chamber], where all the lords come to present themselves, and where strangers who have requests to make are received in audience. He sits here till a quarter of the night or more has passed, and during this time he drinks his three *piyala*, or cups, of wine, taking them successively at regular intervals ... Everyone leaves when the last cup has been drunk, and the King goes to bed. As soon as all the men have left, the Queen

comes with the female slaves, and they undress him, chafing and fondling him as if he were a little child; for his three cups have made him so 'happy' that he is more disposed to rest than to keep awake. This is the time when his wife, who knows so well how to manage him that she obtains whatever she asks for or desires, gets always 'yes', and hardly ever 'no' in reply.[54]

Some might dismiss such an intimate glimpse of the emperor and his favourite wife as bazaar gossip tossed off by a foreigner who would have had no access to the royal chambers. On the other hand Mu'tamad Khan, the courtier entrusted with completing Jahangir's memoir and identified by him as 'a servant who knows my temperament',[55] remarked that the emperor repeatedly let it be known 'that he had bestowed the sovereignty on Nur Jahan Begam, and would say, "I require nothing beyond only a *sir* [0.9 kg] of wine and a half *sir* of meat." '[56] Politics aside, Nur Jahan was deeply devoted to the emperor, as he was to her.[57]

Like Sultan Muhammad bin Tughluq before him, Jahangir made ostentatious displays of his devotion to justice. In his very first order as emperor he established a 'chain of justice' strung between the Agra fort and the Jamuna, with bells attached to it so that anybody seeking justice could shake the chain and expect the government's response.[58] And like his Tughluq predecessor, he was a man of sharp contradictions. He could be almost arbitrarily cruel, as when he had a man nearly beaten to death and imprisoned for life for breaking a china dish.[59] When two bearers and a bush-beater accidently caused a blue bull to run off during a hunt, he ordered the bearers to be hamstrung and the bush-beater killed on the spot.[60] On the other hand, he was capable of great sensitivity. He noticed, for example, that in the winter elephants would shiver when splashing themselves with cold water. Fearing their discomfort, he ordered that lukewarm water be prepared for their use.[61] In the Khyber Pass, he once marvelled at watching a spider the size of a crab seize and kill a snake 1.4 metres in length.[62] He was so struck by the beauty of a falcon and its black markings that he ordered it to be painted by the famous artist Ustad Mansur.[63] And he made a detailed list of the thirty birds that were *not* found in Kashmir.[64] In short, Jahangir's most refined sensibility was aesthetic, especially of the visual sort. But unlike the art patron-ized by Akbar, which depicts the latter engaged in a frenzy of heroic activity – hunting, fighting, directing great projects, and so on – the work patronized by his son was typically contemplative and natural-istic. The contrasting temperaments of father and son could hardly be more stark. And yet he shared with Akbar a fascination with Indian religions, he maintained his father's practice of sponsoring inter-faith debates, and he went out of his way to visit the Hindu ascetic Jadrup, in whose cave near Ujjain he thrice held extended philosophical dis-cussions. Those meetings, too, he ordered to be documented in art [see Fig. 16].

In the last analysis Jahangir, having inherited a finely tuned admin-istrative machine capable of running largely on its own, was able to devote himself to cultivating the sort of cultural projects that only peace and security could afford. He knew that he lived in the shadow of an overachieving father, whom he always honoured despite his youthful rebellion against him. Thus the magnificent tomb in Agra that Jahangir built for Akbar suggests its patron's wish to be remem-bered as the dutiful son, rather than as the impatient prince who had rebelled against his father and arranged for the assassination of his father's revered adviser. Art, literature, architecture, landscaping – especially in his beloved Kashmir – all these were incomparably enriched by Jahangir's refined sensibility and generous patronage. In fact, had he inherited his father's hyperactive side, Jahangir might have waged a lot more wars and overextended the empire to breaking point, as actually did happen under his grandson 'Alamgir. Indeed, Akbar arguably had already overextended the empire with his annex-ation of Kandahar, which lies beyond the subcontinent. All this suggests that, in hindsight, Jahangir was the right man for his time.[65]

## SHAH JAHAN

Jahangir died in late October 1627 while en route from Kashmir to Lahore. Nur Jahan's brother Asaf Khan, who all along had backed the cause of the late emperor's third son, Khurram, now took matters into his own hands, swiftly putting his sister under detention while, as a precautionary measure, removing Khurram's young sons Dara Shukoh and Aurangzeb from her custody. He also sent a courier down to the Deccan to fetch Khurram to north India. While marching to Agra, the prince sent a return courier ordering the execution of other princes who might contest his claim to the throne: his younger brother Shahryar, the two sons of his late brother Khusrau, and two sons of his late uncle Danyal. Khurram was doubtless determined to avoid the sort of messy succession conflict experienced by his father, for which he himself had been responsible. In January 1628 his grisly order was carried out, and soon he triumphantly entered Agra where he was hailed with the title that his father had earlier given him – Shah Jahan. On 4 February 1628, at an hour precisely fixed by his astrologers, he was formally crowned emperor.

Shah Jahan now found himself heading one of the world's mightiest empires at its height of wealth, political clout and cultural attainment. And the empire had found a sovereign who would revel in the most lavish displays of that wealth and glory. The new emperor lost no time in setting the tone for his reign. Upon his coronation, he doled out generous sums to his immediate family: 200,000 gold coins (*ashrafi*) and 600,000 rupees to his favourite wife, Mumtaz Mahal, 100,000 *ashrafi*s and 600,000 rupees to his favourite daughter, Jahanara, and 150,000 rupees to each of his first three sons. He made Asaf Khan the *vazir* of the empire, with a rank of 8,000/8,000. Mahabat Khan was made governor of Ajmer, with the even higher rank of 9,000/9,000, doubtless in recognition of his superior military skills – which Shah Jahan could well appreciate, having been pursued throughout India as a rebel prince and defeated several times by him. By contrast, all Nur Jahan's former power and authority at once drained away from the erstwhile queen, who now sank to a political nonentity. Coins stamped with her name were withdrawn from circulation. Reduced to a pensioned dowager, the once-mighty Nur Jahan quietly lived her remaining eighteen years in Lahore with her daughter, Shahryar's widow. She would be buried next to Jahangir in the magnificent tomb that she had built for her husband outside the city.

Shortly after Shah Jahan assumed the throne, serious rebellions broke out. The Afghan nobleman Khan Jahan Lodi, though a man of mediocre military abilities, had enjoyed high favour under Jahangir, holding governorships first in Gujarat, then in the strip of the northern Deccan under Mughal administration. But in the latter capacity he had handed over much of that strip to the Nizam Shahis of Ahmadnagar in exchange for 300,000 rupees, which he pocketed. On top of that treasonous act, he had backed Shahryar, Nur Jahan's candidate to succeed Jahangir to the throne. Khan Jahan therefore suspected that his prior actions had compromised his status in the new regime. When he failed to pursue the emperor's forward agenda in the Deccan and was transferred to a less prestigious post in Malwa, his insecurity turned to paranoia. And when some of his *jagir*s were resumed, he became so alarmed that he failed to appear in court, as protocol required of *mansabdar*s when in the capital. In October 1629, realizing that his absence had been noticed, he gathered up his household and retainers and fled south. Although an imperial army was sent to pursue the fugitive nobleman, he managed to evade capture and made his way to Daulatabad. Back in the Deccan, he was welcomed by the Nizam Shahi sultan, Burhan III, who placed him in command of his own army in the hope that he could recover parts of his territory which the Mughals had occupied. But in December Shah Jahan, aware that he could not fail this first challenge to his authority as emperor, personally left Agra for Burhanpur, the Mughals' provincial capital in the Deccan, in order to supervise military operations against the rebel. Aware that his sheltering of Khan Jahan had only brought trouble for himself, the Nizam Shahi sultan hinted that his guest should leave. When Mughal pressure drove him from his base, Khan Jahan took the hint and left for the Punjab, but he was abandoned by most of his supporters and ultimately overpowered and beheaded by a detachment of Shah Jahan's Rajput cavalry.

Another early rebellion had its roots in Mughal relations with the Bundela Rajputs of Orchha, located just outside modern Jhansi. In 1627 Jhujhar Singh, the son and successor of Orchha's Raja Bir Singh (r. 1605–27), proceeded to Agra to pay homage to Shah Jahan, who confirmed him with a rank of 4,000/4,000. But in June the next year, after the emperor ordered an inquiry into the unauthorized gains that Bir Singh had made during Jahangir's regime, Jhujhar Singh became alarmed and, like Khan Jahan Lodi, fled Agra. Shah Jahan responded by sending an army that pursued his Rajput vassal to Erachh, the fort in Bundelkhand to which he had fled, sixty-five kilometres north-east of Jhansi. After a successful siege of the stronghold, the rebel Rajput submitted and begged forgiveness for his misdeeds, which the emperor readily granted, restoring him to his original rank. He would soon promote him to an even higher rank as a reward for his service against Khan Jahan Lodi. But in 1634 the Bundela raja reverted to his errant ways. Back in his ancestral capital of Orchha, Jhujhar Singh led an unprovoked attack on the fort of Chauragarh (one hundred kilometres west-south-west of Jabalpur), which belonged to the Gond chieftain Prem Narayan. This siege led to another instance of *jauhar* as Prem Narayan, in extreme desperation, massacred his women and fought to the death with 300 kinsmen, after which Jhujhar Singh occupied the fort.[66] The emperor's response to this egregious act was utterly cynical. While understandably enraged at Jhujhar Singh's grievous behaviour, he did not seek justice or recompense for any of Prem Narayan's surviving kinsmen. Instead, he demanded that Jhujhar Singh pay the court a large indemnity, in effect splitting with his rebel *mansabdar* the loot that the latter had plundered from Prem Narayan.

But Jhujhar Singh, now in full rebellion, refused the emperor's offer and fled further south, into Malwa. In response, in 1635 Shah Jahan sent an army of 20,000 after him, commanded by three veteran generals. On the grounds that the property of a *mansabdar* belonged to the state and was hence liable to confiscation or destruction should its *mansabdar*/patron commit a state crime such as rebellion, Shah Jahan ordered the demolition of the Bundela rajas' dynastic temple at Orchha.[67] But the rebel was not the only target of the emperor's order. The temple had been completed by Jhujhar Singh's father, Bir Singh, mainly to legitimize his irregular accession to the throne, and to atone for the fact that his privileged position as a major courtier at Jahangir's court had been bought through the murder of Abu'l-fazl.[68] Therefore its destruction by Shah Jahan served to undermine the claims to legitimate rule asserted by both the usurper Bir Singh and his rebel son Jhujhar Singh. The emperor also forcibly converted Jhujhar Singh's two sons to Islam, another cynical move since it excluded the rebel's direct descendants from inheriting the rulership of Orchha. Instead, he gave that rulership to a rival branch of the Bundela lineage headed by Raja Debi Singh, a more compliant vassal. As for Jhujhar Singh himself, the fugitive rebel was ultimately driven deep into the forests of Gondwana, where he was slain by a band of Gonds, evidently in revenge for his earlier killing of their king, Prem Narayan.

Shah Jahan also took decisive steps to intensify the governance of provinces that were only loosely brought into the imperial orbit. The aggressive measures he took in 1632 against the Portuguese in lower Bengal transformed much of that region from a zone of political anarchy, favourable for piracy and slaving, to one of orderly government where Bengalis enjoyed a greater degree of security. Further to the north, in 1636 the Mughal ambassador to the Ahom court was murdered by the Assamese, leading to a series of hard-fought battles between the two powers. Although the Ahoms initially overwhelmed the Mughal outpost of Hajo, the Mughals retaliated in late 1637, driving the Assamese back to Darrang, thirty kilometres east of Gauhati. After an Assamese counter-attack the next year, the two powers negotiated a treaty whereby the Ahoms formally acknowledged Mughal control of Kamrup to the west, while the Mughals recognized the independence and territorial integrity of the Ahom kingdom. These operations established the Mughals' ability to adapt to Bengal's riverine terrain, where they had learnt to co-ordinate the use of watercraft and gunboats with cavalry and infantry.

On the other side of the subcontinent, in Sind, the geographical and cultural environment could hardly have been more different. Here, the fertile strip of the Indus abuts a hot, dry pastoral zone inhabited by tribal communities whose raids on trade caravans had caused perennial havoc for the Mughals. In response, Shah Jahan established regular garrisons from which provincial authorities could launch campaigns to collect taxes, in cash, from pastoral tribes. He also sought to integrate tribal chieftains into the Mughal system by defining them as *mansabdar*s governing over territorially bounded pastoral regions that the Mughals called *jagir*s. Lastly, imperial officers gave lucrative land grants to important Sufi shrines that dotted the Indus valley from Sind north to the southern Punjab, and which played important roles in the religious and economic lives of the region's pastoral and agrarian communities. From at least the late fifteenth century, in fact, tribal chieftains had been giving their daughters to descendants of prominent Sufi shaikhs. Shah Jahan therefore treated Sufi shrines as nodes of stability in an otherwise unstable region.[69]

The manner in which Shah Jahan prosecuted these military operations hints at changes in how the emperor began fashioning his public image. Early in his reign, when Jhujhar Singh revolted against imperial authority by fleeing the imperial court, the emperor intended to pursue the fugitive Rajput in person. But the seasoned general Mahabat Khan dissuaded him from doing so, arguing that it was beneath the emperor's dignity to take the field against 'a crowd of peasants and defenceless people'.[70] Heeding the advice, Shah Jahan marched only as far as Gwalior, leaving the command of battlefield operations to his generals. He likewise left the direction of his later military operations to his sons. In this respect Shah Jahan broke from the tradition of his Timurid ancestors, most of whom had personally engaged in battlefield combat. It also pointed to the emperor's gradual withdrawal from direct contact with his subjects, a process actually begun by Akbar, who had institutionalized the use of the *jharokha*. Even when relatively low to the ground, these devices had the effect of removing the sovereign spatially and symbolically from the people, be they commoners or nobility, and of rendering him more an icon to be adored than an administrator with whom one could interact. Settling into his persona as supreme sovereign, Shah Jahan, in sharp contrast to the feisty prince of his earlier days, increasingly projected himself as lofty, distant and majestic.

Such self-fashioning is clearly seen in the emperor's architectural programme. Of all the Mughals, Shah Jahan was the most invested in patronizing grand works of architecture that have become iconic of the entire Mughal era – indeed, of India itself. Even before his accession to power, he had patronized architectural projects in his various postings – for example, quarters inside Kabul fort, the Shahi Bagh in Ahmedabad, a hunting lodge near Burhanpur, the Shalimar garden in Kashmir. But it was an event in the fourth year of his reign that provided a major impetus to express himself through works of monumental architecture. In March 1630 he, his household and his court had reached the Deccan's provincial capital of Burhanpur in order to oversee military and diplomatic operations against the plateau's three remaining independent sultanates: Ahmadnagar, Bijapur and Golconda. This was a happy period for the emperor and his beloved wife, Mumtaz Mahal, who gave birth to a daughter, Husn Ara Begum, a month after the imperial household had reached Burhanpur. This was followed by the good news of the rebel Khan Jahan Lodi's capture and execution.

But in the following year personal tragedy struck. In June 1631, Mumtaz Mahal died giving birth to her fourteenth child, plunging the king into a state of unremitting grief. For a week he refused to appear in public. No business was transacted. From constant weeping he was forced to wear spectacles, so his chronicler reports, and within a matter of days a third of his beard and moustache had turned white.[71] The queen's body was sent to Agra, escorted by their second son, prince Shuja', and buried by the Jamuna on a plot formerly owned by Raja Man Singh. On that spot would rise one of the world's most famous monuments. Work on building the Taj Mahal, a corruption of the queen's name Mumtaz Mahal, began in January 1632 and was completed eleven years later at a cost of five million rupees. Although Europeans of the day – and even colonial British scholars of the twentieth century – were certain it was the work of a European architect,[72] the emperor himself appears to have provided both the inspiration and the overall design, with skilled architects merely carrying out the execution.[73] His aim was to create an earthly replica of the house of Mumtaz Mahal in the Garden of Paradise. For this purpose he took to a monumental scale the kind of riverfront style that was already prevalent among Agra's residential gardens, while also building upon the tradition of Mughal tomb design.[74] Placing any monument over a grave – especially one with a proud, assertive dome – is problematic in Islamic tradition, which stresses humility before God. Babur's grave in Kabul was open to the sky. By contrast Humayun's tomb, built by Akbar, broke with tradition with its prominent marble dome. This was followed by Akbar's and Jahangir's tombs, both of which lack domes. With the Taj, its more daring, more bulbous dome set on a higher drum, surrounded by four smaller domes, Shah Jahan not only reasserted the idea of a domed tomb, but surpassed that of Humayun.

If the Taj Mahal projects an aura of sublime harmony, elegance and simplicity, Shah Jahan's palace complexes convey his vision of a highly centralized, absolute monarchy and of his own exalted place in the cosmos. Notably, the emperor titled himself the 'Second Lord of the Conjunction' (*sahib-i qiran-i thani*), referring to the significance his astrologers attributed to periodic conjunctions of Saturn and Jupiter. In the Persianate world, persons thought to have been born during such an event were considered extraordinary, capable even of ushering in a new age of justice, peace and prosperity. The phrase suggested, in short, a messiah-like figure. Although Timur himself had laid no claim to being a 'Lord of the Conjunction' (*sahib-i qiran*), and in fact denied it, contemporaries across the Persianate world had called him that, while his own soldiers worshipped him as a saint. Shah Jahan's reference to himself as the *second* 'Lord of the Conjunction' therefore reveals how the emperor saw himself in relation to his own, illustrious ancestor. It also reveals a man claiming quasi-divine attributes, destined to play a transformative role in world history – in short, a 'millennial sovereign'.[75] Unlike portraits of Mughal emperors from Babur through to Jahangir, which typically reveal each monarch's humanity, emotions and individual character, those of Shah Jahan present a flawless, unchanging ideal, a face enveloped by a halo, often with small angels above his head, even crowning him. The emperor's official chronicle opens with a frontispiece depicting Timur and Shah Jahan seated on thrones, facing each other, the former presenting the imperial crown to the latter.[76] These were not just artistic fantasies. Revealing how closely he identified with Timur and his legacy, Shah Jahan – alone among Mughal emperors – tried to reclaim for the Mughal empire territory that both Timur and Babur had once ruled. So in the mid 1640s he sent armies across Afghanistan's Hindu Kush Mountains into Central Asia, there to confront his dynasty's ancient enemies, the Uzbeks. Although the invasion failed, the effort shows the emperor's determination to act out his identity as the 'Second Lord of the Conjunction'.

In the first decade of his reign, with a view to aligning his palace architecture with his exalted self-image, Shah Jahan remodelled the forts of the empire's two primary capitals, Lahore and Agra. At both sites, nearly all the structures built by Akbar and Jahangir were dismantled to make room for new palaces that emphasized political hierarchy, a rigid formalization of artistic expression and an obsessive regulation of every detail of courtly life. Shah Jahan's name, after all, means 'king of the world', and a guiding idea pervading his reign was that of the court as a microcosm of the world. It followed that a well-ordered court would radiate outwards, projecting its order into the empire at large. Prior to his reign, imperial *mansabdar*s simply stood in the open courtyards before the emperor's *jharokha*. Shah Jahan, however, built covered audience halls (*chihil sutun*), whose forty evenly spaced columns enabled a precise positioning of courtiers in the imperial hierarchy. *Mansabdar*s stood stiffly at a distance from the *jharokha* corresponding to their relative rank in the imperial hierarchy, their eyes riveted on the emperor seated above them. Probably inspired by audience halls of Persepolis in ancient Iran, these underscored the emperor's centrality in both the cosmos and the empire.[77] In Agra, courtiers faced east towards the emperor's *jharokha*, while directly across the adjacent courtyard was a mosque, whose *qibla* – a niche indicating the direction of Mecca – lay on a direct axis with Jahangir's *jharokha*. Such a design visually expressed a unity of political and spiritual authority and implied the emperor's centrality for both, since contemporary eulogists often praised him as the *qibla* of his subjects.[78]

Remodelling the cramped and crowded forts of Lahore and Agra, however, had its limitations. In order more fully to press architecture and the principles of urban design to serve his expansive political ideals, Shah Jahan resolved to build an entire city–fort complex from scratch. This is Shahjahanabad, today's 'Red Fort' and its adjoining walled city – now Old Delhi – built between 1639 and 1648 at a cost of six million rupees. With its red-sandstone walls rising to a height of thirty-three metres and a perimeter of nearly two and a half kilometres, its eastern side abutting the Jamuna, and with the rest of the perimeter punctuated by stately gateways and encircled by a moat, the fort was intended to be dramatic and imposing, as it certainly is. Moreover, by placing his new capital in the greater Delhi plain, Shah Jahan associated his dynasty more directly with the historical cockpit of north Indian power, and also with the many active shrines of saints – in particular Chishti Sufis – that both the Delhi sultans and the Mughals had patronized. Finally, like Akbar's Fatehpur Sikri, this fort–city gave the emperor a large stage on which to enact his ideals of courtly hierarchy and absolute monarchy. It was in the fort's ornate Hall of Private Audience that Shah Jahan placed his famous Peacock Throne, which took craftsmen seven years to assemble, and whose precious stones were valued at ten million rupees. The French traveller Jean-Baptiste Tavernier visited the court in the winter of 1640–41, when the throne had been built but was still in the court at Agra, as the new capital at Shahjahanabad was then under construction. Himself a gem merchant, Tavernier described a dazzling throne 1.8 metres in length and 1.2 metres wide inlaid with numerous emeralds, rubies, pearls and diamonds, with a canopy surmounted with a peacock, its tail made of blue sapphires, its gold body inlaid with precious stones and an enormous pear-shaped pearl suspended from a large ruby fronting its breast.[79]

Tavernier was hardly the only foreigner struck by the pomp of Shah Jahan's court. Other seventeenth-century travellers like him carried their sense of awe back to Europe, where the very word 'mogul' came to connote grandiose power, as it still does today. Coincidentally, monarchal absolutism and centralized authority, together with a rigid formalization of courtly ritual amplified by elaborate ceremony and monumental architecture, were also being articulated in contemporary Europe. The reign of France's Louis XIV began in 1643, shortly before Shah Jahan formally occupied Shahjahanabad. The French 'Sun King' began enlarging his own dazzling palace–city at Versailles in 1661, just a few years after Shah Jahan's rule had come to an end. By the mid seventeenth century, then, royal absolutism had reached both India and Europe, which is perhaps why contemporary Europeans in India, when beholding Shahjahanabad, seem to have felt a shock of recognition.

# CONCLUSION

India and the Mughals experienced important changes under Jahangir and Shah Jahan. First, the empire grew in both territorial extent and wealth: between 1580 and 1646 its revenue demand more than doubled, growing from 90.7 to 222.3 million rupees, owing largely to territorial annexations, especially in Bengal and the northern Deccan.[80] When Shah Jahan came to power, however, he found a treasury that had been nearly depleted. To remedy this, he increased the amount of the empire's *khalisa* land, or land whose revenues went directly to the central treasury, and decreased its total *jagir* land, whose revenues were allocated to imperial *mansabdars*. Between 1631 and 1646, *khalisa* land increased from 6.6 per cent to 14.3 per cent of the empire's total assessed revenue.[81] Both *khalisa* and *jagir* lands were administered under Akbar's regulation system (*zabt*), according to which government officials made periodic surveys and revenue assessments by measuring land areas and by determining the quality of the fields and their potential crop value. Detailed records of such surveys and assessments were kept in both local and central revenue offices – information that was critical for running the army, since the number of troops a *mansabdar* was expected to maintain had to match the amount of revenue his *jagirs* were expected to produce.

*Mansabdars* of medium or higher rank, by ethnicity[82]

|  | 1595 | | 1656 | |
|---|---|---|---|---|
|  | Number | Per cent | Number | Per cent |
| Iranian | 75 | 26.9 | 139 | 28.4 |
| Turkish | 93 | 33.3 | 123 | 25.1 |
| Afghan | 10 | 3.6 | 34 | 6.9 |
| Indian Muslim | 36 | 12.9 | 59 | 12.0 |
| Rajput | 40 | 14.3 | 87 | 17.8 |
| Other | 25 | 9.0 | 48 | 9.8 |
| TOTAL | 279 | | 490 | |

As the empire's territory expanded, so did its corps of *mansabdars*, both in size and in composition. As the above chart indicates, *mansabdars* holding medium or higher ranks nearly doubled in number between the end of Akbar's reign and the end of Shah Jahan's reign. Throughout this period the nobility's Iranian component remained high and stable, comprising about a quarter of the total. Afghans were poorly represented in Akbar's nobility owing to suspicions of their loyalty, but they fared somewhat better under Jahangir and Shah Jahan, as those suspicions began to dissipate. Whereas the proportion of Indian Muslims in the nobility remained at about an eighth of the total throughout this period, the number of Turkish nobles dropped from a third to a quarter of the total, while Rajputs made a modest gain overall. However, these figures distort the extent of the Rajputs' actual importance in Mughal service, since they tended to have, on average, higher ranks than did other groups.

An important change also occurred in the nature of the *mansabdars*' relationship to the emperor. Under Akbar and Jahangir, powerful *mansabdars* were bound to the emperor by a personality cult in which they were considered disciples of a charismatic ruler. Upon being ceremonially inducted into Akbar's or Jahangir's inner circle, these men received small images of the emperor, which they pinned to their turbans. They also performed full prostration before him. But Shah Jahan did away with the little images, the prostration and the personality cult altogether, replacing them with formalized rituals that established a greater distance between himself and all his subjects. Moreover, with each passing generation, the imperial service became more of an entrenched, hereditary nobility. Instead of instilling an ideological conformity among its ruling elite by instituting something like imperial China's examination system, which was based on a common core of literary classics that applicants had to master, the Mughals recruited new talent through a highly regulated process of nomination. Senior officers recommended candidates whose credentials were then vetted by court officials and, in theory, by the emperor himself. If approved, these recruits were given appointments, typically in the form of *jagir*s. By the end of Shah Jahan's reign, relatives of powerful nobles might enter imperial service not only on the death of their patron-relative, but even during his lifetime. In fact, sons of the highest-ranking *mansabdars* were normally enrolled as *mansabdars* themselves. Although they could not inherit their fathers' status or titles and had to begin their careers with a relatively low rank, such men were marked for promotion and rapid advancement in the system.

Shah Jahan's refinements in his courtly self-fashioning speak of broader changes in royal ideology that had taken place during the early seventeenth century. The century had opened with Akbar, who, despite his vacillations, remained genuinely fascinated with religions of all sorts. Jahangir mostly followed his father in this respect, not only allowing all religions to flourish, but opposing the conversion from any religion to another one.[83] But with Shah Jahan the matter is more complicated. On the one hand, he personally commissioned or initiated the construction of more mosques than any Mughal ruler before or after him. These include Lahore's mosque of Wazir Khan (1635), the mosque at Shaikh Mu'in al-Din Chishti's shrine in Ajmer (1636), and the congregational mosques at Agra (1648), Shah-jahanabad (1656) and Thatta (1657). He also reinstituted the annual pilgrimage to Mecca and issued an edict prohibiting the repair of non-Muslim structures. In view of such acts, his reign has sometimes been called a 'return to an Islamic political culture'.[84]

However, there was a genuine disconnect between Shah Jahan as portrayed in official edicts and court chronicles, and the emperor as portrayed in art and courtly culture. Whereas the former category presents him in the tradition of Islam, the latter portrays him in terms of sacred kingship, messianism, and the cult of Timur as a world-conqueror.[85] At the top of the arched niche behind the *jharokha* in Shahjahanabad's Hall of Public Audience, there is a Florentine image of *Orpheus Playing to the Beasts*. This figure, who in Greek mythology could charm living beings with his music, was identified by the Mughals with the prophet-king Solomon – the font of justice in Middle Eastern lore – who in the context of this throne ensemble was identified with Shah Jahan himself.[86] Cosmic entities also appear differently in paintings of Shah Jahan and his father. Whereas Jahangir is depicted surrounded by superhuman agencies only in paintings in which he is dreaming or imagining something, such as shooting Malik Ambar, those of Shah Jahan often show the emperor surrounded by cosmic beings even while he is engaged in worldly events, as though he were an active millennial figure existing in real time.[87] Furthermore, by titling himself the Second Lord of the Conjunction, the emperor asserted his direct link with Timur, the alleged Lord of the Conjunction. Since Shah Jahan happened to be born in the year 1000 of the Islamic era, he could readily imagine himself as literally a millennial sovereign, a self-perception that appears to have guided his actions. By sending huge armies into Central Asia with the goal of capturing parts of Timur's sovereign territory, the emperor was doing more than just expanding Mughal territory: he was conflating real time with millennial time – he was doing what, to his own thinking, he was born to do.

Important changes in imperial succession also occurred during the reigns of Jahangir and Shah Jahan. The practice that crystallized during their reigns, and which continued down to the year 1712, was unique among the great Persianate states of the day. From around 1600, princes in the Safavid and Ottoman empires were customarily confined to the harem, while the reigning emperor or powerful royal or non-royal actors nominated the next ruler from among those princes. As a result, the new ruler would probably have had little if any experience in the rough-and-tumble world of forging political alliances and networks. By contrast, the Mughals practised an open-ended succession system in which any prince could claim the throne; but he could win it only by defeating his brothers. This principle was conceptualized late in Akbar's reign, and then put to the test in the reigns of his two successors. By denying the throne to his grandson Khusrau, Akbar established a precedent whereby only a sovereign's sons could contend for the throne. This narrowed the eligible princes down to a manageable figure, which in the case of Akbar's own succession was only one: Salim. In addition, Akbar ended the earlier practice of giving semi-independent and semi-permanent holdings to princely heirs. From his reign onwards, princes would receive transferable *jagirs* like any other noble, instead of permanent or semi-permanent power bases on the model of the *iqta*'s of the Delhi sultans. This meant that the Mughals' sovereign realm was no longer thought of as a confederation of semi-independent political territories, but as a single indivisible state. As was revealed in the political manoeuvrings of Khusrau and Salim in the last month of Akbar's life, contenders for power had therefore to vie for the entire empire, and not a portion of it. It was an all-or-nothing contest.

It is sometimes suggested that the sort of bloody, fratricidal contests to which these ideas gave rise were politically destabilizing and detrimental to the long-term health of the Mughal empire, if not, indeed, illustrative of what was once called 'Oriental despotism'. It can be argued, though, that in reality the post-Akbar winner-take-all succession contest fought by a limited number of actors actually contributed to the empire's success and dynamism. Anticipating certain conflict with their brothers in a contest for the throne, princes would spend several decades building up powerful households, resilient alliances and networks of support spanning the entire empire. This sort of princely competition drew new groups into the political system, integrated peripheral areas more closely to the imperial centre, reinforced the foundations of imperial authority and forced princes to articulate a vision of how they might rule. In short, princes had to learn how to be competent political actors, since by this brutal logic the best-networked prince would become the next emperor. Moreover, by backing the right candidate, supporters of the winning prince – many of them from humble origins or from peripheral regions – would be swept into positions of importance. As a result, succession struggles, or even rebellions during a given reign, replenished the empire's body politic with new blood every few decades. At the same time, since supporters of defeated opponents were never considered permanent enemies – an echo of India's ancient *mandala* theory of warfare – victors made a point of forgiving and reintegrating them into the system, which was also a stabilizing influence.[88]

These ideas are nowhere better illustrated than in the bitter and fateful succession struggle that was fought among the four sons of Shah Jahan, an event that occurred about midway in the long life of one of those sons, Aurangzeb. It has been suggested that for sixty years, from the mid seventeenth to the early eighteenth century, the history of India and that of this one individual are practically the same.[89] This claim might be only a slight exaggeration, as we will see in the next chapter.

# 7

# Aurangzeb – from Prince to Emperor 'Alamgir, 1618–1707

I know my fortune in extremes does lie:
The Sons of Indostan must Reign, or die,
That desperate hazard Courage does create,
As he plays frankly, who has least Estate,
And that the World the Coward will despise.
When Life's a Blank, who pulls not for a Prize?

– *John Dryden,* Aureng-zebe: A Tragedy *(written 1675)*[1]


## PRINCE AURANGZEB – FOUR VIGNETTES

On 7 June 1633, Shah Jahan indulged in one of his favourite pastimes: watching two huge male elephants engage in combat. The spectacle was usually performed near the banks of the Jamuna and viewed from a balcony built into the emperor's palace in Agra. At one point on this occasion, the two beasts had grappled with each other directly below the emperor's balcony, preventing him from seeing the action. So he and his three eldest sons – Dara Shukoh, Shuja' and Aurangzeb – went down to the ground level, mounted horses and rode out to have a closer look. Noticing the newcomers, one of the elephants suddenly wheeled, trumpeted loudly and charged the nearest figure in sight, which happened to be the fourteen-year-old Aurangzeb. 'The lion-hearted youth,' records a chronicler of Shah Jahan's reign:

with the greatest courage and intrepidity did not stir from his post; but as soon as the elephant approached, he galloped at it and rose up in his stirrups and hurled his spear with his whole strength against its forehead. The monster, smarting from the wound, again rushed furiously to the attack; and the steed of that 'bold knight on the battlefield of valor' being struck in the flanks by the elephant's trunk rolled over from the violence of the shock. The instant Prince Aurangzeb fell from his saddle on to the ground, he sprang nimbly up, and stood sword in hand, ready to strike.[2]

In the midst of the confusion – the dust, shouting, fireworks, rockets, smoke – the other elephant, seeing his opponent otherwise preoccupied, seized the opportunity to resume the fight, thus sparing any more drama for the prince. By this time Shah Jahan himself had rushed to the scene, where he warmly embraced his son, relieved to find him unharmed.

The event seared deep into the memory of the amazed onlookers. It was also the first time that the court's chroniclers would pay significant notice to Shah Jahan's third son. In fact, the scene was twice memorialized in miniature paintings, the first one made within a few years of the event and included in the *Padshahnama*, the emperor's official chronicle [see Fig. 17].[3] In both images, Aurangzeb is depicted steadying his horse while driving his spear into the brow of the charging tusker, revealing the prince's steely courage in the face of grave danger. By contrast, his elder brother Dara Shukoh – later his sworn enemy – is seen watching the action from a safe distance. The painting affords an early glimpse into the contrasting characters of the brothers.

A year later, Shah Jahan gave Aurangzeb a *mansab* of 10,000, his first position in the Mughal hierarchy. A year after that, in 1635, he was sent off on an imperial campaign to capture and punish the rebel chieftain Jhujhar Singh Bundela. Although the sixteen-year-old prince held only nominal command of the army, the experience gave him his first direct exposure to military strategy, logistics and operations. At the conclusion of this successful campaign he proceeded south to Burhanpur, the seat of government for the Mughal-controlled Deccan. Unlike the older provinces to the north, which had been under imperial administration since the days of Akbar, the Mughal Deccan lay on the cutting edge of a rapidly moving frontier that faced three venerable sultanates: the quickly disintegrating Nizam Shahi kingdom of Ahmadnagar in the north-western Deccan, and two strong and hostile kingdoms to the south, the 'Adil Shahi kingdom of Bijapur and the Qutb Shahi kingdom of Golconda. In early 1636 Shah Jahan marched down to the ancient stronghold of Daulatabad to oversee the empire's forward operations against these three states. Whereas the sultan of Golconda submitted to a show of force and agreed to become a tributary vassal of the Mughals, Sultan Muhammad 'Adil Shah of Bijapur resisted. On reaching a military stalemate, in mid 1636 the two parties concluded an agreement whereby Bijapur would acknowledge the Mughals as overlords but would not be a tributary vassal like Golconda; the two states would divide between them the remaining territory of the kingdom of Ahmadnagar, now formally extinguished; and neither side would try to lure the other's officers into its service.

Having concluded the treaties with the two states, the emperor returned to Agra, leaving Aurangzeb in Burhanpur to govern the Mughal Deccan and to see that the treaty's terms were properly carried out. The governor, still only eighteen years old, soon acquired a taste for extorting as much as he could from Golconda while remaining technically within the terms of the 1636 treaty. He was also eager to annex territory from previously unconquered states in the region, such as Baglana, a strategically important strip of land along the lower Tapti valley. In early 1638 the prince, having obtained his father's permission to pursue this forward policy, sent an army into the region, overwhelming the mountain strongholds of Salhir and Mulhir. He then annexed the whole territory into the empire, absorbed its former rulers into Mughal state service and added Baglana's annual revenue of 400,000 rupees to imperial coffers. The ease with which Aurangzeb accomplished this operation might explain his imagining, much later in life, that conquering the rest of the Deccan would be just as manageable.

Another omen portending Aurangzeb's future operations in the Deccan, which would occupy the last twenty-five years of his life, was the ability of the most talented Maratha commander in the region to elude his grasp. This was Shahji Bhonsle (1594–1664), whose father had been the right-hand man of Malik Ambar, the Ethiopian ex-slave who for two decades had fended off Jahangir's repeated attempts to annex the Nizam Shahi kingdom of Ahmadnagar. After Ambar's death in 1626 and the surrender in 1633 of Daulatabad (the kingdom's capital since 1610) to the Mughals, it was Shahji who picked up the pieces of the crumbling state of Ahmadnagar. This he did by finding and crowning as sultan an eleven-year-old remnant of the Nizam Shahi house, for whom Shahji acted as chief minister and commander-in-chief, or *peshwa*. With 12,000 troops under his command, he managed to recover a number of forts in the old Nizam Shahi territory, boldly running a guerrilla operation against both Bijapur and the Mughals. In 1639 Aurangzeb managed to track down and kill Shahji's first cousin, a former Nizam Shahi officer who had taken to banditry. But he had no such luck with Shahji himself, who by then had abandoned the Nizam Shahi cause and enlisted with Bijapur.

In May 1644 an unexpected event drew Aurangzeb from his posting in the Deccan to the imperial court at Agra. His eldest sister Jahanara, Shah Jahan's favourite daughter, had suffered severe burns when her dress caught fire from a candle in Agra fort, and for weeks her life hung in the balance. As all her siblings were full brothers and sisters born of Shah Jahan and Mumtaz Mahal, the entire royal family responded with affection and concern. Aurangzeb's elder brother Shuja' reached Agra from his post as governor of Bengal, while his younger brother Murad arrived from his as governor of Gujarat. These three brothers had all been governing large provinces and commanding armies. By contrast the firstborn son, Dara Shukoh, had only briefly governed the Punjab in 1635–6, but since then remained in Agra. It seemed to all that, as the emperor's favourite son, he was being kept at court and groomed to succeed Shah Jahan [see Fig. 19]. This was certainly clear to Aurangzeb, who harboured a growing hostility towards Dara. The feeling, moreover, was mutual.

At some point, while the family poured out its sympathy and prayers for the ailing Jahanara, Dara invited his father and brothers to see his newly built mansion in Agra. 'As it was the summer season,' records a contemporary source:

> an underground room had been constructed close to the river . . . Dara conducted Shah Jahan and his brothers to see how the room looked. Muhammad Aurangzib sat down close to the [only] door leading in and out of the room. Dara seeing it winked at the Emperor, as if to say

'See where he is sitting.' His majesty said, 'My child, though I know you to be learned and hermit-like, yet it is also needful to maintain one's rank . . . What necessity is there for you to sit down in the path by which people pass, and in a position below and behind your younger brother [Murad]?' Aurangzib replied, 'I shall afterwards tell you the reason of my sitting here.' After a short time he rose on the plea of performing his mid-day prayer, and went back from the place to his own house without taking the Emperor's permission. When the Emperor heard of it he forbade him the Court, so that the Prince was debarred from the audience for seven months.[4]

More so than Aurangzeb's youthful encounter with the elephant, this vignette speaks of the poisonous relations between Dara and Aurangzeb. The eldest son's knowing wink to their father suggests his privileged status at court, from which the younger brother would soon be expelled for more than half a year. Upon recovering from her burns, Jahanara, the family peacemaker and coolest head, asked Aurangzeb to explain his strange behaviour in the underground room. His reply: he feared that Dara, taking advantage of that unguarded, confined space, might shut the door and dispatch all his brothers by way of ensuring his path to the throne. When Jahanara conveyed this explanation to their father, the emperor summoned Aurangzeb and showered him with favours. But this did nothing to heal the rift between the two brothers, whose relationship had now reached an impasse. Convinced that he and Dara could not be at court at the same time, Aurangzeb approached the prime minister and begged to be posted elsewhere. The minister intervened and the emperor obliged, reassigning him to Gujarat, which he governed from 1645 to 1647.[5]

Meanwhile, Shah Jahan began acting on the grandiose title 'Second Lord of the Conjunction' that he had given himself. Vaguely associated with millennialism, the title also alluded to his dynasty's esteemed ancestor Timur, allegedly the 'Lord of the Conjunction,' and to his vast empire. Shah Jahan therefore aimed to re-establish some sovereign connection with Timur's Central Asian empire, or at least the part of it south of the Oxus – Balkh and Badakhshan – that had belonged to Babur's patrimony. This was the context for the invasion mentioned in the previous chapter. Although Uzbek Turks had dominated the region

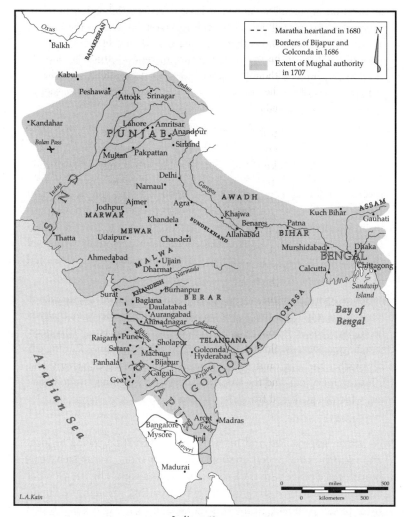

India, 1680–1707

since expelling Babur in the early sixteenth century, by the 1640s they were engulfed in a civil war that, in Shah Jahan's view, invited outside intervention. Short of reclaiming Balkh and Badakhshan by outright annexation, the emperor hoped at least to reduce the region to tributary status. So in 1646 he put his youngest son, Murad, at the head of an army of 50,000 troops that marched over the Hindu Kush Mountains and occupied the city of Balkh. But the young prince soon grew tired of the country's harsh terrain and begged permission to return. When his father refused, he abandoned his command and returned to India in disgrace, leaving his leaderless army behind.

To rescue the crippled Central Asian campaign, the emperor then called on Aurangzeb, who reached Balkh in May 1647. By that time, however, nearly half of Murad's troops had also abandoned the mission, leaving the several Mughal garrisons in Badakhshan and Balkh severely undermanned. Nonetheless, upon learning that a powerful Uzbek force had crossed the Oxus and was pressing on into Mughal-occupied territory, Aurangzeb marched north-west to meet it. When the two armies engaged, the Uzbek commander personally witnessed the Mughal prince's cool courage amidst fierce combat, as recorded in a widely circulated anecdote:

> While the Mughal army was fighting desperately with the vast legions of Abdul Aziz Khan, King of Bukhara, the time for the [noon] prayer [*zuhar*] arrived. Disregarding the prohibitions of his officers, Aurangzeb dismounted from his elephant, knelt down on the ground, and deliberately and peacefully went through all the ceremonies of the prayer, in full view of both the armies. Abdul Aziz on hearing of it cried out, 'To fight with such a man is to ruin one's self,' and suspended the battle.[6]

As winter approached and his army faced starvation owing to local grain scarcities and uncertain supply lines from India, Aurangzeb hastily arranged a peace with the Uzbeks and headed south. By late October his army reached the steep and icy passes cutting through the Hindu Kush range. Although he and his forward units safely reached Kabul before the heavy snows began, the treasure-escort, the supplies and thousands of troops and animals were not so lucky. Between Bamian and Kabul, especially while negotiating the 3,000-metre Shibar Pass, the army lost 5,000 men and as many animals – all buried under the snow. When the snow melted the next spring, piles of bones emerged along the pathways.[7] In the end, the Mughals' two-year campaign accomplished nothing beyond displaying the emperor's vanity. But it did consume forty million rupees, nearly seven times the cost to build Shahjahanabad, and eight times the cost of the Taj Mahal.

The failed Uzbek campaign was soon followed by a crisis with more formidable rivals, the Safavid rulers of Iran, over the strategic stronghold of Kandahar in southern Afghanistan. Having changed hands five times since Babur captured it in 1522, this strategic outpost was seen by each empire as vital for protecting its frontier. In early 1649 a Safavid army again laid siege to the garrison. Determined not to lose it again, the emperor called on Aurangzeb to lead an army of 50,000 to defend the fort. But by the time he arrived that March, it had already fallen, so the prince was ordered to retreat. With Mughal honour now at stake, Shah Jahan devoted the next three years to building up a huge army to mount a second attempt. In May 1652 60,000 troops, again under Aurangzeb's command, arrived before the fort with substantial siege artillery. This time, however, the prince was let down by his incompetent artillerymen, who either blew up their cannon with overloaded powder or fired cannonballs that sank harmlessly into the fort's mud walls. Worse was the interference of Shah Jahan, who had moved up to Kabul to oversee the siege, but whose proximity only enabled him to hector his son about his handling of military operations. With no progress to account for the effort, the emperor ultimately ordered a retreat, and the frustrated prince had to march from Kandahar back to Kabul. En route he received letters in which the emperor challenged his son's military competence, asserting that if he had considered the prince capable of taking the fort, he would not have ordered the retreat. With that swipe, Aurangzeb was instructed to return immediately to the Deccan and take up a second posting there as governor. Compounding his bitterness, Aurangzeb learnt that back in Agra Dara Shukoh, instead of showing support for the Mughal effort at Kandahar, mocked his younger brother, making his failure an object of ridicule.[8]

But the emperor was still not ready to concede failure. In 1653 he ordered a third and final attempt to recover the fort, this time sending

Dara to lead the effort, even though his eldest son had never yet led a major military operation. But that didn't prevent him from boasting that he would easily take the fort within a week, and perhaps even continue westwards and conquer Herat as well. An army of 70,000 men was mobilized, accompanied by a host of heavy artillery, 150,000 kilos of powder and 30,000 cannon balls, some of them weighing up to fifty kilos. But this expedition, lasting from April to September 1653, failed spectacularly. A contemporary account of the campaign portrays the prince as stubborn yet easily swayed by flattery, abusive when thwarted, prone to the use of magic for guidance, insensitive to the suffering of his own troops, and thoroughly incompetent as a commander.[9] In all, the three Kandahar expeditions had cost 120 million rupees, which was more than half of the empire's entire gross annual revenue, or twenty-four times the expense of building the Taj Mahal.[10]

These costly failures only deepened the rift between Aurangzeb and his father. But it had not always been that way. When the sixteen-year-old accompanied the army sent to pursue the rebel Jhujhar Singh and from Bundelkhand, he wrote his father glowing letters of the region's picturesque scenery – its forests, large artificial lakes, hills, wild game, and so on. Shah Jahan was so affected that he made a diversion from his march in order to join the young prince, and together the two made a sightseeing tour of the region's waterfalls and other natural sites.[11] Later, the emperor was genuinely puzzled by Aurangzeb's strange behaviour in Dara Shukoh's underground room in Agra, apparently unaware of the extent of the brothers' mutual animosity. The prince's subsequent banishment from court certainly strained the father–son relationship. Nonetheless, the emperor understood that, of his four sons, Aurangzeb was the ablest commander, which explains his reluctance to give high commands to the other three. The failed second siege of Kandahar, however, marked something of a turning point. In the same letter in which he blamed Aurangzeb for the siege's failure, the emperor advised the prince that he was being deprived of his lucrative *jagir*s in Multan and upper Sind, that his salary was being reduced by 1.7 million rupees, and that – as if to rub salt in his wounds – Dara Shukoh would command the third siege at Kandahar, for which purpose he would receive additional large and fertile *jagir*s in Gujarat.[12] En route to taking up his second posting as governor of the Deccan, Aurangzeb stopped in Delhi for several days, in the course of which he visited his brother Shuja' in the garden of their sister Jahanara's estate. Here the brothers arranged that Aurangzeb's son Muhammad Sultan would marry Shuja''s daughter, thereby cementing an alliance between the emperor's second and third sons.[13] It seems that Aurangzeb was already anticipating a post-Shah Jahan era, for which isolating Dara politically was a first step.

From Delhi Aurangzeb continued down to the Deccan, but instead of taking up his position in a new capital deeper south in the Mughal Deccan, he lingered for nine months – from January to October 1653 – in the old provincial capital of Burhanpur. The reason for the delay was an affair of the heart. Notwithstanding that he was thirty-five and already had several wives and children, Aurangzeb now had his first and only truly romantic relationship, so far as we know. The object of his affections was a young girl of uncommon beauty named Hira Bai Zainabadi, a Hindu slave and singer, skilled in music, who was kept in the household of his maternal aunt's husband. One day the prince happened to notice her as she was strolling, unveiled, by the banks of the Tapti near Burhanpur. He was immediately smitten. In the course of the walk, we are told, Hira Bai:

> saw a mango tree laden with fruit. Without considering the respect due to the Prince, she ran forward joyfully and playfully, and leapt up on the tree and plucked a fruit. This movement was a heart-robbing one and it robbed the Prince of his self-control and his virtue . . . By begging and imploring he obtained possession of her from his indulgent aunt and with all his asceticism and purity he gave his heart to her and used to fill a cup of wine with his own hand and give it to her.
>
> It is stated that she too one day put a cup of wine into the Prince's hand and urged him to drink it. Though he begged and prayed, she had no pity on him and the Prince was helpless, and was about to drink it, when the sly girl drank it off herself, saying: It was to test your love and not to make your palate bitter with the liquor full of evil.[14]

Those months in Burhanpur were surely among the most carefree in Aurangzeb's life – hunting antelope, riding about on horseback, climbing Daulatabad's fort, visiting the caves of Ellora – probably with Hira Bai at his side. We know, too, that word of the prince's dalliance with the singer reached the emperor, who in May 1653 sternly reprimanded his son for his personal conduct. In reply, Aurangzeb protested vehemently that 'the reports recently laid before Your Majesty are a tissue of lies', and asked rhetorically, 'how could I sink to such a depth?'.[15] Inevitably, Dara Shukoh seized on the salacious rumours swirling through the court, saying, 'See the piety and abstinence of this hypocritical knave! He has gone to the dogs for the sake of a wench of his aunt's household.'[16]

Within a year, however, the girl died, which plunged Aurangzeb into a state of anguish and heartbreak. But the affair would have its aftereffects. Niccolao Manucci, a Venetian mercenary who lived in India from 1653 to 1708 and enjoyed close ties to the court, wrote that, long after the girl's death, Aurangzeb 'was accustomed to say that God had been very gracious to him by putting an end to that dancing-girl's life, by reason of whom he had committed so many iniquities, and had run the risk of never reigning through being occupied in vicious practices'.[17] In short, Aurangzeb never forgot his brief but doomed affair with Hira Bai. Nor did he forget her snatching that glass of wine from his willing lips. For she had tested and nearly destroyed his self-control, an attribute that as emperor he would consider absolutely essential for maintaining his grip on power.

From Burhanpur, Aurangzeb moved down to Kirki, the new Mughal provincial capital which the prince renamed Aurangabad, after himself. The next four years he devoted to restoring Mughal administration, as it had fallen into a sorry state since his first governorship in the Deccan. Under a series of corrupt imperial officials, revenues had fallen steeply, cultivators had abandoned their villages, and arable land had lapsed into jungle. This was compounded by problems of security. In his communications with his father, the prince repeatedly stressed that, unlike the empire's interior provinces, or coastal provinces such as Gujarat or Bengal, the Mughal Deccan faced two powerful and rich sultanates, Golconda and Bijapur. Though technically at peace with them since the treaty of 1636, both were hostile and dangerous, requiring substantial troops to keep them in check. But he could collect only a third of the assessed revenue, and in some parts only a tenth, as a result of which the central treasury had to subsidize much of the province's administrative expenses. Yet the emperor, convinced that the province should be self-supporting, and loath to maintain such subsidies, ordered his son to reclaim the lands of unproductive *jagirdar*s. Aurangzeb complied, which only led the dispossessed nobles to intrigue in court against him, persuading the emperor that his son had been enriching himself at their own expense.

Matters did stabilize, however, after Aurangzeb appointed as his revenue minister Murshid Quli Khan, an Iranian migrant who had joined Aurangzeb's staff as paymaster during the Balkh campaign. Whereas revenue assessment in the Deccan had traditionally been calculated simply by counting the number of cultivators' ploughs, the new minister applied the Mughals' *zabt* system of revenue assessment and collection. Murshid Quli Khan oversaw teams of surveyors and assessors who went into the villages, measured the land and prepared detailed records on the basis of which accurate revenue assessments could be made. The minister himself reportedly joined his men, dragging measuring chains across fields with his own hands.[18] As a result, under Aurangzeb's administration villagers regained confidence in the honesty of the government, and as agriculture began to flourish, revenue increased. Yet these administrative successes did not end the prince's feuds with his father. Rather, their quarrels simply shifted to matters of foreign policy. Aurangzeb had always favoured an aggressive posture towards the two remaining Deccan sultanates, Bijapur and Golconda, but felt constrained by the 1636 treaty, which had stabilized Mughal relations with both states, and which the emperor was committed to honouring. Moreover, since Mughal ambassadors to those states reported directly to Shah Jahan, Aurangzeb felt cut out of diplomacy that he regarded as properly belonging in his own domain. But in 1656 events in both states provided the prince with rationales for invading and annexing them, if only his father would sanction such initiatives.

The first to feel Aurangzeb's pressure was Golconda. The prime minister of that kingdom was another Iranian immigrant, Mir Jumla (d. 1663), who had amassed such immense wealth as a gem-merchant that he raised and commanded his own armies, which roused the intense jealousy of his master, the sultan. Upon learning that the sultan sought to ruin him, Mir Jumla made overtures to Aurangzeb about defecting to Mughal service, which the prince warmly welcomed even though the 1636 treaty had banned such intrigues. When the sultan imprisoned Mir Jumla's son on account of improper behaviour in court, Shah Jahan sanctioned Aurangzeb's request to invade if that son were not released. But by the time the sultan set Mir Jumla's son free, Aurangzeb had already sent a Mughal army to invade and plunder Hyderabad, near Golconda fort. The prince now begged his father for permission to annex the southern quarter of the kingdom (extending south to the Palar River), on the grounds that that enormous area had formerly been the *jagir* of Mir Jumla, who had recently defected to Mughal service. He also played upon his father's well-known weakness for jewels, portraying Golconda as a land awash with diamonds and buried treasures, ripe for the picking. In this effort he was helped by Mir Jumla, who presented Shah Jahan with the world's largest diamond, the celebrated Koh-i-Noor.[19] At the same time, Golconda's agents in Delhi, knowing that Dara would do anything to deny his brother the glory of annexing Golconda's territory, lobbied Shah Jahan, through Dara, against annexation. But the emperor's greed, as Aurangzeb correctly calculated, trumped any scruples he might have had. So he approved the annexation.

The year 1656 also proved momentous for Bijapur, the most powerful remaining Deccan sultanate. Because the treaty of 1636 had confirmed his northern frontier with the Mughals, Sultan Muhammad 'Adil Shah was free to send his armies deep into the south, conquering and annexing territory belonging to the scattered and disunited former vassals of the once-mighty Vijayanagara empire, as described in Chapter Four. These included Ikkeri and Bednur in the western peninsula, Bangalore and Mysore in mid-plateau, and the entire Kaveri valley eastwards to the Bay of Bengal, together with the stronghold of Jinji near the Coromandel coast. But Bijapur would not enjoy these new possessions for long. Aurangzeb had planted Mir Jumla in Delhi with a view to tempting the emperor with ever more diamonds and other jewels in both Golconda's and Bijapur's southern territories. In November 1656 the prince's opportunity arrived with the news of Muhammad 'Adil Shah's death, followed by rumours that his eighteen-year-old son was not of legitimate parentage and was therefore barred from lawfully succeeding as sultan. Welcoming such rumours as a gift from heaven, Aurangzeb immediately requested permission to invade and annex the whole of Bijapur on the grounds that it had no legitimate sovereign. Upon receiving his father's sanction, he besieged the former Bahmani capital of Bidar, then under Bijapur's rule, and when it fell in March 1657 he moved on to Kalyana, the other formidable stronghold defending Bijapur's northern frontier. That fort surrendered in August. Seeing that nothing was likely to stop him from besieging and possibly capturing Bijapur's capital itself, Dara Shukoh, driven by a seething jealousy over his younger brother's successes, managed to persuade his father to call off the invasion. Bitterly aware that this was all Dara's doing, Aurangzeb had no choice but to pull back. The stage was set for a decisive moment in Mughal history.

## WAR OF SUCCESSION, 1657–9

On 6 September, within a month of Aurangzeb's withdrawal from Bijapur, Shah Jahan fell ill, so grievously that rumours sped throughout India that he faced imminent death. From an early age Mughal princes were acutely aware that their brothers, though possibly playmates in childhood, would become deadly enemies when their father died. And they well understood that only one of them would survive the struggle to succeed him: according to the well-known Persian proverb, it was 'either the throne, or the coffin' (*ya takht, ya takhta*). The news of the emperor's illness therefore sparked a four-way struggle among Shah Jahan's four sons, India's bloodiest and most notorious war of succession.

If Aurangzeb's disputes with his father frustrated the prince, they were at least limited mainly to matters of public policy, diplomacy and administration. His relationship with Dara Shukoh, by contrast, had deteriorated to a poisonous, mutual hatred. But until the last year of Dara's life, their rivalry had not concerned religion. Both brothers respected and were patrons of spiritual specialists of all traditions. Dara Shukoh famously consorted with Brahmin pundits and eminent

Sufi shaikhs, in particular those of the Qadiri order. Aurangzeb issued dozens of documents between 1659 and 1703 supporting a variety of religious individuals and institutions: Jain saints, sadhus and monasteries (*math*s), temple Brahmins, *gosain*s (wandering ascetics), Jangams (Śaiva priests), Hindu preceptors and yogis.[20] Both brothers had thoroughly imbibed the culture of institutional Sufism. Dara authored three treatises and two biographical dictionaries on the subject, while Aurangzeb throughout his life patronized Sufi shrines and revered holy men.[21] The bitter antagonism between the brothers took a religious turn only once the War of Succession had begun. This was due partly to heightened antagonisms triggered by the war itself, and partly to the evolution of Dara's own religious thinking.

François Bernier, the French physician who briefly served Dara Shukoh during the War of Succession, noticed that the prince was constantly surrounded by Brahmins, to whom he gave large pensions. He also described him as a religious chameleon, outwardly professing Islam, but privately 'a Gentile [Hindu] with Gentiles, and a Christian with Christians'.[22] But the true extent of Dara's religious adventurism lies in his treatises. One of his preoccupations centred on a classic theme of Indian philosophy: the problem of how to reconcile the renunciation of the world, necessary for achieving spiritual liberation, with engagement in the world, necessary for upholding and maintaining a functioning society. Even for ordinary householders, this tension could be a source of anxiety; but for a ruler charged with overseeing the social order of an entire kingdom, the contradiction could be especially acute. For Dara, this anxiety came to a head in late 1653. While returning to north India from Afghanistan, where he had just led a failed effort to recapture Kandahar from the Iranians, he passed through Lahore, where he visited a Punjabi holy man, Baba Lal. In the wake of his stunning defeat at Kandahar, the prince would have been acutely aware of the tension between his spiritual life and the demands of rulership, especially since Shah Jahan had been grooming him for the throne.[23] The questions he put to Baba Lal therefore focused principally on the compatibility of rulership and renunciation.[24] Baba Lal advised Dara that in every religious community a spiritually perfected person stands out from the common mass, and through that person's blessings the community is saved by God.[25] This assertion seems to have furnished Dara with a cogent solution to the renunciation vs engagement dilemma, for in his treatise *Sakinat al-auliya* the prince emphasized that, among Mughal rulers, he alone had been divinely chosen for a special spiritual role.[26] By 1655 he was already referring to himself in exalted terms, including king (*shah*), a highly accomplished saint and 'the perfect manifestation of virtuous conduct'.[27] In short, as the inevitable struggle for succession to the Peacock Throne drew near, an important part of Dara's political calculation appears to have been to present himself as someone who had access to divine secrets unavailable to other mortals.[28]

Dara Shukoh's final intellectual project, completed just months before Shah Jahan fell ill, was the capstone of his religious explorations – an audacious reformulation of the foundations of Islam itself. In a sense, his 'discoveries' of the roots of Islam logically followed from his studies of princely dialogues with ascetics and his fashioning of himself as a spiritually accomplished Perfect Man (a Sufi conception) and an Indian saint-king. In his treatise *Sirr-i akbar* ('The Greatest Secret'), Dara discusses his quest for the roots of monotheism in all human societies. After researching Judaic, Christian, Islamic and Indian traditions, he claims finally to have found such roots in ancient Indian scriptures, namely the Upanishads, which comprise the essence of the four Vedas.[29] In 1656–7 he assembled a group of learned Brahmins of Benares and translated essential parts of the Upanishads into Persian. He also seized upon a Qur'anic passage stating that the Qur'an itself is 'in a hidden Book [that] none but the purified shall touch, a sending down from the Lord of all Being'.[30] Placing this passage side by side with his monotheistic reading of the Upanishads, Dara convinced himself that the 'hidden Book' mentioned in the Qur'an was in fact the Upanishads.[31]

Dara's researches and striking conclusions had unexpected consequences. A copy of his Persian translation of the Upanishads was later acquired by the French Orientalist A. H. Anquetil-Duperron (d. 1805), who in turn translated it into Latin, a copy of which found its way to the library and even the bedside of the German philosopher Arthur Schopenhauer (d. 1860). By such circuitous pathways, interest in ancient Indian philosophy quickened in nineteenth-century Europe.[32] In India, however, Dara's ideas that a full understanding of Islam depended upon the study of the Upanishads, and that those scriptures anticipated Islamic monotheism, were seen by many as theologically deviant. Foremost among these was his younger brother and most dangerous rival. On the conclusion of the War of Succession, and only a year after the *Sirr-i akbar* was completed, Aurangzeb invoked Dara's naming the Vedas a divine book as one of the grounds for his execution.[33]

Leading up to the succession struggle, however, Dara's greatest difficulties were political, as his arrogance and immature behaviour alienated the very nobles whose support he would have needed in his final confrontations with Aurangzeb. He told the Mughals' powerful Rajput ally Jai Singh (d. 1667), the Kachhwaha raja of Amber, that he looked like a musician, a serious insult. The raja remained quiet at the time, but was said to have determined on vengeance, which he would later have. The prince also ridiculed Mir Jumla, ordering his staff to mock the general's gait and gestures; he too would turn against Dara, as would other prominent nobles.[34] Danishmand Khan (d. 1670) resigned as cavalry captain because of Dara's anger at him for upholding Shah Jahan's absolute authority. Owing to some real or imaginary affront, Shaista Khan (d. 1694) greatly disliked Dara and gladly contributed to his downfall. Most seriously, perhaps, Dara on one occasion committed the unforgivable affront of beating Khalil Allah Khan (d. 1662) with his shoe. At a crucial point in the pivotal Battle of Samugarh (1658), the Uzbek commander would take his revenge by advising Dara, for his 'personal safety', to dismount from his elephant and mount a horse. As Khalil Allah expected, Dara's men could no longer see their leader and so, assuming he had been killed, panicked and fled the battlefield.[35]

To be sure, when hostilities eventually broke out, Dara did enjoy the support of Shah Jahan and those nobles present at court. No matter what their private sympathies might have been, the latter were at least nominally loyal to the eldest prince. Residing in Delhi, the empire's geographical and administrative centre, also gave Dara logistical assets such as the ability to control the flow of information to and from the court. But such advantages were offset by his military and political incompetence, in contrast to Aurangzeb's extensive military experience, his known abilities as a commander, his superior skills in political networking and his cool, calculating character. Manucci described Aurangzeb as totally different from his brothers, 'very secretive and serious, carrying on his affairs in a hidden way, but most energetically. He was of a melancholy temperament, always busy at something or another.'[36] And François Bernier: 'Aureng-Zebe . . . was devoid of that urbanity and engaging presence, so much admired in Dara; but he possessed a sounder judgment, and was more skillful in selecting for confidants such persons as were best qualified to serve him with faithfulness and ability.' The Frenchman added that 'his life had been one of undeviating intrigue and contrivance; conducted, however, with such admirable skill, that every person in the court, excepting only his brother, *Dara*, seemed to form an erroneous estimate of his character.'[37]

Accordingly, in the months after September 1657, when news of Shah Jahan's illness sped throughout the realm, Aurangzeb prudently held back from committing himself to a succession struggle, even though by early December his brothers Murad and Shuja' had both impetuously crowned themselves emperor and were mobilizing armies to march on Agra and Delhi. From Bengal Shuja' was the first to advance towards these cities, prompting Dara to send his son Sulaiman Shukoh and top generals down the Ganges valley to check the threat, which they did in February 1658. In Gujarat, meanwhile, Murad had extorted money from merchants of the wealthy seaport of Surat in order to finance his own invasion of the capital. In Delhi, Dara, acting in the name of the ailing Shah Jahan and seeking to defang the brother he feared most, recalled Shaista Khan and Mir Jumla from the Deccan, unaware that both generals secretly supported Aurangzeb. He also persuaded Jaswant Singh, the Rathor raja of Marwar, to lead a Mughal army to check Murad's northward advance from Gujarat. But, as late as March 1658, Aurangzeb held back in Burhanpur, extorting money from Bijapur for his own army while secretly conspiring with Murad to join their two armies, defeat Dara and divide the empire between them. Meanwhile his sister and ally Raushanara was smuggling messages out of Delhi, evading Dara's spies and roadblocks and informing Aurangzeb as to their eldest brother's actions and intentions.

In late March 1658, Aurangzeb finally left Burhanpur for north India – not, ostensibly, as a contender for the throne like Murad and

Shuja', but as the dutiful son piously paying a visit to his ailing father. In mid April his army joined that of Murad south of Ujjain, and several days later, at the Battle of Dharmat, their combined forces of 40,000 completely routed an imperial force of the same size fighting on behalf of Dara. Although Murad fought well in this engagement, it was Aurangzeb's reputation as an accomplished field commander that coursed through the empire's informal networks, much to Dara's dismay. In late May Aurangzeb and Murad crossed the Chambal, cleverly skirting Dara's artillery defences along that river's usual crossing points. At this point Shah Jahan offered personally to go out and persuade the two princes to return to their provincial postings, it being unthinkable that any of his sons would challenge their father in battle. But Dara, ever haughty and over-confident in his military abilities, brushed off his father's offer. The calm eldest sister, Jahanara, also intervened, writing to Aurangzeb that 'according to the Islamic law and convention the elder brother has the status of a father. His Majesty holds the same view.' But this was a flawed argument. The *shari'a* has no law of primogeniture; moreover, as everybody knew, the Turko-Mongol tradition as refined by Akbar gave all sons of a reigning monarch an equal right to inherit the empire. So Aurangzeb wrote to his father, protesting that whereas he merely wished to visit His Majesty, Dara had mobilized a vast army to prevent his progress towards Agra.[38]

But the time for meaningful negotiations had passed. The brothers were bent on war, and on 29 May their armies clashed near the village of Samugarh, thirty-five kilometres south-east of Agra. Although Dara's forces of 60,000 far surpassed in number those of Aurangzeb and Murad, his men, unlike the invaders from Gujarat and the Deccan, had been hastily assembled and were not at all battle-hardened. Worse, some of his leading officers secretly supported Aurangzeb. The battle's progress therefore proved disastrous for Dara, whose forces were swept off the field by late afternoon. The prince himself galloped off to Agra. Too ashamed to face his father after his crushing defeat, a dispirited Dara slipped out of the fort that same night and headed towards Delhi with a handful of supporters. Next came days of tortuous negotiations between Aurangzeb, who now held most of the political cards, and Shah Jahan, still in his palace in Agra but suddenly reduced to the pitiable state of an emperor with no empire. Acting as intermediary, Jahanara conveyed to Aurangzeb the emperor's last-ditch proposal to divide the empire among his four sons.[39] But it was too late for such ideas: the princes all understood that this was a winner-take-all contest. Nonetheless, a direct face-to-face interview between the drama's principal actors was arranged. Aurangzeb had actually saddled up and was riding towards the Agra fort to meet his father when he was handed an intercepted message from Shah Jahan to Dara, in which the emperor advised his eldest son to collect an army in Delhi and stay there while he concluded his negotiations with Aurangzeb. Such evidence of his father's continued collusion with Dara convinced Aurangzeb that he was walking into a trap. So he aborted the intended interview and instead ordered his men to take possession of all royal effects, treasures and so on, and to keep the emperor confined in the palace.[40] Until his death seven years later, Shah Jahan would never again leave the fort.

By 10 June 1658 the War of Succession was effectively over. On that day Aurangzeb felt sufficiently confident of his tightening grip on power to hold in his camp a grand *darbar*, or public audience, where, though not yet crowned, he behaved as though he were already sovereign, presenting himself for public viewing, receiving hosts of courtiers and making appointments. But two obstacles blocked any easy transition to the Peacock Throne. The first was political. Of his three brothers, two were at large – Dara in Delhi, reportedly reassembling an army to challenge the outcome at Samugarh; and Shuja' in Bengal, checked by a Mughal army four months earlier, but said to be preparing to resume his bid for power. Though courageous and successful in combat, his younger brother, Murad, was impetuous, gullible and increasingly unhappy about his role of playing second fiddle to Aurangzeb. Since Murad was near at hand, he was the first to be dealt with. Three days after his *darbar* in Agra, Aurangzeb set off for Delhi in pursuit of Dara, with Murad and his army tagging along several kilometres behind. On the pretext of celebrating their joint victory over Dara, Aurangzeb treacherously invited the unsuspecting Murad to a sumptuous feast, after which his guest was shackled in his slumber and ultimately dispatched to the Mughals' state prison in Gwalior.

Dara, however, would remain a fugitive for the next fourteen months, his condition growing ever more desperate and miserable. Armies that he hastily assembled on the run, using treasures he had either carried with him or seized from former political servants, dwindled progressively towards the vanishing point. Aurangzeb pursued his quarry to Lahore and then to Multan, which he reached in mid September 1658. But Dara stayed just ahead of him, continuing down the Indus valley with an army that rapidly shrank from 14,000 in Lahore to just 3,000. In Multan, Aurangzeb learnt that Shuja', realizing that none of his brothers was occupying Agra or Delhi, had left his base in Bengal and was again marching up the Ganges valley. So Aurangzeb abruptly rushed back to Delhi and thence to what is now Faizabad District, Uttar Pradesh, where he joined the army of his old ally Mir Jumla. At the Battle of Khajwa on 5 January 1659, the allies confronted and defeated Shuja', who for the next four months, pursued by Mir Jumla, fell back into the Bengal forests and finally fled to Burma's Arakan coastal region, where he vanished from historical record.

That left only Dara for Aurangzeb to contend with. While Shuja' was being driven through Bengal, the eldest contender experienced a brief comeback. Having crossed the salt marshes between Sind and Gujarat, he found support for a renewed attempt on the crown in Ahmedabad. Maharaja Jaswant Singh had first fought on Dara's behalf at Dharmat, then switched to supporting Aurangzeb, but then deserted the latter at Khajwa. Now he again offered to help Dara. Although the fugitive prince might have thought better of relying on one with such fickle loyalties, the man was desperate, and so in February 1659 he marched north expecting Jaswant Singh's army to join his own remnants at Ajmer. By the time he got there, though, Aurangzeb had already cautioned the Rajput general against supporting his brother. Like most other Mughal nobles, Jaswant Singh clearly saw which prince it was more prudent to back, and so abandoned Dara to his fate. In mid March Dara bravely staged one last stand at Deorai, just south of Ajmer, but Rajputs fighting with Aurangzeb ultimately outmanoeuvred him. Pursued this time by Maharaja Jai Singh, Dara fled back to Gujarat, retracing his steps across the salt marsh to southern Sind. Reduced to a band of hardly a hundred followers, Dara headed north hoping to find support in Afghanistan. But in early June, near the mouth of the Bolan Pass, a *zamindar* whom Dara thought he could trust betrayed him to Aurangzeb's men, and in August he was taken to Delhi in chains. There he was publicly paraded through the streets and bazaars of Shahjahanabad, wearing coarse cloth and mounted on a miserable, worn-out elephant. François Bernier, who witnessed the spectacle, remarked on the public weeping and lamenting for Dara's wretched fate. Yet nobody made any move to rescue the doomed prince, despite there being hardly any troops guarding him.[41] After a council of clerics drew up a list of charges against him, he was executed on 30 August 1659, and his body was buried in the grounds of Humayun's tomb.[42]

On 13 May, three months before Dara's execution, but several months after that prince's last stand at Deorai, Aurangzeb had staged a grand coronation ceremony in Delhi, officially inaugurating his reign [see Fig. 20].[43] He chose as his imperial title "Alamgir" ('world-conqueror'), apparently in memory of a sword, inscribed with that title, that his father had given him after the decisive Battle of Samugarh a year earlier.[44]

## 'ALAMGIR'S EARLY REIGN

Having trod his bloody path to the Peacock Throne, the new emperor moved swiftly to consolidate his power and assert his claims to legitimacy. First, he richly rewarded the nobles who had aided him during the two years' struggle and pardoned those who had supported any of his brothers. To maintain administrative continuity with Shah Jahan's regime, he retained his father's last finance minister, Raja Raghunath, whom he repeatedly praised for his dedication and competence. To neutralize factions within his immediate family, he arranged marriages between his own children and those of his defeated brothers: two of his daughters were married to Dara's son Sipihr Shukoh and Murad's son 'Izzat Bakhsh after both were released from prison and given official ranks, while his own son Muhammad A'zam was married to Dara's daughter Jani Begum. His success in consolidating his authority is seen in the response to his own serious illness just three years into his reign. Although physicians despaired of his recovery, no prince or noble made any move to restore the still-confined Shah Jahan to power, far less wage another succession war on his own behalf.[45]

For the common population, which had been greatly unsettled by the recent political convulsions, 'Alamgir acted with predictable generosity. 'The doors of the imperial treasuries were opened to all people,' writes a chronicler, adding that the new emperor celebrated his next birthday by indulging in the traditional Indian custom of having himself weighed against gold, which was distributed among the poor.[46] To alleviate suffering from famine, he opened ten additional almshouses in Delhi, twelve more in surrounding districts, and still more in Lahore.[47] Indicating his determination to serve justice, he ordered the public execution of 500 common thieves.[48] For the benefit of merchants, he abolished road tolls on the transit of grain throughout the realm, despite a considerable loss of revenue to the state.[49] And he threw himself into the minutiae of everyday administration with boundless energy. 'Above all,' writes Manucci, 'he prided himself on the number of hours he spent every day in public audience, in the hearing of complaints, and in efforts to suppress the abuses existing in the empire.'[50]

The new emperor also embarked on a vigorous programme of imperial expansion on three frontiers. To the east, where Mughal armies had long since adapted themselves to campaigning in the river-laced forests of the great Ganges delta, 'Alamgir sent his new governor of Bengal, Mir Jumla, up the Brahmaputra River towards Assam. In late 1661 his naval flotillas reached the provincial capital of the Ahom rajas in Kuch Bihar and annexed the surrounding territory. Early the following year his forces continued moving upriver, taking riverside forts one by one, up to the Ahom capital of Garhgaon, which fell to Mir Jumla in March 1662. But torrential rains and poor communication with Dhaka, followed by famine and disease in the imperial camp, forced the Mughals to reach a tributary arrangement with the Ahom raja, similar to those that had been concluded with Rajput chieftains since the days of Akbar. In early 1663 the expeditionary force began its return to Dhaka, but Mir Jumla died en route. Within four years the Ahom kings had renewed the war, pushing Mughal garrisons out of Assam. Despite the Mughals' subsequent attempts to reconquer the upper Brahmaputra valley, by 1681 they had been driven out of Gauhati and Assam for good.

'Alamgir's forces had better luck extending the empire's frontiers in Bengal's south-eastern sector. In 1459 one of the delta's oldest and finest seaports, Chittagong, had been seized from the Bengal sultans by the kings of the Arakan coast. Jahangir's governor in Bengal, Islam Khan Chishti, had managed to recover Bengali territory up to the Feni River seventy kilometres north of Chittagong, but the port itself remained under Arakanese control. What is more, that city was being used as a staging site for Arakanese mariners and renegade Portuguese adventurers to raid lower Bengal for slaves. Therefore, Mir Jumla's successor as Bengal governor, Shaista Khan, renovated the provincial navy, building 300 new boats in order to launch a combined naval and overland expedition to conquer Chittagong. After first seizing the island of Sandwip, in early 1666 a Mughal force of 6,500 wrested the port from the Arakanese, whose capital of Mrauk-U further down the coast had just entered a period of internal disorder, rendering them unable to recover it.

Recalling his father's disastrous campaigns to subdue northern Afghanistan, 'Alamgir adopted more limited goals for the empire's north-western frontier. Protecting vital trade routes, not annexing territory, would be the strategic objective. He also reached political accommodations with the Pashtun clans inhabiting the rugged mountains beyond the Khyber Pass. Early in 'Alamgir's reign, though, several tribal uprisings tested imperial resolve and methods. In 1667, a chieftain of the Yusufzai lineage crowned himself king of the Swat valley and led his tribesmen across the Indus near Attock, attacking government outposts and threatening routes leading into Kashmir. Mughal counter-attacks only drew more frontier tribes into the uprising, which was finally suppressed by Mir Jumla's son, Muhammad Amin Khan. Then in 1672 another lineage, the Afridis, rose up under Acmal Khan, who also crowned himself king, struck coins and declared war on the Mughals. This uprising was more serious, since it was proclaimed in the name of all Pashtuns. Muhammad Amin Khan, now governor of Kabul, recklessly took a huge army into a dangerous part of the Khyber Pass where Afridi tribes ambushed his force, killing 10,000 and enslaving another 20,000. Two years later the Mughals suffered another reverse, in which Indian troops unaccustomed to Afghanistan's bitterly cold winters got caught in the snowy pass leading to Kabul and were again ambushed with heavy losses. After this, 'Alamgir advanced to the Peshawar region, where he spent more than a year personally overseeing Mughal operations. Shrewdly pitting clan against clan, he won over tribal chieftains with gifts, lavish subsidies and promises of productive *jagir*s if they would enter Mughal service. Such policies did stabilize the north-west: Pashtun tribes were mostly pacified, and the caravan routes leading from the Punjab to the Iranian plateau remained open.

On the other hand, 'Alamgir's policies regarding two major Rajput houses – the Rathors of Marwar in western Rajasthan and the Sisodiyas of Mewar in the south – seriously strained Delhi's relations with these long-standing Mughal allies. By mutual agreements, the emperors reserved the right to choose the ruling successor to any Rajput house with which they were tied by treaty, and by custom those choices would conform to Rajput expectations. Problems could arise, however, when a Rajput house was sharply divided over a rightful successor. In late 1678 such a crisis was touched off when Jaswant Singh, raja of Marwar, died with no surviving heir. Indra Singh, a grandson of Jaswant Singh's disinherited elder brother, immediately advanced his claims for the succession, although his candidacy was widely opposed by Rathor clansmen. Word then arrived that in February 1679 a male child named Ajit Singh had been born to one of Jaswant Singh's wives. Not wishing to put Marwar under a regency until the boy had attained majority, 'Alamgir ordered the child placed under imperial custody while naming Indra Singh the state's new raja. Many in Marwar, however, fiercely resisted the emperor's measures, insisting that succession be restricted to direct heirs. They also rejected the emperor's compromise proposal to partition the state between the infant Ajit Singh and Indra Singh. In July 1679 Durga Das, a leading Rathor chieftain, kidnapped Ajit Singh from imperial custody in Delhi and dashed off to Jodhpur, Marwar's capital, where the child was acclaimed the next Rathor raja. Since such defiance of imperial authority amounted to rebellion, in September 1679 'Alamgir moved the imperial court to Ajmer while his troops, following a precedent established in other Rajput states in such circumstances, occupied Jodhpur. The entire kingdom was placed under direct Mughal administration, pending resolution of the succession issue. The emperor also sent in imperial agents to prepare inventories of Jaswant Singh's estate, since the property of any Mughal noble automatically reverted to the state upon his death.

The uprising did not remain confined to Marwar, however. With the Mughals occupying the Rathor capital of Jodhpur, Durga Das with the infant Ajit Singh took refuge in neighbouring Mewar, then ruled by Rana Raj Singh.[51] In response, in November 1679 'Alamgir personally invaded Mewar only to find the Sisodiya capital of Udaipur vacated, as Rana Raj Singh and his entire cavalry had abandoned the plains for the hills. After nearly a year of Mughal–Sisodiya military stalemate, Raj Singh died and was succeeded by Jai Singh, who opposed his clan's continued involvement in the Rathor succession struggle and negotiated a separate peace with 'Alamgir. The emperor, in turn, confirmed Jai Singh in his position as Mewar's raja and made him an imperial *mansabdar* with the rank of 5,000. For the rest of 'Alamgir's reign Mughal relations with Mewar remained cordial, with Sisodiya commanders and troops once again taking up imperial service throughout the empire.[52] Meanwhile the Rathors of Marwar wearily came to accept rule by Mughal governors. But their relations remained strained, as Durga Das kept up a guerrilla resistance for another two decades, albeit with only desultory support from his kinsmen. Ultimately, by 1699 both Durga Das and Ajit Singh, by then an adult, had submitted to Mughal rule and become imperial *mansabdar*s, formally ending Marwar's rebellion against 'Alamgir.[53] But the long struggle had created an air of mutual distrust that lingered for decades.

The Rajput rebellion also led to 'Alamgir's fateful decision not to return to Delhi, but to continue south and conduct military operations in the Deccan. These operations would occupy his remaining twenty-five years of life and permanently alter the course of Mughal history. At the height of the Rajput rebellion, in mid 1680, the emperor had given the command of military campaigns in southern Marwar to his favourite son, Prince Akbar. But the prince, flushed with several battlefield victories and knowing how his father had usurped power from Shah Jahan, made the rash decision to confront

'Alamgir for the Mughal throne. In this he was urged on by 'Alamgir's erstwhile enemies, Durga Das and Rana Raj Singh, who assured him that all Rajputs would certainly rally to his cause. So in early 1681 Akbar, accompanied by his newfound Rajput allies and addled by visions of the gem-studded Peacock Throne, declared himself emperor and marched the 200 kilometres to his father's camp in Ajmer. On the eve of the battle, however, 'Alamgir tricked the Rajputs into believing that Akbar was actually leading them into a trap. As a result, the prince awoke at dawn to find that all his Rajput allies had vanished, leaving him with just a few hundred men to face his furious father. Hastily backtracking, the prince caught up with Durga Das, who was dismayed to learn that 'Alamgir had wiped an entire army off the field without shooting a single arrow. Finding that the Rajputs had no appetite for battling 'Alamgir, Durga Das, together with Prince Akbar, marched south seeking asylum with any anti-Mughal community they could find.

They found that community south of the Vindhya Mountains, where anti-Mughal sentiment had been brewing for several decades. For his part, 'Alamgir had greater plans than merely capturing his rebel son. Back in 1658, before leaving the Deccan to join the War of Succession, he had been on the cusp of annexing both Bijapur and Golconda and checking the nascent power of Maratha chieftains. For more than two decades as emperor, he continued to view these projects as unfinished business. Now, with his rebel son having fled into the arms of one of those adversaries, he had one more reason to pack his tents and, together with the entire court and a good part of the army, shift to the Deccan.

## EMERGING IDENTITIES: THE MARATHAS FROM SHAHJI TO TARABAI

As they crossed the Vindhyas and entered the Marathi-speaking western Deccan, Durga Das and Prince Akbar encountered a political culture very different from the Rajput world they had left behind. By the seventeenth century, sovereign territories in Rajasthan were dominated by members of a single Rajput lineage that claimed descent from a common conqueror–ancestor. Land was parcelled out to *sardars*, who were hereditary leaders of sub-clans and loyal to the clan's ruler, or raja, who was supposed to be the nearest legitimate descendant in direct male line from the state's conqueror–ancestor, and the firstborn of his generation. Because all clan members were morally obliged to support the raja in times of war, and because by this time they had absorbed the martial ideology of the *kshatriya* warrior class, the constituent members of Rajput states could be readily mobilized for collective action, political or military. By 'Alamgir's day, moreover, most Rajput states had submitted to the Mughal empire, symbolized by a raja's acknowledging the emperor's right to apply a vermilion *tika* to his forehead – itself a Rajput political ritual – and by attending the Mughal court. The Rajputs' hierarchically structured polities thus allowed the Mughals access to considerable military manpower, since the submission of any given raja implied that of his entire clan.

The political world of the Marathi-speaking Deccan was very different. Although united since at least the fourteenth century by a common vernacular language and a growing corpus of devotional literature, the mainly agrarian society of the western plateau was fractured politically into *parganas*, each one comprising twenty to 100 villages. Each *pargana* was controlled by a *deshmukh*, who adjudicated disputes, collected revenue and provided local security by maintaining his own retainers and controlling one or more of the hundreds of fortified strongholds that dot the western Deccan's hilly landscape. However, unlike in Rajput states, where a single clan was displaced spatially across a large territory, and where all *sardars* swore loyalty to their raja and claimed descent from a common ancestor–warrior, a *deshmukh*'s political loyalty to anyone beyond his own *desh*, or land, was contractual, not kin-based, and was directed to whichever sultan or warlord could offer him the best deal. In politically volatile times, *deshmukhs* of the western Deccan looked more like 'high-risk rural entrepreneurs and negotiators' than paid bureaucrats.[54] And the mid seventeenth century was an especially volatile time. As the sultanates of the western Deccan were rapidly disintegrating, Maratha *deshmukhs* formerly tied to those kingdoms had to make risky choices about whom to negotiate with and whose patronage to accept. By 1636 the Nizam Shahi sultanate of Ahmad-nagar had already dissolved, its territories divided between the Mughals and the 'Adil Shahi sultanate of Bijapur. Then, in the 1650s and 1660s, Bijapur itself entered a period of decay from which it never recovered.

Amidst this fragmented political environment a new polity emerged in the Marathi-speaking western plateau. Its founder, the charismatic and politically gifted Maratha chieftain Shivaji Bhonsle (1630–80), repeatedly used courage and savvy to outmanoeuvre his adversaries. His ancestral roots, like those of most *deshmukh* families, were embedded in the Deccan's sultanate systems. Shivaji's grandfather, Maloji, had been in the service of Malik Ambar, the powerful Habshi ex-slave and *vazir* of the Nizam Shahi sultanate who held off Jahangir's repeated invasions of the Deccan between 1605 and 1626. Malik Ambar had given land in the western Deccan's Sholapur and Pune region to Maloji's son Shahji, who first tried to prop up the collapsing Nizam Shahi sultanate after Malik Ambar's death, and then briefly entered Shah Jahan's service as a *mansabdar*, before finally defecting to Bijapur in 1636. Leaving his wife and young son Shivaji on his ancestral lands near Pune, Shahji led several 'Adil Shahi military expeditions deep into the southern Deccan, making Bangalore his base. Meanwhile, in 1647 the seventeen-year-old Shivaji used a stratagem to seize the fort of Torna. From the treasure found there he built the fort of Raigarh, from which Bijapur's forces failed to dislodge him. Throughout the early 1650s, while the state of Bijapur was distracted by war with Golconda and the illness of its sultan, Shivaji quietly recruited ever more *deshmukh*s and their retainers to his cause. In 1656 he challenged and defeated in battle the powerful *deshmukh* Chandra Rao More, which gave him access to the Konkan coast. He also acquired more treasure, with which he built another fort, Pratapgarh, in the Western Ghats.

The following year, 1657, Shivaji had his first interaction with Aurangzeb, then the governor of the Mughal Deccan. Recognizing that the Mughal empire, not Bijapur, was the more significant player with which to negotiate, the ambitious Maratha entrepreneur offered his military services to the Mughals if the latter would recognize his rights over the forts he had already seized. Aurangzeb agreed to these proposals, but not to Shivaji's audacious request for recognition of his control of coastal forts, such as Dabhol, that were still in 'Adil Shahi hands. Aurangzeb was already wary of the gathering power of this independent Maratha chieftain. By 1659, when all of north India was preoccupied with the War of Succession, Shivaji commanded a cavalry of 7,000 and controlled some forty forts in the mountains and along the Konkan coast. Meanwhile, Bijapur seized this moment of turmoil over Mughal succession to reassert its grip over its western tracts. In September 1659 that sultanate sent one of its leading generals, Afzal Khan, to punish Shivaji. But the upstart chieftain treacherously killed Afzal Khan during a negotiating session between the two men, after which his cavalrymen poured over the plateau and seized many forts, including Panhala, one of Bijapur's principal strongholds guarding the caravan routes between its capital and the Arabian Sea.[55] Shivaji's power and audacity had reached new heights.

Soon after Aurangzeb had won the throne, he sent his uncle, Shaista Khan, to reassert imperial authority in the Mughal Deccan. But in 1663 Shivaji made a daring night-time raid on the Mughal officer's camp, during which the khan was wounded and his son was killed. An infuriated 'Alamgir immediately recalled him. The next year Shivaji brazenly sacked the port of Surat, the Mughals' principal window on the Arabian Sea. The emperor responded in 1665 by sending his most trusted general, Jai Singh, the Kachhwaha raja of Amber, to the Deccan. After cornering the Maratha chief in his stronghold of Purandar, Jai Singh negotiated an agreement with Shivaji whereby the latter would surrender twenty-three of his thirty-five forts; join Mughal campaigns against Bijapur; give the Mughals a portion of plundered wealth from future conquests of Bijapuri assets; and agree to his son Sambhaji enrolling in Mughal service. Suspecting that the Maratha leader might renege on these provisions, Jai Singh proposed, and 'Alamgir agreed, that Shivaji and Sambhaji should personally appear at the imperial court in Agra. This set the stage for a bizarre spectacle. Wherever it was held, the Mughal court was carefully regulated with respect to protocol and hierarchy. On 12 May 1666, offended at having to stand in court among officers he considered beneath his stature (even though he held no Mughal rank at all), Shivaji made a public scene by falling to the floor, writhing like a wounded animal, then rising and audibly complaining, even threatening suicide.[56] He was immediately hustled out of the audience hall and placed under house arrest, lucky to have escaped with his life for committing such an egregious breach of courtly etiquette. But within several weeks he and his son had managed to escape, probably by bribing guards. Disguised as religious mendicants, they made the long journey back to the Deccan on foot, dodging Mughal patrols.

Shivaji's relations with the Mughals having reached an impasse, and with Bijapur weakened further when in 1672 a four-year-old boy succeeded to the throne, the Maratha chieftain resolved not only to declare his independence from both Bijapur and the Mughals, but also to fashion himself as an explicitly Hindu monarch, one of his titles being *haindava-dharmoddarakla*, 'protector of the Hindu faith'.[57] He would also be a *kshatriya* king, a warrior king according to India's ancient scheme of social hierarchy, thereby raising his moral authority above that of his fellow Marathas and the region's many *deshmukh* families. But this posed a problem. Shivaji's public fiasco at 'Alamgir's court at Agra was more than a breach of courtly protocol. Rajputs standing in his midst perceived him as distinctly alien. Jaswant Singh, the raja of the Rathor Rajputs of Marwar, dismissed him as 'a mere *bhumia*' (petty landholder).[58] To overcome such social barriers, Shivaji arranged for a celebrated Brahmin from Benares, Gagabhat, to come to Maharashtra and authenticate the claim that his family was descended from lapsed Rajputs of the Sisodiya clan who had migrated from Mewar centuries earlier. With that accomplished, in June 1674 he sponsored a lavish and carefully choreographed coronation ceremony at Raigarh, in which he had himself invested with the sacred thread of the twice-born castes, accompanied by elaborate purification rituals, Vedic verses and Brahmanical chants. While Shivaji sat on a golden throne covered with lion and tiger skins, Gagabhat raised the royal umbrella over his head, hailing him Śiva Chhatrapati. The extravagant ceremony, in which thousands of Brahmins were fed and given gifts, cost an estimated five million rupees.[59] The new monarch then embarked on military campaigns to the peninsula's deep south, seizing from Bijapur's control Vellore and Jinji in the Tamil country. Although his reign lasted only five years, he had established Maratha authority over much of the Konkan coast, the western plateau and parts of south India, bequeathing to his male descendants a new, independent polity.

Such was the changed political environment that 'Alamgir found upon his return to the Deccan in early 1682, twenty-four years after he had governed the region as a prince. In those earlier days, Bijapur had been under the firm rule of Sultan Muhammad 'Adil Shah, who commanded the loyalty of most of his client Maratha *deshmukh*s. But now, the 'Adil Shahi throne was occupied by a fourteen-year-old sovereign whose court was riven by feuding ethno-political factions, while Maratha *deshmukh*s formerly loyal to Bijapur had mostly gravitated to the Maratha state's political orbit. Moreover, the possibility of capturing the rebel Akbar disappeared when the prince, shortly after his father's arrival in the Deccan, sailed off to Iran, never to return to India. In these circumstances, the emperor endeavoured to mobilize Bijapur and Golconda into joining the Mughals against the Maratha kingdom. But, when his efforts failed owing to those kingdoms' covert collusion with the Marathas, he instead trained his sights on the two sultanates. Bijapur was the first to fall to the Mughals, which it did in 1686 after an eighteen-month siege. A year later Golconda also fell, thanks to Mughal bribes to the fort's gatekeepers. The territories of both states were swiftly annexed and parcelled out to Mughal officers as *jagir*s.

The Maratha state, ruled since 1680 by Shivaji's first son Sambhaji, now felt the full brunt of Mughal arms. In early 1689 Sambhaji was captured, taken to 'Alamgir's camp and brutally executed. In the Maratha capital of Raigarh Shivaji's second son, Rajaram, was hastily crowned, but the kingdom's leaders, fearful for the young king's security with Mughal armies nearby, arranged for his escape to distant Jinji in the Tamil country. Just months later, Raigarh too fell to 'Alamgir. At this point it seemed that the Maratha state had been crushed. 'Alamgir had captured all Shivaji's remaining treasure, his resplendent golden coronation throne, all the government's records, and the royal horses and elephants. Although Rajaram had eluded their grasp, the Mughals did capture Sambhaji's nine-year-old son Shahu, whom 'Alamgir confined in his mobile court, where he was well treated. He would be raised in Persianate Mughal culture but not converted to Islam, to be saved in the emperor's chess game for future use as a political pawn, albeit a pawn who would ultimately become a king.

The year 1689 marked a turning point for Aurangzeb, for the empire and for India. With the two remaining Deccan sultanates extinguished, their territories annexed and the young Maratha state apparently nipped in the bud, 'Alamgir could easily have returned to north India as a victorious conqueror and, after an absence of ten years, resumed governing the empire from its historic heartland. He could also have taken with him Shivaji's magnificent golden throne as a trophy of war, not to mention the substantial treasure he had seized from Golconda. Some of his advisers actually recommended such a course of action. But in a momentous decision, 'Alamgir rejected such advice. Not only was he determined to complete his subjugation of the Maratha state by seizing Jinji and capturing the fugitive Rajaram; he also coveted the rich lands of southern Karnataka and the Tamil country, long in a state of anarchy since the decline first of Vijayanagara, then of Bijapur. For the next eight years, 1690–98, he would direct the long, laborious operations at Jinji while camped in two sprawling tent cities, first at Galgali by the banks of the Krishna fifty-five kilometres south-west of Bijapur, and then at Machnur by the Bhima River between Sholapur and Pandharpur.

Dominating the Karnatak plain between Arcot and Tiruchirappalli, Jinji is an immense, triangular-shaped stronghold encompassing three steep and well-fortified hills encircled by walls stretching nearly five kilometres in circumference. The challenge of seizing it was given to Zulfiqar Khan, the same general who had brilliantly taken Raigarh. He was joined by the emperor's youngest and favourite son, Kam Bakhsh. But it was a vexed enterprise. The Mughal army soon became bogged down outside Jinji's massive walls, while Maratha cavalry sent down from Maharashtra frequently broke the long supply lines carrying funds, war matériel and vital communications from the emperor's camp. Months passed, followed by years. In 1693, in what appeared a possible restaging of the 1657–9 War of Succession, rumours spread that the emperor was on the verge of death, or had already died. This tempted Kam Bakhsh to patch up a secret settlement with Rajaram and plan a takeover of the imperial army. But the plot was discovered and the prince was sent up to 'Alamgir's camp to be disciplined. While four more years passed with no progress at the siege of Jinji, the emperor endeavoured to draw Maratha chiefs away from the moribund Maratha state by offering them hefty *mansab*s in Mughal service. Many of them agreed; others alternated between Mughal and Maratha service, depending on which side could give them the better deal; still other Maratha families were divided in their loyalties, with different members joining opposing sides.

In late 1697 the Maratha cause revived when dispirited Mughal officers at Jinji, anticipating the need to accommodate the Marathas once the ageing emperor had died, quietly allowed Rajaram to slip out of the fort, which shortly thereafter fell to the Mughals.[60] Reaching Maharashtra in early 1698, Rajaram began rebuilding his father's state, establishing a new capital at Satara and mounting counter-attacks against the Mughals in the northern Deccan. But his efforts would be cut off by an early death, in 1700. Whereas several of his wives nobly committed the ancient rite of *sati*, hurling their bodies on the burning pyre of the deceased raja, two wives declined to do so, each one hoping that her infant son might succeed Rajaram as king. One of these wives was Tarabai, the proud and strong-willed daughter of Shivaji's former commander-in-chief, Hambir Rao Mohite [see Fig. 21]. In the early 1690s, when Rajaram was besieged in distant Jinji, Tarabai, still a teenager, had remained in Maharashtra acquiring administrative skills under the tutelage of senior Maratha officials. Now, following Rajaram's death, she boldly had the sacred thread ceremony performed for her four-year-old son, confirming his ritual status as a *kshatriya* warrior and revealing her intention to crown him king, with herself as regent. This she did in the remote hill fort of Vishalgarh. On hearing this news the Mughal camp was exultant. 'Alamgir ordered the beating of drums, and his officers congratulated each other, convinced, records the chronicler Khafi Khan, 'that it would not be difficult to overcome two young children and a helpless woman. They thought their enemy weak, contemptible, and helpless.'[61]

Though normally shrewd in evaluating his adversaries, 'Alamgir completely misjudged whom he was facing. But not so his adversaries. Prominent Maratha *deshmukh*s now rallied around the twenty-five-year-old Tarabai, recognizing her as the most likely remnant of Shivaji's family to salvage the kingdom's sagging fortunes, despite her gender. The Hindu officer and news writer Bhimsen, then in the Deccan in 'Alamgir's service, bluntly stated that Tarabai 'was a stronger ruler than her husband', adding that after Rajaram's death she 'became all in all and regulated things so well that not a single Maratha leader acted without her order'.[62] From nearby Goa, Portuguese officials referred to her as the 'queen of the Marathas'.[63] Even Khafi Khan, whose chronicle of 'Alamgir's reign glorifies the emperor, admitted that Tarabai showed great powers of command and government, which she had taken into her own hands. 'She won the hearts of her officers,' he wrote, 'and for all the struggles and schemes, the campaigns and sieges of Aurangzeb up to the end of his reign, the power of the Mahrattas increased day by day.'[64]

Nor was Tarabai content with merely holding on to Maratha forts. Shortly before his death, her late husband Rajaram had marched out of Maharasthra into Khandesh and Berar, demanding in certain districts a quarter of the regular imperial revenues as protection money against plundering by his troops. Leaving local Mughal garrisons unharmed, Rajaram initiated a form of dual government in such districts, where the Mughals and Marathas effectively shared land revenues. Tarabai, in turn, built on this policy, expanding it geographically and streamlining it administratively. Very soon after Rajaram's death she boldly sent Maratha armies on military expeditions deep into Mughal domains to the north, well beyond the Deccan. In 1700, even while allowing 'Alamgir to seize some of her own forts, she dispatched 50,000 troops as far north as the Chanderi region in north-western Madhya Pradesh, nearly 1,000 kilometres from the Maratha headquarters in Satara. In 1702 she sent armies into Mughal Khandesh, Berar and Telangana. The next year she attacked cities in Khandesh and Malwa, and in 1706 her generals struck cities in Gujarat.[65] These were not merely raids. As Khafi Khan notes, her plan was to 'cast the anchor of permanence' wherever Marathi armies penetrated. This she did by allocating revenue districts among Maratha administrators, establishing Maratha revenue collectors in conquered districts, and encouraging Maratha invaders to settle down in these districts with their families.[66] Tarabai's energetic leadership not only rescued the Maratha state from disintegration. In her northern invasions she sought to extend that state well beyond the Marathi-speaking Deccan. By striking deep into the Mughal heartland, she anticipated policies her Maratha successors would adopt later in the eighteenth century.

Meanwhile, 'Alamgir's armies continued to plod from fort to fort across the Deccan, trying to mow down the revived Maratha state one fort at a time. But the two sides were asymmetrically matched. Adapted to fighting pitched battles on the flat north Indian plain, 'Alamgir's huge armies lumbered across the plateau with their weighty artillery and heavy cavalry. In 1695 the Mughal camp at Galgali, by the Krishna, measured about fifty kilometres in circumference and contained 60,000 cavalry, 100,000 infantry, 50,000 camels, 3,000 elephants, 250 bazaars and another several hundred thousand servants, merchants and hangers-on.[67] Theirs was hardly an agile or mobile fighting machine. After laboriously taking one fort, a Mughal army would move to another, only to have the first one fall to the Marathas again. Their adversaries, by contrast, avoided pitched battles in the open. Taking advantage of their homeland's hilly terrain, the Marathas used guerrilla tactics that maximized the effectiveness of their swift, light cavalry, luring Mughal units into tight ravines, ambushing Mughal supply caravans and intercepting imperial communications.

The Mughal effort was plagued by other, internal problems. As 'Alamgir approached his ninetieth year of age and his fiftieth year as emperor, many of his veteran generals were dying, leaving him with flattering upstarts much too intimidated by the stubborn octogenarian to dare suggest a change of policy. Petty quarrels and jealousies within his corps of commanders further reduced the Mughals' effectiveness. In this dismal situation 'Alamgir did what came naturally to him: instead of leaving field command to his generals, from 1699 to 1705 he personally oversaw many siege operations. Like the Fool in Shakespeare's *King Lear*, who witnessed his aged lord rage on a barren heath and descend into madness, 'Alamgir's advisers seem to have understood the futility of it all. Bhimsen wrote, 'Emperor Alamgir who is not in want of anything, has been seized with such a longing and passion for taking forts that he personally runs about panting for some heaps of stone [hill forts].'[68]

It was while conducting one of his siege operations – fruitlessly 'panting for some heaps of stone' – that the emperor, a lifelong work-aholic, was finally forced to abandon active military campaigning. In early 1706, in the grip of a severe illness, he was loaded on to a palan-quin and carried to the ancient fort of Ahmadnagar, which he declared his 'journey's end'. He died there the following year. Char-acteristically, he rejected the idea of a grand, ostentatious tomb of the sort that towered over the graves of all his Mughal ancestors save Babur. Instead, he arranged to be buried in a simple grave open to the sky in Khuldabad, a saintly graveyard near Daulatabad. In this final statement, spoken through the medium of architecture, the austere monarch asserted both his personal piety and his lifelong resolve to fashion a legitimacy – and now a legacy – firmly opposed to that of his father. If Shah Jahan had cultivated the aura of a resplendent king, notes one historian, 'Alamgir cultivated one of a renunciate king[69] – a contrast captured for ever in his father's Taj Mahal and in his own humble grave site.

In some ways 'Alamgir's career eerily echoed that of Sultan Muhammad bin Tughluq. A little more than three centuries before Prince Aurangzeb waged successful campaigns in the Deccan, adding new territories to the Mughal empire, Prince Ulugh Khan had led prolonged campaigns in the plateau, successfully adding large tracts of territory to the Delhi sultanate. In 1325 he returned to Delhi and promptly usurped the throne from his father, becoming Sultan Muhammad bin Tughluq. In 1658 Prince Aurangzeb would follow the same path to supreme power. And just as Muhammad bin Tughluq returned to the peninsula towards the end of his reign, never again to see Delhi and destined to spend his last years doggedly trudging from camp to camp, taking personal command of day-to-day military operations while pursuing rebels who ever eluded his grasp, 'Alamgir suffered the same fate. Both men died in the field, far from Delhi. And for both men, prolonged absence from Delhi where day-to-day administration lacked their personal supervision, combined with the drain on the state's treasury owing to costly wars waged far to the south, placed severe stresses on the fiscal and ultimately political sta-bility of their respective empires. As Mark Twain reputedly said: 'History doesn't repeat itself, but it often rhymes.'

# 'ONE POMEGRANATE TO SERVE A HUNDRED SICK MEN'

The last fifteen years of 'Alamgir's reign had seen a bidding war between the emperor and Maratha leaders to court and win the service of powerful *deshmukh*s. Whereas the Marathas could appeal to the legacy of Shivaji or loyalty to the land and culture of Maharashtra, 'Alamgir offered the prestige that came with serving an India-wide empire, and, especially, a high rank in imperial service. For each new *mansab* rank, officials in the Mughal revenue bureaucracy had to find, somewhere in the empire, one or more *jagir*s whose revenue matched a *mansabdar*'s assigned pay. As long as the empire kept acquiring more taxable territory through conquest, there was always land to be made available for assignment as *jagir*s. This additional land could then be granted either to *mansabdar*s who had been promoted to higher *mansab*s or to people newly recruited into the nobility.

In the 1680s, 'Alamgir had induced many powerful nobles of Bijapur and Golconda to abandon those sultanates by offering them high *mansab*s in Mughal service. By 1691 such nobles comprised fully 160 out of the total of 575 Mughal officers holding *mansab*s of 1000 *zat* or higher. That amounted to 28 per cent of the empire's upper nobility.[70] Initially, these men were given *jagir*s in the Deccan itself, but this proved inadequate since the expected revenue for the region had been inflated far beyond its actual capacity. Moreover, the land itself had been ravaged by decades of warfare, as armies devoured the harvest of fields like swarms of locusts. Nor had newly conquered lands in the Karnatak, or the southern Deccan, yet been brought under Mughal control. As a result, it became increasingly necessary to accommodate newly recruited Deccani nobles by assigning them wealth-producing *jagir*s in north India. But this created further problems. Because the imperial domain had not been expanding in north India since 'Alamgir had permanently moved to the Deccan, there were few fresh *jagir*s to distribute to these new nobles. The only practical solution was to reduce or revoke altogether *jagir*s held by the empire's old, established nobility. However, any policy that effectively disenfranchised older sections of the nobility to accommodate new nobles amounted to 'robbing Peter to pay Paul'. In short, there was insufficient unclaimed land to meet the growing demand for *jagirs* owing to the recruitment of new nobles. Or, as the emperor repeatedly, and poetically, wrote on the registers of those claiming new salaries, 'There is only one pomegranate to serve a hundred sick men [*yek anar, sad bimar*].'[71]

This situation worsened after Bijapur and Golconda had been conquered and, after 1689, when 'Alamgir began recruiting Marathas by promising them lucrative *mansab*s as inducements for enlisting in Mughal service. Here again the policy met with success, but only in a narrow sense. In the final twenty-five years of his reign, Marathas comprised 17 per cent of the empire's upper nobility, actually exceeding the Rajputs, who constituted 12.6 per cent.[72] But the influx of these men created problems. First, their loyalty was unreliable. 'Alamgir evidently thought he could deal with Marathas just as Mughal emperors since Akbar had dealt with Rajputs. But, in contrast to the Rajputs, the submission of a Maratha chieftain did not imply that of his entire clan. Furthermore, a deep cultural divide separated north India's Persianized martial classes from the warrior elites of the Deccan, most prominently Telugu *nayaka*s and Maratha *deshmukh*s. This was not a religious issue. Many Rajputs disparaged Maratha chiefs, just as Jaswant Singh had dismissed them as 'mere *bhumia*s'.

The greater problem with 'Alamgir's policy, however, was structural. To pay for the Deccan wars, 'Alamgir classified much of the Deccan's conquered territory as crown land (*khalisa*), whose revenues went directly to the treasury and not to *mansabdar*s in the form of *jagir*s. In north India, fewer *jagir*s were available because so many of them had already been given to Deccanis. All this placed severe strain on the military and fiscal systems and, ultimately, the political system. As *jagir*s became increasingly scarce, it grew more difficult to sustain the established practice of regularly transferring *mansabdar*s every three or four years. Once a *mansabdar* received his transfer notice, he might have to wait four or five years before the revenue bureaucracy could find another *jagir* for him, which meant four or five years without a revenue stream with which to pay his troops.[73] To expedite the transfer process, wealthier and more established *mansabdar*s could employ agents to lobby bureaucrats on their behalf, or simply resort to bribing such functionaries. But *mansabdars* who lacked the means to hire agents or bribe officials were left with nothing. In this way corruption crept into an administrative machine that had operated relatively smoothly ever since Akbar's day. The emperor was well aware of this problem: late in his reign he took the radical step of banning altogether the recruitment of new *mansabdars*.

But by then it was too late. Although the system did not totally collapse in 'Alamgir's reign, all the factors leading to such an outcome were firmly in place. Ultimately, established nobles would simply ignore orders for the transfer of their *jagirs*, since they knew very well that, if they relinquished their hold on their existing *jagirs*, new ones might never be assigned to them. Within a decade of the emperor's death, orders of *jagir* transfers had become mere sheets of paper, as rulers far less disciplined than 'Alamgir continued granting *mansabs* with no corresponding *jagir* to pay for the rank.[74] In short, the entire fiscal–political structure was approaching collapse.

# RELIGION AND SOVEREIGNTY UNDER 'ALAMGIR

In his personal habits, 'Alamgir was notoriously austere and abstemious – traits which converted into a religious sensibility that was pious to the point of puritanical. When he was a prince, some regarded this as an affectation fashioned to mask a secret ambition to power.[75] During his struggle to win the Peacock Throne, his piety served to distance him both from the lavish indulgences of his father – whom one modern historian calls a 'glorified jeweler'[76] – and the religious adventurism of his elder brother Dara. Further defining his religious posture were the events surrounding his actual accession to supreme power. This was because the crisis of 1657–9 was not a typical Turko-Mongol, or even Mughal war of succession in which the princes and their armies engaged in an armed struggle over a vacant throne. The problem this time was that Shah Jahan had not died, even though it was widely believed when war broke out that he already had, or that his death was imminent. By November 1657, just two months after he fell ill, the stricken emperor had fully recovered.

By that time, though, military orders had already been issued, armies had been mobilized, one son had already crowned himself, and another would follow suit a month later. The customary machinery for replacing a deceased sovereign having been set in motion, the inevitable struggle had to be played out to the full, until the drama's final curtain would come down with a new emperor formally installed on the Peacock Throne.

For his part, Prince Aurangzeb had left the Deccan for Delhi genuinely believing that Shah Jahan was at the point of death, if not already dead. But, by the time he reached Agra and found his father in good health, what had begun as a war of succession – he had already defeated Dara's armies twice – suddenly became an act of usurpation, and the usurpation of another person's land or property is prohibited in Islamic law.[77] For a man professing strict observance of that law, the newly crowned emperor suddenly found himself in an untenable position, the more so when experts on canon law refused to sanction his seizure of power since the lawful sovereign, his own father, was still living. In this circumstance Aurangzeb solicited the opinion of 'Abd al-Wahhab, the former *qazi* of Patan, Gujarat, who obligingly decreed that since Shah Jahan was physically unfit to govern (despite evidence to the contrary), the throne was virtually vacant. Aurangzeb's accession as 'Alamgir had therefore not violated Islamic law. As a reward for this valuable hermeneutic service, 'Abd al-Wahhab was made the empire's chief *qazi*; he would go on to become one of the most corrupt chief judges in Mughal history.[78]

The nature of 'Alamgir's rise to supreme power – a bloody usurpation accompanied by the elimination of his brothers and the confinement of his father – had far-reaching consequences. Notwithstanding 'Abd al-Wahhab's whitewashing of the process, the emperor craved legitimacy in the eyes of the wider Islamic world, for which purpose he sought the blessings of the guardian of the holiest shrines in the Muslim world, the Sharif of Mecca.[79] In 1659, shortly after his grand coronation, he sent a considerable sum of money to the Sharif, to be distributed to the needy there. But to his dismay, the authorities in Mecca turned down his gift for the same reason his own jurists had initially rejected his claims to the throne – that he could not legally be sovereign as long as his father was still alive.[80] Undeterred, several years later he sent gifts valued at 660,000 rupees to the Sharif.[81] Finally, in 1666, shortly after Shah Jahan had died, the Sharif sent 'Alamgir a belated congratulations on his accession, together with a sacred relic – the broom and some dust from the Prophet Muhammad's tomb in Medina – which the emperor received with much solemnity.[82]

'Alamgir's relations with his family also influenced his religious posture. During and after the hard-fought succession struggle, it became politically necessary to magnify the differences between himself and Dara Shukoh. In contrast to his elder brother, whom he publicly portrayed as a deviant backslider whose execution was justified partly on religious grounds, Aurangzeb projected himself as a correct Muslim. With Shah Jahan he ratcheted up this posture still higher. In bitter written exchanges with his father, confined to his palace in Agra, the new emperor self-righteously posed as the champion of Islam, stressing that Dara had usurped power and promoted Hinduism during their father's illness. He even claimed that his own victories at Dharmat and Samugarh demonstrated divine sanction for his enterprise.[83] Accordingly, soon after his coronation he ceased participating in courtly functions that conflicted with his understanding of Islam, such as celebrating the Persian New Year's Day (Nauruz), patronizing music and art, appearing at the *jharokha* at sunrise, applying *tika* on the foreheads of subordinate kings, or having himself weighed against gold or silver on his birthday. His abstention from music appears to have been a personal matter that was not imposed on others.[84] Other measures, such as prohibiting gambling or consuming alcohol, were intended to extend beyond the court, but they were blatantly ignored even by his closest courtiers.[85]

To the wider public, meanwhile, he sought to justify – or perhaps atone for – his violent path to power by presenting himself in the guise of a pious and beneficent ruler in the mould of a sultan of Delhi such as Iltutmish or Muhammad bin Tughluq. He ordered that the Islamic confession of faith not appear on Mughal coins, lest the sacred words be intentionally or inadvertently defaced. He replaced the public celebration of the Persian New Year (Nauruz) with that of 'Eid al-Fitr, the feast that ends the fasting in the Muslim month of Ramazan. And he established the office of public censor (*muhtisib*), an official charged with enforcing fairness in the marketplace.[86] He also ordered the abolition of custom duties previously levied on Muslim merchants, leaving in place those imposed on Hindu traders.[87] However, local authorities in Gujarat largely ignored the order and, even when it was briefly enforced, Hindu merchants simply arranged for complicit Muslims to handle their goods for them.[88] Referring to non-Muslim religious practices performed in public, the French physician François Bernier, who visited India during 'Alamgir's first decade of rule, noted that, once in power, 'the Great *Mogol*, though a *Mahometan*, permits these ancient and superstitious practices; not wishing, or not daring, to disturb the *Gentiles* [Hindus] in the free exercises of their religion.'[89] Around 1688 an Englishman travelling through India contrasted what he perceived as the official tolerance during 'Alamgir's reign with the intolerance then prevailing in his own country.[90]

On the other hand, in 1679 'Alamgir issued an order reinstating the discriminatory *jizya* tax, effectively a property tax levied on all non-Muslim males except those in imperial service. The order for this tax, which had never been imposed by a previous Mughal ruler and was only occasionally collected by the Delhi sultans, was definitely carried out. Considering the timing of the decree, it has been suggested that the emperor felt the need to make some dramatic move to rally the empire's Muslims around major political and military initiatives then being contemplated for dealing with deteriorating affairs in the Deccan.[91] Ever since 1663 Shivaji had flagrantly defied Mughal authority, and by the late 1670s, with both Bijapur and Golconda often colluding with the new Maratha kingdom, the emperor's Deccan policy lay in shambles. The order for the *jizya* tax was followed directly by a full-scale invasion of the plateau. To the juridically minded emperor, moreover, non-Muslims living under Mughal rule were, in a narrowly legal sense, a protected population (*dhimmi*) who were obliged to pay this tax to compensate for not serving in the state's armed forces. Curiously, though, to the contemporary Hindu writer Bhimsen, it was not the tax itself that was offensive; rather, it was the corruption of the venal officials who had been recruited from the lower ranks of the Muslim clergy to collect it.[92]

In any event, 'Alamgir himself would not have seen the imposition of the *jizya* tax as politically destabilizing, given the evidence that throughout his reign he scrupulously avoided letting religious considerations threaten the empire's political stability. On one occasion he referred to his chief *qazi* the question of whether captured Hindu rebels should be treated differently from captured Muslim rebels. The *qazi* decreed a light punishment for Muslim rebels, but release for Hindus if they converted to Islam. 'Alamgir, however, returned the decree, ordering that a different ruling should be found, so 'that control over the kingdom may not be lost'. Accordingly, the *qazi* and his learned advisers returned a new judgment, that all the prisoners should be executed regardless of their religion, a decision the emperor accepted.[93] On another occasion, a Sunni Muslim petitioned the emperor for a post as imperial paymaster on the grounds that the two existing paymasters were both Shi'i, and that appointing him would bring sectarian balance to the office. Irritated by the request, 'Alamgir replied:

> What connection have earthly affairs with religion? And what right have administrative works to meddle with bigotry? *'For you is your religion and for me is mine'* [Qur'an 109:6]. If this rule [suggested by you] were established, it would be my duty to extirpate all the [Hindu] Rajahs and their followers. Wise men disapprove of the removal from the office of able officers.[94]

After all, Rajputs, Marathas, Brahmins, Jains, Kayasthas and other non-Muslims were essential for running the empire's vast administrative and military systems. This much is seen in the significant increase in the number of Hindus serving in 'Alamgir's *mansabdari* corps. Under Shah Jahan, Hindus comprised less than a quarter (22.4 per cent) of all nobles holding a rank of 1000 *zat* or higher. By the last years of 'Alamgir's reign that figure had risen to nearly a third (31.6 per cent) of the total.[95]

In keeping with the Mughal and Delhi sultanate precedent of viewing non-Muslim monuments within their sovereign domain as deserving of state protection, 'Alamgir supported temples with cash or land grants. He once ordered officials in Benares to punish miscreants who had been harassing Brahmins in charge of that city's Hindu temples.[96] And he described the temple complex of Ellora, which he visited in the 1650s, as 'one of the marvels of the work of the true transcendent Artisan [God]'.[97] But his treatment of temples patronized by, or associated with, state enemies was another matter. Muslim sovereigns since the late twelfth century, and Hindu rajas since at least the seventh, had looted, redefined or destroyed royal temples of enemy kings as the normal means of detaching defeated rulers from the most prominent manifestations of their former sovereign authority, thereby rendering such rulers politically impotent.[98] For the Mughals, temples formerly patronized by enemy kings became state property once that king had been defeated and his former territory annexed to the empire. However, if a Hindu patron of such a temple rebelled against the state, both he and the temple were liable for punishment. Such a principle would explain 'Alamgir's destruction of temples in Kuch Bihar (north of Bengal) after local rajas there defied Mughal authority in 1661. The same principle accounted for his destruction of the Vishvanath Temple in Benares in 1669: people related to that temple's patron were believed to have facilitated Shivaji's escape from Agra, and hence were state enemies. Similarly, the Keśavadeva Temple in Mathura, which had been supported by imperial grants and was therefore considered state property, was destroyed in 1670 in the wake of a serious Jat rebellion in the region that claimed the life of the city's commandant and patron of its congregational mosque. Moreover, three Brahmins in Mathura had harboured the son of Shivaji shortly after the latter had escaped detention in Agra. In 1679–80 'Alamgir ordered the destruction of prominent temples in Rajasthan – including Khandela, Udaipur and Jodhpur – once it was established that they, too, had been associated with anti-state rebels.[99]

How, then, did non-Muslims view 'Alamgir and his actions regarding religion? Among Rajputs, representations of the emperor could vary enormously, even at the same court. At the Sisodiya court at Udaipur, a text composed just before the rebellion of 1679–81 portrays 'Alamgir as benevolent towards Rana Raja Singh, the raja of Mewar. However, another text, composed during the rebellion while the Sisodiya elite had retreated to the hills and Mughal troops were occupying their capital, vilifies and demonizes the emperor, portraying him as representing a community perennially in conflict with Hindus. But then a third text, completed at the same court shortly after the suppression of the rebellion and the normalization of

Mughal–Sisodiya relations, depicts 'Alamgir as a benevolent ally of the Sisodiya ruler, whom the emperor appreciated and rewarded.[100] Clearly, such varied representations depended on specific historical contexts. Similarly, in today's more religiously polarized climate it is widely believed that Krishna images were forcibly removed from the Braj heartland to Rajasthan in the 1660s and 1670s owing to 'Alamgir's alleged iconoclastic zeal. Contemporary evidence, however, suggests that the images were moved not because of the emperor's alleged iconoclasm but because of insecurity due to local Jat uprisings and threats by sectarian rivals to appropriate them for themselves – conflicts that the emperor himself is said to have mediated.[101]

Taking a much wider perspective, 'Alamgir's India – unlike South Asia in the colonial and post-colonial eras – appears to have been conceptually integrated even while culturally diverse. This much is seen in the memoir of Bhimsen, who portrays the India of his day, the late seventeenth century, as filled with the great cities of the 'heaven-protected' Mughal empire as well as with the seven famous rivers and the seven sacred centres of Hindu mythic geography. At the symbolic centre of that seamlessly interwoven realm, and holding it together conceptually, stood 'Alamgir, sacred king and heir to the spiritual charisma of his Timurid ancestors.[102] Bhimsen describes an incident during the monsoon of 1697 when the Bhima flooded its banks at 'Alamgir's camp at Machnur, drowning many people and bringing its waters to within a metre of the emperor's tent. With the whole camp plunged in a state of distress, the emperor wrote a prayer on a slip of paper and cast it on the river's surface. The water immediately subsided and, records Bhimsen, 'the prayer of the God-devoted Emperor was accepted by God, and *the world became composed again*'.[103] What actually happened on that day we will never know with certainty; but Bhimsen's memoir suggests how Indians of 'Alamgir's own time interpreted the meaning of the great flood of 1697.[104]

Similarly, in 1672 a peasant uprising, the Satnami revolt, broke out in Narnaul (in modern Haryana), in the course of which a prophetess appeared proclaiming that she could use spells to raise an invisible army. When the uprising took an alarming turn, the emperor dispatched a large force with banners on which he wrote prayers and magical figures with his own hand. Fighting magic with magic, 'Alamgir was seen by his contemporary subjects as having bridged the spiritual and mundane worlds. Indeed, he was popularly known as *'Alamgir zinda pir*, 'Alamgir, the living saint.[105] It was even believed that he was capable of making himself invisible whenever he wished, and could instantly appear in Mecca and converse with the Prophet Muhammad. 'From this cause,' noted Manucci, 'the people revere him, and hold him in the greatest respect.'[106] Indians of his day assessed the spiritual status of their leaders by their observed actions. On one occasion, the emperor spent a week in Gulbarga paying respects to the shrine of the Deccan's most renowned Sufi shaikh, Muhammad Gisudaraz, and conversing with reclusive Sufis there. For Bhimsen, the emperor's behaviour was salutary and redemptive, as would be expected of a sovereign perceived as connecting the divine and earthly worlds. By contrast, Shivaji's plundering of the town of Jalna, home of a spiritually gifted holy man named Jan Muhammad, was in Bhimsen's view a reckless act unbefitting a proper sovereign, and the probable cause of the Maratha king's untimely death.[107]

Such contemporary observations highlight a fundamental tension between two opposing conceptions of Mughal sovereignty – the one that 'Alamgir had inherited, and the one that he would promote. By his Indo-Timurid forebears he was bequeathed the identity of a sacred king, a lustrous persona that his father had assiduously cultivated and that his subjects now invested in him. It was also a persona that 'Alamgir occasionally and strategically adopted, as seen in the several episodes cited above. But notwithstanding his popular reputation as a 'living saint', 'Alamgir came to formulate a very different model of sovereignty for himself and for the empire he ruled. In this new dispensation, the kingdom would be governed not by a charismatic, semi-divine king, but by impersonal law – namely, the *shari'a* of Hanafi Sunnis – administered by a reconstituted and vastly empowered judiciary guided by a reformed, thoroughly codified legal system. At the same time, the emperor took dramatic and very public steps to place himself beneath that law. In 1675 he proclaimed that anybody in the empire with a legal claim against him could appeal to specially appointed judicial officials who were sent to every city, province and neighbouring territory of the empire precisely to hear such claims.[108]

It was not only the emperor's puritanical character that led him to embrace such a sweeping agenda for himself and for the empire.[109] Nor was it just the political necessity of distancing himself from his bitter rival Dara Shukoh who, lacking military competence, had wrongly imagined that embracing the Timurid ideology of sacred kingship would elevate him to the Peacock Throne. 'Alamgir's goal of replacing his dynasty's tradition of sacred kingship with an impersonal judicial state actually preceded the War of Succession. Formative in his thinking were the years 1645 to 1647 when, while still a prince, he was sent to govern Gujarat, a province then seething with Shi'i or quasi-Shi'i millennial movements. One of these, the Mahdavi, was initiated by a fifteenth-century charismatic leader, Muhammad Jaunpuri (d. 1505), who had professed to be the Mahdi, a figure who in Shi'i thought will return at the end of the millennium to restore the world to order. When Prince Aurangzeb reached Ahmedabad, he was met by a body of anti-Shi'i and anti-millennial Sunni clerics who, determined to mobilize the new governor's power to suppress a sect they regarded as heretical, arranged to have the Mahdavi leader interrogated in open court. When that leader provoked the Sunni clerics with militant language, Aurangzeb expelled him and his followers from the city.[110] Soon thereafter, Aurangzeb had to deal with a more openly Shi'i group, the Isma'ili Bohras. This was a prosperous merchant community in Gujarat whose leader, or *da'i*, provided spiritual direction for the community until the expected Shi'i messiah, or *imam*, would (re)appear at the end of time to cleanse the world. Again, urged on by vehemently anti-Shi'i clerics, Aurangzeb presided over a religious interrogation in which his Sunni clerics levelled serious charges against the Bohra *da'i*, such as the claim that the sect's veneration of the Prophet's son-in-law 'Ali amounted to idolatry. Under intense pressure by the clerics, the *da'i* ultimately confessed to all the charges and was executed.

As a consequence of his experience governing Gujarat and collaborating with its Sunni clerics in suppressing millennial movements, the prince came to appreciate the use of judicial power not just for dealing with such phenomena – throughout his reign, he persecuted Gujarat's Isma'ili Bohras – but for maintaining public order generally. This, in turn, had several consequences. First and most immediately, once he became emperor, 'Alamgir drew into his inner ruling circle some of the most powerful anti-Shi'i clerics with whom he had cooperated while governor of Gujarat and the Deccan. During his second governorship of the Deccan (1652–9), he had made Qazi 'Abd al-Wahhab, a member of an old family of *qazi*s in northern Gujarat, his legal expert (*mufti*); thereafter he became one of the emperor's closest and most powerful advisers. This was the same man who issued the judgment legitimizing the prince's seizure of the Peacock Throne, for which he was rewarded by being made the empire's supreme judge (*qazi al-quzat*), a post he held until his death in 1675. For forty of 'Alamgir's forty-nine years as emperor, Gujarati clerics held the highest positions in the imperial judiciary. All were anti-millennial and anti-Shi'i.[111]

Throughout 'Alamgir's reign, socio-religious movements of the sort he had earlier confronted in Gujarat repeatedly broke out – some of them Shi'i-based, some not – to most of which he and his judiciary had the same response: investigate, interrogate, then either rectify with persuasion or suppress with fines or violence. Such encounters informed his efforts to place the entire edifice of the Mughal state on a footing that privileged impersonal law above the sacred king. Visually, 'Alamgir's support of the clerical establishment was symbolized by the most ambitious monument he ever patronized: Lahore's splendid Badshahi Mosque (1671–3), for more than three centuries the largest mosque in the world [see Fig. 18]. But a more telling move was his sponsoring the codification and promulgation of the Hanafi Sunni legal code in a single, massive and authoritative compendium: the *Fatawa-i 'Alamgiri*. This comprehensive manual of Islamic jurisprudence, which took a team of nearly fifty scholars eight years to complete (1667–75), streamlined procedures and standardized rulings in what had previously been a chaotic judicial environment. Before its publication, a welter of law books had produced confusion and conflicting rulings by local judges across the empire.[112] The new manual also sought to harmonize the law as applied by India's *qazi*s with the legal norms established by Hanafi jurists of the eighth century. Most importantly, its compilation and dissemination placed the empire under a comprehensive legal code intended to supplant the mystery and majesty of a sacred sovereign. Indeed, the importance 'Alamgir attached to this project compares with the priority his father had given to building the Taj Mahal, except that Shah Jahan's already world-famous tomb and 'Alamgir's *Fatawa-i 'Alamgiri* reflect sharply opposing visions of kingship. If the former portrays Shah Jahan as the resplendent sovereign of a sacred realm, the latter reveals 'Alamgir as the pious, would-be patron of a judicial state.

Given the widespread use of Islamic law by diverse communities in 'Alamgir's India, the emperor's aim of standardizing that legal tradition and using it as a basis of Mughal sovereignty made a certain sense.[113] In the courts of local judges in Gujarat, Hindu artisans, merchants and Brahmins commonly invoked the *shari'a* in transactions pertaining to buying, selling, renting and mortgaging property, or in pursuing litigation in law courts. Hindu women in particular used Islamic law in their attempts to resist patriarchal domination.[114] The same held true further north. In the Punjabi town of Batala, writes the historian J. S. Grewal, 'the *brahmin*, the *khatri*, the goldsmith and the Hindu carpenter frequented the *qazi*'s court as much as the *sayyid* and the Muslim mason'.[115] And in Malwa, the vast majority of attesters in court documents, excepting those dealing with Muslim marriages, were non-Muslims. While acknowledging religious difference, moreover, such courts did not draw legal boundaries around India's ethnic or religious communities. Significantly, the word *shari'a* as used in local courts was not understood as applying to Muslims only, as it is today. Rather, it carried the ordinary and non-sectarian meaning of 'legal'.[116] Until the 1770s, when East India Company officials codified separate legal systems for Muslims and Hindus, Islamic law as it was administered in Mughal courts had functioned as common law. 'Alamgir's project of basing Mughal governance and sovereignty on a standardized codification of that law therefore built upon legal practices that, even though applied differently across the empire, were already in place in the Indian countryside.

However, the Timurid ideology of a sacred sovereign, conspicuously invoked by the emperor's nearest predecessors Shah Jahan, Jahangir and Akbar, could not easily be abandoned. It was too deeply ingrained in the culture of the empire's subjects, despite their various ethnic or religious identities. For generations, such an ideology had conferred an aura of legitimacy on Mughal emperors. Consequently, by enshrining law and empowering the judiciary while playing down the Timurid notion of sacred kingship, the emperor was sawing off the branch on which he sat, for his authority rested on being accepted as a sacred king.[117]

## CONCLUSION

For nearly a half century, the Mughal empire was ruled by one of the most complex and controversial figures in Indian history. 'Alamgir's character was defined by many qualities, some of them contradictory. From an early age he showed remarkable courage, which was repeatedly displayed on battlefields. A steely sense of duty and self-discipline translated into a lifelong commitment to administrative detail, if not minutiae; in modern times he might be called a workaholic. His court historian Muhammad Kazim records that he slept only three hours a night.[118] The Italian traveller Manucci corroborates this observation, adding that he sat up until midnight 'unceasingly occupied' with official business.[119] Yet his devotion to work also prevented him from delegating authority to others and led to meddling in the affairs of his officers and his sons. 'I came to know', he wrote disapprovingly to his second son Mu'azzam, 'that you disregard the soldiers and care more for the highly paid servants.' Or again, to the same son, 'I came to know from a letter of a dear friend that you attend the court with a saffron-like turban on your head.'[120]

In the end, one is left with perhaps the greatest enigma of 'Alamgir's long reign: why did he spend a quarter-century relentlessly pursuing two Deccan sultanates and the Marathas – a futile enterprise that even contemporaries such as Bhimsen knew was running the empire into the ground? One answer lies in his obsessively industrious character. It was due to his focus, dedication, discipline and tenacity that the emperor held court twice daily, micro-managing nearly everything, personally reviewing and signing off on the most routine documents. But the virtue of tenacity could also become the defect of stubbornness, as seen in his refusal to change policy paths or his inability to discern larger geopolitical patterns. 'Alamgir's indefatigable industriousness might have served him well had he been a clerk or middle-level functionary in the Mughals' vast bureaucracy.[121] But good political leadership requires vision, imagination and flexibility, which were not 'Alamgir's strengths. For twenty-five ruinous years he remained trapped in a quagmire of his own making, constitutionally unable to imagine a way forwards beyond his Sisyphean task of doggedly pursuing the Marathas, fort by fort.

Another possible answer to the enigma of 'Alamgir is hinted at by the Italian traveller Giovanni Careri, who in 1695 was granted a private audience with the emperor at one of his Deccan camps. The foreigner afterwards reflected on the underlying reasons for the emperor's long and fruitless Deccan campaign:

> fearing with much reason the perverse Inclination of his Sons, he had continu'd in Arms in the Field for 15 Years; and particularly four Years at *Galgala* [Galgali, on the Krishna], after defeating [Prince] *Akbar*. He said his Father *Sciah-Gehan* [Shah Jahan] had not so much discretion; for he might have learnt by many years' Experience, that the Kings of Indostan when they grow Old, must keep at the head of Powerful Armies, to defend themselves against their Sons.[122]

Haunted by the fear that his sons might do to him what he had done to his own father, 'Alamgir felt compelled constantly to remain in the field, ever at the helm of the army, warily watching them and his grandsons.

John Dryden could hardly have foreseen the morass of the emperor's protracted Deccan campaign, since he wrote his play *Aureng-zebe: A Tragedy* in 1675, five years before that campaign began. Yet he does give his protagonist the telling lines, 'I know my fortune in extremes does lie: The Sons of Indostan must Reign, or die'. The extremes Dryden had in mind were those needed to gain the throne. But gaining the throne, as it turned out, was the easier part of 'Alamgir's lifelong struggle. In order to retain the throne, especially after his sons and even grandsons had reached maturity, he had to resort to extremes of another sort – of remaining constantly engaged in war, personally leading his army while vigilantly watching his own offspring, keeping them in check.

# 8

# Eighteenth-century Transitions

## POLITICAL CHANGES, 1707–48

In accordance with Mughal practice, a deadly struggle between
'Alamgir's three surviving sons – A'zam, Mu'azzam and Kam
Bakhsh – followed the emperor's death. Prince A'zam, at the time in
the Deccan, at once declared his sovereignty and began marching
north towards Agra. Prince Mu'azzam, then posted near Peshawar
on the north-west frontier, also declared his sovereignty and, adopting the title Bahadur Shah, rapidly marched south, beating A'zam in
the race to Agra. In June 1707 he defeated his younger brother, who
died in battle near Agra. After spending nearly a year consolidating
power in upper India, the new emperor marched to the Deccan to
confront 'Alamgir's youngest son, Kam Bakhsh, who had also
declared his sovereignty and established himself in Hyderabad. Badly
outnumbered, however, he too was killed in battle, thereby completing another war of succession, albeit one far less bloody than the war
that had raised 'Alamgir to power.

The succession struggle following 'Alamgir's death differed vastly
from that of 1657–9. Whereas the earlier war had been fought
between powerful princes backed by substantial households and their
allied nobles, the sons of 'Alamgir possessed far smaller households
and fewer resources. This owed in large part to their father's policy
of diverting resources from his sons to himself, for fear that one of
them might overthrow him, as he had overthrown Shah Jahan. It was
therefore the domineering 'Alamgir, not his sons, who was the ultimate arbiter of the fate of their households.[1] Two of his sons spent
long periods in imprisonment, one was driven out of the country, and

none had led any army in the Deccan after 1702. Some of the empire's most powerful nobles simply sat out the struggle between them, defiantly refusing to support any prince. This reflected the quiet drift of real power from princely households to powerful nobles, some of whom felt sufficiently confident in their autonomy to bargain with the new emperor over administrative appointments. And, once in power, they were able to place limits on the emperor's authority. For example, Zulfiqar Khan, the commander who had seized Raigarh from the Marathas and led the siege of Jinji, pressured Bahadur Shah into appointing him both governor of the Deccan and paymaster general (*mir bakhshi*). The latter position authorized him to approve all ranks and promotions, enabling him to thwart the emperor's ability to enlist new nobles into the corps of imperial *mansabdar*s.

By the time Bahadur Shah died in 1712, the institution of princely households had deteriorated even further. All four of his sons were adults at the time their father came to power and, since they all wished to be at the imperial court at the start of the next, inevitable succession struggle, they simply refused to serve in the provinces as governors. For the first time in Mughal history, all princes remained at court for the duration of their father's reign. But doing so compromised their ability to establish independent power bases, build alliances, tap into provincial revenue streams or acquire the administrative experience that might enhance the likelihood of a vigorous and successful reign. Remaining at court for their entire princely lives meant they had much smaller households. Bahadur Shah's eldest son and eventual successor, Jahandar, had only 300 cavalrymen, in contrast to the tens of thousands maintained by princes of the previous century.[2]

Consequently, when Jahandar succeeded to the throne in 1712, he did so mainly because of his lack of political, administrative or military experience or resources, which made him more pliable – and hence attractive – for Zulfiqar Khan, then the empire's most powerful figure. It was he who engineered Jahandar's accession by first forming a troika of Jahandar and two of the prince's brothers against their more experienced and energetic sibling, 'Azim al-Sham, promising that, after the latter was defeated, the empire would be partitioned among the trio. Then, after 'Azim al-Sham had been defeated and killed, Zulfiqar Khan treacherously turned on Jahandar's other two brothers, and when they were disposed of he escorted his royal patron to the Peacock Throne. Most of the followers of Jahandar's three brothers were then imprisoned and their property confiscated, while several prominent nobles were publicly executed. It was the first time that supporters of the losers in a succession struggle were punished instead of being reintegrated into the ruling structure. From this point on, all Mughal emperors would be princes who had little or no experience outside the imperial harem. Clearly, the traditional Timurid mode of handling imperial successions had been corrupted beyond recognition. In the process, the emperor himself had become a virtual puppet of a powerful figure outside the ruling dynasty, in this case Zulfiqar Khan, now the imperial *vazir*.

The relative ease with which Jahandar had been placed on the throne tempted other power brokers to repeat the ploy by advancing the cause of some other prince. The cycle was soon set in motion by two brothers of a well-entrenched clan of Indian Muslims, the Barahas, who had their base in upper India between the Ganges and the Jamuna. These were the so-called Saiyid brothers – Saiyid 'Abd Allah Khan, governor of Allahabad, and Saiyid Husain 'Ali Khan, governor of Bihar. Both men owed their positions to the patronage of Prince 'Azim al-Shan before the latter was killed in the coup that had brought his brother, Jahandar, to the throne. Within months, the ambitious brothers seized on a plan to lift themselves into supreme power by promoting the cause of Farrukh Siyar, the son of their slain patron. In late 1712 a rebel army led by the brothers marched from Bihar up the Ganges valley towards Agra, with Farrukh Siyar in tow. Up to this point Jahandar had been indolently celebrating his rise to power with his musician courtesan, Lal Kunwar, having left administrative affairs to Zulfiqar Khan. But when news arrived of Farrukh Siyar's advancing army, an alarmed court moved frantically to mount a defence. Since the imperial army would not move without pay – and it had not been paid for nearly a year – the desperate court resorted to breaking its vessels of gold and silver, even stripping gold off the roofs of Delhi's imperial palaces. In the confrontation that followed in early 1713, the rebel army routed the hastily organized and faction-ridden imperial army near Agra. Shortly after reaching Delhi, Farrukh Siyar was crowned and forthwith ordered the execution of both Jahandar and Zulfiqar Khan. 'Abd Allah Khan was duly appointed *vazir* and Husain 'Ali Khan paymaster general, the empire's two highest offices.

Farrukh Siyar's reign (1713–19) had hardly begun, however, before struggles broke out over whether the emperor or his highest ministers would have the final word in fundamental issues of state. Long-submerged tensions over the empire's ethnic identity also rose to the surface. On one side were the Saiyid brothers, whose Baraha clan of Indian Muslims was as native to India as were Jats, Rajputs or Marathas. Towards all such communities the two brothers adopted conciliatory policies, abolishing discriminatory measures that 'Alamgir had imposed, such as the *jizya* tax. On the other side was an equally powerful faction of nobles who claimed a Turkic or Iranian ancestry, had enjoyed Mughal patronage for nearly two centuries, and zealously promoted the dynasty's original Timurid character. So poisonous had these factional struggles become that 'Abd Allah Khan needed an escort of up to 4,000 cavalry when he moved through Delhi's streets to attend daily court as *vazir*. When Ajit Singh, the leader of the Rathors of Jodhpur, refused to take up his appointed position as governor of Sind, Farrukh Siyar sent Husain 'Ali Khan with an army to punish the Rajput *mansabdar*. But the emperor also communicated with Ajit Singh, secretly promising him rewards if he would kill Husain 'Ali Khan. Instead, the two men became allies. Similarly, in the course of the Mughals' long struggle with the Marathas, Farrukh Siyar sent secret communications to the Maratha leaders urging them to resist Husain 'Ali Khan's overtures to them. But, again, the two sides simply ignored the emperor, making mutually beneficial agreements that Farrukh Siyar refused to ratify, but which the Saiyid brothers and the Marathas honoured anyway.

Matters came to a head in late 1718 when Husain 'Ali Khan arrived in Delhi from the Deccan with 25,000 cavalrymen, nearly half of them Marathas with whom he was allied. In February 1719, after a fiery verbal confrontation in Shahjahanabad's audience hall between the emperor and the other Saiyid brother, the *vazir* 'Abd Allah Khan, the latter seized control of the Red Fort while Farrukh Siyar, guarded by his armed female slaves, was holed up in the harem. In this political impasse, with armed supporters of both sides already fighting in the streets and a restive urban population on the verge of riot, the Saiyid brothers placed Rafi' al-Darjat, an unsuspecting grandson of Bahadur Shah, on the throne. They then sent their own men to the harem, where Farrukh Siyar was dragged out, blinded and later executed. When the tubercular Rafi' al-Darjat died several months later, the Saiyid brothers, now ruling the empire virtually by fiat, placed the deceased emperor's brother, Rafi' al-Daulah, on the throne. Within weeks he, too, died of tuberculosis, at which point the brothers selected another of Bahadur Shah's grandsons, Muhammad Shah, to be emperor.

Within the single year 1719, then, four emperors had occupied the Peacock Throne in rapid succession, a sure sign of structural instability. However, the dictatorial powers that the Saiyid brothers had assumed, which reduced the emperor to an impotent captive, were vigorously opposed by the empire's older, Turko-Iranian nobility, the so-called *khanazad*s. Their opposition focused not only on the outrage of executing a sitting emperor, Farrukh Siyar, but also on the gains that native Indian Muslims had made thanks to the Saiyid brothers' patronage, which they resented. This old-guard opposition coalesced around the governor of Malwa, Chin Qilich Khan – entitled Nizam al-Mulk (d. 1748) – whom Muhammad Shah secretly implored to help release him from his captors, the Saiyid brothers. Help came in mid 1720, when one of the brothers, Husain 'Ali Khan, was assassinated in a plot engineered by old-guard nobles bitterly opposed to the rise of the Baraha clan and to native Indian Muslims generally. The emperor now eagerly joined an effort to complete the coup by getting rid of the other Saiyid brother, 'Abd Allah Khan, which was duly accomplished later that year.

The problems facing Muhammad Shah's long reign (1719–48), however, were hardly resolved by the eclipse of the Saiyid brothers' two-year incumbency. The first two decades of the eighteenth century saw a deepening of the *jagirdari* crisis that had begun late in 'Alamgir's reign. Successive *vazir*s irresponsibly doled out appointments and ranks to their political followers with no certainty that revenue-producing *jagir*s supporting those ranks could be found. Competition among nobles for such *jagir*s inevitably created tensions and factionalism within the nobility, furthering the divide between old-guard

Iranian or Turkic nobles and newcomers such as Marathas and Indian Muslims. This posed a political problem. Insufficient land earmarked for *jagir*s also reduced *mansabdar*s' ability to generate the levels of revenue needed to pay their cavalry troops. And since soldiers would not take part in campaigns without regular pay, the *mansabdar*s' cavalry contingents fell below required levels. This posed a military problem. Finally, because an increasing number of *mansabdar*s competed fiercely over a shrinking pool of revenue-producing *jagir*s, nobles with substantial land holdings resisted periodic transfers of their *jagir*s, a hallmark of the system since the days of Akbar. As a result, the *jagir*s of many such nobles became hereditary, undermining the entire idea of the Mughal nobility as a service class without permanent landed estates. This posed a systemic problem.

Further undermining Mughal administration, the regime gradually abandoned the *zabt* system of land taxation, whereby revenue assessments were based on measuring individual fields and periodically evaluating the quality of the land and the type of crops sown. In the early decades of the eighteenth century, such systematic management was increasingly overtaken by the practice of revenue farming, as the court simply sold the right of revenue collection to the highest bidders. After remitting the agreed amount of land tax to the government, many revenue farmers enriched themselves by squeezing further 'taxes' from cultivators. Not only did the government in this way lose control of its own revenue administration: such practices fuelled the rural discontent that was exploited by local *zamindar*s, who stood between the Mughal state and revenue-producing village communities. These remnants of ancient royalty, long since pushed down in rural society by successive waves of conquerors, stubbornly clung to their traditional claims of local sovereignty, which they typically manifested by building small, fortified strongholds, maintaining armed retainers, adjudicating disputes and claiming a share of the land revenue. Ever since Akbar's reign it had been Mughal policy to transform these stalwart local elites into state revenue collectors or functionaries, and, if such co-option proved impossible, to forcibly clear the landscape of 'the weeds and rubbish of opposition', as Akbar's minister Abu'l-fazl contemptuously called recalcitrant *zamindar*s.[3] By the early eighteenth century, however, Mughal *mansabdar*s had fewer resources to maintain troopers with which to confront unruly *zamindar*s within their *jagir*s. Further tipping the balance of power in favour of the latter was the diffusion of muskets among the population at large, which considerably narrowed the military advantage that the state had previously enjoyed.[4]

The collapse of the Saiyid brothers' rule in 1720 might have seemed a likely moment for the restoration of the old guard of Timurid *khanazad*s, and possibly for a recovery of Mughal power and authority. In early 1722, in fact, the veteran noble Nizam al-Mulk – already the governor of the Deccan, Gujarat and Malwa – was summoned to Delhi and appointed imperial *vazir*. Having served 'Alamgir with unswerving loyalty since 1688, this commander and administrator naturally evaluated Mughal rule of the 1720s in the light of his former master's austere, disciplined administration. He accordingly dismissed Muhammad Shah as a negligent and weak-minded stooge completely under the influence of his favourite courtiers. Nizam al-Mulk was also aware of the extent to which long-established rules of governance had withered, and how deeply the entry of Marathas and Hindustanis into the nobility had undermined the prestige of his own class of Timurid *khanazad*s. Accordingly, in 1723 he set before the emperor a set of sweeping reforms, which included ending the practice of revenue farming in *khalisa* lands, sacking all nobles ill-fit for the job, redistributing *jagir*s, abolishing *khalisa* lands that had been distributed as *jagir*s, and stamping out the menace of bribery. But Muhammad Shah's favourites at court, fearing the loss of their influence should such proposals be enacted, poisoned the emperor's mind against approving the reforms, which were quietly shelved.[5]

Despairing that the central administration could ever be restored to proper governance, and having been politically marginalized from the court's inner circles since the death of 'Alamgir, Nizam al-Mulk resolved to strike out to the Deccan, the part of India he knew best and where he had the deepest roots. Precipitating his departure was news that his own deputy governor of the Deccan, Mubariz Khan, had in his absence entrenched himself as a practically independent ruler.[6] Departing Shahjahanabad in late 1723 ostensibly for a 'change of air', Nizam al-Mulk reached the Deccan and the next year defeated and killed in battle his rebellious deputy governor, after which Muhammad Shah bestowed on him the exalted title 'Asaf Jah'. The huge block of territory that he carved out, essentially the whole of the Mughal Deccan, would become the state of Hyderabad, effectively launched in 1724 with Mubariz Khan's defeat. After 1763, when its capital was moved from Aurangabad to Hyderabad, Nizam al-Mulk's descendants would be known simply as the Nizams of Hyderabad, and their dynasty as 'Asaf Jahi' – both being titles of the state's founder.

Although he had founded the Mughals' first successor-state on imperial territory, Nizam al-Mulk never formally declared his independence from the Mughals, whom he continued to serve as viceroy of the Deccan. His own coins and those of his successors right up to 1858 continued to bear the emperor's name. By retaining this fictive connection with the regime, the Deccan 'province' offered disaffected northerners the possibility of abandoning Delhi's political chaos while technically continuing their service with the empire. The strategy appears to have worked. Viewing the Deccan as a robust imperial dependency, thousands of administrators, religious scholars, intellectuals, military men and master craftsmen migrated southwards during Nizam al-Mulk's administration, as did, too, talented members of north India's service castes, such as Kayastha accountants and Punjabi Khatri bankers. These northerners were then added to a political system that, under Nizam al-Mulk, had already absorbed a wide spectrum of the Deccan's constituent communities. After 1728 his relations with the Maratha state stabilized to the extent that he was able to recruit Maratha chieftains, Brahmins and low-level revenue officials into his government.[7] He also assimilated restive and potentially hostile Afghans as fort commanders and allowed more than a dozen Telugu kingdoms (*samasthan*s) to subsist within his borders as tributary states, a policy reminiscent of Akbar's accommodative policy towards Rajput states. Other indigenous groups – such as Tamils, Bhils and Gonds – were similarly brought into Nizam al-Mulk's nascent Hyderabad state.[8]

Like Hyderabad, Bengal also became functionally independent in the 1720s, a process traceable to the career of another of 'Alamgir's officers. Kartalab Khan was a Brahmin slave who had been purchased in his youth, converted, brought up and tutored in the intricacies of clerical practices by 'Alamgir's imperial *diwan*, or chief financial officer. In 1698 Kartalab Khan entered Mughal service as the *diwan* of Hyderabad. Recognizing the young man's exceptional talent for administration, in 1701 'Alamgir appointed him the *diwan* of Bengal, a rich but at the time poorly managed province. His mandate was very clear: enhance its revenue and remit its full share to the central government. Soon after reaching Bengal's provincial capital of Dhaka, Kartalab Khan enacted sweeping reforms. First, he reclassified the delta's *jagir* lands as *khalisa* ones and reassigned dispossessed *jagir-dars* from Bengal to *jagirs* on undeveloped lands in neighbouring Orissa, which from 1703 was also placed under his management. As a result, unlike anywhere else in Mughal India, Bengal's provincial government absorbed the whole of the delta's agrarian wealth instead of having to share it with *jagirdars*. Second, he sent surveyors through-out the province to produce accurate figures of local yields. And third, the province's many *zamindars* were made to pay the full amount of assessed revenue or face imprisonment or torture. Under such pressure, *zamindars* with smaller holdings were forced to sell their holdings to larger *zamindars*, with the result that by 1727 just fifteen enormous *zamindari* estates paid nearly half of the province's land revenue. The *diwan*'s reforms also led to the emergence of wealthy banking houses that made enormous profits in interest on loans to *zamindars* unable to pay their stipulated revenue. In this way, by the 1730s the house of the Jagat Seths had become the largest banking firm in Bengal, if not in all India. In effect, these houses served as guarantors that the provincial government would receive its entire revenue demand.[9]

Kartalab Khan's success in enhancing Bengal's revenue proved a boon for the Mughals' central government at a time when the imperial treasury was severely stressed by 'Alamgir's protracted Deccan campaigns. Beginning in 1702 and continuing for the next several decades, the *diwan* annually remitted ten million rupees from Bengal to the central government, which for some time comprised the only consist-ently reliable source of revenue for the whole empire. In 1703 he personally attended 'Alamgir's court in the Deccan, where the emperor awarded him the title Murshid Quli Khan in honour of the fiscal officer of the same title who had served Prince Aurangzeb when he governed the Deccan. 'Alamgir also allowed the *diwan* to rename a city in northern Bengal after his new title – Murshidabad, which became the provincial capital in 1704. In 1717 he was made governor of Bengal in addition to *diwan*. Although this violated Mughal protocols prohibiting one person from occupying both offices, Murshid Quli Khan continued to remit Bengal's large annual share of revenue to the central government until his death in 1727. Succeeding him as Bengal governor was his son-in-law, Shuja' al-Din Muhammad Khan (r. 1727–39), initiating a de facto regional dynasty. Yet Shuja', too, continued to send Bengal's annual revenue to Delhi, in return for which he was allowed to do more or less what he pleased in his province.[10] After his death in 1739, however, authorities in Bengal altogether ceased remitting its substantial revenues to the central government.[11]

In the 1720s and 1730s, still more Mughal provinces acquired de facto independence. In 1722 the emperor appointed Sa'adat 'Ali Khan governor of the central Gangetic province of Awadh, but within just three years he had usurped Delhi's authority by removing imperial *mansabdar*s from their allotted positions and reassigning *jagir*s within the province. The emperor was powerless to enforce his orders or punish the governor. Indeed, Sa'adat 'Ali Khan mobilized local communities around his own banner, entrenching his independent status. Because *jagir*s in Awadh were relatively small, *jagirdar*s lacked substantial power bases, allowing the governor to exert greater authority over them. And, having no sons of his own, he named his nephew and son-in-law Safdar Jung to succeed him as governor of Awadh, thereby launching what amounted to another de facto regional dynasty. He also appointed as his financial officer a Punjabi Khatri who ran the region's finances independently of Delhi's supervision. He, too, passed that office to his son. Further west, the Punjab acquired de facto independence in 1726 when 'Abd al-Samad Khan, who had been appointed governor in 1713, was succeeded by his son.[12]

The ebbing of Mughal power between 1707 and 1750 is seen in other ways, too. Already in Bahadur Shah's reign (1707–12) serious gaps appeared between the assessed revenue and the amount actually collected. Powerful nobles resisted imperial orders to transfer their *jagir*s. Even the Mughal–Rajput alliance showed signs of fraying, as leading Rajput commanders dragged their feet on military campaigns, or abandoned such campaigns altogether. In the reigns of Jahandar and Farrukh Siyar, the practice of farming out revenue collection to the highest bidders, effectively bypassing the official revenue apparatus, became widespread. Jat uprisings in the area west of the Jamuna broke out with increasing frequency and intensity. Jat chieftains plundered trade caravans that moved along routes between Delhi and Agra, and from there east down the Ganges valley or south towards the Deccan. The most notorious and talented Jat leader, Churaman (d. 1721), briefly carved out his own independent state in the Agra region. The Mughals had to expend considerable resources attempting to suppress, or at least contain, such uprisings occurring so close to their imperial capitals.[13] The state's diminished profile is also reflected in the sharp drop in the treasury at Agra, from ninety million rupees in 1707 to just over ten million in 1720. For several more decades the empire continued to receive revenue from Bengal, the sole remaining prop to imperial finances. But, in 1740, it too ceased. By the time of Muhammad Shah's death in 1748 the empire was totally bankrupt, while its former provinces were either practically independent or managed by outsiders from the south. These were the Marathas.

## MARATHA UPRISINGS

Of the various uprisings that challenged Mughal power and authority in the eighteenth century, that of the Marathas was the most sustained and consequential. From 1682 to 1699 the Maratha state had waged a defensive war against 'Alamgir's aggressive campaigns in the western Deccan. But between 1700 and 1707 Tarabai, governing the kingdom as regent for her infant son, co-ordinated the defence of Maratha strongholds against 'Alamgir's armies while establishing a permanent Maratha presence in parts of Khandesh, Malwa and Gujarat. In those provinces her agents extracted a fourth of the revenue normally paid to the Mughals. This levy, called *chauth*, in effect served as protection money against further Maratha raids, which Mughal authorities were powerless to prevent. But, after 1707, many of Tarabai's former supporters drifted to Shahu, the adult grandson of Shivaji whom 'Alamgir had captured in 1689 and held for eighteen years. After the emperor's death, he was strategically released for the purpose of dividing Maratha loyalties. The ploy succeeded. Maratha chieftains soon split between supporters of Shahu, the son of Shivaji's first son Sambhaji, and Tarabai, the widow of Shivaji's second son Rajaram.

Meanwhile, Maratha society and culture became progressively more militarized. From the 1640s, Shivaji had recruited into his service *mavali*s, the men inhabiting the jungles and ravines of the Western Ghats. By the 1680s, 'Alamgir was recruiting the same peoples and deploying them against the Maratha state, creating a bidding war between the Mughals and Shivaji's kingdom over access to the western Deccan's military labour market. The intensity of these bidding wars increased with the entry first of Shahu in 1707 as a rival to Tarabai, and then of Nizam al-Mulk in 1712 as a rival to Shahu. By this time warfare had become so lucrative that enterprising men with no ties to the land or prior *deshmukh* status emerged as chiefs (*sardar*) who enlisted villagers into their war bands. Armed villagers would spend half the year (May to October) working their fields and the other half (October to May) on campaign.[14] The militarization of the western Deccan also transformed the meaning of 'Maratha', which from at least the fourteenth century had referred to Marathi-speaking chiefs and their warrior-clients who offered military services to the Bahmani sultanate or its successor states of Bijapur and Ahmadnagar. The word thereby became associated with a martial ethos. Over time, the term acquired social boundaries and embraced distinctive patterns of dress, diet and codes of conduct. By contrast, caste Hindus not integrated into a sultanate's service elite – such as cultivators, artisans or petty merchants – identified themselves as 'Kunbi'. But in the eighteenth century, as villagers appeared in armies mobilized by the Maratha state, they, too, began to see themselves as Marathas, thereby eroding the distinction between Kunbi and Maratha.[15]

Accompanying the militarization of the western plateau was the rise of the office of *peshwa*, a Persian term for 'prime minister' that the Bahmani sultans had introduced in the fourteenth century and was inherited by the Maratha state. In 1713, in an effort to lure a powerful maritime lord from Tarabai's political orbit into his own, Shahu recruited Balaji Vishvanath, a well-networked Chitpavan

Brahmin from the Konkan coast. To strengthen his negotiating hand, Balaji demanded that he be named the *peshwa* of Shahu's court, to which the Maratha king agreed. Balaji then succeeded in drawing the maritime lord to Shahu's camp, initiating a progressive decline of Tarabai's influence in Maratha politics. The office of *peshwa* soon swelled into the Peshwas – that is, a line of hereditary Brahmin rulers whose authority would ultimately displace that of the Maratha king himself.

At the same time, Brahmins entered the Maratha state's political economy at all levels.[16] Because their troops were paid in cash, *sardar*s had to negotiate loans with bankers at the beginning of each campaign season. And since interest rates on such loans depended on the fiscal stability of the area under a given chief's control, Brahmin accountants (*kulkarni*s, *deshpande*s) would evaluate the fiscal worth of the chief's lands, and hence his creditworthiness. Banking and credit thus provided the hinge by which Brahmins acquired political influence, whether as village moneylenders advancing cash to chiefs and headmen, or as great banking firms financing the Maratha government's large-scale campaigns in Mughal north India.[17] The translation of Brahmins' financial power into political power began with Balaji Vishvanath's appointment as *peshwa* in 1713 and continued as his fellow Chitpavan Brahmins migrated from their native Konkan coast up to the plateau, where they served as tax-collectors, administrators and especially as bankers loaning Shahu money to raise his armies. Upon Balaji's death in 1720, Shahu named Balaji's son Baji Rao (r. 1720–40) as his successor, creating in effect a dynasty of hereditary Brahmin Peshwas.

From 1713 on, Maratha armies ranged ever deeper into the older imperial provinces to the north. Typically filling the vacuum left by the Mughals' decaying local administration, these raids were manned by Maratha–Kunbi peasant-soldiers, directed by the Peshwas and financed by Brahmin financial credit and the levy of *chauth*. After 1735, their armies began to remain in north India through the monsoon season without returning to Maharashtra. But this hindered agricultural operations in the Maratha heartland, since so many soldiers were cultivators. Efforts to compensate by mobilizing landless peasants to cultivate state lands and wastelands only reduced government revenues, since landless peasants paid few or no land taxes.[18] On the other hand, attempts to bring peasant-soldiers back to Maharashtra for agricultural purposes left the armies in the north strapped for manpower. To meet the deficit, the government enlisted non-Maratha mercenaries, including Pashtun Afghans, Arabs and north Indians.[19] This further diluted the character of 'Maratha' armies, a process that had already begun with the incorporation of Kunbi villagers in the Peshwas' infantries.

The growth of Maratha power in north India proceeded by stages. In 1716 Balaji audaciously asked Farrukh Siyar to grant him the right to collect *chauth* everywhere south of the Narmada, proposing in effect a dual government in which Marathas and Mughals would share the collection of revenue. The emperor angrily rejected the proposal. But in 1719, after Farrukh Siyar was overthrown by the Saiyid brothers, the latter, with whom the Peshwa was then allied, consented to the deal. This agreement served as a charter for subsequent Maratha claims to the Deccan's revenues, and as a blueprint for access to the revenues of older Mughal provinces in the north. Under Baji Rao, Maratha raids into Malwa became more regular and more lucrative, culminating in 1728 when the Peshwa defeated Nizam al-Mulk just thirty-two kilometres west of the latter's capital of Aurangabad. From there he continued marching further north to Ujjain, defeating its Mughal defenders. This threw all of western Malwa open to Maratha plundering. After these reverses, Nizam al-Mulk granted the Peshwa what Delhi had already granted the Maratha leader, namely the latter's right to collect *chauth* throughout the Deccan. By the 1730s Baji Rao was raising ever larger armies and sending them further afield, through Malwa both north into Rajasthan and east into the Gangetic plain. By 1737 his armies managed to drive north as far as Delhi itself. Neither Muhammad Shah's decaying government in Delhi nor Nizam al-Mulk's in Aurangabad could halt the Peshwa. By January 1739 Nizam al-Mulk had acknowledged the Marathas' complete sovereignty in Malwa and in all lands between the Narmada and the Chambal River, which runs a mere forty-five kilometres south of Agra.

Later that year the Persian warlord Nadir Shah marched through the Khyber Pass with 150,000 cavalry, defeated a much larger Mughal army and sacked a supine, defenceless Delhi. Like Timur more than three centuries earlier, he chose not to remain in India, returning to

Iran with caravans laden with looted gold, silver and jewellery worth 1.5 million rupees, including the famed Koh-i-Noor, and, not least, Shah Jahan's priceless Peacock Throne. With such celebrated symbols of imperial glory for ever stripped from Indian soil, the Marathas were suddenly awakened to the reality that the Mughals were not, in fact, their enemy. Rather, they now saw the house of Babur as the key symbol of Indian sovereignty, to be defended from foreign invaders at all costs. To this end, Baji Rao proposed that all the powers of north India join a confederation to protect India's Timurid dynasty, making the Peshwa almost resemble a proto-nationalist figure. For several decades, a cornerstone of Maratha policy was to pose as the Mughals' truest defenders, at least at the imperial level.

At the grass-roots level, however, the Peshwa's *sardar*s continued to chip away at Mughal sovereignty. In older provinces such as Malwa, Khandesh or Gujarat, independent bands of up to 5,000 light cavalry would raid and plunder the countryside, avoiding pitched battles with imperial armies.[20] Mughal authorities in these provinces might still control major fortified urban centres, but they were no longer drawing revenue from their rural hinterlands. The transition from Mughal to Maratha authority between the 1730s and 1750s was therefore barely perceptible, not only because it occurred so gradually, but also because the Marathas continued to use Mughal administrative procedures and practices, mitigating a sense of a political rupture.[21] Yet Maratha rule was patchy and irregular across much of central India in those decades, some regions being fully administered by the Peshwa's men and others only thinly administered, and populated by recalcitrant *zamindar*s who managed to defy Maratha authority from behind walled strongholds.

Under Baji Rao's son Nana Saheb (r. 1740–61), Maratha conquests briefly encompassed almost all of north India. These included six devastating raids on Bengal between 1741 and 1751. But, by the late 1750s, the Marathas had become more than simply the guarantors of Mughal authority. As their strategic objective shifted from defending their mountainous homeland to plundering and then governing north India's wide plains, they also adopted Mughal military culture. In the days of Shivaji, Maratha forces had consisted of small, mobile bands of swift cavalry and lightly armed infantry, appropriate for the sort

Fig. 12: Vrindavan: interior of the Govinda Deva Temple (completed 1590)

Fig. 13: Nur Jahan loading a musket.
Painting attributed to Abu'l-Hasan (1620)

Fig. 14: Jahangir taking aim at the head of Malik Ambar. Painted by Abu'l-Hasan (1616)

Fig. 15: Amritsar: Harmandir, or Golden Temple (1589)

Fig. 16: Jahangir conversing with Jadrup. Painted by Govardhan (c.1616–20)

Fig. 17: Prince Aurangzeb attacking a raging elephant. Painting in the *Padshah-nama* (1633)

Fig. 18: Lahore: Badshahi Mosque (1671–73)

Fig. 19: Shah Jahan enthroned, with his son Dara Shukoh. Watercolour and gold on paper, by Govardhan (c.1630–40)

Fig. 20: Prince Aurangzeb, probably painted while governor of the Deccan (1653–57)

Fig. 21: Kolhapur, Kavala Naka Square: equestrian statue of Tarabai (erected 1981)

of guerrilla warfare that Malik Ambar had pioneered in the Ahmadnagar sultanate's final decades. By contrast, the great Maratha armies of the 1740s and 1750s, which numbered up to 40,000 mainly uniformed infantry, lumbered across the land like moving cities, moving no faster than the bullocks that dragged their long trains of baggage and heavy artillery. By mid-century, too, the Maratha ruling elite, owing to its prolonged exposure to north India's ways, had acquired a taste for the refinements of Mughal culture. This in turn created a demand in urban Maharashtra for Kashmiri shawls, Bengali silks, ivory craft, metalwork in silver, copper and brass and so on, while administrators in the Maratha capital in Satara, and after 1750 in Pune, patronized north Indian styles of painting and music.[22]

Because they had become so deeply enmeshed in north Indian affairs, it was Maratha generals who in 1759 negotiated with Ahmad Shah Abdali, an Afghan ruler whose army had entered the Punjab and asserted Afghan territorial claims to the province. With a major showdown between the Marathas and Afghans in the air, in December the next year the Peshwa, Nana Saheb, began moving his own army northwards, aiming to join the main Maratha force then camped at Panipat, the historic battlefield north of Delhi. But he never got there. In mid January 1761, an estimated 50,000 Marathas were slaughtered at Panipat in one of the greatest military debacles in Indian history. For the Peshwa personally, the disaster represented a bitter indictment of decades of his and his predecessors' forward policy in north India. Upon hearing the news while still en route to join the battle, the Peshwa turned round and headed back to Pune, a disillusioned and broken man. Within six months he was dead. The entire Maratha project north of Maharasthra had become either stalled or reversed.

## SIKH UPRISINGS

The other formidable challenge to Mughal authority in the eighteenth century was mounted by the Sikhs. Unlike the Marathas, who contested Mughal power throughout India, the Sikh rebellion was confined to the Punjab. And whereas the Marathas initially resisted the Mughals but ended up defending the crippled empire, with the

Sikhs it was the reverse. The movement launched by Guru Nanak had emerged in the sixteenth century within the matrix of the Mughal imperium, with which it was once on generally good terms. But over time relations between the two grew increasingly hostile. How and why, then, did the Sikhs' militantly anti-Mughal posture incubate and grow?

We have seen that following Jahangir's execution of Guru Arjun, the latter's son and successor, Guru Hargobind, adopted a distinctly martial profile. Claiming both temporal and spiritual authority over the Sikh community, he built a fort at Amritsar, where he also established a court and 'immortal throne' (Akal Takht). Suspicious of others adopting the trappings of sovereignty within his domain, Jahangir had him imprisoned for twelve years. Even while relations with the Mughals continued to deteriorate, the Sikhs faced formidable internal threats, as collateral descendants of the fourth guru fiercely contested successions to that office. Guru Hargobind's authority was challenged by his uncle, whose own son and later his grandson set themselves up as an alternative line of gurus. Owing to such internal challenges, combined with periodic skirmishes with Mughal forces, Guru Hargobind withdrew from Amritsar and established his court in the Himalayan foothills in the Siwalik range to the north-east, beyond directly administered Mughal territory. There, among the hill rajas, the last five of the ten Sikh gurus spent most of their time. Yet relations with the Mughals continued to worsen. In 1675, imperial authorities interpreted the activities of the ninth guru, Tej Bahadur (G. 1664–75), as threatening and had him arrested and executed.[23]

Although residence in the hills had minimized the gurus' direct contact with Mughal authorities, it also cut them off from the bulk of the growing Sikh community, which dwelt on the plains of the eastern Punjab. As a result, dissenting factions outside the lineage of the tenth guru, Gobind (G. 1675–1708), were able to take control of Amritsar and the sacred precincts of the Golden Temple. What is more, many of his *masand*s – the institutional link between the gurus and the bulk of their followers – were appropriating power for themselves, appointing their own deputies for collecting offerings from the faithful, following rival claimants to the guruship, and interfering in succession struggles. In these circumstances, Guru Gobind concluded that radical reforms were needed to reassert his sole authority over the Sikh community and to end the divisive succession disputes.

His solution was dramatic. In 1699 he declared that the lineage of gurus would end with himself, thereby resolving the issue of any future succession struggles, and that his spiritual authority would henceforth be invested in a new, self-governing corporate body, the Khalsa, sworn by rites of initiation and dedicated to undertaking certain reforms. Initiates would leave their hair and beards unshorn, disavow previous caste identities, renounce the use of tobacco, cease patronizing *masand*s, collectivize the community's material resources and visit the guru bearing arms. Guru Gobind took this drastic initiative in order to resist Rajput incursions into Sikh domains, halt dissenting groups from encroaching on the Sikh community, and eliminate the many *masand*s that stood between the guru and the larger Sikh community.[24] The importance of the last concern is seen in the very name Khalsa. In Mughal usage, the familiar category *khalisa* – an administrative term derived from the Arabic *khalis* meaning 'pure' or 'unmediated' – denoted land whose wealth flowed directly to the state, unmediated by *jagirdar*s. Similarly, Guru Gobind understood the Khalsa as a family of faith whose loyalty was unmediated by *masand*s or other human agents, such as rival claimants to the guruship.

The Mughal government's position towards these developments was generally benign but wary. In 1689 Guru Gobind had established himself in Anandpur, in the Siwalik range seventy kilometres north-east of Ludhiana. Ten years later, immediately after the Khalsa was formed, substantial numbers of volunteers, arms and funds began pouring into the region. In response, 'Alamgir ordered local officials to leave the guru alone as long as he adopted a modest lifestyle like other spiritual mendicants, but to make him submit and pay taxes if he imitated kingly ways.[25] At that time, the guru's most immediate adversaries were not Mughal authorities but neighbouring hill rajas who presided over hierarchically ordered societies and Brahmin-dominated royal courts that clashed with the Sikhs' egalitarian social vision and guru institution. Moreover, to accommodate the host of followers who had arrived from the plains, the Sikhs at Anandpur had been raiding richer, nearby villages for supplies. This, in turn, angered the hill rajas, who in 1704 (or 1705) subjected Anandpur to a protracted siege.[26] The rajas also appealed to the Mughals to intervene in the conflict.[27]

As a consequence of the siege, Guru Gobind and his followers were ultimately forced to abandon the town and its forts. But in the confusion that followed, Mughal authorities captured and killed the guru's two youngest sons, notwithstanding the government's sworn promise to ensure the Sikhs' safe passage from Anandpur. The aggrieved guru then appealed directly to 'Alamgir for redress, using an extraordinary medium – a long Persian poem in which he defiantly censured the Mughals for their perfidy. He also demanded a personal meeting with the emperor to obtain justice and, more generally, to sort out Sikh–Mughal relations.[28] 'Alamgir agreed and ordered his officials in the Punjab to arrange for the guru's safe passage to his court in the Deccan. After Guru Gobind left the Punjab, however, news arrived that in March 1707 'Alamgir had died. But the guru proceeded anyway, meeting Bahadur Shah in Delhi as he was consolidating his power there, and then accompanying the new emperor to the Deccan. There, in 1708, the guru himself died, leaving the community momentarily leaderless so soon after the Khalsa institution had been launched.[29]

In this fluid atmosphere, before the idea of shared Sikh governance had had time to take root, in 1709 a mysterious, charismatic figure named Banda Bahadur appeared on the scene claiming to be the guru's chosen representative and promising to lead the still-fractured Sikh community into glory. His followers, consisting mainly of Khalsa Sikhs drawn from small *zamindar*s and Jat farmers of rural east Punjab, grew tenfold within a year or so, from 4,000 to 40,000.[30] For the next six years, until 1715 when he was captured by Mughal authorities, this quasi-millennial figure led his supporters against wealthy cities, plundering and gathering strength. The rebellion initially targeted the prosperous Mughal city of Sirhind in south-eastern Punjab, the base of the imperial officer who had betrayed Guru Gobind, killing members of his family. The movement thus had a specifically anti-Mughal basis from the start. It then spread to larger Mughal centres, notably Lahore, disrupting the functioning of provincial government generally. Although Bahadur Shah sent armies to suppress the revolt shortly after it had begun, further imperial energies were sapped with that emperor's death in 1712, followed by three years of factional turmoil in Delhi during the reign of Jahandar and the coup that brought Farrukh Siyar to power.

Banda's successes also built on a century of material prosperity in the Punjab, as lineages of Jat farmers opened up new tracts for settlement and cultivation. On the one hand, this spurt in rural prosperity enabled many villagers to afford more and better weapons with which to participate in the Punjab's growing military labour market. On the other hand, the establishment of the Khalsa presented an attractive alternative to participation in that market. Initiation into the community conferred on every male Sikh the prestigious name 'Singh', a title hitherto claimed only by aristocratic Rajputs, who were rulers or landholders, or in some cases by Khatris, the dominant commercial class.[31] For prosperous Jat agriculturalists, then, becoming not just Sikhs but members of the Khalsa constituted a rise in social status commensurate with the greater prosperity that they and the Punjab generally were experiencing. Shunning the idea of fighting for money as opposed to fighting for community and religion, Khalsa Sikhs joined Banda Bahadur's military movement rather than participate in the cash-driven military labour market.

All this lent socio-religious force to Banda's rebellion, which inflicted damaging attacks on Mughal centres across the Punjab, especially in the east, where most of Banda's supporters were rural Jats recently absorbed into the Khalsa. But the rebellion cannot be reduced to neat binaries, such as Sikhs versus Muslims, or peasants versus feudal landholders. Banda's most proximate adversaries were hostile neighbours such as the Ranghar Rajputs, the Mein Rajputs and the Qasur Afghans, just as Guru Gobind's immediate adversaries at Anandpur had been neighbouring hill rajas. Because *zamindar*s varied enormously in the amount of land they controlled, they never formed a single class. As a result, they too were found on both sides of the rebellion. The uprising also exposed rifts within the Sikh community, most importantly between Khatris – the caste to which Guru Nanak and subsequent gurus had belonged – and Khalsa Sikhs, who never comprised more than a tenth of the total community. Many Khatri Sikhs were big cloth and textile merchants who opposed the disruptions to business caused by Banda's plundering raids.

Others were revenue farmers who, being closely tied to the imperial administrative system, supported Mughal efforts to suppress the rebellion. Still others held high *mansabs* in Mughal officialdom, appearing in imperial literary works as notables or even nobles. They also served as agents or clerks for imperial *jagirdars*, in which capacity they maintained their own aristocratic establishments, including elephants, workshops and servants. Such Khatri Sikhs, too, were inclined to defend the existing order.[32] Nor did Banda's efforts to project his movement as a holy war (*dharma yudha*) find favour among Hindus, even those who had their own grievances against the Mughals.[33] In short, Banda's fiercely anti-Mughal rebellion elicited anything but a unified response across Punjabi society.

But this soon changed. When the Mughals finally managed to crush the uprising, they did so harshly, culminating in 1716 with the execution of Banda and more than 700 of his followers in Delhi. This public episode was spectacularly brutal: the rebel leader was first made to kill his own son and then was torn to pieces.[34] What provoked the Mughals' violent suppression of the movement was not just its seizure of de facto control of virtually all the Punjab east of Lahore. Equally serious was Banda's minting of his own coins – a sign of independent sovereignty – and establishing his own calendar, vaguely projecting the rebel as a millennial figure.[35] Neither of these could be tolerated by the Mughal state: the former challenged the regime's claims to sole sovereignty in the Punjab, and the latter its monopoly of sacred kingship.

The rebellion had far-reaching consequences. With the abandonment of the guru's court in the Himalayan foothills, Amritsar and the Golden Temple's sacred precincts once again became the primary locus of the Sikhs' religious and political aspirations. Second, as the Mughals' harsh suppression of the revolt polarized the Punjab's population between supporters of the regime and those of the Khalsa Sikhs, the latter grew more militant and more implacably opposed to the state. Ever since Banda's rebellion, and in a sense building on it, Khalsa Sikhs had begun organizing themselves into war bands called *misals*, which sought to replace Mughal sovereign territory with their own. Using light cavalry and guerrilla tactics not unlike those of the Marathas in the early days of Shivaji or Tarabai, these bands and their *sardar*s filled the political and military vacuum created by the ebbing of Mughal authority throughout the central, eastern and southern Punjab. By the middle of the century, twelve such bands controlled those regions. By that time, there had also appeared within the Sikh community a genre of texts called *rahit-nama*s, which drew clear lines between Sikhs and other religious communities, often demonizing Muslims. On the other hand, once individual *misal* chiefs acquired control of territory, the practical business of governance compelled them to cut deals with Afghans, Marathas or even Mughals, ignoring the advice of the *rahit-nama*s. Depending on the political realities of the moment, *misal* chiefs might join the campaigns of any of those groups, or hire Muslims in their own service just as the Mughals hired Sikhs in theirs.[36]

It was overland invasions from the west, however, that destroyed what little remained of Mughal power in the Punjab. Nadir Shah's 1739 raid on north India and sacking of Delhi clearly exposed the Mughals' increasingly feeble condition under Muhammad Shah.[37] Then in 1748 Ahmad Shah Abdali, the powerful Afghan ruler, made the first of seventeen annual raids on north India. Although the Mughals repulsed the first of these, just four years later matters had deteriorated such that the Mughal governor of the Punjab agreed to send his land revenue to Ahmad Shah rather than to Delhi. This effectively removed the province administratively from the Mughal empire. As discussed above, in 1761 the Afghan ruler crushed an immense Maratha army at the Third Battle of Panipat, thereby ending the Marathas' bid to control the Punjab. Within six years of that battle, with the Afghans in no position to collect revenue in the province, a loose confederation of Sikh *misal*s gained control over the greater part of the Punjab plains. By this time, though, the Mughals had sunk to little more than onlookers from the political sidelines.

## EMERGING IDENTITIES: MUSLIMS IN BENGAL AND PUNJAB

At the very time that the Mughal empire's central institutions had reached an advanced state of decay, India's largest Muslim community was emerging along the empire's eastern frontier.[38] Bengali Muslims, most of whom inhabit present-day Bangladesh, comprise the world's second-largest ethnic community of Muslims. Their appearance was actually one dimension of a larger transformation of the region's politics and economy, which coincided with the delta's shifting geomorphology. The story of the growth Bengal's Muslim population therefore begins with the land itself.

By depositing rich silt that made possible the cultivation of wet rice, Bengal's many rivers had for centuries provided the material basis of the delta's society and culture. But owing to the land's flat surface, those slow-moving rivers never remained fixed in place. Upon silting up their channels, they repeatedly jumped their own banks and gravitated ever eastwards between the twelfth and eighteenth centuries (see Maps 5, 7 and 8). In the 1570s the Ganges had already divided into two branches in present-day Malda District, one branch flowing south towards Satgaon (near Kolkata) and the other flowing east towards Sonargaon (near Dhaka). By 1666 the former branch had become altogether unnavigable.[39] Having abandoned its former channels in western and southern Bengal, the Ganges system then linked up with the Padma and other rivers, cutting through the heart of the eastern delta in present-day Bangladesh. These riverine movements carried the centre of Bengali civilization eastwards, as formerly thriving population centres in the western delta became moribund when the rivers abandoned them. Meanwhile, pioneers in the delta's more ecologically active eastern regions cut virgin forests, throwing open a widening zone for field agriculture.[40] Deposited over an expanding area of the eastern delta during annual flooding, greater volumes of silt permitted intensified cultivation along the larger rivers where rice cultivation had already been established, and an extension of cultivation into those parts of the interior not already brought under the plough. As a result, in the seventeenth and eighteenth centuries Bengal achieved remarkable levels of rice production: by the 1630s more than 100 vessels laden with rice were embarking annually from Bengal, bound for ports around the Bay of Bengal as far east as Sumatra.[41]

Bengal's riverine changes and subsequent agricultural boom coincided not only with the rise of Mughal power in the province, but also with the growth in overland and maritime trade that linked Bengal ever more tightly to the world economy. In the last two decades of the sixteenth century, while Mughal troops pushed into the heart of the active delta and established their provincial headquarters in Dhaka, the Portuguese built the port of Hooghly adjacent to modern Kolkata, expanded their community in Chittagong and planted mercantile colonies in and around Dhaka. In the early seventeenth century the Dutch and English trading companies gradually replaced the over-extended Portuguese as the dominant European merchants in Bengal's port cities, and by the end of that century the export of raw silk and cotton textiles had grown so rapidly that Bengal emerged as Europe's single most important supplier of goods in all Asia.[42] Stimulating this manufacturing boom were substantial quantities of silver that poured into the province from overseas. In the 1550s the Portuguese were shipping so much treasure into Bengal that the value of silver currency in Goa actually fluctuated with their sailing seasons to Bengal and Malacca.[43] Between 1709 and 1717 the Dutch and English East India companies together shipped into Bengal cargoes averaging 4.15 million rupees in value annually, 85 per cent of which was silver.[44] Advanced to Bengali agents, merchants or weavers, this treasure was quickly absorbed into the regional economy, adding considerably to the stocks of rupee coinage already in circulation.[45] Yet Bengal experienced no price inflation in the seventeenth and eighteenth centuries, since the production of agricultural and manufactured goods, together with the population base, grew at levels high enough to absorb the expanding money supply created by the influx of foreign silver. Newly minted silver percolated freely throughout Bengali society, penetrating ever lower levels and facilitating the kinds of land transfers and cash advances that typically accompany an expanding agrarian frontier.

These geographical, political and economic changes in eastern Bengal coincided in time and place with the earliest recorded appearance of a Bengali Muslim peasantry. In 1567 a Venetian traveller noted that the entire population of Sandwip, a large island in Bengal's south-eastern corner opposite Chittagong, was Muslim, and in 1599 a Jesuit missionary, touring the rural districts near Narayanganj in south-eastern Dhaka District, noted that 'the people are nearly all Mahometans'.[46]

In 1638, the Mughal governor of Bengal mentioned large Muslim communities inhabiting eastern Bengal's Noakhali coast.[47] Significantly, prior to the advent of Mughal rule in the delta, the masses of eastern Bengal were not firmly integrated into a Hindu socio-religious order.[48] This suggests that, when the growth of Islam did occur in this region, its population did not migrate from a Hindu to a Muslim identity. Rather, the religious culture of the fishing, hunting and slash-and-burn farming communities of pre-Muslim eastern Bengal was saturated with local forest cults that focused especially on female deities such as Manasa or Chandi. On the other hand, the western portion of the delta, where Islam made little headway, was at the time of the Mughal conquest already populated by settled, wet-rice-cultivating communities of hierarchically ordered Hindu castes.[49]

From at least the sixteenth century, the arduous business of forest-clearing and land reclamation in the eastern delta was associated with the activities of enterprising men who were popularly – and often retroactively – identified as holy men. In local memory, some of these men swelled into vivid, mythico-historical figures whose lives served as metaphors for the expansion of both religion and agriculture. They endured precisely because, in collective memory, their careers captured and telescoped a complex historical socio-religious process whereby a land originally forested and non-Muslim became arable and mainly Muslim. A Bengali poem composed around 1590 associates Muslim pioneers with the clearing of forests and the establishment of local markets.[50] And a late-sixteenth-century Bengali biography of the Prophet Muhammad and other prophets of Islam, the *Nabi-Bangsa*, characterizes the patriarch Abraham as a man who, born and brought up in a forest, travelled to Palestine, where he attracted tribes from nearby lands, mobilized local labour to cut down the forest and built a holy place – Jerusalem's Temple – for offering prayers to God.[51] In this way, the main themes of Abraham's life as recorded in this epic precisely mirrored the careers of the hundreds of pioneers who, during the sixteenth to eighteenth centuries, mobilized local clients in the Bengali countryside for just such activities.

This literary evidence corroborates data found in seventeenth- and eighteenth-century Mughal documents referring to pioneers who opened up virgin forest for rice cultivation by mobilizing labour, advancing capital and clearing the land's thick forests prior to launching rice-cultivation operations. From a local *zamindar* who might have had claims to the land, these entrepreneurs acquired authorization for clearing the forest, and from mainly Hindu bankers or moneylenders they obtained finances with which to pay their labour force. The pioneers then organized local labourers to clear and ultimately cultivate the land, which Mughal authorities subsequently declared tax-free.

Notably, it was never the state's intention to promote a Muslim society on the Bengal frontier. Rather, by outsourcing community and economic development to enterprising pioneers, whether Hindu or Muslim, government officials endeavoured to secure a loyal and stable society on an otherwise unruly frontier, while also expanding the amount of arable land within their domain. As Mughal revenue documents stipulate, all pioneers regardless of their religious identity were required to 'assiduously pray for the survival of the powerful state'. Loyalty, stability and agrarian productivity, not religious affiliation, were the state's overriding concerns. As a condition for receiving a grant that authorized the development of a tax-free tract of forest, a Hindu pioneer had to build a temple and a Muslim pioneer had to build a mosque, either of which would have provided a measure of institutional focus and local stability. But because most pioneers were Muslims, more mosques appeared in the eastern delta than temples. Consequently, more indigenous peoples were exposed to Muslim than to Hindu religious culture.

As a result of these measures, the primitive mosques of bamboo and thatching built by Muslim pioneers constituted the earliest Muslim institutions in what had hitherto been dense, thinly populated forests. Shortly after the Mughals annexed the heavily forested Chittagong region in 1666, mosques and shrines began proliferating throughout the area, as provincial officers issued written orders (*sanads*) to local functionaries ordering them to transfer jungle lands from the royal domain – or from *zamindars* claiming proprietary rights – to enterprising pioneers. These tax-free grants set in motion far-reaching socio-economic processes: forest lands became rice fields, while local hunters, fisherfolk or slash-and-burn farmers became wet-rice-cultivating communities. They also became clients of the pioneers who had opened up particular tracts of land, and since these grants were renewable, subsequent generations were clients of the descendants of those pioneers. Over time, many of the original pioneers came to be venerated as Muslim holy men, or even as spiritually powerful Sufi shaikhs, and their grave sites as shrines. This is why in Bengal, unlike elsewhere in India, local saints are often associated with both the propagation of Islam and the introduction of wet-rice agriculture.

The growth of Muslim communities along the Bengal frontier was thus a by-product of interconnected political, economic and ultimately geomorphological processes. Having assisted the grantee in clearing the forests, the latter's dependants continued to serve the institution the grantee had established by cultivating the lands included in the grant. Each new mosque in the forest thus became the nucleus for a new community of Muslim cultivators. Even while the Mughals' imperial centre was sinking into irreversible decay, along the state's peripheries the government's bureaucratic machinery continued to grind forwards out of sheer inertia of motion, issuing land grants that allowed enterprising pioneers to clear jungle land and establish permanent wet-rice cultivation. Indigenous peoples in this way became cultivators of the land, over time acquiring the religious identity associated with those original pioneers and their humble mosques.

A similar combination of peasantization and Islamization occurred in the western Punjab, a process that began in the thirteenth century but was not complete until the eighteenth. Like eastern Bengal, western Punjab had for centuries lain on the margins of expansive, Delhi-based empires. And like the indigenous communities of eastern Bengal, Jat pastoralists in the western Punjab had been only partially incorporated into a Hindu socio-religious world at the time of their earliest contact with Muslims. Finally, as in eastern Bengal, the growth of Islam in the western Punjab occurred in tandem with a transition to settled agriculture – specifically, as Jat clans began to abandon full-time pastoralism and take up settled wheat-farming. However, whereas Islamization in eastern Bengal had been launched and sustained by hundreds of humble, thatched mosques established by forest-clearing developers, in the Punjab this role was played by large, state-supported shrine complexes that had been built over the grave sites of renowned Sufi shaikhs. Located along the banks of the southern and western Punjab's rivers – the Indus, Jhelum, Chenab, Ravi and Sutlej – these shrines were socio-cultural magnets, attracting large numbers of Jat communities for whom they provided a range of socio-economic and religious services. The spiritual power (*baraka*) of eminent Sufi shaikhs buried at these shrines was, and is, widely believed to adhere to the physical shrines and their immediate precincts. Like many other such shrines in western Punjab, that of Shaikh Farid al-Din Ganj-i Shakar, popularly known as Baba Farid, attracted rural folk from across the region seeking the blessings and intercession of a saint believed capable of mediating the human and divine worlds. Located in Pakpattan by the banks of the Sutlej River, Baba Farid's shrine attracted the patronage of political actors at the highest levels. Sultan Muhammad bin Tughluq built an imposing structure over the shaikh's grave site and granted endowments for the upkeep of his shrine and its large public kitchen. Sultan Firuz Tughluq conferred robes of honour on the saint's descendants and confirmed their land holdings. Ibn Battuta, Timur and Akbar all paid their respects to the shrine.

The predominant clientele of the Punjab's great shrines, however, were Jat communities who by the eleventh century had migrated from Sind up the Indus valley into the southern Punjab, where they were described as 'low Sudra' cattle-owners. By the thirteenth century they were reported in the western Punjab, and by the late sixteenth they had taken up settled agriculture. By that time the charismatic authority of major shrines had long been preserved and nurtured by the descendants of their respective founders. These men not only supervised and led the rituals associated with the shrines; they also patronized the chiefs of Jat clans, just as they themselves were patronized by Mughal authorities. In Pakpattan, Jat chiefs gave their daughters in marriage to the sons of the leader of Baba Farid's shrine, whereas the leader's own daughters were kept within the extended family, thereby replicating the same sort of marital practices and alliances that the Mughals had established with politically subordinate Rajput clans. As Jat clans entered into political, religious and marital relations with shrines such as that of Baba Farid, the names they gave their children reveal a gradual adoption of an Islamic identity. As early as the fifteenth century, Muslim names began to appear among Jat tribes associated with Baba Farid's shrine, but they did not become dominant among those tribes until the early eighteenth, indicating a very slow and apparently unconscious process of Islamization.[52]

Quite significantly, these socio-religious movements in eastern Bengal and western Punjab created the two largest Muslim communities in pre-British India, which would ultimately comprise the core of two post-British states: Bangladesh and Pakistan. The two communities shared a similar historical trajectory in that, in both, the evolution of an Islamic religious identity was associated with a transition to sedentary agrarian life among communities only lightly touched by Hindu culture. These were not, however, the only instances in which changes in socio-economic status led to new cultural identities. We have seen that rising social status resulting from participation in India's military labour market also drove new cultural identities, as in the case of Kunbi farmers of Maharashtra becoming Marathas, Gujarati pastoralists becoming Rajputs, or Jats of eastern Punjab becoming Sikhs. All these cases indicate how cultural identities were never fixed or immutable, but contingent upon, and shaped by, larger processes specific to particular historical contexts.

## EARLY MODERN GLOBALIZATION

Partly responsible for these changes in cultural identity were powerful, interconnected transregional forces. These included the movement of pastoral communities into agrarian zones, the expanding geographical and social reach of cash, and the growing integration of India's economy and society with wider networks of commerce. Such forces were part of a quickened, worldwide exchange of ideas, commodities, technologies, peoples, diseases and cultural traditions that transformed all participants, not least the Mughal empire.

In early December 1572, during his first attempt at conquering Gujarat, Akbar visited the ancient seaport of Cambay, at the time the region's principal window on the outside world. Upon being welcomed at a pleasant spot by a delegation of foreign merchants – Turks from the Ottoman world, Persians from Safavid Iran, possibly some Portuguese – the emperor and a select body of men embarked on a ship. This brief excursion out on the water had no military or commercial purpose. It was made, records Abu'l-fazl, merely 'to witness the spectacle of the ocean'.[53] Never before had any ruler in Akbar's direct line of descent, going back to Timur himself, seen the ocean. But from this moment on, the Mughals would learn what peoples in coastal India had long known: that the sea was a source of wealth and power. Appropriating existing ports or establishing new ones, owning ships and investing in trade would open up to the Mughals a much wider world than the one they had previously known. In a larger sense, Akbar's direct encounter with the open sea symbolized the joining of the land-based Mughal imperium with transoceanic commercial networks. To obtain direct access to the sources of spices, pepper and textiles, fifteenth-century Portuguese navigators had already pioneered an all-maritime route from the North Atlantic Ocean to India, where they established a series of fortified trading enclaves along the coasts of the peninsula, Gujarat and Bengal.

Although Portuguese strategists imagined that they had 'conquered' large parts of the Indian Ocean world, they were actually accommodating themselves to a dense web of maritime commerce that had been built up over many centuries by a mix of seafaring peoples – Arabs, Gujaratis, Malays, Iranians, Tamils, Swahilis, Chinese. Yet, soon after Vasco da Gama lowered anchor at Calicut in 1498, and especially after the Estado da India's grand strategist Afonso d'Albuquerque established a permanent, colonial enclave at Goa in 1510, the Portuguese enterprise introduced new commodities, ideas and technologies to India. A vigorous Catholic mission in Goa carried religious ideas to Akbar's court in Agra. New crops that the Portuguese brought from America – for example potatoes, maize, chillies, squash and tomatoes – utterly transformed the Indian diet. Europe's direct maritime connection with India also facilitated technological transfers, as when Deccani engineers applied the idea of swivel cannon, which the Portuguese had mounted on their ships' gunwales, to the massive cannon that were then positioned atop the Deccan's hill forts.

By the dawn of the seventeenth century, other European enterprises had reached the Indian Ocean: the Dutch East India Company, founded in 1602, and its smaller counterpart, the English East India Company, founded in 1600. Unlike Portugal's Estado da India – a royal endeavour in which soldiers, merchants and clergy all worked for the king – these were joint stock companies launched by independent merchants in Amsterdam and London. Although they enjoyed the support of their respective governments, the companies were primarily responsible to their investors. Private merchants working for them would pool their resources, buy and equip ships and launch overseas 'ventures' in which stockholders shared profits or losses – an early instance of global capitalism. These two north European operations, followed somewhat later by Danish (1616) and French (1664) overseas trading companies, established a number of trading posts that paralleled the network of Portuguese enclaves already scattered around the Indian Ocean rim. By 1700 European companies were importing annually over 877,000 untailored pieces of cotton cloth from India.[54] And yet, because the Mughals controlled the ports in textile-rich Gujarat and Bengal, Europeans were in no position to dictate the terms of commerce. Rather, they had to petition imperial authorities for permission to establish trading enclaves. Even then, they could conduct business only on Mughal terms.

Nonetheless, Europe's new commercial connection with Indian markets had profound effects on the subcontinent's economy, as reflected in India's currencies. Prior to the Mughal era, only Gujarat possessed a reliable and stable silver coinage, based on the high volume of maritime commerce that had attracted silver from the Middle East ever since the early centuries AD.[55] Other Indian regions, lacking extensive silver mines of their own and not enjoying Gujarat's volume of overseas trade, relied on other media for their coinage, such as copper, gold, billon or cowrie shells. All this changed in the late sixteenth century. The Indian economy being largely self-sufficient, in order to purchase Indian goods Europeans had to export silver, the one foreign item that the Mughals lacked and wanted, apart from war-horses. Luckily for the fledgling overseas companies in England and the Netherlands, Spain's plundering of rich silver mines in Mexico and Peru from about 1550 was followed by the diffusion of tons of silver into northern Europe, driven largely by Spain's costly wars there between 1568 and 1648. That money, in turn, allowed both the Dutch and English companies literally to buy themselves into India's export markets.[56] Between 1586 and 1605, overseas silver flowed into the Mughal heartland at the stunning rate of about 185 metric tons a year.[57] 'India is rich in silver,' noted the English merchant William Hawkins in 1613, 'for all nations bring coyne and carry away commodities for the same.'[58] American silver arriving in India was immediately minted into silver rupees, which became the Mughals' principal currency medium from about 1580. In 1615 one observer estimated the Mughals' annual revenue at 120 million silver coins, compared to forty-five million for the Ottoman empire and just fifteen million for neighbouring Iran.[59] In fact, between 1600 and 1800 India absorbed about 20 per cent of the precious metals produced throughout the world.[60]

By the beginning of the seventeenth century, then, the Mughals had experienced two fundamental economic transformations. First, their conquest of north India and subsequent rule in the sixteenth century completed a long-term process that had been initiated by the Turkish invasions of upper India in the late twelfth century, whereby the warrior institutions of semi-pastoral Central Asia merged with the revenue institutions of agrarian India.[61] By the end of the sixteenth century the Mughal empire had undergone a second transformation as it became integrated with a global economy, symbolized by Akbar's capture of Gujarat, India's most highly commercialized subregion. In the seventeenth and eighteenth centuries, most imported silver was no longer carried to India by the Portuguese Estado da India, but by the Dutch, English and French trading companies. These north European companies, however, were not content with merely establishing enclaves where they would receive and ship to Europe finished goods that Indian merchants brought to their coastal warehouses. Rather, needing to maximize profits for their investors and stockholders back home, the managers of these companies endeavoured, wherever possible, to reduce costs by gaining direct or indirect control over the factors of production – the land, labour and capital – that went into making the goods.

The economic and political objectives of the English company would prove decisive in this respect. Ever since the mid sixteenth century (with much earlier antecedents), the English Parliament had been passing laws giving the state and employers coercive powers over English workers, while setting limits on their wages and controlling their mobility. Passed in 1563 and remaining on the books until 1813, the Statute of Artificers stipulated, among other things, that English workers could not leave an employer until after at least one year's labour for him, that workers seeking new employment required a termination certificate from a former employer, and that workers' wages would be set by government officials.[62] Measures of this nature aligned with prevailing mercantilist thought that obliged the state to take any necessary steps to keep domestic manufactures competitive at home and abroad. And when Queen Elizabeth gave the East India Company a monopoly on England's trade with the Indian Ocean region, company officials took such ideas with them to India. For a century and a half after its founding in 1600, however, the Company was in no position to intervene coercively in the economic factors that had created the goods in greatest demand at home, namely India's finely woven and world-renowned cotton textiles, whether plain, printed, painted or patterned on the loom.

By contrast, neither the Mughals nor other Indian states with which the English company dealt claimed the right, or ever wished, to intervene directly in the production process. For officials of the Mughal empire and those of the English East India Company occupied very different moral universes. In 1778, for example, officers of the English company asked the nawab (ruler) of Arcot in the Tamil country to round up and forcibly return weavers who had fled from a company-controlled manufacturing centre. Astonished at the request, the nawab replied that such a thing was 'contrary to custom and it was never done before'.[63] Even taxation had its limits. Since the supply of arable land in pre-colonial India surpassed that of labour, villagers always had the option of simply abandoning their fields and establishing new settlements elsewhere if their taxes became too onerous. Aware of this, states sought non-coercive means to keep villagers productive. Emperor 'Alamgir, for example, ordered that if any cultivator abandoned his fields, local revenue officers 'should ascertain the cause and work very hard to induce him to return to his former place'.[64] Such an order hardly suggests a ruler governing from a position of overwhelming strength vis-à-vis India's labour force. For the Mughal empire was no mighty juggernaut, crushing everything in its path. On the contrary, despite its image as an absolute monarchy, Mughal officials co-operated with numerous stakeholders, making alliances with, and working through, countless petty *zamindars* and other local elites.[65] Such officials were in no position to coerce merchants or others with whom they shared de facto sovereignty.[66] Far less did they establish strict production schedules for labourers, impose maximum wages for producers or restrict their mobility. Yet these were the very kinds of mercantilist measures that employees of the English East India Company considered fundamental for maximizing their profits.

It was in India's textile-manufacturing sector that such ideas most closely engaged with Indian economic realities. And for good reason. Because their northern location and temperate climate prevented them from cultivating cotton, Europeans for centuries had clothed themselves in wool or linen. Spanish Arabs introduced cotton to Europeans in the tenth and eleventh centuries – the English word for the fibre is derived from the Arabic *qutun* – and from the twelfth century northern Italy supported a modest textile industry based on raw cotton imported from across the Mediterranean Sea. A strong demand for cotton products did not take hold in northern Europe, however, until after the establishment of direct maritime contact with India, which had been the world's leading manufacturer of cotton for more than five millennia.[67] This demand grew steadily through the seventeenth century. In 1664 alone, the English East India Company imported a quarter of a million pieces of cloth, nearly half of them from Coromandel, a third from Gujarat and less than a fifth from Bengal. Twenty years later the Company was annually importing 1.76 million pieces of Indian textiles to England, which represented 83 per cent of the Company's total trade.[68] This was the height of the so-called 'calico craze', when India's cotton textiles were in feverish demand in England and across Europe generally. Indeed, England's sustained commercial connection with India is seen in the many textile-related Indian words that entered the English language in this period – for example, dungaree, chintz, seersucker, calico, pyjamas, shawl, khaki, cummerbund, taffeta, jaconet and bandana.

Nor was this just an English craze. Indian textiles occupied the centre of a global phenomenon that transformed the economies and societies of five continents. By the dawn of the eighteenth century, India's cotton textiles had displaced rice and spices as the principal item of trade in the Indian Ocean. And by the mid eighteenth century, when more than three-quarters of all the English East India Company's imports from India consisted of textiles, Asia, Europe, Africa and the two Americas were all tightly integrated by the white fibre and the textiles spun from it. To obtain slaves for their transatlantic plantations, Europeans purchased captives from West Africa using mainly Indian textiles, which were in great demand among African merchants and political elites.[69]

However, in order to obtain the Indian textiles that were in such high demand in Europe and Africa, European payments to Indian merchants and producers had to be made mainly in treasure. This posed a serious problem, since, according to prevailing mercantilist thought, states should be hoarding silver and gold in their national treasuries, not exporting such precious metals for overseas purchases. Only by restricting the flow of silver bullion to India, and by reducing the cost of overseas purchases, could the Company align its commercial policies with mercantilist objectives. By acquiring political authority in India's major textile-producing regions – Coromandel, Bengal and Gujarat – the Company achieved both objectives. Two factors allowed this to occur. One was the fierce competition between European powers over access to India's textile-manufacturing sector, which led ultimately to armed conflict between Europeans. This, in turn, militarized the Company, which by the 1760s had a private army of 20,000, a figure that would grow to about 260,000 by 1803.[70] Second, from the mid eighteenth century, Indian rulers, in order to advance their own fortunes on an increasingly fragmented political stage, willingly surrendered revenue-collection rights in return for access to European weapons and/or European-trained soldiers. Such rights became the principal mechanism by which the English company would leverage its commercial operations into outright domination over Indian territory.

These processes began quietly enough in the 1750s along the Coromandel coast. There, rivalry between the French and English companies

intensified when each company backed opposing claimants to succeed as the nawab of Arcot, a remnant of 'Alamgir's conquests in
the south-eastern Deccan. In 1763, after armed forces of the British
East India Company defeated those of the French company for commercial hegemony in the region, the British-backed nawab became
heavily indebted to his European sponsors and surrendered to the
British company the revenue-collecting rights to lands adjacent to its
base at Madras. Later called Chingleput District, this region was
styled the Company's *jagir*. The use of this Mughal administrative
term suggested that the British were merely servants of the nawab of
Arcot, who in theory ruled under the authority of the nizam of
Hyderabad, who governed the Deccan theoretically as governor (*sub-
ahdar*) of the emperor in Delhi. In this way the Company inserted
itself on India's political map, albeit at the bottom of a largely fictitious chain of political authority that stretched from Delhi down to
Chingleput.

Secure in their position as the legitimate collectors of revenue in
their *jagir*, officers of the British company soon aligned their commercial operations with mercantilist ideals. By 1766, the Company
was using its authority to order weavers in its *jagir* to accept advances
only from Company merchants, thereby creating a monopoly of the
textile trade in its territory. Company officials also began advancing
loans directly to the weavers, thereby circumventing the merchants
who had been doing that for generations. Placing the looms in their
*jagir* under the supervision of a Commercial Resident, the Company
was then in a position to reject any cloth that did not meet its stringent standards, impose minimum quotas of cloth to be produced per
loom per month, reduce the amount of cash advanced to weavers,
and insist upon prompt deliveries of goods to meet its tight shipping
schedules, which were governed by monsoon winds. The Company
also used its judicial power to enforce contracts made with producers, and its military power – in the form of Company-trained Indian
soldiers, or *sepoy*s – to prevent weavers from absconding with cash
advances.[71] By the 1760s, then, the profile of the Company had
changed dramatically from what it had been for more than a century
and a half. In short order, the political complexion of India, too,
would change.

Similar developments took place in Mughal Bengal. In 1756 the British company had refused to obey the provincial nawab's orders to cease building fortifications, which were driven, again, by Anglo-French rivalry. In response, the impetuous twenty-three-year-old nawab seized the British company's base of Calcutta. The following year Robert Clive, a military officer who had already played a leading role in the Company's territorial acquisitions in Coromandel, was ordered to sail from Madras and recover the city. After accomplishing that goal, Clive, being well beyond the reach of Company or Parliamentary checks on his ambition, exceeded the terms of his authorized mission by conspiring with the nawab's disaffected commander-in-chief to overthrow the unpopular nawab. In June 1757 he defeated the nawab's forces 150 kilometres north of Calcutta and then installed his native co-conspirator as Bengal's new Mughal nawab, who then became in effect a Company puppet.

After its troops defeated a coalition of Mughal armies at Buxor (thirteen kilometres west of Patna) in 1764, the East India Company tightened its de facto authority in Bengal. In the following year Clive personally met the virtually powerless Mughal emperor, Shah 'Alam II (r. 1759–1806), who signed a document – the so-called Diwani of Bengal (August 1765) – formally giving Company officers the right to assess and collect the province's revenue. As in Coromandel, the Company swiftly made use of its newly won political authority to enact mercantilist policies in eastern India. Company officials seized textiles woven for their Dutch rivals and obliged all weavers in Bengal to work exclusively for them. In 1767, pieces being made for the French were cut off the looms and their weavers made subject to bodily and monetary punishments. The Company also coerced intermediary merchants and weavers to work for them on terms far below the market, forcing many weavers to abandon their craft altogether.[72] Merchants who refused to sign papers agreeing to the Company's harsh terms were caned or jailed. In a poignant application of the new regime's economic philosophy, in 1767 one merchant who appeared before Company officials with a piece of cloth fifty centimetres shorter than the required length was made to rub his nose on the ground several times for that exact distance.[73]

Such disciplinary measures came more slowly where the Company still lacked political power or where, as in Gujarat, it was forced to share power with other actors.[74] Nonetheless, the 1765 Diwani of Bengal had set a precedent for what would subsequently happen elsewhere in India: the acquisition of de facto governing authority not through outright conquest but through mutual agreements concluded between regional powers and an overseas trading company – albeit a company authorized not just to monopolize trade but to mint coins, exercise justice and wage war. Moreover, the Company's acquisition of Bengal's public finance meant that it could use that province's revenues to help pay for its investments in the region's goods for export, thereby sharply reducing its reliance on silver bullion shipped from Britain to India.[75] As a result, between 1760 and 1829 silver accounted for only 18.6 per cent of the value of goods that the Company sent to Asia, a significant drop from the period before 1756, when that metal accounted for 70–85 per cent of those exports.[76]

## CONCLUSION

As signs of Mughal decline, it is easy to conjure up striking images of foreign invaders pillaging the north Indian countryside. One can readily visualize Nadir Shah, having sacked Delhi in 1739, marching through the Khyber Pass with long columns of pack animals loaded with looted treasures that included Shah Jahan's Peacock Throne and the Koh-i-Noor diamond. A more accurate image of imperial decline, however, would be of the empire being undermined from within and below, in the way that termites silently hollow out the base of a wooden structure. Across eighteenth-century India, local power holders were able to challenge imperial authority with resources ultimately derived from the higher volume of cash that circulated throughout Indian society as a result of the commercialization of the entire Indian Ocean region. As merchant wealth expanded, new market centres were established, boosting development in both agrarian and manufacturing sectors. Land use was greatly intensified, as happened when pioneers in Bengal used cash to mobilize labour for transforming dense jungle into arable fields for the cultivation of food crops.

Although coastal tracts first felt the impact of imported silver, the coined metal quickly diffused into India's hinterland, owing, among other things, to the overall structure of the textile industry. Whereas cloth was woven, bleached, dyed and printed in coastal regions, the raw cotton was grown, harvested, cleaned and spun into yarn deep in the interior. Bengal depended on yarn from Gujarat, Coromandel acquired its cotton from the Deccan, Gujarat relied on raw silk transported from Bengal. The cotton grown on the black soils of the central Deccan was brought 400 kilometres to Coromandel by nomadic clans – the Banjaras – on huge caravans of 10,000–40,000 bullocks each.[77] The entire hinterland of Madras was devoted to supplying rice to coastal markets and their weaving communities.[78] As a result, the growth of maritime commerce stimulated India's land-based economy both in the hinterland and along the coast.

But the diffusion of cash-based commerce into India's interior also had political consequences. Since access to India's military labour market was predicated on the availability of money, as more cash flowed from the coasts to the interior, provincial Mughal governors acquired greater means to mobilize standing armies with which to challenge or resist imperial demands. This also held true for intermediary orders of Indian society, including large and small *zamindars*, transregional merchants, Sikh chieftains, powerful bankers and revenue farmers, among others. Especially prominent were *zamindars*, India's ancient class of hereditary, quasi-royal landholders who, with their armed retainers, their legacies of former sovereignty (real or imagined) and their claims to a share of a territory's wealth, commanded respect and some legitimacy among rural folk. Neither the Mughals nor any other power had ever fully suppressed or co-opted them. Now, thanks to the waves of mobile wealth that washed over the Indo-Gangetic plain in the eighteenth century, *zamindars*, always ready to reassert their ancient political claims, could challenge imperial authority by tapping into the military labour market.[79]

Ultimately, what enabled growing European influence in the second half of the eighteenth century in India was local demand for European weaponry or mercenaries, which Europeans happily supplied. A single incident suggests the general trend. In April 1758 the acting governor of Portuguese Goa wrote to Tarabai, at that time the aged dowager of the Maratha kingdom, that he would be most pleased to supply her with the 2,000 guns she had ordered, provided she paid for them before delivery.[80] Tarabai duly furnished the cash, drawn from the accumulated stocks of silver that had been flowing into Indian coasts for the previous two and a half centuries.

Did such deals constitute a significant break with the past? Many historians have seen the mid eighteenth century as a major – if not *the* major – point of rupture in the flow of Indian history. Yet the entry of Europeans as political actors was built upon long-established Indian institutions. One of these were the well-developed revenue-extracting bureaucracies that were still operating at local levels, even if the Mughal central government was not receiving those revenues. Another was India's long-standing and extensive military labour market. For centuries before the mid 1700s, ambitious Indian rulers or would-be rulers had been buying into indigenous markets of military labour in order to advance their claims to political authority. From the mid eighteenth century onwards, however, those same figures began contracting European-trained military labour or, as in the case of Tarabai's dealings with the acting governor of Goa, European weaponry. Yet the reverse also occurred, as both Frenchmen and – more successfully – Englishmen tapped into India's indigenous military labour market. 'British conquest', writes the historian C. A. Bayly, 'often meant no more than the slow drift to the East India Company of soldiers, merchants and administrators, leaving the Indian rulers with nothing more than a husk of royal grandeur.'[81]

In both moral and economic terms, then, the advent of a ruthlessly mercantilist ideology carried to South Asia by the East India Company certainly did represent a radical break with the Indian past. And yet neither that ideology nor its carrier – the English company – could have taken root and flourished without the pre-existing institution of India's military labour market.

# Conclusion and Epilogue

## INDIA IN THE PERSIANATE WORLD

India has never been isolated. Jutting into the heart of the Indian Ocean – the world's oldest maritime zone – and connected to the Iranian plateau by several strategic mountain passes, the Indo-Gangetic plain and the great peninsula to its south have long been a major crossroads of transregional movement and exchange. Pathways leading to and across the subcontinent have carried a wide range of global flows, while migrating populations brought or took away diverse cultural traditions embracing statecraft, architecture, warfare, cuisine, religion and much more. Although some of these flows had very deep roots in time, they all moved with a quickening pace between the eleventh and eighteenth centuries, the period of this book's concern.

As a subset of these transregional flows, Persian texts and Persian-speakers circulated through West, Central and South Asia from the eleventh century in expanding and increasingly dense networks. Artisans, mercenaries, Sufi shaikhs, slaves, poets, scholars, adventurers, diplomats, migrants, pilgrims and merchants all travelled along the maritime and overland routes that both undergirded and constituted the Persianate world. For most of these peoples, whatever their ethnic background or geographical origin, facility in Persian was an acquired skill. Yet even rudimentary acquaintance with the language exposed them to a stable canon of Persian texts, together with the sensibilities and norms of sociability they elaborated. In the present age, when South Asia has been absorbed in an Anglophone world, it is easy to forget India's central place in an earlier, Persophone world. For centuries Persian had been the pre-eminent language of diplomatic discourse in India. Even before the Mughal age, Lodi rulers had employed members of Hindu scribal communities and issued bilingual revenue documents in Persian and Hindavi.[1] During the Afghan interregnum that followed the Mughal conquest, Sher Shah appointed two writers (*karkun*s) for each district, one for Persian and one for Hindavi.[2]

The big breakthrough, however, came in 1582 when Akbar, with the apparent aim of promoting a political culture that would arch over the Mughal realm's diverse religious and cultural communities, established Persian as the official language. It was to be used at every level of the Mughals' bureaucracy, from the imperial capitals down to the most remote settlements in the rural hinterland.[3] Within a few generations, India had become a major centre of the Persian-speaking or -reading world. An Italian who travelled through Gujarat in 1623 considered that in Mughal territories Persian was more commonly used than vernacular languages.[4] By 1700 India was probably the world's leading centre for the patronage of Persian literature and scholarship, with an estimated seven times more people literate in Persian than in Iran.[5] For scribal castes that had traditionally served state bureaucracies such as the Kayasthas or Khatris, facility in Persian was a practical necessity. Gaining proficiency in it, moreover, was no more traumatic than acquiring English during the British Raj, since Persian, notwithstanding its extensive use in Sufi writings of all sorts, was not tied to liturgical or scriptural Islam, as was Arabic. Rather, in seventeenth-century north India it was viewed as an unproblematic, neutral language of everyday correspondence, literary expression and social mobility.[6]

Partially meeting the growing demand for a working knowledge of Persian was the system of schools, or *madrasa*s, that Akbar had reformed.[7] Village schools, or *maktab*s, also introduced India's scribal castes to basic Persian literacy. From the age of four, children of the Kayastha caste were taught practical skills such as accounting (*siyaqi*), enabling them to tabulate rent rates and audit revenue accounts. Manning the lower tiers of the Mughal revenue machine, Kayasthas typically served as land registrars (*qanungo*) and village accountants (*patwari*), providing the institutional mortar of the whole governing edifice. Higher up in the system, Kayasthas served as news writers, revenue reporters, petition writers, surveyors or even court readers. In all these capacities, it was their facility in Persian that gave them not only employment in the Mughal bureaucracy but status in the larger Persianate world, for a *maktab* curriculum invariably included classics drawn from the Persian literary cannon, such as Sa'di's *Gulistan* or Firdausi's *Shahnama*. In the process, Kayasthas gradually became acculturated to Persianate norms, adopting Persian pen names and attending musical rituals (*qawwali*) at Sufi shrines in centres like Allahabad or Lucknow.[8]

In addition, from at least the fourteenth century versified bilingual wordbooks circulated throughout the Persian-speaking world. Known as *nisab*s, these simplified, rustic dictionaries interpreted words from an unfamiliar language to a familiar one. Prior to the mid sixteenth century such books had explained Hindavi terms for Persian-knowing immigrants to India.[9] From the mid sixteenth century onwards, however, they had the opposite aim of interpreting Persian words for Hindavi-speakers. After Akbar had made Persian the sole language for all levels of the Mughal bureaucracy, such wordbooks proliferated, their numbers exploding in the eighteenth century. Many of them were intended for children of groups occupying the social space between the labouring and ruling classes, particularly scribal castes, with a view to socializing them into the Mughal world from a tender age. For such groups, *nisab*s provided an introduction to the language of power and an avenue to higher education, and hence to the vast horizons afforded by the financial, political and cultural cosmopolitanism of the Persianate world.[10] In short, Persian in the Mughal period was not just a bureaucratic medium. Bilingual wordbooks served as guides for accessing courtly culture. It is not coincidental that the Persian word for 'dictionary', *farhang*, also means 'good breeding', 'greatness' or 'education'.[11] In eighteenth-century Bihar, Hindu and Muslim *zamindar*s established *madrasa*s where Hindu literati taught the language, and where students studied classic texts such as the poetry of Sa'di.[12] All descriptions of the educational attainments of Bengali aristocrats of the seventeenth and eighteenth centuries emphasize their proficiency in Persian, which was even accorded the status of a *shastra* – that is, a formal intellectual discipline, and not just a practical medium to be used for keeping revenue accounts or composing government petitions.[13]

Whereas Persian–Hindavi word-books, *madrasa*s and *maktab*s helped make Persian the language of ordinary governance across north India and the Deccan, the Mughal court had loftier aims. A 'classical' canon of Persian literature as we know it today had been consolidated and stabilized under Timurid patronage in centres such as late-fifteenth-century Herat, a city that both Babur and Humayun visited in the twilight of that city's Timurid glory.[14] Having begun their imperial career in India just as their Timurid kin had ended theirs in Central Asia, the Mughals therefore inherited a Persian literary past that was already coherent, systematized and available.[15] The Mughal court then not only lavishly patronized that canon, but endeavoured to place India at the centre of the wider Persophone world. It was to this end that Akbar commissioned the compilation of a comprehensive Persian dictionary, the *Farhang-i Jahangiri*, so called because it was completed in 1606 during Jahangir's reign. The compilers of this work of some 9,000 entries consulted forty-four dictionaries in the course of its making, thereby seeking to consolidate all previous lexicographical efforts and embrace the entirety of the Persian language.

Contemporary accounts of the Mughal court suggest how its cosmopolitan atmosphere overlapped with the Persianate world. Chandar Bhan Brahman (d. *c*.1666/70), who enjoyed a long career as imperial secretary for Jahangir, Shah Jahan and 'Alamgir, described one of Shah Jahan's assemblies as including:

> Tajiks, Kurds, Georgians, Tatars, Russians, Ethiopians, Circassians and various others from the lands of Rum, Egypt, Syria, 'Iraq, Arabia, 'Ajam, Persia, Gilan, Mazandaran, Khurasan, Transoxiana, the Qipchaq steppes, Turkistan, Georgia and Kurdistan, each in their respective places.
>
> So too with the various communities of Hindustan, from among the masters of excellence and perfection, and men of the sword and the pen, such as *sayyids* of pure ancestry, martial *shaikh-zadas*, Afghan tribes [*alusat*] like the Lodis, Rohillas, Khweshgis, Yusufza'is and others, not to mention various classes of Rajputs, Ranjas, Rajas, Raos, and Rais, among them the Rathors, Sisodias, Kachwahas, Hadas, Kurus, Chauhans, Jhalas, Chandrawats, Jaduns, Tonwars, Baghelas, Baiswaras, Gujars, Pawars [Paramaras], Bhadauriyas, Singhis, Bundelas, Shagarwals, and other attendees from the rest of India.[16]

Inasmuch as all the sites mentioned were centres of Persianate cultural production, Chandar Bhan Brahman was implicitly aligning the court's geographical reach with that of the Persianate world, while placing the Mughal court in its conceptual centre.[17] Many Rajputs certainly saw themselves as sharing in that world. The *Manacharita*, a vernacular biography written in 1585, falsely credits the Rajput *mansabdar* Man Singh with Mughal victories far beyond India, including in Kirghizstan, Samarqand, Merv, Khurasan, Hormuz, Baghdad, Isfahan and Tabriz.[18] In the author's fertile imagination, the territorial extent of the Mughal empire overlapped much of the Persianate world, and in this reading it was a Rajput general who had brought it about.

In the end, what sustained this universe was the circulation of people along established transregional networks that connected key centres of Persianate cultural production. The moral authority underpinning this universe derived from a canon of classical texts that circulated along those same networks, providing peoples of diverse ethnic or religious backgrounds with a common point of reference. The texts comprising this canon were never fixed. Chandar Bhan Brahman compiled his own list of texts that he considered fundamental for shaping a well-rounded, cultured person, and which he recommended for his own son to study and absorb.[19] Yet some literary genres remained constant over time, including advice literature, poetry of all sorts (epic, lyric, mystical), biographies, histories, treatises, narratives, even proverbs. Certain authors regularly appeared in the canon, such as Firdausi, Sa'di, Nizami, Amir Khusrau, Tusi and Jami.[20] Taught in *madrasa*s and other educational outlets at both elite and non-elite levels, works by these writers were read, reread, memorized, recited and quoted so often and so widely that to varying degrees their readers or listeners internalized their values and sentiments.[21]

Owing to the extent of Persian literacy among India's non-elite classes, considerable Persian vocabulary penetrated India's vernacular languages, even as those languages were attaining their own status as literary vehicles. It is telling that, shortly after his coronation in 1674, Shivaji commissioned the compilation of a Persian–Sanskrit glossary, the *Rajavyavaharakosa*, intended to help government administrators find Sanskrit equivalents for Persian lexical items already in common use among Marathi-speaking clerks, accountants and revenue officials.[22] The very attempt to purge the spoken language of Persian vocabulary indicates the degree to which the western Deccan had become absorbed into the Persianate world during the previous several centuries.[23] Persian vocabulary even entered Indian religious thought, with the Sikh tradition absorbing such key lexical items as *hukm* ('grace of God'), *langar* ('communal meal'), *khalsa* ('community of sworn initiates') and the term by which Guru Nanak referred to himself – *tabl-i baz*, or 'herald'.[24] Persian literary culture also entered Indian thought streams via translations, commentaries and adaptations of canonical works in India's vernacular languages. The Tamil 'tellings' of the popular text *The Book of One Thousand Questions* (*Ayira Macala*) claimed Persian origins traceable to sixteenth-century south India.[25] Between the fifteenth and eighteenth centuries Persian romance narratives, especially Nizami's *Layli va Majnun* and Jami's *Yusuf va Zulaykha*, enjoyed numerous translations in vernacular languages.[26] In this way values and sensibilities embedded in works of the Persian canon were absorbed by Indian populations having no facility in the Persian language.

The case of Burma's Arakan coastal region illustrates this process. Between the mid fifteenth and early seventeenth centuries the region's Buddhist kings, seeking to integrate themselves with a maritime world saturated with Persian culture, adopted Persian royal titles and issued coins in the Perso-Arabic script, as well as those of Sanskrit and Arakanese. By the mid seventeenth century Arakanese was used as the language of the ruling elite, Sanskrit that of the court's Brahmins, Pali that of the Buddhist canon, Bengali that of the kingdom's sizeable Muslim population (the ancestors of today's Rohingya community) and Persian that of administration and diplomacy. Connecting the Buddhist court with the Persianized maritime world beyond Arakan were literati such as the poet-translator Alaol (fl. 1651–71), one of thousands of Bengalis whom Arakanese pirates had seized from lower Bengal, enslaved and taken to labour at the Arakanese capital of Mrauk-U. With the help of powerful patrons, Alaol rose in courtly circles and adapted such Persian classics as Nizami's *Haft Paykar* and *Sikandar-nama* to vernacular Bengali, thereby conveying a high, transregional Persianate tradition into a local idiom.[27] Whereas the poet had got to Arakan via established slave routes, Persian literary motifs reached Arakan via commercial routes that crossed the Bay of Bengal. Whenever a Persian literary theme or motif was adopted in Dakani – the dialect of Hindavi spoken in the Qutb Shahi sultanate of Golconda – that same motif would appear several years later in Bengali texts composed in Arakan by Alaol or other poets.[28] In this way, routes of literary transmission were mapped on existing migration corridors and commercial networks.

## THE MUGHALS IN THE SANSKRIT WORLD

The Persianate was not the only cosmopolitan tradition that flourished in the Mughal period. More than any of the Indian sultanates that preceded them, the Mughals staked their claims to sovereignty by engaging with Sanskrit literary traditions. By appropriating a culture deeply rooted in India's pre-Persianate past, they saw themselves as Indian kings and wished to be seen as such by others. It is therefore hardly surprising that both Brahmin and Jain scholars maintained a significant presence in the Mughal court in the latter decades of Akbar's reign and continuing through those of Jahangir and Shah Jahan.[29]

Such a policy did have precedents. In fifteenth-century Kashmir Sultan Zain al-'Abidin had patronized the production of successive local histories, the *Rajatarangini*s, by the Sanskrit writers Śrivara and Jonaraja. But Akbar and Jahangir made more significant moves in this direction, ordering some fifteen Sanskrit works to be translated into Persian, which enabled court literati unfamiliar with that language to engage with Sanskrit thought.[30] Meanwhile, Jain and Brahmin intellectuals who served in the Mughal court as astrologers, translators, religious guides and political negotiators inevitably drew the Mughals into their own world. Padmasundara (fl. 1569), an early Jain visitor to the imperial court, accommodated the Mughal world to Sanskrit literary theory and placed Akbar at the centre of Sanskrit aesthetics. The Jain monk Śanticandra (fl. 1580s) mapped the Mughal empire on to the topography of a timeless India as imagined in Sanskrit literature, portraying Akbar as a Jain king and his military exploits as a classically Indian 'conquest of the quarters' (*digvijaya*).[31] In the late sixteenth century Akbar commissioned Vihari Krsnadasa to write *Parasiprakaśa*, which was both a thesaurus-like list of common words in both languages and a Sanskrit grammar of Persian in which the author aimed to explain Persian to Sanskrit intellectuals.[32]

Among such inter-cosmopolitan projects, the most ambitious were the court-commissioned Persian translations of the great Sanskrit epics, the *Mahabharata* and the *Ramayana*, which Akbar sponsored from the 1580s. Here the overriding effort was to emphasize the epics' political character and to accommodate Indian deities to Persianate sensibilities. Thus, a translation of the *Ramayana* was refashioned into a meditation on Mughal sovereignty, associating Akbar with the epic's hero, Rama, and suggesting that the emperor was an incarnation of Vishnu.[33] A translation of the *Mahabharata*, entitled *Razm-nama*, preserved hundreds of Sanskrit words, Indian imagery, *avatar*s and Indian deities while conveying the idea of a monotheistic deity, identifying Brahma with the generic Persian term for 'god' (*khudavand*). The epic's most specifically religious section, the *Bhagavad Gita*, occupies just a few pages of the Persian translation, in contrast to 700 pages of the Sanskrit text.[34] Rather than adhering to the Sanskrit text's emphasis on establishing cosmic and social order (*dharma*) in the world, the Persian translation emphasizes the proper virtues of the king. In his preface to the translation, Akbar's principal spokesman Abu'l-fazl framed the work within the kingly advice genre of classic Persian literature. His brother, the court's poet laureate Fayzi, went further, transforming parts of the *Mahabharata* into Persian literature, even poetry. The Iranian immigrant Muhammad Tahir Sabsavari, who was active at the courts of Akbar and Jahangir, included another version of the *Mahabharata* story in his universal history *Rauzat al-Tahirin*, assimilating the Indian epic into a wider history of the human race and linking the Mughals with India's ancient kings.[35]

Among all spheres of culture, it was perhaps in the sciences that knowledge passed most freely between the Persianate and Sanskritic worlds. In the field of medical theory, Greco-Islamic doctrines inherited from the Persian polymath Ibn Sina (Avicenna, d. 1037) differed radically from India's Ayurvedic tradition regarding the number and nature of bodily humours. But the fourteenth-century Indo-Persian scholar Shihab al-Din Nagauri, whose treatise on the subject circulated widely among both Hindu and Muslim physicians, sought to reconcile these differences by assimilating Ayurvedic understandings of physiology into the Avicennian framework. Most Persian writing on Indian medicine, however, focused on practice, not theory. Since the Avicennian tradition had evolved in the dry Middle Eastern environment, many diseases and therapies integral to that tradition were not relevant in wetter, tropical India. This required Indo-Persian physicians and scholars to engage closely with Sanskrit works on pharmacology and native Indian plants. By 'Alamgir's reign, Avicenna's theories had become Indianized as Hindus who had learnt Persian engaged with them. At the same time, Ayurvedic medicine became Persianized as it gained influence in the courts of the Deccan and north India.[36]

Interaction between Indic and Persianate views on astronomy also gathered momentum in the Mughal age. If Indo-Persian writers had taken the initiative accommodating Indian medicine to Persian medical theory and practice, with astronomy the reverse was the case. In the Mughal period Brahmin pundits – not without considerable controversy among themselves – gradually assimilated Greek models of planetary movements as originally formulated by Aristotle, Euclid, or Ptolemy, and as refined and mediated by medieval Arabo-Persian scientists. Prominent among the latter was the Persian polymath Nasir al-Din Tusi, who persuaded his Mongol overlords to support the construction of a massive observatory at Maragheh (1259), in north-west Iran, together with a library and teams of scholars, to test Greek principles against empirical observation. In 1429 Timur's grandson, Ulugh Beg (d. 1449), built another such observatory in Samarqand, modelled on that at Maragheh. He, too, assembled teams of scholars who in turn tested, wrote commentaries on, and refined the astronomical theories of Tusi and other Arabo-Persian scientists. The assimilation of these ideas by Indian scholars, however, was slow. One problem was the smugly insular stance of Sanskrit scientific literature which, refusing to recognize the authority of non-Indian science, remained for centuries wilfully ignorant of its competitors. There were also profound differences over cosmology.

The medieval Arabo-Persian tradition, following the ancient Greeks, believed in the uniformity of nature over time and space, whereas the classical Indian view saw the universe as decaying over time. Moreover, Greco-Islamic physics assumed that planets move by Aristotelian ideas of natural motion, whereas Indian cosmology postulated planetary movement by material forces such as wind or demons. Finally, any transmission of ideas required proper dictionaries, and the first Persian–Sanskrit dictionary only appeared in the late sixteenth century, with Krsnadasa's *Parasiprakaśa*. In 1643 Shah Jahan patronized the compilation of another dictionary with the same title.[37]

Thanks to such dictionaries, and the patronage of Brahmins and Brahmanical knowledge at the Mughal court, the self-imposed walls of Brahmanical orthodoxy regarding astronomy began to crack. In 1628 the first pundit to absorb Arabo-Persian astronomical influence, Nityananda, translated from Persian into Sanskrit the tables that had been prepared for Shah Jahan predicting the location and movements of the planets. These tables were based on those prepared by Ulugh Beg in fifteenth-century Samarqand, which in turn had built on those of Nasir al-Din Tusi in thirteenth-century Iran. In 1639 Nityananda composed another Sanskrit translation in which, in order to gain its acceptance by orthodox Brahmins, he offered the pretext that the Arabo-Persian astronomy it contained had been derived from the revelation of an Indian deity.[38] Despite such camouflage, the work led to fierce disputes in Benares, the bastion of Brahmanical learning, which split into opposing camps over the compatibility of Arabo-Persian astronomy with received Indian tradition. One camp was led by Kamalakara, who in 1658 authored a Sanskrit treatise that agreed with the Ptolemaic notions of the structure of the planetary system as confirmed by the observations at Ulugh Beg's observatory.[39] Although his ideas were vigorously opposed in some quarters of orthodox opinion, by 'Alamgir's reign Persianate notions of astronomy had stimulated considerable intellectual ferment in Sanskrit circles, forcing scholars either to defend, modify or reject their inherited tradition.

Ulugh Beg's observatory in Samarqand also inspired Jai Singh II (r. 1700–43), the Rajput raja of Amber and high-ranking Mughal *mansabdar*, to build a number of his own observatories, including those in Delhi and Jaipur, the eponymous capital city he founded.

Unlike the pundits at Benares, who were divided over the acceptability of non-Indian astronomy, Jai Singh enthusiastically studied Brahmanical and Perso-Arabic systems and patronized scholars of both traditions at his court. In Jaipur between 1728 and 1732, just as Mughal central authority was dissolving and provincial governments were assuming de facto independence, a Persian scholar collaborated with a Brahmin pundit in translating the works of Tusi, Ptolemy and Euclid from Persian or Arabic into Sanskrit, through the medium of their common tongue, Hindavi.[40] Jai Singh himself wrote texts on astronomy in both Persian and Sanskrit, and his direct observations led him to modify astronomical calculations of Ulugh Beg, his Timurid predecessor.[41] Although the raja's modifications of Perso-Arabic astronomical theory hardly represented a scientific breakthrough, his close engagement with Persianate science is nonetheless impressive, as is the stunning effect of his observatories, with their sweeping curves, on the landscapes of Delhi and Jaipur.

## THE LOTUS AND THE LION

When considering the pre-colonial evidence in such fields as architecture, art, language, literature, religion or the sciences, one might ask whether the Sanskritic universe had assimilated its Persianate counterpart, or whether it had been the other way around. But perhaps the question is misplaced. At the moment of their initial encounter, to be sure, each literary tradition and the fields it elaborated were mutually opposed in nearly every respect. That was certainly how it seemed to the eleventh-century Persian polymath Abu Rayhan al-Biruni (d. 1048), who registered one of the most thoughtful and articulate responses to the Sanskrit world ever voiced by an educated Persian. Having travelled extensively in north India, learnt Sanskrit and immersed himself in the study of all aspects of Indian culture, Biruni wrote a comprehensive survey of Indian knowledge, *Kitab ta'rikh al-Hind*, at the dawn of the encounter between the Persianate and Sanskritic worlds. The book's very first chapter emphasized the stark opposition he perceived between the Indian scholarly and cultural universe and his own, which had synthesized Greek, Arabic and

Persian intellectual traditions.[42] And yet already in 1027 Biruni's own patron, Mahmud of Ghazni, minted coins bearing a Sanskrit translation of the Islamic confession of faith in which the Prophet Muhammad was presented as an *avatar* of God, translated as *avyaktam*, 'the Unmanifested'.[43] By using Sanskrit terms that roughly approximated the meaning of the Arabic, Mahmud was already blurring two very different theological spheres.

Six hundred years later, however, the process of mutual acculturation had proceeded to the extent that many ordinary Indians reflexively combined these worlds in their ritual practices. In the early seventeenth century, Jahangir noted that 'crowds on crowds of the people of Islam' travelled long distances to bring offerings and pray at the stone image in the temple of Bajreśwari Devi near the Kangra fort in present-day Himalchal Pradesh.[44] In the same century, it was natural for educated elites to view India's history and material culture through the prism of universal kingship, rather than that of specific religions. Chandar Bhan's seventeenth-century history of the kings of Delhi seamlessly connected the Mughals and Delhi sultans to their north Indian royal predecessors, something Biruni could never have imagined.[45] Shortly after 1596 Bijapur's ambassador to Ahmadnagar, the Iran-born Rafi' al-Din Shirazi, visited the famous rock-cut temples and monasteries at Ellora in the north-western Deccan. Comparing the site to the palaces of Persepolis, the ceremonial capital of ancient Persian emperors that he knew from having grown up nearby, Shirazi viewed Ellora's monuments as a past record of dynastic royalty, the same way that Chandar Bhan perceived Indian history. Accordingly, the ambassador understood the Kailash Temple to be a monument depicting the court life of some ancient Indian king, and its statue of Śiva to be a stone portrait of a royal figure.[46]

Works of architecture and literature also reflect the extent to which, from the late sixteenth century onwards, the Persianate and Indic cultural spheres lost the stark polarity that had seemed so obvious to Biruni. The kingdom of Orchha had been a tributary state of the Mughals since the 1570s. As a Rajput chief assimilated into the Mughal ruling class, Orchha's ruler, Bir Singh, lavishly incorporated Indo-Timurid, Vaishnava and Rajput motifs into the monuments he patronized, such as the Keśavadeva Temple in Mathura or the Jahangir Mahal in Orchha itself. Meanwhile, Akbar's alliance with Rajput houses, and the presence of high-ranking Rajput women in the Mughal harem, had brought the dialect of Hindavi spoken in the region south of Delhi – Brajbhasha (or Braj) – into the heart of the imperial court. By the late sixteenth century, both Hindu and Muslim poets of Braj enjoyed Mughal patronage.[47] A pivotal figure in this movement was Bir Singh's court poet, Keshavdas (fl. 1580–1612), who, instead of writing in Sanskrit as his ancestors had done, pioneered a refined, courtly style of Braj that incorporated protocols and genres from classical Sanskrit literature.

As seventeenth- and eighteenth-century writers of Braj literature moved from court to court seeking patrons across the Mughal realm, their dialect of Hindavi became increasingly cosmopolitan in nature. And since courtliness in India was largely an imitative behaviour, courts naturally responded to what other, higher-status courts were doing. So when the Mughals, as north India's supreme lords, began promoting distinctive styles in domains such as manuscript painting, architecture or courtly Braj literature, their Rajput allies, who served as imperial *mansabdar*s across north India and the Deccan, imitated those same styles.[48] In this way, the Mughals' patronage and stamp of excellence proved critical for the success of classical Hindi, meaning that the Rajput–Mughal alliance was as much a literary as a political phenomenon.[49] On the other hand, the success of vernacular Braj as a literary form carried serious implications for the patronage and usage of Sanskrit. Keshavdas and his many successors in seventeenth- and eighteenth-century India contributed to a larger process by which Braj, by appropriating Sanskrit style, began to encroach upon the cultural space that Sanskrit had once monopolized, eventually usurping its place and rendering the classical language increasingly irrelevant.[50]

Persian in India would experience a fate similar to that of Sanskrit, though somewhat later and for very different reasons. Critical to this process was the reception of Europe's 'one nation, one language' ideology in nineteenth-century Iran and India, and the rise of nationalist movements in both countries. In Iran, Persian was vigorously promoted as that country's national language, for which purpose classical poets such as Firdausi were appropriated as proto-national Iranian poets. This seriously compromised Persian's former status as a trans-regional, cosmopolitan medium, thereby eroding an historic cultural bridge between India and Iran. In India, meanwhile, Persian experienced a precipitous drop in patronage following the final collapse of the Mughal empire in 1858 and the subsequent rise of Indian nationalism. Unlike Persian in Iran, Sanskrit could not be nationalized since it was not commonly spoken anywhere. However, as Delhi's economic and political importance continued to decline after the mid eighteenth century, many of the city's poets migrated to the empire's former provinces – Bengal, Bihar, Awadh, Punjab, Hyderabad – where they acquired students wishing to emulate the new metropolitan poetic style called *rekhtah*. Written in Persian script and appropriating Persian literary models, this new style was composed in the vernacular dialect of the Delhi region and evoked the lustre of the Mughals' remembered, glorious past. In particular, it was associated with the prestige of their imperial capital in Delhi, or *urdu*, by which name the language would be known.[51]

In this way, between the mid eighteenth and the late nineteenth centuries, two great transregional languages, which for centuries had defined the Sanskritic and Persianate worlds, became artefacts in India, eclipsed in the north by new literary genres in dialects of spoken Hindavi – prominently Braj and Urdu.[52] And yet, although the patronage of Sanskrit and Persian literature and the usage of the two languages receded dramatically, the values, sentiments and ideas sustained through their respective literary traditions had become deeply enmeshed over the course of nearly a millennium of mutual interaction. It would take the efforts of later generations to reverse that process.

## TOWARDS MODERNITY

Contrary to the claims of British imperial propagandists or apologists, modernity in India did not commence with the arrival of European merchants or colonial rulers. That story goes back to their Mughal predecessors. The reigns of two Mughal emperors in particular – Akbar and 'Alamgir – saw distinctive, but very different, harbingers of what people in the twenty-first century might call modernity. Akbar's reign exhibited a spirit of rational self-control and a nearly obsessive preoccupation with order in all spheres of experience, especially in governance and administration. Abu'l-fazl's monumental imperial gazetteer, the *A'in-i Akbari* or 'Institutes of Akbar' (*c.*1595), shows a determined effort to standardize and impose the most minute regulations over nearly everything: the manner of cleaning matchlock firearms, the daily allowance for feeding mules, the wages for imperial glass-cutters, the rearing and care of pigeons, the expenses for the maintenance of different classes of war-horses, etc. Every plot of the empire's cultivated area was subjected to careful surveys using standard units of measurement. Corruption, while endemic in most large state systems, was minimized by the Mughals' promoting an ethic of efficiency, while standard monetary units – the silver rupee, the gold *muhr* and the copper *dam* – helped regularize the most basic of governmental functions: the collection of revenue. Record-keeping from Akbar's reign onwards was meticulous, as strict rules were established for maintaining data and auditing accounts. Soldiers under the charge of a *mansabdar* were listed by name, place of residence, age, race and physical descriptions; war-horses were carefully identified by their types and their distinguishing features – all with a view to promoting military efficiency.[53]

The imperial court's endeavour to set the tone for an empire-wide ethos of discipline and rational order is neatly epitomized by a water-clock that Akbar maintained in his palace in Fatehpur Sikri. There, orderlies would strike loud bronze gongs as each quarter-hour had elapsed. 'These water-clocks', noted a Jesuit Father then residing at the court:

> consist of a brazen vessel filled with water, and a hollow bronze cone of such a size that exactly a quarter of an hour is taken for the water to fill it through a small hole in the bottom. This cone is placed on the top of the vessel filled with water, and the water runs in through the hole in its bottom. When the cone is full, it sinks, and thus shows that a quarter of an hour has elapsed. *Everything that goes on in the palace is regulated by this clock.*[54]

The preoccupation with efficient management of time, with discipline and with control suggests an attempt to impose an ethos of rational order on the world. Accompanying this sensibility was a new sort of secularism. Sultanates dating to ninth-century Central Asia had in principle divided a state's political and religious spheres between the sultan and the caliph respectively. But chronicles going back to the reigns of the Delhi sultans had nonetheless manipulated historical anecdotes to show a deep divine intervention in human affairs. In the writings of prominent Mughal literati from the late sixteenth century onwards, however, human agency was understood as having replaced divine agency. Only the Mughals rationalized their empire by applying this secular outlook to the religious traditions of their subjects.[55]

Despite such indicators of modernity, however, Akbar immersed himself in the cult of sacred kingship inherited from his Timurid patrimony.[56] In this view it was the Mughal emperor, endowed with semi-divine attributes, who conceptually linked the mundane world of everyday life to the spiritual world. Akbar's messianic identity was reinforced by the atmosphere of anticipation leading up to the close of the first Islamic millennium, which occurred in 1591, the thirty-fifth year of his reign. By that time, the emperor was presenting himself as a charismatic millennial sovereign, as well as the Perfect Man as elaborated in Sufi discourse, reinforced by his association with light, Illuminationist philosophy and Zoroastrian thought. All this meant that, paradoxically, Akbar's regime exhibited both the premodern sensibility of sacred kingship *and* the modern sensibility of a rationally ordered universe, as manifested in his court's culture and administration.

In contrast, 'Alamgir rejected, at least in principle, the cult of sacred kingship inherited from his Timurid predecessors. As prince, Aurangzeb had commanded a large Mughal army sent deep into Central Asia to fulfil his father's fantasy of conquering the heartland of Timur's former empire, thereby affirming the emperor's claim to being the 'Second Lord of the Conjunction'. But the expedition failed spectacularly, owing mainly to the logistical impossibility of holding territory so far from India. Although this failure did not shake Shah Jahan's belief in his own sacred status, it was his son who had to trudge through bitter winter snows high in the Hindu Kush Mountains, where 5,000 soldiers under his command froze to death. In the first instance, the debacle contributed to the prince's growing estrangement from his father. More fundamental was his rejection of the ideology of sacred kingship that had informed his father's policies, including the Central Asian campaign. Aurangzeb also had to distance himself politically and ideologically from his brother Dara Shukoh, his bitter rival for the Peacock Throne. Lacking military competence or administrative experience, Dara had enthusiastically embraced his father's potent ideology of sacred kingship, which he mistakenly felt would carry him to power in the 1658–9 War of Succession. Most decisive, however, was Aurangzeb's conviction, formed already while governor of Gujarat, that the cult of sacred kingship was incapable of countering or absorbing anti-state movements that were millennial in nature.

After winning the throne, therefore, 'Alamgir endeavoured to replace Dara's and his ancestors' cult of sacred kingship with something entirely new in Mughal history. Instead of a state that pivoted on a charismatic, sacred emperor, he tried to establish an impersonal polity governed by the rule of law, for which purpose he gave sweeping powers to the Mughal judiciary and patronized the production of the *Fatawa-i 'Alamgiri,* a comprehensive and authoritative legal compendium of Hanifi Sunni Islam that was promulgated throughout the empire. This effort not only marked a radical departure from the past; it also had a decidedly modern ring to it, since such a state would have effectively desacralized a world believed to be charged with spiritual presence and energy.[57] But the emperor's lofty project ultimately failed. For one thing, the sort of judicial state he apparently envisioned could be successfully implemented only by efficient and honest subordinates, and 'Alamgir was served by all-too-human officials who, like the venal functionaries who collected *jizya* taxes, were immersed in local politics, petty power struggles, bribery and corruption.

Moreover, any transition from the idea of sacred kingship to the rule of law was too drastic a move to have been accomplished even in 'Alamgir's long reign. Most of his subjects yearned for a sovereign who mediated human and sacred realities. In fact, the emperor himself occasionally found it expedient to draw upon the deep reservoir of sacred kingship that was his inheritance, as when he was thought to have calmed a raging river by casting on it pieces of paper on which he had written prayers, or when his troops faced down rebels with banners on which he had personally inscribed prayers and magic symbols. Perceiving such actions as miraculous, ordinary subjects hailed him as a living saint (*'Alamgir, zinda pir*). In short, the emperor could not shake off a ruling ideology so deeply entrenched among his dynastic predecessors and his own subjects. Yet he had at least envisioned a break with the sacred kingship of the premodern past, wherein lay the seeds of modern statehood. In this way his efforts prefigured modern movements of political Islam; they would go on to have a profound effect on South Asian modernity.[58]

In very different ways, then, the long, half-century reigns of both Akbar and 'Alamgir set India on a path towards modernity well before European colonial rule took hold in South Asia. The former sovereign established principles of efficiency, discipline and rational order at every level of governance, and the latter laid out a vision of a state run by the impersonal rule of law rather than the whims of a sacred sovereign. Yet, for all its rationality, Akbar's reign remained deeply invested in the premodern mould of the sacred king, and for all his dedication to the principle of a judicial state, 'Alamgir was let down by his own corrupt officials, and on occasion found it expedient to invoke his inherited status as sacred king.

Still, by the beginning of the eighteenth century critical foundations of modern South Asia had been put in place. Also in place by then, of course, was India's highly advanced textile-manufacturing sector, which was already clothing much of Europe, Africa and Asia. That sector would soon draw India into ever-tighter economic and political relationships with the rest of the world, and with the rest of world history.

# Notes

## INTRODUCTION

1. D. S. Richards (trans.), *The Chronicle of Ibn al-Athir for the Crusading Period from al-Kamil fi'l-Ta'rikh* (Aldershot: Ashgate, 2006–8, 3 vols), vol. 3, p. 13.

2. *Economist* (12 Dec. 1981), p. 48. Cited in Faisal Devji, *Muslim Zion: Pakistan as a Political Idea* (Cambridge, MA: Harvard University Press, 2013), p. 4.

3. Cynthia Talbot, *The Last Hindu Emperor: Prithviraj Chauhan and the Indian Past, 1200–2000* (New York: Cambridge University Press, 2016), pp. 35–6.

4. Ibid., p. 42; idem, 'Inscribing the Other, Inscribing the Self: Hindu-Muslim Identities in Pre-Colonial India', *Comparative Studies in Society and History* 37, no. 4 (1995), pp. 704–10. For contemporaries it was not religion that ordered the world, but a heightened awareness of insider vs outsider. Such a perspective demonized foreigners in much the same way that ancient Greeks had demonized non-Greek-speakers, in the process inventing, for Europeans, the notion of the barbarian Other. See Romila Thapar, 'The Image of the Barbarian in Early India', *Comparative Studies in Society and History* 13, no. 4 (Oct. 1971), pp. 408–36.

5. Sir Henry M. Elliot, *Bibliographical Index to the Historians of Muhammedan India* (1850; repr. Delhi: Idarah-i Adabiat-i Delli, 1976), Preface, p. xvii. This Preface was reproduced in H. M. Elliot and John Dowson (eds), *The History of India as Told by Its Own Historians* (1867–77; repr. Delhi: Kitab Mahal, 1964, 8 vols), vol. 1, p. xxi.

6. Elliot, *Bibliographical Index*, pp. viii, xx; Elliot and Dowson (eds), *History*, vol. 1, pp. xvi, xxii.

7. James Mill, *The History of British India* (London: Baldwin, Craddock and Joy, 1817).

8. Manan Ahmed Asif, *A Book of Conquest: The* Chachnama *and Muslim Origins in South Asia* (Cambridge, MA: Harvard University Press, 2016), p. 7.

9. Aditya Behl, ed. Wendy Doniger, *Love's Subtle Magic: An Indian Islamic Literary Tradition, 1379–1543* (New York: Oxford University Press, 2012), p. 3.

10. The same pattern extends to archaeology, a discipline bedevilled by the assumption that a given artefact indicates a particular religious identity, and that the use of such an artefact, once identified as 'Hindu' or 'Muslim', was confined to a particular historical period, such as 'Rajput' or 'Sultanate'. See Supriya Varma and Jaya Menon, 'Archaeology and the Construction of Identities in Medieval North India', *Studies in History* 24, no. 2 (2008), pp. 173–93.

11. See Behl, *Love's Subtle Magic*.

12. Sheldon Pollock, 'The Sanskrit Cosmopolis, AD 300–1300: Transculturation, Vernacularization, and the Question of Ideology', in J. E. M. Houben (ed.), *Ideology and Status of Sanskrit: Contributions to the History of the Sanskrit Language* (Leiden: Brill, 1996), p. 230; idem, *The Language of the Gods in the World of Men: Sanskrit, Culture, and Power in Premodern India* (Berkeley: University of California Press, 2006), pp. 10–19, 226–36, 274–80. See also Yigal Bronner, Whitney Cox and Lawrence McCrea (eds), *South Asian Texts in History: Critical Engagements with Sheldon Pollock* (Ann Arbor: Association for Asian Studies, 2011).

13. 'Persianate' is an adjectival construction analogous to Germanic, Latinate, Italianate, Hellenic, Indic, Hispanic, etc., all of which refer to the wide range of culture derived from, or based on, a particular language or literary tradition. Its acceptance in academic and publishing circles is seen in the many book, series and journal titles that have appeared since around 2010, and which foreground the term.

14. See Owen Cornwall, 'Alexander and the Persian Cosmopolis, 1000–1500' (PhD dissertation, Columbia University, 2016). 'Whereas the medieval European Alexander romance traditions were about faraway places,' notes Cornwall, 'the Persian Alexander epics were about home and the process of making home into the world. Many of the cities Alexander founded were in the Persian cosmopolis. Alexander's journeys, therefore, had immediate referents and political consequences. For medieval European readers, Alexander's encounters with Brahmins in India would have seemed impossibly far away. In medieval India, on the other hand, Muslim rulers encountered Brahmins every day.' Ibid., p. 12.

15. Rebecca K. Gould, 'How Newness Enters the World: The Methodology of Sheldon Pollock', *Comparative Studies of South Asia, Africa, and the Middle East* 28, no. 3 (2008), p. 547.

16. David Morgan, 'Persian as a Lingua Franca in the Mongol Empire', in Brian Spooner and William L. Hanaway (eds), *Literacy in the Persianate World: Writing and the Social Order* (Philadelphia: University of Pennsylvania Museum of Archaeology and Anthropology, 2012), pp. 161, 166.

17. Ann K. S. Lambton, 'Justice in the Medieval Persian Theory of Kingship', *Studia Islamica* 17 (1962), p. 100.

18. Vasundhara Filliozat, *l'Épigraphie de Vijayanagara du début à 1377* (Paris: École française d'Extrême-Orient, 1973), pp. 134–6. *Mysore Archaeological Reports*, no. 90 (1929), pp. 159 ff.

19. Khaliq Ahmad Nizami, *Royalty in Medieval India* (New Delhi: Munshiram Manoharlal, 1997), p. xi.

20. Phillip B. Wagoner, *Tidings of the King: A Translation and an Ethnohistorical Analysis of the* Rayavacakamu (Honolulu: University of Hawaii, 1993), p. 95.

21. The notion of justice found no exact counterpart in Sanskrit. The term for 'justice' used by Baddena is *nyaayam*, a Sanskrit term usually used in the sense of 'logic', 'reason' or 'principle'. It can carry the sense of 'justice' in *dharma-śastra* literature when court cases and lawsuits are discussed. But these seem to be secondary, more specialized meanings. Until Baddena, the term was never elevated to the status of *the* fundamental principle of statecraft.

22. Daud Ali, 'The Historiography of the Medieval in South Asia', *Journal of the Royal Asiatic Society* 22, no. 1 (Jan. 2012), p. 11.

## CHAPTER 1: THE GROWTH OF TURKIC POWER, 1000–1300

1. Richard Davis, *Lives of Indian Images* (Princeton: Princeton University Press, 1997), pp. 51–93 *passim*.

2. Edward Sachau (trans.), *Alberuni's India: An Account of the Religion, Philosophy, Literature, Geography, Chronology, Astronomy, Customs, Laws, and Astrology of India, about AD 1030* (New Delhi: S. Chand & Co., 1964, 2 vols in 1), vol. 2, p. 103.

3. For a survey of how Mahmud's raid on Somnath has been treated by successive generations over the past millennium, and by different literary and religious traditions, see Romila Thapar, *Somanatha: The Many Voices of History* (London: Verso, 2005).

4. Davis, *Lives*, pp. 201–10.

5. *Kautilya's Arthaśastra*, trans. R. Shamasastry (5th edn, Mysore: Śri Raghuveer Printing Press, 1956), ch. 16, p. 340; *The Laws of Manu*, trans. G. Buhler (Oxford: Clarendon Press, 1886), ch. 7:202, p. 249.

6. H. Krishna Sastri (trans.), *South Indian Inscriptions* (Madras: Government of India, 1920, 37 vols), vol. 3, part 3, no. 205: Tiruvalangadu Copper Plate Inscription, verse 122, p. 425.

7. See *Kautilya's Arthaśastra*, book 6, ch. 2, pp. 289–92; *Laws of Manu*, ch. 7:156–60, p. 241.

8. David Shulman describes Kautilya, the author of the famous second-century manual of Indian statecraft, the *Arthashastra*, as a 'hyper-Machievellian theorist' who 'inhabits a dog-eat-dog kingdom ('fish eat fish' is the usual Indian metaphor) in which no one is above suspicion and everyone is vulnerable to sudden assassination by the vast, shadowy army of secret agents and informers that keeps the state going; ruthless utility in such cases overrides all possible ethical scruples. A principle of unabashed craftiness driven by self-interest applies to all levels of political life; truthfulness is seen, in general, as a mostly irrelevant virtue (or even a fault)'. David Shulman, 'Off with their Heads', *New York Review of Books* 65, no. 6 (5 April, 2018), p. 31.

9. The game of chess also appears to have reached Sasanian Iran from India in the sixth century. Edward G. Browne, *A Literary History of Persia* (1902; repr. Cambridge: Cambridge University Press, 1969, 3 vols), vol. 1, p. 110.

10. R. Champakalakshmi, 'Urbanization from Above: Tanjavur, the Ceremonial City of the Colas', in idem, *Trade, Ideology and Urbanization: South India 300 BC to AD 1300* (New Delhi: Oxford University Press, 1996), pp. 424–41.

11. Sastri (trans.), *South Indian Inscriptions* vol. 3, part 3, no. 205: Tiruvalangadu Copper Plate Inscription, verses 109–10, p. 424.

12. Y. Gopala Reddy, 'The Feudal Element in the Western Chalukyan Polity', in M. S. Nagaraja Rao (ed.), *The Chalukyas of Kalyana (Seminar Papers)* (Bangalore: The Mythic Society, 1983), pp. 115–20.

13. Referring to the imperial Cholas, Upinder Singh writes, 'There is an inverse correlation between the power of kings and the inscriptional references to chieftains. In the early 11th century, at the midpoint of Rajaraja Chola's reign, an increase in centralization led to a corresponding decline in inscriptional references to chiefs. In the late 11th century, especially after the reign of Kulottunga I (1070–1122), there was a rise in the number of such references, indicating an increase in their power

as the Chola monarchy declined.' Upinder Singh, *A History of Ancient and Early Medieval India: From the Stone Age to the 12th Century* (Upper Saddle River, NJ: Pearson Education, 2008), p. 562.

14. P. Arundhati, *Royal Life in Manosollasa* (Delhi: Sundeep Prakashan, 1994), p. 66.

15. Davis, *Lives*, pp. 51-83 *passim*.

16. See Romila Thapar, Harbans Mukhia and Bipan Chandra, *Communalism and the Writing of Indian History* (Delhi: People's Publishing House, 1969), pp. 14, 31; Michael Willis, 'Religion and Royal Patronage in north India', in Vishaka N. Desai and Darlielle Mason (eds), *Gods, Guardians, and Lovers: Temple Sculptures from North India, 700-1200* (New York: Asia Society Galleries, 1993), p. 59. The same pattern continued after the Turkish conquest of India. In the 1460s, Kapilendra, the founder of the Suryavamshi Gajapati dynasty in Orissa, sacked both Śaiva and Vaishnava temples in the Kaveri delta in the course of wars of conquest in the Tamil country. See Phillip B. Wagoner, *Tidings of the King: A Translation and Ethnohistorical Analysis of the* Rayavacakamu (Honolulu: University of Hawaii, 1993), p. 146. Somewhat later, in 1514, Krishna Raya looted an image of Bala Krishna from Udayagiri, which he had defeated and annexed to his growing Vijayanagara state. See Davis, *Lives*, pp. 65, 67.

17. Willis, 'Religion and Royal Patronage', p. 59.

18. Cited in J. D. Latham, 'The Archers of the Middle East: The Turco-Iranian Background', *Iran* 8 (1970), p. 97.

19. André Wink, *al-Hind: The Making of the Indo-Islamic World*, vol 2: *The Slave Kings and the Islamic Conquest, 11th-13th Centuries* (Leiden: Brill, 1997), pp. 80-84.

20. India was not the only object of Mahmud's plundering raids, however. When he captured Ray, near modern Teheran, his army carried off 260,000 dinars of coined money, 30,000 dinars' worth of gold and silver vessels and half a million dinars' worth of jewels. C. E. Bosworth, *The Ghaznavids: Their Empire in Afghanistan and Eastern Iran, 994-1040* (1963; repr. Delhi: Munshiram Manoharlal, 1992), pp. 78-9.

21. John S. Deyell, *Living Without Silver: The Monetary History of Early Medieval North India* (Delhi: Oxford University Press, 1990), p. 57.

22. 'In modern parlance,' writes Ilker Evrim Binbaş, 'an informal intellectual network is based on personal contact, communication, or correspondence between the participants. The members of an informal network often share similar philosophical, political, ideological,

religious, and aesthetic sensibilities. The exchange of letters or pamphlets, the commitment to a methodological principle or to the bonds of friendship and family ties, the occasional attention of a particular patron, as well as not infrequent actual encounters among members kept such networks together and functioning . . . Such cases of informal networks . . . are defined mainly by peer-to-peer relationships, hence displaying little or no hierarchical stratification. They were interregional and not territorially bound, a feature that made their participants true cosmopolitans.' Ilker Evrim Binbaş, *Intellectual Networks in Timurid Iran: Sharaf al-Din 'Ali Yazdi and the Islamicate Republic of Letters* (Cambridge: Cambridge University Press, 2016), pp. 8–9.

23. C. E. Bosworth, *The Later Ghaznavids: Splendour and Decay* (New York: Columbia University Press, 1977), p. 66.

24. Ibid., p. 117.

25. Ibid., pp. 65, 101.

26. Ibid., p. 99.

27. Bosworth, *Ghaznavids*, pp. 101, 107, 110.

28. Bosworth, *Later Ghaznavids*, pp. 57–8. A cache of coins found in and near a cave in Pakistan's Mardan District points to the dynasty's desire to integrate Hindu temples into its fiscal and commercial networks. These small copper coins, which were derived from earlier, Hindu Shahi prototypes but also bore Arabic legends referring to Ghaznavid sultans, were locally minted for the evident purpose of enabling pilgrims to make offerings to a temple complex dedicated to the goddess Bhima Devi. Taxes levied on this complex, which was located near a major trade route, would have provided a steady source of revenue for the Ghazanavid state. See Waleed Ziad, ' "Islamic Coins" from a Hindu Temple', *Journal of the Economic and Social History of the Orient* 59 (2016), pp. 618–59.

29. As the renowned political theorist Nizam al-Mulk (d. 1092) succinctly put it, 'One obedient slave is better than three hundred sons; for the latter desire their father's death, the former his master's glory.' Nizam al-Mulk, *The Book of Government, or Rules for Kings: The* Siyar al-muluk, or Siyasat-nama *of Nizam al-Mulk*, trans. Hubert Darke (2nd edn, London: Routledge & Kegan Paul, 1978), p. 117.

30. Mahmud of Ghazni was the first ruler actually to style himself 'sultan', which he did from 1002 onwards. Although his royal predecessors in Central Asia and the Middle East had been titled '*amir*' or '*malik*', the ideology of the sultan had already been formulated by those predecessors, especially the Samanid *amir*s of Bukhara.

31. Fakhr al-Din Razi, *Jami' al-'ulum*, ed. Muhammad Khan Malik al-Kuttab (Bombay: Matba'-i Muzaffari, 1905), p. 207.

32. Ahmet T. Karamustafa, *God's Unruly Friends: Dervish Groups in the Islamic Later Middle Period, 1200–1550* (Salt Lake City: University of Utah Press, 1994).

33. Sunil Kumar, *The Emergence of the Delhi Sultanate, 1192–1286* (New Delhi: Permanent Black, 2007), p. 49.

34. G. Le Strange (trans.), *The Geographical Part of the Nuzhat al-Qulub, Composed by Hamd-Allah Mustaufi of Qazvin in 740 (1340)* (1919; repr. London: Gibb Memorial Trust, 2017), p. 151.

35. 'Abd al-Malik 'Isami, ed. and trans. Agha Mahdi Husain, *Futuhu's Salatin* (Bombay: Asia Publishing House, 1967, 3 vols), vol. 1, p. 148.

36. Owing to the significance of the Chauhan dynasty's defeat at the hands of Muhammad Ghuri, the life of Prithviraj has been the subject of many different tellings over the centuries. For a study of these different constructions of his life, and what they tell us about South Asian history, see Cynthia Talbot, *The Last Hindu Emperor: Prithviraj Chauhan and the Indian Past, 1200–2000* (Cambridge: Cambridge University Press, 2016).

37. Kumar, *Emergence*, p. 51.

38. D. S. Richards (trans.), *The Chronicle of Ibn al-Athir for the Crusading Period from al-Kamil fi'l-Ta'rikh* (Aldershot: Ashgate, 2006–8, 3 vols), vol. 3, p. 48.

39. The earliest historian to identify the sultan in such terms was Minhaj al-Din Juzjani, but he was not writing until 1260, six decades after the conquest. More importantly, he was writing in the immediate aftermath of the Mongol holocaust, which had driven countless traumatized refugees like himself out of Central Asia to the security of India. For him, India was construed as a 'Muslim territory', made so by the religio-military exertions of Muhammad Ghuri, who was thus retroactively construed as a *ghazi*. Michael O'Neal, 'The Ghurid Empire: Warfare, Kingship, and Political Legitimacy in Eastern Iran and Northern India' (Master's thesis, Tel Aviv University, 2013), p. 215.

40. See Richard M. Eaton, 'Temple Desecration and Indo-Muslim States', in Sunil Kumar (ed.), *Demolishing Myths or Mosques and Temples? Readings on History and Temple Desecration in Medieval India* (New Delhi: Three Essays, 2008), pp. 93–139. There is no evidence that the Ghurids carried off religious images as war trophies, as Mahmud of Ghazni had done at Somnath, or as Indian rajas often did after defeating their Indian rivals.

41. O'Neil, 'Ghurid Empire', p. 213.
42. Kumar, *Emergence*, p. 113.
43. Finbarr B. Flood, *Objects of Translation: Material Culture and Medieval 'Hindu-Muslim' Encounter* (Princeton: Princeton University Press, 2009), pp. 111, 119.
44. Richards (trans.), *Chronicle of Ibn al-Athir*, vol. 3, pp. 59–60.
45. Flood, *Objects*, p. 117.
46. Similarly, whereas the dynasty's monuments in Afghanistan and the Indus valley conformed to the architectural conventions of that region (baked brick, blue glazes, stucco), those they patronized in north India followed the region's building traditions – carved stone, post-and-beam construction rather than arches and domes, embellishments of carved ornamentation, vegetal motifs, etc. This was due, in part, to the employment of Indian stonemasons on the worksites of sultanate monuments. Architects commissioned by Muhammad Ghuri, his slave commanders and their successors also deployed in their monuments newly carved stone columns that emulated those that were reused from Hindu or Jain structures. This suggests that these rulers consciously adapted themselves to north India's aesthetic environment. Ibid., pp. 137, 164, 180.
47. Unlike his contemporaries in Delhi, Lahore or Multan, Bakhtiyar Khalaji had not been one of Muhammad Ghuri's slaves. In fact, the conqueror of Bengal was not even one of the Ghurids' leading commanders. Hailing from a humble, pastoral background in southern Afghanistan, Bakhtiyar Khalaji actually failed to pass muster by the sultan's recruiters both in Ghazni and in Delhi. Yet in the early thirteenth century the political situation in the Gangetic plain was so unstable, the demand for armed personnel so great, and Bengal so remote from the centre of Ghurid operations in upper India, that someone of even middling abilities or of relatively low standing in the Ghurids' social world could make a mark for himself. When news of Bakhtiyar Khalaji's successes in eastern India reached his Afghan homelands, Khalaji kinsmen joined him and provided him with yet more resources. Finally, in 1204 he surprised and defeated the most prominent ruler in the Bengal delta, Lakshmana Sena, handing the Ghurid leadership yet another conquest in the Indian theatre. Kumar, *Emergence*, pp. 71–3.
48. One of these chroniclers was 'Ali Kufi, who completed his regional history of Sind, the *Chachnama*, in 1226. This Persian chronicle has been read as an attempt to legitimize Turkish authority in India generally,

and specifically Qubacha's independent sultanate based on Uch, which lasted until his death in 1228. See Manan Ahmed Asif, *A Book of Conquest: The* Chachnama *and Muslim Origins in South Asia* (Cambridge, MA: Harvard University Press, 2016).

49. Actually, his rise to power echoed that of the slave Sabuktigin, founder of the Ghaznavid sultanate, who married the daughter of his former master, Alptigin – a precedent that Iltutmish's contemporaries would have remembered. Such matrimonial measures lent both Sabuktigin and Iltutmish at least a semblance of dynastic continuity between their former masters and themselves.

50. 'Isami, *Futuhu's Salatin*, vol. 2, pp. 220–21. Cf. A. S. Usha (ed.), *Futuhus-Salatin by Isami* (Madras: University of Madras, 1948), p. 110. Notwithstanding these arguments made to Yildiz, Iltutmish himself would strenuously endeavour to start a dynasty by leaving the throne of Delhi to his own progeny.

51. Nilanjan Sarkar, 'An Urban Imaginaire, ca. 1350: A Capital City in Ziya al-Din Barani's Fatawa-i Jahandari', *Indian Economic and Social History Review* 48, no. 3 (2011), p. 408.

52. Kumar, *Emergence*, pp. 196–7.

53. Ibid., p. 201.

54. Sunil Kumar, 'Transitions in the Relationship between Political Elites and the Sufis: The thirteenth- and fourteenth-century Delhi Sultanate', in N. Karashima (ed.), *State Formation and Social Integration in Pre-Modern South and Southeast Asia: A Comparative Study of Asian Society* (Tokyo: Toyo Bunko, 2017), p. 210. For example, deep in central Punjab and far from the court in Delhi, a government official tried to prohibit the use of music and dance at the lodge of Shaikh Farid al-Din, but failed owing to the Sufi's immense influence among the local population.

55. Flood, *Objects*, pp. 248–50.

56. Kumar, *Emergence*, pp. 243–63.

57. The relationship between the two men was complex, not least because Nasir al-Din had married Ulugh Khan's daughter, making the sultan the son-in-law of his own slave!

58. Ibid., pp. 286, 335–7.

59. Mohammad Habib (trans.), *The Political Theory of the Delhi Sultanate (Including a Translation of Ziauddin Barani's* Fatawa-i Jahandari, *Circa 1358–9 AD* (Allahabad: Kitab Mahal, *c.*1965), p. 48.

60. Pushpa Prasad, *Sanskrit Inscriptions of Delhi Sultanate, 1191–1526* (Delhi: Oxford University Press, 1990), pp. 3–15.

61. Amir Hasan Sijzi, who resided in Delhi between 1308 and 1322, wrote: 'The son of Khwaja Rukn al-din, the venerable Chishti saint ... was taken captive during the onslaught of the infidel Mongols ... During the Mongol onslaught, the infidels of Chinghiz Khan turned toward India. At that time, Qutb al-din counseled his friends, "Flee, for these people will overpower you". When the Mongols reached Nishapur, its ruler summoned Shaykh Farid ad-din 'Attar ... and asked the Shaykh to petition God ... It was then that I heard the report from Ghazna: the Mongols had reached that city and martyred my mother, father, and all of my close relations ... As the Lahore traders were making their way home, they were informed *en route* that the Mongols had invaded their city and reduced it to rubble.' Bruce B. Lawrence (trans.), *Morals for the Heart: Conversations of Shaykh Nizam ad-din Awliya, recorded by Amir Hasan Sijzi* (New York: Paulist Press, 1992), pp. 99, 101, 142, 165, 216.

62. The decline had already set in by the middle of the first millennium across India. Although some Buddhist pilgrimage centres persisted in the south and west until as late as the fifteenth century, by the year 1000 monastic Buddhism had been eclipsed and replaced by Hindu and Jain institutions. In the north-west, too, most Buddhist monasteries and pilgrimage sites had been abandoned by that time. Lars Fogelin, *An Archaeological History of Indian Buddhism* (New York: Oxford University Press, 2015), pp. 218–19.

63. Around AD 400 the pilgrim Faxian counted twenty-two monasteries in Tamralipti, a seaport on the Bay of Bengal. By around 637, Xuanzang counted ten monasteries there. By 685, that figure had dropped to just five or six, as recorded by a third Chinese pilgrim, Yijing. Samuel Beal (trans.), *Chinese Accounts of India: Translated from the Chinese of Hiuen Tsiang* (Calcutta: Susil Gupta, 1958, 4 vols), vol. 4, pp. 403, 407, 408; J. Takakasu (trans.), *A Record of the Buddhist Religion as Practiced in India and the Malay Archipelago (AD 671–695) by I-tsing* (Delhi: Munshiram Manoharlal, 1966), p. xxxiii.

64. See Wink, *al-Hind*, vol. 2, pp. 146–8, 334–51. By the eleventh and twelfth centuries, these kings gradually withdrew their patronage from these institutions, favouring Hindu temples instead. During those centuries, most of the art patronized by kings of the Pala dynasty was Brahmanic in subject matter, with Vaishnava themes outnumbering the rest three to one. Susan L. Huntington, *The 'Pala-Sena' Schools of Sculpture* (Leiden: Brill, 1984), pp. 155, 179, 201.

65. Those that escaped attack – such as Somapura in Bengal, or Lalitagiri, Udayagiri and Ratnagiri in Orissa – were soon abandoned by their

resident monks owing to disruptions in the flow of land revenues on which they had grown dependent. Fogelin, *Archaeological History*, p. 222. For a provocative analysis of the issue, which argues that Brahmanical classes took advantage of the Turkish conquest in order finally to defeat their ancient Buddhist rivals, see Giovanni Verardi, *Hardships and Downfall of Buddhism in India* (New Delhi: Manohar, 2011). See also Audrey Truschke, 'The Power of the Islamic Sword in Narrating the Death of Indian Buddhism', *History of Religions* 57, no. 4 (May 2018), pp. 406–35.

66. Flood, *Objects*, p. 108.

67. Wink, *al-Hind*, vol. 2, pp. 125, 155.

68. Browne, *Literary History*, vol. 1, pp. 340–41.

69. See Julie Scott Meisami, *Persian Historiography to the End of the Twelfth Century* (Edinburgh: Edinburgh University Press, 1999), pp. 29, 39.

70. Browne, *Literary History*, vol. 2, pp. 145–6.

71. Bahram Shah also patronized the translation of a widely popular collection of animal fables, illustrating an early, fruitful encounter between the Sanskrit and Persian worlds. Composed originally in Sanskrit, the *Panchatantra* had been translated into Middle Persian in the sixth century, then in the eighth century from Middle Persian into Arabic as *Kalila va Dimna*, and around 1145 from Arabic into modern Persian as the *Fables of Bidpai*. Since this occurred just as the Ghaznavid court was about to shift to Lahore, the *Panchatantra* effectively returned to India, though in a Persian guise. See Bosworth, *Later Ghaznavids*, p. 109. Browne adds: 'Few books in the world have achieved so great a success as that of *Kalila and Dimna*, or have been translated into so many languages.' Apart from Arabic and both Middle and Modern Persian, these include Greek, Hebrew, Latin, Spanish, Italian, Slavonic, Turkish, German, English, Danish, Dutch and French. Browne, *Literary History*, vol. 2, p. 350.

72. The fifteenth-century biographer of Persian poets Daulatshah Samarqandi relates that Mahmud was regularly attended by 400 poets, presided over by the poet laureate. Bosworth, *Ghaznavids*, p. 131.

73. By the mid thirteenth century works in that canon included, in addition to those just mentioned that were produced under Ghaznavid patronage, the advice literature of Kai Ka'us (d. 1087), Nizam al-Mulk (d. 1092), and Nizami Aruzi al-Samarqandi (d. 1161), the panygeric poetry of Anvari (d. 1189), the romance literature of Nizami Ganjavi (d. 1209) and the mystical poetry of 'Attar (d. 1221). During Balban's reign there appeared, among other such works, the ethical literature of

Nasir al-Din Tusi and the moral poetry of Sa'di (d. 1291). Although the canon of Persian literature continued to grow, for centuries the works of these important literati continued to be copied in libraries, taught in *madrasa*s and in some cases committed to memory.

74. Solomon I. Baevskii, trans. N. Killian and rev. John R. Perry, *Early Persian Lexicography: Farhangs of the Eleventh to the Fifteenth Centuries* (Folkstone: Global Oriental Ltd, 2007), p. 69.

75. This was *Lubab al-albab*, compiled in 1222 at Uch by Sadid al-Din Muhammad 'Aufi (d. *c.*1252). Browne, *Literary History*, vol. 2, p. 478.

## CHAPTER 2: THE DIFFUSION OF SULTANATE SYSTEMS, 1200-1400

1. The Chola army that marched from the Tamil country north to Bengal in 1025, mentioned in the previous chapter, avoided the Vindhyas by hugging the low, eastern coastline.

2. 'It is advisable', he said, 'that during this year, the sublime standards should be put in motion for the purpose of ravaging and carrying on holy war in the extreme parts of the territory of Hindustan, in order that ... booty may fall into the hands of the troops of Islam, and means to repel the infidel Mughals [Mongols], in the shape of wealth, may be amassed.' Minhaj-ud-Din, trans. H. G. Raverty, *Tabakat-i-Nasiri* (1881; repr. New Delhi: Oriental Books Reprint Corp., 1970, 2 vols), vol. 2, p. 816.

3. Ziya al-Din Barani, trans. Ishtiyaq Ahmad Zilli, *Tarikh-i Firoz Shahi* (Delhi: Primus Books, 2015), pp. 172-4, 186.

4. Ziya al-Din Barani writes: 'Sultan Ala ud Din succeeded in completely eradicating the Mongol menace and because of the price stability of goods required by the army, the troops were well maintained and territories of the kingdom in all the four corners were brought under complete control with the help of trusted *malik*s and sincere servants, while the rebels and recalcitrant turned obedient. Revenue according to measurement and house tax as well as grazing tax came to be fully accepted by subjects. Rebellions, idle talk and wishful thinking was entirely removed from people.' Ibid., pp. 197-8.

5. Richard M. Eaton and Phillip B. Wagoner, *Power, Memory, Architecture: Contested Sites on India's Deccan Plateau, 1300-1600* (New Delhi: Oxford University Press, 2014), pp. 44-8.

6. Ibn Battuta, trans. Mahdi Husain, *The Rehla of Ibn Battuta* (1953; repr. Baroda: Oriental Institute, 1976), p. 47.

7. Richard M. Eaton, *A Social History of the Deccan, 1300–1761. New Cambridge History of India*, vol. I:8 (Cambridge: Cambridge University Press, 2005), pp. 16–22.

8. On Ulugh Khan's alleged parricide, see Agha Mahdi Husain, *The Rise and Fall of Muhammad bin Tughluq* (Delhi: Idarah-i Adabiyat-i Delli, 1972), pp. 66–74.

9. Eaton and Wagoner, *Power*, pp. 57–61.

10. For Muhammad bin Tughluq's failed schemes, see Barani, *Tarikh*, pp. 291–4.

11. Ibn Battuta, *Rehla*, p. 83. On another occasion an eminent Hindu brought a claim against the sultan that he had killed the plaintiff's brother without just cause. When summoned to appear before the *qazi*, the sultan walked unarmed to the *qazi*'s court, saluted and bowed, having previously sent orders that the *qazi* should not stand up for him upon his arrival. At the court, the sultan stood before the judge, who ordered him to recompense the Hindu plaintiff for having killed his brother, and he did so. Ibid.

12. Ibid., p. 56.

13. Simon Digby, 'Before Timur Came: Provincialization of the Delhi Sultanate through the Fourteenth Century', *Journal of the Economic and Social History of the Orient* 47, no. 3 (2004), p. 309.

14. Ibn Battuta, *Rehla*, p. 45.

15. Digby, 'Before Timur', p. 314.

16. Ibid., p. 306.

17. Ibid., pp. 309–13.

18. Barani, *Tarikh*, p. 117. Curiously, the Persian source that recorded this event referred to these criminals as 'thugs', which is the first time that term is known to have appeared in writing.

19. Shamsud-Din Ahmed (ed. and trans.), *Inscriptions of Bengal,* vol. 4: (*being a Corpus of Inscriptions of the Muslim Rulers of Bengal from 1233 to 1855 A.C.*) (Rajshahi: Varendra Research Museum, 1960), pp. 31–3.

20. *The Book of Marco Polo*, trans. and ed. Henry Yule and Henri Cordier (3rd edn, Amsterdam: Philo Press, 1975, 2 vols), vol. 2, p. 115.

21. Shams-i Siraj 'Afif, *Tarikh-i Firuz Shahi*, in H. M. Elliot and John Dowson (eds), *The History of India as Told by Its Own Historians* (1867–77; repr. Allahabad: Kitab Mahal, 1964, 8 vols), vol. 3, pp. 295, 296.

22. Naseem Ahmed Banerji, *The Architecture of the Adina Mosque in Pandua, India: Medieval Tradition and Innovation*, Mellen Studies in Architecture, vol. 6 (Lewiston, NY: Edwin Mellen Press, 2002).

23. Ahmed, *Inscriptions of Bengal*, p. 20.

24. Ibn Battuta, *Rehla*, p. 44.

25. 'Now,' writes Duncan Derrett, 'acts of terrorism were frequent, patronage had suffered a severe blow, and the land-holders were obliged to oppress the cultivators.' J. Duncan M. Derrett, *The Hoysalas: A Medieval Indian Royal Family* (Madras: Oxford University Press, 1957), p. 148.

26. Ibn Battuta, *Rehla*, p. 96.

27. 'Abd al-Malik 'Isami, ed. and trans. Agha Mahdi Husain, *Futuhu's Salatin* (Bombay: Asia Publishing House, 1967, 3 vols), vol. 3, p. 902.

28. *Vidyaranya Kalajnana*, cited in Phillip B. Wagoner, 'Harihara, Bukka, and the Sultan: the Delhi Sultanate in the Political Imagination of Vijayanagara', in David Gilmartin and Bruce B. Lawrence (eds), *Beyond Turk and Hindu: Rethinking Religious Identities in Islamicate South Asia* (Gainesville: University Press of Florida, 2000), pp. 312-20.

29. Malabar, derived from the Malayalam *mala-baram* (side of a hill), refers to the peninsula's south-western coast along the Arabia Sea, whereas Coromandel, derived from the Tamil *cholamandalam* (realm of the Cholas), refers to its south-eastern coast along the Bay of Bengal.

30. Ibn Battuta, *Rehla*, p. 180.

31. Vasundhara Filliozat, *l'Épigraphie de Vijayanagara du début à 1377* (Paris: École française d'Extrême-Orient, 1973), pp. 134-6. *Mysore Archaeological Reports* no. 90 (1929), pp. 159ff.

32. Filliozat, *l'Épigraphie*, pp. 25-8.

33. Ibid., pp. xxxii, 39-42.

34. 'Ali Tabataba, *Burhan-i ma'athir* (Delhi: Matba'-i Jami'a-yi Dihli, 1936), p. 12.

35. 'Isami, *Futuhu's Salatin*, vol. 3, p. 687.

36. Ibid., vol. 1, p. 13. See also Carl W. Ernst, *Eternal Garden: Mysticism, History, and Politics at a South Asian Sufi Center* (Albany: State University of New York, 1992), p. 119.

37. 'Isami, *Futuhu's Salatin*, vol. 1, p. 13. It is kept in a glass trunk at Zain al-Din Shirazi's shrine in Khuldabad and is brought out for public viewing once each year, on the occasion of the Prophet Muhammad's birthday.

38. Phillip B. Wagoner, 'From "Pampa's Crossing" to "The Place of Lord Virupaksa": Architecture, Cult, and Patronage at Hampi before the Founding of Vijayanagara', in D. Devaraj and C. S. Patil (eds), *Vijayanagara: Progress of Research, 1988-1991* (Mysore: Directorate of Archaeology and Museums, 1996), pp. 141-74.

39. This is seen, especially, in their title *hindu-raya-suratrana*, 'sultan among Indian kings'. See Chapter Four below.

40. Christopher Chekuri, '"Fathers" and "Sons": Inscribing Self and Empire at Vijayanagara, Fifteenth and Sixteenth Centuries', *Medieval History Journal* 15, no. 1 (2012), p. 149. Vijayanagara's assimilation in the Persianate world is further discussed in Chapter Four below.

41. Although of foreign origin, the calendar was made to seem indigenous by simply calling it the *Kashmiri sanah*, or Kashmiri Year. R. K. Parmu, *History of Muslim Rule in Kashmir, 1320–1819* (Delhi: People's Publishing House, 1969), p. 90.

42. Mohammad Ishaq Khan, 'Islam, State and Society in Medieval Kashmir: A Revaluation of Mir Sayyid Ali Hamadani's Historical Role', in Aparna Rao (ed.), *The Valley of Kashmir: The Making and Unmaking of a Composite Culture?* (New Delhi: Manohar, 2008), pp. 152–3.

43. Mohibbul Hasan, *Kashmir Under the Sultans* (Calcutta: Iran Society, 1959), p. 52.

44. Ibid., p. 59. The gesture recalls the tradition of Deccani shaikhs who placed a crown on the head of new Bahmani sultans, an act expressing the belief that worldly sovereignty was the prerogative of spiritually powerful Sufis to dispense to ordinary rulers.

45. Jayalal Kaul, *Lal Ded* (New Delhi: Sahitya Akademi, 1973), p. 131, no. 130.

46. Ibid., p. 110, no. 66.

47. Chitralekha Zutshi, *Kashmir's Contested Pasts: Narratives, Sacred Geographies, and the Historical Imagination* (Oxford: Oxford University Press, 2014), p. 251; Mohammad Ishaq Khan, 'The Impact of Islam on Kashmir in the Sultanate Period (1320–1586)', in R. M. Eaton (ed.), *India's Islamic Traditions: 711–1750* (New Delhi: Oxford University Press, 2003), p. 350.

48. Kaul, *Lal Ded*, p. 61.

49. 'Siva abides in all that is, everywhere; Then do not discriminate between a Hindu or a Musalman. If thou art wise, know thyself; That is true knowledge of the Lord.' Ibid., p. 107.

50. Samira Sheikh, *Forging a Region: Sultans, Traders, and Pilgrims in Gujarat, 1200–1500* (New Delhi: Oxford University Press, 2010), p. 5.

51. S. A. I. Tirmizi, *Some Aspects of Medieval Gujarat* (Delhi: Munshiram Manoharlal, 1968), p. 8.

52. Elizabeth Lambourn, '"A Collection of Merits . . .": Architectural Influences in the Friday Mosque and Kazaruni Tomb Complex at Cambay, Gujarat', *South Asia Studies* 17, no. 1 (2001), p. 136.

53. D. C. Sircar, 'Veraval Inscription of Chaulukya-Vaghela Arujuna, 1264 AD', *Epigraphia Indica* 34 (1961–62), pp. 141, 150.

54. Lambourn, 'Collection of Merits', p. 124.
55. 'The reason', he continued, 'is that the majority of its inhabitants are foreign merchants, who continually build there beautiful houses and wonderful mosques – an achievement in which they endeavor to surpass each other.' Ibn Battuta, *Rehla*, p. 172.
56. S. C. Misra, *The Rise of Muslim Power in Gujarat: A History of Gujarat from 1298 to 1442* (New York: Asia Publishing House, 1963), p. 102.
57. Digby, 'Before Timur', p. 300.

## CHAPTER 3: TIMUR'S INVASION AND LEGACY, 1400–1550

1. Peter Jackson, *The Delhi Sultanate: A Political and Military History* (Cambridge: Cambridge University Press, 1999), p. 323.
2. Simon Digby, 'After Timur Left', in Francesca Orsini and Samira Sheikh (eds), *After Timur Left: Culture and Circulation in Fifteenth-Century North India* (New Delhi: Oxford University Press, 2014), p. 51.
3. Dirk H. A. Kolff, *Naukar, Rajput and Sepoy: The Ethnohistory of the Military Labour Market in Hindustan, 1450–1850* (Cambridge: Cambridge University Press, 1990), p. 32.
4. S. H. Askari, 'The Correspondence of Two Fourteenth-Century Sufi Saints of Bihar with the Contemporary Sovereigns of Delhi and Bengal', *Journal of the Bihar Research Society* 42, no. 2 (1956), p. 187.
5. See Richard M. Eaton, *The Rise of Islam and the Bengal Frontier, 1204–1760* (Berkeley: University of California Press, 1993), pp. 50–53.
6. Ibid., pp. 53–4.
7. Ziauddin Desai, 'Some New Data Regarding the Pre-Mughal Muslim Rulers of Bengal', *Islamic Culture* 32 (1958), p. 204; Abdul Karim, *Corpus of the Muslim Coins of Bengal, down to AD 1538*, Asiatic Society of Pakistan Publication no. 6 (Dacca: Asiatic Society of Pakistan, 1960), p. 77.
8. Shamsud-Din Ahmed (ed. and trans.), *Inscriptions of Bengal*, vol. 4 (Rajshahi: Varendra Research Museum, 1960), p. 45; Karim, *Corpus*, p. 170.
9. Ma Huan, trans. J. V. G. Mills, *Ying-yai Sheng-lan: 'The Overall Survey of the Ocean's Shores'* (Cambridge: Cambridge University Press, 1970), p. 161.
10. Niharranjan Ray, 'Mediaeval Bengali Culture', *Visva-Bharati Quarterly* 11, no. 2 (Aug.–Oct. 1945), p. 54; Md. Enamul Haq, *Muslim Bengali Literature* (Karachi: Pakistan Publications, 1957), pp. 38–9.

11. Nizamuddin Ahmad, trans. Brajendranath De, *Tabaqat-i Akbari* (1939; repr. Delhi: Low Price Publications, 1992, 3 vols), vol. 3, p. 648; Jonaraja, *Rajatarangini*, ed. S. L. Sadhu, trans. J. C. Dutt (New Delhi: Atlantic Publishers & Distributors, 1993), p. 54. It is impossible to know the extent of such desecrations. Writing in 1623, the Mughal emperor Jahangir, who was well acquainted with the valley owing to his own visits there, wrote that 'the lofty temples of Kashmir which were built before the manifestation of Islam are still in existence, and are all built of stones, which from foundation to roof are large, and weigh 30 or 40 mounds, placed one on the other'. Henry Beveridge (ed.), Alexander Rogers (trans.), *The Tuzuk-i-Jahangiri; or, Memoirs of Jahangir* (2nd edn, New Delhi: Munshiram Manoharlal, 1968, 2 vols), vol. 2, p. 150.

12. Michael Witzel, 'The Kashmiri Pandits: Their Early History', in Aparna Rao (ed.), *The Valley of Kashmir: The Making and Unmaking of a Composite Culture?* (New Delhi: Manohar, 2008), p. 91.

13. The Sanskrit poet Jonaraja (d. 1459) is explicit, however, that Sikandar acted only at the instigation (*prerana*) of Suha Bhatta. Jonaraja, notes Luther Obrock, 'carefully absolves the sultan of all guilt and places it upon one man, a man with a peculiar conflict of identity'. Luther Obrock, 'Translation and History: The Development of Kashmiri Textual Tradition from *c.*1000–1500' (PhD dissertation, Berkeley: University of California, 2015), p. 90.

14. Luther Obrock, 'History at the End of History: Śrivara's Jainatarangini', *Indian Economic and Social History Review* 50, no. 2 (2013), pp. 231–2.

15. Rattan Lal Hangloo, 'Mass Conversion in Medieval Kashmir: Academic Perceptions and People's Practice', in Rao (ed.), *Valley of Kashmir*, p. 130.

16. Stan Goron and J. P. Goenka, *The Coins of the Indian Sultanates* (New Delhi: Munshiram Manoharlal, 2001), pp. 467–8.

17. Yigal Bronner, 'From Conqueror to Connoisseur: Kalhana's Account of Jayapida and the Fashioning of Kashmir as a Kingdom of Learning', *Indian Economic and Social History Review* 50, no. 2 (2013), pp. 171–2.

18. Satoshi Ogura, 'Linguistic Cosmopolitanism, Political Legitimacies, and Religious Identities in Shahmirid Kashmir (1339–1561)', Third Perso-Indica Conference, Delhi University (3–4 Sept. 2015), p. 2.

19. Ibid., p. 3. Unfortunately, none of these Persian translations has survived.

20. N. A. Baloch and A. Q. Rafiqi, 'The Regions of Sind, Multan, Baluchistan, and Kashmir', in A. H. Dani and V. M. Masson (eds), *History of Civilisations of Central Asia* (Paris: UNESCO, 1992–2005), vol. 4, part 1, p. 316.

21. Jami's literary classic narrates the passionate love of Zuleikha for Joseph, the biblical patriarch, when the latter was in Egypt as a slave of Zuleikha's husband – a story that in Sufi circles represented the human soul's intense longing for God.

22. *Indian Economic and Social History Review* 50, no. 2 (2013), p. 129.

23. Ogura, 'Linguistic Cosmopolitanism', p. 6.

24. Chitralekha Zutshi, *Kashmir's Contested Pasts: Narratives, Sacred Geographies, and the Historical Imagination* (Oxford: Oxford University Press, 2014), pp. 31, 58.

25. Mohammad Ishaq Khan, 'The Impact of Islam on Kashmir in the Sultanate Period (1320–1586)', in R. M. Eaton (ed.), *India's Islamic Traditions, 711–1750* (New Delhi: Oxford University Press, 2003), p. 350.

26. Braj B. Kachru, 'The Dying Linguistic Heritage of the Kashmiris: Kashmiri Literary Culture and Language', in Rao, *Valley of Kashmir*, p. 310.

27. Ibid.

28. Persian biographies and histories in Kashmir were written in close dialogue with the valley's pre-sultanate mythic history as recorded in Sanskrit traditions. For example, the *Dastur-i salatin*, a mixed prose and verse praise of a certain Shaikh Hamza written in 1554, drew on Sanskrit texts such as the *Nilamata Purana* and Kalhana's *Rajatarangini*, which described the Kashmir valley as originating from a body of water through the divine intervention of the great gods Brahma and Vishnu, with the emergent land being adorned by goddesses in the shape of rivers and pilgrimage sites scattered across the landscape. While the *Dastur* did not specifically mentioned those Hindu deities, it is replete with images of the valley's bodies of water and their resident spirits (*jinn*s), just as pre-Islamic Kashmiri religious beliefs had focused on a landscape littered with sacred springs associated with snake deities (*naga*s), to which nearby pilgrimage sites were dedicated. Zutshi, *Kashmir's Contested Pasts*, p. 39.

29. Sheldon Pollock (ed.), *Literary Cultures in History: Reconstructions from South Asia* (Berkeley: University of California Press, 2003), p. 93.

30. Samira Sheikh, *Forging a Region: Sultans, Traders, and Pilgrims in Gujarat, 1200–1500* (New Delhi: Oxford University Press, 2010), pp. 6, 64.

31. Ibid., pp. 70–71.
32. Ibid., p. 16.
33. Ibid., pp. 91–4.
34. Ibid., pp. 83–4, 118, 148–51.
35. Ibid., pp. 15–16, 68–9.
36. Ibid., p. 130.
37. Ibid., pp. 143, 166, 174.
38. Udayaraja asserted that Mahmud's munificent and prosperous court surpassed in brilliance even those of the gods Indra, Vishnu and Kama, on account of which the goddess Saraswati, after descending to earth, had no desire to return to her heavenly abode. Aparna Kapadia, 'The Last Chakravartin? The Gujarat Sultan as "Universal King" in Fifteenth Century Sanskrit Poetry', *Medieval History Journal* 16, no. 1 (2013), pp. 63–88. See also idem, *In Praise of Kings: Rajputs, Sultans and Poets in Fifteenth-century Gujarat* (Cambridge: Cambridge University Press, 2018), pp. 114–28.
39. In 1423 Hoshang Shah seized the fort of Gagraun after a spectacular instance of the harrowing rite of *jauhar*. Just before the fort fell, its defenders realized their doom and the queens of the fort's chieftain, together with thousands of other women, sacrificed their lives in a fire pit while the men sallied out in a final, desperate fight to their own deaths. Upendra Nath Day, *Medieval Malwa: A Political and Cultural History, 1401–1562* (New Delhi: Munshi Ram Manohar Lal, 1965), p. 50.
40. Ibid., p. 353.
41. Ibid., p. 371. Such dictionaries include the *Adat al-fudala* (1419), *Farhang-i zafanguya u jahanpaya* (1423) and the *Miftah al-fudala* (1468). Dilorom Karomat, 'Turki and Hindavi in the World of Persian: Fourteenth- and Fifteenth-Century Dictionaries', in Orsini and Sheikh (eds), *After Timur Left*, pp. 130–65.
42. Stefano Pellò, 'Local Lexis? Provincializing Persian in Fifteenth-Century North India', in Orsini and Sheikh (eds), *After Timur Left*, p. 170.
43. Razieh Babagolzadeh, 'On Becoming Muslim in the City of Swords: Bhoja and Shaykh Changal at Dhar', *Journal of the Royal Asiatic Society* 22, no. 1 (Jan. 2012), p. 124.
44. Day, *Medieval Malwa*, pp. 213–14.
45. This mosque is commonly known as the 'Bhojsala', reflecting a myth that it had originally been a 'Hall of Sanskrit Learning' erected by the famous ruler of the Paramara dynasty, Bhoja (r. *c*.1000–1055). However, the earliest reference to such a hall dates to 1902. Owing partly to nineteenth-century Orientalist stereotypes about Muslim iconoclasm

in India, and partly to their own spectacular ineptitude, British imperial officers came to the mistaken belief that the mosque had been King Bhoja's Sanskrit college, complete with a shrine and statue of Saraswati, the goddess of learning. See Michael Willis, 'Dhar, Bhoja and Sarasvati: From Indology to Political Mythology and Back', *Journal of the Royal Asiatic Society* 22, no. 1 (Jan. 2012), pp. 136–49.

46. Dhar also had spiritual connections with north India. At the time of the Khalaji conquest in the early fourteenth century Kamal al-Din Malawi (d. 1330), a Sufi shaikh of the Chishti order, migrated to Dhar and was patronized by its first governor. As a disciple of two of India's foremost Sufi shaikhs, Farid al-Din Ganj-i Shakar (d. 1265) and Nizam al-Din Auliya (d. 1325), he, too, represented Delhi's hegemonic presence in the region, for in Malwa, as in other provinces, the diffusion of the sultanate's power had been accompanied by a diaspora of Chishti Sufis. See ibid., pp. 134–5.

47. See Thomas W. Lentz and Glenn D. Lowry, *Timur and the Princely Vision: Persian Art and Culture in the Fifteenth Century* (Los Angeles: Los Angeles County Museum of Art, 1989), pp. 42–3.

48. Michael Brand, 'The Sultanate of Malwa', in Abha Narain Lambah and Alka Patel (eds), *The Architecture of the Indian Sultanates* (Mumbai: Marg Publications, 2006), pp. 85–90; Day, *Medieval Malwa*, p. 386.

49. Brand, 'Sultanate', p. 91.

50. In his *Ma'athir-i Mahmudshahi* (1468), the chronicler Shihab Hakim boasted that the sultanate's artisans had come from north India and Khurasan, then the heartland of Timurid culture. Ibid.

51. The book's accompanying miniature paintings also reveal a hybridized Iranian and central Indian style that anticipated artistic traditions in the sixteenth-century Deccan. Norah M. Titley, *The Ni'matnama Manuscript of the Sultans of Mandu: The Sultan's Book of Delights* (London: Routledge, 2004).

52. The earliest known illustrated manuscript produced in India is another copy of the *Kalpa Sutra*. Dated 1411, this text was also produced in the Malwa sultanate, at Karakara, 150 kilometres north-west of Bhopal. See Milo Cleveland Beach, *Mughal and Rajput Painting. New Cambridge History of India*, vol. I:3 (Cambridge: Cambridge University Press, 1992), pp. 8–9, 229.

53. Daljeet, V. K. Mathur and Rajeshwari Shah, *Fragrance in Colour: Indian Miniature Paintings from the Collection of the National Museum, New Delhi* (New Delhi: National Museum, 2003), pp. 17–18.

The art historian Milo Beach writes that Mandu became indisputably the most active identified centre of book-painting in India until as late as the early sixteenth century. Beach, *Mughal and Rajput*, p. 120.

54. In the prologue (*praśasti*) to this work the author writes: 'Mahmud, the king (*narendra*), the destroyer of the enemy-like mass of darkness, as if with the rays of magnificent sun, who is just like the moon of the sea of Khilchi dynasty, he is victorious.' http://www.jainworld.com/literature/jainhistory/chapter15.asp

55. Often projected back to the twelfth century or even earlier, the term 'Rajput' has been called a 'well-established anachronism'. Jackson, *Delhi Sultanate*, p. 9.

56. Michael B. Bednar, 'Conquest and Resistance in Context: A Historiographical Reading of Sanskrit and Persian Battle Narratives' (PhD dissertation, University of Texas at Austin, 2007), pp. 161–86. Cited in Cynthia Talbot, *The Last Hindu Emperor: Prithviraj Chauhan and the Indian Past, 1200–2000* (Cambridge: Cambridge University Press, 2016), p. 120.

57. These include the *Shajarat al-ansab* by Fakhr-i Mudabbir and the *Tabaqat-i Nasiri* of Juzjani. See Jackson, *Delhi Sultanate*, p. 9.

58. See Michael Boris Bednar, 'Mongol, Muslim, Rajput: Mahimasahi in Persian Texts and the Sanskrit *Hammira-Mahakavya*', *Journal of the Economic and Social History of the Orient* 60, no. 5 (2017), pp. 585–613.

59. Kolff, *Naukar*, pp. 6–7.

60. Ibid., pp. 3, 7.

61. Although north Indian states had regularly recruited mounted archers from beyond India, much larger numbers of infantry or auxiliaries were recruited locally, with the ratio of infantry to cavalry varying from 3:1 to as many as 6:1. See ibid., pp. 22, 51.

62. The pattern persisted even into the twentieth century. During the First World War, Hindu landholders who enlisted in the British Indian Army became Sikhs merely by the act of enlisting, while those who stayed at home remained 'Hindus'. As a British recruiting officer in the Punjab noted at that time, 'It was an almost daily occurrence for – say – Ram Chand [i.e. a Hindu] to enter our office and leave it as Ram Singh – Sikh recruit.' Ibid., p. 58.

63. Sheikh, *Forging*, pp. 15–16.

64. Tanuja Kothiyal, *Nomadic Narratives: A History of Mobility and Identity in the Great Indian Desert* (New Delhi: Cambridge University Press, 2016), p. 97.

65. Bardic sources dating to fifteenth-century Gujarat depict the 'Rajput' in multiple guises: as valorous warriors, as men constituting the retinue of such warriors, and as any itinerant men having access to weapons. These different meanings point to the fluidity of the category itself. See Aparna Kapadia, *In Praise of Kings: Rajputs, Sultans and Poets in Fifteenth-century Gujarat* (Cambridge: Cambridge University Press, 2018), p. 153.

66. Ramya Sreenivasan, 'Warrior-Tales at Hinterland Courts in North India, *c.*1370–1550', in Orsini and Sheikh (eds), *After Timur Left*, pp. 242–6.

67. Importantly, works that are today designated Hindi or Urdu were formerly called Hindavi, or a variant of that word, regardless of their script or their authors' religious identity. The choice of script for a given literary work depended entirely on the predilections of the scribe or his patron, not their presumed religious affiliation. Recent scholarship has rejected the practice of categorizing texts and authors by their supposed religious identity, seeing instead an era of a shared landscape with multilingual genres. Orsini and Sheikh (eds), *After Timur Left*, p. 22. As used by contemporary chroniclers in the Deccan, 'Hindavi' referred to neither Hindi nor Urdu, but to local vernaculars such as Marathi or Kannada.

68. Imre Bangha, 'Early Hindi Epic Poetry in Gwalior: Beginnings and Continuities in the Ramayan of Vishnudas', in Orsini and Sheikh (eds), *After Timur Left*, pp. 365–402.

69. Aditya Behl, ed. Wendy Doniger, *Love's Subtle Magic: An Indian Islamic Literary Tradition, 1379–1545* (Oxford: Oxford University Press, 2013).

70. The earliest text of this genre was *Chandayan*, written by Maulana Daud in 1379, followed by *Mirigavati* by Qutban (1503), *Padmavat* by Muhammad Jayasi (1540) and *Madhumalati* by Manjhan (1545).

71. Early-twentieth-century Indian nationalists, trapped in their binary categories of Hindi/Hindu/*nagari* script versus Persian/Muslim/Arabic script, had difficulties fitting this hybridized genre into their dichotomized and polarized understanding of culture. In 1929 Ramchandra Shukla wrote a study linking language, national consciousness and history in an evolutionary scheme. But what to do with Muslims in the evolution of modern standard Hindi? The Islamic identity of *premakhyan* poetry was for him a difficulty and an embarrassment. See Behl, *Love's Subtle Magic*, pp. 11–12.

72. Maulana Daud was patronized in Awadh by a local functionary of the Tughluq dynasty, Qutban was patronized by Sultan Husain Shah Sharqi of Jaunpur after Sultan Bahlul Lodi of Delhi had driven him

into exile in Bihar, and both Jayasi and Manjhan were patronized by Afghan rulers whose political bases were also in Bihar.

73. Nor were Sufi poets like Jayasi the only ones composing such stories at this time. In order to bolster their claims to royal status, petty rulers or chieftains in central India, claiming Rajput status, patronized poets who wrote romance literature very similar in narrative style and substance to the *premakhyan* texts, and also in the emerging Hindavi written language. See Sreenivasan, 'Warrior-Tales', pp. 242–72.

74. Orsini and Sheikh (eds), *After Timur Left*, pp. 18, 23.

75. Muzaffar Alam, 'The Culture and Politics of Persian in Precolonial Hindustan', in Pollock (ed.), *Literary Cultures in History*, p. 157.

76. K. Lakshmi Ranjanam, 'Telugu', in H. K. Sherwani and P. M. Joshi (eds), *History of Medieval Deccan (1295–1724)* (Hyderabad: Government of Andhra Pradesh, 1974, 2 vols), vol. 2, p. 147.

77. Phillip B. Wagoner, 'The Multiple Worlds of Amin Khan: Crossing Persianate and Indic Cultural Boundaries in the Qutb Shahi Kingdom', in Navina Najat Haidar and Marika Sardar (eds), *Sultans of the South: Arts of India's Deccan Courts, 1323–1687* (New York: Metropolitan Museum of Art, 2011), p. 94.

78. John Briggs (trans.), *History of the Rise of the Mahomedan Power in India* (1829; repr. Calcutta: Editions Indian, 1966, 4 vols), vol. 3, pp. 47–8; Muhammad Qasim Firishta, *Tarikh-i Firishta* (Lucknow: Neval Kishor, 1864–5, 2 vols in 1), vol. 2, p. 27.

79. Hiroshi Fukazawa, *The Medieval Deccan: Peasants, Social Systems and States, Sixteenth to Eighteenth Centuries* (Delhi: Oxford University Press, 1991), p. 5.

80. See Richard M. Eaton, *A Social History of the Deccan, 1300–1761. New Cambridge History of India*, vol. I:8 (Cambridge: Cambridge University Press, 2005), pp. 145–50.

81. Mukundaram, ed. Srikumar Bandyopadhyay and Visvapati Chaudhuri, *Kavikankana Candi* (Calcutta: University of Calcutta, 1974), p. 346.

82. See P. K. Gode, 'Migration of Paper from China to India, AD 105 to 1500', in K. B. Joshi, *Paper Making (as a Cottage Industry)* (Wardha, India: V. L. Mehta, 1947), pp. 198–214; Jeremiah P. Losty, *The Art of the Book in India* (London: British Library, 1982), pp. 10–12; Jonathan M. Bloom, *Paper Before Print: The History and Impact of Paper in the Islamic World* (New Haven and London: Yale University Press, 2001), pp. 41–2; Nile Green, *Indian Sufism Since the Seventeenth Century: Saints, Books and Empires in the Muslim Deccan* (New York: Routledge, 2006), p. 65.

83. For expressive purposes, written Kannada appeared from the eleventh century and Marathi from the late thirteenth. See Sheldon Pollock, *The Language of the Gods in the World of Men: Sanskrit, Culture, and Power in Premodern India* (Berkeley: University of California Press, 2009), pp. 288–9.

84. For a discussion of an early 'public sphere' in the Marathi world in the thirteenth and fourteenth centuries, see Christian Novetzke, *The Quotidian Revolution: Vernacularization, Religion, and the Premodern Public Sphere in India* (New York: Columbia University Press, 2016).

85. Referring to Rabindranath Tagore's description of the literary output of the poet-saint Raidas, the religious historian Jack Hawley argues that the *bhakti* impulse created a 'storm of songs' in the mother tongues of the masses. John Stratton Hawley, *A Storm of Songs: India and the Idea of the Bhakti Movement* (Cambridge, MA: Harvard University Press, 2015), pp. 2, 6–7.

86. For debates on the role *bhakti* played in the rise of vernacular literatures, see ibid., esp. pp. 311–12.

87. Kolff, *Naukar*, pp. 91–103.

88. At the courts of sultanates, Hindus, Jains and Muslims all patronized Sanskrit inscriptions. Orsini and Sheikh (eds), *After Timur Left*, pp. 20, 201.

89. Aparna Kapadia, 'The Last Chakravartin? The Gujarat Sultan as "Universal King" in Fifteenth Century Sanskrit Poetry', *Medieval History Journal* 16, no. 1 (2013), pp. 63–88.

90. Aparna Kapadia, 'Universal Poet, Local Kings: Sanskrit, the Rhetoric of Kingship, and Local Kingdoms in Gujarat', in Orsini and Sheikh (eds), *After Timur Left*, pp. 213–41.

91. Imre Bangha, 'Early Hindi Epic Poetry in Gwalior: Beginnings and Continuities in *Ramayan* of Vishnudas', in Orsini and Sheikh (eds), *After Timur Left*, p. 367.

92. Stefano Pellò, 'Local Lexis? Provincializing Persian in Fifteenth-Century North India', in Orsini and Sheikh (eds), *After Timur Left*, pp. 167–8.

93. Ibid., pp. 182–3.

94. Dungar Singh Tomar (d. 1459), the Rajput chief of Gwalior, noted Sultan Firuz Tughluq's 'sincere graciousness' towards Jains who were living in Delhi. Eva de Clercq, 'Apabhramsha as a Literary Medium in Fifteenth-Century North India', in Orsini and Sheikh (eds), *After Timur Left*, p. 362.

95. An example is the popular Sanskrit work *Purusha Pariksha* by Vidyapati (d. 1448). Sunil Kumar, 'Bandagi and Naukari: Studying Transitions in

Political Culture and Service under the North Indian Sultanates, Thirteenth–Sixteenth Centuries', in Orsini and Sheikh (eds), *After Timur Left*, pp. 94, 97.

96. J. T. O'Connell, 'Vaisnava Perceptions of Muslims in Sixteenth-Century Bengal', in Milton Israel and N. K. Wagle (eds), *Islamic Society and Culture: Essays in Honour of Professor Aziz Ahmad* (New Delhi: Manohar, 1983), pp. 298–302.

97. Sebastião Manrique, trans. E. Luard and H. Hosten, *Travels of Fray Sebastien Manrique, 1629–1643* (Oxford: Hakluyt Society, 1927, 2 vols), vol. 1, p. 77.

98. Percy Brown, *Indian Architecture, Islamic Period* (5th edn, Bombay: D. B. Taraporevala, 1968), p. 38.

## CHAPTER 4: THE DECCAN AND THE SOUTH, 1400–1650

1. Writing around 1600, the historian Firishta recorded that a Deccani was once asked whom he considered the greater person, the Prophet Muhammad or the shaikh. The Deccani replied, with some surprise at the question, that although the Prophet was undoubtedly a great man, Gisudaraz was a far superior order of being. John Briggs (trans.), *History of the Rise of the Mahomedan Power in India* (1829; repr. Calcutta: Editions Indian, 1966, 4 vols), vol. 2, pp. 245–6.

2. Muhammad 'Ali Samani, ed. S. N. Ahmad Qadri, *Siyar al-Muhammadi* (1427; Hyderabad: Matbu'ah I'jaz Printing Press, 1969), pp. 22–32.

3. Briggs (trans.), *History*, vol. 2, p. 234.

4. These no longer exist, but were described by the Spanish ambassador Gonzalez de Clavijo in 1404. See Guy le Strange (trans.), *Clavijo: Embassy to Tamerlane, 1403–1406* (New York: Harper & Brothers, 1928), p. 208.

5. George Michell and Richard Eaton, *Firuzabad: Palace City of the Deccan* (Oxford: Oxford University Press, 1992), pp. 80–82.

6. Phillip B. Wagoner, ' "Sultan among Hindu Kings": Dress, Titles, and the Islamicization of Hindu Culture at Vijayanagara', *Journal of Asian Studies* 55, no. 4 (Nov. 1996), p. 862.

7. Ibid., p. 863.

8. Such borrowing, however, was by no means universal across India. While noting that courtiers at Vijayanagara had avidly adopted the cosmopolitan Persianate dress code, Shah Rukh's ambassador was shocked to see that upper-class men along India's coasts went bare-chested in

public, which to his Central Asian sensibility rendered them virtually naked. In 1433, a Chinese visitor noted that people in Sri Lanka and the Malabar coast walked in public bare to the waist, as did elite Muslims of the nearby Maldive islands. Wearing elite Persianate apparel – long-sleeved tunics and tall headgear – was a matter of affiliating with a known, transregional style, regardless of one's religious identity. See ibid., pp. 859, 865–6.

9. These are the Mahanavami Dibba and the Ramachandra Temple. See John Fritz, George Michell and M. S. Nagaraja Rao, *Where Kings and Gods Meet: The Royal Centre at Vijayanagara, India* (Tucson: University of Arizona Press, 1984), pp. 99–102; Anna L. Dallapiccola, et al., *The Ramachandra Temple at Vijayanagara* (New Delhi: Manohar, 1992), pp. 83–5.

10. 'More than half of the more than 100 male figures depicted here', writes George Michell, 'are shown with prominent eyes, long noses and pointed beards; long ribbons in their hair flow outwards at either side. They wear pointed faceted caps with upturned rims, and upper garments with long sleeves, "cloud-collars" with multi-curved profiles, and waist belts hung with various items; their shoes have pointed ends.' George Michell, 'Migrations and Cultural Transmissions in the Deccan: Evidence of Monuments at Vijayanagara', in Laura E. Parodi (ed.), *The Visual World of Muslim India: The Art, Culture and Society of the Deccan in the Early Modern Era* (London: I. B. Tauris, 2014), p. 80. See also Anna L. Dallapiccola, *The Great Platform at Vijayanagara: Architecture & Sculpture* (New Delhi: Monahar, 2010), pp. 36–7.

11. T. V. Mahalingam, *Administration and Social life under Vijayanagar, Part II, Social Life* (2nd edn, Madras: University of Madras, 1979), p. 211; Briggs (trans.), *History*, vol. 3, p. 47.

12. Robert Sewell, *A Forgotten Empire, Vijayanagara: A Contribution to the History of India* (1900; repr. New Delhi: Publications Division, 1962), p. 329.

13. Michell, 'Migrations', pp. 84–5.

14. Briggs (trans.), *History*, vol. 2, p. 302.

15. Haroon Khan Sherwani, *The Bahmanis of the Deccan* (2nd edn, 1977; repr. New Delhi: Munshiram Manoharlal, 1985), p. 217.

16. Richard M. Eaton and Phillip B. Wagoner, *Power, Memory, Architecture: Contested Sites on India's Deccan Plateau, 1300–1600* (New Delhi: Oxford University Press, 2014), pp. 126–33.

17. Ibid., p. 134.

18. Deborah Hutton, *Art of the Court of Bijapur* (Bloomington: Indiana University Press, 2006), pp. 64-5, figure 2:12, plate 4; Emma Flatt, 'The Authorship and Significance of the *Nujum al-'ulum*: A Sixteenth-Century Encyclopedia from Bijapur', *Journal of the American Oriental Society* 131, no. 2 (2011), pp. 226, 235; idem, *Courts of the Deccan Sultanates: Living Well in the Persian Cosmopolis* (Cambridge: Cambridge University Press, 2019), ch. 5.

19. Eaton and Wagoner, *Power*, pp. 208-11.

20. Ibid., pp. 211-13.

21. Ibid.

22. Apparently hoping to strike it rich, the founding fathers of Golconda, Illinois (named in 1817) and Golconda, Nevada (fl. 1898-1910) certainly made this association. As the first town's website proudly declared, 'Golconda sparkles like a diamond on the banks of the mighty Ohio River.'

23. An example of the *nayakwaris*' mobility and integration with Persianate culture is Jagadeva Rao. A member of the party of *nayakwari* chieftains who had facilitated Ibrahim Qutb Shah's return to Golconda and accession to the throne, Rao became the prime minister of the Qutb Shahi sultanate before moving first to Berar to take up service with the Imad Shahi sultan, and from there to Vijayanagara, where he became a commander. See H. K. Sherwani, *History of the Qutb Shahi Dynasty* (New Delhi: Munshiram Manoharlal, 1974), pp. 86, 88-91, 97, 99-104.

24. Eaton and Wagoner, *Power*, pp. 214-30.

25. George Michell, *The Vijayanagara Courtly Style: Incorporation and Synthesis in the Royal Architecture of Southern India, 15th-17th Centuries* (New Delhi: Manohar, 1992), pp. 65-9.

26. Ajay Rao, 'A New Perspective on the Royal Rama Cult at Vijayanagara', in Yigal Bronner, Whitney Cox and Lawrence McCrea (eds), *South Asian Texts in History: Critical Engagements with Sheldon Pollock* (Ann Arbor: Association for Asian Studies, 2011), pp. 29-30.

27. Ibid., p. 30.

28. Deeds authenticated before Vitthala occurred sporadically, in 1408, 1493 and 1503. After 1516 they grew in frequency, keeping pace with those authenticated before Virupaksha, until 1544, after which all deeds were authenticated before Vitthala. Anila Verghese, *Religious Traditions at Vijayanagara as Revealed through Its Monuments* (New Delhi: Manohar, 1995), appendix A, pp. 141-54.

29. A. V. Narasimha Murthy, *Coins and Currency System of Vijayanagara Empire* (Varanasi: Numismatic Society of India, 1991).

30. Kathleen D. Morrison, 'Naturalizing Disaster: From Drought to Famine in southern India', in Garth Bawden and Richard M. Reycraft (eds), *Environmental Disaster and the Archaeology of Human Response* (Albuquerque: Maxwell Museum of Anthropology, 2001), p. 30.

31. Narasimha Murthy, *Coins*.

32. Sanjay Subrahmanyam, *The Political Economy of Commerce: Southern India, 1500–1650* (Cambridge: Cambridge University Press, 1990), pp. 94–8.

33. Vijaya Ramaswamy, 'Artisans in Vijayanagar Society', *Indian Economic and Social History Review* 22, no. 4 (1985), p. 435.

34. Ibid., pp. 427, 435.

35. Carla M. Sinopoli, *The Political Economy of Craft Production: Crafting Empire in South India, c.1350–1650* (Cambridge: Cambridge University Press, 2003), pp. 285–90.

36. Noboru Karashima, *Towards a New Formation: South Indian Society under Vijayanagar Rule* (New Delhi: Oxford University Press, 1992), pp. 49–50, 59, 64–5, 152–64; Venkata Raghotham, 'Religious Networks and the Legitimation of Power in 14th c. South India: A Study of Kumara Kampana's Politics of Intervention and Arbitration', in Madhu Sen (ed.), *Studies in Religion and Change* (New Delhi: Books and Books, 1983), pp. 154–5.

37. Burton Stein, *Vijayanagara. New Cambridge History of India*, vol. I:2 (Cambridge: Cambridge University Press, 1989), p. 51.

38. Ibid., pp. 89–90.

39. Briggs, *History*, vol. 3, p. 47.

40. Henry Heras, *The Aravidu Dynasty of Vijayanagar* (Madras: B. G. Paul & Co., 1927), pp. 29–38.

41. Eaton and Wagoner, *Power*, pp. 85–9.

42. Cesare Federici, 'Extracts of Master Caesar Frederike his Eighteene Yeeres Indian Observations', in Samuel Purchas, *Hakluytus Posthumus, or Purchas his Pilgrimes* (1625; repr. Glasgow: J. MacLehose and sons, 1905–7, 20 vols), vol. 10, pp. 92–3, 97.

43. See Michael Roberts, 'The Military Revolution, 1560–1660', in idem (ed.), *Essays in Swedish History* (Minneapolis: University of Minnesota Press, 1967); Geoffrey Parker, *The Military Revolution: Military Innovation and the Rise of the West* (Cambridge: Cambridge University Press, 1988); Clifford J. Rogers (ed.), *The Military Revolution Debate: Readings on the Military Transformation of Early Modern Europe* (Boulder: Westview, 1995); Jeremy Black, *Beyond the Military Revolution: War in the Seventeenth-Century World* (New York: Palgrave Macmillan, 2011).

44. Rainer Daehnhardt, *The Bewitched Gun: The Introduction of the Firearm in the Far East by the Portuguese* (Lisbon: Texto Editora, 1994), pp. 38–9.

45. Richard M. Eaton and Phillip B. Wagoner, 'Warfare on the Deccan Plateau, 1450–1600: A Military Revolution in Early Modern India?', in *Journal of World History* 25, no. 1 (2014), pp. 1–46.

46. Eaton and Wagoner, *Power*, pp. 251–2.

47. Ibid., pp. 254–68.

48. Eaton and Wagoner, 'Warfare', pp. 22–34.

49. Heras, *Aravidu Dynasty*, pp. 221–2.

50. The state's most famous and successful king, Krishna Raya, even issued gold coins with an image of Venkateśvara on one side and his own name on the other.

51. The Aravidu kings were also following a path blazed by earlier migrations of Telugu-speakers southwards. From the early fifteenth century onwards, martial, mercantile and cultivating castes had been moving from the dry upland plateau of Andhra south into the Tamil country. These aggressive, mobile and land-hungry pioneers generally avoided the most densely populated areas of the south, preferring to open up uncultivated regions for growing rice, millets and dry crops that used the same sort of tank irrigation that characterizes the drier northern Deccan. Migrations extending from the mid fifteenth to the late eighteenth centuries left their mark on subsequent demographic patterns. By the late nineteenth century Telugu-speakers comprised from 15 per cent to nearly a quarter of the population in some parts of the Tamil south. Subrahmanyam, *Political Economy*, pp. 16–17.

52. See Velcheru Narayana Rao, David Shulman and Sanjay Subrahmanyam, *Symbols of Substance: Court and State in Nayaka Period Tamilnadu* (Delhi: Oxford University Press, 1992), pp. 57–82.

53. Lennart Bes, 'Heirs of Vijayanagara: Court Politics in Early-Modern South India' (PhD dissertation, Radboud University, Nijmegen, 2018), pp. 305–6.

54. Arguments in this paragraph are drawn from Phillip B. Wagoner, *Tidings of the King: A Translation and Ethnohistorical Analysis of the* Rayavacakamu (Honolulu: University of Hawaii Press, 1993), pp. 10–50.

55. Subrahmanyam, *Political Economy*, p. 23.

56. The following is based on A. Sauliere, SJ, 'The Revolt of the Southern Nayaks', part 1: *Journal of Indian History* 42, no. 1 (April 1964), pp. 93–104; part 2: 44, no. 1 (April 1966), pp. 164–6.

57. Sauliere, 'Revolt', part 1, p. 95.

58. See Thomas R. Trautmann, *Elephants and Kings: An Environmental History* (Chicago: University of Chicago Press, 2015), esp. pp. 44–9, 68–70.

59. The king's career had a shadowy coda. According to Jesuit testimony, Śriranga III led a miserable life in Mysore, and around 1653 Kanthirava Narasaraja, having grown tired of his troublesome guest, left the king to his fate. Early the next year the latter managed to return to Vellore, but Tirumala, *nayaka* of Madurai, was so upset upon seeing that he 'was again raising his head' that he encouraged the sultan of Bijapur to drive him out of that city, which 'Adil Shahi forces did in August 1654. 'After wandering for six years in foreign states and alienating the neighbouring princes,' recorded a contemporary missionary, the 'poor' king 'withdrew into the last corner of his dominions still left to him'. That was Bednur, in the western plateau, where the *nayaka* of Ikkeri sheltered the powerless emperor, evidently hoping to use the latter's nominal imperial status to help prosecute his own wars against his enemy to the south, the ruler of Mysore, one of Śriranga III's former hosts. The last inscriptions issued in the name of Śriranga III are dated 1660, 1661 and finally 1669, just over a century after the Battle of Talikota. See Sauliere, 'Revolt', part 2, pp. 164–5, 169; K. D. Swaminathan, *The Nayakas of Ikkeri* (Madras: P. Varadachary & Co., 1957), pp. 90–92, 213; R. Sathyanatha Aiyar, *History of the Nayaks of Madura* (Madras: University of Madras, 1980), p. 98; H. K. Sherwani and P. M. Joshi (eds), *History of Medieval Deccan (1295–1724)*, vol. 1 (Hyderabad: Government of Andhra Pradesh, 1973), p. 137.

60. Bes, 'Heirs of Vijayanagara', pp. 280, 294, 314.

61. This was based on a type of land tenure geared towards furnishing the ruler with troops recruited and maintained by an *amaranayaka*, or the noble granted such a land holding. The term *amara* is derived from the Arabic–Persian *amr*, in the sense of 'command'. *Amr* is also the root of *amir*, or commander. See Wagoner, *Tidings*, pp. 198–200.

62. Bes, 'Heirs of Vijayanagara', p. 293.

63. Russell Shorto, *The Island at the Center of the World: The Epic Story of Dutch Manhattan and the Forgotten Colony That Shaped America* (New York: Vintage, 2005).

64. Henry Yule and Henri Cordier (trans.), *The Book of Ser Marco Polo* (1871; repr. London: John Murray Ltd, 1975, 2 vols), vol. 2, pp. 204, 235. Manned by 200 crewmen, each ship could carry up to 6,000 baskets of black pepper. Ibid., p. 250.

65. In the mid fifteenth century Calicut collected a 2.7 per cent charge on the sale of all goods leaving its port. This rate was doubtless kept low

by the availability of pepper at rival ports along the coast, rendering all of Malabar a buyer's market. Stephen F. Dale, *Islamic Society on the South Asian Frontier: The Mappilas of Malabar, 1498–1922* (Oxford: Clarendon Press, 1980), p. 14.

66. The poet, Tayan-Kannanar, was referring to Roman traders in Malabar. Andrew Dalby, *Dangerous Tastes: The Story of Spices* (Berkeley: University of California Press, 2000), p. 91.

67. Susan Bayly, *Saints, Goddesses and Kings: Muslims and Christians in South Indian Society, 1700–1900* (Cambridge: Cambridge University Press, 1989), pp. 243–57.

68. Malabar's only seaport blessed with a natural harbour is Cochin, down the coast from Calicut. Ibn Battuta's views on Calicut must be taken seriously. Unlike Marco Polo, he was not prone to exaggeration, and, having already visited ports throughout the Mediterranean, the Indian Ocean, and the South China Sea, he certainly had some basis for evaluating Calicut's relative size.

69. Sebastian R. Prange, *Monsoon Islam: Trade and Faith on the Medieval Malabar Coast* (Cambridge: Cambridge University Press, 2018), pp. 167–81; S. M. Mohamed Koya, 'Matriliny and Malabar Muslims', *Proceedings of the Indian History Congress* 40 (1979), pp. 419–31.

70. This divided source of authority would generate dissension and violence for the next several hundred years. Bayly, *Saints*, p. 269.

71. This was the *Tuhfat al-mujahidin* by Zain al-Malabari. See Prange, *Monsoon Islam*, pp. 143–7, 197; Dale, *Islamic Society*, pp. 50–56.

72. Prange, *Monsoon Islam*, pp. 221–2.

73. Sewell, *Forgotten Empire*, p. 1.

74. Phillip B. Wagoner, 'Money Use in the Deccan, *c.*1350–1687: The Role of Vijayanagara *hon*s in the Bahmani Currency System', *Indian Economic and Social History Review* 51, no. 4 (2014), p. 472.

75. Ibid., p. 477.

76. Eaton and Wagoner, *Power*, chs 3 and 4.

## CHAPTER 5: THE CONSOLIDATION OF MUGHAL RULE, 1526–1605

1. Wheeler M. Thackston (trans. and ed.), *The Baburnama: Memoirs of Babur, Prince and Emperor* (Washington DC: Freer Gallery of Art, 1995), p. 350. On the other hand, he asserted that 'when the mango is good, it is really good'. Ibid., p. 343.

2. Ibid., pp. 354–5.

3. Stephen Frederic Dale, *Babur: Timurid Prince and Mughal Emperor, 1483–1530* (New Delhi: Cambridge University Press, 2018), p. 28.

4. The British would later describe the acculturation of their own people in South Asia as 'browning in the Indian sun'. But the contrasts between the Mughal and British imperial enterprises in this respect are instructive. Whereas earlier generations of East India Company servants had, in the seventeenth and eighteenth centuries, adopted a wide spectrum of Indian culture, in the course of the early nineteenth century they became progressively more distant from their colonial subjects. With the Mughals it was the other way around, as an originally foreign dynasty over time became progressively more indigenized.

5. See Lisa Balabanlilar, *Imperial Identity in the Mughal Empire: Memory and Dynastic Politics in Early Modern South and Central Asia* (New York: I. B. Tauris, 2012), pp. 18–36.

6. Thackston, *Baburnama*, pp. 373–6, 387.

7. Muzaffar Alam, 'The Mughals, the Sufi Shaikhs, and the Formation of the Akbari Dispensation', *Modern Asian Studies* 43, no. 1 (2009), pp. 137–51.

8. Balabanlilar, *Imperial Identity*, p. 35. Ebba Koch, *Mughal Architecture: An Outline of Its History and Development (1526–1858)* (rev. edn, New Delhi: Primus Books, 2014), p. 33.

9. H. Beveridge (trans.), *The Akbar Nama of Abu'l-fazl* (1902–39; repr. New Delhi: Ess Ess Publications, 1979, 3 vols) vol. 1, p. 277.

10. A fourth son, Hindal, was only seven years old at the time of Babur's conquest in 1526.

11. Dirk H. A. Kolff, *Naukar, Rajput and Sepoy: The Ethnohistory of the Military Labour Market in Hindustan, 1450–1850* (Cambridge: Cambridge University Press, 1990), pp. 48–68, *passim*.

12. He would later reward the wife of the man who saved him from drowning by letting her wet-nurse his son, the future Emperor Akbar.

13. Catherine B. Asher and Cynthia Talbot, *India Before Europe* (Cambridge: Cambridge University Press, 2006), p. 122.

14. Khwandamir, trans. Baini Prashad, *Qanun-i Humayuni* (Calcutta: Royal Asiatic Society of Bengal, 1940), cited in Munis D. Faruqui, *The Princes of the Mughal Empire, 1504–1719* (Cambridge: Cambridge University Press, 2012), p. 63.

15. Eva Orthmann, 'Court Culture and Cosmology in the Mughal Empire: Humayun and the Foundations of the Din-i Ilahi', in Albrecht Fuess and Jan-Peter Hartung (eds), *Court Cultures in the Muslim World, Seventh to Nineteenth Centuries* (New York: Routledge, 2011), pp. 202–21.

16. Vincent A. Smith, 'The Death of Hemu in 1556, after the Battle of Panipat', *Journal of the Royal Asiatic Society* 48, no. 3 (July, 1916), pp. 527–35.

17. Norman P. Ziegler, 'Rajput Loyalties during the Mughal Period', in John F. Richards (ed.), *Kingship and Authority in South Asia* (Delhi: Oxford University Press, 1998), p. 269.

18. Ruby Lal, *Domesticiy and Power in the Early Mughal World* (Cambridge: Cambridge University Press, 2005), p. 166.

19. Cynthia Talbot, 'Justifying Defeat: A Rajput Perspective on the Age of Akbar', *Journal of the Economic and Social History of the Orient* 55 (2012), pp. 329–57.

20. Ramya Sreenivasan, 'Rethinking Kingship and Authority in South Asia: Amber (Rajasthan), circa 1560–1615', *Journal of the Economic and Social History of the Orient* 57, no. 4 (2014), p. 572.

21. Ibid., p. 559.

22. The founder of his Kachwaha lineage had been a devotee of the Ramanandi sage Krishnadas Payohari of Galta, a relationship that prefigured the royal devotionalism that would soon sweep through many kingdoms of western India as Rajput rulers began to embrace Vaishnavism. Allison Busch, 'Portrait of a Raja in a Badshah's World: Amrit Rai's Biography of Man Singh (1585)', *Journal of the Economic and Social History of the Orient* 55, no. 2/3 (2012), p. 300.

23. Catherine B. Asher, 'The Architecture of Raja Man Singh: A Study of Sub-Imperial Patronage', in Barbara Stoler Miller (ed.), *The Powers of Art: Patronage in Indian Culture* (New Delhi: Oxford University Press, 1992), pp. 184–5. See also Margaret H. Case (ed.), *Govindadeva: A Dialogue in Stone* (New Delhi: Indira Gandhi National Centre for the Arts, 1996).

24. Rulers of those states had understood Vaishnava Hinduism as less political and hence less threatening, unlike India's many Śaiva cults, which had a long history of underwriting Hindu royal sovereignty.

25. Sreenivasan, 'Rethinking', p. 577. The same was true in Orissa. In 1589, after a successful campaign in which local Afghan landholders (*zamindars*) in coastal Orissa were dislodged from power, a temple to the regional deity Jagannath in Puri was rebuilt – according to Kachwaha chronicles, by Man Singh, the conquering Mughal officer; and according to local Oriya chronicles, by a local chief. In any event, Man Singh claimed the city and its temple for Mughals, who administered revenues from the temple and the city. Ibid., pp. 575–6.

26. Ibid., p. 555.

27. Ziegler, 'Rajput Loyalties', p. 284, n.95.

28. This preoccupation was already becoming visible earlier in the sixteenth century, when legends circulated that clans such as the Chauhans, the Chalukyas, the Paramaras and the Pratiharas had been born in a sacrificial fire pit on Mount Abu in western Rajasthan, thereby distinguishing them from other clans of the warrior class, or *kshatriya*s.

29. Tanuja Kothiyal, *Nomadic Narratives: A History of Mobility and Identity in the Great Indian Desert* (New Delhi: Cambridge University Press, 2016), pp. 93–6.

30. Cynthia Talbot, *The Last Hindu Emperor: Prithviraj Chauhan and the Indian Past, 1200–2000* (Cambridge: Cambridge University Press, 2016), pp. 119, 144.

31. J. F. Richards, 'The Formulation of Imperial Authority under Akbar and Jahangir', in idem (ed.), *Kingship and Authority*, p. 287.

32. Rosalind O'Hanlon, 'Kingdom, Household and Body: History, Gender and Imperial Service under Akbar', *Modern Asian Studies* 41, no. 5 (2007), pp. 891–4, 905.

33. Architecturally, one sees this most clearly in the Atiya mosque in modern Tangail District, Bangladesh. Built by Afghan patrons in 1609, this mosque, with its complex terracotta façade, its ringed corner towers and its curved cornice, is a highly evolved elaboration of the much older Bengal sultanate style, itself modelled on building practices and aesthetics of Bengali folk culture.

34. Abu'l-fazl 'Allami, trans. H. Beveridge, *Akbar-nama* (1902: repr. Delhi: Ess Ess Publications, 1977, 3 vols), vol. 3, p. 95.

35. One contemporary observer wrote that 'the cavalry is regarded as in every way the flower of the army', adding that Akbar 'spared no expense in order to maintain an efficient, and as far as possible, perfectly-equipped force of cavalry to guard the empire.' *The Commentary of Father Monserrate, S.J., on his Journey to the Court of Akbar*, trans. John Hoyland (London: Oxford University Press, 1922), pp. 88–9.

36. S. Inayat Ali Zaidi, 'Ordinary Kachawaha Troopers Serving the Mughal Empire: Composition and Structure of the Contingents of the Kachawaha Nobles', *Studies in History* 2, no. 1 (1980), pp. 58, 60.

37. For an elaboration of the idea and practice of *fitna*, see André Wink, *Land and Sovereignty in India: Agrarian Society and Politics under the Eighteenth-century Maratha Svarajya* (New York: Cambridge University Press, 1986).

38. Abu'l-fazl 'Allami, *Akbar-nama*, vol. 3, pp. 170, 173.

39. When a Portuguese diplomat was presented to the court of Sultan Nasir al-Din Nusrat Shah in 1521, the sultan, in the words of the for-

eigner, 'turned to me and ordered that I be given a robe that he had worn'. Genevieve Bouchon and Luis Filipe Thomaz (trans. and eds), *Voyage dans les deltas du Gange et de l'Irraouaddy: Relation portugaise anonyme (1521)* (Paris: Centre culturel portugais, 1988), p. 333.

40. Abu'l-fazl 'Allami, *Akbar-nama*, vol. 3, p. 185.

41. Audrey Truschke, *Culture of Encounters: Sanskrit at the Mughal Court* (New York: Columbia University Press, 2016), p. 268, n.174.

42. Pankaj Kumar Jha, 'Literary Conduits for "Consent": Cultural Groundwork of the Mughal State in the Fifteenth Century', *Medieval History Journal* 19, no. 2 (2016), p. 335.

43. As he wrote, 'People travel in all directions from islands to mountains and seas to meet the Ranas and Rauts, but you would find all of them together here at the door [of the Sharqi court] . . . [Rajaputs from] Telanga, Vanga, Cola, and Kalinga were all there. They, rajaputas and brahmanas [*pandia*] alike, shivered with fear, gathered courage and made submissions in their own languages *ni-a bhasa* [before the Sultan's court].' Quoted in ibid., p. 337. The passage comes from Vidyapati's *Kirttilata*, which was composed in Avahatta, an early stage in the evolution of eastern Indian languages such as Bengali, Maithili, Assamese and Oriya.

44. 'Permanence of dominion' is the phrase found in early-nineteenth-century British discourse regarding the East India Company's rapid expansion of power in India. See, for example, Francis G. Hutchins, *The Illusion of Permanence: British Imperialism in India* (Princeton: Princeton University Press, 1967).

45. Farhat Hasan, *State and Locality in Mughal India: Power Relations in Western India, c.1572–1730* (Cambridge: Cambridge University Press, 2004), pp. 41–3.

46. Ibid., pp. 36–8.

47. As Hasan put it, 'Since the political system required a continuous partaking of "shares" in sovereignty in favour of the local power holders, the Mughal state was continually undermined by its own beneficiaries.' Ibid., p. 126.

48. Abu'l-fazl 'Allami, trans. H. S. Jarrett, *A'in-i Akbari* (1948; 2nd edn, repr. New Delhi: Oriental Books Reprint Corp., 1978, 3 vols), vol. 3, p. 429.

49. Ibid., vol. 3, p. 433.

50. Iqtidar Alam Khan, 'Akbar's Personality Traits and World Outlook – a Critical Appraisal', in Irfan Habib (ed.), *Akbar and his India* (New Delhi: Oxford University Press, 1997), p. 84.

51. André Wink, *Akbar* (Oxford: Oneworld, 2009), p. 89.

52. Khan, 'Akbar's Personality Traits', p. 87. For a contemporary account of these meetings by one of his Muslim critics, see 'Abdu'l-Qadir ibn-i-Muluk Shah al-Badaoni, trans. W. H. Lowe, *Muntakhabu't-Tawarikh* (1899; repr. Delhi: Idarah-i-Adabiyat-i-Delli, 1973, 3 vols), vol. 2, pp. 262–9.

53. O'Hanlon, 'Kingdom', pp. 902, 905.

54. Badaoni, *Muntakhab*, vol. 2, pp. 276–7.

55. Ibid., vol. 2, p. 279, vol. 3, pp. 128–31.

56. Ibid., vol. 2, p. 281.

57. Hoyland (trans.), *Commentary*, p. 142.

58. Ibid., pp. 155–6.

59. Ibid., p. 173.

60. Sanjay Subrahmanyam, 'Connected Histories: Notes towards a Reconfiguration of Early Modern Eurasia', *Modern Asian Studies* 31, no. 3 (1997), pp. 735–62. See pp. 746–55.

61. Hoyland (trans.), *Commentary*, p. 129.

62. A. Azfar Moin, *The Millennial Sovereign: Sacred Kingship and Sainthood in Islam* (New York: Columbia University Press, 2012), p. 137.

63. Najaf Haider, 'Disappearance of Coin Minting in the 1580s? A note on the Alf Coins', in Habib (ed.), *Akbar*, p. 58.

64. John F. Richards, *The Mughal Empire. New Cambridge History of India*, vol. I:5 (Cambridge: Cambridge University Press, 1993), p. 72.

65. Moin, *Millennial Sovereign*, p. 145.

66. Harbans Mukhia, 'Time in Abu'l Fazl's Historiography', in Harbans Mukhia, *Exploring India's Medieval Centuries: Essays in History, Society, Culture, and Technology* (Delhi: Aakar Books, 2010), pp. 6–7.

67. Hoyland (trans.), *Commentary*, p. 184.

68. Moin, *Millennial Sovereign*, p. 151.

69. Hoyland (trans.), *Commentary*, p. 203.

70. Truschke, *Culture of Encounters*, p. 152.

71. As Abu'l-fazl wrote, 'Akbar exercises upon himself both inward and outward austerities, though he occasionally joins public worship, in order to hush the slandering tongues of the bigots of the present age.' Abu'l-fazl 'Allami, trans. H. Blochmann, *The A'in-i Akbari* (1927; 2nd edn, repr. New Delhi: Oriental Books Reprint Corp., 1977, 3 vols), vol. 1, p. 163.

72. See Richard M. Eaton, *The Rise of Islam and the Bengal Frontier, 1204–1760* (Berkeley: University of California Press, 1993), pp. 179–83.

73. As Monserrate observed, 'The King has the most precise regard for right and justice in the affairs of government.' Hoyland (trans.), *Commentary*, p. 209.

74. Ibid., p. 210.

75. See Faruqui, *Princes*, pp. 12–21.

76. The 'Lord of the Conjunction' was an astrologers' term for the divine blessing believed to have been conferred by being born under a conjunction of Jupiter and Saturn.

77. Moin, *Millennial Sovereign*, pp. 133–4.

78. Cited in Truschke, *Culture of Encounters*, p. 153.

79. Faruqui, *Princes*, pp. 141–2.

## CHAPTER 6: INDIA UNDER JAHANGIR AND SHAH JAHAN, 1605–1658

1. Henry Beveridge (ed.), Alexander Rogers (trans.), *The Tuzuk-i-Jahangiri, or Memoirs of Jahangir* (2nd edn, New Delhi: Munshiram Manoharlal, 1968, 2 vols), vol. 1, p. 375.

2. Ibid., vol. 1, p. 332

3. Ibid., vol. 1, p. 308.

4. Ibid., vol. 2, p. 246.

5. Beni Prasad, *History of Jahangir* (5th edn, Allahabad: Indian Press, 1962), p. 344.

6. M. I. Borah (trans.), *Baharistan-i-Ghaybi* (Gauhati: Government of Assam, 1936, 2 vols), vol. 2, pp. 707, 710, 721.

7. Munis Faruqui, *The Princes of the Mughal Empire, 1504–1719* (Cambridge: Cambridge University Press, 2012), pp. 208–15.

8. Ibid., pp. 12–21.

9. Borah, *Baharistan*, vol. 1, p. 6.

10. Ibid., vol. 1, p. 43.

11. Ibid., vol. 1, p. 236.

12. Ibid., vol. 2, pp. 632–33.

13. Ibid., vol. 1, p. 146, vol. 2, p. 635.

14. Ibid., vol. 1, p. 27.

15. Ibid., vol. 1, pp. 27–8, vol. 2, pp. 799–800. Musa Khan's base covered most of the former British districts of Comilla, Dhaka and Mymensingh.

16. Ibid., vol. 1, pp. 248–53, 292.

17. Richard M. Eaton, *The Rise of Islam and the Bengal Frontier, 1204–1760* (Berkeley: University of California Press, 1993), pp. 188–91.

18. After Mughal arms had reimposed imperial rule in Kamrup, a Mughal revenue agent misappropriated 700,000 rupees of government revenue. Fearing an official investigation into his misdeeds, he made overtures to the Ahom raja of neighbouring Assam to the east, treasonously

offering to submit to Ahom overlordship if the raja would recognize him as the ruler of the Kuch region. Borah, *Baharistan*, vol. 2, p. 443.

19. Ibid., vol. 1, pp. 156–7.
20. Ibid., vol. 1, p. 18.
21. Ibid., vol. 1, pp. 97–8.
22. Ibid., vol. 1, p. 32.
23. Ibid., vol. 2, pp. 596–7.
24. Ibid., vol. 1, pp. 196–7.
25. Ibid., vol. 1, pp. 120, 205.
26. Ibid., vol. 1, pp. 213–14.
27. Ibid., vol. 1, pp. 439–40.
28. Ibid., vol. 2, pp. 594, 599.
29. Ruby Lal, *Domesticity and Power in the Early Mughal World* (New York: Cambridge University Press, 2005), p. 170.
30. Ellison Banks Findly, *Nur Jahan, Empress of Mughal India* (New York: Oxford University Press, 1993), pp. 124–6.
31. Navina Najat Haidar and Marika Sardar (eds), *Sultans of Deccan India, 1500–1700: Opulence and Fantasy* (New York: The Metropolitan Museum of Art, 2015), pp. 74–5.
32. William Foster (ed.), *Early Travels in India 1583–1619* (Delhi: S. Chand & Co., 1968), p. 138.
33. James Grant Duff, ed. J. P. Guha, *History of the Mahrattas* (New Delhi: Associated Publishing House, 1971, 2 vols), vol. 1, p. 36.
34. Gunther-Dietz Sontheimer, trans. Anne Feldhaus, *Pastoral Deities in Western India* (Delhi: Oxford University Press, 1993), pp. 163, 30, 158, 159.
35. Stewart Gordon, *The Marathas, 1600–1818. New Cambridge History of India*, vol. II:4 (Cambridge: Cambridge University Press, 1993), p. 34.
36. Radhey Shyam, *Life and Times of Malik Ambar* (Delhi: Munshiram Manoharlal, 1968), p. 147.
37. John Stratton Hawley, *A Storm of Songs: India and the Idea of the Bhakti Movement* (Cambridge, MA: Harvard University Press, 2015), pp. 295–312.
38. David Shea and Anthony Troyer (trans.), *The Dabistan or School of Manners* (Washington and London: M. Walter Dunne, 1901), p. 284.
39. J. S. Grewal, *The Sikhs of the Punjab. New Cambridge History of India*, vol. II:3 (Cambridge: Cambridge University Press, 1990), p. 38.
40. Gurinder Singh Mann, *The Making of Sikh Scripture* (New York: Oxford University Press, 2001), pp. 5–9.
41. Ibid., p. 12.

42. Harjot Oberoi, *The Construction of Religious Boundaries: Culture, Identity, and Diversity in the Sikh Tradition* (Chicago: University of Chicago Press, 1994), p. 54.

43. Mann, *Making*, pp. 102, 120.

44. Oberoi, *Construction*, pp. 55–6. See also W. H. McLeod, *Guru Nanak and the Sikh Religion* (New Delhi: Oxford University Press, 1996).

45. Shea and Troyer (trans.), *Dabistan*, p. 287.

46. Irfan Habib, 'Jatts of Punjab and Sind', in Harbans Singh and N. G. Barrier (eds), *Punjab Past and Present: Essays in Honour of Dr. Ganda Singh* (Patiala: Punjabi University, 1976), pp. 94–8. See also Gurinder Singh Mann, 'Guru Nanak's Life and Legacy, an Appraisal', in Anshu Malhotra and Farina Mir (eds), *Punjab Reconsidered: History, Culture, and Practice* (New Delhi: Oxford University Press, 2012), pp. 136–8.

47. Grewal, *Sikhs of the Punjab*, p. 51.

48. Mann, *Making*, p. 19.

49. H. Beveridge (trans.), *The Akbar Nama of Abu'l-fazl* (1902–39; repr. Delhi: Ess Ess Publications, 1977, 3 vols), vol. 3, p. 1115.

50. Grewal, *Sikhs of the Punjab*, pp. 42, 56.

51. Beveridge (ed.) and Rogers (trans.), *Tuzuk*, vol. 1, p. 72.

52. Jahangir described Guru Arjun as a Hindu 'in the garments of sainthood and sanctity' who had 'captured many of the simple-hearted of the Hindus' as well as Muslims. Ibid.

53. Mu'tamad Khan, *Iqbalnama-yi Jahangiri*, cited in H. M. Elliot and John Dowson (eds), *The History of India as Told by Its Own Historians* (1867–77; repr. Allahabad: Kitab Mahal, 1964, 8 vols), vol. 6, p. 405.

54. W. H. Moreland and P. Geyl (trans.), *Jahangir's India: The Remonstrantie of Francisco Pelsaert* (Delhi: Idarah-i Adabiyat-i Delli, 1972), p. 53.

55. Beveridge (ed.) and Rogers (trans.), *Tuzuk*, vol. 2, p. 246.

56. Mu'tamad Khan, *Iqbalnama-yi Jahangiri*, vol. 6, p. 405.

57. Rejecting the role of 'seductive vamp' that appears in Bollywood cinema or novels, Ellison Banks Findly notes that Nur Jahan was already middle-aged when she met Jahangir, with whom she formed a mature, political partnership. She also proposes that Nur Jahan fulfilled the emperor's ideal of motherhood, as is suggested in his well-documented attraction to the Christian image of the Madonna and Child. See Findly, *Nur Jahan*, pp. 84–6.

58. Beveridge (ed.) and Rogers (trans.), *Tuzuk*, vol. 1, p. 7.

59. Foster (ed.), *Early Travels*, p. 109.

60. Beveridge (ed.) and Rogers (trans.), *Tuzuk*, vol. 1, p. 164.

61. Ibid., vol. 1, p. 410.

62. Ibid., vol. 1, p. 117.

63. Ibid., vol. 2, p. 108.

64. Ibid., vol. 2, pp. 168–9.

65. Findly, *Nur Jahan*, p. 64.

66. Banarsi Pasad Saksena, *History of Shahjahan of Dihli* (Allahabad: Central Book Depot, 1968), p. 84.

67. A. R. Fuller (trans.), W. E. Begley and Z. A. Desai (eds), *The Shah Jahan Nama of 'Inayat Khan* (Delhi: Oxford University Press, 1990), p. 161. As his chronicler 'Abd al-Hamid Lahauri wrote in the *Padshah-nama*, the emperor's actions against Jhujhar Singh were intended to 'set an example to all other short-sighted individuals who did not appreciate their own well-being'. Milo Cleveland Beach and Ebba Koch, trans. Wheeler Thackston, *King of the World: The Pad-shahnama, an Imperial Manuscript from the Royal Library, Windsor Castle* (London: Azimuth Editions, 1997), p. 88.

68. Heidi Pauwels, 'A Tale of Two Temples: Mathura's Keśavadeva and Orchha's Caturbhujadeva', *South Asian History and Culture* 2, no. 2 (2011), p. 290.

69. Richard M. Eaton, 'The Political and Religious Authority of the Shrine of Baba Farid', in Barbara D. Metcalf (ed.), *Moral Conduct and Authority: The Place of Adab in South Asian Islam* (Berkeley: University of California Press, 1984), pp. 333–56.

70. Dirk H. A. Kolff, *Naukar, Rajput and Sepoy: The Ethnohistory of the Military Labour Market in Hindustan, 1450–1850* (Cambridge: Cambridge University Press, 1990), p. 139.

71. Fuller (trans.), *Shah Jahan Nama of 'Inayat Khan*, p. 70.

72. Vincent A. Smith, *The History of Fine Art in India and Ceylon* (Oxford: Clarendon Press, 1911), pp. 417–18. W. H. Sleeman, *Rambles and Recollections of an Indian Official* (London: H. Milford, 1915), p. 385.

73. Ustad Ahmad Lahouri, who laid the foundations for the Red Fort in Delhi, is credited by his son with building the Taj. The chronicler Lahauri mentions Mir 'Abd al-Karim as the supervisor of the project. See Ebba Koch, *The Complete Taj Mahal and the Riverfront Gardens of Agra* (London: Thames & Hudson, 2006), pp. 83, 89.

74. Ibid., p. 103.

75. A. Azfar Moin, *The Millennial Sovereign: Sacred Kingship and Saint-hood in Islam* (New York: Columbia University Press, 2012), pp. 23–31, 54.

76. This is the Windsor Castle *Padshah-nama* of 'Abd al-Hamid Lahauri. Beach and Koch, *King of the World*, pp. 26–7.

77. Ebba Koch, 'Diwan-i 'Amm and Chihil Sutun: The Audience Halls of Shah Jahan', in idem, *Mughal Art and Imperial Ideology: Collected Essays* (New Delhi: Oxford University Press, 2001), pp. 239–49.

78. Ebba Koch, *Mughal Architecture: An Outline of Its History and Development (1526–1858)* (rev. edn, New Delhi: Primus Books, 2014), p. 110.

79. Jean-Baptiste Tavernier, trans. V. Ball, *Travels in India* (1889; repr. Lahore: al-Biruni, 1976, 2 vols), vol. 1, pp. 381–4.

80. Irfan Habib, *The Agrarian System of Mughal India, 1556–1707* (2nd rev. edn, New Delhi: Oxford University Press, 1999), pp. 454–5.

81. Habib, *Agrarian System*, pp. 314–15.

82. Tabulated from data in M. Athar Ali, *The Apparatus of Empire: Awards of Ranks, Offices and Titles to the Mughal Nobility (1574–1658)* (Delhi: Oxford University Press, 1985), p. xx.

83. Thomas Coryat, the eccentric Englishman who walked from Jerusalem to India in 1614–15 and for two years moved with Jahangir's court between Ajmer, Agra and Mandu, observed that 'The King likes not those that change their religion; hee himselfe being of none but of his owne making, and therefore suffers all religions in his kingdome.' Foster (ed.), *Early Travels*, p. 280.

84. John F. Richards, *The Mughal Empire. New Cambridge History of India*, vol. I:5 (Cambridge: Cambridge University Press, 1993), p. 121.

85. Moin, *Millennial Sovereign*, pp. 214, 225.

86. Ebba Koch, 'Shah Jahan and Orpheus: The Pietre Dure Decoration and the Programme of the Throne in the Hall of Public Audiences at the Red Fort of Delhi', in idem, *Mughal Art and Imperial Ideology: Collected Essays* (New Delhi: Oxford University Press, 2001), pp. 61–129.

87. In one such painting, which shows the emperor receiving a gift from his *vazir* Asaf Khan, a very worldly activity, angels above play musical instruments while God Himself casts a shaft of light from the heavens on to the halo that surrounds the emperor's head. Moin, *Millennial Sovereign*, p. 233.

88. Faruqui, *Princes*, pp. 12–21.

89. Jadunath Sarkar, *History of Aurangzib* (1912; repr. New Delhi: Orient Longman, 1973, 5 vols), vol. 1, p. xi.

## CHAPTER 7: AURANGZEB – FROM PRINCE TO EMPEROR 'ALAMGIR, 1618–1707

1. John Dryden, *Aureng-zebe: A Tragedy* (London: J. Tonson, 1735), p. 44.
2. A. R. Fuller (trans.), W. E. Begley and Z. A. Desai (eds), *The Shah Jahan Nama of 'Inayat Khan* (Delhi: Oxford University Press, 1990), p. 96.
3. An image painted within a few years of the event, titled 'Prince Awrangzeb facing a maddened elephant named Sudhakar', is found in Milo Beach and Ebba Koch, *King of the World: The Padshahnama, an Imperial Mughal Manuscript from the Royal Library, Windsor Castle* (London: Azimuth Editions, 1997), pp. 72–7. Another painting, drawn in the mid seventeenth century, is held in the Royal Asiatic Society and is reproduced in A. Schimmel, *Empire of the Great Mughals* (New Delhi: Oxford University Press, 2005), p. 54, plate 17.
4. Jadunath Sarkar (trans.), *Anecdotes of Aurangzib and Historical Essays* (Calcutta: M. C. Sarkar & Sons, 1917), pp. 36–7.
5. Ibid., p. 37.
6. Ibid., pp. 3–4. See also Saqi Must'ad Khan, trans. Jadu-Nath Sarkar, *Maasir-i-'Alamgiri* (Calcutta: Royal Asiatic Society of Bengal, 1947), p. 317.
7. Arminius Vambery, *History of Bokhara* (1873; repr. New York: Arno Press, 1973), p. 322. The disaster compares with the British retreat from Kabul towards the end of the First Afghan War. In January 1842, 4,500 British troops and 12,000 civilians perished in that operation.
8. Jadunath Sarkar, *History of Aurangzib* (1912; repr. New Delhi: Orient Longman, 1973, 5 vols), vol. 1, p. 92.
9. Munis Faruqui, *The Princes of the Mughal Empire, 1504–1719* (Cambridge: Cambridge University Press, 2012), pp. 176–7.
10. Sarkar, *History*, vol. 1, pp. 92–3.
11. Banarsi Prasad Saksena, *History of Shahjahan of Dihli* (Allahabad: Central Book Depot, 1968), p. 90.
12. Vincent J. A. Flynn, 'An English Translation of the *Adab-i 'Alamgiri*: The Period before the War of Succession, being the Letters of Prince Muhammad Aurangzib Bahadur to Muhammad Shihabu'd-din Shah Jahan Sahib-i Qiran-i Sani, Emperor of Hindustan' (PhD thesis, Australian National University, 1974), letter 36, pp. 33–9.
13. Ibid., letter 47, p. 181.

14. Shah Nawaz Khan and 'Abdul Hayy, trans H. Beveridge, *Maathir-ul-Umara* (1911–14; repr. Patna: Janaki Prakashan, 1979, 3 vols), vol. 1, pp. 806–7.

15. Flynn, *Adab-i 'Alamgiri*, letter 52, pp. 200–01.

16. Sarkar (trans.), *Anecdotes*, p. 45.

17. Niccolao Manucci, trans. William Irvine, *Storia do Mogor* (1907; repr. New Delhi: Oriental Books Reprint Corp., 1981, 4 vols), vol. 1, p. 222.

18. Sarkar, *History*, vol. 1, p. 106.

19. François Bernier, trans. Archibald Constable, *Travels in the Mogul Empire* (2nd edn, Delhi: S. Chand & Co., 1968), p. 22.

20. See B. N. Goswamy and J. S. Grewal, *The Mughals and the Jogis of Jakhbar* (Simla: Indian Institute of Advanced Study, 1967), pp. 32–4; Jnan Chandra, 'Aurangzib and Hindu Temples', *Journal of the Pakistan Historical Society* 5, no. 4 (Oct. 1957), pp. 247–54; idem, "Alamgir's attitude towards non-Muslim institutions', *Journal of the Pakistan Historical Society* 7, no. 1 (Jan. 1959), pp. 36–9; idem, "Alamgir's Tolerance in the Light of Contemporary Jain Literature', *Journal of the Pakistan Historical Society* 6, no. 4 (Oct. 1958), pp. 269–72. Satish Chandra, 'Some Religious Grants of Aurangzeb to maths in the State of Marwar', in Satish Chandra, *Mughal Religious Policies, the Rajputs, and the Deccan* (New Delhi: Vikas Publishing House, 1993), pp. 190–93.

21. As a prince he invariably addressed his father in his correspondence as *murshid* (Sufi teacher) and himself as 'this *murid*', or disciple. Flynn, *Adab-i 'Alamgiri*, p. xix.

22. Bernier, *Travels*, p. 6. Manucci notes: 'When with Mahomedans, he praised the tenets of Muhammad; when with Jews, the Jewish religion; in the same way, when with Hindus, he praised Hinduism.' Manucci, *Storia do Mogor*, vol. 1, p. 214.

23. Rajeev Kinra, 'Infantilizing Baba Dara: The Cultural Memory of Dara Shekuh and the Mughal Public Sphere', *Journal of Persianate Studies* 2 (2009), p. 173.

24. Dara's interactions with Baba Lal fit into an ancient literary genre found in both Indo-Persian works and in much older Indian literature, namely, the dialogue between the princely seeker and the spiritual teacher. Supriya Gandhi, 'The Prince and the *Muvahhid*: Dara Shikoh and Mughal Engagements with Vedanta', in Vasudha Dalmia and Munis D. Faruqui (eds), *Religious Interactions in Mughal India* (New Delhi: Oxford University Press, 2014), pp. 71–5.

25. Ibid., p. 71.

26. Ibid., p. 77.

27. Muzaffar Alam, 'In Search of a Sacred King: Dara Shukoh and the Yogavasisthas', *History of Religions* 55, no. 4 (May 2016), p. 450.

28. Munis Faruqui, cited in Sunil Khilnani, *Incarnations: A History of India in Fifty Lives* (New York: Farrar, Straus and Giroux, 2016), p. 133. In 1655, just two years before that succession struggle began, Dara translated (or commissioned) a Persian version of the *Yogavasistha*. Probably composed between the ninth and twelfth centuries, this Sanskrit text consists of dialogues between the troubled youth Rama, who would become the divine hero of the *Ramayana* epic, and the ascetic Vasistha Muni. Once again, the text's central theme is the young Rama's dilemma of reconciling disengagement with engagement with the world. In these dialogues, Vasistha relates to Rama the famous episode from the *Mahabharata* epic, in which the warrior Arjuna baulks at the prospect of killing his own relatives on the battlefield. Haunting both Arjuna and Dara was the question of how a spiritually accomplished person could engage in a war of succession against his own brothers. While working on this text, Dara knew that he would soon be facing the same dilemma faced by Arjuna. See Gandhi, 'The Prince', p. 73; Alam, 'In Search of a Sacred King', pp. 455-9.

29. Bikrama Jit Hasrat, *Dara Shikuh: Life and Works* (2nd edn, New Delhi: Munshiram Manoharlal, 1982), p. 261.

30. Qur'an 56:77-80.

31. 'Hereby,' he concluded, 'things unknown to this *faqir* became known, and things incomprehensible became comprehensible.' Hasrat, *Dara Shikuh*, p. 263. My translation.

32. The book so impressed Schopenhauer that he named his dog Atma, or 'world soul'. David E. Cartwright, *Schopenhauer: A Biography* (Cambridge: Cambridge University Press, 2010), pp. 150-51.

33. Sarkar, *History*, vol. 1, p. 170.

34. Manucci, *Storia*, vol. 1, pp. 216-17.

35. Bernier, *Travels*, pp. 48-56; Manucci, *Storia*, vol. 1, p. 269.

36. Ibid., vol. 1, p. 220.

37. Bernier, *Travels*, p. 10.

38. Aqil Khan Razi, ed. Khan Bahadur Maulvi Haji Zafar Hasan, *Waqiat-i-Alamgiri* (Delhi: Aligarh Historical Institute, 1946), pp. 9-11.

39. Ibid., p. 28.

40. Ibid., pp. 28-30.

41. Bernier, *Travels*, pp. 98-9.

42. The charges against Dara were both political and religious in nature. On the second day after he reached Delhi's southern suburb of Khizrabad, riots broke out among the 'rabble of the city', and his execution

was ordered 'according to the demands of the well-being of state and rule'. But he was also charged with studying and translating the Vedas, which he was accused of regarding as divine speech, ancient scripture and the holy book. He was additionally charged with wearing jewellery inscribed with the Sanskrit word *Prabhu* ('Lord'). Muhammad Kazim, ed. Hadim Husayn and 'Abd al-Hayy, *'Alamgirnama* (1865–8; repr. Osnabrück: Biblio Verlag, 1983), 1983), pp. 34–5. See Sarkar, *History*, vol. 1, pp. 169–70, and Craig Davis, 'Dara Shukuh and Aurangzib: Issues of Religion and Politics and their Impact on Indo-Muslim Society' (PhD dissertation, Indiana University, 2002), pp. 236, 238.

43. Technically, this was a second coronation. On 21 July 1658, shortly after winning the Battle of Samugarh and confining his father, he had hastily and unceremoniously crowned himself in Delhi before setting off for the Punjab in pursuit of Dara.

44. Must'ad Khan, *Maasir-i-'Alamgiri*, p. 3.

45. All nobles, wrote Bernier, knew that to open Shah Jahan's door 'would be to unchain an enraged lion'. *Travels*, p. 124.

46. Must'ad Khan, *Maasir-i-'Alamgiri*, pp. 13, 15.

47. Ibid., p. 20.

48. Manucci, *Storia*, vol. 2, p. 2.

49. Must'ad Khan, *Maasir-i-'Alamgiri*, p. 16.

50. Manucci, *Storia*, vol. 2, p. 16.

51. By inserting his house into Marwar's succession dispute, Rana Raj Singh evidently saw an opportunity once again to exert Sisodiya influence over the greater part of Rajasthan. Indeed, he had supported Marwar's cause even before Ajit Singh was born.

52. Robert C. Hallissey, *The Rajput Rebellion against Aurangzeb: A Study of the Mughal Empire in Seventeenth-Century India* (Columbia, MO: University of Missouri Press, 1977), pp. 71, 75.

53. Ibid., p. 81.

54. Stewart Gordon, *The Marathas, 1600–1818. New Cambridge History of India*, vol. II:4 (Cambridge: Cambridge University Press, 1993), p. 34.

55. For the notorious Afzal Khan incident see S. Moinul Haq (trans.), *Khafi Khan's History of 'Alamgir* (Karachi: Pakistan Historical Society, 1975), pp. 122–4. See also Surendranath Sen (trans.), *Extracts and Documents Relating to Maratha History*, vol. 1: *Siva Chhatrapati, being a Translation of the Sabhasad Bakhar, with Extracts from Chitnis and Sivadigvijaya, with Notes* (Calcutta: University of Calcutta, 1920), pp. 11–22.

56. Haq (trans), *Khafi Khan's History*, p. 193; Sen (trans.), *Extracts*, pp. 61–4.

57. Satish Chandra, *Medieval India, from Sultanat to the Mughals, part two: Mughal Empire* (6th edn, New Delhi: Har-Anand Publications, 1999), p. 326.

58. Jadunath Sarkar, *House of Shivaji* (Calcutta: M. C. Sarkar & Sons, 1955), p. 159.

59. Sen (trans.), *Extracts*, vol. 1: *Śiva Chhatrapati*, pp. 113–18. See also John F. Richards, *The Mughal Empire. New Cambridge History of India*, vol. I:5 (Cambridge: Cambridge University Press, 1993), p. 213.

60. André Wink, *Land and Sovereignty in India: Agrarian Society and Politics under the Eighteenth-century Maratha Swarajya* (Cambridge: Cambridge University Press, 1986), pp. 60–63.

61. Khafi Khan, *Muntakhab al-lubab*, in H. M. Elliot and John Dowson (eds), *The History of India as Told by Its Own Historians* (1867–77; repr. Allahabad: Kitab Mahal, 1964, 8 vols), vol. 7, p. 367.

62. V. G. Khobrekar (ed.), Jadunath Sarkar (trans.), *Tarikh-i-Dilkasha (Memoirs of Bhimsen Relating to Aurangzib's Deccan Campaigns)* (Bombay: Department of Archives, Government of Maharashtra, 1972), pp. 232, 256.

63. Appasaheb Pawar (ed.), *Tarabaikalina Kagadpatre* (Kolhapur: Sivaji Vidyapitha, 1969, 3 vols), vol. 1, p. 103.

64. Elliot and Dowson (eds), *History*, vol. 7, p. 374.

65. Brij Kishore, *Tara Bai and Her Times* (Bombay: Asia Publishing House, 1963), pp. 71–93.

66. Elliot and Dowson (eds), *History*, vol. 7, p. 374.

67. Surendranath Sen (ed.), *Indian Travels of Thevenot and Careri* (New Delhi: National Archives of India, 1949), p. 218.

68. Khobrekar (ed.), *Tarikh-i-Dilkasha*, p. 223.

69. Munis Faruqui, ed. Gudrun Kramer et al., 'Awrangzib', *Encyclopaedia of Islam, Three* (Leiden: Brill, 2014) p. 71.

70. M. Athar Ali, *The Mughal Nobility Under Aurangzeb* (Bombay: Asia Publishing House, 1968), p. 28.

71. Ibid., p. 92.

72. At that time Marathas comprised ninety-six of the 575 nobles holding ranks of 1,000 *zat* or higher, whereas Rajputs comprised seventy-three of the total at that level. Ibid., pp. 25, 30.

73. Haq (trans.), *Khafi Khan's History*, p. 395.

74. Ali, *Mughal Nobility*, pp. 93–4.

75. According to Bernier, while governing the Deccan for the second time, Aurangzeb caused it to be believed that his most cherished wish 'was

to pass the rest of his days in prayer or in offices of piety, and that he shrank from the cares and responsibility of government'. Bernier, *Travels*, p. 10. Manucci writes: 'Above all, for a long time he pretended to be a faquir [faqir] a holy mendicant, by which he renounced the world, gave up all claim to the crown, and was content to pass his life in prayers and meditation.' Manucci, *Storia*, vol. 1, p. 220.

76. Ellison Banks Findly, *Nur Jahan, Empress of Mughal India* (New York: Oxford University Press, 1993), p. 63.

77. Qur'an 4:29; *Sahih al-Bukhari*, vol. 3, book 43, hadith 632.

78. Sarkar, *History*, vol. 3, p. 48.

79. Such a blessing would have amounted to the closest approximation to the robes of honour or certificates of political authority that the caliphs of Baghdad used to confer on the sultans of India – until, that is, the thirteenth century, when the office of caliphate itself was abolished.

80. Manucci, *Storia*, vol. 2, p. 1.

81. Must'ad Khan, *Maasir-i-'Alamgiri*, p. 32.

82. Manucci, *Storia*, vol. 2, pp. 106–7.

83. Sarkar, *History*, vol. 3, pp. 86–8. 'Alamgir protested to Shah Jahan that he had taken up 'the perilous load of the crown out of sheer necessity and not from free choice', and that by doing so had done his father the favour of removing the burden of rulership from his shoulders.

84. Katherine Butler Brown, 'Did Aurangzeb Ban Music? Questions for the Historiography of his Reign', *Modern Asian Studies* 41, no. 1 (Jan. 2007), pp. 77–120.

85. Manucci claims to have personally supplied a daily bottle of spirits to no less than the empire's chief *qazi*, 'Abd al-Wahhab, 'which he drank in secret, so that the king could not find it out'. Manucci, *Storia*, vol. 2, p. 3.

86. Must'ad Khan, *Maasir-i-'Alamgiri*, pp. 13–14.

87. Chroniclers writing after the emperor's death, and motivated to paint him in a rigidly puritanical light, recorded that head clerks and accountants who were Hindus were ordered to be replaced by Muslims. But even if such an order were issued, we are told that such a discriminatory measure was never carried out. In any event, such a measure is contradicted by the emperor's own statement in the matter. Ibid., p. 314; Haq (trans.), *Khafi Khan's History*, pp. 252, 255.

88. The order proved to be such a farce that it was formally withdrawn in 1681. Farhat Hasan, *State and Locality in Mughal India: Power Relations in Western India, c.1572–1730* (Cambridge: Cambridge University Press, 2004), p. 117.

89. Bernier, *Travels*, p. 303. As Aurangzeb wrote to a Rajput leader during the War of Succession, 'men belonging to various communities and different religions should live in the vale of peace and pass their days in prosperity, and no one should interfere in the affairs of another'. M. Athar Ali, 'Towards an Interpretation of the Mughal Empire', in Hermann Kulke (ed.), *The State in India, 1000–1700* (New Delhi: Oxford University Press, 1995), p. 269.

90. The Mughal government, he noted, 'takes no notice of [the people's] various Opinions and Casts [*sic*], one more than another. But the [government's] powers are equally extended alike to all, for their Safety and Protection . . .'. Quoted in Rajeev Kinra, 'Handling Diversity with Absolute Civility: The Global Historical Legacy of Mughal Sulh-i Kull', *Medieval History Journal* 16, no. 2 (2013), p. 258. The writer was contrasting India under 'Alamgir with the religious turmoil in England between the Civil War (1642–51), the Protectorate of Oliver Cromwell (1653–58) and the Revolution of 1688.

91. Satish Chandra, 'Jizya and the State in India during the Seventeenth Century', *Journal of the Economic and Social History of the Orient* 12, part 3 (Sept. 1969), pp. 322–40.

92. 'What shall I write of the violence and oppression of the *amin*s appointed to collect the *jaziya* that has been [newly] imposed, as they are beyond description? They realise crores of rupees and pay only a small portion of it into the treasury.' Khobrekar (ed.), *Tarikh-i-Dilkasha*, p. 231.

93. Sarkar (trans.), *Anecdotes*, p. 141.

94. Ibid., p. 99.

95. Athar Ali, *Mughal Nobility*, p. 31.

96. *Journal of the Asiatic Society of Bengal* (1911), pp. 689–90.

97. Faruqui, 'Awrangzib', p. 73.

98. Richard M. Eaton, 'Temple Desecration and Indo-Muslim States', in David Gilmartin and Bruce B. Lawrence (eds), *Beyond Turk and Hindu: Rethinking Religious Identities in Islamicate South Asia* (Gainesville: University Press of Florida, 2000), pp. 246–81. See esp. pp. 254–6.

99. Catherine B. Asher, *Architecture of Mughal India. New Cambridge History of India*, vol. I:4 (Cambridge: Cambridge University Press, 1992), pp. 254, 278. Heidi Pauwels, 'A Tale of Two Temples: Mathura's Keśavadeva and Orchha's Caturbhuvadeva', *South Asia History and Culture* 2, no. 2 (2011), pp. 288–90.

100. Cynthia Talbot, 'A Poetic Record of the Rajput Rebellion, *c*.1680', *Journal of the Royal Asiatic Society* 28, no. 3 (July 2018), pp. 461–83.

101. One vernacular text even portrays 'Alamgir as an ardent, though uncouth, devotee of Krishna. Heidi Pauwels and Amelia Bachrach, 'Aurangzeb as Iconoclast? Vaishnava Accounts of the Krishna Images' Exodus from Braj', *Journal of the Royal Asiatic Society* 28, no. 3 (July 2018), pp. 485–508.

102. Taymiya R. Zaman, 'Nostalgia, Lahore, and the Ghost of Aurangzeb', *Fragments: Interdisciplinary Approaches to the Study of Ancient and Medieval Pasts* 4 (2015), p. 11.

103. Khobrekar (ed.), *Tarikh-i-Dilkasha*, p. 215. Emphasis mine.

104. Perceptions of 'Alamgir have changed dramatically since the seventeenth century. A story circulating in 1990 in Machnur appears to be a memory of the same flood. In this version, 'Alamgir built a ditch in an attempt to divert the river at Machnur so that it would destroy the local temple. But, instead, the river outwitted the emperor and, leaving the temple unharmed, washed away his entire camp. Anne Feldhaus, *Water and Womanhood: Religious Meanings of Rivers in Maharashtra* (New York: Oxford University Press, 1995), pp. 42–3.

105. Haq (trans.), *Khafi Khan's History*, p. 257; Sarkar, *History*, vol. 3, pp. 198–9.

106. Manucci, *Storia do Mogor*, vol. 3, p. 247.

107. S. A. A. Rizvi, *Muslim Revivalist Movements in North India in the Sixteenth and Seventeenth Centuries* (Agra: Agra University, 1965), p. 375; Khobrekar (ed.), *Tarikh-i-Dilkasha*, p. 127; Zaman, 'Nostalgia', p. 13.

108. Haq, *Khafi Khan's History*, pp. 251, 255.

109. According to one account, probably exaggerated, 'Alamgir would spend forty days a year retiring in penitence, sleeping on the ground, fasting and giving alms. Manucci, *Storia*, vol. 2, p. 309.

110. Samira Sheikh, 'Aurangzeb as seen from Gujarat: Shi'i and Millenarian Challenges to Mughal Authority', *Journal of the Royal Asiatic Society* 28, no. 3 (July 2018), pp. 559–65.

111. Ibid., pp. 565–73.

112. Alan M. Guenther, 'Hanafi *Fiqh* in Mughal India: The Fatawa-i 'Alamgiri', in Richard M. Eaton (ed.), *India's Islamic Traditions, 711–1750* (New Delhi: Oxford University Press, 2003), pp. 209–30.

113. There is evidence that both Akbar and Jahangir had similar such aspirations, though these remained unrealized until 'Alamgir's reign. See Corrine Lefèvre, 'Beyond Diversity: Mughal Legal Ideology and Politics', in Thomas Ertl and Gijs Kruijtzer (eds), *Law Addressing Diversity: Pre-modern Europe and South Asia in Comparison (13th–18th Centuries)* (Berlin: De Gruyter, 2017), pp. 124–37.

114. Hasan, *State*, pp. 72-6.
115. 'This may explain,' he continues, 'among other things, the continuation of the *qazi*'s office at Batala during the Sikh period.' J. S. Grewal (ed.), *In the By-Lanes of History: Some Persian Documents from a Punjab Town* (Simla: Indian Institute for Advanced Study, 1975), p. 32.
116. Nandini Chatterjee, 'Reflections on Religious Difference and Permissive Inclusion in Mughal Law', *Journal of Law and Religion* 29, no. 3 (Oct. 2014), pp. 408-10. Chatterjee notes: 'it was the need for secure commercial transactions, the smooth functioning of the state, and the resultant creation of entitlements, as well as a shared culture of Indo-Persian legal forms, that brought litigants into the ambit of these formally Islamic courts. This legal culture survived until the late eighteenth century, and only then, with crucial, British-inspired shifts in ideals of sociopolitical existence and legal governance, was *shari'a* turned into "Mahomedan law" – or personal status laws for Muslims in British-ruled India.' Ibid., p. 403.
117. Sheikh, 'Aurangzeb', p. 559.
118. Sarkar (trans.), *Anecdotes*, p. 184, citing the *Alamgir-nama* of Muhammad Kazim.
119. Manucci, *Storia*, vol. 2, p. 309.
120. Jamshid H. Billimoria (trans.), *Ruka'at-i-Alamgiri, or Letters of Aurangzebe* (1908; repr. Delhi: Idarah-i Adabiyat-i Delli, 1972), pp. 7, 9.
121. Chandra, *Medieval India*, p. 348.
122. Sen (ed.), *Indian Travels*, p. 239.

## CHAPTER 8: EIGHTEENTH-CENTURY TRANSITIONS

1. Munis Faruqui, *The Princes of the Mughal Empire, 1504–1719* (Cambridge: Cambridge University Press 2012), pp. 284-9.
2. Ibid., pp. 312-13.
3. Henry Beveridge (trans.), *The Akbar Nama of Abu'l-fazl* (1902-39; repr. New Delhi: Ess Ess Publications, 1977), vol. 3, pp. 143, 169, 376.
4. Satish Chandra, 'The Jagirdari Crisis: A Fresh Look', in Meena Bhargava (ed.), *The Decline of the Mughal Empire* (New Delhi: Oxford University Press, 2014), pp. 16, 20.
5. Satish Chandra, *Parties and Politics at the Mughal Court, 1707–1750* (2nd edn, New Delhi: People's Publishing House, 1972), pp. 174-5.
6. Munis Faruqui argues that he abandoned Delhi more from a position of weakness than from one of strength. Having been used by 'Alamgir as a political counterweight to the emperor's own sons, Nizam al-Mulk

had never been assimilated into any of those sons' households. As a result, he refused to take part in the war of succession following 'Alamgir's death in 1707. This, in turn, froze him out of the inner circle of that war's victor, Bahadur Shah. And by sitting out of the succession wars that followed the reigns of both Bahadur Shah and Jahandar, Nizam al-Mulk remained politically marginalized at the end of Farrukh Siyar's reign (1713–19) and beyond. See Munis D. Faruqui, 'At Empire's End: The Nizam, Hyderabad and Eighteenth-Century India', *Modern Asian Studies* 43, no. 1 (2009), pp. 13–18.

7. Ibid., pp. 27, 35–8.

8. Ibid., pp. 29, 32.

9. Philip B. Calkins, 'The Formation of a Regionally Oriented Ruling Group in Bengal, 1700–1740', in Bhargava (ed.), *Decline*, pp. 169–80.

10. Ibid., p. 176.

11. M. Athar Ali, 'The Passing of the Empire: The Mughal Case', in Bhargava (ed.), *Decline*, p. 136.

12. Unlike in Awadh, though, the larger size of *jagir*s in the Punjab gave more power to its *jagirdar*s, which imposed limits on the governor's authority within the province. Muzaffar Alam, 'The Crisis of Empire in Mughal North India: Awadh and the Punjab, 1707–1748', in Bhargava (ed.), *Decline*, pp. 181–203.

13. William Irvine, ed. Jadunath Sarkar, *Later Mughals* (1921–2; repr. New Delhi: Oriental Books Reprint Corp., 1971, 2 vols in 1), vol. 1, pp. 321–7.

14. To high-born members of the Mughal nobility who commanded professional archers, lancers or swordsmen mounted on heavy steeds, the peasant-soldiers they encountered in the Deccan appeared as little more than rabble. In 1740 one Mughal aristocrat described his Maratha adversaries as 'unendowed with the excellence of noble or illustrious birth'. Yet he conceded that 'as they undergo all sorts of toil and fatigue in prosecuting a guerrilla warfare, they prove superior to the easy and effeminate troops of Hind [north India], who for the most part are of more honourable birth and calling'. Nawab Ibrahim Khan Bahadur, *Tarikh-i Ibrahim Khan*, in H. M. Elliot and John Dowson (eds), *The History of India as Told by Its Own Historians* (1867–77; repr. Allahabad: Kitab Mahal, 1964, 8 vols), vol. 8, pp. 262–63.

15. See Satish Chandra, 'Social Background to the Rise of the Maratha Movement during the 17th Century in India', *Indian Economic and Social History Review* 10, no. 3 (Sept. 1973), pp. 214–16. Put another way, the meaning of Maratha was expanding to include all those

participating in the Maratha state's northern campaigns, in the same way that, several centuries earlier, villagers of eastern India's military labour market became Rajputs by virtue of their recruitment by Rajput middlemen for service in extended campaigns far from their homes.

16. Stewart Gordon, *Marathas, Marauders, and State Formation in Eighteenth-Century India*. New Cambridge History of India, vol. II:4 (New Delhi: Oxford University Press, 1994), pp. 43–4, 56–7.

17. André Wink, *Land and Sovereignty in India: Agrarian Society and Politics under the Eighteenth-century Maratha Svarajya* (Cambridge: Cambridge University Press, 1986), p. 337.

18. Hiroshi Fukuzawa, *The Medieval Deccan: Peasants, Social Systems, and States, Sixteenth to Eighteenth Centuries* (New Delhi: Oxford University Press, 1991), pp. 183–9.

19. Sumit Guha, *Environment and Ethnicity in India, 1200–1991* (Cambridge: Cambridge University Press, 1999), p. 87n. As early as 1738, the Peshwas were seeking to recruit Arab soldiers into their armies.

20. Stewart Gordon, *The Marathas, 1600–1818*. New Cambridge History of India, vol. II:4 (Cambridge: Cambridge University Press, 1993), pp. 127–9, 140–43.

21. 'Taxes were called by Mughal terms,' writes Gordon, 'assessed in a Mughal manner, paid in the customary Muslim months. The Marathas even retained the Mughal differential transit duties, which charged Hindu traders double their Muslim counterparts. Maratha demands never exceeded the pre-existing Mughal settlement . . . When the Marathas established the basic apparatus of law and order – courts, rural and urban police – both the terminology and function resembled their Mughal counterparts.' Ibid., pp. 143–4.

22. Ibid., p. 145.

23. Purnima Dhavan, *When Sparrows Became Hawks: The Making of the Sikh Warrior Tradition, 1699–1799* (New York: Oxford University Press, 2011), p. 33.

24. Ibid., pp. 40–44, following mainly Sainapati's *Gursobha*, composed c.1708.

25. Ibid., p. 39.

26. Louis E. Fenech, *The Sikh Zafar-Namah of Guru Gobind Singh* (New York: Oxford University Press, 2013), p. 14.

27. Revealing the gathering concern with community identity and social boundaries typical of the later eighteenth century, a text dating to that period contends that the rajas' appeal for Mughal intervention was made on the grounds that the Sikhs' creation of the Khalsa, by liqui-

dating the fourfold Hindu class system, had represented a threat to social order. In other words, 'Alamgir was asked to intervene in order to preserve the Hindu social hierarchy. Anne Murphy, 'Thinking Beyond Aurangzeb and the Mughal State in a Late Eighteenth-Century Punjabi Braj Source', *Journal of the Royal Asiatic Society* 28, no. 3 (July 2018), pp. 548–9.

28. See Fenech, *Zafar-Namah*.

29. Guru Gobind either died from wounds he had earlier sustained, or was assassinated by an Afghan mercenary reputedly hired by the guru's enemies in the Punjab. See ibid., p. 20; Dhavan, *Sparrows*, p. 45.

30. Muzaffar Alam, *The Crisis of Empire in Mughal North India: Awadh and the Punjab, 1707–1748* (Delhi: Oxford University Press, 1986), p. 145.

31. Ibid., p. 144.

32. Ibid., pp. 151–75.

33. Ibid., p. 153.

34. Dhavan, *Sparrows*, p. 51.

35. Ibid., p. 55.

36. Ibid., pp. 74–96.

37. Before Nadir Shah left India with his caravans of Mughal loot, the governor of Punjab ceded part of the western Punjab to the Iranian warlord, and upon his death in 1745 his sons fought over the remainder as though it were a family heirloom.

38. The following paragraphs are derived from Richard M. Eaton, *The Rise of Islam and the Bengal Frontier, 1204–1760* (Berkeley: University of California Press, 1993).

39. Beveridge (trans.), *Akbar Nama*, vol. 3, p. 153. Jean-Baptiste Tavernier, trans. V. Ball, *Travels in India* (1889; repr. Lahore: Al-Biruni, 1976, 2 vols), vol.1, p. 125.

40. Since the cultivation of wet rice, a labour-intensive crop, was the region's major income-producing activity, Mughal land revenue statistics reflect changes in the relative population density of different sectors within the delta. Between 1595 and 1659 the revenue demand for the north-eastern and south-eastern parts of the delta increased by 97 per cent and 117 per cent respectively, whereas that for north-western Bengal, the most moribund part of the delta, actually declined by 13 per cent. Eaton, *The Rise of Islam*, p. 199.

41. Sebastian Manrique, trans. E. Luard and H. Hosten, *Travels of Fray Sebastien Manrique, 1629–1642* (Oxford: Hakluyt Society, 1927, 2 vols), vol. 1, pp. 54, 56.

42. Om Prakash, *The Dutch East India Company and the Economy of Bengal, 1630–1720* (Princeton: Princeton University Press, 1985), p. 75.

43. Sanjay Subrahmanyam, 'Notes on the Sixteenth-Century Bengal Trade', *Indian Economic and Social History Review* 24, no. 3 (1987), pp. 269, 279.

44. Prakash, *Dutch East India Company*, pp. 162–3.

45. Susil Chaudhuri, *Trade and Commercial Organization in Bengal, 1650–1720* (Calcutta: Firma K.L.M., 1975), pp. 100–25.

46. Cesare Federici, 'Extracts of Master Caesar Frederike his Eighteene Yeeres Indian Observations', in Samuel Purchas (ed.), *Hakluytus Posthumus, or Purchas his Pilgrimes* (1625; repr. Glasgow: James MacLehose & Sons, 1905, 20 vols), vol. 10, p. 137; H. Hosten, 'Jesuit Letters from Bengal, Arakan and Burma (1599–1600)', *Bengal Past and Present* 30 (1925), p. 59.

47. S. H. Askari, 'Mughal–Magh Relations Down to the Time of Islam Khan Mashhadi', *Indian History Congress, Proceedings*, 22nd Session, Gauhati, 1959 (Bombay: Indian History Congress, 1960), p. 210.

48. Writing in 1595, at the dawn of the Mughal age in Bengal, Abu'l-fazl 'Allami, the foremost spokesman for Mughal imperial ideology, wrote that the indigenous peoples of the eastern delta were of dark skin, had little or no beard, and practised a religion 'said to be different to that of the Hindus and Muhammadans'. Abu'l-fazl, trans. H. S. Jarrett, ed. Jadunath Sarkar, *A'in-i Akbari* (1949; 2nd edn, repr. New Delhi: Oriental Books Reprint Corp., 1978, 3 vols), vol. 2, p. 132.

49. As was noted by Father Martin SJ, who toured the Hooghly region of west Bengal in 1699, 'nearly the whole country is given to idolatry'. H. Hosten, 'The Earliest Recorded Episcopal Visitation of Bengal, 1712–1715', *Bengal Past and Present* 6 (July–Dec. 1910), p. 217.

50. Muslims directing forest-clearing operations are said to have come from the west, in contrast to aboriginals who came from within the delta. Chanting the name of a Muslim holy man, 2,000 Muslim labourers were led by one Zafar Mian, evidently the group's organizer. The poem can be read as a grand epic dramatizing the process of civilization-building in Bengal and the eastward movement of the delta's ecological frontier as agrarian civilization pushed into formerly forested lands. Kavikankan Mukundaram Chakravarti, *Chandimangal*, trans. Edward M. Yazijian (Gurgaon: Penguin Random House, 2015), pp. 81–2.

51. Saiyid Sultan, ed. Ahmed Sharif, *Nabi-Bangsa* (Dhaka: Bangla Academy, 1978, 2 vols), vol. 1, pp. 348, 420–21.

52. Richard M. Eaton, 'Reconsidering "Conversion to Islam" in Indian History', in Andrew C. S. Peacock (ed.), *Islamisation: Comparative*

*Perspectives from History* (Edinburgh: Edinburgh University Press, 2017), pp. 384–7.

53. Beveridge (trans.), *Akbar Nama*, vol. 3, pp. 13–14.

54. Sven Beckert, *Empire of Cotton: A Global History* (New York: Vintage Books, 2014), p. 42.

55. John S. Deyell, *Living Without Silver: The Monetary History of Early Medieval North India* (Delhi: Oxford University Press, 1990), p. 240.

56. André Gunder Frank, *ReOrient: Global Economy in the Asian Age* (Berkeley and Los Angeles: University of California Press, 1998), pp. 139–60.

57. Shireen Moosvi, *Economy of the Mughal Empire, c.1595: A Statistical Study* (New Delhi: Oxford University Press, 1987), p. 376.

58. William Foster (ed.), *Early Travels in India, 1583–1619* (New Delhi: S. Chand & Co., 1968), p. 112. In 1647 an Ottoman official made a similar observation: 'So much cash treasury goes for Indian merchandise that . . . the world's wealth accumulates in India.' Cited in Beckert, *Empire of Cotton*, p. 18.

59. The figures come from the eccentric Englishman Thomas Coryat, who walked from Jerusalem to India in 1614–15. Along the way he recorded revenue figures he acquired from authorities in Istanbul, Isfahan and Jahangir's court. Foster (ed.), *Early Travels*, p. 246. While most imported silver stayed in India (as appeared to be the case to Hawkins), between 1581 and 1590 nearly three million silver coins flowed from India to Iran and Central Asia, mainly for purchasing war-horses. Moosvi, *Economy*, p. 379.

60. Prasannan Parthasarathi and Giorgio Riello, 'The Indian Ocean in the Long Eighteenth Century', *Eighteenth-Century Studies* 48, no. 1 (2014), p. 5. The high volume of silver imports also had political consequences, since it enabled the Mughals to elaborate a hierarchy of imperial *mansabdar*s whose ranks were based on cash salaries. Monetizing political status in this way had the effect of eroding traditional loyalties that had been based on ethnic, kinship or religious solidarities. Cash salaries had become the new standard of status.

61. See André Wink, *al-Hind: The Making of the Indo-Islamic World*, vol. 2: *The Slave Kings and the Islamic Conquest, 11th–13th Centuries* (Leiden: Brill, 1997), pp. 382–3.

62. Prasannan Parthasarathi, *The Transition to a Colonial Economy: Weavers, Merchants and Kings in South India, 1720–1800* (Cambridge: Cambridge University Press, 2001), p. 122.

63. Ibid., p. 126.

64. Jadunath Sarkar, 'The Revenue Regulations of Aurangzeb', *Journal of the Asiatic Society of Bengal*, n.s., 2, no. 6 (June 1906), pp. 234-5.

65. Farhat Hasan, *State and Locality in Mughal India: Power Relations in Western India, c.1572-1730* (Cambridge: Cambridge University Press, 2004), p. 102.

66. Lakshmi Subramanian, 'The Political Economy of Textiles in Western India: Weavers, Merchants and the Transition to a Colonial Economy', in Giorgio Riello and Tirthankar Roy (eds), *How India Clothed the World: The World of South Asian Textiles, 1500-1850* (Leiden: Brill, 2013), p. 259.

67. Cotton was first spun and woven in the Indus valley, where fragments of cotton textiles have been found dating to between 3250 and 2750 BC. Beckert, *Empire of Cotton*, p. 7.

68. Nick Robins, *The Corporation that Changed the World: How the East India Company Shaped the Modern Multinational* (2nd edn, London: Pluto Press, 2012), p. 48.

69. Indian textiles comprised about a third of the value of goods used to purchase African captives. Joseph E. Inikori, 'English versus Indian Cotton Textiles: The Impact of Imports on Cotton Textile Production in West Africa', in Riello and Roy, *How India Clothed the World*, pp. 103, 106.

70. William Dalrymple, 'The East India Company: The Original Corporate Raiders', *Guardian*, 4 Mar. 2015.

71. Parthasarathi, *Transition*, pp. 83-93.

72. Om Prakash, 'From Market-Determined to Coercion-Based: Textile Manufacturing in Eighteenth-Century Bengal', in Riello and Roy, *How India Clothed the World*, pp. 224-41.

73. Ibid., p. 247.

74. In Gujarat's coastal entrepôt of Surat, where Mughal authority had already been usurped by Marathas, the Company had to share control of the port with Maratha chiefs. It was only after the annexation of the city in 1800 that the Company was able to remove intermediaries between its own agents and weaving communities, prevent non-Company buyers from engaging in trade, or using armed soldiers to enforce its measures. Lakshmi Subramanian, 'The Political Economy of Textiles in Western India: Weavers, Merchants and the Transition to a Colonial Economy', in Riello and Roy, *How India Clothed the World*, pp. 275-80.

75. There was actually a bit of charades being played here. In order to prevent the British king from getting his hands on Bengal's revenues, the House of Commons preferred that they be kept with the Company,

which in turn pretended to be passing those revenues on to an Indian king who everybody knew would never see them.

76. H. V. Bowen, 'Bullion for Trade, War and Debt-Relief: British Movements of Silver to, around, and from Asia, 1760–1833', *Modern Asian Studies* 44, no. 3 (2010), pp. 446, 461.

77. Joseph J. Brennig, 'Textile Producers and Production in Late Seventeenth Century Coromandel', in Sanjay Subrahmanyam (ed.), *Merchants, Markets and the State in Early Modern India* (Delhi: Oxford University Press, 1990), p. 69.

78. David Washbrook, 'The Textile Industry and the Economy of South India, 1500–1800', in Riello and Roy, *How India Clothed the World*, p. 185.

79. M. Athar Ali, 'Recent Theories of Eighteenth-Century India', in P. J. Marshall, *The Eighteenth Century in Indian History: Evolution or Revoltion?* (New Delhi: Oxford University Press, 2003), p. 94.

80. Appasaheb Pawar (ed.), *Tarabaikalina Kagadpatre* (Kolhapur: Shivaji Vidya Pitha, 1969, 3 vols), vol. 3, p. 122.

81. C. A. Bayly, *Rulers, Townsmen, and Bazars: North Indian Society in the Age of British Expansion, 1770–1870* (Cambridge: Cambridge University Press, 1983), p. 6.

## CONCLUSION AND EPILOGUE

1. Francesca Orsini and Samira Sheikh (eds), *After Timur Left: Culture and Circulation in Fifteenth-Century North India* (New Delhi: Oxford University Press, 2014), p. 9.

2. 'Abbas Khan Sarwani, ed. S.M. Imamuddin, *The Tarikh-i Sher Shahi* (Dacca: University of Dacca, 1964), p. 210.

3. Muzaffar Alam, *The Languages of Political Islam: India 1200–1800* (Chicago: University of Chicago Press, 2004), pp. 133–40.

4. Edward Grey (ed.), *The Travels of Pietro della Valle in India: From the Old English Translation of 1664, by G. Havers* (London: Hakluyt Society, 1892; repr. New York: B. Franklin, n.d., 2 vols), vol. 1, pp. 96–7.

5. Juan R. I. Cole, 'Iranian Culture and South Asia, 1500–1900', in Nikki R. Keddie and Rudi Matthee (eds), *Iran and the Surrounding World: Interactions in Culture and Cultural Politics* (Seattle: University of Washington Press, 2002), p. 18.

6. Rajeev Kinra, *Writing Self, Writing Empire: Chandar Bhan Brahman and the Cultural World of the Indo-Persian State Secretary* (Berkeley: University of California Press, 2015), p. 25.

7. Alam, *Languages*, p. 129.

8. Hayden Bellenoit, 'Between Qanungos and Clerks: The Cultural and Service Worlds of Hindustan's Pensmen, *c.*1750–1850', *Modern Asian Studies* 48, no. 4 (2014), pp. 881–7.

9. The *Qasideh dar Lughat-i Hindi*, written at this time, gave Persian equivalents for Hindavi terms, indicating that it presupposed an audience familiar with Persian, but not with Hindavi. Walter Hakala, 'On Equal Terms: The Equivocal Origins of an Early Mughal Indo-Persian Vocabulary', *Journal of the Royal Asiatic Society* 25, no. 2 (April 2015), p. 226.

10. Ibid., p. 225.

11. In modern Persian, in fact, *farhang* denotes 'civilization' as well as 'dictionary'.

12. Kumkum Chatterjee, 'Scribal Elites in Sultanate and Mughal Bengal', *Indian Economic and Social History Review* 47, no. 4 (2010), pp. 459–62.

13. Ibid., p. 462. This helps explain the appearance of Hindus as authors of Persian treatises in the seventeenth and eighteenth centuries. Whereas only six works of Persian literature are known to have been authored by Hindus in seventeenth-century India, in the eighteenth century that figure rose to at least forty-nine, authored by thirty-two different writers. M. Athar Ali, 'The Passing of the Empire: The Mughal Case', in Meena Bhargava (ed.), *The Decline of the Mughal Empire* (New Delhi: Oxford University Press, 2014), p. 138.

14. Paul E. Losensky, *Welcoming Fighani: Imitation and Poetic Individuality in the Safavid-Mughal Ghazal* (Costa Mesa, CA: Mazda, 1998), pp. 134–64.

15. Prashant Keshavmurthy, *Persian Authorship and Canonicity in Late Mughal Delhi: Building an Ark* (London: Routledge, 2016), p. 14.

16. Rajeev Kinra, 'Handling Diversity with Absolute Civility: The Global Historical Legacy of Mughal Sulh-i Kull', *Medieval History Journal* 16, no. 2 (2013), pp. 253–4. For flow, I have made slight changes in this extract's orthography.

17. Even something as mundane as the fruits prepared for Shah Jahan's breakfast suggest the court's imagined participation in a wider, conceptually unified field: melons from Balkh, plums from Kashghar and Ghur, pears from Samarqand, pomegranates from Yazd and Thatta, fruits from Hindustan, mangoes from Gujarat and the Deccan, watermelons from Kashmir. Kinra, *Writing Self*, p. 109.

18. Allison Busch, 'Portrait of a Raja in a Badshah's World: Amrit Rai's Biography of Man Singh (1585)', *Journal of the Economic and Social History of the Orient* 55, no. 2/3 (2012), p. 318.

19. His list included the collected letters of Jami (d. 1492), *Gulistan* and *Bustan* of Sa'di, *Akhlaq-i Nasiri* of Nasir al-Din Tusi, *Akhlaq-i Jalali* of Jalal al-Din Dawani (d. 1502), *Akhlaq-i Muhsini* of Husain Wa'iz Kashifi (d. 1504), *Habib al-Siyar* of Muhammad Khwandamir (d. 1534), *Rauzat al-Safa'* of Mir Khwand (d. 1498), *Rauzat al-Salatin* of Muhammad Fakhri Haravi (fl. 1487), *Tarikh-i Guzida* of Hamd Allah Qazvini (d. 1349), and *Zafar-Nama* of Sharf al-Din 'Ali Yazdi (d. 1454). See Kinra, *Writing Self*, p. 61.

20. Nearly everyone in India who knew Persian was familiar with Jami's works, which were usually included in the standard *madrasa* curriculum. Muzafar Alam, 'Scholar, Saint, and Poet: Jami in the Indo-Muslim World', in Thibaut d'Hubert and Alexandre Papas (eds), *Jami in Regional Contexts: The Reception of 'Abd al-Rahman Jami's Works in the Islamicate World, c.9th/15th–14th/20th Century* (Leiden: Brill, 2018), p. 98.

21. Works from that canon served as reference points in their daily thought. The earliest surviving manuscript of one of the most popular works in the canon of Hindavi literature, Jayasi's *Padmavat* (composed in 1540), was copied in 1674 by a scribe named Muhammad Shakir. As he was making his copy, certain episodes from Jayasi's Hindavi poem sparked his memory of fragments of the poetry of Hafiz, which he then scribbled in the margins of the manuscript. Shantanu Phukan, 'The Rustic Beloved: Ecology of Hindi in a Persianate World', *Annual of Urdu Studies* 13 (2000), p. 6.

22. Audrey Truschke, 'Defining the Other: An Intellectual History of Sanskrit Lexicons and Grammars of Persian', *Journal of Indian Philosophy* 40, no. 6 (Dec. 2012), p. 660. See Ramesh Bharadwaj (ed.), *Rajavyaharakosha of Raghunatha Pandit: Persian-Sanskrit Phraseology* (Delhi: Vidyanidhi Prakashan, 2007).

23. A similar instance would be the attempts of the Académie française (whose motto is 'To immortality') to purge French of English and other foreign words.

24. The last phrase suggests how the founder of Sikhism saw himself in relation to the tradition he founded. He used neither *peyghambar* nor *rasul*, the respective Persian and Arabic terms for 'messenger', far less the Sanskrit *avatar* (incarnation of a deity) or *paramesvar* (lord). Rather, *tabl-i baz* denotes the drum beaten by hunters that would rouse aquatic birds to be captured by a falcon. Grewal plausibly renders it as 'herald'. J. S. Grewal, *The Sikhs: Ideology, Institutions, and Identity* (New Delhi: Oxford University Press, 2009), p. 14.

25. Ronit Ricci, *Islam Translated: Literature, Conversion, and the Arabic Cosmopolis of South and Southeast Asia* (Chicago: University of Chicago Press, 2011), pp. 41, 132.

26. Alam, 'Scholar', p. 120.

27. Thibaut d'Hubert, 'Pirates, Poets, and Merchants: Bengali Language and Literature in Seventeenth-Century Mrauk-U', in Thomas de Bruijn and Allison Busch (eds), *Culture and Circulation: Literature in Motion in Early Modern India* (Leiden: Brill, 2014), pp. 47–74.

28. Ibid., pp. 65–6.

29. Audrey Truschke, *Cultures of Encounters: Sanskrit at the Mughal Court* (New York: Columbia University Press, 2015), p. 19.

30. Ibid., p. 37.

31. Ibid., pp. 69–77.

32. Ibid., p. 93.

33. Ibid., pp. 204–5.

34. Ibid., p. 116.

35. Ibid., pp. 137–9.

36. See Fabrizio Speziale, 'Les Traités Persans sur les Sciences Indiennes: Médecine, Zoologie, Alchimie', in Denis Hermann and Fabrizio Speziale (eds), *Muslim Cultures in the Indo-Iranian World during the Early-Modern and Modern Periods* (Berlin: Klaus Schwartz Verlag, 2010), pp. 403–47; idem, 'Introduction of Galenic Medicine and Sufism in the Sultanates of India', *East and West* 53, no. 1/4 (Dec. 2003), pp. 149–78; idem, 'The Encounter of Medical Traditions in Nur al-Din Shirazi's Ilajat-i Dara Shukohi', *Journal of Indian Medicine* 3 (2010), pp. 53–67; idem, *Culture persane et médecine ayurvédique en Asie du Sud* (Leiden: Brill, 2018).

37. David Pingree, 'Indian Reception of Muslim Ptolemaic Astronomy', in F. Jamil Ragep and Salley P. Ragep (eds), *Tradition, Transmission, Transformation* (Leiden: Brill, 1996), pp. 471–5, 484.

38. Ibid., p. 477.

39. Takanori Kusuba and David Pingree (eds and trans.), *Arabic Astronomy in Sanskrit: al-Birjandi on Tadhkira II, Chapter 11 and its Sanskrit Translation* (Leiden: Brill, 2002), p. 5.

40. Ibid., p. 6.

41. David Pingree, 'Indian and Islamic Astronomy at Jayasimha's Court', *Annals of the New York Academy of Sciences* 500, no. 1 (June 1987), pp. 313–28.

42. Edward C. Scahau (trans.), *Alberuni's India: An Account of the Religion, Philosophy, Literature, Geography, Chronology, Astronomy,*

*Customs, Laws and Astrology of India, about AD 1030* (1910; repr. Delhi: S. Chand & Co., 1964, 2 vols), vol. 1, pp. 17-26.

43. D. C. Sircar, *Studies in Indian Coins* (Delhi: Motilal Banarsidass, 1968), p. 19.

44. Henry Beveridge (ed.), Alexander Rogers (trans.), *The Tuzuk-i-Jahangiri; or, Memoirs of Jahangir* (2nd edn, New Delhi: Munshiram Manoharlal, 1968, 2 vols), vol. 2, p. 224.

45. Kinra, *Writing Self*, p. 97.

46. Carl W. Ernst, 'Admiring the Works of the Ancients: the Ellora Temples as Viewed by Indo-Muslim Authors', in David Gilmartin and Bruce B. Lawrence (eds), *Beyond Turk and Hindu: Rethinking Religious Identities in Islamicate South Asia* (Gainesville: University Press of Florida, 2000), pp. 98-120.

47. Allison Busch, *Poetry of Kings: The Classical Hindi Literature of Mughal India* (New York: Oxford University Press, 2011), p. 165.

48. Ibid., p. 169. In 1749 even the raja of Kutch, in Gujarat, founded a school of Braj, indicating the language's transregional character within India. Ibid., p. 199.

49. Ibid., pp. 165, 187.

50. Ibid., p. 129.

51. Walter Hakala, *Negotiating Languages: Urdu, Hindi, and the Definition of Modern South Asia* (New York: Columbia University Press, 2016), pp. 100-05.

52. There were many names for what were dialects of Hindavi, or proto-Hindi-Urdu, including Avadhi, Brajbhasha, Gujri, Rajasthani, Pingal, Sadhukkari, Hindustani, Dihlavi, Purbi Zaban, Dakani, Rekhta. Busch, *Poetry*, p. 8.

53. André Wink, *Akbar* (Oxford: Oneworld, 2009), pp. 52-61.

54. *The Commentary of Father Monserrate, S.J., on his Journey to the Court of Akbar*, trans. John S. Hoyland (London: Oxford University Press, 1922), p. 211. Emphasis mine.

55. The historian Nizam al-Din Ahmad (d. 1594), author of *Tabaqat-i Akbari*, treats fate and its agents – usually Sufi dervishes – nearly contemptuously, since in his view humans possess power over their actions and destiny. Ali Anooshahr, 'Author of One's Fate: Fatalism and Agency in Indo-Persian Histories', *Indian Economic and Social History Review* 49, no. 2 (2012), pp. 200-01.

56. A. Azfar Moin, *The Millennial Sovereign: Sacred Kingship and Sainthood in Islam* (New York: Columbia University Press, 2012), pp. 130-69.

57. Nearly a century after 'Alamgir's death and half a world away, Britain's American colonies, having successfully rebelled against King George III, debated what to call their new head of state. Instead of reigning over the United States as an absolute monarch, George Washington, it was eventually decided, would merely uphold the laws enacted by the government at which he presided, and therefore be called 'president'.

58. Samira Sheikh, 'Aurangzeb as Seen from Gujarat: Shi'i and Millenarian Challenges to Mughal Authority', *Journal of the Royal Asiatic Society* 28, no. 3 (July 2018), p. 581.

# Index

ALLEN LANE
*an imprint of*
PENGUIN BOOKS

## Also Published

John Tierney and Roy F. Baumeister, *The Power of Bad: And How to Overcome It*

Greta Thunberg, *No One Is Too Small to Make a Difference: Illustrated Edition*

Glenn Simpson and Peter Fritsch, *Crime in Progress: The Secret History of the Trump-Russia Investigation*

Abhijit V. Banerjee and Esther Duflo, *Good Economics for Hard Times: Better Answers to Our Biggest Problems*

Gaia Vince, *Transcendence: How Humans Evolved through Fire, Language, Beauty and Time*

Roderick Floud, *An Economic History of the English Garden*

Rana Foroohar, *Don't Be Evil: The Case Against Big Tech*

Ivan Krastev and Stephen Holmes, *The Light that Failed: A Reckoning*

Andrew Roberts, *Leadership in War: Lessons from Those Who Made History*

Alexander Watson, *The Fortress: The Great Siege of Przemysl*

Stuart Russell, *Human Compatible: AI and the Problem of Control*

Serhii Plokhy, *Forgotten Bastards of the Eastern Front: An Untold Story of World War II*

Dominic Sandbrook, *Who Dares Wins: Britain, 1979-1982*

Charles Moore, *Margaret Thatcher: The Authorized Biography, Volume Three: Herself Alone*

Thomas Penn, *The Brothers York: An English Tragedy*

David Abulafia, *The Boundless Sea: A Human History of the Oceans*

Anthony Aguirre, *Cosmological Koans: A Journey to the Heart of Physics*

Orlando Figes, *The Europeans: Three Lives and the Making of a Cosmopolitan Culture*

Naomi Klein, *On Fire: The Burning Case for a Green New Deal*

Anne Boyer, *The Undying: A Meditation on Modern Illness*

Benjamin Moser, *Sontag: Her Life*

Daniel Markovits, *The Meritocracy Trap*

Malcolm Gladwell, *Talking to Strangers: What We Should Know about the People We Don't Know*

Peter Hennessy, *Winds of Change: Britain in the Early Sixties*

John Sellars, *Lessons in Stoicism: What Ancient Philosophers Teach Us about How to Live*

Brendan Simms, *Hitler: Only the World Was Enough*

Hassan Damluji, *The Responsible Globalist: What Citizens of the World Can Learn from Nationalism*

Peter Gatrell, *The Unsettling of Europe: The Great Migration, 1945 to the Present*

Justin Marozzi, *Islamic Empires: Fifteen Cities that Define a Civilization*

Bruce Hood, *Possessed: Why We Want More Than We Need*

Susan Neiman, *Learning from the Germans: Confronting Race and the Memory of Evil*

Donald D. Hoffman, *The Case Against Reality: How Evolution Hid the Truth from Our Eyes*

Frank Close, *Trinity: The Treachery and Pursuit of the Most Dangerous Spy in History*

Richard M. Eaton, *India in the Persianate Age: 1000-1765*

Janet L. Nelson, *King and Emperor: A New Life of Charlemagne*

Philip Mansel, *King of the World: The Life of Louis XIV*

Donald Sassoon, *The Anxious Triumph: A Global History of Capitalism, 1860-1914*

Elliot Ackerman, *Places and Names: On War, Revolution and Returning*

Jonathan Aldred, *Licence to be Bad: How Economics Corrupted Us*

Johny Pitts, *Afropean: Notes from Black Europe*

Walt Odets, *Out of the Shadows: Reimagining Gay Men's Lives*

James Lovelock, *Novacene: The Coming Age of Hyperintelligence*

Mark B. Smith, *The Russia Anxiety: And How History Can Resolve It*

Stella Tillyard, *George IV: King in Waiting*

Jonathan Rée, *Witcraft: The Invention of Philosophy in English*

Jared Diamond, *Upheaval: How Nations Cope with Crisis and Change*

Emma Dabiri, *Don't Touch My Hair*

Srecko Horvat, *Poetry from the Future: Why a Global Liberation Movement Is Our Civilisation's Last Chance*

Paul Mason, *Clear Bright Future: A Radical Defence of the Human Being*

Remo H. Largo, *The Right Life: Human Individuality and its role in our development, health and happiness*

Joseph Stiglitz, *People, Power and Profits: Progressive Capitalism for an Age of Discontent*

David Brooks, *The Second Mountain*

Roberto Calasso, *The Unnamable Present*

Lee Smolin, *Einstein's Unfinished Revolution: The Search for What Lies Beyond the Quantum*

Clare Carlisle, *Philosopher of the Heart: The Restless Life of Søren Kierkegaard*

Nicci Gerrard, *What Dementia Teaches Us About Love*

Edward O. Wilson, *Genesis: On the Deep Origin of Societies*

John Barton, *A History of the Bible: The Book and its Faiths*

Carolyn Forché, *What You Have Heard is True: A Memoir of Witness and Resistance*

Elizabeth-Jane Burnett, *The Grassling*

Kate Brown, *Manual for Survival: A Chernobyl Guide to the Future*

Roderick Beaton, *Greece: Biography of a Modern Nation*

Matt Parker, *Humble Pi: A Comedy of Maths Errors*

Ruchir Sharma, *Democracy on the Road*

David Wallace-Wells, *The Uninhabitable Earth: A Story of the Future*

Randolph M. Nesse, *Good Reasons for Bad Feelings: Insights from the Frontier of Evolutionary Psychiatry*

Anand Giridharadas, *Winners Take All: The Elite Charade of Changing the World*

Richard Bassett, *Last Days in Old Europe: Triste '79, Vienna '85, Prague '89*

Paul Davies, *The Demon in the Machine: How Hidden Webs of Information Are Finally Solving the Mystery of Life*

Toby Green, *A Fistful of Shells: West Africa from the Rise of the Slave Trade to the Age of Revolution*

Paul Dolan, *Happy Ever After: Escaping the Myth of The Perfect Life*

Sunil Amrith, *Unruly Waters: How Mountain Rivers and Monsoons Have Shaped South Asia's History*

Christopher Harding, *Japan Story: In Search of a Nation, 1850 to the Present*

Timothy Day, *I Saw Eternity the Other Night: King's College, Cambridge, and an English Singing Style*

Richard Abels, *Aethelred the Unready: The Failed King*

Eric Kaufmann, *Whiteshift: Populism, Immigration and the Future of White Majorities*

Alan Greenspan and Adrian Wooldridge, *Capitalism in America: A History*

Philip Hensher, *The Penguin Book of the Contemporary British Short Story*

Paul Collier, *The Future of Capitalism: Facing the New Anxieties*

Andrew Roberts, *Churchill: Walking With Destiny*

Tim Flannery, *Europe: A Natural History*

T. M. Devine, *The Scottish Clearances: A History of the Dispossessed, 1600-1900*

Robert Plomin, *Blueprint: How DNA Makes Us Who We Are*

Michael Lewis, *The Fifth Risk: Undoing Democracy*

Diarmaid MacCulloch, *Thomas Cromwell: A Life*

Ramachandra Guha, *Gandhi: 1914-1948*

Slavoj Žižek, *Like a Thief in Broad Daylight: Power in the Era of Post-Humanity*

Neil MacGregor, *Living with the Gods: On Beliefs and Peoples*

Peter Biskind, *The Sky is Falling: How Vampires, Zombies, Androids and Superheroes Made America Great for Extremism*

Robert Skidelsky, *Money and Government: A Challenge to Mainstream Economics*

Helen Parr, *Our Boys: The Story of a Paratrooper*

David Gilmour, *The British in India: Three Centuries of Ambition and Experience*

Jonathan Haidt and Greg Lukianoff, *The Coddling of the American Mind: How Good Intentions and Bad Ideas are Setting up a Generation for Failure*

Ian Kershaw, *Roller-Coaster: Europe, 1950-2017*

Adam Tooze, *Crashed: How a Decade of Financial Crises Changed the World*

Edmund King, *Henry I: The Father of His People*

Lilia M. Schwarcz and Heloisa M. Starling, *Brazil: A Biography*

Jesse Norman, *Adam Smith: What He Thought, and Why it Matters*

Philip Augur, *The Bank that Lived a Little: Barclays in the Age of the Very Free Market*

Christopher Andrew, *The Secret World: A History of Intelligence*

David Edgerton, *The Rise and Fall of the British Nation: A Twentieth-Century History*

Julian Jackson, *A Certain Idea of France: The Life of Charles de Gaulle*

Owen Hatherley, *Trans-Europe Express*

Richard Wilkinson and Kate Pickett, *The Inner Level: How More Equal Societies Reduce Stress, Restore Sanity and Improve Everyone's Wellbeing*

Paul Kildea, *Chopin's Piano: A Journey Through Romanticism*

Seymour M. Hersh, *Reporter: A Memoir*

Michael Pollan, *How to Change Your Mind: The New Science of Psychedelics*

David Christian, *Origin Story: A Big History of Everything*

Judea Pearl and Dana Mackenzie, *The Book of Why: The New Science of Cause and Effect*

David Graeber, *Bullshit Jobs: A Theory*

Serhii Plokhy, *Chernobyl: History of a Tragedy*

Michael McFaul, *From Cold War to Hot Peace: The Inside Story of Russia and America*

Paul Broks, *The Darker the Night, the Brighter the Stars: A Neuropsychologist's Odyssey*

Lawrence Wright, *God Save Texas: A Journey into the Future of America*

John Gray, *Seven Types of Atheism*

Carlo Rovelli, *The Order of Time*

Mariana Mazzucato, *The Value of Everything: Making and Taking in the Global Economy*

Richard Vinen, *The Long '68: Radical Protest and Its Enemies*

Kishore Mahbubani, *Has the West Lost It?: A Provocation*

John Lewis Gaddis, *On Grand Strategy*

Richard Overy, *The Birth of the RAF, 1918: The World's First Air Force*

Francis Pryor, *Paths to the Past: Encounters with Britain's Hidden Landscapes*

Helen Castor, *Elizabeth I: A Study in Insecurity*

Ken Robinson and Lou Aronica, *You, Your Child and School*

Leonard Mlodinow, *Elastic: Flexible Thinking in a Constantly Changing World*

Nick Chater, *The Mind is Flat: The Illusion of Mental Depth and The Improvised Mind*

Michio Kaku, *The Future of Humanity: Terraforming Mars, Interstellar Travel, Immortality, and Our Destiny Beyond*

Thomas Asbridge, *Richard I: The Crusader King*

Richard Sennett, *Building and Dwelling: Ethics for the City*

Nassim Nicholas Taleb, *Skin in the Game: Hidden Asymmetries in Daily Life*

Steven Pinker, *Enlightenment Now: The Case for Reason, Science, Humanism and Progress*

Steve Coll, *Directorate S: The C.I.A. and America's Secret Wars in Afghanistan, 2001 - 2006*